Y0-BED-837
9/23

The Waite Group's
MS-DOS®
Papers

HOWARD W. SAMS & COMPANY
HAYDEN BOOKS

Related Titles

**The Waite Group's
MS-DOS® Developer's Guide,
Revised Edition**
John Angermeyer and Kevin Jaeger

**The Waite Group's
Understanding MS-DOS®**
Kate O'Day and John Angermeyer

**The Waite Group's
Tricks of the MS-DOS®
Masters**
*John Angermeyer, Rich Fahringer,
Kevin Jaeger, and Dan Shafer*

**The Waite Group's
Discovering MS-DOS®**
Kate O'Day

**Hard Disk Management
Techniques for the IBM®**
Joseph-David Carrabis

**IBM® PC AT User's
Reference Manual**
Gilbert Held

**IBM® PC & PC XT User's
Reference Manual,
Second Edition**
Gilbert Held

**The Waite Group's
Desktop Publishing Bible**
*James Stockford, Editor,
The Waite Group*

**Personal Publishing with PC
PageMaker®**
Terry Ulick

Micro-Mainframe Connection
Thomas Wm. Madron

**The Waite Group's
Modem Connections Bible**
*Carolyn Curtis, Daniel Majhor,
The Waite Group*

**The Waite Group's
Printer Connections Bible**
*Kim G. House, Jeff Marble,
The Waite Group*

*For the retailer nearest you, or to order directly from the publisher,
call 800-428-SAMS. In Indiana, Alaska, and Hawaii call 317-298-5699.*

The Waite Group's
MS-DOS®
Papers

Edited by The Waite Group

HOWARD W. SAMS & COMPANY

A Division of Macmillan, Inc.
4300 West 62nd Street
Indianapolis, Indiana 46268 USA

©1988 by The Waite Group, Inc.

FIRST EDITION
FIRST PRINTING—1988

All rights reserved. No part of this book shall be reproduced, stored
in a retrieval system, or transmitted by any means, electronic,
mechanical, photocopying, recording, or otherwise, without
written permission from the publisher. No patent liability is
assumed with respect to the use of the information contained
herein. While every precaution has been taken in the preparation
of this book, the publisher and author assume no responsibility for
errors or omissions. Neither is any liability assumed for damages
resulting from the use of the information contained herein.

International Standard Book Number: 0-672-22594-8
Library of Congress Catalog Card Number: 88-60990

From The Waite Group, Inc.
Development Editor: *Mitchell Waite*
Editorial Director: *James Stockford*
Content Editor: *Harry Henderson*
Technical Reviewer: *Blair Hendrickson*

From Howard W. Sams & Company
Acquisitions Editor: *James S. Hill*
Development Editor: *James Rounds*
Editor: *Albright Communications, Incorporated*
Cover Artist: *Ron Troxell*
Illustrator: *Wm. D. Basham*
Indexer: *Ted Laux*
Compositor: *Shepard Poorman Communications Corporation*

Printed in the United States of America

To our families

Contents

Preface   **xiii**

Acknowledgments   **xv**

Introduction   **xvii**

Section One
Extending the MS-DOS User Interface

1 A Guided Tour inside MS-DOS   **5**

Harry Henderson

The Challenge of Change   5
Overall Structure of MS-DOS   6
The User Level   11
The Applications Level   21
The Hardware Level   29
The Future of MS-DOS   30

2 Searching the File Tree with `whereis`   **35**

Frank Whaley

Tree-Structured Directories   35
Searching: The Recursive Solution   36
Directory Search Functions   37
Using Options for Power and Flexibility   38
The `whereis.c` Program   39
Compiling `whereis`   52
Conclusion   53

3 Adding UNIX Power with PCnix   **55**

R. Edward Nather

Why PCnix?   55
Our Strategy   57
Tweaking MS-DOS   58
Improving MS-DOS Operation   61
Using Batch Files to Create PCnix Commands   62
Using Batch File Helpers to Increase Flexibility   67
The Software Toolkit   75
MS-DOS Wildcards Are Not UNIX Metacharacters   86
Epilogue   88

4 Adding Power to MS-DOS Programming   **91**

Douglas O. Adams

Setting Up Your Operating Environment   92
Using Extended Batch Language for Real Power   94
Programming Screen Control Facilities   99
Key File Access Systems   107
Summary   112

5 Advanced MASM Techniques   **117**

Michael Goldman

Records   117
Structures   120
Include Files   125
Data Macros   126
Code Macros   129
Interrupt Tips   136
Parting Shots   140

Section Two
Programming Tools and Techniques

6 Undocumented MS-DOS Functions   **147**

Raymond J. Michels

Program Segment Prefix   148
File Handles   152
The Environment Segment   155

PSP Functions   158
Memory Management   160
Other Undocumented Functions   169
Undocumented Interrupts   178

7 Safe Memory-Resident Programming (TSR)   185

M. Steven Baker

Why Are TSRs Useful?   185
The Origin of Memory-Resident Programs   186
Well-Behaved Memory-Resident Programs   190
A Simple Memory-Resident Program   198
A Closer Look at TSRs   208
Complex TSR Programs That Make MS-DOS Function Calls   209
An UNSPOOL TSR Program   211
Programming Guidelines for TSR Programs   213
The Bottom Line   214

8 Data Protection and Encryption   217

Asael Dror

Three Levels of Unauthorized Data Access   217
MS-DOS Data Structure and Access   219
Hiding Your Data   221
Protecting Files Using the Read-Only Attribute   224
Password Protection   225
Data Encryption   227
Loopholes in MS-DOS Data Security   237
Summary   238

9 Inside Microsoft Windows   241

Michael Geary

Who's in Charge Here?   241
Windows and Messages   242
Window Styles: Overlapped, Popup, Child   248
Window Classes   250
Graphics Programming in Windows   252
Memory Management   255
Resources   256
The Spy Program   257
Conclusion   270

Section Three
Working with the Hardware Interface

10 Developing MS-DOS Device Drivers   **303**

Walter Dixon

DOS Data Structures   304
What Is a Driver and How Is It Used?   307
Using the DOS INT 21H Application Services Interface   310
The Boot Process   312
The INT 21H Dispatcher: Processing Application Requests   321
Using FCBs and Handles   323
Working with the SFT   324
From Driver Request to Call   325
Writing Background Programs   336
Debugging a Driver   338
Conclusion   344

11 Writing a SOUND Device Driver   **347**

Walter Dixon

Setting up the SOUND Driver   347
SOUND Driver Commands and Musical Notation   349
Using the SOUND Driver   353
Hardware Review   355
Programming Techniques   359
DOS Internals   366
Prototype Driver   369
Sound Generation Hardware   373
Overview of the SOUND Driver   375
SOUND Driver Finite State Machine   376
SOUND Driver Coroutines   378
Synchronization and Circular Buffers   378
Speeding up the System Clock   379
New Clock Interrupt Service Routine   379
Driver Performance   381
Adding Refinements   382
Finishing Touches   383
Conclusion   385

12 Programming the Enhanced Graphics Adapter   **435**

Andrew Dumke

Inside the EGA   435
The egacheck.c Program and Macros   440

A Print Screen Routine with Dithering   461
Conclusion   474

13 Programming the Serial Port with C   **477**
Nabajyoti Barkakati

Basics of Asynchronous Data Communications   477
Taming the UART   484
Specifications for Our Serial Communications Package   493
Conclusion   502
Program Listings and the Makefile   502

14 Understanding Expanded Memory Systems   **535**
Ray Duncan

Lotus, Intel, Microsoft EMS   535
What Is Expanded Memory?   536
Expanded Memory Manager   538
Testing for Expanded Memory   540
Using Expanded Memory   542
C Interface to Expanded Memory   550

Index   **563**

Preface

MS-DOS Papers is the latest in The Waite Group's contributed series on programming languages and operating systems. This particular collection of essays focuses on the MS-DOS operating system and brings together a far flung variety of MS-DOS programmers. In choosing these essays, we have strived to reflect the real world of MS-DOS programming rather than the more traditional approach of textbooks and software manuals. Thus, you will find in this book subjects not usually covered, in a way not usually found, in the trade literature:

- secrets and tricks of coding
- use of MS-DOS internal structures
- tools
- utilities

None of the original designers of MS-DOS expected it to be used for a wide variety of applications, nor could they have anticipated the needs that users now present. In the early 1980s, the designers revised the system by providing new functions, interrupts, and other internal services, and they protected their revision process by secrecy and documentation that often offered no more explanation than "reserved." But give them credit for a good design! MS-DOS has survived tremendous changes, although to a large degree the operating system itself has become something of a kludge—a set of patches, fixes, device drivers, and add-ons. And all the while, application programmers have been busy disassembling, uncovering, and sharing the mysteries one by one.

Although the operating system is now quite mature, the revisions to MS-DOS are coming more slowly, while the market is screaming for more performance. New generations of software need more than 640K memory, higher resolution graphics, faster calculations, and multitasking on a single-tasking system. Obviously MS-DOS has hit a performance wall. In order to answer these new market demands, enhancements are coming not from further improvements of the operating system internals but from external sets of ad hoc conventions that define such standards as Expanded Memory Specification (EMS), Enhanced Graphics Adapter (EGA), and Terminate and Stay Resident (TSR) programs, and such extensions as device drivers and C libraries.

So long as MS-DOS continues to flourish in this "pruning" and "patching" way, MS-DOS programmers must learn to work outside of the operating system as well as within it. This means learning not only the standards of EMS, EGA, MS Windows, and other external environment additions, but also the conventions of programming lore—which registers to use, which functions to call, how to share the use of system services with unknown applications, how to test the IN _DOS flag, upper interrupt areas (INT 60H to 67H), PSP, and other MS-DOS data structures. For example, if different applications are to share memory, the program designers must agree on the allocation and use of that common memory space, or one program may write over the other. As another example, programmers must know how to test for, save, and restore any existing screen contents if their application is to overwrite an area of the display. To make the point, a TSR program that disables other TSRs, or that overwrites a screen and then disappears without restoring that previous screen, is likely to get poor recommendations from disgruntled users. Anticipation of possible problems and awareness of well-behaved manners are critical to a designer's ability to create a successful MS-DOS application today.

In the increasingly complex MS-DOS operating system environment, many programming rules, conventions, and good manners are shared by word of mouth, over telecommunications networks, and in special journals. We have tried to capture much of this hard-to-find lore inside this book. We have asked the authors to explore what MS-DOS areas they know best. It is our hope that you find this a readable, rich collection of wisdom that adds to your experience and skill as an MS-DOS programmer.

Acknowledgments

The Waite Group wishes to acknowledge the help of the many people who have contributed to this book. Our first acknowledgment is to the authors of these essays; thank you for sticking with this project complicated with deadlines, rush mail, late night phone calls, rewrites to perfect the essays, and corrections for typesetting. Secondly, we could not have done this without Harry Henderson, our editor, for whose patience and insight we are again deeply grateful. Many thanks to Blair Hendrickson, who provided technical reviews for all the papers, to Cynthia Pepper for her help through most of the development cycle, and to Scott Calamar for his help during the production phase. Thanks to James Stockford for managing the project, for the Introduction to the book, and for development work on Overview of MS-DOS, PCnix, MS-DOS Power, and Device Driver Basics.

We wish to thank Sams production members Wendy Ford, Kathy Ewing, and Don Herrington for management and Nancy Albright for editing. Thanks to Ron Troxell for his Genie on the cover and to Glenn Santner for keeping the Genie in the bottle. Thanks to Jim Rounds for constant support in development and to Jim Hill for his faith in the book from the beginning.

Mitchell Waite

Trademarks

All terms mentioned in this book that are known to be trademarks or service marks have been appropriately capitalized. Neither The Waite Group nor Howard W. Sams & Company can attest to the accuracy of this information. Use of a term in this book should not be regarded as affecting the validity of any trademark or service mark.

Apple is a registered trademark of Apple Computer, Inc.

AT&T is a registered trademark of American Telephone and Telegraph.

Concurrent and Concurrent PC-DOS are trademarks, and CP/M is a registered trademark of Digital Research Inc.

CRAY is a registered trademark of Cray Computer, Inc.

Epson is a registered trademark of Epson America, Inc.

Framework and dBASE II are registered trademarks of Ashton-Tate.

GEM is a trademark of Digital Research Inc.

IBM, IBM AT, PC-DOS, Personal Computer AT, OS/2, IBM PC, IBM XT, and IBM 9370 are registered trademarks of International Business Machines Corporation.

Intel, Intel 80286 and 80386 are trademarks of Intel Corporation.

Lotus, 1-2-3, and Symphony are registered trademarks of Lotus Development Corporation.

Macintosh is a registered trademark of McIntosh Laboratory, Inc., licensed by Apple Computers, Inc.

MS-DOS, Microsoft, Microsoft Windows, and XENIX are registered trademarks of Microsoft Corporation.

The Norton Utilities is a trademark of Peter Norton Computing, Inc.

PostScript is a registered trademark of Adobe Systems, Inc., licensed by Apple Computer, Inc.

ProKey is a trademark of RoseSoft, Inc.

SuperCalc is a registered trademark of Sorcim Corporation.

ThinkTank is a trademark of Living Videotext, Inc.

Turbo BASIC, Turbo Lightning, Turbo Prolog, Turbo Pascal, SideKick, Superkey, and Reflex are registered trademarks of Borland International.

UNIX is a registered trademark of American Telephone and Telegraph.

VAX, VAX/VMS are registered trademarks of Digital Equipment Corporation.

WordPerfect is a registered trademark of WordPerfect Corporation.

WordStar is a registered trademark of MicroPro International Corporation.

Introduction

In the course of studying programming in MS-DOS, you may have noticed that people seem to have markedly different approaches, even to the point of contradiction. Indeed, one quickly discovers that the MS-DOS world is one of short-cuts and trickery of remarkable range, where anything that works is fair game. Finding these important tricks, insider techniques, and bottom line facts is extremely tedious because they are spread out in so many places—from technical networks to obscure articles in programming magazines. *The Waite Group's MS-DOS Papers* brings you the most important of these ideas, tips, and techniques in a single reference source.

Our purpose in this collection of essays on MS-DOS programming is to create a forum for many professional points of view so that you can pick and choose among techniques and inspect the major advanced extensions of MS-DOS through many different windows. This is not a training book showing users how to use MS-DOS; rather, the essays in this book show programmers how to arm themselves to manipulate the operating system and to write better performing software. As usual, speed is a major goal, so many of these essays reveal slick techniques to speed up the user interface and access hardware. If you have any interest in understanding the inner workings of the MS-DOS operating system, this book is for you.

The Waite Group's MS-DOS Papers is divided into three topic areas:

> sophisticated use of the user interface (manipulating directory structures, using libraries and batch files)

> techniques for programming (working with functions and internal data structures of the operating system to control application programs such as Terminate and Stay Resident programs)

> control of the system hardware (understanding interrupts, functions, and data structures to manipulate hardware such as the serial port, Enhanced Graphics Adapter, Enhanced Memory Specification, and more)

It goes without saying that MS-DOS programmers must be fluent in both the C language and assembly language, especially MASM 5.0. They must be facile users of the compilers and software development tools. Indeed, much of the work programmers do is spent setting up their systems for maximum efficiency. They must be practiced users of the operating system's commands and underlying environment. These skills are the focus of essays in the first section.

MS-DOS programmers must contend with an increasingly extended environment, and this is the background for the second and third sections. MS-DOS, despite its age, is still growing and expanding, so most MS-DOS systems are beginning to suffer from overpopulation of large application programs, memory-resident programs that are squeezing the interrupt system, and constraints of managing huge amounts of data. The effect is that after several major revisions, the MS-DOS operating system has reached a state of maturity that now requires working programmers to be familiar with all the system's interrupts and functions and several sets of services beyond those of MS-DOS itself.

Essays in the second section deal with understanding undocumented functions, learning to write Terminate and Stay Resident programs that work predictably without interfering with other applications also loaded in memory, creating data protection and encryption schemes for file security, and inspecting the behavior of the MS Windows operating environment.

Essays in the third section focus on hardware—how to write device drivers, control the serial port, program high-resolution color screens controlled by the EGA display cards, and use large amounts of memory provided by the EMS hardware and software.

This Book and Other Waite Group Books

The Waite Group's MS-DOS Papers is a follow up to other Waite Group books: *MS-DOS Developer's Guide*, a detailed examination of the MS-DOS operating system; *Tricks of the MS-DOS Masters*, a collection of techniques for advanced users; *MS-DOS Bible*, a complete reference book with tutorials for intermediate users; and *Discovering MS-DOS* and *Understanding MS-DOS*, both of which are introductions to the MS-DOS operating system for beginners.

What You Have to Know to Read *MS-DOS Papers*

You must, at a bare minimum, know how to operate MS-DOS well enough to copy files between subdirectories, install drivers and other commands in the CONFIG.SYS file, and use the standard internal and external commands. You must also understand generally how the 8088/86 central processing unit (CPU) works, the limitations of the MS-DOS 640K memory scheme, and the relationship between peripheral devices, ports, and the I/O channel slots. Building upon this basic knowledge, you will learn what structures make up MS-DOS and how they behave and gain an understanding of modern enhancements to the system.

Intermediate programmers, with professional user-level skills and some knowledge of either assembly language or the C programming language, will find useful details of MS-DOS services as well as usable program listings with complete explanations of the design of the code.

Advanced programmers, familiar with both 80X86 assembler and C as well as MS-DOS system calls, have in this book a sophisticated treatment of many of the important topic areas that underlie the major marketing features of modern applications, namely, control of the Enhanced Graphics Adapter (EGA), use of Expanded Memory Specification (EMS), operation of memory-resident programs (TSRs), examination of the Microsoft Windows operating environment, and much more.

Organization of *MS-DOS Papers*

MS-DOS Papers begins with an overview of the inner structure of MS-DOS, followed by sections that roughly parallel the three conceptual areas of MS-DOS itself: the user interface shell; the kernel; and access to hardware through the BIOS, ports, and device drivers. The following is a description of the essays in this book.

Section One: Extending the MS-DOS User Interface

MS-DOS is composed of three modules: the user shell `COMMAND.COM`; the kernel and the main services, `MSDOS.SYS`; and the hardware access routines `IO.SYS`. This division provided the inspiration for the section divisions of this book. The fact of this modularity of MS-DOS has allowed for the upgrade of each module without respect to the others and also for manipulation and even replacement of one of the modules without disturbance to the others.

A Guided Tour inside MS-DOS

Essay 1 offers a rare, comprehensive overview of the insides of MS-DOS with suggestions for modifications for increasing user-level speed and functionality. Of special note, this essay contains a great number of references to the other essays in this book and serves to tie all of the papers together.

Searching the File Tree with `whereis`

The MS-DOS file system is built around a hierarchical file system of directories and subdirectories, yet it does not include a feature with which to find and act on a file without first setting a PATH specification or invoking the correct subdirectory. In other words, in order to find a file, first you have to know where it is—not good. Essay 2 presents a search tool written in C called `whereis`. The `whereis` utility combines two essential features: the ability to search for matching files within the whole file tree (not just within one directory) and the ability to use MS-DOS commands or programs to manipulate the files it finds.

Adding UNIX Power with PCnix

PCnix is a homespun set of public domain utilities, batch files, and imaginative patches that augment the MS-DOS `A>` prompt interface. By adding PCnix to your MS-DOS system, you get such UNIX-like features as command-editing and a "history" capability to the MS-DOS user interface, the use of UNIX syntax, and a toolkit of UNIX-style commands for managing files and text. Essay 3 presents a highly entertaining description of the process of tweaking interrupts and "fooling DOS" to attain important UNIX-like power while preserving MS-DOS compatibility. PCnix is available on three diskettes.

Adding Power to MS-DOS Programming

The first order of business for a professional C programmer is to set up applications and files for fast, easy access. This means developing a library of routines and having a way to invoke them quickly. Essay 4 examines a popular third-party interface extension, Enhanced Batch Language (EBL), a powerful batch language facility with increased variables and commands, as well as two C library packages, the C-INDEX, which provides detailed file-search capabilities, and Vitamin C, a set of library routines that automate the creation of screens and windows and provide B-tree file indexing.

Advanced MASM Techniques

Nearly all working programmers must use assembly language at least occasionally, and yet, constructing a program at the machine instruction level is painstaking at best. It's easy to lose track of bits, frustrating to retype code, and tedious to construct database records and fields. Essay 5 examines features of Microsoft's Macro Assembler (MASM) version 5.0 from the standpoint of using names to set up and control bits within a byte and bytes and words within data structures. It explores the uses of directives, Macros and subroutines (and when each is appropriate), how to handle hardware interrupts, and more.

Section Two: Programming Tools and Techniques

While Microsoft and IBM have discouraged use of many "undocumented" services within the operating system, the programming community has relied on just those services to push performance to the limits. Essays in this section focus on how to work with the operating system itself.

Undocumented MS-DOS Functions

Essay 6 explains the Program Segment Prefix (PSP), a data structure that MS-DOS creates and loads as a header to .COM and .EXE programs. It then shows how to: use file handles to customize redirection; access and manipulate the environment segment from batch files; use PSP function calls from within TSRs; allocate and deallocate memory; inspect the Memory Control Block chain; and get MS-DOS busy flag, switch char, DOS variables, and more.

Safe Memory-Resident Programming (TSR)

Terminate and Stay Resident (TSR) programs (known to many users as "popups") have come into respectability despite their use of undocumented functions. Essay 7 discusses the skills of safe TSR design that have become a staple in many working programmers' bags of tricks. It begins with a history of TSRs in CP/M, 86-DOS, and MS-DOS, then describes problems in handling hardware and software interrupts, noting differences between INT 27H (terminate but stay resident interrupt, originally used in 86-DOS), INT 21H Function 31H (Keep Process Call, first used in MS-DOS 2.X), and INT 2FH (Multiplex Interrupt, developed in MS-DOS 3.X). Also included is discussion of how to use INT 21H Function 34H (IN_DOS Flag Call), INT 28H (background process function), and INT 21H Function 50H (how to save the PSP of the foreground program), all of which allow multiple TSRs to exist in memory. Finally, there is an examination of the TSRs provided with MS-DOS: GRAPHICS, ASSIGN, and PRINT utilities. You'll also find a TSR to toggle the print screen function and a review of the newest Microsoft TSR guidelines.

Data Protection and Encryption

Data protection, meaning protecting your data from loss or unauthorized encroachment, is often ignored by the application programmer or implemented as an afterthought. Essay 8 provides a complete tutorial on MS-DOS data security programming techniques. You see how each programmer can hide data by using nonstandard names and characters, by using an assembly language program to toggle the hidden attribute, and by using the read-only attribute. The author shows how to use a password protection scheme in the AUTOEXEC.BAT file, in a device driver, installed on an add-on card, or with a TSR to capture INT 21H calls to verify password status. Finally we see how to encrypt the data itself by using code book, keytape, and DES and RSA key algorithm systems.

Inside Microsoft Windows

The Microsoft Windows operating environment, after several years of development, extends MS-DOS functionality into the complex and powerful realm of multitasking and windowing similar to the Macintosh and OS/2 systems. Essay 9 introduces the major programming concepts of MS Windows, messages, and queues that make for an event-driven, modeless environment. It illustrates the message stream from the mouse, keyboard, and other software sources and shows how to use Windows functions to manipulate that stream. It explains new concepts and terms such as overlapping and popup windows, child windows, classes, coordinate systems, regions, memory management including global and local heaps, resources, and the new Windows functions that are associated. It also presents complete explanation and source code for an examination utility that traces through running Windows applications and reports back details on their behavior and resources.

Section Three: Working with the Hardware Interface

The five essays in this section focus on controlling the hardware environment and extracting the maximum speed from RAM memory, board-level registers, and MS-DOS services.

Developing MS-DOS Device Drivers

Device drivers are the critical software between custom hardware and applications that run under the operating system. The key to programming successful device drivers lies in knowing what MS-DOS services come into play and how they work. The trouble is this involves nearly all MS-DOS kernel internal structures, which makes a tangle of relationships and a need for a half-dozen books, tables, and manuals. Essay 10 presents all the workings of these MS-DOS data structures: stacks, the System File Table, File Control Blocks and file handles,

Device Control Blocks, Current Directory Structure, Program Segment Prefix with the device driver strategy, and interrupt structures. The author uses a small applications program that simply lists a file at the console to exemplify the basic kernel behavior. As the essay progresses, the author shows such details as checking both the IN_DOS flag and the critical error flag to avoid disrupting non-reentrant procedures, using file handles instead of the File Control Block, using IOCTL requests, and more.

Writing a SOUND Device Driver

Following the previous essay on device driver theory, Essay 11 explains the operation of a real-world device driver that lets an operator use the PC for manipulating tones, sounds, and special effects. This sophisticated driver mimics the BASIC PLAY statement down to its detailed command language. The driver code depends upon such computer science concepts as circular buffers, coroutines, finite state machines, and more. In its simplest form, you can create a file composed of commands for the driver, then COPY the file to the driver. With just a small amount of additional code, you can open the device from within an application, then write to it, thus playing a tune from within your spreadsheet, word processor, data capture application, or whatever. The essay concludes with a complete listing for a driver named SOUND.

Programming the Enhanced Graphics Adapter

The resolution offered by the Enhanced Graphics Adapter (EGA) is the current preferred standard for color displays. But program control of the EGA is markedly different from that of its predecessors, especially in the way in which one keeps track of writes and rewrites to the registers. Essay 12 begins with a thorough discussion of the EGA, its registers, and its latches. After showing how to use macros to control the bit mask and map mask, the author presents a very fast line-drawing routine based on Bresenham's algorithm, a macro PEEK and POKE directive, a hard-to-find dithering algorithm for a laser printer, and more techniques to write colored images to the screen. The author also shows how to read the EGA memory and how to use the EGA's data rotate register to perform Boolean operations on the EGA bit maps.

Programming the Serial Port with C

The serial port has become overloaded with peripherals—mice, pads, and cameras, as well as modems and printers. It is no wonder that control of the serial port is a chief target of concern of hardware programmers. Essay 13 begins with a complete, fast-moving overview of the conventions of serial data flow and shows how to control the serial port hardware, including the UART and a modem. The discussion covers error-checking, flow control, buffers, and use of the 8259 to manage the serial adapter interrupts, and ends with discussion of a circular data buffer. Finally, the author offers an explanation of commented source code in C for a complete communications package.

Understanding Expanded Memory Systems

Expanded memory systems depend on a scheme of switching various banks of memory in and out of the 640K MS-DOS main memory address structure defined by MS-DOS. The bank-switching process is controlled by a driver called the Enhanced Memory Manager (EMM) designed by Lotus, Intel, and Microsoft. Essay 14 shows how the EMM behaves and notes differences between the three existing systems: Expanded Memory Specification (EMS) version 3.2, EEMS (the extra E for Enhanced), and EMS version 4. The essay begins with a discussion of bank-switching and the genesis of EMS. It then shows two ways to test for the presence of an EMS device. The first uses Function 3DH (open file or driver-request) specifying the guaranteed name, EMMXXXX0, then uses subfunctions of Function 44H to check further. The second uses INT 67H to check for the ASCII string of that same guaranteed name. The author includes a table of error codes, a summary of relevant functions for both EMS 3.2 and EEMS, a simple eight-step strategy for using EMS, and much more.

Disks Available

Some authors are offering disks with source code; ordering information is given at the end of Essays 3, 8, 11, and 13.

Inside the Book

Each essay begins with a synopsis and a list of keywords, and ends with a biography of the author and a list of related essays. As noted earlier, within each essay, where appropriate, you will find references to other essays. The purpose is for you to determine your own reading path through the book.

We suggest that you begin with the first essay, "A Guided Tour inside MS-DOS" (by our editor Harry Henderson). In this essay, Harry mentions all the other essays within the book as he explores the internal operations of the MS-DOS operating system. From there you can jump to essays that meet your interests.

EXTENDING THE MS-DOS USER INTERFACE

The MS-DOS operating system, depending on which version you may be using, provides roughly two dozen internal commands that allow only the most elementary inspection and manipulation of files and directories. Its accompanying utility programs, otherwise known as the external commands, provide sufficient power for necessary housekeeping, but in a painfully inelegant manner. Using the MS-DOS system by itself, a programmer must work slowly, chore by chore. At the operator level, the MS-DOS operating system provides just enough capability to load and run application programs and store their files. It seemed like a good system at first, but most active users have outstripped it, as a youngster outgrows a pair of pants.

Working programmers, especially, must develop a flexible set of tools to manage complex file relationships and to invoke a rapid succession of utilities. Most programmers have developed a colorful mix of third-party patches—some of their own invention, some from bulletin boards, and some from the pages of magazines—to fill the gaps of a user interface that seems increasingly inadequate. The artful use of batch files shows the skill with which inventive minds can bootstrap the limitations of the batch file commands. An inspection of an extensive `CONFIG.SYS` file reveals the soul of system flexibility with a list of names that are as technical and arbitrary as the cards that sit in the internal slots of the machine.

This section of *MS-DOS Papers* contains five essays illustrating the authors' creations for improving the limited features of the MS-DOS user interface.

A Guided Tour inside MS-DOS

The first essay, by Harry Henderson, introduces you to the inner structure of MS-DOS. It is a rare overview with suggestions for increasing user-level speed and functionality. The author also includes many references to all the other essays, thereby tying together the entire book.

Searching the File Tree with `whereis`

In the second essay of this section, Frank Whaley explains how he created a powerful file and subdirectory finder, `whereis`, written in C, that lets you search, match, and manipulate files using MS-DOS commands.

Adding UNIX Power with PCnix

Ed Nather presents a wild set of utilities and routines that provide an expansive UNIX-like environment, with command editing, file and directory manipulation, and a running commentary explaining a slightly topsy-turvy view of the MS-DOS interrupt and function scheme.

Adding Power to MS-DOS Programming

The fourth essay, by Doug Adams, presents a quick overview tutorial of the use of the Extended Batch Language (EBL) utility and C libraries that streamline mundane programmer's chores such as the creation of menus, windows, indexed files, and more.

Advanced MASM Techniques

In the fifth essay, Michael Goldman shows us tricks to using MASM 5.0 labels, directives, and macros to reduce bit-level errors and speed data constructs as well as to handle hardware interrupts.

Keywords

► user interface

► MS-DOS kernel

► BIOS

► MS-DOS file system

► programming environments

► commands and utilities

Essay Synopsis: MS-DOS has three basic parts: a user interface (normally provided by `COMMAND.COM`), a system kernel containing data structures and function calls needed by programmers, and a hardware-oriented BIOS. This essay points out the significant features of MS-DOS at each of these levels, and highlights the strengths and weaknesses of each for power users and programmers. MS-DOS is more than just an operating system, however. It is also an environment that can be expanded and customized by the addition of new shells, utility programs, programming environments, and device drivers. This essay shows how these products can be used to overcome many of the shortcomings of MS-DOS, and explores current and future trends in MS-DOS use and programming.

A Guided Tour
inside MS-DOS

Harry Henderson

MS-DOS has many faces—like the fabled elephant, it can look very different depending on one's point of view. Users need to be able to configure their environment, set up their applications programs and programming tools, and manage megabytes worth of directories and files. Applications programmers must learn how to use the many MS-DOS system services that their programs need to manage system resources. Many of these services are poorly documented, and many rely on an understanding of internal DOS tables or data structures. Systems programmers need to write device drivers to enable programs to use a new printer or mass storage device. In addition, programmers frequently need to learn specialized programming interfaces such as those for the serial port, Enhanced Graphics Adapter (EGA), Expanded Memory Specification (EMS), or Microsoft Windows.

The Challenge of Change

MS-DOS programmers live in a complicated and ever-changing world. Those who want to be competitive must keep one eye on today's needs and the other on those of the future. Consider the life cycle of a simple application program. Beginning as one programmer's "quick and dirty" tool for performing some calculations, the program is given to a team whose mission is to turn it into a commercial product. The original program provided only a text display, but the marketing department convinces the programmers that there is a demand for color graphics. The IBM Color Graphics Adapter (CGA) display doesn't provide enough resolution or colors for most graphic needs, however, so it's time to learn how to program the EGA.

   The first version of the product is marketed. Users quickly request more features—such as the ability to move from writing a report to calculating a spreadsheet to consulting a database, with instant access to any or all of these features. Now we have an "integrated software package," but the users are complaining that the program takes up too much memory and doesn't allow them to run their favorite memory-resident utilities. It's time to learn how to break the "640K barrier" imposed by DOS, by using EMS to handle larger amounts of data and conserve precious space in main memory. Next, the users say they want Post-Script output and the ability to use a new laser printer. Oh, and by the way, larger customers are starting to ask when the network version will be ready. It's time to learn everything about device drivers.

Now the program is powerful but it's hard to use. Perhaps it should be re-written to run in the Microsoft Windows environment, and provide a graphic user interface, and update the spreadsheet every time a change is made in the database . . .

Overall Structure of MS-DOS

Before we can find out how to improve MS-DOS and our programming environment, we have to understand its design and the way its parts fit together.

There are three modules that make up MS-DOS: the user shell, the system kernel, and the hardware interfaces, including the Basic Input-Output System (BIOS) routines.

MS-DOS is, at bottom, a program loader and file handler with roots in the CP/M operating system developed in the late 1970s. MS-DOS has, of course, become much more than that after going through two major (and numerous minor) revisions since Microsoft and IBM first made it available in 1982. It has had to accommodate hard disks and other new storage media, RAM disks, new display standards, mice, memory-resident programs, expanded memory, and networks, to mention just a few of the developments.

The most important aspect of the structure of MS-DOS is its modularity. The division of MS-DOS into three parts—a command processor, a system kernel, and a hardware-specific BIOS—is what has made it possible to add features in response to the development of new hardware, and to accommodate the differences in the underlying hardware of PC clones and compatibles. Because only the BIOS module is hardware-dependent, the user interface and system kernel do not have to be revised to accommodate new hardware.

MS-DOS contains a standard character-oriented user interface that is similar to those found on most mainframe operating systems. Because this interface is a separate module, however, it can be replaced or supplemented with a different one such as Microsoft Windows or a UNIX-like shell.

The MS-DOS kernel contains the compiled code for the internal services (such as file management and I/O) needed to execute both MS-DOS commands and applications programs. This kernel is essentially hardware-independent, so a hardware vendor does not need to rewrite it to get MS-DOS to run on a new machine. Furthermore, the installation of new devices requires only that a device driver be written and linked into a list of drivers maintained by the kernel.

Finally, the BIOS contains the hardware-specific code, the code that deals with devices on a low level. Because the hardware details are hidden from the rest of the operating system, additions at the BIOS level make it possible to add support for new devices, such as hard disk support in MS-DOS 2.X and support for 720K 3½″ floppies in MS-DOS 3.2, without having to make extensive changes to services in the kernel.

System Files and DOS Modules

The MS-DOS distribution disk provides the operating system itself in the form of three files that correspond to the three modules or interfaces that we have mentioned:

▶ COMMAND.COM, a program that provides the standard MS-DOS user interface and a prompt, and interprets user commands

▶ MSDOS.SYS, the MS-DOS kernel with many services that is called upon by application programs and provides the applications interface (this level is invisible to the user)

▶ IO.SYS, containing the BIOS with hardware-specific code, including a collection of built-in device drivers (some or all may be stored in ROM)

In IBM PC-DOS, the kernel is called IBMDOS.COM and the BIOS is called IBMBIO.COM.

How has the development of new versions of MS-DOS affected the three DOS modules or interfaces? It is interesting to compare two significant revisions of MS-DOS in order to see what has grown and by how much (see Table 1-1).

Table 1-1.   Comparison of Two MS-DOS Revisions

Module	DOS 2.0	DOS 3.3
Size of System Files		
COMMAND.COM	17664	25307
IBMDOS.COM	4608	22100
IBMBIO.COM	17152	30159
Total	39424	77566
Number of External Commands		
	23	35

PC-DOS 2.0 was the first "modern" version of MS-DOS, with such features as a hierarchical tree-structured system of directories and subdirectories, hard disk support, and installable device drivers. Its generic equivalent, MS-DOS 2.11, has been the operating system normally distributed with PC compatibles. MS-DOS 3.0 and the minor revisions that followed added support for new media types (the 1.2MB AT disk, and then 3½" 720K and 1.44MB disks) and for networking. It also added several useful new utility commands.

The table shows that the size of the user interface code COMMAND.COM has grown by roughly 50 percent, that of the kernel IBMDOS.COM has exploded by about five times, and that of the BIOS has nearly doubled. The number of external commands has also grown by about 50 percent.

It is hard to draw precise conclusions from this byte length comparison because, for example, a significant improvement between versions at the user interface level might be reflected mainly by addition of certain system services in the kernel or the development of special-purpose external programs rather than by an increase in the size of COMMAND.COM itself. Nevertheless, the table does reflect what has been the general experience of MS-DOS users: although the operating system has grown considerably in size in moving from the 2.X level to the 3.X level, most new features have been in the areas of internal routines (system services in the kernel) and in special device support. There has not been much added to user interface, batch processing capabilities, or external utility commands.

DOS Startup and Configuration

The best way to begin to understand how the modules that make up MS-DOS work is to go through the highlights of what happens when the system is booted or started up. You will see that by the time you see A> on your screen, MS-DOS has already been hard at work. It has installed itself in several parts of memory, created many important data structures, configured system resources, and installed several device drivers. (See Essay 10, Developing MS-DOS Device Drivers, by Walter Dixon, for more detailed information on the MS-DOS boot process.)

From the user point of view, MS-DOS is a series of layers going down from the user interface to the kernel and then the BIOS. The boot process goes in the opposite direction, however, from the most hardware-specific operations below even the BIOS all the way up to the user prompt level. Figure 1-1 is a schematic of the overall process.

In the IBM PC and most other MS-DOS systems, once the built-in ROM hardware-checking routines (the POST or Power On Self Test) finishes running, *bootstrap* code in ROM triggers the loading process. This code "knows" just enough about the disk to try to read first drive A:, sector 1, track 0, referred to as the *boot sector* in MS-DOS. If there is no disk in drive A: (which is typical of many systems today), it tries to read the same location on the hard disk, drive C:.

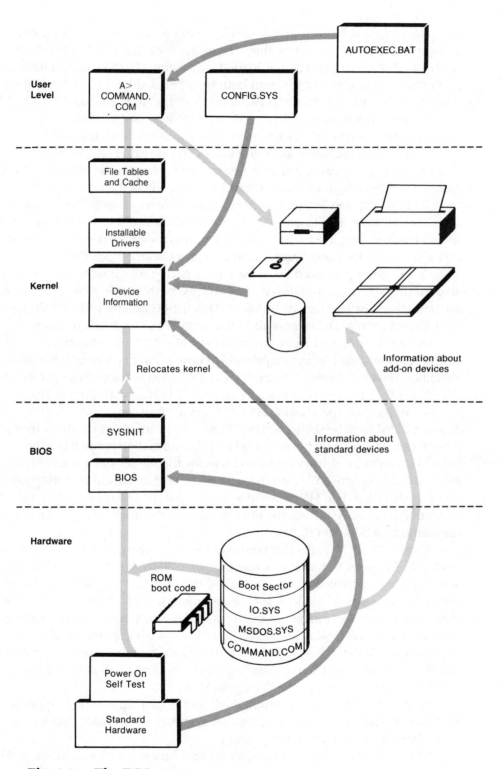

Fig. 1-1.   The DOS startup process.

The code that has now been read from the boot sector enables the loading process to continue. Assuming they are in the root directory of the boot disk, IO.SYS and then MSDOS.SYS are loaded. (In some MS-DOS implementations, IO.SYS loads MSDOS.SYS rather than both being loaded by the boot sector code.) The IO.SYS file actually contains two modules: the BIOS and SYSINIT. The BIOS contains the built-in device drivers that allow standard communications with the computer's keyboard, screen, printer, serial ports, and disk drives.

SYSINIT is responsible for a number of coordinating efforts. First, it determines the configuration of available memory and relocates the DOS kernel so that it goes down from high memory. Second, it calls code in the now loaded MS-DOS kernel MSDOS.SYS that builds important data structures or tables MS-DOS will need in order to be able to use devices correctly. Each of the resident device drivers is initialized, and, in turn, returns information about the device that is put into a data structure for each device called a Device Control Block (DCB).

DCBs make up a linked list (a list where each item contains the starting address of the next item), and the starting address of this list is recorded in a global list (sometimes called the List of Lists). This list eventually will contain further information such as the largest allowable sector size for block devices.

Once the built-in drivers are initialized, SYSINIT will attempt to read the CONFIG.SYS file. This file, as you probably know, contains user specifications for installable device drivers—drivers that can be added to those already resident in MS-DOS. These drivers are normally contained in files with the .SYS extension. If, for example, you specify DEVICE=VDISK.SYS in your CONFIG.SYS file, the virtual disk (RAM disk) will be set up. SYSINIT then collects information about the available devices. As an installable driver is loaded, information about it is added to the linked list of device drivers that also includes the names of built-in drivers. Tables for tracking active files and the structure of the current directory are also set up at this time. The MS-DOS cache (buffer for file I/O) is also set up based on information obtained during the boot process as modified by any user BUFFERS= command found in CONFIG.SYS.

Finally, SYSINIT loads the command interpreter, or shell, normally COM-MAND.COM. (If there is a SHELL= statement in CONFIG.SYS, the specified shell is loaded instead of COMMAND.COM. The size of the DOS "environment" is also determined by the value found in a SHELL= statement in CONFIG.SYS or set to the default. The DOS environment consists of a number of standard variables such as PATH, which we will look at later, as well as room for user-specified variables such as those used in batch files. Finally, any AUTOEXEC.BAT file is executed. Entries in this file are commonly used to install memory-resident programs and sometimes to start a session with a particular application.

Once all of this is accomplished, either an application specified in AUTOEXEC.BAT has been started and is now running, or COMMAND.COM alone is running, showing the familiar DOS prompt.

The startup process tells us several important things about MS-DOS. First, the process moves from the hardware-specific level (ROM code, absolute disk sectors, and so on) through the installation of the standard MS-DOS drivers and then to user-installable drivers. We thus move from the necessary and built-in components to the optional and flexible add-ons such as user-supplied device drivers. Next, MS-DOS, as part of the startup process, "learns" many important things about the system, and sets up data structures to hold both this information and information that will be obtained in subsequent operations. Finally, these structures are flexible enough that any device that can provide the required information via a driver can be "hooked in" to the system.

Now we will look at the top of the iceberg that has emerged from our startup process—the user level—in more detail.

The User Level

The user interface or shell is the MS-DOS module that is responsible for accepting, interpreting, and acting upon the command lines typed at the keyboard by the user. Every operating system has to communicate with the user, and much of our time is spent dealing with the user interface. It is thus worthwhile to see if we can improve the interface so we can get more work done more easily. Remember, programmers are users whenever they type an MS-DOS command to change directories or delete a file.

For each command line, the shell must figure out what command or program is to be run, what files it is to use, and what options have been specified. It must then load the program, provide it with the required information, run the program, and return ready to execute the next command.

COMMAND.COM: The Standard MS-DOS Shell

As we noted earlier, the standard MS-DOS interface is provided by a program called COMMAND.COM. This program is called a *shell* because it (metaphorically) surrounds the operating system proper (the kernel and BIOS layers) and is the means by which users can give commands to be run. Any time we see the user prompt (such as A>, COMMAND.COM is running. We will now look at how user commands are processed.

Finding Commands and Programs

Figure 1-2 provides a schematic of how COMMAND.COM responds to commands. We will suppose we have just typed CD. COMMAND.COM first parses (breaks into significant parts) the command line and then attempts to load and run the item specified, which can be any one of the following:

- ➤ an internal MS-DOS command (for example, `DIR`)
- ➤ a `.COM` program
- ➤ an `.EXE` program
- ➤ a `.BAT` (batch) file

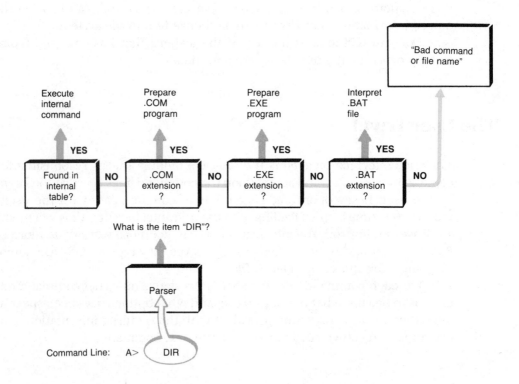

Fig. 1-2.   How `COMMAND.COM` responds to commands.

`COMMAND.COM` looks for the name of the item within a table within its code to see if it is an internal command. The routines for executing internal commands are included in `COMMAND.COM` itself—in memory so they are executed quickly just by jumping to the appropriate routine. In the case of our example command line, since `CD` is an internal MS-DOS command, it is found in the table. Since we didn't type any filenames or options on the command line, the `DIR` command can be run right away. Many MS-DOS command lines are more complicated, however. If the item is not found in the table, it is assumed to be something external to `COMMAND.COM`—an external command, an application program, or a batch file. In this case, `COMMAND.COM` searches the disk drives for `.COM` programs, then `.EXE` programs, and finally `.BAT` files. The search begins in the current drive and directory unless the program's path (directory location) is specified on the command line. Additional drives and directories are searched if they have been specified as part of the search path. The ability to specify a search path is an important feature because it would be very inefficient for MS-DOS to have to search through dozens of directories on several drives in search of a particular program. By using the SET PATH command to give a sequence of drives and directories to be searched, the user can specify that the most frequently used directories be searched first, making the process much more efficient. Most MS-DOS users therefore specify their PATH in the AUTOEXEC.BAT file.

If the item is found in one of the directories on the search path, COMMAND.COM sets up the environment needed to load and run the program (more on this later). If the program is not found, the user sees the familiar message Bad command or file name.

Organizing Resources

The PATH variable gives MS-DOS more flexibility by telling it how the user has arranged resources (programs). It solves only part of the problem, however, because "resources" also include the data (source code, documents, spreadsheets, databases, or whatever) the user wants to work with. Indeed, as users, we are really saying to ourselves, "now I want to revise this letter," not, "now I'll run WordPerfect." The MS-DOS path, however, is searched only for executable program or batch files, not the data files to be used with our applications. Later versions of MS-DOS provide the APPEND command in an attempt to help track data files, but MS-DOS has not yet developed a coherent way of looking at resources. There is no linkage, for example, between a document and the word processor that was used to create it.

Many software designers feel that users are more comfortable when abstractions such as files and directories are represented by physical objects (icons) that can be moved around. Examples of this approach to accessing resources, graphical interfaces such as those used by the Macintosh or provided by Microsoft Windows, have emerged as an alternative to the traditional command-line interface. Linking of needed files (but not the use of icons) is also offered to programmers in an integrated programming environment such as the Borland Turbo or Microsoft Quick languages, where the files needed to edit, compile, and link a program are brought together automatically. Such links could be implemented in a revision of the standard command-line interface, however, and future add-on utilities might offer them.

Parsing, Expansion, and Redirection

Besides figuring out what command or other program is to be executed, COMMAND.COM also parses the remainder of the command line and uses the specifications found there to find matching filenames and to specify a program's input and output. For example, consider this command line:

```
DIR C:\TABLE? | SORT > LIST
```

The internal `DIR` command is given the file specification `C:\TABLE?` and run. Because a *wildcard* character `?` is used in the file specification (pathname), `COM-MAND.COM` searches the specified directory and passes to the `DIR` command all filenames that consist of `TABLE` plus any one other letter. In other words, the compact pathname with wildcards is "expanded" so that it represents all matching file or path names.

Besides expanding wildcards, `COMMAND.COM` also looks for symbols that tell it to redirect input and output from their normal channels. The `¦` or *pipe* symbol is conceptually a pipeline (connection) between two operations (the internal `DIR` command and the external `SORT` command in our example) so that the output of the first operation becomes the input to the second. (Redirection and piping were implemented starting with MS-DOS 2.0.) In our example, first `COMMAND.COM` redirects the output of `DIR` from the default standard output (the screen) to a temporary pipe file. `DIR` then generates its output, which is put in the pipe file. `SORT` then runs with its input redirected to take data from the pipe file. The `>` (greater than) symbol following `SORT` causes `COMMAND.COM` to redirect the output of this command to the file `LIST`. (The distinction here is that piping connects a program with another program, while redirection with the `>` and `<` operators directs the output or input respectively to a file.)

Finally, `COMMAND.COM` also looks on the command line for *option switches*, and makes them available to the program to be run. For example, the command `DIR /w` means "print a directory listing in wide (multicolumn) format." This facility is not limited to MS-DOS commands, however. When any program is run, MS-DOS constructs a block of data called the Program Segment Prefix (PSP) and puts the remainder of the command line that invoked it (that is, everything but the program name itself) into the PSP, so any program can access its command line and check for option specifications. PSP is called a prefix because it consists of the first 256 bytes of the 64K segment that either contains or begins the program code. Figure 1-3 summarizes the steps that `COMMAND.COM` takes in parsing the command line and preparing to load the specified program.

These features benefit programmers and power users in several ways. Most programming languages support redirection and piping, so it is easy to write *filter* programs that perform useful chores such as stripping out the high bits in WordStar files. Several filters can be connected together with pipes, which allows the programs to be used in whatever combination or order makes sense. The ability of MS-DOS to pass command-line parameters or switches to a program enables the desired behavior of each tool to be specified when it is used in a command or batch file.

When combined with the batch file facility, filename expansion, redirection, piping, and command-line options allow quite a lot of work to be done automatically—compiling, linking, and running a program, or processing text files in converting between formats.

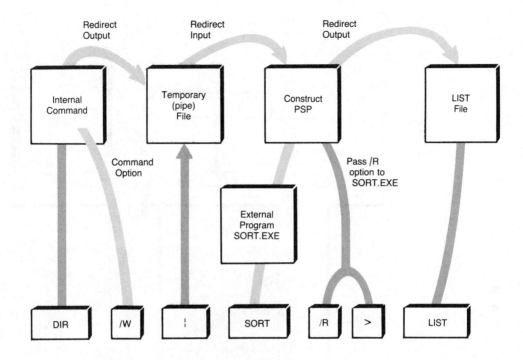

Fig. 1-3.   Command-line parsing.

There are some shortcomings to these command-line features, however. One of the most annoying is that most commands will not accept multiple filenames. For example, you can't say, `del *.bak *.old temp?`. Nor can you specify several commands on the same command line, except when joining them with a pipe. Additionally, the support for wildcards is not uniform throughout the MS-DOS command set. For example, you can't say `type report?` to list `report1` through `report9`. In general, the revisers of MS-DOS have paid much more atten- tion to adding new commands than they have to increasing the utility and con- sistency of the existing ones. We will look at some possible ways to improve this situation later.

Program Execution

Once `COMMAND.COM` finishes parsing the command line, the specified program must be loaded and run (see Figure 1-4). `COMMAND.COM` actually has two parts: a permanent part and a temporary part. The permanent or resident part contains code that monitors for user interrupts (breaks), critical errors, and for a signal indicating that the current program has terminated. It also contains code that is used to load the temporary or transient part of `COMMAND.COM` back into memory. The transient part contains all of the rest of `COMMAND.COM`—the command-line parser, batch file facility, internal commands, and so on.

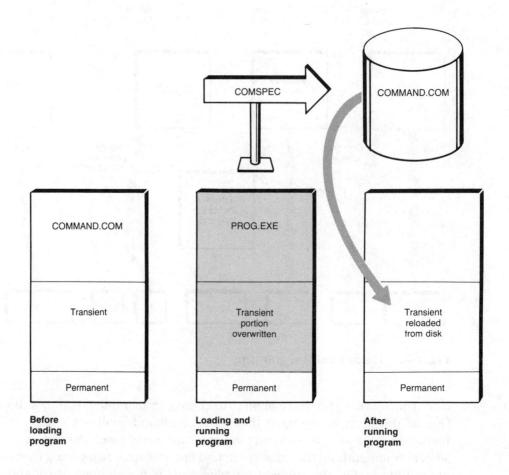

Fig. 1-4. **How COMMAND.COM runs a program.**

Thus, when a program is run, it is loaded into upper memory where it frequently overwrites part of COMMAND.COM's transient portion. When the program is terminated, the resident portion does a checksum in order to find out if the transient portion is intact. If it is not, a fresh copy is loaded from disk. (The variable COMSPEC can be used to tell COMMAND.COM where to look for it.) In floppy-based systems, this sometimes requires disk swapping after running an application.

The reason for having only a minimal part of the shell in permanent residence goes back to the fact that, in its earliest incarnation, MS-DOS had to run on machines that had only 64K of memory. If all of COMMAND.COM were kept in memory, the amount of memory available to application programs would be correspondingly reduced. Since the size of the user interface continues to grow and applications tend to want all available memory, this feature is probably still useful.

Running Multiple Shells

Note that COMMAND.COM itself, since it is actually "just a program," can be run like any other program from an existing copy of COMMAND.COM. Thus at the DOS prompt, you can type command /c dir and get a directory. The /c is a switch that tells the new COMMAND.COM to execute the rest of the line as a command. The real use of this, however, is to have a batch file run another batch file. (In DOS 3.3, there is a CALL statement that provides a more straightforward way to do this.) You can also have an applications program run a batch file by using a system call (the EXEC function), to invoke a new COMMAND.COM with the appropriate command line placed in memory.

Batch Processing

Another powerful feature of MS-DOS is the ability to put a series of command lines in a batch file that can be executed by naming it, in the same way an MS-DOS command or other program is run. Indeed, a batch file is a program consisting of MS-DOS command lines and some rudimentary branching and control structures. Batch files are typically used for such tasks as configuring the system at startup, installing new software, and assembling or compiling programs. The power user columns of popular PC magazines are filled with batch files that perform a number of other chores such as setting a serial port or printer. Because they are ordinary text files, batch files can be created with whatever editor is handy.

Much of the power of batch files comes from the fact that they can be given general placeholders that can be filled in from the command line when the batch file is called. For example, if a batch file called BACKIT.BAT contains the line COPY %1 %1.BAK, typing BACKIT LETTER results in the command COPY LETTER LETTER.BAK being executed.

Unfortunately, the MS-DOS batch facility, despite the creative uses to which it has been put, is very limited as a programming language. There is an IF but no ELSE, for example. There is a FOR statement, but it accepts only lists and is not able to use a counter. Long batch files (such as those used to install software) are hard to read and maintain because of the lack of good control structures and the inability to use subroutines. In addition, the MS-DOS batch-processing language has no facility for performing arithmetic, doing anything other than a literal comparison to a string, or even for getting input (other than pausing for a key-press) from the user.

There are several approaches that can be taken to improve MS-DOS batch processing. One is to write short utilities that can extend the versatility of the batch facility. (See Essay 3, Adding UNIX Power with PCnix, by Edward Nather, which describes the use of batch files to implement UNIX-style utilities in

MS-DOS. He also describes batch file helpers—short programs that can, for example, check user input in a batch file.)

Another place to look for more power and ease in batch programming is among the many menu-generation programs, some of which are public domain or shareware. These programs allow you to set up a nested series of menus to guide beginning users, and, in some cases, include batch facilities as well.

A more comprehensive solution is a product called EBL (Extended Batch Language) that provides the many features missing in the MS-DOS batch language, yet is compatible with regular DOS batch files. This is a shareware product available on many bulletin boards. (See Essay 4, Adding Power to MS-DOS Programming, by Doug Adams, for a detailed overview of EBL with examples.)

Finally, there are a number of products that provide implementations of UNIX shells for MS-DOS, offering what is, in effect, a general-purpose macro programming language. (The Korn shell, `ksh`, is the most comprehensive one.) UNIX shells offer programmers more (and more flexible) variables, better control structures, and many more conditions that can be tested. Such shells are definitely more complex than `COMMAND.COM`, but this will not dismay people who are already programmers or power users of MS-DOS. The UNIX shells for MS-DOS vary in quality. The best I have found is in a product called the MKS Toolkit. It provides a very full implementation of the new UNIX Korn shell with many UNIX utilities besides. This product is compatible with the rest of the MS-DOS environment, including memory-resident programs. It can be run either instead of `COMMAND.COM` or from it.

The MS-DOS File System

Readers of this book are likely to be quite familiar with the use of pathnames, directories, and subdirectories to navigate among files under MS-DOS. Of course, it is not easy for even a power user to type a pathname like `c:\c5\bin\graphics\ega` without errors. The significant milestone in the MS-DOS file system was the implementation of a tree-structured (hierarchical) file structure starting with MS-DOS 2.0. Such a system of directories and subdirectories was, of course, made necessary by the advent of hard disks with space for hundreds of files. The syntax used is very similar to that of UNIX, except that MS-DOS uses \ to separate parts of a file path, while UNIX uses /. On the other hand, MS-DOS uses / for command options, while UNIX uses -. This is a continuing frustration to people who use both operating systems daily. (See Essay 3, Adding UNIX Power with PCnix, by Edward Nather, for a discussion of ways to modify MS-DOS to accept the UNIX conventions.)

The difficulty many people have in visualizing their place in the file tree has led to a number of developments. Numerous commercial DOS shells (which are not really shells, since they don't replace `COMMAND.COM`) offer users a graphic depiction of their file structure and easy selection of files for inspection, copying, or removal. More radically, graphic environments that follow the Macintosh philosophy (such as GEM and MS Windows) replace directories and subdirectories with folders. These are designed to be more intuitive, especially for beginning users, but some graphic interfaces (notably that of the Macintosh) do not allow one to use command lines where appropriate. A command line using wildcards enables us to act globally (on a whole set of files or a directory) with a single command.

Another shortcoming that is keenly felt by most MS-DOS users is the limitation of filenames to eight characters plus a three-character extension. One wonders how many person-hours have been lost trying to come up with a way to name a document so that you can find it again without having to examine other similar files. One solution is to use several layers of subdirectories to specify the meaning of a name by its position in the hierarchy. In other words, since you can't use `report.income.1987.fall`, you can use `\reports\income\1987\fall`. Although there are times when such an organization makes sense conceptually (perhaps if you have many similar files), it usually substitutes the problem of directory navigation mentioned earlier for the problem of incomprehensible filenames. Disappointingly, there appears to be no provision in planned new releases of MS-DOS or OS/2 to allow longer filenames.

As usual, the market has responded to users' needs, however—in this case, by providing MS-DOS shell or file manager programs (often memory-resident) that allow you to associate a longer name or phrase (or keywords) with a filename. When your application asks you for a filename, you can pop up the utility and use it to find the right name and then invoke the application.

Going beyond these relatively superficial problems, the MS-DOS file system also suffers from a structural problem. Conceptually, one should be able to get from any part of the file tree to another, simply by searching recursively. In this case, recursive searching means searching the first directory, then searching any subdirectories in that directory, searching each of *its* subdirectories, and so on. Indeed, MS-DOS provides system functions that allow programs to navigate through the directory hierarchy, but the user commands generally aren't recursive. That is, they can't operate on the current directory and all its subdirectories and all *their* subdirectories. You can't, for example, copy or delete a directory and all of its subdirectories in the way you can in UNIX. (MS-DOS 3.2 provides a new command called `xcopy` that is recursive and copies subdirectories, however.)

While it can be argued that such recursion increases the chances of accidents, it is needed to take full advantage of the file system structure. MS-DOS has most of the pieces of the needed facility. For example, starting with DOS 2.0, MS-DOS provides a command called `tree` that displays the directory tree starting at a specified point. Unfortunately, there is no command that will search through this tree and show you the path to a specified file. Nor is there a command in standard MS-DOS that allows you to find matching files in the tree and

apply an MS-DOS command to them (for example, to find the file `REPORT8` somewhere in the depths of your `ACCOUNTS` directory and `TYPE` it to the screen, or to
`DELETE` all files with the extension `.BAK` regardless of their position in the hierarchy). In UNIX, this function is performed by the powerful `find` command,
which is not to be confused with the MS-DOS `FIND` command. The latter doesn't
find files, but rather finds words *in* a file.

Again, enterprising programmers have come to the user's rescue by providing a utility that will find matching files anywhere in the file tree, and optionally
apply an MS-DOS command to them. (See Essay 2, Searching the File Tree with
`whereis`, by Frank Whaley, for a very complete implementation of this utility.)

Strategies for Improving the User Interface

A "better" interface means two things that are often hard to reconcile: more
powerful and easier to use. Figure 1-5 shows stylized learning curves for three
environments: "classic" MS-DOS, the Macintosh-style interface, and UNIX. Each
plots power along the vertical axis and ease of learning and use along the horizontal. (These are not meant to be exact quantifications.)

Classic MS-DOS has a pretty steep learning curve that eventually levels off
as the user learns features. Unfortunately, the power also levels off quickly due
to the systemic shortcomings of elements such as the batch-processing and file
systems and the lack of commands for many functions.

The Macintosh-style interface offers a more shallow learning curve (it is easier to learn) and a higher initial level of power, but the power does not grow significantly over time. It is a bit like the hare and the tortoise: on the average, as a Mac
user, you will be able to do much more with the operating system in the first
couple of months than will the MS-DOS (or UNIX) user, but the lack of global commands and batch processing means that you will not be able to do much more in
the operating system after six months than you were able to do after one.

Finally, UNIX offers a learning curve that tends to remain fairly steep, but
with power that continues to increase. The MS-DOS power user who obtains a
UNIX-style shell and utilities may be able to accomplish many things the other
two kinds of users cannot, though any shell scripts created cannot be run on
another system without also providing a copy of the shell (and probably other
programs).

It should be clear that there is a place for both the easy-to-learn graphical
interface and the power user's command-line interface. Fortunately, both are
available today. With the use of a product such as Microsoft Windows, a user can
have access to both worlds, with many other benefits besides. (See Essay 9, Inside Microsoft Windows, by Michael Geary.) In addition, integrated programming environments usually offer a graphic-style windowed interface, access to
MS-DOS from within the program, and batch-mode compile and link options.

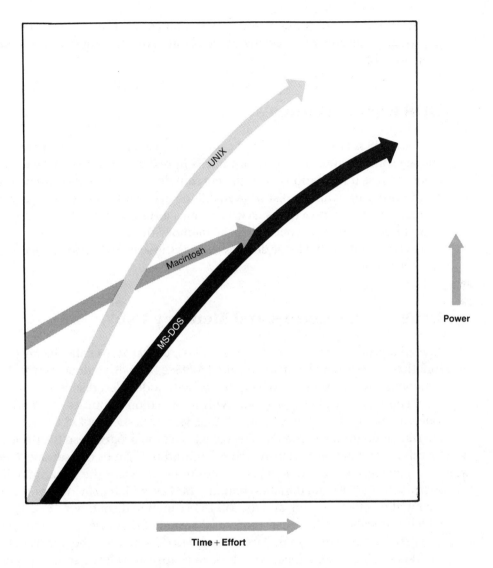

Fig. 1-5.   Learning ease of use vs. power.

Programmers and power users may have a bewildering variety of choices these days, but with thought and planning they can have both power and ease of use.

The Applications Level

At the applications level, we move from what the user needs to what a programmer must do. The programmer's interface to MS-DOS is the applications services level—the system kernel, which is loaded from the MSDOS.SYS file (IBMDOS.COM in

PC-DOS). The kernel contains the data structures and service routines that applications programs must access correctly in order to function in the MS-DOS environment.

DOS Kernel Features

The MS-DOS kernel serves an applications program in two general ways. First, it manages information the program needs in order to interact with its environment, such as information about the current directory, the files assigned for use by the program, and the list of available devices and how they organize data. Second, the kernel provides service routines (often called MS-DOS functions or interrupts) that handle such things as memory management, file management, and I/O for built-in character devices such as the screen, keyboard, parallel port, and serial port.

Program Structure and Memory Use

To load a program (either a `.COM` or an `.EXE`), `COMMAND.COM` calls the kernel's `EXEC` function `INT 48H`, which constructs the PSP. (See Essay 6, Undocumented MS-DOS Functions, by Ray Michels, which begins with a detailed discussion of the PSP.)

The PSP provides a program with information about its current environment, including the values of current DOS variables such as `PATH`. It also contains the remainder of the command line used to call the program, so the program can search for and act on option switches and find the names of user-specified files.

The PSP also contains the addresses of key services the program will need, such as the MS-DOS termination handler `INT 22H`, which provides for the orderly termination of a program, and the MS-DOS function dispatcher `INT 21H`, through which requests for disk operations and various I/O services are sent. The PSP also provides information that can be used to determine if the program has allocated enough memory for its needs or perhaps can release some memory.

The PSP thus provides a private copy of the environment for each program. Although only one program can be active at a time, there can be several PSPs and associated programs in memory. The PSP for each program serves to identify it as a process. This allows the maintenance of multiple memory-resident programs. Beyond that, the PSP structure is useful for developing task-switching and the provision of variable amounts of processor time for different processes—in other words, a form of multitasking, since each process can be maintained with its own PSP. While Microsoft has chosen not to exploit this line of development (opting for the much more sophisticated approach in OS/2), other vendors have created multitasking versions of DOS or task-switching that run under DOS.

.COM *Program Structure*

As all users learn, there are two types of executable programs that run under MS-DOS. The simplest type is the .COM program, identified by this file extension. A .COM program is an exact image (copy) of binary program code. It is always loaded just after the PSP, and it cannot be relocated. A .COM program is limited to one segment (64K), minus the space for the PSP (256 bytes) and the minimum stack (2 bytes). The compensation for this inflexibility is that .COM programs are compact and load fast, since multiple segments do not have to be accessed.

Most .COM programs found these days are usually either old programs (perhaps originally ported from CP/M) or small utility programs. The first generation of languages on PCs often produced only .COM programs, but most compilers can now use large-memory models and produce .EXE files.

.EXE *Program Structure*

Larger programs and those that need to be able to allocate and release memory as needed are constructed as .EXE programs (using that file extension). The key features of an .EXE program, as compared to a .COM program, are that it can use as many segments of memory as are available, and it can be relocated after loading. Separate segments can be devoted to program code, data, and the stack. Figure 1-6 compares the structures of .COM and .EXE programs.

Unlike the case with .COM programs, which are always loaded as a block, MS-DOS must know a lot of information about an .EXE program to be able to load it into memory and allocate whatever extra memory is needed. Each .EXE program has a header that includes information such as the location and size of the program's code, data, and stack segments. Other header fields tell MS-DOS how much more memory the program must have in order to run, and how much more the program would like to have if available. An .EXE program can also call functions that release memory that is no longer needed. Thus, .EXE programs, at the expense of additional overhead, are much more flexible than are .COM programs.

In the early days of MS-DOS, flexible memory allocation and the ability to deallocate unneeded memory were not very important. Normally there would be only one program in memory at a time. The advent of memory-resident programs changed all of this. An "ill-behaved" program that grabs all available memory freezes out memory-resident programs that expect to be able to allocate some memory as needed. Today, most programs that are intended to be used in a typical MS-DOS environment should be able to release and reclaim memory as needed. In addition, .EXE programs that follow certain rules can run under MS-DOS, OS/2 (MS-DOS compatible) mode, or OS/2 protected mode.

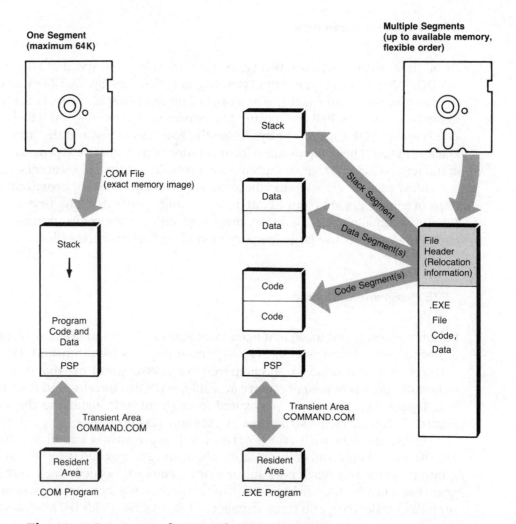

**One Segment
(maximum 64K)**

**Multiple Segments
(up to available memory,
flexible order)**

.COM File
(exact memory image)

Stack

Data

Data

Code

Code

PSP

Stack Segment

Data Segment(s)

Code Segment(s)

File
Header
(Relocation
information)

.EXE
File
Code,
Data

Stack

↓

Program
Code and
Data

PSP

Transient Area
COMMAND.COM

Transient Area
COMMAND.COM

Resident
Area

Resident
Area

.COM Program

.EXE Program

Fig. 1-6.   Structure of `.COM` and `.EXE` programs.

Memory-Resident Programs

The story of the development of memory-resident programs (usually called TSR for Terminate and Stay Resident programs) is a fascinating one. (See Essay 7, Safe Memory-Resident Programming (TSR), by Steven Baker, for both history and a very detailed discussion of the workings of TSRs and potential pitfalls.) A feature apparently intended by Microsoft only for reconfiguring access to devices (such as the MODE command) or spooling printer output (the PRINT command) was unearthed by eager developers and exploited to bring us SideKick and dozens of other utilities that are available at the touch of a key. Indeed, one of the biggest problems for serious users today is deciding how many of these attractive programs can be fit into the 640K of total available memory while still leaving room for an applications program.

As noted earlier, there can be multiple programs, each with its own PSP, in memory at the same time. Normally an MS-DOS program is removed from memory (or more precisely, its memory is released) after it terminates. When a TSR program first runs, it calls a function (usually `INT 21H, Function 31H` that tells MS-DOS to maintain the program in memory even after it has exited. By using the interrupt mechanism, a TSR can set things up so it is triggered when an event such as a specific keypress is encountered. Problems occur when two TSRs are set to respond to the same keypress, or a TSR does not pass on the keystrokes it examines so other TSRs can check them.

In essence, the TSR facility, because it allows multiple programs (processes) to exist simultaneously, provides the capability of task-switching. Since several programs are in memory and each can be selected by a particular keypress, the user can switch "instantly" between them. Memory-residency potentially supports an object-oriented, event-driven approach where a program could be constructed of modules that can respond to "messages" sent to them by various events. Programmers can explore the possibility of implementing an application as a group of memory-resident modules. The drawbacks are considerable however. Many important functions relating to TSRs have only been documented recently, some are still undocumented. MS Windows and ultimately OS/2 are much better environments for developing such event-driven programs, but there is still room for exploiting memory-resident programming in the standard MS-DOS environment.

Accessing System Services through Interrupts

The basic mechanism by which programs request the services of the MS-DOS kernel is the *software interrupt*. There are basically two kinds of interrupts in the PC environment: hardware interrupts and software interrupts. Hardware interrupts originate from the hardware controlling devices, and programs must respond appropriately to them. Remember, there is nothing traumatic or unusual about hardware interrupts in the MS-DOS world. Many are nothing more than a device saying that it has completed the requested I/O operation.

Software interrupts are used by programs to obtain such services as file management (creating, writing, and reading files, creating directories, and so on), memory management (allocating or releasing memory), reading the keyboard, displaying text or graphics, or running a program from the current program.

Interrupts are referred to as `INT XXH` where `XX` is a hexadecimal number. `INT` is also the name of the assembly language instruction used to call an interrupt.

Software interrupts can access the BIOS for low-level operations, and this is sometimes done for speed reasons. For example, INT 10H is a general-purpose interrupt used to access the BIOS video services. In general, however, the most compatible way to request DOS services is through the software interrupts that call code within the MS-DOS kernel. An interrupt with special significance here is INT 21H. This interrupt is a general dispatcher used for calling most of the MS-DOS kernel's system services. Aproximately 100 different functions are available through INT 21H, called by putting the hexadecimal number of the specified service into the AH register, loading other registers with codes that specify the desired processing, and then using the INT 21H instruction.

The INT Instruction

Software interrupts are activated by executing the INT assembly language instruction. The form of the instruction is INT n, where n is the hexadecimal interrupt number. Before the INT statement is executed, CPU registers must be loaded with appropriate values as specified in the description of the interrupt. When the interrupt returns control to the program, return values, as appropriate, are provided in the registers.

The INT instruction first directs the CPU to save the current contents of the code segment (CS) and instruction pointer (IP) registers onto the stack. This must be done so that the program that was interrupted can be started up where it left off. New values are then loaded into these registers using the values found in the Interrupt Vector Table in the first 1024 bytes of memory. The interrupt number serves as an index into the table. The CPU then executes the code found at the locations now specified by the CS and IP registers, and, when done, restores the original CS and IP values from the stack. Execution of the interrupted program now resumes.

Because values in the Interrupt Vector Table can be replaced by the programmer with other values, software designers can substitute their own code for handling a particular interrupt by putting appropriate values in the table for that interrupt number. This is how, for example, a TSR can intercept a keyboard interrupt with code that checks for certain keystrokes.

Using MS-DOS Data Structures

The use of the many system functions (or interrupts) involves not only an understanding of how a particular interrupt works, but frequently how it uses internal MS-DOS data structures. For example, a number of MS-DOS functions have to do with file management: creating, writing, reading, closing, and removing files. Internally, MS-DOS uses a System File Table (SFT) and individual data blocks called File Control Blocks (FCBs) to manage files. The SFT keeps track of the status of all files that are currently open. Each file has its own FCB, which contains the file's name, status, history (when it was last accessed), as well as pointers to the location within the file that was last accessed.

Constructing FCBs used to be a tedious process because all of this information had to be obtained by the program and inserted one field at a time. But MS-DOS (starting with version 2.0) has provided an alternate and preferable way for applications to handle files, the file handle. The programmer obtains a file handle by passing the address of a string containing the pathname of the file to the file creation or file-opening function. The handle that is returned is a 16-bit value that identifies that file. All further references to the file use only the handle, and MS-DOS keeps track of the file's FCB without further ado. The use of file handles makes it easy to find a file anywhere in the file system hierarchy, redirect input and output, and control the use of files and records in a network environment.

The file handle example is typical of a problem with learning how to program with MS-DOS. In the interest of compatibility with earlier versions, many MS-DOS facilities do not replace the functions they are intended to supplant. It is up to the programmer to learn what the preferred techniques are. (See Essay 10, Developing MS-DOS Device Drivers, by Walter Dixon, and Essay 6, Undocumented MS-DOS Functions, by Ray Michels, for discussions of the use of the SFT, FCB, and file handles.)

Problems in Interrupt Handling

While the interrupt mechanism is conceptually simple, in practice, many problems can occur in managing interrupts. As the name implies, an interrupt "interrupts" whatever program was running when it was triggered, so the handler for the interrupt must properly save and restore the interrupted program's register values. The programmer must also be concerned with preventing interrupts from interrupting themselves.

The interrupt mechanism worked well in the environment for which it was designed (only one program running at a time). The use of interrupt-driven TSR programs complicates the issue—the problem is that there is no way to protect the system from the misbehavior of one process or from an improperly handled interrupt. In most multitasking operating systems such as UNIX or OS/2, programmers request system services and access memory only through the operating system, not by means of interrupts. The operating system is an ever-present monitor, not just a program loader. The OS protects each program's memory from unauthorized access. This kind of memory management and the use of protected mode (on the 80X86) means that an errant program can commit suicide, but cannot murder another program. (See Essay 10, Developing MS-DOS Device Drivers, by Walter Dixon, for a detailed discussion of the interrupt mechanism. See Essay 5, Advanced MASM Techniques, by Michael Goldman, for techniques and tips for proper handling of interrupts.)

New Programming Tools and Techniques

Applications programming requires good tools as well as knowledge and techniques. The last few years have seen the emergence of powerful and versatile tools for programmers, and of integrated programming environments that make it easier to use them. The new programming tools also make it easier for beginning programmers, traditionally introduced to BASIC, to move directly to using C or other languages that are better designed for professional programming.

Integrated Programming Environments

Borland International started a small revolution with the introduction of its fast, cheap, and easy to use Turbo Pascal product. Instead of a tedious write-compile-link-run-debug-revise cycle, programmers could now write code in an editor, have it compiled, linked, and run automatically, and immediately invoke the editor to fix any errors that emerge. The control of all aspects of the programming process from the same interface provided an integrated programming environment.

Since then, Borland and Microsoft have brought out products that add power while retaining the easy-to-use pull-down menus and dialog windows. Microsoft C 5.0 is particularly noteworthy in that it offers an integrated environment (QuickC) that is fully compatible with the full-fledged command-line driven compiler, linker, and librarian, and provides a subset of its CodeView debugger commands from within the integrated environment.

The significance of integrated environments is that they help programmers concentrate on the design and coding of the program rather than the mechanics of keeping track of include files, compiler options, "make" files, and other housekeeping details.

A further step toward programming ease has recently been taken by Microsoft, starting with its QuickBASIC 4.0 product. By using a "threaded" mechanism for linking compiled code sections, this integrated environment makes it possible in many cases to recompile and relink just the parts of the program affected by the most recent edit.

Another trend that is seen especially in the Microsoft and Borland products is the provision of a uniform interface that allows programs created using one language to call routines created using another language. This is mainly a matter of having the compiled code from each language pass parameters on the stack using the same sequence. This "multilanguage programming" provides flexibility in using existing resources and allows the programmer to choose the language best suited for a given task.

C Function Libraries

The general acceptance of C as the premier higher-level language for MS-DOS programming has resulted in the development of numerous commercial and public-domain libraries of C functions for nearly everything one might want to do with an MS-DOS system and its hardware. (Two good examples on a small scale are the serial communications routines in Essay 13, Programming the Serial Port with C, by Naba Barkakati, and the EGA graphics routines in Essay 12, Programming the Enhanced Graphics Adapter (EGA) by Andrew Dumke. Essay 4, Adding Power to MS-DOS Programming, by Doug Adams, describes the features and gives examples of the use of two commercial C libraries: Vitamin C, a screen generator, and C-INDEX, an indexed file-retrieval system.

The Hardware Level

Finally we come to the lowest (but certainly not least important) level of MS-DOS, the interface to hardware. When all is said and done, a program must communicate effectively with the outside world. From lowest to highest level, there are three ways a program can control devices: direct access, BIOS calls, and device drivers.

Direct access involves directly manipulating the registers or memory locations associated with devices connected with the system, or directly accessing memory buffers associated with the devices. In general, this is usually done for speed—in the case of the video display, for example, to provide high-speed drawing and animation. The drawback of this approach is that it depends on exact hardware compatibility, which is not the same as the "functional compatibility" advertised particularly by the early PC-compatibile vendors. Most software developers avoid this approach, except in some games.

The BIOS

In our discussion of interrupts we mentioned the BIOS calls available through INT 10H. Since the calls for device services through the BIOS have to be translated into specific register or memory changes, this approach is slower than direct access. On the other hand, now that very highly compatible BIOS chips for PC compatibles are widely available, the BIOS approach guarantees a high degree of compatibility.

Communicating with Devices

The third approach to communicating with hardware is the device driver. A device driver is a program that is installed by MS-DOS in memory where it waits for control sequences directed at a particular device. The driver translates these commands into the low-level instructions needed to get the device to perform the required function. MS-DOS comes with a number of built-in device drivers for the devices that are built into every PC, such as the keyboard, disk drives, and parallel and serial ports.

Installable Device Drivers

The open architecture of the IBM PC and its compatibles rapidly led to the proliferation of add-on devices. In the area of the video display, IBM offered the EGA and the Video Graphics Array (VGA) and other adapters to provide more resolution and color. Meanwhile, Hercules established its own display "standard." Modifying the BIOS or the MS-DOS kernel to keep up with these new devices would have led to a logistical nightmare. Instead, MS-DOS 2.0 added the capability for users to install their own device drivers.

As we mentioned in the discussion of the DOS boot process, MS-DOS builds a list of device drivers that starts with its own built-in drivers. MS-DOS also provides some optional drivers, such as `ANSI.SYS` (a console driver) and `VDISK.SYS` (a RAMdisk driver). These or drivers written by other programmers can be installed (hooked into the MS-DOS driver list), and a `DEVICE=` statement naming the driver in the `CONFIG.SYS` file then tells MS-DOS to install the driver at system startup. (See Essay 11, Writing a SOUND Device Driver, by Walter Dixon, for a complete minicourse on designing, using, and testing installable device drivers.)

The installable device driver is one of MS-DOS's outstanding successes. In addition to accommodating new devices such as laser printers or CD drives, device drivers can even be used to intercept file accesses and provide password protection. (See Essay 8, Data Protection and Encryption, by Asael Dror.)

The Future of MS-DOS

Microsoft Windows, with the recent release of version 2.0, represents several fundamental extensions of the MS-DOS environment without sacrificing the underlying MS-DOS kernel. For users, it provides a graphical user interface with most of the features popularized by the Macintosh. For programmers, however, the real significance of MS Windows is that it provides a new model for thinking about and designing programs. This is the model that is often called *object-oriented programming*. Instead of an application being written as a collection of functions that are called according to the logic of the main program, each Windows function is designed to handle specified inputs (messages) and send messages in return to the central dispatcher. Events such as mouse movements thus become input to the function controlling each window.

In a traditional program, the user is put in the position of an applicant who must fill out a series of forms (navigate menus) in order to get to the point of being able to do some work. In an object-oriented, "modeless" program, the user picks up the desired tool and the tool responds in a way that seems natural for the intended work. While in practice, Windows may not be this seamless, it provides a taste of things to come. (See Essay 9, Inside Microsoft Windows, by Michael Geary, for more discussion on the Windows interface and programming environment.)

Expanded Memory

The proliferation of TSRs, the overhead involved with environments such as MS Windows, and the sheer amount of data that applications are now called upon to handle often leads to a shortage of usable memory. Remember, MS-DOS allows only 640K of memory to be addressed directly. The ultimate solution is an operating system that takes advantage of the "protected mode" of the 80286 and 80386 to address many megabytes of memory, such as OS/2 or UNIX. Meanwhile, EMS, a workable if not ideal solution, allows access to memory beyond 640K under MS-DOS. Portions of the 640K main memory are treated as windows into which chunks of memory from a memory expansion board can be mapped as needed. While this technique is slower than being able to directly address the extra memory (and involves housekeeping), it is much faster than using the hard disk for swapping code or data in and out. Increasing numbers of applications are being written or revised to take advantage of EMS or its successors, Enhanced Extended Memory Specification (EEMS) and EMS 4.0. (See Essay 14, Understanding Expanded Memory Systems, by Ray Duncan, for a conceptual and practical understanding of expanded memory and how a program can use it.)

OS/2

Even granting its shortcomings and limitations, by any standard, MS-DOS has been a remarkable success. Microsoft has added significant features to the operating system on several occasions, and has been innovative in the areas of operating environments (MS Windows) and programming tools (of which Codeview and the "Quick" integrated environments are most notable). Perhaps the real driving force behind the success of MS-DOS, however, is the community of developers who have discovered and exploited features such as memory-resident programming to meet an increasingly demanding market.

It is traditional in the computer industry to want to be where the action is—the latest wave rather than the tried and true. There is no doubt that in the long run OS/2 is the successor to MS-DOS, providing multitasking, a new user interface (Presentation Manager), and a new programming environment.

On the other hand, there is a huge installed base of PCs and XTs that will never be upgraded to run OS/2. Also, OS/2 is significantly more expensive than MS-DOS, especially considering its hefty memory requirements and the cost of replacing all applications in order to take full advantage of OS/2, rather than merely running in a slightly degraded fashion in a compatibility mode. Further, it will take time to rewrite significant applications to take advantage of OS/2, and until new applications are conceived that take full advantage of multitasking in their design, there will be limited incentive for most ordinary users to learn OS/2 instead of using a combination such as MS-DOS, Windows, and EMS. Thus it is likely that, for at least the next several years, there will be a significant market for MS-DOS applications and considerable room for innovation in the MS-DOS world.

Reading List

Angermeyer, J., R. Fahringer, K. Jaeger, and D. Shafer/The Waite Group. 1987. *Tricks of the MS-DOS Masters*. Indianapolis: Howard W. Sams & Company.
► Full of tips that turn users into power users, including ways to enhance MS-DOS with add-on products.

Angermeyer, J., and K. Jaeger/The Waite Group. 1986. *MS-DOS Developer's Guide*. Indianapolis: Howard W. Sams & Company.
► Contains many strategies and techniques for program development under MS-DOS including real-time programming, the 8087 coprocessor, and network support.

Duncan, R. 1986. *Advanced MS-DOS*. Redmond, Washington: Microsoft Press.
► A very thorough guide to MS-DOS internal structures and system functions with numerous examples in assembly language.

Mortice Kern Systems. 1986. *MKS Toolkit*. Waterloo, Ontario, Canada.
► Describes the MKS toolkit, a product that provides a very UNIX-like environment under MS-DOS, including the Korn shell.

Simrin, S./The Waite Group. 1985. *MS-DOS Bible*. Indianapolis: Howard W. Sams & Company.
► Guide to MS-DOS features for power users and programmers.

Harry Henderson is a freelance technical writer and editor specializing in operating systems and programming languages. He has worked on numerous books for The Waite Group and Sams Publications, including their UNIX series, and is technical editor for MS-DOS Papers. He also works with his wife, Lisa Yount, on educational writing, under the close supervision of three cats.

Related Essays

2 Searching the File Tree with `whereis`
3 Adding UNIX Power with PCnix
4 Adding Power to MS-DOS Programming
9 Inside Microsoft Windows

Keywords

- ▶ tree-structured directories
- ▶ recursive search algorithms
- ▶ filename matching
- ▶ `whereis` (utility)
- ▶ `find` (UNIX utility)

Essay Synopsis: Most MS-DOS users are familiar with the concept of tree-structured directories. Unfortunately, MS-DOS does not provide user commands for finding particular files in the file tree and processing them. Additionally, many programmers are not aware of the techniques needed to enable programs to traverse the directory tree and search for files that match particular criteria. Because subdirectories are nested, a recursive algorithm allows programs to access the subdirectories within a given directory, the subdirectories of these subdirectories, and so on. This essay discusses the algorithms and proper DOS calls to use for a program to access to the MS-DOS file system. As an illustration, a very powerful utility called `whereis`, written in Microsoft C, is provided and fully explained. This utility allows you to search for files throughout the directory tree and automatically apply MS-DOS commands or other programs to matching files.

Searching the File Tree with
whereis

Frank Whaley

The more recent releases of MS-DOS (versions 2.0 and above) provide a very useful feature that can be a tremendous aid to organizing disk files—Tree-Structured Directories (also known as a hierarchical file system). However, users and programmers are often confused about how to use this feature properly. While we will assume that you possess a working knowledge of MS-DOS directories (including the commands for directory creation, deletion, and other maintenance activities), we will review the basic concepts of MS-DOS directories and show why directory searching is a required task of many programs.

The directory search program `whereis` searches all of the directories on a disk for a given set of filenames provided on the command line. The `whereis` program also contains a number of options which turn it into a useful file utility program that can move, delete, copy, or perform other operations on the located files. As you study `whereis`, you will learn how to access and best use the MS-DOS file system. In addition, this program contains a number of valuable subroutines that may be clipped out and used in other programs.

`whereis` is actually very similar to the UNIX command `find`, but has been slightly modified to be more like the `FileFind` program from Peter Norton's *The Norton Utilities*. These alterations allow for simpler command lines (at least for the simpler commands) and give `whereis` more of a regular MS-DOS flavor. We could not use the name `find`, as this is the name of the standard MS-DOS text pattern-matching program.

Tree-Structured Directories

Just as a hierarchy of offices, filing cabinets, file drawers, and folders can be used to organize paperwork, the tree-structured directories provided by MS-DOS allow us to organize our disk files into a hierarchical structure. A practical application of such a system would be organizing your disk files so you could have subdirectories for each subcategory of your work (for example, all files pertaining to material purchases in one directory, and all files pertaining to equipment purchases in another). This approach has many advantages:

▶ Related files are kept in the same area, and their names can be seen together in a single directory listing.

▶ More significant characters become available for creating unique and meaningful filenames (compare DPCMJN with DETROIT\PROD\COSTS\MATERIAL\JUNE).

▶ Files containing similar information may have the same name, provided they are kept in different directories (APRIL\SALES and MAY\SALES).

▶ MS-DOS requires less search time to find a given file if there are fewer files in the current directory.

One shortcoming of this type of directory structure, however, is that files may become lost. They may be created in the wrong directory, or you may simply forget where a file was put. A tool for automatic directory searching becomes very useful, particularly when you have a hard disk with dozens of directories and hundreds of files. It is for this reason that we selected whereis as a method for demonstrating some of the principles of directory searching.

Searching: The Recursive Solution

As with most computer programs, there are several methods that we could use to search directories. Seemingly straightforward methods involving nested loops require a considerable amount of housekeeping code—stacks of directory information must be maintained.

One of the definitions of a directory is "an object which may contain files or other directories." Since this definition is self-referential (or recursive), it would seem that a recursive algorithm might be used for directory search. In fact, recursive methods are the most common methods used with tree-oriented data structures, because they allow for simplification of the code required to examine each branch of the tree. For example, our whereis program revolves around a very simple algorithm:

1. Find all plain files in this directory.
2. Repeat for all subdirectories in this directory.

This method of searching is very much different from what is required by most commercial programs. For example, finding a help message file typically involves appending the name of the file to each element of a list of directories, and testing for the presence of each constructed filename. Some programs can get away with assuming that all pertinent files exist in the current directory, and that any other condition is cause enough to abort the program.

The method used by whereis is most aptly suited to cases where all instances of a certain class of file must be operated on at one time. These files may be selected either by name, type, attributes, or some other condition or combination of conditions.

Directory Search Functions

MS-DOS was not the first, nor is it the only, operating system to provide tree-structured directories. While there is a remarkable similarity between the appearance of MS-DOS directories and those used by other systems, MS-DOS provides one of the simplest methods for finding files and information about these files.

MS-DOS directories are viewed as special files, and can only be accessed via two special function calls through INT 21H: Search For First (Function 4EH) and Search For Next (Function 4FH). (In truth, the actual disk sectors that contain the directory information may be read via the Absolute Disk Read interrupt (number 25H), but this method requires much more programming and is usually considered appropriate only for programs which help recover data after a major disk failure.) Although these function calls are primarily designed for finding files, they actually provide more information than similar functions in other operating systems.

The First/Next function calls perform wildcard matching (? and *) and deposit information about the matched file into a predefined data area. This data area is described by the following C structure:

```
typedef struct  /*  Directory Information  */
    {
    char      r[21];    /*  data area reserved by MS-DOS    */
    char      attr;     /*  attribute (system,hidden,etc.)  */
    unsigned  time,     /*  time stamp                      */
              date;     /*  date stamp                      */
    long      size;     /*  file size in bytes              */
    char      name[13]; /*  actual file name                */
    }
    DIRINFO;
```

MS-DOS uses the concept of a Data Transfer Area (DTA) for passing blocks of data which are too large to be contained in registers. The current DTA is used by MS-DOS to return the `DIRINFO` structure shown above. The current DTA must be set before each First/Next function call. This process is handled by the `SETDTA()` macro.

The First/Next function call pair allows the controlling loop of a directory search routine to be reduced to just a few lines, as shown in the pseudocode below:

```
if (a first match can be found)
    {
    process the matched file
    while (subsequent matches are found)
        process the matched file
    }
```

Examine the `Search()` subroutine within the `whereis` program (listed at the end of this chapter) for another example of this technique.

Using Options for Power and Flexibility

Options are what allow simple programs to perform more than one task, thereby increasing both their power and utility. While it may sometimes be enough to be able to say

```
whereis thisfile
```

to find all of the various versions of `thisfile`, adding a few options like

```
whereis -r -b-5000 -t+30 thisfile
```

uses the same program to find all of the occurrences of `thisfile` that are read-only, less than 5000 bytes long, and more than 30 days old.

`whereis` searches all directories on the current drive for files which match both the selected options (or defaults) and one of the file specifications (*filespecs*). In the option descriptions given in Table 2-1, the argument *n* is expected to be a decimal integer where + *n* means more than *n*, *n* means less than *n*, and *n* means exactly *n*. For options that have parameters, the parameter may be given either as part of the option argument -t+10 or as the next argument -o \bin.

filespecs may be any list of ambiguous filenames. If *filespecs* is not provided, `*.*` (all files) is assumed. The following are a few ways that we can use `whereis`.
To find all .h files:

```
whereis *.h
```

Table 2-1.   **Options for** whereis

Option	Function
advshr	Match files with given attribute bit set (Archive [a], Directory [d], Volume-label [v], System [s], Hidden [h], and Read-only [r]). Each attribute must be specified separately (as −a −s −r).
b n	Match files *n* bytes long.
t n	Match files whose date stamps are *n* days before today.
o dir	Begin searching at the directory dir instead of the root directory.
e cmd	Execute the command cmd for each matched file, substituting the current filename for any '$' found in cmd. Multiple e commands may be included, and each will be executed in the order encountered. The commands should be quoted (as "dir $") since most commands contain spaces.

To show the directory hierarchy:

```
whereis −d ¦ sort
```

To find all program files that are also marked System, Hidden, and Read-Only:

```
whereis −s −h −r *.com *.exe *.bat
```

To delete all .wks files that are more than 30 days old:

```
whereis −t+30 −e "del $" *.wks
```

To copy all .arc files to a floppy disk:

```
whereis *.arc −e "copy $ a:"
```

To create an archive of all .txt files marked Archive and then delete the .txt files:

```
whereis −a *.txt −e "echo (ARCHIVE: $) >>archive"
    −e "type $ >>archive" −e "del $"
```

The whereis.c Program

The whereis program is a fairly self-contained module—except for library sub-routines, all of the code is contained in a single file, whereis.c. As is typical in C programs, the first section contains some identification and some constant definitions. This version of whereis is coded to conform to the standards of the Microsoft C compiler, releases 3.0 and 4.0.

Includes and Constants

The source listings shown on the next several pages comprise the entire text of the whereis program. You may create your own copy of this source code by entering all of the blocks of text shown in computer font.

```
/*
 *    whereis.c ->    find files
 */
#define    LINT_ARGS        /* strict type checking */
#include <stdio.h>
#include <ctype.h>
#include <dos.h>
#include <direct.h>
#include <signal.h>


    /* constants */
#define ARC      0x20        /* attribute bits   */
#define DIR      0x10
#define VOL      0x08
#define SYS      0x04
#define HID      0x02
#define RDO      0x01
    /* match plain files */
#define PLAIN    (SYS | HID)
    /* match subdirectories */
#define SUBDIR   (DIR | SYS | HID | RDO)
```

These constants refer to the file attribute flags contained within a directory entry (the attr element of the DIRINFO structure). Note that these values are used to specify which types of files to match.

Directory Information Structure

As stated earlier, the First/Next function calls fill in a data area providing some information about the currently matched file. This information can be used to help select the appropriate file:

```
    /* data types */
typedef struct /* Directory Information */
    {
    char        r[21];    /* reserved data    */
```

```
char       attr;       /*  attribute found  */
unsigned   time,       /*  time mark        */
           date;       /*  date mark        */
long       size;       /*  file size        */
char       name[13];   /*  file name        */
}
DIRINFO;
```

Macros and Functions for MS-DOS Access

Let's look next at the interface between our whereis program and MS-DOS.
Three macros are provided to allow for relatively easy modification to fit the
library functions provided by your favorite C compiler. The Microsoft C library
contains many functions to interface to MS-DOS, but whereis requires a connection that is not provided in a simple fashion. The First/Next function calls expect
input parameters in the CX and DX registers, and they return a flag in the AL
register. There is no MS-DOS interface function in the Microsoft C library that
passes data in exactly this way, so we have included an interface function which
serves exactly our purpose.

```
/*
 *       macros
 */
#define SETDTA(d)    dos(0x1A, d)        /*  set DTA         */
#define FIRST(f,a)   !dos(0x4E, f, a)    /*  search for first */
#define NEXT()       !dos(0x4F)          /*  search for next  */
/*
 *    dos() ->   connect to MS-DOS
 */
unsigned char dos (ah, dx, cx)
    unsigned char    ah;
    char             *dx;
    unsigned         cx;
    {
    union REGS       r;
    r.h.ah = ah;
    r.x.dx = (unsigned)dx;
    r.x.cx = cx;
    intdos (&r, &r);
    return (r.h.al);
    }
```

Note that the First/Next function calls return zero if a matched file is found, and nonzero if no match was found. In order to make the function usage semantically correct (`FIRST()` returns TRUE if a match is found), we must reverse the sense of the functions with the `!` operator.

The fourth macro `AddFile()` is included only as a shorthand definition of a simple function that adds a single file specification to the list of file specifications.

```
#define AddFile(f)   FileList[nFiles++]=f /*  add filespec    */
```

Next we see the global data used by the program.

```
      /*  global data  */
char *Exec[32],          /*  execute commands, from -e     */
     *FileList[32],       /*  the list of filespecs         */
     StartDir[128],       /*  initial directory             */
*TopDir = "\\";           /*  start directory, from -o      */

int  AttrMask = 0,        /*  mask for attribute search     */
     ByteFlag = 0,        /*  controls size searching       */
     DateFlag = 0,        /*  controls date searching       */
     DateStamp = -1,      /*  date stamp to match           */
     nExecs = 0,          /*  number of execute commands    */
     nFiles = 0,          /*  number of filespecs given     */
     Today;               /*  today's date stamp            */
long ByteCount = -1;      /*  file size to match            */
        /*  offsets of "first of month" from "first of year"  */
int  months[] = {  0, 31,  59,  90, 120, 151,
              181, 212, 243, 273, 304, 334 };
```

Both `ByteFlag` and `DateFlag` control the sense of comparison (1,0,1 represents $\langle , = , \rangle$), and `DateStamp` and `ByteCount` contain the data to compare against.

Note that both the `Exec` and `FileList` arrays have 32 elements at most. This means that there is a maximum of 32 'execute' commands and 32 file specifications allowed on the command line. There is no overflow checking in the `whereis` program—we assume that the user will always enter less than 32 of either item.

Forward Declarations

In general, C programs are coded in a top-down fashion, with the main routine appearing as the first function. This is usually done to show the basic structure of the program. Therefore the functions that do not return integers must have forward declarations. (They must be described before they may be used.) This forward declaration informs the compiler that these functions do not return the default data type (integer), and prevents the compiler from complaining when it later finds the formal definitions of these functions:

```
int   GracefulDeath(void);
void  Handle(DIRINFO *),
      ParseCommandLine(int, char **),
      Search(void);
```

Note that even though the GracefulDeath() function does return an integer value, its name is used as a function parameter (see the call to signal() in the next section), and must be declared before use to prevent confusing the compiler.

The Main Program

As the leading comment says, the program proper begins with "good old main":

```
/*
 *    good old main
 */
int main(argc, argv)
    int    argc;
    char  *argv[];
    {
    /* get today's day number */
    Today = SysDate();
    /* pick options and filespecs from command line */
    ParseCommandLine(argc, argv);
    /* save initial directory */
    getcwd(StartDir, sizeof(StartDir));
    /* set the interrupt handler */
    signal(SIGINT, GracefulDeath);
    /* move to starting directory */
    chdir(TopDir);
    /* any filenames given ?? */
    if (!nFiles)
        AddFile("*.*");      /* a nice default */
    /* search for named files */
    Search();
    /* pop back to initial directory */
```

```
chdir(StartDir);
/* successful return */
return (0);
}
```

Handling Interrupts Gracefully

Before any directory searching can begin, we want to be certain that we have a
safe environment. The next function serves as the interrupt handler for whereis.
Because whereis uses the standard library function chdir() to move through the
directory tree, aborting the program may cause the program to leave the users
in some directory other than where they started. This is a typical source of lost
files—some program leaves the user in a different directory than was intended,
and files are created there never to be found again. It would be unforgivable to
allow our file finder program to make a mistake like that, so let us ensure that
whereis dies a graceful death:

```
/*
 *    GracefulDeath() ->    clean-up upon interrupt
 */
int GracefulDeath()
    {
    chdir(StartDir);
    exit(1);
    }
```

The Directory Search Function

Now that we have taken care of potential interrupts, we move to the starting directory. We use any file specifications that were given on the command line. If
there were none, *.* (all files) is used as the default. The Search() subroutine is
called to perform most of the work:

```
/*
 *    Search() ->    search for files
 */
void Search()
  {
  DIRINFO  info;
  int      i,
           first;
```

```
/*   search current directory for all filenames   */
for (i = 0; i < nFiles; i++)
   {
   first = 1;
   while (Scan(FileList[i], &info, PLAIN ¦ AttrMask, first))
      {
      first = 0;
      if (info.name[0] != '.') /*  skip "." and ".."  */
         Handle(&info);
      }
   }
/*   search all subdirectories   */
first = 1;
while (Scan("*.*", &info, SUBDIR, first))
   {
   first = 0;
   /*   search only directories and skip "." and ".."   */
if ((info.attr & DIR) && (info.name[0] != '.'))
      {
      /*  pop into that directory  */
      chdir(info.name);
      /*  search for the filenames  */
      Search();
      /*  back to where we were  */
      chdir("..");
      }
   }
}
```

Search() performs the recursive search described earlier. The major variation is that the search is repeated for each of the file specifications given on the command line. This function depends heavily on the Scan() function, which proves to be very simple:

```
/*
 *  Scan() ->  find a matching file
 */
int Scan(name, info, attr, first)
   char     *name;
   DIRINFO  *info;
   int      attr;
   int      first;
   {
   SETDTA(info);
```

```
        return (first ? FIRST(name, attr) : NEXT());
        }
```

This is the only occurrence of the three compiler-dependent macros shown earlier. Scan() could also be implemented as a macro, but is shown as a function here to simplify debugging and copying to another program.

With the exception of the Handle() function (which decides whether some action should be performed on the current file), most of the whereis program has already been described. Before the various options can be applied to any matched files, let us see how the options are parsed from the command line.

Parsing Command-Line Options

As we saw in good old main, the argument count argc and argument string vectors argv are passed to the ParseCommandLine() function.

```
/*
 *      ParseCommandLine() ->      pick our options and filespecs
 */
#define    NEXTARG()        {if(!*++argp){argp=(*argv++);argc--;}}
void ParseCommandLine(argc, argv)
    int     argc;
    char    **argv;
    {
    char    *argp;
    argc--;         /* skip argv[0] */
    argv++;
    while (argc--)
        {
        argp = *argv++;
        if (*argp != '-')
            AddFile(argp);
        else
            {
            argp++;
            switch (tolower(*argp))
                {
                case 'a' :    /* archive bit */
                    AttrMask |= ARC;
                    break;
                case 'd' :    /* directory bit */
                    AttrMask |= DIR;
```

```
                        break;
            case 'v' :      /*  volume label  */
                AttrMask |= VOL;
                break;
            case 's' :      /*  system bit  */
                AttrMask |= SYS;
                break;
            case 'h' :      /*  hidden bit  */
                AttrMask |= HID;
                break;
            case 'r' :      /*  read-only bit  */
                AttrMask |= RDO;
                break;
            case 'b' :      /*  byte count  */
                NEXTARG();
                if ((*argp == '-') || (*argp == '+'))
                    ByteFlag = (*argp++ == '-') ? -1 : 1;
                ByteCount = PickVal(&argp);
                break;
            case 't' :      /*  time stamp  */
                NEXTARG();
                if ((*argp == '-') || (*argp == '+'))
                    DateFlag = (*argp++ == '-') ? -1 : 1;
                DateStamp = Today - PickVal(&argp);
                break;
            case 'o' :      /*  origin directory  */
                NEXTARG();
                TopDir = argp;
                break;
            case 'e' :      /*  execute  */
                NEXTARG();
                Exec[nExecs++] = argp;
                break;
            default :
                fputs("Usage : whereis [-advshr] [-b<n>]\ [-t<n>] [-
e<command>] [-o<dir>] [files]...\n",
                    stderr);
                exit(1);
            }
        }
      }
    }
```

The cryptic `NEXTARG()` is a very useful macro which allows for flexible specification of the parameters of options. In essence, this macro states, "if there was no parameter given as part of the option string, move the argument pointer to the next argument." It is included within the `ParseCommandLine()` block to facilitate copying to another program. `ParseCommandLine()` uses only one other interesting function `PickVal()`, which converts an ASCII string to a long integer representation:

```
/*
 *    PickVal() ->    pick an integer from a string
 */
long PickVal(p)
    char  **p;
    {
    long  v;

    for (v = 0; isdigit(**p); ++*p)
        v = (v * 10) + (**p - '0');
    return (v);
    }
```

Handling Matched Files

Now we are ready for the `Handle()` function:

```
/*
 *    Handle() ->     handle a matched file
 */
void Handle(info)
    DIRINFO    *info;
    {
    char  theFile[128];
    int   i;
    /*  attributes ??  */
    if ((info->attr & AttrMask) != AttrMask)
        return;
    /*  byte  count  */
    if (ByteCount >= 0)
        switch (ByteFlag)
            {
            case -1 :
                if (info->size >= ByteCount)
                    return;
```

```
                        break;
                case 0 :
                    if (info->size != ByteCount)
                        return;
                    break;
                case 1 :
                    if (info->size <= ByteCount)
                        return;
                    break;
                }
    /*  date stamp  */
    if (DateStamp >= 0)
        switch (DateFlag)
                {
                case -1 :
                    if (FileDate(info->date) <= DateStamp)
                        return;
                    break;
                case 0 :
                    if (FileDate(info->date) != DateStamp)
                        return;
                    break;
                case 1 :
                    if (FileDate(info->date) >= DateStamp)
                        return;
                    break;
                }
    /*  a match, build the complete filename  */
        /*  first the pathname  */
    getcwd(theFile, sizeof(theFile));
        /*  add trailing '\' if required  */
if (*(theFile + strlen(theFile) - 1) != '\\')
        strcat(theFile, "\\");
        /*  add the filename  */
    strcat(theFile, info->name);

    /*  execute any -e commands, otherwise print  */
    if (nExecs)
        for (i = 0; i < nExecs; i++)
            Execute(Exec[i], theFile);
    else
        puts(theFile);
        }
    }
```

There are a couple of interesting points within the Handle() function: The comparisons inside the ByteCount and DateStamp checks are opposite. This is because the "more than" tests have opposite meaning—greater than a certain size or before (less than) a certain date. The filenames matched are not printed if the "execute" option was selected. This is done purely for cosmetic reasons, so the filename does not interfere with the output of the executed program.

Executing Commands on Matched Files

For the actual execution of a command, the Execute() function handles the substitution of the current filename for any occurrence of the '$' character:

```
/*
 *    Execute() ->      execute command, substituting filename
 */
void Execute(cmd, name)
      char *cmd,
           *name;
      {
      char  command[128],
            *cp,
            *np;
      cp = command;
      while (*cmd)
            if (*cmd == '$')
                  {
                  np = name;
                  while (*np)
                        *cp++ = *np++;
                  cmd++;
                  }
            else
                  *cp++ = *cmd++;
      *cp = 0;
      system(command);
      }
```

Handling Dates

MS-DOS provides two formats of a date—one format for describing the date stamp of a file, and another for describing the current date. The last two functions of whereis convert these two date formats into absolute integers which can be compared. Both of these functions could be made considerably shorter. They are shown in this fashion only to demonstrate how to extract the date information:

```
/*
 *     FileDate() ->    return file date as absolute integer
 */
int FileDate(d)
    unsigned    d;
    {
    int   days,     /*  days  */
          mons,     /*  months  */
          yrs;      /*  years  */
    yrs = d >> 9;
    mons = (d >> 5) & 0x0F;
    days = d & 0x1F;
    if (yrs % 4)    /*  handle leap years  */
        days++;
    return ((yrs * 365) + months[mons - 1] + days);
    }
```

The Microsoft C library provides a number of time and date handling functions. However, they are all very general routines and as such consume a considerable amount of code. The following function uses the intdos() function to get the current system date directly from MS-DOS, saving several hundred bytes of code. This function also converts the system date to an absolute integer compatible with dates returned by FileDate():

```
/*
 *     SysDate() ->    return system date as absolute integer
 */
int SysDate()
    {
    int              days,
                     mons,
                     yrs;
    union REGS       r;

    r.h.ah = 0x2A;
    intdos(&r, &r);
    days = r.h.dl;
    mons = r.h.dh;
    yrs = r.x.cx - 1980;
```

```
if (yrs % 4)    /* handle leap years */
    days++;
return ((yrs * 365) + months[mons - 1] + days);
}
```

Neither of these functions is exactly correct, because they do not handle all of the variations of leap-year calculations. However, they probably will last well past the point where MS-DOS becomes obsolete, and thus may be considered "good enough."

Compiling whereis

Due primarily to the simplicity of the program, compilation is also very simple. For the Microsoft C 3.0/4.0 compilers, the command line

```
cl whereis.c
```

is sufficient to produce a working version of whereis. If you desire an optimized version, I would suggest the following command, which provides maximum optimization:

```
cl -Ox whereis.c
```

Note that it is not necessary to include *wildcard expansion* subroutines (contained in the SSETARGV.OBJ file), because those are handled by the directory search functions, and we want them to receive exactly what was typed on the command line.

You may have noticed that whereis was written without using either the printf() or scanf() functions. While it may have made for some cumbersome code in one spot (the end of the Handle() function), including even the "no floating-point" version of printf() would have caused whereis.exe to be at least 2000 bytes larger.

This version of whereis makes no effort to handle any disk drive other than the current drive. It would be relatively simple to replace the chdir() function with a ChangeDriveAndDirectory() function that would allow the -o options to include a drive specifier.

It was mentioned earlier that the filenames matched are not printed if the execute option was selected. The UNIX program find has a -print option which controls whether matched filenames are printed, regardless of any other options. Sometimes it is essential that the matched filenames be printed before a program is executed. It would be a rather simple programming exercise to add a -p option, indicating that matched filenames should always be printed.

Conclusion

This chapter has shown you some techniques for accessing directory entries, and for navigating around tree-structured directories. We have also used both normal and alternate methods of calling MS-DOS from within a C program.

The whereis program evolved in the same fashion as its UNIX counterpart find—out of a desire to find files and to do something about them when they were found. Professional programmers have found that whereis has become a useful file utility program—although it is small and simple, its power and versatility will allow you to perform tasks never before thought possible.

Reading List

Card, S., T. Moran, and A. Newell. 1983. *The Psychology of Human-Computer Interaction*. Hillsdale, New Jersey: Lawrence Erlbaum Associates.

Myers, G. 1976. *Software Reliability*. New York: John Wiley & Sons, Inc.

After several years of developing code for WordStar and WordStar 2000, **Frank Whaley** has retired to a life of contract programming in Southern California.

Related Essays

1 A Guided Tour inside MS-DOS
3 Adding UNIX Power with PCnix
4 Adding Power to MS-DOS Programming

Keywords

- ► UNIX
- ► directories and files
- ► software tools
- ► batch processing
- ► text processing
- ► command editing

Essay Synopsis: The UNIX operating system has had considerable influence on the design and development of MS-DOS, and is thus a good source of ideas for extending its power and flexibility. This essay presents PCnix, a set of modifications, batch files, and public domain programs that adds much of the functionality of UNIX to MS-DOS systems, without any sacrifice of compatibility with your regular MS-DOS software. As you explore PCnix, you will learn more about MS-DOS as well as about some of the basic features of UNIX. This essay gives you a fascinating glimpse of the thought process that went into the development of PCnix, the relevant DOS internals, the key decisions, and their consequences. As a practical benefit, you will gain new power to control and manage the MS-DOS environment, including improved batch file processing, command editing and recall (history), and a variety of file and text-handling tools.

## 3

Adding UNIX Power
with PCnix

R. Edward Nather

The UNIX operating system was designed by computer programmers Ken Thompson and Dennis Ritchie for their own use, to provide a comfortable working environment in which to write computer programs. Nonprogrammers find it hard to learn—it takes a while to get used to its terse, powerful commands and to get in tune with its underlying unity. Many critics of UNIX, who find it less than the ideal environment for business operations or secretarial work, seem to forget its original purpose. In my view, UNIX has been remarkably successful in achieving its original goal. It's the most convenient operating system I've ever used. This view is shared by many other programmers. I have yet to meet anyone who has become completely comfortable in a UNIX environment who prefers to use any other. If you've already used MS-DOS, installing PCnix on your computer can offer you a relatively painless way to learn more about UNIX and the real power it offers—and more about MS-DOS as well.

Why PCnix?

When I first got access to an IBM PC running MS-DOS (version 2.0), I was struck by the number of familiar UNIX-like features: command-line arguments, I/O redirection, a hierarchical file system with directories, pipes, interpreted text scripts (batch files), a set of included software tools, etc. UNIX has clearly had a strong (but often unacknowledged) influence on MS-DOS—but so has another operating system: CP/M. The latest version of MS-DOS (3.3 at this writing) remains an unhappy hybrid of the two systems, with many UNIX-like features but with vestiges of CP/M as well. These seem awful to UNIX users—not necessarily because they *are* awful, but because they are different. The formal name for this problem is Semantic Confusion. The net result is that going back and forth between UNIX and MS-DOS can be dangerous to your mental health.

There were several versions of "cut-down UNIX" available at the time I first got access to an IBM PC, so I tried two of them and learned a great truth: the 8088 is not a speedy microprocessor on the best of days, and, burdened with an operating system not hand-crafted to make best use of it, the result was unbearably slow. Also, most of the neat new software was being written in garages, haylofts, and universities for the MS-DOS operating system, and I wanted to be able to use it, while still enjoying a UNIX-like environment.

Things are somewhat better today: the 80286 is a faster engine, and some commercial products offer a UNIX-like shell and a reasonable selection of software tools—but they can't run all MS-DOS programs, and in particular are often baffled by memory-resident programs (TSRs). In general, they force you to give up your MS-DOS environment to get UNIX power into your PC. This is a sacrifice most PC users cannot afford to make. In addition, PCnix has the advantage that, unlike the commercial "UNIX for MS-DOS" products, it is fully customizable since you are provided with the source code for the system and most of its utilities.

The PCnix system—essentially a collection of software tools that use the (unmodified) MS-DOS kernel—is my attempt to remove as many irritating differences as possible, and to provide a comfortable working environment in which to write computer programs on the IBM PC. This design approach has some real advantages:

► Complete MS-DOS compatibility is retained. (If you really prefer to use the DIR command rather than the UNIX command ls you can do it—just don't tell me about it.)

► It is fast even on floppy-based 8088 machines with enough memory for a modest-sized RAMdisk.

► It offers the most-used UNIX software tools, and can be easily expanded by the user. New commercial and public domain versions of UNIX tools are continually being written and they can be easily added to PCnix.

► Source code (in the C language) is available for almost all of the tools, so you can tinker with them as you choose and perhaps learn about C, UNIX, and MS-DOS in the process.

To comply with government-sponsored truth in labeling, the disadvantages are:

► Since it uses the MS-DOS shell COMMAND.COM, it can interpret MS-DOS batch files, but lacks the ability to interpret UNIX-style shell scripts.

► It does not attempt to provide multitasking capability.

► Some C programs developed under UNIX must be changed to run properly under PCnix, where the system calls differ.

Overall, I think the advantages outweigh the disadvantages—but I may not be completely objective about it. In any event, let's explore what we must do to bend MS-DOS nearer to our heart's desire.

Our Strategy

Our mission is to provide MS-DOS with the "look and feel" of UNIX without serious compromises in response time, and without mucking about in the MS-DOS kernel. Let's first look at the basic problem we must face before we leap into action.

UNIX supports a rich set of software tools, and people who use the system begin to think of problems in terms of the tools they have available to them—the richer the set, the more options they have in finding a solution. "To the man with only a hammer, everything looks like a nail." We must be prepared to add the most-used UNIX tools to those supplied with MS-DOS. This is quite possible: only a few operations are internal to the MS-DOS shell `COMMAND.COM`; most are external commands, i.e., executable programs. We can replace any MS-DOS external command by replacing it with a program of the same name, or add a new command by providing a program with a different name. However, the way commands operate under UNIX differs from what is possible under MS-DOS—UNIX is multitasking and MS-DOS is not.

The UNIX toolkit is designed around the idea of pipes, where a string of separate tools works in sequence on a data stream, each tool doing its own thing and passing the result along to the next tool in line. For example, the command sequence

```
cat names phones ¦ more
```

will first invoke the `cat` command (concatenate the text files `names` and `phones` end-to-end); its output stream becomes input to the `more` command, which pages the text onto the display screen, pausing so the text doesn't run off the top of the screen before it can be read.

This command sequence, running under UNIX, will have both tools active at the same time—whenever there is any usable output from `cat` it is passed along to `more` right away, and immediately appears on the display screen. Under MS-DOS, which cannot handle more than one task at a time, `cat` must run to completion, storing its output in a temporary disk file. When `cat` is finished, the temporary file is read back from disk into `more`, whose output is (finally!) sent to the display screen. It may not take forever, but it feels like forever if you're used to UNIX. PCnix can't solve this problem in a general way, but we can design tools with a primitive `more` built into them so that they won't need to use a pipe, and can give much faster response. In general, we'll need to tailor our tools to the MS-DOS environment in which they must run.

As a matter of principle, we want to do as little work as possible, so we will choose the simplest way we can find to provide any particular tool. If MS-DOS already provides the appropriate tool (e.g., `format`) we'll use it unchanged; if not, we'll explore enhancing the tool's operation (and perhaps changing its name) by including it in a batch file (e.g., `copy`). If that doesn't work, we'll try to find a suitable tool in the public domain. If all else fails, we'll write it ourselves, using the C language to code it in, and calling on the available MS-DOS services where necessary.

Let's do the easy things first.

Tweaking MS-DOS

In addition to providing enhanced, more UNIX-like tools for MS-DOS, we must make a few changes in the way it looks to the user. This involves getting MS-DOS to accept a more UNIX-like syntax.

The simplest change to "raw" MS-DOS is to change the prompt. The command

```
prompt %%
```

in the `AUTOEXEC.BAT` file turns the `A>` prompt into a UNIX-like `%` that already feels better—UNIX Bourne shell users might prefer `$`—but it has an awkward flaw: you can't tell what drive you're on.

UNIX has no notion of drive, since the complete file system looks like one huge inverted tree to the user. MS-DOS inherited the idea of drives from CP/M and still uses them, and it's important to know where you are in the file system, since it affects how you refer to a file you want to work on. If the file is not on the current drive, you must begin the name with the drive designator (e.g., a:) or MS-DOS can't find it. As our first of many compromises, we use

```
prompt $n%%
```

in the `AUTOEXEC.BAT` file to get the prompt `C%` if we are on drive C, `A%` on drive A, etc.

Next we must change the path separator character from \ to / or every pathname will look jarringly different from its UNIX counterpart. MS-DOS, like CP/M before it, normally uses the / character to indicate a command-line option, or "switch," as in the MS-DOS command

```
DIR /P
```

where the option P asks that the `DIR` command pause at the end of the screen so you can read what it told you. UNIX, contrariwise, uses the / character to separate pathnames, and the character - to indicate a command-line option. Fortunately, someone at Microsoft knew about this, and arranged MS-DOS so it can use either / or \ as a path separator, and you can change the switch character `SWITCHAR` if you know how.

We first change the value of `SWITCHAR` that `COMMAND.COM` uses in parsing the command lines we type. By default, that character is /. If we use some other character to designate a switch, almost all of MS-DOS will let us use / in pathnames. The obvious choice is – which UNIX uses as a switch designator, but that choice has problems, too.

Many PC programs use the – character as part of their names—PC-Write, for example. If we substitute – for the switch character, the parser in `COM-MAND.COM` looks for a file called `pc` and prepares to hand it the switch -W as an argument—not what we want. We can avoid this problem by referring to the filename as PC?WRITE but that subterfuge is too ugly to tolerate. We'll have to rename files that have – in their name.

Alternatively, we can substitute \ as the switch character, in effect reversing the meaning of the forward and reverse slash characters. We'll have to remember to use \ as a switch designator for those (few) MS-DOS programs that need a switch and that can't accept – instead. This is the solution I prefer, but either way will work. MS-DOS 2.X allowed the switch character to be changed by including the line

```
SET SWITCHAR=\
```

in the `CONFIG.SYS` startup file, but MS-DOS 3.X doesn't. Undaunted, we use the (undocumented) Function 37h to fix things up; this works on all versions of MS-DOS starting with 2.0. A small program called `INT37.COM` does this job right away in the `AUTOEXEC.BAT` startup file, so all subsequent pathnames can use / as the separator. Like UNIX, / by itself designates the root directory.

Finally, since we want batch files to appear to execute the same as any other kind of executable command, we must do something about the `ECHO` operation, which decrees that all batch file commands are echoed to the console screen as they are executed. This gabbiness is particularly offensive to UNIX users, who come to appreciate the quiet way UNIX tools do their job. Even the mechanism provided to shut up this chatty behavior is flawed: the command `ECHO OFF` in a batch file is, itself, echoed to the screen, instantly betraying that a batch file, rather than some other type of command, is being executed. The latest version of MS-DOS (3.3) recognizes the ə character at the beginning of a line to mean "don't echo this line"; earlier versions must be patched.

Each version of `COMMAND.COM` has a pair of flag characters that govern the behavior of the `ECHO` operation, and by default, they are set ON. We want to set them OFF by default. Note that this still permits batch file commands to be echoed if that is desirable. Just include the command `ECHO ON` as the first command. The change only has to be done once to a copy of `COMMAND.COM`, and only the initial values of two internal flags are modified; `COMMAND.COM` is otherwise unaffected.

Using debug Scripts

When PCnix is first installed on a hard disk, the installation program (a batch file) calls on debug to fix COMMAND.COM, handing it a debug script with instructions about where the flags are and how to set them. What's a debug script? Glad you asked.

The MS-DOS program debug can be used to create or modify executable files as well as to debug them. A few simple one-character commands, with arguments attached, is all we need to make a copy of COMMAND.COM into a friendlier and quieter shell. We can do it from the keyboard, of course—or we can prepare a set of commands, store them in a file, and call debug with standard input redirected so it comes from the file instead of the keyboard. The only tricky thing about writing such scripts is to note that debug understands the CR (carriage-return) code as a line ending, but is baffled by LF, the line-feed code. Scripts prepared by any self respecting MS-DOS editor will have their lines ended by CR/LF, the ill-chosen MS-DOS convention, so you'll have to take out all the LF codes (and comments) before debug will be happy with it. Not a terrible job, but annoying. If you have a working copy of PCnix, you can remove the offending codes, and run the debug script, with the single command line

```
tr -d \012 < file.dbs ¦ debug newfile.com
```

since the option -d tells the UNIX-like utility tr (transliterate) to delete octal code 12, the line feed.

The debug script used to modify COMMAND.COM in MS-DOS version 3.1 follows, with each command shown on a separate line:

```
e 105b 2          ;change hex location 105b to the value 2
e 1967 0          ;change hex location 1967 to the value 0
w                 ;write the modified file
q                 ;quit
```

If this script is stored in a file called fixcom.dbs (with all LF codes and comments removed, and lines ended by a single CR code), then the command

```
debug command.com < fixcom.dbs
```

will make COMMAND.COM a less irritating shell, automatically. A more extensive patch job is needed for DOS 2.X.

The following procedure is used to shut up ECHO OFF in MS-DOS 2.X:

1. Copy COMMAND.COM and debug.com onto a work disk.
2. Execute debug command.com from that disk. At the - prompt, type

3. s 0 7fff 01 00 00 01; write down found_address + 3 as `flag`.
   Type

4. s 0 7fff 61 6E 64 20 70; write down found_address as `patch`.
   Type

5. s 0 7fff B9 0A 00 E8; write down found_address as `jmp`.
   Type

6. u `jmp` [substitute value found in step 5 for `jmp`].

7. First instruction is `MOV CX,000A`, second is `CALL` yyyy - record yyyy value.

8. a `jmp+3`
   CALL `patch+1`

9. a `patch`
   DB 24
   ES:
   MOV BYTE PTR [`flag`], 00
   JMP yyyy

10. w

11. q

Values found for different DOS versions are listed in Table 3-1.

Table 3-1.   Values for DOS Versions

Value	DOS 2.0	DOS 2.1	DOS 2.11
flag	96E	96E	9B7
patch	364A	365D	3886
jmp	171D	1730	17E3
yyyy	1E6D	1E80	2A10

Improving MS-DOS Operation

MS-DOS supports a system call of unusual power, Terminate and Stay Resident (TSR), Function 31h. It allows an executable program to remain in active memory after it has been loaded, and protects it from being overwritten by other programs. (See Essay 7, Safe Memory-Resident Programming (TSR), by Steven Baker, for a detailed discussion.) The program can remain in memory throughout any computing session, up to the next computer reboot, ready to leap into action if called upon. We can use small programs of this type to add facility to the way MS-DOS does things without changing the MS-DOS innards in any way. There are lots of these additions available; PCnix uses two of them.

Much of the operation of MS-DOS is controlled by interrupts, and a table of pointers (interrupt vectors) is resident in low memory during normal operation. Any program can, at its own risk, replace one of these vectors so it will get called into action by the associated interrupt, then terminate but remain in memory. The program springs to life again whenever the chosen interrupt is triggered.

The keyboards normally supplied with IBM computers or their clones allow almost any keystroke to be repeated automatically just by holding the key down. Unfortunately, the repetition rate is very slow, chosen so novice users would not be frightened. This unfortunate hardware design choice can, fortunately, be corrected in software.

The program `qk.com` is a version of the program `quickeys.asm`, written by Dan Rollins and published in *PC Tech Journal* (September 1986). It has been slightly modified for PCnix in order to remove a bug. Its only job is to watch for interrupts from the keyboard (one for each key action) and, when a key is pressed (and after a suitable pause), generate identical keystrokes at a much faster pace than the glacial rate provided by the PC keyboard itself, until the key is released. It is a small thing, but it makes any program requiring keyboard input seem much peppier. It works particularly well with PC-Write, the shareware editor. It is loaded automatically on bootup by the command `qk` in the `AUTOEXEC.BAT` file.

The second TSR program, `keydo.com`, does much more, providing both a command history mechanism (like the UNIX C shell does) and a direct and simple way to edit the command line. Previous commands can be recalled by the up- or down-arrow keys on the PC keypad, while the other arrow keys move the cursor back and forth. The Home key puts the cursor at the start of the command line, the End key puts it at the end, and the Del key deletes characters. Any printable character typed is inserted in front of the cursor position. The ⟨RETURN⟩ key calls `COM-MAND.COM` to execute the command no matter where the cursor is. Commands are stored in a circular buffer for prompt recall—they can be modified, or executed as is. Once you get used to it, you feel crippled without it. The public domain version used in PCnix was written by IBM programmer J. Gersbach, and is installed on bootup by the command `keydo` in the PCnix `AUTOEXEC.BAT` file.

Using Batch Files to Create PCnix Commands

Text files whose filenames end in `.BAT` are interpreted by `COMMAND.COM` as executable commands, providing it can understand them. Although this facility is much more limited than the shell programming provided by the UNIX shells, it can still provide simple and useful services if two basic rules are followed in writing batch files:

1. Keep it short.
2. No, it's too long; make it shorter.

The COMMAND.COM interpreter is rudimentary but reasonably fast. It is often defeated, however, by a curious self-inflicted wound: whenever it finds a batch file line that is an external program to be run, it runs it—overwriting the batch file in the process, which must then be reloaded before it can examine the next line. Keeping the batch files in a RAMdisk helps but is awkward to arrange. Still, if a batch file runs fast enough, it's often the easiest way to add a simple command to the repertoire.

Changing Names to Protect the Innocent

The UNIX C shell provides a simple but powerful "alias" facility which allows you to rename a command anything you like. For example, novice UNIX users often complain about the terse and cryptic commands, such as ls or grep. Some users prefer to rename the commands to something they can remember more easily. Batch files can provide a simple alias facility as well. For example, the PCnix du command displays current disk usage via the batch file

```
ls -asR %1 %2 %3 %4 %5 %6 %7 %8 %9
```

simply by calling the ls command with suitable switch parameters.

Commands Can Be Repeated

Batch files are capable of far more than just calling a command by another name. They can improve the way a command operates to make it more useful. For example, the UNIX rm file-removal command can be approximated by a batch file that calls on the MS-DOS (internal) command DELETE in a loop until it runs out of filenames to erase:

```
:loop
if "%1" == "" goto end
del %1
shift
goto loop
:end
```

This emulation is simple, but not perfect. It permits deletion of a series of filenames, but it lacks the ability to delete subdirectories and their contents that the UNIX command rm-r * provides. Some may consider this an improvement rather than a defect, considering the havoc that can be wreaked from careless use of the UNIX rm.

Batch Files Can Be Subroutines

If one of the commands in a batch file is the name of a second batch file, every-thing works, but in a chaining fashion; control is transferred to the second batch file but never returned to the first. This behavior has led several technical writ-ers to insist (erroneously) that you can't call a batch file as a subroutine from another batch file. MS-DOS version 3.3 has a CALL command for this purpose, but earlier versions can get the same effect by simply invoking a new copy of COMMAND.COM to run the second batch file. Control returns to the original batch file when the second has finished:

```
command \c second.bat
```

Remember, PCnix reverses the / and \ characters, so \c designates a switch, telling the new COMMAND.COM to quit when it has finished running its argument as a command—in this case, the second batch file. A copy of the current MS-DOS envi-ronment variables are passed along to the second batch file subroutine, but the copy is erased when it finishes, so it can't just use the MS-DOS SET command to return strings to the calling batch file. There are ways, but they are ugly.

Commands Can Be Combined

As another example of a PCnix batch file command, one of the most-used opera-tions in UNIX (or MS-DOS) is to move to a new working directory (cd) and then display a listing of the files located in the new directory (ls). These two opera-tions are used so often it's worth combining them into a single command (ch). The UNIX command

```
alias ch 'cd \!*; ls -aFC ¦ more'
```

defines this new command in terms of known ones; the cryptic notation \!* is C-shell shorthand for "all arguments on the command line." In PCnix we do this same job with a batch file:

```
if "%1" == "a:" goto fix
if "%1" == "b:" goto fix
if "%1" == "c:" goto fix
if "%1" == "d:" goto fix
if "%1" == "e:" goto fix
if "%1" == "" goto fix
ls %1
cd %1
```

```
goto end
:fix
cd %1/
ls %1
:end
```

Most of the verbiage in our batch file arises from the desire to allow the command to change the working directory on a designated drive as well as on the current working drive—a concept not present in UNIX. For example, if the batch file above is invoked with the command

```
ch a:/usr/bin
```

it will execute the PCnix commands

```
ls a:/usr/bin
cd a:/usr/bin
```

which will first list all the files in the directory a:/usr/bin, and then change the working directory on drive a: to /usr/bin. If the batch file is invoked with the name of a drive but no path, then the root directory is understood to be the target, and the batch file provides the cd command with the root directory designator /. The command also returns you to the root directory on the current drive when used with no argument at all, just as the UNIX cd command with no argument returns to the user's home directory.

The most ambitious batch file command in PCnix emulates the UNIX cp command:

```
if "%2" == "" goto err
if not "%2" == "" set INTO=%2
if not "%3" == "" set INTO=%3
if not "%4" == "" set INTO=%4
if not "%5" == "" set INTO=%5
if not "%6" == "" set INTO=%6
if not "%7" == "" set INTO=%7
if not "%8" == "" set INTO=%8
if not "%9" == "" set INTO=%9
:loop
if %1 == %INTO% goto end
copy %1 %INTO%
shift
goto loop
:err
echo Use: cp fromfile tofile
```

```
echo   or   cp fromfile [fromfile ...] todir
:end
set INTO=
```

The first line enforces the UNIX convention that `cp` must have at least two arguments. The MS-DOS convention that the second argument can be missing to designate the current directory "." is confusing in practice. The next series of tests scans the argument list, setting the environment variable `INTO` according to the last argument it finds. By UNIX convention, this should be a directory if more than one filename precedes it. The batch file hopes it is, but doesn't check. (It is possible to check, using a "batch file helper," but that slows things down too much for simple copies.)

Once the last argument is found, the MS-DOS `copy` command is called to copy the files, one at a time, into the file or directory represented by the string in `INTO`. The syntax `%INTO%` is known to the batch file interpreter, which substitutes the actual environment string for its name before executing the resulting command. When the loop runs out of arguments, it terminates. The final line erases `INTO` as a matter of cleanliness. Again, the UNIX recursive copy `cp-r *` is not emulated. Some day . . .

Batch Files Provide On-Line Help

PCnix also contains a built-in help system with a simple syntax: `help` alone gets a list of commands, and `help xx` displays a short description of command `xx` by searching a known directory for `xx.doc`. It is made up entirely of text files and a batch file driver `help.bat`:

```
if "%1" == "" goto noarg
if exist c:/help/%1.doc cls
p c:/help/%1.doc
goto end
:noarg
if exist c:/help/help.doc cls
p c:/help/help.doc
:end
```

The command `p` is the PCnix equivalent of the UNIX `more` command. Without arguments or redirection, it just sends the file to the screen, pausing after 22 lines to keep things in view. The 〈RETURN〉 key gets one more line, 〈SPACE〉 gets one more screenful. It displays an error message if it can't find the file.

PCnix contains a help file for each command. It shows the syntax—what you should type to make it work—then explains available options, describes in general terms how the command works, and finally gives an example or two of its operation. Each text file attempts to fit within one screen and is successful for the simpler commands. As an example of the format of the help documents, the following shows the text of the file tail.doc, which is displayed if you type the command helptail.

```
tail - display the tail end of a text file's contents
Syntax:   tail [-####] filename [filename ...]
With only the filename as an argument, 'tail' displays
the last eleven lines in a text file. With more than one
filename, it displays the last eleven lines of each file
successively. Two will just fit on one screen display; this can
be handy in comparing two versions of a text file. With a numeric
argument, 'tail' displays the number of requested lines
at the end of the designated file(s). By default, output is
displayed on the console screen, with a pause every 22 lines.
<RETURN> displays one more line, any other key displays the
next screenful. The pause does not occur if output is redirected
to a file or device. A huge numeric argument will display the
complete text file. Binary files give a funny looking display but
nothing burns.
Examples:
tail text              Display the last 11 lines of "text."
tail -123 xx > yy      Extract the last 123 lines of file "xx"
                       and deposit them into a file called "yy."
```

Using Batch File Helpers to Increase Flexibility

Batch files have no direct mechanism for making system calls to MS-DOS, but since they can run an external program (at some cost in time) we can add this capability. All that is required is a short program to make the needed system call and a way of returning the result so the batch file can test it. MS-DOS provides a crude return mechanism: if the program exits via the interrupt Function 4Ch, the value in the AL register is preserved and can be tested by the if errorlevel construct.

Creating Short Programs

Probably the simplest way to write a short program is to use debug interactively to create it as a .COM file. Here's the procedure to use:

1. debug newfile.com (Debug responds File not found and creates it)

2. a (Debug now accepts commands to assemble)

3. Type the commands in sequence (addresses will start at 0100h)

4. Type ⟨RETURN⟩ to make an empty line

5. rcx (Debug responds CX 0000 bytes, then prompts with ":")

6. Type the (hex) number of the empty line address (line 4), after subtracting 100h.

7. w

8. q

As an example, here's what your screen shows when you create INT37.COM to set the SWITCHAR variable to / as described earlier (except for comments following ";"):

```
debug int37.com
File not found            ; Debug creates int37.com, grumpily
-a                        ; start to assemble
1166:0100 mov dl,5C       ; put '\' code into register DL
1166:0102 mov ax,3701     ; Function number 37h to AH, 1 to AL
1166:0105 int 21          ; AL == 1 means set SWITCHAR from DL
1166:0107 mov ax,4C00     ; Exit with errorlevel set to 0
1166:010A int 21
1166:010C                 ; empty line tells Debug to stop assembly
-rcx                      ; examine the CX register
CX 0000                   ; Debug response: current value is 0
:C                        ; empty_line_address - 100h
-w                        ; write number of bytes in CX
Writing 000C bytes        ; Debug response
-q                        ; quit.
```

If you are adept at using the assembler MASM, you might prefer to write batch file helpers in assembly code, which is easier to document and maintain. They are usually so short, though, that using debug is much faster.

Taming the SUBST Command

Many useful programs for the PC were written when MS-DOS was young, before it knew about directories; these programs assumed everything was available directly on one of the drives. In UNIX parlance, all the files were stored in the root directories. This was tolerable before hard disks entered the scene, but with 10MB or more of storage available, a `DIR` command became a real adventure. The hierarchical directory system, eerily similar to the one used in UNIX, was added to MS-DOS 2.0. This solved one problem but created another: the older programs only worked if the directory they were stored in was the default, an awkward requirement to realize with a single (hard disk) drive. Since we want to be able to use these older programs under PCnix (and have them look just like the newer ones), we must solve this problem somehow.

MS-DOS 3.0 provided a partial solution in the form of the `SUBST` command. This command allowed any directory to be designated as an honorary drive, defined by its pathname. Now the older programs could be located anywhere, and a batch file could be designed to make them operate as if they understood about directories. It almost worked.

Let's examine how to write a batch file to call the IBM program Wordproof into action. This excellent program looks up words in its dictionary and stops on any it can't identify, letting the user verify or change the spelling. It can suggest possible spellings (or synonyms) on request. For convenience, we'll put Wordproof in the directory /edit/spell. We can use `SUBST` to call this directory drive e:, for example, so when we want to proofread the file we've been working on in our current directory, c:/propose/draft, we can say

```
cd e:
```

to go to /edit/spell. Now we want to call the Wordproof program into action with `draft` as an argument, so . . . oops. That file is on the drive c, the one we just came from, not drive e. Can't do it that way.

Well, OK, let's call the program from our working directory, with the command

```
e:wp draft
```

so Wordproof can find it—but now Wordproof can't find its own dictionary, because it looks only on the default drive when it starts up.

We could assume we'll always be working from drive c and wire that idea into the controlling batch file, but that means we can't proofread a file that is on a floppy disk in drive a.

The right way to do it, of course, is to find out what drive we are on *before* we go to our mythical drive e, then use that information to tell Wordproof where to find the file to proofread. We can then return to our original working directory when we are done. MS-DOS knows what drive we are using, and even has a function call to tell us—if we could make such a call from our batch file. With a batch file helper, we can. Consider this small program:

```
; drv - return current drive number as errorlevel
    mov ax,1900    ; get current drive number (function 19h)
```

```
int 21
mov ah,4C          ; return AL as errorlevel (function 4C)
int 21             ; int 21h does almost everything ...
```

MS-DOS Function 19h returns the current drive number (0 = a, 1 = b, etc.) in the AL register, just where Function 4C expects to find the errorlevel value. If we create this program as drv.com using debug, we can include it in our batch file proof.bat:

```
drv
if errorlevel 0 set DRV=a:
if errorlevel 1 set DRV=b:
if errorlevel 2 set DRV=c:
if errorlevel 3 set DRV=d:
subst e: c:\editp\spell
e:
wp %DRV%%1
%DRV%
set DRV=
subst e: -D
```

First we call drv.com, then put the name of our current drive in the environment variable DRV. (The errorlevel test is a bit strange: if errorlevel 1 tests true if the errorlevel value is equal to *or less than* 1. Reversing the test order would leave the wrong value in DRV.) Next we create our phantom drive and go there, where Wordproof lives. The string %DRV% will be replaced by the string we stored in the environment, so if we typed the command

```
proof draft
```

the command that calls Wordproof into action becomes

```
wp c:draft
```

if our original working drive was drive c. Similarly, after Wordproof finishes its job, the next line will be

```
c:
```

which returns to the directory draft is in. As a final bit of cleanliness, we remove DRV from the environment and delete the connection between e: and c:/edit/spell.

Syntactic note: the shiny new SUBST command stubbornly refuses to look at SWITCHAR for its switch character, so it insists on \ as a pathname separator. To delete the established connection, it demands the D switch (and requires that it be uppercase!). But it will accept neither \ nor / as the switch character if SWITCHAR has been changed. It *does* accept - however, a fact missing from the MS-DOS documentation.

How Many Drives Are Out There?

PCnix can run comfortably on a two-floppy system, providing it has enough memory to hold a RAMdisk of reasonable size—640K is nice. The most-used commands are written to the RAMdisk on system startup, with the help files and less popular commands residing in directories on floppy drive a. Startup is a bit slow, but if the RAMdisk is the default directory, most commands take less time to run than from a hard disk. A lot of floppy-swappy goes on, though, if you try to do something serious such as run a compiler. A hard disk is better if you can afford one.

PCnix uses a public domain RAMdisk system written by Nat White; it has the advantage of being able to be removed (well, set to zero capacity) without rebooting. The driver, ram.sys, must be included in the CONFIG.SYS file used during startup. It does need to know the name of the drive it pretends to be, though, and this depends on how many real drives are installed in front of it. Here's the batch file helper used to find out about the drives present:

```
; ldrv - return index of last valid drive
mov     bl,20        ; assume no more than 32 drives
mov     ax,4404      ; IOCTL call, read from block device
mov     cx,0000      ; number of bytes to read (none)
int     21
dec     bl           ; count down in BL
cmp     al,0F        ; IOCTL returns 0F if drive invalid
jz      0102         ; if so, try the next smaller one
mov     al,bl        ; else BL now has the index
mov     ah,4C        ; return with index as errorlevel
int     21           ; 0 means A, 1 means B etc.
```

The portion of the AUTOEXEC.BAT file that creates the RAMdisk and then fills it with commands from the floppy disk looks like this:

```
;find out drive name for RAMdisk
ldrv
if errorlevel 2 set RD=C
```

```
if errorlevel 3 set RD=D
if errorlevel 4 set RD=E
path %RD%:/;a:/bin;a:/system
echo Creating a RAMdrive as drive %RD%: ...
setram %RD%: 256
echo Copying the most-used commands to drive %RD%: ...
copy a:/toram/*.* %RD%: > nul
set comspec=%RD%:\command.com
```

Note that MS-DOS will insist you have two drives even if there is only one physical drive installed. This is actually ingenious, since two drives are simulated by the system by using the one real drive alternately. The command

```
copy a: a:
```

works just fine, prompting you to change source and target disks as needed. In any event, ldrv will never return 0 or 1 as the last valid drive index if ram.sys has been loaded.

Once the drive name is known (and stored in the environment as RD), the name %RD% can be used wherever the drive name is needed—as the first directory searched (after the current one) via the PATH command, as the target of the copy command, and as the location for COMMAND.COM, should the latter get overwritten and need to be reloaded.

Taming the MKDIR Command

PCnix installs itself onto a hard disk from a batch file, which creates directories (bin, help, etc.) on the hard disk to hold everything. Should the directory already exist, the installer should quietly put files into it—without complaint. The MS-DOS command MKDIR, however, gets upset if the directory already exists, and complains with an error message that cannot be redirected into the NULL file— the usual way of shutting things up. In this case, we need to know whether a particular name is already present as a directory, so we create a batch file helper to tell us:

```
; fd - find out if arg string is the name of a subdirectory
mov     bx,0081          ; psp address of arg string start
add     bl,[0080]        ; number of chars in string
mov     byte ptr [bx],00 ; null-terminate the string
mov     dx,0082          ; point to 1st non-blank char
mov     ax,4300          ; get filename attribute
int     21
```

```
mov     ax,4C00                 ; return errorlevel exit
cmp     cx,+10                  ; is it a directory?
jnz     011B                    ; if no, return 0
inc     AX                      ; if yes, return 1
int     21
```

We assume that the string was given to the fd command as an argument, and has been installed by COMMAND.COM in the usual place for the first command-line argument. The string format is different from that expected by MS-DOS Function 43h. (Naturally—consistency is a virtue of the small mind.) So, we must first convert it, then call on the system to see if it is the name of an existing directory. We convert the returned attribute into a yes/no answer and return it as a testable errorlevel.

Here's a portion of the PCnix file install.bat that uses this helper, reading from a floppy disk in drive a: and installing the system onto drive c:

```
a:/bin/fd c:bin
if not errorlevel 1 mkdir c:bin > nul
echo Filling directory "bin" with PCnix executable files ...
copy a:bin bin > nul
```

Is There a Clock in the House?

As a final example, PCnix tries to read the clock/calendar via its AUTOEXEC.BAT file on bootup. In a brave attempt to be independent of the hardware that might be present, it tries several "readclock" routines for different types of hardware. It depends on a batch file helper to find out if it has been successful in reading the clock. If not, it keeps trying until it runs out of things to try. If it is successful, it writes a short code string into the environment to tell other routines what kind of clock is present, in case they need to know. It knows it's running on a PC/AT clone if the clock is correctly set before it tries anything.

Here's the helper that finds out if the (internal, MS-DOS) clock has been properly set:

```
; tclk - test to see if clock/calendar has been set
mov     ah,2A           ; Get date
int     21
mov     ax,4C00         ; 0 -> AL, "return errorlevel" -> AH
cmp     cx,07C3         ; is date less than 1987?
jl      010E            ; if yes, clock is not set
inc     ax              ; else mark it as set
int     21              ; return AL as errorlevel
```

Figure 3-1 summarizes our discussion of the design of PCnix by showing how the parts of a typical PCnix system are arranged. Notice how the batch files and software tools used by PCnix fit into the MS-DOS environment. (See Essay 1, Harry Henderson's Guided Tour inside MS-DOS, for a discussion of how the parts of MS-DOS interact.)

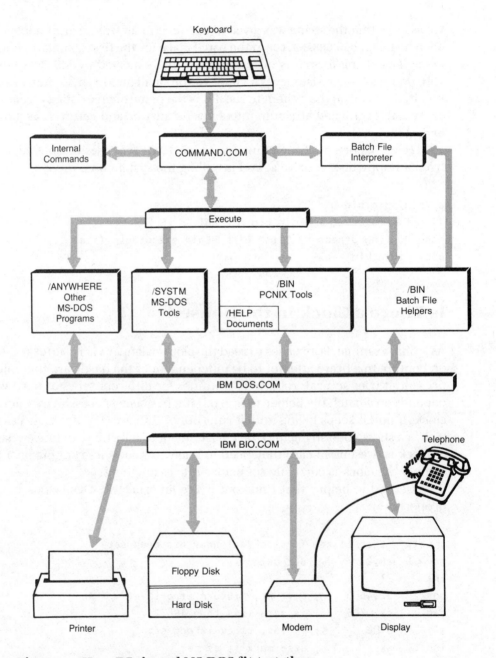

Fig. 3-1.   How PCnix and MS-DOS fit together.

The Software Toolkit

We've created our basic PCnix environment and the easy support routines; now we have some *real* work to do. MS-DOS provides several software tools that are specific to its own file system. We can adopt those tools that do a good and useful job (FORMAT, DISKCOPY, CHKDISK, SYS), and we can scour the public domain for others. Even so, we'll fall far short of the nifty tools provided by UNIX—so we'll just have to write them. We'll adopt the C language as the most portable and UNIX-like, using a commercial compiler (Microsoft C or Borland's Turbo C) as the closest approximations to the Portable C compiler (cc) that comes with our particular UNIX system, Berkeley UNIX 4.3bsd.

Tools for Dealing with Text

Our plan is to avoid slavishly copying the UNIX toolkit in every detail. We must take into account the different operating environment provided by MS-DOS, and use its services as much as possible to make things speedy. We'll start by dividing the tools into groups, and we'll tackle first those tools concerned mostly with manipulating text—the primary medium of exchange between the various UNIX software tools. Table 3-2 lists those in PCnix.

Table 3-2.   Text Tools

Tool	Function
ed	PC-Write, a powerful, modeless editor for word processing
diff	Find minimal differences between two text files
eline	Enforce MS-DOS line-ending convention on a text file
grep	Search text files for patterns, print all lines that match
p	Display files, optionally with visible control codes
pr	Page and print text files, optionally in multiple columns
split	Split a long file into shorter segments, gracefully
sr	Search and replace multiple text patterns in parallel
str	Find the ASCII strings in a binary file
tail	Display the tail end of a file's contents
tr	Transform a series of (single) character codes into others
uniq	Remove (or print) duplicate lines in a text file
wc	Count lines, words, and characters in a text file

We'll need an editor to create and edit text files. PCnix really doesn't care what editor you use, so long as it creates normal ASCII text and runs under MS-DOS. The shareware editor PC-Write is a good one, and a PC version of the Berkeley UNIX editor vi is available commercially. PCnix also uses the nansi.sys public domain replacement for the MS-DOS display driver `ANSI.SYS`, written by Dan Kegel, because it's faster.

Some of the text tools do the same jobs, and therefore bear the same names, as their UNIX counterparts: `diff`, `grep`, `pr`, `tail`, `tr`, `uniq`, and `wc`. A few are different, or have different features, in order to cope better with MS-DOS. For example, text lines under UNIX are ended with a single code `LF`. MS-DOS requires two: `CR/LF`. CP/M uses only one: `CR`. The `eline` tool can cope with alien line endings, substituting the MS-DOS `CR/LF` convention for whatever it finds. If no line-ending convention is found, it word-wraps at the end of a line whose length can be specified (default 80 columns). Its ability to word-wrap (but without any attempt at hyphenation) makes it a useful companion to the `pr` program, which can produce two (or more) columns of text, but chops the ends off text lines that are too long.

The `p` (pager) program has a couple of hidden talents in addition to paging text to the display screen. It can strip out high-order character bits inserted by some other text programs, most notably WordStar, thus converting the output to a printable form. If its output is redirected into a disk file, it behaves like the UNIX `cat` command. It can also substitute printable codes for the eight codes not normally printed by the `nansi.sys` screen driver (Null, Tab, Bell, Backspace, `CR`, `LF`, Escape, Rubout), so you can see what they are. It uses intensified characters to distinguish them from their unintensified look-alikes. Printing a binary file to the screen is quite entertaining but the results are not terribly informative.

In a more practical vein, the `str` program searches through binary files and displays any text strings it finds. This action is similar to the UNIX program `strings` except it knows about the various different kinds of text strings found in MS-DOS. UNIX, bless it, has only one style. Strange things can sometimes be found in executable files. For example, if you scan a new program fresh from a BBS and encounter a string like `HA HA, GOTCHA!!!!!`, don't run the program.

Now, let's choose one of the text tools and examine it in some detail. The C language encourages a program architecture consisting of many separate functions, each of which does a logically complete job. If these functions are written with some attention to modest generality, they can often be used unchanged in subsequent programs. Since we've already seen the `help.doc` file describing `tail` let's see how that command works. Here are the separate routines in outline form:

```
tail - display the tail end of a text file's contents
    allnum - examine a string for numeric characters exclusively
    toscreen - find out if output is to the console screen
    filecopy - copy the last part of a file to stdout
        stak - a circular data storage & retrieval structure
            size - set the modulus size of the circular stack
            push - overwrite the oldest stack entry
            pull - extract the oldest available stack entry
```

(pop - extract the youngest stack entry)
endlin - end a line and watch for screen overflow

The main routine, tail.c, processes the command line options—in this case only one option may be present, the one to set the number of lines to be printed. It calls on allnum.c for help with that chore. It also calls toscreen.c to see if the output is going to the display screen or not. If it is, tail.c sets a global flag (tsc) so the output will pause after each screenful of text. tail.c next opens any files on the command line it can find, calling on filecopy.c to do the dirty work for each one of them:

```
/* toscreen - find out if output is to console screen */
#include <dos.h>
toscreen()
{
union REGS r;
r.x.ax = 0x4400;                    /* get IOCTL status code */
r.x.bx = 1; intdos(&r, &r);
return((r.x.dx & 1) && (r.x.dx & 0x80));    /* isdev && iscin */
}
```

The function toscreen.c shows the way C can be used to make MS-DOS system calls and return the result. The #include file dos.h is a header file that defines REGS to match the registers available in the 8088 microprocessor. All C compilers available under MS-DOS have this facility, but there is no standardization, so the PCnix tools try to isolate this activity, minimizing the number of routines that have to be changed if some other compiler is used. ANSI, where are you?

The filecopy.c routine makes use of a very UNIX-like feature of MS-DOS. Files are treated as simple strings of bytes; with text files, one character is stored in each byte. System calls allow the pointer that indicates the next character to be moved around—just like a memory pointer. The file characters need not be read-only in the order they are stored. By putting the file pointer to the file's end, filecopy.c can determine how many characters the file holds, and can then move back the number of lines requested and display them.

There is one complication: how many characters (bytes) are there on each line? It varies with the text—in fact, some files may not be text files at all, so we'd best be careful here. If we want to move back 11 lines from the end (the default value), we can move back 880 characters and be reasonably safe, since we display at most 80 characters on a line. Now we'd like to move forward in the file, watching for line-endings and counting them until we come to the end again. If we keep track of just where we found each one, we can go immediately to the start of the eleventh line from the end and print from there.

The filecopy routine calls on a circular storage buffer to do this last job, setting its length to the number of requested lines—in our example, eleven. It then proceeds to examine the file one character at a time, using the push() operation to store a character count for each line-ending found. If there are more than 11 lines, as there may well be, the oldest counts are overwritten. When the end-of-file is found, the desired character count will be the eleventh count from the end. The pull() operation extracts it since it is the oldest value present. (The pop() operation—extract the most recent value—is included for completeness but is not used here.)

```c
#define FHOME 0                    /* symbolic constants for fseek */
#define FHERE 1
#define FEND 2
/* filecopy - copy the last part of an open file to stdout */
filecopy(fp)
FILE *fp;
{
extern long lines;
int c, lc = 0;
long nchars, guess, acnum;
long pull();
size(lines + 2);       /* size stack, allow for trailing newline */
guess = lines * 80;   /* estimate no. of chars this represents */
fseek(fp, 0l, FEND);
acnum = ftell(fp);            /* find how many there really are */
if(acnum <= guess)
     guess = acnum;                    /* use the smaller number */
fseek(fp, -guess, FEND);            /* rewind to that point */
nchars = ftell(fp);
while((c = fgetc(fp)) != EOF) {            /* and run forward */
     nchars++;
     if(c == '\n') {
          lc++;                       /* counting text lines */
          push(nchars);      /* and save corresponding char no. */
     }
}
if(lc >= lines)
     fseek(fp, pull(), FHOME);   /* rewind to requested point */
else
     fseek(fp, -guess, FEND);        /* or to best guess */
while((c = fgetc(fp)) != EOF)           /* and send it out */
     if(c == '\n' && endlin())    /* watching for display pause */
          continue;
     fputc(c, stdout);
     }
}
```

Under UNIX, we could just pipe the output through more to page it one screenful at a time, but that's much too slow under MS-DOS. Instead, we'll include the subroutine endlin.c in each tool we write that sends text to the screen.

```
#define SCRSIZ 22
/* endlin - end a line and watch for screen overflow */
static int lc = 0;                          /* line counter */
endlin()
{
extern int tsc;                    /* true if output is to screen */
register int c;
if(tsc && ++lc >= SCRSIZ) {       /* pause if output is to screen */
    fputs("\r\n\033[7m--More--", stdout);    /* and a screenful */
    c = bdos(7) & 0xFF;                      /* get a keystroke */
    fputs("\033[0m\r\033[K", stdout);
    switch(c) {
        case '\r':                 /* <RETURN> - show 1 more line */
            lc = SCRSIZ - 1;
            break;
        case 'q':                  /* quit with "q" or "ctrl-C" */
        case '\003':
            exit(0);
        default:
            lc = 0;                /* else show another screenful */
            break;
        }
    return(1);                     /* yes, we ended this line */
    }
return(0);                         /* no, we didn't end it */
}
```

The strange codes in the fputs function are understood by the MS-DOS screen driver nansi.sys; they paint --More-- in reverse video, on a line of its own below the text lines. The function then waits for a keystroke, which it examines to see what to do next. When it finds one, it either quits or returns a code indicating whether it had to stop (and thence end the last displayed line) or not, and erases the --More-- from the screen. The caller must supply the line-ending codes if the subroutine did not.

An external flag (tsc) indicates whether the output is going to the screen or not. This is very useful to many tools. If output is redirected into a disk file, or to the printer, it can be passed to them uninterrupted. The flag can be set correctly for any execution of the tool by calling toscreen() once, as was done here by tail.c.

If you are curious about the circular storage buffer, it's surprisingly simple:

```c
/* stak - a circular data storage & retrieval structure */
#define EMPTY -1
long *s = NULL;                         /* holding stack */
unsigned int lp = 0;                        /* lifo index */
unsigned int fp = 0;                        /* fifo index */
unsigned int endm = 0;                  /* modulus limit */
/* size - set the mod size of the stack & allocate space */
size(i)
int i;
{
if((s = (long *)malloc(i * sizeof(long))) != NULL)
    endm = i;
}

push(x)                 /* overwrite the oldest stack entry */
long x;
{
s[lp++] = x;
if(lp >= endm)
    lp = 0;
if(lp == fp)
    fp = ++fp % endm;
}
long pull()      /* extract the oldest available stack entry */
{
long j;
if(lp == fp)
    return(EMPTY);
j = s[fp];
fp = ++fp % endm;
return(j);
}
long pop()              /* extract the youngest stack entry */
{
if(lp == fp)
    return(EMPTY);
if(--lp < 0)
    lp += endm;
return(s[lp]);
}
```

Dealing with Files

The PCnix toolkit also includes a set of software tools for listing, finding, and manipulating files. Table 3-3 lists the current repertoire.

Table 3-3.   PCnix File Tools

Tool	Function
arc	Compress and archive files, or decompress files
dog	Reorganize your hard disk for fastest access
chmod	Change the mode of a file to/from system, hidden, etc.
chn	Change the name of a file, directory, or volume label
du	Summarize disk usage in a part of the file hierarchy
ffind	Find path(s) to filename(s) on the designated drive
ls	List filenames in a directory, in many nice ways
mv	Move files or directories to another location
pwd	Print full path to current working directory on a drive

The file compressor/archiver/decompressor `arc` is a shareware program, distributed by System Enhancement Associates, that first examines a file, then chooses one of several compression techniques depending on what it finds. Text or binary files can be compressed 30 percent to 50 percent, a helpful saving if the file is destined for transmission over phone lines.

The disk organizer `dog`, written by G. Allen Morris III, is also distributed as shareware. It explores your hard disk and then, with your permission, reshuffles the way storage clusters (clumps of disk segments) are ordered on the disk to paste together all the files that have become fragmented (stored in several pieces) by the MS-DOS storage system. This can speed up subsequent disk-intensive operations dramatically. It can take a long time to run, but it keeps you entertained with a slightly breathless account of how the job is progressing. Run it during lunch break.

The UNIX program `find` can be dispatched into the file system to look for (and perhaps modify) files you name or describe on the command line. It is a very powerful tool only UNIX gurus use, because the syntax is unbelievably painful. It's a superb example of a program that tries to do too much. Our PCnix program `ffind` has a much more modest mission: it explores a file system on a designated drive recursively, peeking into each subdirectory and listing the complete pathname to any file we tell it to watch for. It can accept the MS-DOS wildcard characters, so we can find all the batch files on drive c, for example, with the command

```
ffind c:*.bat
```

It's marginally useful on floppy disks and almost essential on hard disks with

20MB or more of storage—it's amazing how easy it is to misplace files even in a well-organized directory system. (See Essay 2, Searching the File Tree with whereis, by Frank Whaley, for a utility more like the complete UNIX find command.)

What's in a Name?

MS-DOS 2.X had a curious limitation: its rename command, which called on Function 56h, worked on files but not on directories. To change a directory name, you first had to create a new (empty) directory with the chosen name, copy all the files from the old one into the new one, delete the old files, and then delete the old directory. On a floppy disk, you would always run out of space about halfway through. Yet, MS-DOS Function 17h could rename directories. It did not, however, understand about pathnames. Our PCnix chn command is a short program that calls Function 17h, accepting the limitation that the designated file must be in the current directory of one of the drives.

MS-DOS 3.0 quietly introduced a new version of Function 56h that can rename directories (without, of course, mentioning that fact in the documentation). Our mv command can use this new capability to rename directories, but it can't do so under MS-DOS versions before 3.0. We'll also teach mv about drives. If a file or directory is moved to another location on the same drive, only the File Allocation Table (FAT) need be changed, and Function 56h will do that for us. Moving files or directories to another drive requires that everything be copied to the new, then (if the copy is successful) erased from the old. mv does it that way.

What's in a Directory?

Perhaps the most-used command in either UNIX or PCnix is the ls command, which tells us the names of files in one or more directories, and as much about them as we ask for—unlike DIR, which tells everything it knows whether we ask or not, shouting at us in UPPERCASE. The ls command has (perhaps too many) options available to control what it does:

```
ls - a UNIX-like directory listing program for MS-DOS

Syntax: ls [-acilrstuR] [(path)name ... ]

Options may appear in any order, grouped or separated; if
separate, each must be preceded by a dash. The name(s) may refer
to files or directories. If no name is given, the current
directory is listed. MS-DOS wildcards are graciously accepted.
```

```
Options:
(none)    Show filenames (only) sorted alphabetically
 -a       all: include system files, hidden files, "." and ".."
 -c       columnar: change how many columns are used in the listing
 -i       identify: change whether directory pathname is shown
 -l       long listing: include file's size, date, time, attributes
 -r       reverse the sorting direction
 -s       report size(s) only
 -t       sort by time of last file modification
 -u       include actual disk use, with totals & available space
 -R       recursively list all subdirectories
```

The default settings for most of these options can be changed, so ls can be sweetened to taste. For example, some people like to have the name of the current directory shown, along with its contents, when ls is invoked without arguments—in effect, UNIX pwd followed by ls. Others find this offensive. If it matters to you, you can change one or more of the "customizing constants" in the program to change the default settings from those normally supplied:

```
/* customizing constants */
#define ID     1          /* always identify directory if 1 */
#define ALL    0          /* show hidden files by default if 1 */
#define LONG   0          /* long listing by default if 1 */
#define SCOLM  0     /* 1-column short listing by default if 1 */
#define LCOLM  1     /* 1-column long listing by default if 1 */
#define RSORT  0          /* reverse sort by default if 1 */
#define TSORT  0          /* time sort by default if 1 */
#define DU     0          /* include disk use by default if 1 */
```

Since ls has to poke around in the MS-DOS file system, much of its operation involves making system calls to learn things, and reformatting the result (e.g., transforming filenames to lowercase) for display. In outline form, here are the various routines that make up the whole, with MS-DOS function calls identified in parentheses:

```
ls - a UNIX-like directory listing program for MS-DOS
main - process input options
toscreen - find out if output is to console screen          (44h)
setps - set pathname separator to MS-DOS switchar value     (37h)
curdrv - get name of current default drive                  (19h)
curpath - get path to directory on default drive            (47h)
search - search 'path' for filename or directory
```

```
find_first - find first file in chosen directory   (1Ah, 4Eh)
    comp - compare size of two entries for quicksort
    gcdate - get current date (months) for comparison   (2Ah)
    getcl - get cluster size & space left on A drive   (36h)
    abspath - get absolute path into search path buffer
find_next - find the next file in this directory   (1Ah, 4Fh)
    (calls the same routines as find_first)
shortlist - print a list of names in up to 5 columns
    putname - convert name to lower case and print
    endlin - end a line and watch for screen overflow
longlist - list everything about files in one or two columns
    fill - fill long list structure with file information
    mname - convert month number to month name
    putname - convert name to lower case and print
    endlin - end a line and watch for screen overflow
```

Table 3-4 lists a few other tools to complete our toolkit. Fortunately, a complete version of the wonderful UNIX utility make for MS-DOS has been distributed as shareware by its author, D. G. Kneller—it is superior to the "professional" version distributed by Microsoft with its C compiler. We'll add the touch command to work with it, calling Functions 2Ah and 2Ch to get the current time and date, then calling Function 57h to insert them into the file's time-stamp.

Table 3-4.   Hacker Tools

Tool	Function
make	Compile, link a C program from separate files, minimally
tglob	Transform global definition file into extern decl file
touch	Mark the time-stamp of a file with the present date/time
kermit	Terminal emulator and file transfer utility
uuencode	Encode a binary (executable) file as ASCII text
uudecode	Recover the original binary from encoded text files
now	Display the current day, date, and time
switch	Display or change DOS SWITCHAR character (default is \)
xp	Expand wildcards in filenames and display all that match

We'll use the excellent Kermit protocol for file transfer to and from our Vax (running UNIX, of course) written by Frank da Cruz, and distributed at cost by Columbia University. We can make use of its MS-DOS version to pretend our PC is actually a smart terminal—Kermit has terminal emulation built in. We'll also use the public domain programs uuencode and uudecode, written by Mark Horton, so we can send binary files over phone lines. Kermit handles binary files correctly, but many electronic mail programs get serious indigestion from nontext code combinations. The uuencode program transforms a binary file into an encoded text file, and `uudecode` recovers the original binary file at the other end. The original filename is preserved. By convention, `beerbust.uue` is an encoded file and should be fed to `uudecode`, which might produce `beerbust.arc` as its output. The command

```
arc x beerbust.arc
```

will extract the individual files from the transmitted archive, binary or otherwise.

Our miscellaneous category includes `now`, which tells you what now is, `switch` that permits changing `SWITCHAR` as a last resort in getting a program to run, and `xp`, an MS-DOS version of the UNIX `ECHO` command. The UNIX shell programs expand the metacharacters `?` and `*` for each program they invoke, but `COMMAND.COM` does not. Under UNIX, the command

```
echo *.txt
```

will echo to the screen all filenames in the current directory that end in `.txt`, so you can see what will happen if you use, instead,

```
rm *.txt
```

The `xp` command does this same job for MS-DOS.

But what is that program called `tglob`? Well, it's a programmer's tool—a bit specialized, perhaps, but handy when we write large C programs like `ls`. The C language demands that global filenames be defined, and optionally initialized, in only one place. The normal convention is to `#include` them in the `main.c` program. All separate subroutines must know about them to use them, however, so they need the same list of names, but listed as external declarations. Keeping two name lists is both tedious and error-prone. The final goody in our "friendly programming environment" project PCnix is the help file for `tglob`:

```
tglob - transform global definition file into extern decl file

Syntax:  tglob [filename] > outfile

Global variables may only be defined in one place in a C program,
but must be referenced as "extern" declarations in all other
files that use them. "tglob" acts as a filter, to transform a
global definition file into another file with the necessary
"extern" declarations present, and with any initializing
values removed, so only the definition file need be maintained.
With no filename present "tglob" reads its standard input; it
always writes to stdout. Using a makefile, the following
```

dependence entries will create a new declaration file from the
definition file, automatically:

```
sglob.h : glob.h
     tglob glob.h > sglob.h
```
where "glob.h" is the definition file, and "sglob.h" is
the resulting declaration file. The main program file should
contain #include "glob.h"
and all separate subroutine files should contain
#include "sglob.h"

Example: Before (input to tglob):
```
================================================================
/* individual field lengths for full and reduced display */
int box1 = 4;
char ffmax[]={0,8,9,0,19,19,19,19,19,0,8,19,2,0,6,6,6,6,0,3,0,0};
unsigned char wbuf1[] =
"              *******************************\r\n\
               *         02:07:13 UT         *\r\n\
               *         23 Jan 87           *\r\n\
               *******************************\r\n";
char *mo[] = {
    "Jan","Feb","Mar","Apr","May","Jun","Jul","Aug","Sep","Oct",
    "Nov","Dec"
    };
int ftime[40];               /* filter change time array */
================================================================
After (output from tglob):
================================================================
/* individual field lengths for full and reduced display */
extern int box1 ;
extern char ffmax[] ;
extern unsigned char wbuf1[] ;
extern char *mo[] ;
extern int ftime[];          /* filter change time array */
================================================================
```

MS-DOS Wildcards Are Not UNIX Metacharacters

Although the wildcard characters ? and * in MS-DOS (and hence in PCnix) are, at
first glance, the same as the ? and * metacharacters in UNIX, there are real differences that can cause you grief. Basically, the filenames in MS-DOS consist of 8-

character (max) filenames, optionally followed by a dot (.) and a 3-character (max) extension:

```
wildcard.doc (longest possible filename in MS-DOS)
```

If you move a file from UNIX, be sure the name follows MS-DOS rules. As an ugly example, if you copy a UNIX file called `wildcard.doc2` to MS-DOS, it becomes `wildcard.doc`. The extension is truncated to 3 characters and the file may overwrite one called `wildcard.doc` if one is present in your working directory.

The `?` metacharacter in UNIX matches any one filename character, just as in MS-DOS. In UNIX, however, `???` matches any 3-character name but not any one- or two-character names. In MS-DOS, `???` matches all filenames with one, two, or three characters. Thus, the construction `????????` will match any name in MS-DOS that has no extension, and the construction `????????.???` matches any possible name.

The `*` metacharacter in UNIX matches any sequence of filename characters, as it does in MS-DOS, but there is an important difference. Wherever `*` is found in a filename, MS-DOS replaces it with as many `?` characters as will fit, up to the dot character or to the end of the extension. If you are in the habit of using `*` on UNIX to avoid typing long filenames, look out. The UNIX command `rm *ff` would remove any filename that ends in `ff` but in MS-DOS the same command removes all files that lack an extension. Similarly, the UNIX command `rm *ff.*gg` removes only those filenames that end in `ff` and have an extension ending in `gg`. In MS-DOS, the same command removes all files in the current directory! In these cases, the `*` is encountered first and is replaced by `????????` in front of the dot character and `???` afterward, so the `ff` and `gg` exceed the allowed filename length and are truncated and thrown away.

The danger is that some things work the same on both operating systems and some do not. For example, `rm abc*` removes only those files that start with `abc` on both systems, and have no dot or extension. But `rm *.*` removes all files in the current directory in MS-DOS, and leaves those files in UNIX that do not have the dot character in their name somewhere. MS-DOS does warn you by asking `Are you sure (Y/N)?` whenever it encounters `????????.???` (perhaps expanded from `*.*`), so if you get this warning when you were not expecting it, say NO.

Table 3-5 lists some MS-DOS examples, and what they mean.

Table 3-5. MS-DOS Examples

Command	Function
rm ???.*	Remove all files with one-, two-, or three-character filenames, with or without an extension
rm ?.???	Remove all files with one character filenames, with or without an extension
rm *any.???	Remove all files in the current directory

Epilogue

PCnix is not UNIX, and doesn't try to be. It adopts, with grateful acknowledgment, many of the really good programming ideas embodied in the UNIX operating system and its accompaniment of software tools. It brings a comfortable UNIX-like environment to the IBM PC and its clones. It has been embraced by many who go back and forth between a UNIX system and a PC—and, surprisingly, by a few who have never used UNIX.

So what is the UNIX operating system? Is it a kernel surrounded by software facilities to provide multitasking capabilities to a large number of users simultaneously? If so, PCnix isn't even in the same ballpark. Yet PCnix feels a lot like UNIX to a user—in a blind test, a UNIX guru worked away for over 20 minutes before he discovered he was really talking to MS-DOS. (He was furious.)

So perhaps UNIX—or the heart of UNIX—is just a collection of software tools that work well together, and provide a comfortable and convenient working environment on a computer. PCnix has no pretensions beyond that modest goal.

> The PCnix software collection will be available in two formats: executable code only, which takes up about three 360K floppy disks; and executables plus all available source code, which needs about six. The current system loads itself onto a hard disk and runs comfortably under MS-DOS version 3.1; other versions of MS-DOS or other computer configurations may take some setup work on your part. For more information, contact R. E. Nather; P. O. Box 27007; Austin, TX 78731.

Reading List

Angermeyer, J., R. Fahringer, K. Jaeger, and D. Shafer/The Waite Group. 1987. *Tricks of the MS-DOS Masters*. Indianapolis: Howard W. Sams & Company.

Baker, P. 1987. Pipes and filters. *Byte Extra Edition: Inside the IBM PCs* 12, no. 12:215.

Claff, W. 1987. Better batch files through assembly language. *Byte Extra Edition: Inside the IBM PCs* 12, no. 12:159.

Kernighan, B., and R. Pike. 1984. *The UNIX Programming Environment*. Englewood Cliffs: Prentice-Hall, Inc.

R. Edward Nather is the Rex G. Baker and McDonald Observatory Centennial Research Professor of Astronomy at the University of Texas. He designs and builds computer-controlled instruments for the automatic collection, recording, and display of astronomical data, which he uses to study exploding stars called novae, burnt-out stars called white dwarfs, and other cosmic exotica.

Related Essays

1 A Guided Tour inside MS-DOS
2 Searching the File Tree with `whereis`
4 Adding Power to MS-DOS Programming
6 Undocumented MS-DOS Functions
7 Safe Memory-Resident Programming (TSR)

Keywords

- Extended Batch Language
- screen generation
- Vitamin C
- windows
- C-INDEX
- keyed index files
- B + trees

Essay Synopsis: Every programmer is aware of the amount of repetitive and tedious work involved in developing an MS-DOS application. Menus, help screens, data entry screens, and perhaps dialog boxes and windows all have to be designed and implemented. Routines for indexing and accessing data have to be written. MS-DOS itself offers little help in these areas, since it provides only a rudimentary batch-processing capability and no screen generation, windowing, or data management facilities. In recent years, however, many products have been developed to add power to MS-DOS programming. This essay looks at three representative products in detail and shows you how they can solve programming problems. Extended Batch Language (EBL) provides sophisticated batch processing to automate programming tasks, and amounts to a full-featured programming language in its own right. Vitamin C makes it easy for C programmers to do the attractive screens and windows users expect today. Finally, C-INDEX uses indexed files with easy-to-use data management routines that can be used with any C program.

4

Adding Power to MS-DOS Programming

Douglas O. Adams

With each new version, MS-DOS has become a more powerful operating system, but many programmers do not use its features to the best advantage. There are many techniques and tools you can use under MS-DOS that will make programming faster and more convenient. We will look at some typical problems encountered by the MS-DOS programmer and show how to overcome them. Since the C language is becoming the primary PC programming language, we will use C for our examples. If you are not a C programmer, similar tools are available for other programming languages.

Once the environment is set up and running, how do you run a group of commands or programs consecutively as a batch? Most operating systems allow users to put a group of commands into a file so they will be executed consecutively or conditionally. This feature allows commonly needed operations such as compilations and file backups to be performed without repetitive typing. On UNIX systems, this is called shell programming and on large IBM systems it is called C Scripts. MS-DOS currently supports a similar, but more limited, facility called batch or .BAT files.

Most operating systems for larger computers provide support for screen generation and data entry for application programs, but as recent as several years ago, few such tools were available for personal computers, and PC programmers had to write their own screen and data entry code for each project. Due to their speed and single-user support, very fast screen operations are possible on a PC, but programming PC screens in most languages is a very time-consuming and error-prone process.

Organized information storage presents specific challenges: a list of names needs to be available alphabetically, invoices need to be accessible by number, scientific weather data may need to be ordered by date and time. Early computer systems sorted massive amounts of data to achieve this accessibility. A newer technique, indexes, provides a way to order and select data in a much more efficient manner.

Setting up Your Operating Environment

Many users want their computers to set certain parameters and install device drivers each time the system is booted. As you probably know, a CONFIG.SYS file allows you to do this. This file is executed by MS-DOS automatically each time the system is booted, and can include instructions to add additional devices and modify certain DOS defaults. Such a file might include

DEVICE = MOUSE.SYS (turn on mouse driver)

DEVICE = VDISK.SYS 128 /E (set up RAMdisk memory)

FILES = 20 (allow more open files)

BUFFERS = 20 (increase disk buffers)

The mouse device driver will work as soon as the system is started. The second line in the file defines a virtual disk using extended memory beyond the 640K size limit to simulate a disk drive. The MS-DOS default for the maximum number of open files is 8 files. Since this is not enough for many compilers to operate, we extend the number of open files to 20 by including FILES=20. Buffers are used for holding information being read from or written to disk files.

The DOS command BUFFERS= lets you set the buffer size from 1 to 99, with each number equaling 528 bytes. The default setting is BUFFERS = 2 or 1024 bytes. For an XT class machine, the setting should be BUFFERS = 6. For an AT class machine, BUFFERS = 20 is generally suggested. Although this means the DOS will use more memory, file operations will generally run much faster.

Using AUTOEXEC.BAT to Get Started

As you probably know, DOS provides AUTOEXEC.BAT, a special batch file which should be placed in the main directory along with COMMAND.COM, and will automatically be executed when you boot your system. It is usually used to execute a series of programs that you want to run each time you start up the system. For example:

```
PATH=\;\MW\PROG;\UTIL\DISK\DOS;\UTIL\MISC;\UTIL\SH\NC
PROMPT $p$g
RETRIEVE
CD \UTIL\DO
```

```
DO
MENU
CD\
```

The first line sets the path with a list of subdirectories. Any program or .BAT file in the listed subdirectories may now be run from any other subdirectory. This is useful for frequently used utility programs or a word processor that may use text files in many different subdirectories. The second line changes the prompt to display the current path (name of the drive and subdirectory now active), making it easier to keep track of where you are in the directory hierarchy. Next, a memory-resident program RETRIEVE is run. This program maintains a stack of DOS commands for later use and also lets you edit the DOS command line.

Some programs, including many compilers, need to access overlays or data files in order to run. Since the PATH command does not establish access to any data files, the line CD \UTIL\DO is used to change the current path to another subdirectory where the program DO is run. DO is a calendar-scheduling program called Daily Organizer that runs automatically each time the computer is turned on. The program is necessary to change the current directory so DO can find the data files it uses and expects. The last program run before changing the path back to the main directory is a customized MENU program.

Benefits of the Menu System

Using a menu program to run commonly used applications has three benefits. First, it saves having to remember the exact name of each program and type it. Second, it saves having to awkwardly change the current directory. Finally, it makes it possible for people with little knowledge of MS-DOS to use the computer effectively. For example, the following batch file is named MENU.BAT:

```
CD \UTIL\MENU
MENU
CD\
```

This simply changes the subdirectory, runs a program named MENU.COM, and then returns to the main directory. If MENU.BAT is placed in a subdirectory that is listed with the PATH command, it can be run from any current subdirectory. Incidentally, if you use such batch programs, be sure to place them in a subdirectory included in the PATH so they will always be available. Many powerful menu programs are available if you should choose to use one. Figure 4-1 summarizes the use of the files and programs we have discussed for setting up your environment. (Harry Henderson's Essay 1, A Guided Tour inside MS-DOS, evaluates the MS-DOS user interface and programming environment and has further suggestions for improving it.)

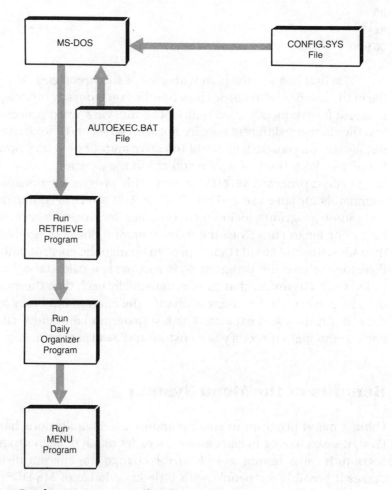

Fig. 4-1. Setting up your environment.

Almost everything described will work with any version of MS-DOS that is 2.0, or later, but version 3.0 adds the VDISK.SYS command and version 3.3 adds APPEND. The latter allows access to data files similar to the way the PATH command provides access to programs.

Using Extended Batch Language for Real Power

Extended Batch Language (EBL) is a program from Seaware Corporation of Delray Beach, Florida. It offers the following features:

▶ operating batch files faster
▶ accepting messages from the user

▷ creating attractive DOS screens

▷ creating help screens using DOS

▷ passing information on to programs

▷ performing arithmetic expressions and assignments

▷ parsing strings for special handling

▷ searching for files to see if they exist

DOS processes batch files by reading them from the disk one line at a time. Each line is executed and another disk access is required for the next line. This results in very slow processing. EBL speeds up the processing of batch files by reading the entire batch file into memory before its execution, allowing you to set a buffer size that can be as large as 64K. This buffer is then used to hold all batch files currently in use.

The batch command set is considerably expanded, and additional commands allow you to provide a number of operations beyond the minimal ones offered by MS-DOS. While many of these commands are very easy to use, a 366-page manual and a bulletin board service are available for assistance from the program's developers. Let's begin with a simple example using EBL:

```
BAT CALL HELP.TXT
BAT PAUSE
BAT CLS
```

The first line uses CALL to display a regular text file. This can include instructions, warnings, or any other information you want to present to the user. PAUSE is a regular DOS batch command which will hold the text on the screen until the user presses a key, and CLS, of course, clears the screen. The BAT at the beginning of each line identifies it as an EBL command.

EBL provides full control over the screen to create an attractive and helpful user interface. You can create menus, display text and help screens, draw boxes, and change colors—all with ease. While DOS batch commands do not allow any user responses, EBL lets you ask the user questions or make selections. This is very important when you need to accept a selection or filename from the user. Another simple example would be to read in a filename to execute with your word processor:

```
BAT /P
TYPE Enter the name of the file to process:
READ %7
WORD %7
```

Notice that we began the program this time with /P after the BAT. We can now eliminate the BAT prefix to all the other commands. TYPE is standard DOS.

But the READ command is new. It allows us to read a string from the keyboard and assign it to the variable %7. MS-DOS allows batch variables in the range from %0 to %9. EBL extends the batch variables by adding the range from %A to %O. The last line of our example starts Microsoft Word with the file specified in %7. This example may seem trivial, but you can devise much more complex sets of instructions that require user input to carry out a sequence of operations.

String-handling operations, arithmetic expressions, and assignments can be performed on the user responses. File searches can be conducted and program return codes can be checked. All these operations allow you to branch to the appropriate part of your batch program and to provide error messages when needed.

EBL Commands

The basic EBL commands are listed in Table 4-1. They are used in batch files to display data, accept keyboard data, and control the logic flow of the batch program. Each command performs a simple operation, defined beside the command. They are used in a similar way to the language used in C and Pascal.

Table 4-1.   Basic EBL Commands

Command	Function
BEEP	Sound speaker
BEGIN/END	Delimit block of commands
BEGSTACK/.END	Add data to keyboard stack
BEGTYPE/END	Display text
CALL	Invoke another batch file
CLS	Clear the display screen
COLOR	Change text color
EXIT	Leave batch program
GOTO	Branch to a label
IF/THEN . . . ELSE . . .	Conditional statement
INKEY	Accept single keystroke
LEAVE	Stop EBL and continue DOS
PARSE	Separate string into variables
READ	Accept response, assign to variable
READSCRN	Get variables from screen
READ.PARSED	Read and parse
READSCRN.PARSED	Readscreen and parse
RETURN	Return from a CALLed subroutine
SHELL	Execute DOS command
SKIP	Skip number of lines specified
STATEOF	Check for existence of a file
STACK	Pass input to a program
STACK.LIFO	Put messages on stack
TYPE	Display messages or variables
*	Batch file line is a comment

Control functions and directives (see Table 4-2) provide additional control over EBL batch files. They are used to determine how EBL will operate.

Table 4-2.   EBL Control Functions and Directives

Function or Directive	Operation
CALL.PURGE	Clear CALL/RETURN stack
STACK.ON	Turn stack on
STACK.OFF	Turn stack off
STACK.PURGE	Clear user response stack
TRACE.ON	Turn on debugging mode
TRACE.OFF	Turn off debugging mode
⟩file	Write file
⟩⟩file	Append file
⟩	Close write
⟨file	Read file
⟨⟨file	Reopen file
⟨	Close read
/K	Kill EBL batch processing
/L	LEAVE default
/P	No BAT Prefix
/Q	Permit strings to use quote marks
/R	Run new file
/S	SHELL default
/U	Uppercase
BIOS or RAM	Set display writing mode

EBL expands the number of variables from the 10 provided by DOS to a total of 26 under EBL (see Table 4-3). It also provides additional special purpose variables.

Table 4-3.   EBL Variables

Variable	Function
%0 to %9	DOS variables
%A to %O	EBL Global User variables
%Q	Returns stack status
%R	Stores MD-DOS return code
%S	Space Literal
%V	Default Drive
%%	"%" Literal
%NAME%	Environment variables

Error-recovery processing is made possible by two commands which allow you to provide special instructions or processing when an error occurs during the operation of an EBL batch file: -ON.ERROR indicates branch to label if an error occurs; RESUME indicates branch to line number on the error.

EBL provides an additional 25 external functions for the advanced programmer. They are called external because they reside in three separate .COM programs that can be activated if needed. These functions provide advanced string-handling, system-status inquiries, low-level system control, and floating-point arithmetic.

Unlocking Your Storage with EBL

Imagine a fairly typical problem: you have several disk drives and you know that your word processor and a text file are somewhere on the system. But where are they actually stored? The following EBL program (supplied by Seaware Corporation when you purchase EBL) will find them for you and begin execution. The program first locates which diskette the editor is on, then locates the file you want to edit, and finally starts the editor with the appropriate file. Lines starting with an asterisk (*) are comments. Begin with

```
A> EDIT MYFILE.DOC
```

EDIT will invoke a batch file named EDIT.BAT. MYFILE.DOC is the name of the word processing data file that you want to edit. If the EDLIN editor were on drive A and the file MYFILE.DOC was on drive B, this EBL program would create the following DOS command:

```
A> EDLIN B:MYFILE.DOC
```

The listing for the EBL batch file follows:

```
BAT /p
* LISTING OF "EDIT.BAT"
* Enter here the name of editor to call:
%0 = EDLIN

* Make sure editor is somewhere
STATEOF %0.COM%c
IF %R <> 1 SKIP 4
STATEOF %0.EXE%b
IF %R <> 1 SKIP 2
TYPE The %0 editor could not be found on any drive!
EXIT

* Setup drive # where editor really is:
```

```
IF %R <> 0 %0 = %R:%0

* Search for the file to be edited...
%C =
STATEOF %1%C
IF %R <> 9  SKIP 3
   TYPE The filename to edit is invalid.
   TYPE Reenter command . . .
   EXIT
IF %R <> 1 %1 = %C
STACK %0 %1 %2 %3 %4 %5 %6 %7 %8 %9
EXIT
```

First, assign the name EDLIN to a variable %0. Next, the STATEOF command looks for a prefix of EDLIN and a suffix of .COM or .EXE. The IF statement checks for a valid return code. The return code after performing a STATEOF command is always returned in the variable L%R. If a file is not found, the return code will be equal to 1. The program will fall through to the TYPE command which will display an error message. If the file is found, the program will SKIP to EXIT. If the editor is found on another drive, the drive is changed in the IF %R <> 0 %0 = RR:%0 line. Next, we look for the file to be edited, using the STATEOF command once again. Note that if %R equals 9, the filename is invalid. This could occur with an incorrect disk drive designation or with a filename which did not follow the MS-DOS conventions. A %R return code of 1 indicates that the filename was valid but that the file was not found. In this case, the argument is set to %C which is blank. The editor will be started but no file will be opened with it. The STACK command passes data to MS-DOS as though it came from the keyboard. Here, it is used to actually execute the edit program with the specified file. Using this command eliminates the need to return to the batch file after the editing is completed.

In summary, EBL is a fairly complete programming language that lets you quickly write batch files that can take the place of compiled programs. Since they do not require compiling, they are much faster to write and test. EBL commands also offer system-level features which other programming languages do not.

Programming Screen Control Facilities

Early computers used a teletype machine as the terminal. It operated exactly like a typewriter, handling one character at a time. CRT display screens were very rare. Today, with the universal use of CRT display screens capable of displaying many lines of data at a time, new techniques for screen display are necessary. We want increasingly powerful capabilities on our display screens—windows, color, and simple editing of data fields.

You may have discovered that the C language (and most other languages on personal computers) has no built-in facilities for handling data fields on the screen. Most computer systems larger than PCs offer features to simplify the development of display screens. These features may be part of the operating system or add-on packages. The IBM System/36, for example, offers as part of its Control Program (operating system) the ability to create a menu system and information display screens that edit and format.

Larger computer systems use a variety of packages to offer these features. On IBM mainframes, CICS (Customer Information Control System) is widely used to develop such screens, serving as an interface between the programming language and the operating system. It reduces the amount of code the programmer has to write, and even more importantly, provides a standard interface between different programs, thus making program changes and maintenance easier. CICS also provides a consistent interface to make it easier for users to learn new applications. Other hardware manufacturers offer similar facilities for their systems.

Taken a step further, Fourth Generation languages exist both on PCs and large computers. Programs such as Paradox for PCs and IDMS for mainframes offer fast ways to develop screens, once you have mastered the tools. These programs both include database facilities, however, which may not be required or suitable for your application.

There are simpler, still very powerful, tools for PC screen development. These work in conjunction with another programming language such as C, Pascal, or COBOL. Since we are focusing on the C language, we will discuss one particular C screen tool: the Vitamin C (VC) library.

Libraries for the C Programmer

C was developed with the specific goal of making it a general purpose language that could be easily used on many different computers. This portability was achieved by providing a small language with no input or output facilities. In itself, such a language would be useless, of course, but the implementers of C determined that all input and output would be done by linking the C code with code from an easy-to-use library for each specific machine. These I/O library functions can be used within a C program like any other function. All C compilers are shipped with a standard I/O library for some computer, provided for by the `#include stdio.h` instruction in the C program. The emerging ANSI standard for C specifies the minimal set of functions each compiler should provide.

The standard I/O library is very limited in its capabilities by today's standards. The VC library is much more powerful than the one shipped with your compiler and just as easy to use. Simply incorporate the VC functions into your C source code program, using an `#include` statement. While you link your program to the C libraries, you include the VC object code libraries in your command to the MS-DOS linker. The linker locates the necessary VC functions and incorporates them into the object code (see Figure 4-2). VC is an excellent product for program development using the C language.

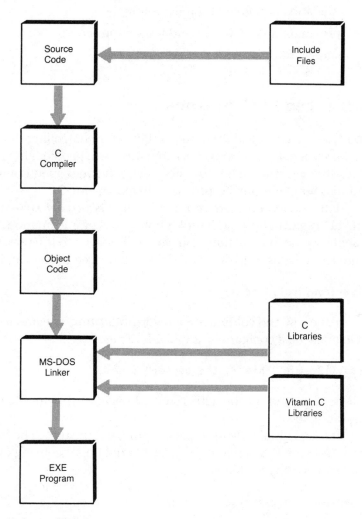

Fig. 4-2.   Using Vitamin C.

Features of Vitamin C

VC offers many features. Some of them you may use every time you write a program and some you may use rarely, if at all. The following are available with VC:

▶ creating a data entry or display field

▶ using the standard IBM editing keys for data input

▶ providing the user with a request for data

▶ providing help screens linked to fields

▶ controlling color and other text attributes

▶ validating and formatting data input

▶ providing up to twelve windows on the screen

▶ simple, but powerful text editing

Advanced I/O Routines

The C language provides limited facilities for controlling the placement of data on the screen. How do you overcome this basic problem in order to create data fields that are easy to edit by the user? You could spend months writing these routines yourself, but VC provides them for you.

Information entered into a computer is usually structured into fields of data or freeform text. VC handles both types of information. Fields of data represent specific information, and can be displayed to the user or used to request input from the user. To display a field on the screen you would use the command

```
atsay(row, col, string);
```

where the row and column are integers indicating placement on the screen. The string may be a constant or a variable. Thus

```
atsay(12, 40, "This is the center");
```

will be displayed on the 12th row and begin in the 40th column, printing the message shown.

It is equally simple to request input from the user. The following command uses `field` for the name of the variable holding the string and `picture` for optional formatting of that string:

```
atget(row, col, field, picture);
```

The next problem is how to make sure that the user has entered the correct type of data. The picture part of the command allows you to build a template of acceptable input. The following symbols, used in the picture, indicate which type of data is acceptable:

x = any key

X = any key with uppercase alpha conversion

a = only alpha

A = only alpha with uppercase conversion

9 = numbers entered from left to right

= numbers entered from right to left

The # sign lets the display act like an adding machine with the digits moving to the left as each digit is entered. You can also include formatting characters in the picture template. To bring this all together, let's use a simple example where we want the user to enter a telephone number, making sure only digits are entered. We also want to supply the parentheses for the area code and the hyphen for the local number automatically. The following code will do all this:

```
atget(6,20,phone,"(999)999-9999";
```

Special characters such as a decimal point, comma, floating dollar sign, or asterisk-filled field can be used for money amounts. The entire set of symbols gives you a lot of flexibility.

Now comes the best part of all. If you create a form on the screen, all the special keys on the IBM keyboard work just the way you would expect (see Table 4-4).

Table 4-4. Key Functions in VC

Key	Function
LEFT ARROW	Move cursor left
RIGHT ARROW	Move cursor right
INSert	Toggle insert mode
DELete	Delete character at cursor
UP ARROW	Move cursor up
DOWN ARROW	Move cursor down
Home	Move to the first field
End	Move to the last field
Pgdn	Move to the next page
PgUp	Move to the previous page
F1	Display help text for field
F2	Move or adjust window size
ESC	Quit input and lose data

Moving through the form to the last field ends the input normally, allowing the program to save the data. All of the values above can be changed by the programmer if you have special data entry requirements. However, these default operations can save you a lot of special coding and provide your programs with an excellent user interface. Since the keys will always work the same way throughout your programs, the user will learn how to use them much faster and find them easier to use.

A character's *attribute* indicates how it is displayed. Attributes include color, underlining, and blinking. The setattr() function can be used at any time to change or add attributes.

Although it is easy to create a form with labels, a label of just the word "Date:" might not be meaningful to the user. What date is requested and what format is required? Vitamin C allows you to provide instructions for each field on a special status line using the xatget() function. When the cursor is moved into a field, the status line provides additional information on the field. We will use date in the following example:

```
xatget(6,0,name,"99/99/99",NULL,
                "Enter date of purchase",
                NULL, vc.dft, vc.dft);
```

The format (slashes) will appear in the screen field, and the message "Enter date of purchase" will be displayed whenever the cursor is within this field. The descriptive information can be provided for each data field on the screen with no extra programming—all cursor management is handled for you by VC. The string constant can also be a pointer to a string assigned elsewhere in your program. In this example, NULL and vc.dft are defaults for other optional control fields. Since we do not now want to use these special features, we fill the arguments with default values. An optional function isblank() will require the user to enter something into the field before continuing on to the next field.

Usually, the picture will provide sufficient control over the data being entered. However, a validation capability also gives the ability to provide your own data-editing functions. If we substitute editdate() for the first NULL in the command above, our function editdate() will be called when the user exits the field. Thus, we have the capability for any type of editing needed if we are willing to write the editing functions.

Since MS-DOS does not currently allow multitasking, is there any way to perform more than one function at a time? One of the more amazing abilities of VC is *loop functions*. They give the appearance of a multitasking system by allowing a function to execute repeatedly while the computer is awaiting input from the keyboard. For example, the following code fragment incorporated in your input function will execute continuous updating of the time on the display screen:

```
int timeloop();
PFI oldloop, setloop();
oldloop = setloop(timeloop);
```

The first line declares the name of your function to display the time as `timeloop()`. The second line uses a special typedef `PFI` (Pointer to a Function). The driver `setloop()` is supplied in the library ⟨vcstdio.h⟩ to simplify your programming. The third line actually executes `timeloop()` while your input function is waiting for data from the keyboard.

Far more complex work can be carried out. The VC demo disk has a program that continuously displays a text file while another form is being filled in by the user—and, these multiple displays are very easy to program.

Developing User Help Screens

It is considered almost mandatory to provide some kind of online "help system" for programs today, but most are seriously inadequate, plunging the user into a lot of information that may or may not be relevant. The best help systems are said to be context-sensitive, which simply means that the help you get is the help you need, depending upon what you are doing. However, context-sensitive help systems are difficult to program. Is there an easy way?

VC provides the ability to provide help for any input statement by including a keyword for the help message. When the user presses the F1 function key, a help window opens up displaying the text you want displayed. Pressing the F1 key again removes the help window. This is provided in the following example:

```
xatget(6,0,name,"99/99/99",NULL,
            "Enter date of purchase",
            "Datehelp", vc.dft, vc.dft);
```

Notice that the keyword `"Datehelp"` has been added to the example that we previously used. Simple, isn't it? Of course, the text for the help screen has to come from somewhere, and this is where VC is really helpful to you.

First, you create a help file with any word processor. The file uses the following format:

```
@@DATEHELP
Enter the date that the purchase actually took place.
The date should be entered in the month, day, and year
format. Thus January 12, 1988, would be entered as
01/12/88. You do not need to type in the slashes as
they will be supplied by the program.
@@NEXTHELP
```

`@@DATEHELP` and `@@NEXTHELP` are arbitrary keywords which you assign. They are used to index the data entry field to the help message file. The `@@` is used to indicate the presence of a keyword. All the help messages are stored in one file, and since the file is independent from your program, you can change the help messages without changing your program. This is a great advantage, since the messages often need clarification later.

Next, VC provides a utility program called HELPGEN.EXE to build an index to the help file. When you change the text in your help file you just run HELPGEN again and an updated index is created.

Finally, VC lets you provide default help messages, so that the user always gets a message when the F1 key is pressed. The default messages can be changed throughout your program.

Creating Windows the Easy Way

Multiple windows on the screen seem to be the user's delight and the programmer's horror—the amount of coding can be overwhelming. Witness the years of development of Microsoft Windows by teams of skilled programmers. Once again, VC provides a simple solution to this problem, by allowing you to open up to twelve windows on the screen at the same time. The windows can be placed wherever you wish, thus allowing overlapping windows. The following code opens a window:

```
int win1;
win1 = wopen(3,10,18,34,"First Window");
win2 = wopen(10,5,12,65),"Second Window");
win3 = wopen(23,1,24,79),"Command Window");
```

This indicates that the window we have optionally called win1 will be a rectangle beginning at row 3, column 10 and ending at row 18, column 34. The text "First Window" will be displayed as a title in the window's border. Using exactly the same format, we can now continue to open another eleven windows if we wish.

Everything in VC works exactly the same, with or without windows. The only difference is that all data is written to or taken from the current window. The last window opened is current by default. You can also make a window opened earlier current with the following command:

```
ret = wselect(win1);
```

The ret is a variable used to capture the return code from the wselect() function to test for correct operation. You can close a window and include error-checking by using this statement:

```
if(ret=wclose(win1)) == -1)
   atsay(0,0,"That window is not open.");
```

There are many other options for windows available. You can set the attributes for each window, hide or unhide windows, and have a *virtual window*, one that is actually larger than the physical size displayed. You can scroll horizontally or vertically to display the hidden data just as you can scroll using Lotus 1-2-3. You can also write to hidden windows, and when they are redisplayed, something new will appear to the user. This is a useful trick for presenting relevant information without cluttering up the screen.

VC comes with the complete source code, written in C, for all the libraries. This allows you to customize the functions or move them to other computer systems by recompiling the code. It is also furnished with a set of demonstration programs. They should be studied carefully, since they can be used as templates for building your own applications. The most interesting example is a menu system which uses pull-down windows like the Apple Macintosh or Microsoft Windows. The current version of VC does not provide mouse support or scroll bars, however. Thus, it is a simpler product with the virtue of running quickly on any PC and being simple to program. VC is a stunning example of clever programming, and can be used to speed up your program development time.

Key File Access Systems

Once you enter data into a computer system, you want to store it on a disk file and be able to retrieve it quickly. Most operating systems provide a variety of ways to access disk files. Early model computers, including PCs, provided only limited facilities. The four types of file access available today are sequential files, random files, keyed-index files and database files. Sequential files just read or write starting at the beginning of the file and continue until they reach the end. They are used today for copying entire files or for making backups of files. The standard DOS COPY command uses this technique.

Random files allow you to select a record from within a file based upon the physical record number. For most business applications, this approach is inadequate. A later development, hashing, allows identifiers such as customer name or number, date, or invoice number to be converted into a record number, but this approach has its own problems in efficiently using disk space and handling duplicate identifiers.

During the 1960s, the index sequential file was invented and incorporated into most operating systems. Using this technique, a list is created of the identifier and the corresponding physical record number. Various tricks are used to speed to the list processing to locate and obtain the desired record more quickly.

In the early 1970s, computer scientists produced a new technique called the B + tree. This provides for very efficient records searching. A version of B + tree-indexing is available for most computers today (called VSAM on large IBM computers). All database management systems make use of B + trees internally, but you don't need to purchase a $700 package to use these techniques. You can purchase file access libraries to incorporate the B+ record indexing within your own programs.

Using a B+ Tree Library for Your Own Programs

We have selected C-INDEX+ from Trio Systems as our example of a file access library. C-INDEX will allow you to add powerful indexing capabilities to your programs with a minimum of extra work. It offers the following features:

▶ variable length keys and data

▶ storage using multiple keys

▶ data and keys in the same file

▶ advanced B+ tree implementation

▶ multiuser capabilities with record-locking

▶ full source code provided in C

▶ no royalties on developed applications

Let's look at each of these features and find out what they really mean. Many file access programs will accept only fixed length fields. This means wasting disk space. C-INDEX will automatically compress the data, wasting no space. If a field is left blank by the user, it takes up no disk space at all. You can define up to 20 key fields for each record in the standard version.

Most file access systems require a separate DOS file for each indexed field. C-INDEX is completely flexible in this regard. It lets you store all the indexes and the data together in one MS-DOS file, if you choose, making it much easier for you to back up data files and reducing the disk space overhead that occurs with each separate MS-DOS file. On the other hand, if you really want to keep your index files separate, you can do so.

C-INDEX uses advanced B+ tree-indexing. This is a Third Generation product which has been tested on many types of computers. It has also been run under UNIX should you ever want to move your program up to the UNIX operating system. The user manual even mentions use on the CRAY supercomputer, using UNIX.

Functions are provided for use with multiuser systems and local area networks. While this does require some changes to individual programs, these changes appear to be minimal. Here, however, the most important feature is record-locking. Many other multiuse systems require the user to lock everyone else out of the whole file while adding or deleting records. With C-INDEX, this severe limitation is overcome by locking only the individual record being changed. Thus, other users can continue their work on other records in the same file without interference.

Finally, the full source code is provided in C, with instructions for recompiling and testing the libraries under other compilers. This means the library (and your programs) should not become obsolete as new products come along. No royalties are required, so if you plan to sell your programs, this is an important consideration.

Let's See How It Actually Works

C-INDEX provides seven basic functions to allow you to create, open, update, and close files. Let's use a simple example where the data is stored in the following structure:

```
/* structure for phonelist and notes */
struct nap {
        char lastname[10];
        char firstname[20];
        char phone[20];
        char notes[240];
} naprec;
```

The structure name nap is an arbitrary name standing for name and phone. naprec is the name of the record using this structure. Now we need to tell C-INDEX how to use each of these fields. This is done by creating a "datalist," describing the type of data and indicating whether it is a key field. The simplest way to do this is by initializing the structure with the following code:

```
FIELD naplist[] = {
        STRING, STRING, DUPKEY, 10, 1, naprec.lastname,
        STRING, STRING, NONKEY, 20, 0, naprec.firstname,
        STRING, STRING, NONKEY, 20, 0, naprec.phone,
        STRING, STRING, NONKEY, 240, 0, naprec.notes,
LASTFIELD
);
```

The first line includes STRING twice since both the key and the data are of the type string. DUPKEY indicates the field is a key field to be indexed and that duplicates are allowed. (After all, some people do have the same last name.) The field has a maximum length of 10 characters, and the key is kept in index 1. For example, we could have one index based on last name and another based on first name and last name. In that case, the format would be:

```
STRING, STRING, DUPKEY, 30, 2, naprec.lastname, naprec.firstname
```

This is a function most databases don't provide.

Finally, we indicate the variable `naprec.lastname` to store the data. The next three lines are similar except that they are not key fields, hence, the `NONKEY` label with an index number of zero.

Does it seem to you that each record will be 294 bytes long? This would take a lot of disk storage, most of which might be unused. However, remember that C-INDEX only stores the data actually input. We have a system using true variable-length records and a record might be only 30 bytes long. That's why we have allowed such a large size for notes.

`LASTFIELD` lets the compiler know the record definition is complete. Note, we said the compiler. Since we have initialized an array of pointers, this definition is only performed at compile time—it is not repeated each time the object program is run.

Using the "Magic 7" Functions

Let's begin by creating the DOS files:

```
ret = dcreate(&napfile, "nap.dat", workbuf, 294);
```

`ret` is a variable for the return code. Each function always returns a code telling us that everything went okay or an error occurred. There is an extensive list of error codes to tell us what went wrong. For the function `dcreate()`, we first pass a pointer to the definition `&napfile`, then the DOS filename `nap.dat`, the buffer name, and finally the buffer size (294 since it has to be large enough to hold the longest possible record).

Now we want to open the file for use. The following code does the trick. You can see that it is exactly the same except for the name of the function:

```
char workbuf[294];

ret = dopen(&napfile, "nap.dat," workbuf, 294);
```

Closing a file is even easier:

```
ret = dclose(&napfile);
```

Of course, what we really want to do next is add some records to the file. The following little function will add records:

```
addrec();                    /* add a record to the file */
```

```
{
        int ret;   /* return code for possible errors */

        getdata(naplist); /* your function to get data */
        ret = dadd(&napfile, naplist);
        if (ret != 0) printf("Error -  Record Not Added.);
}
```

Your own function `getdata()` puts the data into the structure called naplist. You could (and probably should) use VC data entry functions to create your input function. The function `dadd()` then puts it into the file, providing automatic indexing of the last name. Note that we also check the return code and display an error message if an error occurs.

Now that we have a file of useful information, we are ready to find a record. The function `dfind()` does just that:

```
ret = dfind(&napfile, 1, "SMITH", STRING, EQUAL);
```

Once again, &napfile is the pointer to the file, and 1 is the index number we are using. "SMITH" is the last name we are looking for and we want to find a record EQUAL to that name. We also could have specified any of these choices:

EQUAL (find only equal matches to the key)

GREATEQ (find anything equal or greater)

GREAT (find anything greater than)

LESS (find anything less than)

LESSEQ (find anything less than the key)

Since we have this much flexibility, the user does not need to know how to spell the name exactly. We can write the program, using GREATEQ, so if only the first letter was entered, the program will page through the file. To do this, we use another command that will let us get the next record:

```
ret = desq(&napfile, 1, NEXT);
```

This function lets us move through the file sequentially. Thus, we can find the next record from wherever we happen to be. We can also look for the previous record, first record, or last record, instead of the next record. Now that we have found the record that we were looking for, we read it into the structure:

```
ret = dread(&napfile, naplist);
```

Deleting a record is done with `ddelete()`, as you probably have guessed by now. You must first use dfind() to find the record, and then ddelete() to delete it. "LOSEIT" is the keyword value in the record that we will delete:

```
/* first find the name to delete */
ret = dfind(&napfile, 1, "LOSEIT" STRING, EQUAL);
if (ret == 0)
  ret = ddelete(&napfile, naplist);
if (ret == 0)
  fprint("Record has been deleted.");
```

One final function allows us to update an existing record: dupdate(). To update the record for "JONES", we could use the following code:

```
/* first find the record in the file */
ret = dfind(&napfile, 1, "JONES" STRING, EQUAL);
if (ret == OK)
  ret = dread(&napfile, naplist);
if (ret == OK)
{
        displayrec(naplist);      /* display old data */
        getdate(naplist);                    /* get new data */
        ret = dupdate(&napfile, naplist);
        if (ret == OK)
           printf("Update Successful");
```

Note that we always check the return code to make sure that the operation was successful. We now have a complete set of seven functions for handling keyed files. The syntax is uniform and usage is consistent. Of course, we have not covered the many advanced features of C-INDEX. The 154-page user manual provides much additional information, but you have already learned the fundamentals for using the system.

The concepts of using keyed files is very important for most computer applications today. I hope the example given above has shown how easily they can be implemented using good systems software.

Summary

Effective programming today consists of using a consistent set of well-matched tools. The tools selected for this tutorial were very carefully evaluated. They are all well-designed, well-documented, and continually updated. They all work with the Microsoft C compiler and recent versions of MS-DOS. While there are other products on the market, you should examine any tools carefully before making a decision that will commit you to using them for a major project. Figure 4-3 summarizes a possible integrated programming environment.

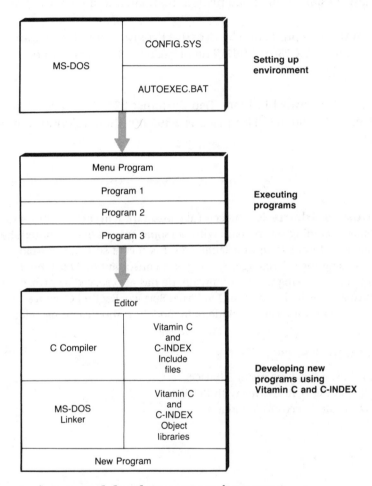

Fig. 4-3. An integrated development environment.

If you are an individual programmer, your work will become more fun and creative by following these guidelines. If you are working on program development for your company or for commercial sale, the approach described herein can save your firm hundreds of hours of development time.

Programs

RETRIEVE is available from IBM Personally Developed Software on their Utilities I disk. The price is $19.95; it can be ordered by calling 800/426-7279.

EXTENDED BATCH LANGUAGE is available as shareware from BBSs and user groups. It may be registered by calling Seaware Corporation in Delray Beach, Florida at 305/392-2046. The price is $69.95. They will send you the latest program version, a 366-page printed manual, and a password for their user BBS.

VITAMIN C is published by Creative Programming Consultants, Inc.; Box 112097; Carrollton, TX 75011-2097. The price is $149.95; you can order by phone by calling 214/245-6090.

C-INDEX is available from Trio Systems; 2210 Wilshire Blvd.; Suite 289; Santa Monica, CA 90403. The price is $395.00; their telephone number is 203/394-0796.

Douglas Adams is a successful consultant with nearly 20 years of computer experience, including seven years with personal computers. Although he has used more than 10 different computer languages, his recent software development has been done using the C language. Serving as a consultant to AT&T, he developed C programs that are now being used nationwide. He has also served as project manager for large organizations including the U.S. Postal Service, Bechtel Corporation, and Wells Fargo Bank. Current interests include data modeling and designing relational databases.

Related Essays

1 A Guided Tour inside MS-DOS
3 Adding UNIX Power with PCnix
9 Inside Microsoft Windows

Keywords

- records (assembly language)
- bit fields
- structures (assembly language)
- include files
- data macros
- code macros
- interrupt processing

Essay Synopsis: If you are new to assembly language programming, it is easy to do things the hard way because you don't know how to take advantage of the advanced features of the Microsoft Macro Assembler (MASM). If you are an experienced assembly language programmer, you've probably developed an impressive bag of tricks—but have you updated it lately? This essay covers the advanced features of MASM 5.0. You will learn how to use records and structures to provide assembly language programs with data structures similar to those used in C and Pascal. You will also learn how to use include files for better organized programs with less typing. A complete discussion of macros takes you from the simplest data macros to macros that provide great flexibility and power in generating program instructions. Finally, you will learn how to handle interrupts safely.

## 5

Advanced MASM Techniques

Michael Goldman

If you have been writing assembly language code, you know that what most often trips you up is the detailed repetitive work, having to recode every BIOS call every time you want to do some simple task like reading the keyboard. Microsoft's MASM, version 5.0, like many good assemblers, offers many powerful features to make coding assembly language as easy and error-free as a good higher-level language. We will look at the following MASM features which can help you as a programmer:

 ▶ records (setting up and manipulating bit-oriented data using meaningful names)

 ▶ structures (creating relationships between pieces of data similar to those found in C or Pascal)

 ▶ include files (saving time and typing, improving program organization)

 ▶ macros (creating flexible, powerful "super instructions")

Records

Records are very convenient templates for setting up bit-oriented data structures. They save time, and by automating the process, help us avoid errors in setting our data bits. For example, in a byte used for setting up the line control register for the Asynchronous Communications Element (ACE) (i.e., COM1 or COM2) bits 0 & 1 set the word length, bit 2 the number of stop bits, bits 3 through 5 the parity, bit 6 the break conditions, and bit 7 is the Data Latch Access Bit. To work with all these parameters in one byte, we can define a record called LineCtrlBits as follows:

```
LineCtrlBits    RECORD  DLAB:1, BREAK:1, PARITY:3, STOP:1, LEN:2
```

`LineCtrlBits` is the name of the record, which represents one byte (8 bits). `DLAB`, `BREAK`, and so on represent fields in the record, and are followed by the number of bits for each field. Note that this definition merely gives names to the bits in a byte, it doesn't create a byte with those bits set or cleared. Just as `MyWord dw 1234` creates a word with the value 1234, so we create a record for particular combinations of bit settings with the following statements in the DATA segment of the program:

```
LcrOnEven27 LineCtrlBits<DLABon,BreakOff,EvenParity,stop2,length7>
LcrOffOdd18 LineCtrlBits<DLABoff,BreakOff,OddParity,stop1,length8>
```

Note that the name of the specific record (such as `LcrOnEvn27`) is followed by the name of the record definition used (`LineCtrlBits` in this case) and then the names of bit values.

In the equates section of our program we have defined:

```
DLABoff         equ     0B      ; Data Latch Access Bit off
DLABon          equ     1B      ; Data Latch Access Bit on
BreakOff        equ     0B      ; set break is disabled
BreakOn         equ     1B      ; xmit data line forced to space
                                ; (logical 0) as long as bit is one
NoParity        equ     000B    ; bit setting for parity off
OddParity       equ     001B    ; bit setting for odd parity
EvenParity      equ     011B    ; bit setting for even parity
MarkParity      equ     101B    ; bit setting for mark parity
SpaceParity     equ     111B    ; bit setting for space parity
stop1           equ     0B      ; 1 stop bit
stop2           equ     1B      ; 2 stop bits if word 6, 7, or 8 bits
length5         equ     00B     ; 5-bit character length
length6         equ     01B     ; 6-bit character length
length7         equ     10B     ; 7-bit character length
length8         equ     11B     ; 8-bit character length
```

We can now write an instruction such as `MOV AL,LcrOffOdd18` in our program as if we had defined a byte as follows:

```
LcrOffOdd18     db      00001011b ; ACE bit settings
```

Note that we cannot write `MOV AL,NoParity` since `NoParity` is not a byte but rather just the value of an equate. Likewise, if we write `MOV AL,BREAK`, what we find in `AL` is not a bit moved into bit 6 but the *number* 6, which is the position of `BREAK` in the record.

Manipulating Bit Fields

So far, it may appear that records are just a convenient way to define bit-oriented data, but there is more we can do. The TEST instruction allows us to do with bits what CMP (COMPARE) does with bytes and words. The Intel logical instructions AND, OR, XOR, and the MASM directive NOT allow us to manipulate the bit fields. The NOT directive changes 1s to 0s, and 0s to 1s.

Use the bit fields in the record LineCtrlBits as above, so we can use the MASM directive MASK to define what are called (naturally enough) masks. The MASK operator tells MASM to create a binary constant with a bit set to 1 for the bit positions defined in the record by that record field and a zero for all the other bit positions. For example:

```
DLABmask        =        MASK DLAB      ; = 10000000B
BREAKmask       =        MASK BREAK     ; = 01000000B
PARITYmask      =        MASK PARITY    ; = 00111000B
BIT2            =        MASK STOP      ; = 00000100B
LENmask         =        MASK LEN       ; = 00000011B
```

We've called the mask defined for the STOP bit BIT2 to show there's no restriction on what you name the mask. Now we wish to change the parity setting in LcrOffNo18 from off to even, i.e., from 000 to 011. We'll use the MASK operator to help, for instance, NOT PARITYmask = 11000111b (NOT works only at assembly time, not run time).

```
and     LcrOffNo18,NOT PARITYmask   ; LcrOffNo18 = 00000011b
mov     al,LcrOnEven27  ; al = 00011110b, even parity setting, etc.
and     al,PARITYmask   ; al = 00011000b, all but parity bits cleared
or      LcrOffNo18,al   ; LcrOffNo18 = 00011011b, even parity setting
```

The use of symbolic constants helps control bits of records in MASM. In the first line of the example, LcrOffNo18 is a data record for the Line Control Register on the serial port, and is followed by the MASM NOT instruction. PARITYmask is the mask created with MASM's MASK directive. LcrOnEven27 means Line Control Register, with Break On, Even parity, 2 stop bits, 7 bits long.

A reminder about AND, OR, and NOT operations: these are called "logical" operations because they obey the rules of Boolean logic. They work as follows:

1 and 1 = 1,   1 and 0 = 0,   0 and 1 = 0,   0 and 0 = 0

1 or 1 = 1,   1 or 0 = 1,   0 or 1 = 1,   0 or 0 = 0

not 1 = 0,   not 0 = 1

So, the first instruction in the example ANDs 11000111b (NOT PARITYmask) with 00000011b (LcrOffNo18) to produce 00000011b. The purpose of this is to clear out the parity bit settings so that we can put new settings in there with the OR instruction later. The next instruction loads al with 00011110b (LcrOnEven27). We then AND the 00011110b in al with 00111000b (PARITYmask) to obtain 00011000b. The PARITYmask masks (zeros) out all the bits in al except the parity bits so that al is left with only the bit setting for even parity. Now we OR LcrOffNo18 with al which will put the bit settings we want into the parity bit positions. Note that had we not done the and al,PARITYmask, there might have been some bits from the previous setting which would come through the OR operation.

Thus, we have succeeded in changing the 3 parity bits without affecting the other bits. Just as we might use a CMP instruction to see if two bytes are the same, so we can use the TEST instruction to see if any of the parity bits are set, for example:

```
test    ax,PARITYmask    ; parity bits set in ax ?
jz      BlankParity      ; if zero flag, blank parity field
```

Records can be created and used on preexisting data. So, for example, we could have defined the byte

```
anybyte db     01001111b        ; no thought of records here
```

and then at some later time in our programming define the record LineCtrlBits as above. We could also refer in the same program to the same word with a different record definition such as

```
Simple  RECORD  Begin:2,Middle:3,End:3
```

and do the same bit manipulations as previously with the three parity bits, referring to them as Middle instead of Parity. The point is that, at any time, we can create ways of referring to data in whatever way is appropriate in the context. The record is a template to fit over data. Figure 5-1 shows a typical use of records. DLAB indicates the Data Latch Access Bit, and LEN refers to character length. BREAK, PARITY, and STOP bits are also shown.

Structures

Structures are the next level up from records in imposing order on our data. They are assembler directives that enable you to build complex data formats composed of bytes, words, etc., in ways that make them much more meaningful and accessible to you. They are very similar to C structures and Pascal records.

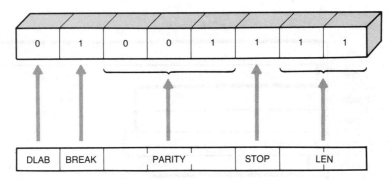

Fig. 5-1.   Records as templates.

They differ in that, in MASM, indexing is harder and nesting is not allowed. As an example, suppose you are making a membership list in which every member is listed with name, address, and phone number. Here's how you can create a structure for this entity:

```
Member  STRUC
        LastName   DB20 DUP (?)        ; 20 characters
        MidInit    DB?                 ; 1 character
        FirstName  DB12 DUP (?)        ; 12 characters
        Street     DB12 DUP (?)        ; 12 characters
        City       DB 'San Francisco'  ; 13 characters
        StateAbbr  DW?                 ; 2 characters
        PhoneNumb  DB'415' 7 DUP (?)   ; 10 characters
Member  ENDS
```

City, PhoneNumb, etc., are called field names" for the Member structure (see Figure 5-2). You can now allocate space for the officers and members of your organization with

```
President       Member  <,,,,,'CA',>
VicePresident   Member  <,,,,,'CA',>
Treasurer       Member  <,,,,,'CA',>
MembrList       Member  100 DUP (<,,,,,'CA',>)
```

which reserves space for 103 members. At 70 bytes/member, this is 7210 bytes for our membership list. Each member's city is initialized by default to San Francisco in the structure definition, and each state is initialized to CA in the structure declaration. The places where we have commas are blank field names that you can fill in with data later, at run time, reading in from a keyboard or disk, etc.

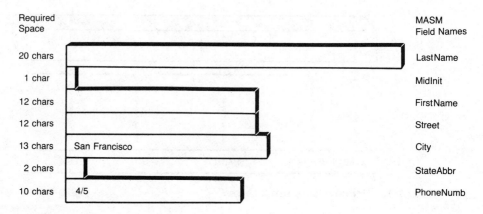

Required Space — MASM Field Names

Required Space		MASM Field Names
20 chars		LastName
1 char		MidInit
12 chars		FirstName
12 chars		Street
13 chars	San Francisco	City
2 chars		StateAbbr
10 chars	4/5	PhoneNumb

Fig. 5-2.   Structure layout.

This is a good time to point out that in MASM, the following are equivalent ways to refer to the address in register di plus 10:

```
[10][di]
[di + 10]
[di].10
[di] + 10
```

Therefore, since the structure is really just giving mnemonics to displacements, you can now refer to the membership list by the field names, just as you might in C or Pascal. For example:

```
cmp     Treasurer.FirstName,'A'
```

is equivalent to

```
cmp     [Treasurer + 21],'A'
```

which compares the first byte of the FirstName field of the Treasurer's name. For example, if we wish to scan the entire list of members for the first member with last name beginning with A we would code

```
        mov     di,MemberList    ; get address of list
        mov     cx,100           ; length of list for looping
        mov     bx,70            ; length of structure
CmpLup: cmp     [di].FirstName,'A' ; is the first letter = 'A' ?
        je      ExitLup          ; yes, search done
        add     di,bx            ; set pointer to next structure
        loop    CmpLup           ; scan the entire list of members
ExitLup:...
```

Using Multiple Structures to Address Data

It is possible to add to the options in addressing the data by defining another structure for the same data:

```
NewMembr        STRUC
Name    DB      33 DUP (?)
Address DB      27 DUP (?)
Phone   DB      10 DUP (?)
NewMembr        ENDS
```

Without reentering the old data, we can now refer to it by the `NewMembr` structure names as well as the `Member` structure names. We could write this comparison loop:

```
CmpLup: cmp     [di].LastName,'A'
        je      ExitLup
        add     di,bx
        loop    CmpLup
ExitLup:cmp     [di].Phone,'4'
        jne     ...
```

    The key to understanding structures is to realize that MASM simply replaces the names you give to the structure elements with numbers. Specifically, MASM will reference the number of bytes from the beginning of the structure. Thus, `[di].FirstName` is the same as `[di+20]`. The name you give it is for your easy use.

    One very useful feature of using structures is that you can rearrange or add to the structure definition at any time and the names you gave the elements will be automatically updated when you reassemble. For example, let's change the `Member` structure above to interchange `FirstName` and `LastName` and add the element `Country`:

```
Member  STRUC
FirstName       DB      12 DUP (?)          ; 12 characters
MidInit         DB                          ; 1 character
LastName        DB      20 DUP (?)          ; 20 characters
Street          DB      12 DUP (?)          ; 12 characters
City            DB      'San Francisco'     ; 13 characters
StateAbbr       DW                          ; 2 characters
Country         DB      6  DUP (?)          ; 6 characters
PhoneNumb       DB      '415' 7 DUP (?)     ; 10 characters
Member  ENDS
```

To see what this does, here are the "before" and "after" equivalencies:

```
BEFORE                            AFTER
[di].LastName  = [di+0]           [di].LastName  = [di+13]
[di].MidInit   = [di+20]          [di].MidInit   = [di+12]
[di].FirstName = [di+21]          [di].FirstName = [di+0]
[di].Street    = [di+33]          [di].Street    = [di+33]
[di].City      = [di+45]          [di].City      = [di+45]
[di].StateAbbr = [di+58]          [di].StateAbbr = [di+58]
------                            [di].Country   = [di+60]
[di].PhoneNumb = [di+60]          [di].PhoneNumb = [di+66]
```

The nice thing about having used structure names in our code is that
[di].LastName still points to the last name even though we've rearranged the
data. So, code referring to data by structure name needn't be rewritten. Note,
however, that if we have data in our file using the old structure definitions, we
must realign that existing data to conform to our new structure. Rearranging
the structure doesn't rearrange the existing data, only the relative positions declared for it. We have to ensure that the actual data corresponds to the data
structure declaration on our own.

Using Structures with Existing Data

You can also apply a structure you define to a data set that you had no hand in
creating. For example, the first 22 bytes of the PSP that MS-DOS puts at the beginning of executable files could be accessed via the following structure:

```
PSP      STRUC
         INT32      DB      2 DUP (?)       ; 2 bytes
         MemSize    DW      (?)             ; 1 word
         Reserved   DB      (?)             ; 1 byte
         DOSCall    DB      5 DUP (?)       ; 5 bytes
         TermVctr   DW      2 DUP (?)       ; 2 words
         BreakVctr  DW      2 DUP (?)       ; 2 words
         ErrorVctr  DW      2 DUP (?)       ; 2 words
PSP      ENDS
```

The PSP can now be accessed as in the following code fragment:

```
mov      di,0             ; PSP begins at offset zero
push     cs               ; PSP segment is in cs
pop      ds               ; PSP segment -> ds
mov      si,[di].MemSize ; program memory size -> extra segment
```

Note that, unlike C, structure definitions cannot contain other structures.

Include Files

The simplest way to avoid retyping "boilerplate" lists of equates, code, or segment declarations is to use include files with these where you would otherwise
put your text. You simply put your frequently used constructs in a standard DOS
file as ASCII text and tell MASM to insert the text from that file in your procedure. To use an include file, you specify

```
include myfile.xyz
```

where you would otherwise have put the equates, definitions, etc. MASM brings
in the contents of these files at assembly time and treats them as text as if you
had typed everything in the include file in that spot in your program. Include
files can contain other include files. Figure 5-3 illustrates the idea of bringing in
files to insert in your source file. Use "greeking" (nonsense) text in the include
files to represent codes.

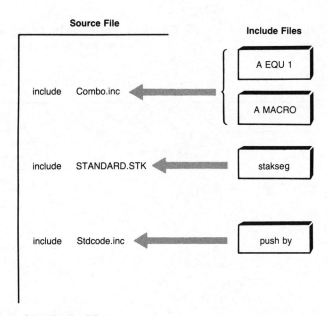

Fig. 5-3.   Use of include files.

For example, if your standard stack declaration is

```
stakseg SEGMENT STACK 'STACK
DB    16 DUP ('STACK  ) ; MAKE STACK EASY TO FIND IN DEBUG
stakseg ENDS
```

then simply put this into a file called `STANDARD.S TK` or some such, and then `include STANDARD.STK` where you would normally type in your stack declaration. Finally, having an include file for each set of related definitions promotes modular organization and helps make programs easier to maintain, especially when several programmers are involved.

Data Macros

Macros are a very flexible way of having the assembler do a lot of the tedious work for you. Macros can be used to generate both data and actual MASM code. Much of their power comes from their ability to accept parameters and do conditional testing. Setting up tables, creating labels, and checking for errors can all be done by macros that you create to meet your needs. We'll cover code macros later but remember that everything used for data macros can be used for generating code as well. Data macros are instructions to the assembler to create certain data based on parameters we give it (see Figure 5-4). The simplest example of this is when we create 10 bytes of data with

```
TenBytes        DB        10 DUP 4  ; reserve 10 bytes with the
                                    ; number 4 in them
```

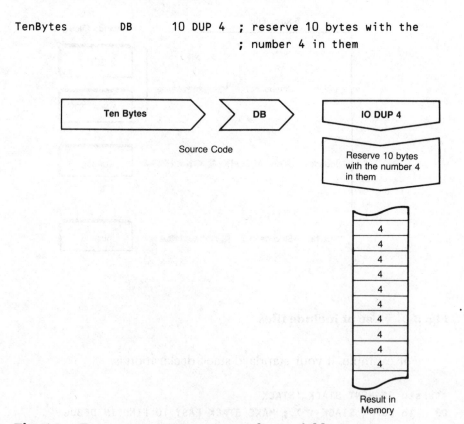

Fig. 5-4.   Data macros reserve space for variable names.

This is of limited use since it is more likely that we want a variety of numbers as in an indexing set. For example, let's reserve N bytes of data with the set of squares of the numbers from 1 to N as follows:

```
@squares MACRO   N                    ; Define a macro with parameter N
         NUMB  =       0              ; Initialize the number
         REPT    N                    ; Repeat the following N times
                 NUMB = NUMB+1        ; INCREMENT INDEX
                 DB        NUMB * NUMB ; Define a byte with NUMB squared
         ENDM                         ; End REPT command
ENDM                                  ; End Macro
```

Note that we have an `ENDM` to match every `MACRO` directive.

The `REPT` directive is a looping structure like "do . . . while" in higher-level languages. Just bear in mind that you are programming MASM to create constants. You are not programming the computer to loop at execution time.

If we put the squares macro definition at the top of our program and then in our data segment, we have

```
@squares        4
```

MASM will assemble 4 bytes as seen in the following listing:

```
94                @squares 4
95 0004   01    2 DB   NUMB * NUMB   ; Define a byte with NUMB squared
96 0005   04    2 DB   NUMB * NUMB   ; Define a byte with NUMB squared
97 0006   09    2 DB   NUMB * NUMB   ; Define a byte with NUMB squared
98 0007   10    2 DB   NUMB * NUMB   ; Define a byte with NUMB squared
```

The invocation of our macro is on line 94 of our listing. The next 4 lines show that byte 4 of our data segment has 1 squared = 1, byte 5 has 2 squared = 4, etc. Note that the numbers are given in hex. The 2 before the `DB` is the line number of the macro listed. We could, of course, have used a number other than 4 as well.

We need a label to use to refer to this list of squares. We don't want to type a label every time we use the macro so we'll use the Substitute operator `&` to have MASM make our label for us:

```
@squares   MACRO     N                    ; Define a macro with parameter
N
Sqr1to&N   label     byte                  ; Define a label
           NUMB    =       0               ; Initialize the number
           REPT      N                     ; Repeat the following N times
                   NUMB = NUMB+1           ; Increment index
```

```
                              DB       NUMB * NUMB ; Define a byte with NUMB
squared
              ENDM                              ; End REPT command
ENDM                                            ; End Macro
```

Now the list file shows our macro as follows:

```
93                   @squares 4
94 0004         1 Sqr1to4   label byte    ; Define a label
95 0004   01    2 DB  NUMB * NUMB  ; Define a byte with NUMB squared
96 0005   04    2 DB  NUMB * NUMB  ; Define a byte with NUMB squared
97 0006   09    2 DB  NUMB * NUMB  ; Define a byte with NUMB squared
98 0007   10    2 DB  NUMB * NUMB  ; Define a byte with NUMB squared
```

&in the macro definition told MASM to substitute the value of N used in the macro invocation. But still we're not satisfied. (We never are!) Having only one label for the list of squares will force us to use an index to access the list since there is only one access point. What we'd like is a label for every item. The expression operator % will enable us to take the value of each of our numbers and use it as part of a label. So we rewrite our macro as the two macros below:

```
@sqr     MACRO   NAM,NUM          ; NAM for our label, NUM for the data
SqrOf&NAM       DB      NUM * NUM ; Define a byte with NUMB squared
         ENDM                     ; End Macro

@squares       MACRO   N          ; Define a macro with parameter N
         NUMB    =       0        ; Initialize the number
         REPT    N                ; Repeat the following N times
             NUMB = NUMB+1        ; Increment index
             @sqr %NUMB,NUMB      ; Create a byte of NUMB * NUMB
         ENDM                     ; End REPT command
ENDM                              ; End Macro
```

Now when we look at the listing file, we find each byte in our list of squares (below) has an appropriate label for our use:

```
97                   @squares 4
98 0004   01 3 SqrOf1  DB  NUMB * NUMB ; Define a byte with NUMB squared
99 0005   04 3 SqrOf2  DB  NUMB * NUMB ; Define a byte with NUMB squared
100 0006  09 3 SqrOf3  DB  NUMB * NUMB ; Define a byte with NUMB squared
101 0007  10 3 SqrOf4  DB  NUMB * NUMB ; Define a byte with NUMB squared
```

We can create sophisticated tables in this way. If we have some formula such as (N * M) / ((P+Q) MOD T), we can let MASM create our table for us instead of doing it by hand and typing in the results.

We could and should check for overflow by including the following in our macro code:

```
IFE    ((NUM * NUM) LE 255)    ; bigger than a byte can hold ?
       DB           NUM * NUM    ; ok, small enough for a byte
ELSE
       %OUT       ERROR IN SQUARES MACRO
```

%OUT sends your message to the screen at assembly time, in this case ERROR IN SQUARES MACRO.

So far, we have always used parameters as individual items separated by commas. It is also possible to have a set of items be a single parameter to the macro for repetitive data creation. For example, if we want to set up a list of strings of messages to display, we could code a macro as follows:

```
@OptDisp       MACRO   OptType,Options  ; OptType -> label, Options =
list
OptType&List   db      Options
ENDM                            ; End Macro
```

and then use it in the data segment as follows:

```
@OptDisp                LineSpeed,<'1200','2400','4800'>
```

LineSpeed will be substituted in the label and each string in the angle brackets will be put in a db directive, just as if we'd typed in

```
LineSpeedList   db      '1200'
                db      '2400'
                db      '4800'
```

There's much more you can do with macros to generate data but these are a good idea of the possibilities. The same techniques can be used to generate code as well as data.

Code Macros

Macros are a very powerful way of getting the assembler to do some programming for you. Just as you can write a BASIC program to make the computer do some work for you, so you can write a MACRO program to make the

ASSEMBLER program, MASM, do some of the most tedious aspects of programming for you.

A simple example of what we mean is the following macro designed to get a character from the "standard input device" (usually the keyboard).

```
@INCHR  MACRO            ; Tell MASM we're defining a macro named INCHR
        MOV     AH,1     ; STANDARD INPUT WITH ECHO
        INT     21H      ; DOS CALL
        ENDM             ; Tell MASM the macro definition is ended
```

Now, instead of retyping the MOV and INT instructions whenever we want to get a character from the standard input, we can use INCHR where we would otherwise have written the code:

```
@INCHR           ; MASM substitutes MOV AH,1 & INT 21H here
```

You could do the same thing with a subroutine but making short pieces of code into subroutines is inefficient. The difference between a macro and a subroutine is that the macro inserts the desired code right where our macro is placed in the source file, whereas a subroutine resides elsewhere and we have to jump to that location to execute the code. We use a macro instead of a subroutine for the same reason we call someone on the phone for a short conversation instead of going across town to visit—the time lost in going to another location isn't justified given the brevity of our task. Thus, code macros tend to be very short since they take up space every time they are used. If they get too long, they should be recoded as a subroutine. How long is too long? That depends on the overhead needed to invoke the subroutine, how often you use the function, and the relative value of memory versus speed for your application. Macros are faster since they don't require saving registers, pushing parameters, etc., but a lot of repetitions of short macros can start taking up space in your object and executable files. Make the code a macro at first and if it seems to be getting out of hand, recode it as a subroutine. Later, we'll see how you can even code the subroutine call as a macro.

Suppose we want to have a macro for standard input with no echo. We could write another macro like the one above but calling DOS for standard input with no echo, or we could expand our original macro by adding an argument to determine if we want echo or not. For example:

```
@inchrif MACRO  EKOFLAG ; define macro INCHRIF with argument EKOFLAG
   IFIDN  <EKOFLAG>,<EKO>    ; if the argument EKOFLAG is IDENTICAL to
                             ; the 3 letters EKO, assemble the next line
            mov     ah,1     ; DOS function - standard input with echo
   ELSE                      ; if the argument EKOFLAG is NOT IDENTICAL to
                             ; the 3 letters EKO, assemble the next line
```

```
        mov     ah,8    ; DOS function - standard input with no echo
ENDIF                   ; end condition testing
        int     21h     ; dos call
        ENDM            ; Tell MASM the macro definition is ended
```

In this case, MASM looks at the argument `EKOFLAG` to determine whether to insert `mov ah,1` or `mov ah,8`. It would be used as shown below:

```
@inchrif EKO      ; MASM substitutes MOV AH,1 & INT 21H here
         .        ; because the argument is identical to EKO
         .
         .

@inchrif NOEKO    ; MASM substitutes MOV AH,8 & INT 21H here
         .        ; because the argument is NOT identical to
         .        ; EKO
         .
```

Note that instead of `NOEKO` in the example, we could have used `PHUBAH` or anything else since the important thing is that the argument not be `EKO`. If it were, it would leave open the possibility we would forget our odd spelling and mistakenly write `@inchrif ECHO`. This would give us no echo because we wrote `ECHO` instead of `EKO`. We can eliminate this error possibility by limiting ourselves to either `EKO` or `NOEKO` and by providing error-checking as follows:

```
@inchrif MACRO  EKOFLAG ; define macro INCHRIF with argument EKOFLAG
IFIDN   <EKOFLAG>,<EKO>    ; if EKOFLAG = EKO, assemble the next line
        mov     ah,1    ; standard input with echo
ELSE                    ;     otherwise...
IFIDN   <EKOFLAG>,<NOEKO> ; if EKOFLAG = NOEKO, assemble the next line
        mov     ah,8    ; standard input with no echo
ELSE                    ; if the argument doesn't match either then
        .ERR            ; generate an assembly error
ENDIF                   ; end condition testing
        int     21h     ; dos call
ENDM                    ; Tell MASM the macro definition is ended
```

Nested Macros

The macros we have been defining use the DOS function to get a character from the standard input by waiting for input. But we don't want to wait forever. Instead, we may wish to check if input is there first, and if not, continue on. DOS Function 0Bh will check if a key has been struck, returning `AL = OFF` (hex) if a character is available and AL = 00 if a character is not available. We can write a macro chkchr and call it from our macro inchrif as follows:

```
@chkchr MACRO              ; define macro CHKCHR
        mov     ah,OBH     ; check standard input
        int     21h        ; dos call
        ENDM               ; Tell MASM the macro definition is ended


@inchrif MACRO  WAITFLAG,EKOFLAG ; 2 arguments: WAITFLAG, & EKOFLAG
        LOCAL   bye                 ; define a dummy address
IFNB    <WAITFLAG>                  ; if the field for WAITFLAG is not
                                    ; blank, assemble the following
        @chkchr         ; see if a character is waiting
        cmp     al,0    ; al = 0 => no character waiting
        je      bye     ; if no character, continue on
ENDIF                   ; end condition testing
IFIDN   <EKOFLAG>,<EKO>         ; if EKOFLAG = EKO, assemble the next line
        mov     ah,1    ; standard input with echo
ELSE                    ;   otherwise...
    IFIDN <EKOFLAG>,<NOEKO> ; if EKOFLAG = NOEKO, assemble next line
        mov     ah,8    ; standard input with no echo
    ELSE        ; if the argument doesn't match either then..
        .ERR            ; ...generate an assembly error
    ENDIF                       ; end condition testing
        int     21h     ; dos call
bye:
ENDM                    ; Tell MASM the macro definition is ended
```

This newest version of inchrif has several features worthy of discussion. The LOCAL directive tells MASM that the label bye is a "dummy" label which MASM is to replace with a different one every time the macro is invoked within a program. This is to avoid having the same label used twice in one program, generating an assembly error. MASM will assemble the macro using ??0000 the first time in a module, ??0001 the second time, etc., through ??FFFF (hex) should you care to invoke the macro 65,536 times in one program. Note that the LOCAL directive must be the very first thing after the MACRO directive—not even comments can be placed before it!

The IFNB WAITFLAG tells MASM to assemble the 3 lines following only if the argument WAITFLAG is not blank. Otherwise, the code is not included and the first line assembled will be one of the lines governed by IFIDN. This gives us the option of generating either code that will wait for input forever or code that will just check the keys and go on if nothing's there. The IFNB checks for existence of WAITFLAG, not for spelling, so we could invoke the macro by any of the following:

```
@inchrif WAIT,EKO
@inchrif WAITE,EKO
@inchrif NoWate,EKO
@inchrif FOOBAH,EKO
```

and still generate code that does *not* wait for input. Note also that we have nested our macros, one macro invoking another.

More Macro Features

Instead of using only the WAITFLAG to determine whether to assemble the code for waiting, we might also make it a global option that we can choose at assembly time. For example, we might like it to wait for a key if we're debugging or if the WAITFLAG is set, but not wait otherwise. While we're extending this macro, we'll throw in some other new stuff. The new macro definition is

```
@inchrif MACRO   WAITFLAG,EKOFLAG
         LOCAL   bye      ; define a dummy address
;; Macro to get a character from the standard input
;;  2 arguments: WAITFLAG, & EKOFLAG determine whether to wait for a
;;  character, and whether to echo the input
x        =       0        ; x will be our indicator
IFNDEF   DEBUG            ; if the parameter DEBUG is not defined,
x        =       1        ; flag = 1
ENDIF                     ; end condition testing
IFNB     <WAITFLAG>       ; if the field for WAITFLAG is not blank
x        =       2        ; flag = 2
ENDIF                     ; end condition testing
IF       (x eq 1) or (x eq 2) ; if either DEBUG is not defined, or
                         ; WAITFLAG is not blank
         @chkchr          ; see if a character is waiting
         cmp     al,0     ; al = 0 => no character waiting
         je      bye      ; if no character, continue on
ENDIF                     ; end condition testing
IFIDN    <EKOFLAG>,<EKO>     ; if EKOFLAG = EKO, assemble the next line
         mov     ah,1     ; standard input with echo
ELSE                     ;    otherwise...
   IFIDN <EKOFLAG>,<NOEKO> ; if EKOFLAG = NOEKO, assemble next line
         mov     ah,8     ; standard input with no echo
   ELSE                   ; if the argument doesn't match either then
         .ERR             ; ...generate an assembly error
         %OUT ; Error in INCHRIF MACRO - EKOFLAG not found
```

```
        ENDIF                   ; end condition testing
    ENDIF                       ; end condition testing
            int     21h         ; dos call
    bye:
            .CREF               ;; restore cross-referencing
    ENDM                        ; Tell MASM the macro definition is ended
```

Now at assembly time we can use the /d option to define DBUG:

```
MASM  myprgm,,,; /dDBUG
```

and all the invocations of inchrif will generate code to wait for input.

We have used a flag (with = instead of equ since we redefine it in the next two IF statements) to determine whether or not we wait for a character. Instead of (x eq 1) or (x eq 2), we could have coded x gt 0 or x ne 0 since any value other than our initial value of 0 is valid.

Note that we also added a few new directives. The ;; tells MASM the comment should not be in the assembly listing. The .XCREF saves assembly time and cross-reference listing space by telling MASM not to clutter up our cross-reference listing with the names used only in the macro. .CREF restores cross-referencing or it would be off for the rest of the listing. We have also added the %OUT directive which will write to the screen the error message given.

Though there's plenty more we could do to it, this has become a pretty fearsome macro, so we'll leave it here and let you figure out all the complications left to add.

As promised earlier, we'll now show you how a generic subroutine call can be coded as a macro. The task is to push some parameters on the stack and call the subroutine. Pretty simple, except that we want a variable number of parameters, and we want to allow for byte and word parameters. The word parameters are easily handled, we simply push them. But byte variables have to be converted to words first. The macro below takes care of this problem:

```
@FcnCall MACRO  Fnctn,ParmList  ; subroutine, & list of parameters
IRP     N,<ParmList>            ; indefinite repeat (see below)
  IF ((.TYPE N) NE 22H)         ; is N data-related and defined ?
    push        N               ; if so, done
  ELSE
  IF ((TYPE N) EQ 2)            ; if 2-byte parameter
    push        N               ; push it
  ELSE
    IF ((TYPE N) EQ 1)          ; if 1-byte parameter
        mov     ah,0            ; clear upper byte of ax
        mov     al,N            ; parameter now a word...
        push    ax              ; ...so we can push it
```

```
      ELSE
           .ERR
      ENDIF
    ENDIF
   ENDIF
   call Fnctn
   ENDM                    ; Tell MASM the IRP is ended
  ENDM                     ; Tell MASM the macro definition is ended
```

We have used the TYPE operator which will return a 1 if the parameter is a byte, and a 2 if the parameter is a word. We also introduced the .TYPE operator to make it work with registers. Don't confuse this with the TYPE operator. There's a "." as the first character of this new operator. Using .TYPE allows the macro to handle a register such as BX as well as a data word or byte. .TYPE x returns a byte with the bits set according to the following scheme:

Bit 0 = 1 if x is code related, 0 otherwise

Bit 1 = 1 if x is data related, 0 otherwise

Bit 5 = 1 if x is defined, 0 otherwise

Bit 7 = 1 if x is external, 0 local or public

All other bits are zero.

For example, if x is data-related, defined, and local, .TYPE x returns 00100010b (22 hex) (bit 1 is set and bit 5 is set). Since we want to allow the use of registers (which are code related) as parameters, we will use the .TYPE operator to tell us if we have data-related parameters.

We've introduced IRP, the indefinite repeat macro directive. This tells MASM to repeat the instructions once for each element of the list enclosed by <>, substituting each element of the list for the dummy variable. For example:

```
IRP     y,<1,2,3>

db      y

ENDM
```

will generate

```
db      1
db      2
db      3
```

The nice thing about IRP for our purposes is that we don't have to specify in advance how many parameters we wish to send to the subroutine until we call it. We could call one routine with 3 parameters and another routine with 2 parameters. For example:

```
@FcnCall Fcn1,<word1,word2,byte3>
@FcnCall Fcn2,<word1,byte3>
```

and so on with virtually unlimited numbers of parameters for any subroutine call we wish.

Structures As Subroutine Parameters

While this FcnCall macro has been very instructive as a way of demonstrating MASM operators and directives, the best way to pass parameters to a subroutine is via a structure address. As an example, let's pass to our subroutine the data in one of the elements of our member list defined in our discussion of structures. Addresses are always the segment and offset. If we use a label of our data structure, such as Treasurer, then we can code

```
push    offset Treasurer
push    segment Treasurer
call    Fcn1
```

If we have a label of a list, such as MembrList in the example on structures, and an index displacement from that label, we use [MembrList + di] instead of Treasurer.

   If we want to send only one element of the structure, such as the phone number, we use [MembrList + di].PhoneNumb where we had Treasurer originally. So now the macro to make subroutine calls and pass parameters is simple enough that I can leave you with those immortal words, "It is left as an exercise for the reader"!

Interrupt Tips

If you have done much assembly language programming on the IBM PC, you have probably used software interrupts like INT 21 to make a DOS call, or INT 13 to make one of many BIOS calls. There are also hardware interrupts that can be of use when using the communications ports (COM1 or COM2), the keyboard, or the timer. Unfortunately, the proper techniques for writing an interrupt service routine (ISR) can be tricky. Let's look at the basic considerations.

There are three routines needed to handle interrupts: one to install the ISR, the ISR itself, and one to remove the ISR.

The ISR install routine simply uses DOS Function 35h to get the address of the current ISR for the interrupt in question, and DOS Function 25h to set the current ISR address. The following routine installs ISR CHKINT to respond to interrupt 4:

```
data        segment PARA public     'data'  ;define segment
OldVectorAdr        label   dword   ; double word for lds instruction
OldVectorOff        dw      0       ; offset of old vector
OldVectorSeg        dw      0       ; segment of old vector
NewVectorAdr        label   dword   ; double word for lds instruction
NewVectorOff        dw      offset CHKINT   ; offset of ISR = New vector
NewVectorSeg        dw      seg CHKINT      ; segment of New vector
data        ends
                    .
                    .
                    .
mov         ax,350ch            ; ah=35h = DOS "get current int vector"
                                ; int 0ch (= 4 * interrupt number) -> al
int         21h                 ; dos call returns vector in es:bx
lea         si,OldVectorOff ; get offset adr of where to put old int vctr
mov         [si],bx             ; store offset of old vector
mov         [si+2],es           ; store segment of old vector
push        ds                  ; need ds for new int vctr seg adr
lds         dx,NewVectorAdr ; load offset:seg of new int vctr in ds:dx
                                ; vectored to when the 8259 interrupts
mov         ax,250ch            ; 0Ch=int #(4-1) * 4
                                ; (4 bytes=segment:offset)
                                ; code the 8259 places on
                                ; data bus for 8088
                                ; ah= 25 hex = dos fcn to
                                ; set interrupts
int         21h                 ; dos call
pop         ds                  ; restore ds
in          al,IMR              ; IMR=21h=8259 bus address, get current masks
and         al,0EFh             ; reset IRQ4 mask (bit 4=0=>unmasked=enabled)
out         IMR,al              ; and store the new mask settings
cli                             ; disable (clear) interrupts
mov         al,20h              ; nonspecific EOI (if interrupts enabled)
out         20h,al              ; send it
                    .
                    .
                    .
```

The ISR differs from most MASM routines in stack segment addressing and in precautions needed for the ISR interrupting itself. The problem with the stack that can occur when writing ISRs is not having a stack available when the interrupt fires off. This can happen if the interrupt occurs when the system is executing BIOS code in ROM, or the DOS stack is close to its limit. You might think this is not a problem because we can create our own stack, but where do you save the segment registers, and how do you load the new ones? The following example solves this problem.

```
stkchk  SEGMENT PUBLIC
DB      32 DUP ('STACKCHK')        ; STACK SEG EASY TO FIND IN DEBUG
stksp   equ     $               ; define beginning of stack for chkint
stkchk  ENDS
DATA    segment PARA public     'data' ;define segment
  reges dw      (?)     ; don't use stack - save it here
  regss dw      (?)     ; don't use stack - save it here
  regsp dw      (?)     ; don't use stack - save it here
  spadr dw      stksp
DATA    ends
CHKCODE SEGMENT PARA PUBLIC
ASSUME  CS:CHKCODE,DS:CHKCODE,ES:CHKCODE,SS:CHKCODE
PUBLIC  CHKINT
CHKINT  PROC    FAR     ;define interrupt service procedure
jmp     short SetSeg    ; jump over our local storage area
ChkTmpAX        dw      (?)
ChkTmpDS        dw      (?)
SetSeg  label   near    ; establish data addressability
mov     cs:ChkTmpAX,ax  ; save ax, ds, & dx in the only segment we
mov     cs:ChkTmpDS,ds  ; can address right now - the code segment
mov     ax,dgroup       ; now we establish the addressability of our
mov     ds,ax           ; data segment
ASSUME  DS:DGROUP
mov     dgroup:reges,es ; we can now save the other segment registers
mov     es,ax           ; in the data segment
ASSUME  ES:DGROUP
mov     dgroup:regss,ss
mov     dgroup:regsp,sp
mov     ax,stkchk       ; get the address of the stack segment
mov     ss,ax           ; put it in the ss register
mov     sp,dgroup:spadr ; get the address of the stack top
ASSUME  SS:STKCHK
push    bp              ; finally we can use our stack
```

Let's start our examination of this example with the code segment. We will jump over some data space reserved in our code segment because, until we can put the address of our data segment in the ds register, the only thing we can rely on is that the code segment is in the cs register. When the interrupt fired off to get to our program, the current address was pushed on the existing stack, and the cs register was loaded with the place to jump to—CHKINT in this case.

We then save ax so we can use it as a scratch register, and ds so we can give it our own data segment address. Then we load ds with the data segment address and now we can store things in our data segment. We still haven't established our stack, so we save the remaining two segment registers in the data segment. Now we can load the stack segment and stack pointer registers. We didn't want to do this before, because we had interrupted some other program in midstream, which had no chance to save its stack registers. We want to be a good citizen and restore the interrupted program's stack. Notice that we load sp *immediately* after we load ss. The reason is that the 8088 and later CPUs of the Intel line automatically inhibit all interrupts for one instruction after the ss register is loaded. This enables us to load the sp register right after loading the ss register without fear that another program will interrupt our program in between, wreaking havoc because we still have an old sp. For example, if our ss:sp will be 1000:100, our code segment 1000:200, and the last ss:sp was 2000:0220, then, after we load ss but before we load sp, the ss:sp address will be 1000:220. If an interrupt program executes a push instruction now, it will overwrite our code. Not every interrupt program is as nice as ours and sets up its own stack. Many assume there's one available and use it without so much as a "by your leave," hence, the immediate mov sp,dgroup:spadr while interrupts are disabled.

There may be some cases where the interrupt can fire off while you are in the middle of the ISR. Then the ISR interrupts itself. This is like everyone crowding onto a boat without letting anyone out. In a short while, there's no room for anyone else and the boat sinks.

The system will crash due to stack overflow if too many ISRs are started before any can finish. The solution is to check a flag when the ISR begins, and if it is set, exit immediately. Otherwise, set it and reset it when the ISR is done.

Removing the ISR is simple:

```
lds     dx,dgroup:OldVectorAdr  ; load offset:seg of old int vctr in
                                ; ds:dx`vectored to when the 8259 interrupts
mov     ax,250ch                ; 0Ch=IRQ no.(4)+initialized base(8)=int type
                                ; code the 8259 places on data bus for 8088
                                ; dos fcn to set interrupts
int     21h                     ; dos call
pop     ds                      ; restore ds
in      al,21h                  ; 21h=8259 bus address, get current masks
or      al,10h                  ; set IRQ4 mask (bit 4=1 => masked=disabled)
out     21h,al                  ; and store the new mask settings
```

Parting Shots

The *Programmer's Guide* of version 5.0 of MASM may not be your idea of light reading, but there are some interesting new features that make it worthwhile. In particular, take a thorough look at Chapter 5 which introduces some new ways to deal with segments, the model declarations in particular. One of the most useful for me is the set of predefined equates discussed in Section 5.1.5 of the *Guide*. This allows you to set up general-purpose macros for segment naming based on the segment name, or filename. The new documentation provides some very nice examples which I won't try to elaborate on here.

I was also pleased with the "Communal" declaration described in Section 8.4. This feature allows you to declare variables as Communal in a single include file instead of having to declare it public in the procedure it is defined in and then external in the procedures it is referenced in.

One of the most useful new features of MASM 5.0 is the inclusion of the Codeview debugger. This window-oriented debugger has many desirable features. It allows you to view your source code (including comments and assembler directives) as you debug. It also allows you to declare some memory locations (by name or address) to be "watch" variables which means they will appear in a separate watch window so that you can observe any changes as they happen. It supports debugging of Expanded Memory Specification (EMS), overlay programs, and library modules. And for the first time, it allows you to see the 8087 coprocessor stack and status registers. There are many more features of Codeview which make it a very worthwhile debugger, although it lacks several features, such as tracing backwards, creating your own window features through macro scripts, and saving your session to disk for later review. Don't let the fact that Codeview is better than Debug preclude you from considering other debugging tools.

Finally, looking forward to an exciting future, we have the ability to assemble 80386 and 80387 code in both real and privileged (protected) modes.

There is much more to macros, interrupts, etc., than we could cover here but this leaves the thrill of discovery to you. Nothing in programming is beyond you if you have your own PC and an attitude of "What if I try this . . . ?" After all, the worst that can happen is that you have to power off and then on again.

Reading List

Biggerstaff, T. 1986. *Systems Software Tools*. Englewood Cliffs: Prentice-Hall, Inc.
   ▶ This contains readable descriptions of interrupt and communications
      hardware and software on the IBM PC.

Dunford, C. 1983/84. Interrupts and the IBM PC. *PC Tech Journal.* (November/ December, January).

▶ This contains an interrupt-driven communications program in assembler as an example.

Intel Corporation. 1985. *iAPX 286 Programmer's Reference Manual.* Santa Clara, California.

▶ This contains 80286/80287 details and assembly programs.

————. 1986. *Microsystem Components Handbook.* Santa Clara, California.

▶ Go to the source! Not light reading but invaluable.

Michael Goldman wrote his first program in 1964 when response time was days. He wrote his second program in 1972. While waiting for response time to improve, he received a B.S. in physics and an M.A. in mathematics from the University of Wisconsin. He now writes systems-level programs in C and assembly language in Silicon Valley. Only assembly language feeds his insatiable appetite for ever-faster response time.

Related Essays

4 Adding Power to MS-DOS Programming
13 Programming the Serial Port with C

PROGRAMMING TOOLS AND TECHNIQUES

To compete in the 1990s, MS-DOS programmers not only must thoroughly understand the MS-DOS operating system, they must learn how to use many undocumented functions that were meant to be reserved for the operating system. Also, they must master new standards of functionality such as popup utilities and background-processing TSRs, data security, and interfacing with the Microsoft Windows operating environment.

At this stage in its history, the MS-DOS operating system is generally recognized to be mature, with expected revisions not likely to exceed version 3.5. Therefore, more and more programmers are cautiously ignoring the warning that undocumented functions are reserved for future features. In fact, many reserved functions and interrupts have been used by Microsoft to implement some of the earliest external command utilities, and neither these functions nor any of the others are likely to be changed. Everything inside the system is now fair game for exploitation.

The name of the game is mastery. The four essays in this section revolve around the topic of developing the skill to manipulate—even customize—the way in which the MS-DOS kernel handles application programs and their files.

Undocumented MS-DOS Functions

This essay leads the section, and in it, author Ray Michels brings together explanations of most of the important undocumented functions, including those that let you examine and manipulate the Program Segment Prefix (PSP), allocate and deallocate memory, and inspect the MS-DOS busy flag. With these techniques, you can take real control of the internal MS-DOS data structures and services.

Safe Memory-Resident Programming (TSR)

The second essay in this section, by M. Steven Baker, shows how to use documented and undocumented interrupts and functions to create stable memory-resident programs that do not contend with other memory-resident applications. He examines some MS-DOS memory-resident programs such as PRINT and GRAPHICS and presents an example of a handy memory-resident utility that lets you disable and reenable the PRINT SCREEN key combination.

Data Protection and Encryption

Asael Dror, in this third essay, discusses the problem of protecting data from unauthorized access. He shows simple methods of using nonstandard characters and manipulating file attributes as well as the limitations of those methods. He discusses more advanced protection schemes, closing with techniques for effectively using RpublicS encryption algorithms. Ultimately, the software designer must assume that the encroacher is as smart, technically well-equipped, and intimately informed as the authorized users, and yet still must be locked out of the encryption scheme.

Inside Microsoft Windows

In this section's fourth and final essay, Michael Geary explains the fundamental concepts behind the Microsoft Windows multitasking operating environment. He shows how to use functions to examine the Windows message stream, the important circulation of information between the applications and devices that inhabit the Windows environment. Finally, he presents his now-famous SPY code, a tracing utility that reports details of applications as they run under Windows.

Keywords

- MS-DOS internals
- undocumented MS-DOS functions
- Program Segment Prefix (PSP)
- file handles
- Environment Segment
- environment variables
- memory management
- Drive Parameter Block

Essay Synopsis: Even after all these years, there are many parts of the MS-DOS internals that are poorly documented or not documented at all. In some cases (such as TSR-related functions), the lack of documentation may have been intended to discourage use of certain features. Because many undocumented functions are nevertheless useful, knowledge of them has sometimes been jealously guarded. In other cases, undocumented functions can be dangerous to use, and there is, of course, no guarantee they will be supported by future versions of DOS. Learning about these undocumented functions highlights important DOS internals and increases your understanding of operating system design and Intel processor architecture. This essay is your guide through the labyrinth of DOS functions and data structures.

6

Undocumented MS-DOS Functions

Raymond J. Michels

The MS-DOS Operating System, which has been available now for over seven years in several versions of increasing functionality, remains in many ways an undocumented system. Dozens of features, interrupts, and internal calls have remained secret within Microsoft or known only to a few MS-DOS developers. This paper explains some of the more useful DOS functions that have been neglected in the documentation. Though some of these functions are used internally by DOS, their operations can be useful to application programs.

I have documented the following areas of MS-DOS:

▶ Program Segment Prefix (PSP)

▶ MS-DOS File Handles

▶ Program Environment Segment

▶ MS-DOS Memory Management

▶ MS-DOS System Variables

There are still several MS-DOS functions that are either poorly documented or not documented at all. The process of documenting all of the "foggy" areas of MS-DOS has been an ongoing project of mine for the last four years. Much of what I've learned is the result of calling undocumented functions and observing the results, and disassembling the MS-DOS code itself. A "break-out switch" debugger (a resident debugger that can be activated with a special hardware switch) proved to be one of the best tools for doing this type of work, because it allows you to stop the machine and examine the computer system state at any time.

These MS-DOS "secrets" can be utilized in many different ways. By understanding how MS-DOS works, you can write better programs that take advantage of all of MS-DOS' internal functions. It is also possible to extend the function of MS-DOS by adding your own functions and utilities. With the advent of OS/2 and also fast computers (i.e., 80286 and 80386) multitasking functions that emulate OS/2 could be a very desirable feature. In addition, I think that just snooping inside of DOS is a fun way to learn about 8086 architecture and operating system concepts.

Much of the information contained herein is not documented in the Microsoft manuals. This implies that this information may not apply to future versions of MS-DOS. However, all existing DOS 2.00 to 3.20 versions should work (unless stated otherwise). So far, Microsoft has not removed any functions or tables from DOS, but if you use undocumented features be sure to test your code with every new version of MS-DOS to be sure. The fact that certain functions are undocumented also implies that they may be destructive if used in the wrong way. Be very careful when tampering with the MS-DOS system tables and memory blocks described in this paper. The wrong operation can crash your system and can even result in loss of file data!

I have made two assumptions about your level of expertise: You have a basic knowledge of 8086 assembly language and have some experience in writing programs in it, and you understand how to perform MS-DOS functions via Interrupt 21h.

In several of the examples presented in this chapter, I make use of the following common subroutines:

- char__out: output a character in the AL Register
- string__out: output string addressed by DS:DX
- hex__to__ascii: output word in ascii hex format
- hexb__to__ascii: output byte in ascii hex format

These routines can be found at the end of this paper.

We'll start by examining both documented and undocumented aspects of the Program Segment Prefix (PSP).

Program Segment Prefix

PSP is a 256-byte block of memory reserved by MS-DOS at program execution time. For each program run, a unique PSP is created. Since it contains control information related to the associated program, the PSP can also be considered to be a Process Data Block (a unique block of data that stores specific system and program data for the associated program). MS-DOS file and memory operations rely upon having access to the data in the PSP and also use the value of the physical PSP segment (its actual segment address in memory) as a unique process identifier.

In this section, we will examine each section of the PSP. Those of you familiar with CP/M may recognize sections of the PSP, since much of the same structure of the CP/M program header was retained when MS-DOS was developed using CP/M as a guide. This was to minimize the translation of 8-bit CP/M software to 16-bit MS-DOS software. Some of the structures in the PSP are reserved by MS-DOS and are also undocumented, so be very careful when changing such structures in the PSP. A wrong address or data value can send your program into the trash can.

The PSP segment address for a program can be found easily at startup. For COM files, the PSP is the value in the CS register. For EXE files, the PSP is the value in both the ES and DS registers. The offset address of the PSP is always zero. Since the DS register can change when an EXE file is run, it is important that your program save its value for later access to the PSP and its related fields. Figure 6-1 shows the PSP in relation to a program.

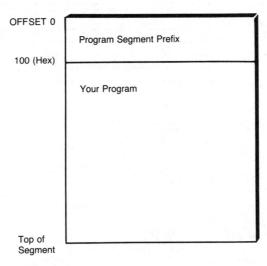

Fig. 6-1.   PSP and your program.

The PSP structure is identical for both COM and EXE programs. Finding the start of a PSP located outside of your program's environment, such as the PSP of a Terminate and Stay Resident program (TSR), is more difficult. (See Essay 7, Safe Memory-Resident Programming (TSR), by Steven Baker.) A technique for finding these PSPs will be described later in the section on MS-DOS Memory Management. Figure 6-2 shows the layout of a PSP presented in tabular format and in the form of an assembly language MASM listing. You may find it useful to run the MS-DOS DEBUG program so you can examine the values in your PSP. Simply type D 0 100 at the DEBUG prompt –. This will display the entire PSP of the program that you are debugging. Even if you have not loaded a program, DEBUG still sets up a default PSP.

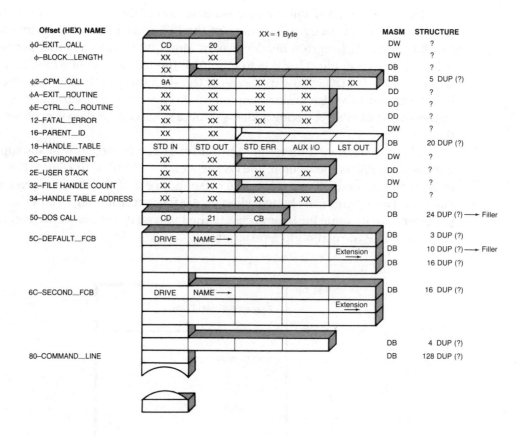

Offset (HEX) NAME						MASM	STRUCTURE
				XX = 1 Byte			
φ0–EXIT_CALL	CD	20				DW	?
φ–BLOCK_LENGTH	XX	XX				DW	?
	XX					DB	?
φ2–CPM_CALL	9A	XX	XX	XX	XX	DB	5 DUP (?)
φA–EXIT_ROUTINE	XX	XX	XX	XX		DD	?
φE–CTRL_C_ROUTINE	XX	XX	XX	XX		DD	?
12–FATAL_ERROR	XX	XX	XX	XX		DD	?
16–PARENT_ID	XX	XX				DW	?
18–HANDLE_TABLE	STD IN	STD OUT	STD ERR	AUX I/O	LST OUT	DB	20 DUP (?)
2C–ENVIRONMENT	XX	XX				DW	?
2E–USER STACK	XX	XX	XX	XX		DD	?
32–FILE HANDLE COUNT	XX	XX				DW	?
34–HANDLE TABLE ADDRESS	XX	XX	XX	XX		DD	?
50–DOS CALL	CD	21	CB			DB	24 DUP (?) ⟶ Filler
5C–DEFAULT_FCB	DRIVE	NAME ⟶				DB	3 DUP (?)
					Extension ⟶	DB	10 DUP (?) ⟶ Filler
						DB	16 DUP (?)
6C–SECOND_FCB	DRIVE	NAME ⟶				DB	16 DUP (?)
					Extension ⟶		
						DB	4 DUP (?)
80–COMMAND_LINE						DB	128 DUP (?)

Fig. 6-2.   PSP structure.

Overview of the PSP

Let's take a look at the contents of the PSP and try to make some sense of it.

The first 2 bytes of the PSP are machine codes to generate an INT 20H which is the interrupt used to terminate a program. Thus, calling address 0 any time from within your program will cause it to execute the INT 20H. Your program will terminate and return to MS-DOS. This is a holdover from CP/M where a jump to address zero of your program would exit you to the system prompt A>. This method of program exit is not advised in MS-DOS since MS-DOS versions 2 and above provide better ways to terminate a program by using Function 4Ch via INT 21H, the main MS-DOS function interrupt. This DOS function allows you to set a return code that can be examined in a batch file or from a calling program. It may also perform better housekeeping and cleanup when your program terminates.

The next word in the PSP is called block length and contains the total amount of memory available in paragraphs in this PC. One paragraph is 10h bytes. Reading this address can be useful for quickly determining if there is enough memory available for your program's needs. If, for example, you know your program needs 512K bytes of memory and the PSP block length field reports only 256K bytes, appropriate action can be taken (such as reporting there is not enough memory available).

Byte number five of the PSP contains machine code to perform MS-DOS functions. Calling this location (similar to the old CP/M `Call`) is equivalent to performing an `INT 21H`. The function number is placed in the CL register prior to calling offset 5. Note that this differs from the traditional `INT 21H` convention of placing the function number in the AH register. Other registers may be needed but they vary for each function. This is another holdover from CP/M and is referred to among MS-DOS aficionados as the "ancient system call." MS-DOS functions should never be performed in this manner and don't use this value, but it allowed easy porting from CP/M to MS-DOS.

Starting at offset 0Ah are three double-word (32-bit) pointers, each in the form of an offset address and a segment address. They are pointers to the `Exit` routine, the `Control-C` routine, and the `Fatal Error` routine. These are copies of Interrupts 22h through 24h from the standard interrupt vector table in the base page of memory (segment 0,offset = 0). When your program exits back to MS-DOS, these values will be copied back to the interrupt vector table. This is done just in case your program modified these values for its specific needs (such as installing its own Critical Error Handler).

The next two components of the PSP are undocumented. The first contains the Process Id of the parent process. What this means is that this word, starting at 16h, points to the PSP of the program that initiated the "current" program. (The original program will still be in memory.) By using the documented Function 4Bh, one program can initiate another. The second component is a table of 20 bytes starting at 18h in the PSP. These locations are used to manage file handles. Remember, a handle in MS-DOS is a method of file access. The size of this table is the reason that one program can only open 20 files at a time.

The environment pointer for our program starts at offset 2Ch in the PSP. This is the segment address of the program's environment-each program in memory has a unique environment.

The double word at offset 2Eh is used by DOS to store the caller's stack segment and stack pointer when DOS switches to an internal stack during `INT 21H` processing.

The two components starting at offset 32h deal with the File Handle Table (FHT). The word at offset 32h contains the maximum number of file handles and the FHT's size for the program. Offset 34h contains a `DWORD` (double-word) pointer to the FHT. DOS does not seem to be affected by changing these values. They can be used when you need the number of file handles and the address of the handle table.

Starting at offset 50h are machine instruction bytes to perform a DOS function call INT 21H and RETF. If you set up your registers properly and perform a FAR call to location PSP:50h, the INT 21H will be executed (performing the desired DOS function) and when DOS returns, the RETF will return back to your code.

Three well-documented sections of the PSP are at locations 5Ch, 6Ch, and 80h. Offset 5C contains an unopened File Control Block (FCB) if a file was specified as a program parameter on the command line, as in DIR FILE1. If a second file was specified (COPY FILE1 FILE2), its associated FCB will be found at 6C. These FCBs at 5C and 6C are yet another CP/M holdover. Location 80 contains the entire command line following the program name. This can be useful when passing program switches such as the /P in DIR *.* /P. Your program can examine the data at offset 80 and recover this information. Since locations 5C and 6C only create FCBs, location 80 is needed if full pathnames (such as \SYSTEM\FILE) are used as command-line file parameters.

The PSP can be considered the heart of your program. It controls your file access and also is used for memory allocation. It paves the way for a multitasking environment since it could be used as a unique process identifier and control mechanism. Let's move on and look more closely at the File Handle Table and the Environment Pointer sections of the PSP.

File Handles

One of the major changes in MS-DOS with the release of version 2.00 was the introduction of file handles to the operating system. A handle is a byte value assigned to an opened file. All subsequent operations performed on the file only require the handle number and not a full FCB. MS-DOS keeps track of the FCB for you in its own System File Table (SFT).

As we have seen, the FHT, located at offset 18 (hex) in the PSP segment, is a table of 20 bytes. When an operation that uses a file handle is performed, DOS uses the handle number to index into this table. DOS then uses the number retrieved from the table to locate the actual file in the SFT. (See Essay 10, Developing MS-DOS Device Drivers, by Walter Dixon.) The following handles are opened for you when your program is loaded:

0- Standard Input

1- Standard Output

2- Standard Error Output

3- Standard Auxiliary I/O

4- Standard Printer Output

The remaining 15 bytes of the FHT are available for your program's data files. This table size is what limits your program to using 20 files (five of which are already used). The `FILES=nn` in the `CONFIG.SYS` file sets up how many file blocks are available for the entire system. If `FILES=40`, a TSR can use 20 files and your program can use 20 files. Figure 6-3 descibes how DOS uses the file handle number to get to its internal SFT.

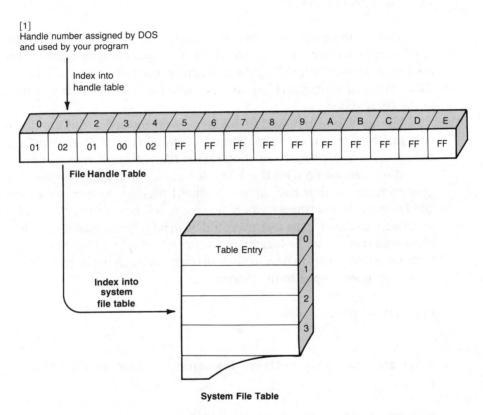

Fig. 6-3.   File handles in action.

What does this method of file access achieve? Since, in MS-DOS, the Console Input and Output are opened as file handles (remember that these are numbers and not names), it is very easy to substitute an actual disk file for console output or input. (Standard Error, COM1 and LPT can also be accessed through file handles.) This is exactly what DOS does during a request for I/O redirection: `DIR *.*> file`. A disk file is opened with a file handle and the console output handle is replaced by the disk file handle. The UNIX operating system (where this idea came from) uses a similar concept for managing its files. Since the first five file handles are already open, it is very easy to perform I/O on these devices by just using the appropriate handle number in the documented MS-DOS file output Function 40h:

```
mov   ah,40H        ;write to a file with handle function
mov   bx,1          ;Standard Output handle
```

```
        mov  cx,7            ;write 7 bytes to Standard Output
        mov  dx,offset msg   ;DS:DX points to data to output
        int  21H             ;

msg  db   'Hello',13,10
```

This example would write the message Hello (defined with db) to the standard output (either the Console Output or the current redirection device).
MS-DOS Function 3Fh will perform a similar operation except that it will input
data (rather than output) from the specified file handle to the specified address
in the DS register.

File handles also moved DOS a step closer toward a multitasking operating
system. The actual file information is maintained by MS-DOS. This enables multiple programs to gain access to the same file without any conflicts.

What can we do with this PSP File Handle Table? It is possible, under program control, to alter this table to redirect files on your own. Redirection is a
good feature, but at times it would be nice to be able to turn it on and off during
program execution. This feature could be used to print screens to files for documentation use, for error-logging or for program-debugging. The following code
fragments demonstrate how to change from printing, to the console, to redirecting the console output to the printer:

```
redirect     proc     near


;
;this procedure will redirect the console output to the printer
;

;assumes DS:BX points to start of PSP segment

        les     bx,[bx+34h]      ;get handle table address
mov al,es:[bx+1]                 ;get current std output handle
mov save_console,al              ;save it
mov al,[bx+4]                    ;get current print output
mov [bx+1],al                    ;put it in console spot

;
;now all output to the standard output will be directed to the
;printer

redirect     endp



cancel_redir     proc     near
```

```
;
;this procedure will cancel the redirection set up in redirect
;
;assumes ES:BX points to file handle table

mov   al,save_console ;get original console value
mov   [bx+1],al        ;put it back

;
;redirection is now canceled
;

cancel_redir    endp

save_console    db      (?)
```

In this example, we can change the I/O direction of any file just by altering the FHT. Make sure you remember to save the original table entry before any changes are made.

The Environment Segment

In our earlier discussion of the PSP, we mentioned that it contains a pointer (at offset 2Ch) to the program's environment. This address is a segment number with an offset of 0. As its name implies, the environment identifies specific parameters that can be used by the associated program. The environment is sparsely documented in the *IBM DOS Technical Reference*. Let's look at it more closely.

Variables in the Environment

The environment contains a series of ASCIIZ strings (a string of ASCII characters terminated by a null (0) byte). Each of these strings can have specific meaning either to DOS or your own program. An environment string is set up at the command prompt by entering a command with the form SET VARIABLE = (String parameter), for example, SET PATH = \SYSTEM. This will place the string following the SET command into the next available environment slot. MS-DOS reserves three environment variables, COMSPEC, PATH and PROMPT. The COMPSEC variable is always set by MS-DOS at boot time and it defines the path and name of the command processor (usually COMMAND.COM, but a custom command processor could also be used). The COMSPEC variable can be useful to the application program when executing another program or MS-DOS commands such as DIR or ERASE (by using the MS-DOS EXEC Function 4Bh where COMMAND.COM is being used to execute a command). The PATH variable identifies the current search path for command execution, so when you type a command, MS-DOS knows which directory paths to search for it. PROMPT is used for generating a user-defined prompt. Both the PATH and PROMPT commands are well-documented in the DOS Reference Manual. Additional variables can be set up for application program use.

A good use of environment variables is to allow the user to identify where application specific data or parameter files are located at the time a program is run. Using this method, files accessed by your program that would otherwise have had to be in a predefined place (either in a specific directory or in the current directory) can be placed in a directory chosen by the user. This feature could be used to support multiple, unique data sets that can be accessed by a single program. A batch file can change the environment variable to point to the desired data. In Microsoft C, a function called GETENV is provided (and documented) in version 4.0 to gain access to environment variables. For other languages, you will have to search the environment space to locate the specific variable of interest.

A null byte follows the last ASCIIZ string defining variables. For MS-DOS versions 2.XX, the environment ends here. In version 3.00 and above, this is followed by a word called a byte count. However, I have always found this to be "one." An ASCIIZ string specifying the full PATH name of the current application is next. For example, if the program name were ENVI.COM and its path C:\SYSTEM\UTIL, the string will contain C:\SYSTEM\UTIL\ENVI.COM. It will be terminated by one null to end the program name string. This single null byte also marks the end of the environment data. We will use this string later in an example that prints out a memory map of resident programs.

Using the Environment in Batch Files

A feature of environment parameters (undocumented until DOS 3.30) is that they can be easily accessed from and used within a batch file. For example, suppose that you have issued the command SET USER=NOVICE at the MS-DOS command line. The value of the variable USER can be obtained from inside a batch file by enclosing it in percent symbols. The following line:

```
IF %USER% == "NOVICE" TYPE HELP.TXT ¦ MORE
```

could be used inside a batch file to output a special help file through the MS-DOS MORE filter. The ¦ (pipe) instructs MS-DOS to take the standard output from the first program and use it as data to the standard input for the second program. MORE displays a screenful of text and waits for a key to be hit before continuing.

Another interesting batch file trick is to use environment variables in such a way as to allow callable subroutines within a batch file. These routines can be called and then return control to a specified label in the batch file. It is really just an intelligent GOTO. The following batch file example describes this technique:

```
SET RETURN=ONE                  Set up a 'return' label
GOTO SUBROUTINE                 Perform the subroutine


:ONE                            Subroutine will 'return' here
SET RETURN=TWO                  Set up a 'return' label
GOTO SUBROUTINE                 Perform the subroutine


:TWO                            Subroutine will 'return' here
GOTO END                        Exit this batch file


:SUBROUTINE                     Subroutine to call
ECHO INSIDE OF SUBROUTINE       Subroutine Body
GOTO %RETURN%                   'Return' to caller

:END
```

Environment variables thus add a new dimension to batch file programming by moving the batch language close to a real programming language. DOS 3.30 has added the capability of having one batch file call another as though it were a subroutine.

Expanding Environment Space

When setting environment variables, the error message OUT OF ENVIRONMENT SPACE may be encountered. The size of the initial environment for the command processor sets the environment size of all subsequent programs. The default size varies by DOS level and MS-DOS distributor and it can be changed by specifying a shell program in the CONFIG.SYS file. The default shell is COMMAND.COM. We will still use COMMAND.COM in the example, but by using the documented SHELL statement in the CONFIG.SYS file, we can alter the size of the initial environment. The syntax of the statement is as follows:

```
SHELL = C:COMMAND.COM /P /E:nn
```

The first parameter /P tells COMMAND.COM to become permanent (be kept in memory) as the top-level process, and cause the AUTOEXEC.BAT file, if present, to be executed. The second parameter /E:nn defines the environment size, and applies to MS-DOS versions 3.00 and above only. For versions 3.00 and 3.10, the nn defines the number of paragraphs to allocate (one paragraph equals 16 bytes) and this value can be from 10 to 62 (giving environment sizes from 160 to 992 bytes). For MS-DOS 3.20 and 3.30, the nn defines the absolute number of bytes to allocate to the environment, from 160 to 32768. Remember, each program in memory gets its own environment so setting a large environment will waste memory if a number of TSRs are used.

When COMMAND.COM executes a program, it makes a copy of its own environment (the one affected by the SET command) and attaches this environment to the new program. When the program terminates, its environment, along with the PSP and executable image, is returned to free memory (unless it is a TSR). This is an important fact since programs that alter the environment are only accessing a COPY of the master and any changes will only be in effect while the current program is executing and has not terminated. This also applies to a program executed or started from a program other than COMMAND.COM (as in a child process).

PSP Functions

Table 6-1 lists the five functions useful for manipulating the PSP segment. The last three are undocumented. Let's briefly examine the documented functions first.

Table 6-1.   PSP Functions

Function	Operation
Function 26h	Create PSP Block
Function 50h	Set Current PSP
Function 51h	Get PSP Segment
Function 55h	Duplicate PSP Block
Function 62h	Get PSP Segment (DOS 3.00 and above)

Function 26h Create PSP Block

MS-DOS Function 26 will create a PSP block at the memory segment address specified in the DX register. Prior to the EXEC call's (Function 4Bh) being available (starting with DOS 2.0), Create PSP Block was a way to have one program "chain" to another (that is to create a child process). It is up to the main program to create/allocate the memory space required for the new program. Function 26 should be avoided since the EXEC Function 4B now does a much better job.

Function 62h Get PSP Segment

Function 62 will return the current PSP segment in the BX register. This function is not available prior to MS-DOS version 3.00. In version 2.XX, the undocumented Function 51h performs the same operation and it is still available in later versions. It is rumored that Function 51 has a bug when used from a resident program, so use Function 62h whenever this service is required. The bug is that DOS switches to the wrong internal stack. This will cause problems if called from a TSR during an interrupt 28h.

Function 50h Set Current PSP

Function 50 (along with Function 62) is best used from within a TSR. Since the PSP segment is unique for every program, it is used as a Process ID by DOS for file handling and memory allocation. Function 50, Set Current PSP, is called with the AH register equal to 50h and the BX register equal to the desired PSP segment number (Process ID). We'll say more about these soon.

Function 55h Duplicate PSP Block

This function is almost identical to Function 26. The new PSP segment is passed in the DX register and, on return, a new PSP is initialized. The major difference is that the Parent ID portion of the PSP is set up by MS-DOS. Function 55 is used by Function 4B when executing a new program. It could be useful to you if you need to execute a program but want total control (as in a multitasking environment). The following steps could be used to develop a method to execute a program:

1. Allocate memory for the PSP and program code.
2. Duplicate the PSP.
3. Load your code into newly allocated segment above the PSP.
4. Save current PSP.
5. Set PSP to newly duplicated one.
6. Jump to start of code.

Undocumented TSR and PSP Secrets

The two most useful PSP functions are 50h, Set Current PSP, and 51h (or 62h), Get PSP Segment. They are generally used from inside a TSR.

In MS-DOS, each process can only have a maximum of 20 files open at one time. If a process terminates with open files, they will automatically be closed by MS-DOS. This can cause confusion if a TSR uses files without adjusting the program segment. For example, if a TSR opens a file, DOS will use the File Handle Table in the current (foreground) PSP, which does not belong to the TSR but to the program the TSR interrupted. This could cause the foreground process to run out of file table space since it didn't expect a TSR to be using its files. It can be even more disastrous if the foreground process terminated since this would close the TSR's file as well! A TSR-performing memory allocation/deallocation can cause similar problems since it may be modifying the foreground process memory pool instead of its own. Because of this, a TSR needs to save its PSP segment during initialization for later use during file operations and/or memory allocation/deallocation.

Another useful idea using the Get PSP call is that a TSR can access the foreground program's environment. Different TSR operations could be run based on an environment variable's setting.

Memory Management

One of the major features that DOS 2.00 added to 1.00 was the ability to allocate and deallocate memory as needed. The concepts used are similar to those used in the UNIX operating system (and other multiuser systems). Each program in memory can get a block of memory and shrink or expand it based on its needs.

There are documented MS-DOS functions available that deal with memory management (listed in Table 6-2). The MS-DOS manual does not explain these fully, especially for a novice programmer.

Table 6-2. Memory Management Functions

Function	Operation
Function 48h	Allocate Memory
Function 49h	Free Memory
Function 4Ah	Adjust Block Size

Memory Allocation Blocks are referenced in paragraphs and one paragraph equals 16 bytes. To convert a memory value in bytes to a memory value in paragraphs in a program, just add 16 to the value and binary shift the result to the right four times. This rounds the value up by one paragraph and divides by four. To convert back, binary shift it to the left four times. Let's briefly take a look at these memory management calls.

Function 48h Allocate Memory

Allocate Memory requests a block of memory from the MS-DOS pool of free memory. Place the Function number 48h in the AX register and the number of paragraphs required in the BX register. On return, if the `Carry Flag` is set, then BX contains the maximum number or paragraphs available. Note that no actual allocation takes place in this case. To allocate memory, you must call the function again with BX less than or equal to the total amount available. If the `Carry Flag` is clear, the memory is allocated, and AX contains the segment address of the allocated space. If you want to allocate as much memory as possible, call this function with BX equal to FFFFh. This request will never be granted but it will return the maximum amount of memory available for allocation.

Function 49h Free Memory

Free Memory is the opposite of allocate. It will return the specified block of memory back to the system memory pool. You must free the entire segment allocated by a Function 48h call. Place Function 49 in the AX register and the segment address of the memory block to free in the ES register. On return, if the `Carry Flag` is set, the operation failed and AX will contain the DOS error code. An error is usually caused by specifying a segment of memory that does not belong to your program.

Function 4Ah Adjust Block Size

Adjust Block Size is a request to change the size of a currently allocated block of memory. You can shrink or expand a previously allocated memory block with this function. Place Function 4A in the AX register, the segment address of the block to modify in the ES register, and the new block size (in paragraphs) in the BX register. If the `Carry Flag` is set, BX will contain the maximum number of paragraphs available; otherwise, the operation was successful. To find the maximum amount of memory available use the same technique described for Function 48 (call with `BX = FFFFh`).

In MS-DOS, when `COMMAND.COM` loads your program, all the available system memory is allocated to that program, so if the program is a TSR, it will need to deallocate all that extra memory before terminating. MS-DOS programs also have the ability to call other MS-DOS programs, but if another program is to be loaded, some memory must be freed up to make room for the new program. The MS-DOS EXEC Function 4Bh is used to execute other programs. For those of you familiar with Pascal, MS-DOS memory functions are similar to the NEW and DISPOSE functions.

Now that we have briefly touched upon the MS-DOS memory functions, let's take a look at the undocumented physical structure of these memory blocks that can be created. By understanding how these blocks are organized, it is possible to write a program that reports the status of all allocated memory blocks that can be very handy for debugging purposes. As an example, we will describe a technique for printing out a map of all programs currently in memory.

Every official memory block created by MS-DOS has a 10h byte (one-paragraph) Memory Control Block (MCB) physically preceding it. (Since both the environment and the PSP segments are allocated by MS-DOS, they each have an MCB.) Thus, any memory blocks that your application program allocates for holding data will have an associated control block. To find the MCB for a specific segment, simply subtract one from the segment address. This will be the allocated block's corresponding MCB. (Since segment numbers are the leftmost four digits of a five-digit value, subtracting one is the same as subtracting 10h). The following is a MASM data structure for an MCB. These control blocks are linked together to form a chain of MCBs.

```
MCB Signature   db   0 ;(MCB = Memory Control Block)
MCB Owner       dw   0 ;(Segment of owner - Usually PSP
                       ; segment)
MCB Size        dw   0 ;(in paragraphs)
```

The byte called signature can be either 4Dh or 5Ah. A 4D signifies that this is an MCB. Because the MCBs are a linked list, the 5A signifies the last block in the allocated chain.

Owner specifies which segment owns this block, and is generally the owner's PSP segment address. Remember, the PSP is used as a unique process ID. By using the Owner field, DOS can ensure that one program (such as a TSR) does not attempt to alter the size of another program's memory block. This protection is only valid when using DOS memory allocation/deallocation functions.

Size specifies how many paragraphs are contained in this block. By adding the size value to the segment address of the MCB and then incrementing the result by one, you are able to access the next block in the chain (provided that the current signature is not 5ADh, indicating the end of the chain). Figure 6-4 shows a chain of Memory Control BLocks.

There is no way to go backward in the MCB chain. This makes it tough for a program to find out information about any TSR installed or a parent process. But there exists an undocumented way to get to the start of the MCB chain. DOS

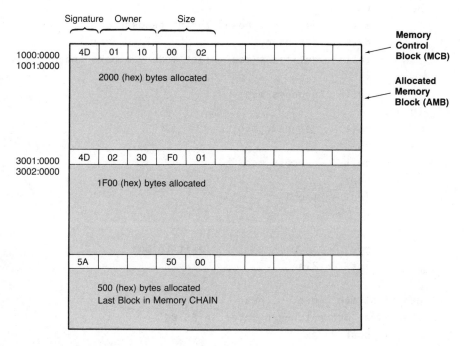

Fig. 6-4.   A memory control block chain.

Function 52h returns a pointer to a number of special DOS variables. One of these variables happens to be a pointer to the first MCB. Using this value, we can create a program that will start at the beginning of the MCB chain, trace through all allocated blocks, identify PSP segments, and generate a memory map of the system. The environment segments can be found from the environment pointer in the PSP segments. The following is a MASM module that will print out selected information about allocated memory. It works in this manner:

1. Get memory block.
2. If it is a PSP, print its MCB's segment address.
3. Print PSP's segment address.
4. Print size of PSP in paragraphs (from MCB).
5. Print program name (from environment).
6. Print PSP's parent name (from Parent ID).

```
mcb       struc
          signature      db      0
          owner          dw      0
          size           dw      0
mcb       ends
```

```
begin:
        mov     dx,offset head0 ;print headers
        call    string_out
        call    get_first_mcb   ;get memory blocks and process

        call    process_mcb
loop1:
        call    get_next_mcb
        pushf
        call    process_mcb
        popf
        jnc     loop1


        mov     ah,0            ;exit to dos
        int     21h

get_first_mcb   proc    near
;get first mcb returns pointer in ES:BX
        push    ax
        mov     ah,52h          ;get DOS Variables
        int     21h
        sub     bx,2            ;get first MCB pointer
        mov     ax,es:[bx]
        mov     es,ax
        xor     bx,bx
        clc
        pop     ax
        ret
get_first_mcb   endp

get_next_mcb    proc    near
;get next mcb
;assumes ES:BX pointer to current MCB
;
        push    ax
        mov     ax,es           ;get MCB segment address
        inc     ax              ;point to actual allocated
                                ;   memory block
        add     ax,es:[bx.size] ;add in block size
        mov     es,ax           ;now we point to next block
        cmp     es:[bx.signature],4dh
        je      get_all_ok
        stc                     ;flag end of chain
```

```
        jmp      get_exit
get_all_ok:
        clc
get_exit:
        pop      ax
        ret


get_next_mcb      endp



process_mcb  proc    near
;Print pertinent field of device driver header
;Input: ES:BX points to device driver header
;Output: None

        push     ax                 ;save registers
        push     bx
        push     cx
        push     dx
        push     si

        cmp      byte ptr es:[bx+16],0CDh ;Is It PSP?
        je       isipsp
        jmp      process_exit
ispsp:
        mov      dx,es
        call     hex_to_ascii
        mov      cx,4

l0:
        mov      al,' '
        call     char_out
        loop     l0

        mov      dx,es:[bx.owner]
        call     hex_to_ascii
        mov      cx,4

l1:
        mov      al,' '
        call     char_out
        loop     l1

        mov      dx,es:[bx.size]
```

```
                call    hex_to_ascii
                mov     cx,4
        l2:
                mov     al,' '
                call    char_out
                loop    l2

                push    es
                call    extract_prog_name

process_loop:
                push    ds
                push    es
                pop     ds
                xor     cx,0

process_loop1:
                lodsb
                inc     cx
                call    char_out
                cmp     byte ptr [si],0
                jne     process_loop1

                mov     ax,13
                sub     ax,cx
                mov     cx,ax

        l3:
                mov     al,' '
                call    char_out
                loop    l3

                pop     ds
                pop     es

                push    es
                push    bx
                push    ds

                mov     ax,es:[bx+26h] ;get PID
                dec     ax             ;point to MCB
                mov     bx,0
                mov     es,ax
                call    extract_prog_name
```

```
        push    es
        pop     ds
        xor     cx,cx
process_loop3:
        lodsb
        inc     cx
        call    char_out
        cmp     byte ptr [si],0
        jne     process_loop3

        mov     ax,13
        sub     ax,cx
        mov     cx,ax

l4:
        mov     al,' '
        call    char_out
        loop    l4

        pop     ds
        pop     bx
        pop     es
        mov     dx,offset crlf
        call    string_out


process_exit:
        pop     si              ;restore registers
        pop     dx
        pop     cx
        pop     bx
        pop     ax
        ret
process_mcb  endp

extract_prog_name proc    near
;
;es:bx -> psp
;returns es:si -> prog name
        push    ds
        push    es
        pop     ds
```

```
                mov       ax,es:[bx+3ch] ;get environ segment
                cmp       ax,0
                jne       extract_cont
                pop       ds
                push      ds
                pop       es
                mov       si,offset command
                ret

extract_cont:
                mov       ds,ax
                xor       si,si

not_found:
                cmp       word ptr [si],0
                je        found
                inc       si
                jmp       not_found

found:
                add       si,4

not_found1:
                cmp       byte ptr [si],0
                je        found1
                inc       si
                jmp       not_found1


found1:
                dec       si
                cmp       byte ptr [si],''
                jne       found1
                inc       si
                push      ds
                pop       es
                pop       ds
                ret

extract_prog_name endp

;
;data
;
```

```
head0 label word

   db 149,' MCG      PSP     PROG (PARAGRAPHS)                    ',13,10
   db ' SEG     SEG    SIZE          NAME        PARENT   ',13,10
   db '----     ----   ----   ------------ ------------',13,10

crlf    db      2,13,10
command db      'COMMAND.COM',0
```

The following is a sample of the output produced by the preceding program:

```
MCB     PSP     PROG (PARAGRAPHS)
SEG     SEG     SIZE          NAME         PARENT
----    ----    ----   ------------ ------------
0D34    0D35    00C3   COMMAND.COM   COMMAND.COM
0E0F    0E10    005B   SYSTEM        COMMAND.COM
0E73    0E74    0037   KBDFIX.COM    COMMAND.COM
0EB2    0EB3    18ED   SK.COM        SK.COM
27A8    27A9    0040   GRAPHICS.COM COMMAND.COM
27F1    27F2    780E   PMCB.COM      COMMAND.COM
```

Other Undocumented Functions

The following functions don't really fall into a definitive group so they have been placed in this section. They are:

▶ Numerous Dummy Functions

▶ Function 37h Set Switch Character

▶ Function 52h Get MS-DOS Variables

▶ Function 1Ch and 32h Get Disk Parameters

▶ Function 45h and 46h Duplicate File Handles

Functions 45 and 46 are documented but have some undocumented side effects.

MS-DOS Dummy Functions

The following functions are not used by MS-DOS:

▶ 18h

▶ 1Dh

▶ 1Eh

▶ 20h

Many of the lower numbered functions of MS-DOS have an equivalent CP/M counterpart. These CP/M functions were not implemented by MS-DOS but were probably left in to ease the porting of CP/M to MS-DOS based software by keeping the succeeding function numbers the same. These are described in MS-DOS manuals as "reserved."

Function 34h Get MS-DOS Busy Flag

After performing an INT 21H with AX equal to 34h, ES:BX will point to a byte called the MS-DOS busy flag. When this byte is nonzero it indicates that MS-DOS is in use. This function is generally used by a TSR to make sure that it is safe to perform MS-DOS functions. Since MS-DOS is not reentrant, calling DOS while it is busy will usually corrupt its stack and cause a system crash. You should not call MS-DOS every time a flag check is needed. The proper procedure is to call this function once and store the value returned in ES:BX for use during the current activation of the TSR. When a later check on this flag is required, use the previously stored ES:BX value to examine the flag value. If the flag is nonzero when your TSR is activated, it means that you have interrupted the main (foreground) program performing a DOS function.

Function 37h Get/Set Switch Char

The Switch Char is the character that precedes command-line switch (hence the name). In the command DIR /P, the character / is called a switch character. The directory structure of MS-DOS was patterned after the UNIX operating sytem, but with one small (and sometimes frustrating) difference. In UNIX, /BIN/FILE is a legal filename. In MS-DOS, it would have to be called \BIN\FILE. Notice that the filename separators are reversed. This is because the / was already used. At one time, there existed a command that could be put in the CONFIG.SYS file that could alter the switch character. Many people prefer to use – for a command-line switch and / for directory separators. By changing the switch character from /, the directory separator will revert to the UNIX format. Though this command has been removed in DOS 3.XX, you can still change the switch character through Function 37h. When the switch character is changed from /, the directory path can use either \ or / as a separator.

Function 52h Get DOS Variables

Function 52 returns a pointer to block of data values that can be called DOS variables, also referred to as List of Lists (see Essay 11). These variables either point to or contain relevant system information about the disk drives, file system, device drivers, and a few other items. The returned pointer will be in the ES:BX register set.

The following MASM structure describes the layout of the table:

```
VARS  STRUC

          dpb_ptr    dd    0    ;BX+0
          sft_ptr    dd    0    ;BX+4
          clock_ptr  dd    0    ;BX+8
          con_ptr    dd    0    ;BX+0CH
          max_sec    dw    0    ;BX+10H
          cache      dd    0    ;BX+12H
          drive_inf  dd    0    ;BX+16H
          fcb_ptr    dd    0    ;BX+1AH
          unknown    dd    0    ;BX+1EH
          nul_dev    dd    0    ;BX+22H

VARS      ENDS
```

The order of this table seems to vary with versions of DOS and OEM implementation. The preceding table was taken from DOS 3.20.

The first element in the table, at offset BX + 0, is a pointer to the Drive or Device Parameter Block (DPB). The DPB is a block of data that contains specific information about each MS-DOS physical disk drive. We will examine the DPB in detail a little later.

The second element, at offset BX + 4, is a pointer to the MS-DOS SFT, containing information about all open files. There is another file table pointer at offset 1Ah which points to a table of files opened with the older style FCB access.

The third and fourth elements, at offsets BX + 8 and BX + 0C (hex), are pointers to the Clock and Console Device Drivers, respectively.

The next element, at offset BX + 10h, is a maximum sector size value. This is set to the largest sector size being used internally by MS-DOS prior to loading block device drivers. After device driver initialization, this value is compared to the sector size returned by the device driver. If the device driver's sector size is greater, MS-DOS prints an error message `Sector Size Too Large` and the driver is not installed into DOS.

Offset BX + 12h contains a pointer to the MS-DOS cache buffer head. I have not been able to decipher the buffer structure.

At offset BX + 16h is a pointer to a series of blocks containing such drive information as the current directory of a particular drive. The last element, at offset BX + 22h, is the start of the NUL device driver. The first two words of a device driver is a pointer to the next driver. Since the NUL device is always first, we can follow the device driver chain until these first two bytes are FF FF (− 1) in the last device driver. When debugging device drivers, it can be very helpful to know where in memory they are located. Using this information, you can examine data inside the driver. With the proper debugging tools, you can even set a break point in the driver code itself.

An item that is not actually part of the DOS variable table can be found at BX-2. This word points to the first MCB. Remember, we used this value to display information about all of the MCBs. Again, it should be stressed that any values found in the variables table, or data pointed to from the table, should not be altered. They are best used in a read-only mode. These values control many important operations of MS-DOS such as file I/O, Device Handling, and Memory Management.

Drive Parameter Blocks

The Drive Parameter Block (DPB) is a table created by MS-DOS during system initialization. Every logical drive has an entry in this table. (Logical is used to access each drive, A: B:, but may not be a physical disk drive. It could be a RAMdisk or one hard disk with multiple drives.) These entries describe all parameters necessary for MS-DOS to maintain a file system on the disk drives. The following MASM structure defines the layout of the DPB:

```
dpb          struc

logical_num  db        ?
drive_num    db        ?
sector_size  dw        ?
spa          db        ? ;sectors per allocation unit (cluster)
shift        db        ? ;shift factor (2^shift)-1 = spa
reserved     dw        ?
number_fats  db        ?
number_dirs  dw        ?
data_start   dw        ?
alu          dw        ? ;number of allocation units
fat_size     db        ?
dir_start    dw        ?
device_drv   dd        ?
media        db        ?
dirty_flag   db        ?
next_dpb     dd        ?
dpb_unknown  dw        ?
dpb          ends
```

The first entry, `logical_num`, is the logical drive number (A = 0, B = 1 . . .). This is used to identify the table entry if searching for a specific disk drive.

The next entry, `drive_num`, is the drive unit within the associated device driver. Since device drivers can control multiple units (drives), each unit is assigned a sequential unit number within the driver. DOS will need this number to "talk" to the device driver.

`sector_size` is the sector size in bytes. The next entry, `spa`, contains the number of sectors per allocation unit. An allocation unit, or cluster, is the smallest unit that DOS can allocate for a file.

`reserved` is the number of reserved sectors before the File Allocation Table (FAT). Usually this is a one, reserving a sector for the `BOOT` information. If the device is not bootable, such as a RAMdisk, its value will be zero so that no sectors will be wasted.

`number_fats` defines how many FATs are contained on the disk drive. Most MS-DOS implementations keep two copies of the FAT table for data integrity.

`number_dirs` defines how many directory entries can reside in the `ROOT` directory.

`data_start` defines what sector the file data begins. This comes directly after the FATs and the directory. `alu` defines how many allocation units make up the disk drive. Dividing `alu` by `spa` gives you the total number of sectors available for data.

`fat_size` defines the size of each FAT in sectors. `dir_start` defines the starting sector of the directory. `device_drv` is a pointer to the device driver that controls this disk drive. Using this value, MS-DOS can "talk" to the disk device through the device driver.

`media` is the media descriptor byte. This is usually the first byte in the MS-DOS FAT and usually identifies the current disk type. This is especially useful for identifying floppy drives where you can insert single and double-sided floppies.

The DPB can be used when a program needs to know where the FAT starts, or where the directory is located. Usually these programs will of be a diagnostic type. A program that scans a disk containing data for bad sectors and then reports what files contain bad sectors would require most of the information in the DPB table. The scope of this paper does not allow us to develop an extensive program but the following MASM code fragments describe how the data in the DPB can be utilized:

```
load_fat      proc      near

;load the fat into memory starting at address DS:SI
;make sure you have a large enough buffer
;Call this procedure with ES:BX pointing to a DPB
;On return if Carry Set then an error occurred
;This routine will use the Documented MS-DOS Interrupt 25 (hex)
```

```
;   Absolute Disk Read

        push    ax
        push    bx                      ;save registers
        push    cx                      ;int 25h uses a lot of regs
        push    dx
        push    bp
        push    di
        push    si
        push    es
        push    ds

        mov     dx,es:[bx.reserved]     ;get starting FAT sector
        mov     cx,es:[bx.fat_size]     ;number of secs to read
        mov     al,es:[bx.logical_num]  ;drive number to read
        mov     bx,si                   ;target offset for FAT read
        int     25h                     ;do the disk read
        jnc     good_exit

error_exit:

        popf                            ;pop flags left on stk by int 25
        stc                             ;flag carry as error
        jmp     final_exit

good_exit:

        popf                            ;pop flags left on stk by int 25
        clc

final_exit:

        pop     ds                      ;restore registers
        pop     es
        pop     si
        pop     di
        pop     bp
        pop     dx
        pop     cx
        pop     bx
        pop     ax

load_fat     endp
```

```
read_all_sectors  proc    near

;
;this procedure will read all data sectors
;(starting after reserved,fat and dir sectors)
;call with es:bx pointing to DPB

        push    ax                      ;save registers
        push    bx                      ;most destroyed by int 25
        push    cx
        push    dx
        push    bp
        push    di
        push    si
        push    ds
        push    es


        mov     ax,es:[bx.dir_start]    ;get directory start
        mov     bx,es:[bx.number_dirs]  ;number of dir entries
        mov     cl,8                    ;
        shl     bx,cl                   ;multiple by 32
        add     ax,bx                   ;ax is data start sector
        push    ax                      ;save start sector
        mov     cx,es:[bx.spa]          ;sectors per alloc unit

        inc     ax
        mov     ax,es:[alu]             ;# of alloc units
        mul     cx                      ;get # of sectors
        mov     cx,ax                   ;put in cx for loop
        pop     dx                      ;get data start sector
        mov     al,es:[bx.logical_num]  ;drive to read


read_loop:


        push    cx
        mov     cx,1                    ;read 1 sector
        push    dx
        mov     bx,offset sector_buffer
        push    ax                      ;register are not
        push    bx                      ;saved by INT 25
```

```
                push    cx
                push    dx
                int     25h
                jc      read_error
                popf
                pop     dx
                pop     cx
                pop     bx
                pop     ax
;
;process sector data here
;
                pop     dx
                inc     dx              ;increment sector to read
                pop     cx              ;restore loop counter
                loop    read_loop
                clc
                jmp     exit

        read_error:                     ;here if error on read

                pop     dx
                pop     cx
                pop     bx
                pop     ax
                stc

        exit:

                pop     es              ;restore registers
                pop     ds
                pop     si
                pop     di
                pop     bp
                pop     dx
                pop     cx
                pop     bx
                pop     ax


        read_all_sectors  endp

        sector_buffer       db      512 dup (?)
```

Functions 1Fh and 32h

Undocumented functions 1F and 32 return pointers to the DPB. There are two major differences between using these functions and getting to the DPB via the DOS variables:

1. These functions need to access the disk drive when called. This can be inconvenient if it is an empty floppy drive since you will get an "Abort, Retry, Ignore" type error.

2. The table pointer returned is based on a specific drive, whereas the DOS variable DPB pointer places you at the start of the table. Function 1F returns information on the currently logged disk drive while Function 32 allows you to specify a disk drive.

When calling these functions, place the function number in AH. For Function 32, place the drive number in DL (0 = default, A = 1 . . .). On return, DS:BX will point to the appropriate table entry. It may be easier to use these functions than the DOS variable pointer when dealing with specific disk drives since you don't need the extra code to search for the specific table entry. The DPB examples given in the previous section will work just as well with these functions.

Functions 45h and 46h: Duplicate Handles

These two functions are documented in MS-DOS reference guides but they have some additional undocumented uses. Function 45h duplicates an existing file handle into another file. The BX register contains an open file handle and, on return, the AX register contains a new duplicate handle. This gives you two separate file handles referencing the same files. Function 46 takes two different file handles and forces them both to refer to the same file. Register BX contains the file handle to duplicate and CX contains a handle that will be force duplicated. If the original file in CX is open before the INT 21H call, it will be closed first.

The directory and FAT information are not updated for an open file handle until that file handle is closed. If you have large amounts of data to process and the system crashes in the middle of a file output process, all output is pretty much lost. (You could rebuild pieces of the file sector by sector but that could take a long time.) The obvious solution is to close the file periodically to update the directory entry and FAT, but all of this opening and closing means a lot of DOS overhead. In DOS 3.3, Funtion 68h is called Commit File and will flush the file's buffers and update the disk.

The best solution is to use Function 45h to create a duplicate of your open file handle. Whenever you want to update the file information, simply close the duplicate file. The next time an update is needed, open and close a duplicate handle again. Just keep in mind that this additional file handle reduces the number of files that you can have open (15 files after the MS-DOS default files are opened).

In the PSP section, we discussed altering the file handle table to affect redirection. Function 46h can also change redirection. Since Function 46 takes two file handles and makes them one, we can create a redirection. For example, suppose we want to redirect the console output to a file that we have opened. Let's call the console FILE_CON and the opened disk file FILE_DISK. First we want to make a duplicate of FILE_CON. Since we are going to be changing the standard output file, we want to save it for restoration later. Let's call the duplicate FILE_SAVE. By doing this, we would call Function 45h with BX containing 1 (the file handle for Standard Output). On return, save the value of the AX register. This will be our FILE_SAVE. Next we will call Function 46h to force the FILE_CON to be a duplicate of FILE_DISK. For this operation, load the BX register with the file handle number of FILE_DISK and the CX register with 1. After processing the INT 21H request, all output to the standard output file FILE_CON will go to the disk file FILE_DISK. To restore things to the way they were before the redirection, we need to put the old console output FILE_SAVE back. Again we will call Function 46h. Load the BX register with the handle value store as FILE_SAVE and the CX register with 1. When the function is complete, all is restored. (Don't forget to close the file FILE_DISK.) (For all those out there still using FCB open calls instead of file handles, you can see that you can do much more with a file handle.)

Undocumented Interrupts

There are three undocumented MS-DOS interrupts that can be useful to programmers. They are:

- ▶ Interrupt 28h DOS Safe Interrupt
- ▶ Interrupt 29h Console Device Output
- ▶ Interrupt 2Eh Back Door To Command Processor

Interrupt 28h DOS Safe Interrupt

I call this function the DOS Safe Interrupt because, when this interrupt is issued by MS-DOS, it is safe to use Functions 0Ch and above-if the DOS Busy Flag is not greater than 1. It only appears to be called when DOS is waiting for keystrokes (as the command processor COMMAND.COM is waiting for keystrokes at the system prompt). As soon as the first key is hit, this interrupt is no longer called. This enables resident programs to take advantage of the fact that the system is sitting idle. A resident process that operates concurrently with the foreground process could use this as a flag that the system is not being used and "steal" more time away from the foreground. The only MS-DOS program that uses this interrupt is the background print spooler `PRINT.COM`. This interrupt is generally used in conjunction with DOS Function 34h (DOS Busy Flag) to perform background operations.

Fast Console Output

Interrupt 2Ah appears to be a back door into the console output device driver. The character in AL is output to the console when this interrupt is performed.

Back Door to Command Processor

MS-DOS provides a method for one program to execute another through the `EXEC` Function 4Bh. Though this function is very useful, there also exists a "fast and dirty" method of executing commands. The undocumented Interrupt 2Eh appears to be a back door into the command processor `COMMAND.COM`. To execute an MS-DOS command, simply shrink memory down to make room for the new program (as in Function 4B) and perform an Interrupt 2E with the DS:SI register set pointing to a parameter string. This string has its length as the first byte, the command to perform (such as `DIR *.*`), and a carriage return (0Dh) to terminate the string. The carriage return is counted as part of the string length. On return, make sure you reset your stack again since this interrupt may not save the SS:SP values. The following MASM fragment will execute a `DIR *.*` command from within a program:

```
mov   bx,end_of_code      ;set to end of our code space
mov   cx,4                ;shift count
shr   bx,cl               ;divide by 16
inc   bx                  ;a little extra
mov   ah,4ah              ;adjust memory block
int   21h
mov   si,offset parameter ;get command string
int   2eh                 ;do command
push  cs                  ;reset stack
pop   ss
cli
mov   sp,offset stack
sti
```

```
parameter db    8,'DIR *.*',0dh

end_of_code     equ $
```

Common Subroutines

We have examined many documented and undocumented MS-DOS features that will enable you to write better, more efficient programs. The following are the common subroutines promised at the beginning of this paper:

```
char_out proc near

;
print character in al to the standard output device using
;MS-DOS funtion #2

        push    dx                  ;save register used to
                                    ;       output character
        mov     dl,al               ;set up for DOS function call
        mov     ah,2
        int     21h                 ;call MS-DOS
        pop     dx                  ;restore register
        ret

char_out        endp


string_out      proc    near

;print a string pointed to by DS:DX
;first byte of passed string is string length

        push    ax                  ;save registers used
        push    bx
        push    cx
        push    dx
        mov     ah,40h              ;MS-DOS Write To File Handle
        mov     bx,dx               ;get string address in BX
        inc     dx                  ;point to actual text of string
        xor     ch,ch               ;zero out ch register
        mov     cl,[bx]             ;get length byte of string
        mov     bx,1                ;standard output handle
```

```
        int     21h             ;call DOS
        pop     dx              ;restore registers used
        pop     cx
        pop     bx
        pop     ax
        ret

string_out      endp


hex_to_ascii    proc    near
;
;output word value in DX as a 4-digit ASCII HEX Number
;to the standard output

        push    cx              ;save registers
        push    ax
        mov     cx,4            ;loop Counter (4 hex digits)

hex1:

        push    cx              ;save loop counter
        mov     cl,4            ;rotate count
        rol     dx,cl           ;swap high word and low word of
                                ;DX
        mov     al,dl           ;get byte
        and     al,0fh          ;turn into nibble (4 bits)
        daa                     ;create printable ASCII character
        add     al,0F0h         ;(0-9 or A-F)
        adc     al,040h
        call    char_out        ;output the character
        pop     cx              ;restore loop counter
        loop    hex1            ;go back for more
        pop     ax              ;restore registers
        pop     cx
        ret

hex_to_ascii    endp


hexb_to_ascii   proc    near
;
;output byte value in DX as a 2-digit ASCII HEX Number
;to the standard output
```

```
        push    cx              ;save registers
        push    ax


        mov     cx,2            ;loop Counter (2 hex digits)

hex2:

        push    cx              ;save loop counter

        mov     cl,4            ;rotate count
        rol     dl,cl           ;swap high and low nibble of DX
        mov     al,dl           ;get byte
        and     al,0fh          ;turn into nibble (4 bits)
        daa                     ;create printable ASCII char
        add     al,0f0h         ;(0-9 or A-F)
        adc     al,040h
        call    char_out        ;output the character

        pop     cx              ;restore loop counter
        loop    hex1            ;go back for more

        pop     ax              ;restore registers
        pop     cx
        ret

hexb_to_ascii   endp
```

Reading List

Duncan, R. 1986. *Advanced MS-DOS*. Redmond, Washington: Microsoft Press.

Norton, P. 1986. *Inside the IBM PC*. New York: Brady Communications Co.

Raymond J. Michels has been working with the MS-DOS operating system since its introduction. He is a senior programmer at CES Corporation in Maryland, writing application software for the remittance processing industry. Ray is also an independent consultant specializing in MS-DOS application and system programs.

Related Essays

2 Searching the File Tree with `whereis`

3 Adding UNIX Power with PCnix

7 Safe Memory-Resident Programming (TSR)

10 Developing MS-DOS Device Drivers

Keywords

► TSR

► memory-resident programs

► desk accessories

► well-behaved programs

► interrupt vectors

► `PRINT.COM`

► print screen function

Essay synopsis: In MS-DOS, only one program can actually run at a given time. A program can, however, be told to Terminate and Stay Resident (TSR). Such programs remain in memory, ready for instant activation by a keystroke or other event. MS-DOS itself contains several examples of TSRs, including a print spooler. Because of the convenience offered by TSR "desk accessories" and other programs that can be accessed from any application, TSRs are in widespread use today. This essay will show you how to program TSRs, and how to avoid the many pitfalls and create "well-behaved" TSRs that can coexist with other programs.

7

Safe Memory-Resident Programming (TSR)

M. Steven Baker

The ability to support memory-resident programs is an interesting and useful feature of MS-DOS. An ordinary MS-DOS program is loaded from disk on each execution and removed from memory after its operation is terminated. If you want to run the program again, you must reload it from disk. A memory-resident program remains in memory even when it is no longer running. Thus, such programs are often called Terminate and Stay Resident (TSR) programs.

A TSR program can be reactivated at any time, even while another program is running. This is usually done by typing a specified character sequence at the keyboard. Some TSR programs are reactivated by other events, such as the movement of a mouse, a specific time event, or information from some other hardware event. Reactivating a TSR program suspends the execution of whatever other program is running. When the TSR program is exited, it becomes dormant again and the program that was running resumes. Several TSRs can be in memory at the same time, although this can sometimes cause conflicts, depending on how the programs were implemented and how they are activated.

Why Are TSRs Useful?

Perhaps the most familiar type of TSR in use today is the *desk accessory* program, such as Borland's SideKick or Lotus's Spotlight. These programs fulfill the need for computerized desk accessories by providing facilities such as a notepad editor, calendar, calculator, phone list (similar to a rolodex), phone dialer, and so on. Most of the utility of such a program comes from the fact that its functions are available at the touch of a key or two, regardless of what you are doing at the time. For example, you can activate a calculator desk accessory while in the midst of writing a letter using your favorite word processor. Then you can perform some calculations and "paste" the results of the calculation back into your letter, all without leaving the word processor. If the calculator were not a TSR, you would have to exit your word processor, run the calculator program and save the results to a temporary file, exit the calculator program, restart your word processor, and finally read in the file with the results in it.

In addition to the desk accessories, some other popular examples of commercial TSR programs include ProKey, Turbo Lightning, and Ready. ProKey is typical of many keyboard macro programs that allow the user to program a series of keystrokes onto a single keystroke for convenience. Other similar TSR keyboard programs include Superkey and Smartkey. Turbo Lightning includes a spelling checker and thesaurus available at the touch of specified keys. The spelling checker can be set up to automatically beep at you if a misspelled word is typed. Ready is a sophisticated outline processor which can be activated in the middle of another program. Popup graphics programs such as Graph in a Box make it easy to graph data in a spreadsheet or database. Programs such as Instant Recall provide freeform database features.

TSRs in MS-DOS

Another type of TSR is actually installed as an extension to the hardware environment or the operating system. These TSRs include keyboard macro programs, mouse driver programs, networking hardware support, hardware cards for communication with IBM mainframes, print spoolers, and the like.

You have probably used a number of TSR programs in your everyday use of MS-DOS, perhaps without realizing it. The MS-DOS operating system comes with several TSR utility programs. Starting with the earlier versions of DOS, these include `MODE`, `PRINT`, `GRAPHICS`, and `ASSIGN`.

TSR programs can be found for a diverse range of other applications and offer two main advantages to the user:

▶ the ability to extend or enhance some features of MS-DOS (for example, replace a long string of key commmands with a few keystrokes)

▶ the convenience of having several programs accessible at virtually the same time (within the limitation of MS-DOS' being able to actually run only one program at a time)

Today, many PC users would feel lost without their favorite assortment of TSRs supporting their work environment.

The Origin of Memory-Resident Programs

The MS-DOS operating system has its roots in the CP/M-80 operating system written by Digital Research for 8-bit microcomputers based on the Intel 8080,

8085, and Zilog Z80 microprocessors. The early versions of MS-DOS were very similar to CP/M-80. However, one large difference stands out between these earlier 8-bit microcomputers and the IBM PC. The older machines can only directly address 64K bytes of memory, while the IBM PC-based machines can address 1024K. (Actually, the IBM PC has only 640K of memory available for user programs, since memory above this point is used or reserved for the video display adapters, hard disks, ROM BIOS, and other purposes.) Any way you look at it, a lot more memory is available for programs on the PC than with the previous generation of machines. Under CP/M, memory was precious.

CP/M Programs

Any enhancements to CP/M (i.e., keyboard macros or function keys) were normally incorporated into the machine specific part of the operating system (the BIOS) written by the computer manufacturer. These enhancements were limited by how much memory they could take from the basic 64K. If the operating system grew in size, less memory would be available to run your favorite applications such as WordStar, SuperCalc, and dBASEII. Since these features were chosen by the manufacturer, the user could not customize them. However, even under CP/M, some memory-resident programs were developed and used even at the expense of the memory required. Three popular TSRs under CP/M were Smartkey (a keyboard macro program), Uniform (a utility to allow reading and writing various CP/M disk formats), and Unspol (a public domain print spooler similar to PRINT under MS-DOS).

Early MS-DOS Features

A TSR feature was incorporated with the earliest version of MS-DOS. Seattle Computer Products (SCP) was the original author of MS-DOS. The earliest commercial release of 86-DOS version 0.3 (as it was called then) offered a TSR function well over a year before the operating system was purchased by Microsoft and became MS-DOS. The purpose of this operating system function call was to allow extensions to DOS to be added easily to the operating system, particularly user-written interrupt handlers. A program could be loaded that enhanced MS-DOS and then remained resident in memory. New enhancements or device support could be added to MS-DOS without rewriting the operating system. This was all made possible by the ability to address and use more memory. But memory only seemed to be less precious under MS-DOS than it had been under CP/M. Soon we were complaining about the "640K barrier."

The version of MS-DOS customized and sold by IBM was called PC-DOS, version 1.0. PC-DOS versions before version 2.0 did not have the option of user-installable device drivers, but TSR programs provided a somewhat equivalent feature. For example, early multifunction cards by AST and other manufacturers would come with TSR programs for the realtime clock, RAMdisk and print spoolers.

The only TSR program distributed with PC-DOS and MS-DOS version 1.XX was the MODE program, which incorporates several video and device control features. The memory-resident part of MODE allows output to the DOS parallel printer to be redirected to the serial port. Why was it necessary to incorporate this feature as a TSR? In fact, this reveals one of the major deficiencies of MS-DOS from its beginning—the operating system was designed with very poor support for printers.

Under PC-DOS and most versions of MS-DOS, the printer device is assumed to be a parallel port (designated LPT#1). However, a user might have a serial printer or plotter instead or even two printers—a dot matrix draft printer and a letter quality printer. The MS-DOS operating system did not support sending printer output to anything but this one parallel port device. The MODE program provides a mechanism to redirect output normally sent to a parallel printer port to be sent to one of the serial ports instead.

Why was the MODE program written as a TSR? The inconvenient alternative would have been for every program written for MS-DOS to have an installation procedure and support routines to send any printer output to either the MS-DOS parallel printer device or to serial ports (on the IBM PC, designated COM1 and COM2). Another possibility would have been to invoke something similar to MODE as part of each program you used. Clearly, the TSR mechanism makes more sense. When TSRs are used, the changes in configuration remain in memory and operate transparently—no application program has to be changed, and nothing else has to be reloaded.

Later MS-DOS Programs

With the introduction of MS-DOS version 2.0 by Microsoft, several TSR utility programs were included with the operating system for the IBM PC:

- ▶ PRINT.COM
- ▶ MODE.COM
- ▶ GRAPHICS.COM
- ▶ ASSIGN.COM

PRINT is a memory-resident print spooler of limited usefulness. It is similar to the earlier public domain UNSPOL program used under CP/M-80. PRINT allows a file to be printed in the background while another application is operating.

While MS-DOS is waiting for keyboard input or while noncritical functions are happening, PRINT can send a text file to the printer as a background task. This program assumes that the file to be printed is an ASCII text file.

PRINT expands any tabs in a file based on tab settings every eight spaces and considers the 1AH character (the old CPM end-of-file character) to mark the end of file. Binary or nontext files can be sent to the printer properly as long as they don't contain any embedded TAB (09) or EOF (1Ah) characters, but it isn't easy to guarantee such files don't have these characters. Effectively, this precludes using PRINT to spool graphics files to the printer, many formatted text files to daisy wheel printers, or font files to laser printers. The TAB or EOF character in these files may mean which pin to fire on a dot matrix graphics dump, or may be part of the character definition in a font file.

Why does PRINT need to be a TSR? A print spooler needs to be memory-resident so that it can function even though several other applications are started and stopped.

Three other simpler TSRs were included with MS-DOS 2.X. The MODE program, which we have discussed, allows redirecting parallel printer output to the serial ports. GRAPHICS is a memory-resident addition to the PRINT SCREEN function. This program allows full screen dumps to an IBM graphics printer or compatible printer from a graphics image on an IBM Color Graphics Adapter (CGA) or compatible adapter and display. This program is only of use when the display is in one of several possible graphics video modes. For convenience, since GRAPHICS was written as a TSR, it only needs to be invoked once.

ASSIGN is a memory-resident utility that assigns logical disk drives to actual drives in a system. The ASSIGN command provides the ability to run programs on a hard disk system even though they were written assuming only one or two floppy disk drives are available. ASSIGN maps calls through a logical disk (A through H) to another physical disk. This utility modifies disk calls passed to the operating system.

Microsoft and TSRs

The background print spooler showed, for the first time, the appearance of accessing two programs at the same time and provided an example of its implementation. MS-DOS is still a single-user system, but the sense of task-switching was demonstrated. This "simulated multitasking" naturally attracted the interest of software developers, but as with other aspects of the operating system, Microsoft provided only limited details on the 8086 interrupts and DOS function calls that support these new TSR system features. Thus TSR-supporting features were discovered by programmers trying to emulate and extend the features embodied in the TSRs supplied with MS-DOS. The result, as we have seen, has been the development of a considerable variety of TSR programs.

At the same time, Microsoft expressed a general policy of not supporting the concept of TSR programs. Why would Microsoft incorporate TSR features in MS-DOS and not document them and support them? The most likely reason is that they conflict with long-term goals of making MS-DOS into a true multitasking operating system like OS/2. Most TSR programs are not "well-behaved" and depend on taking control of some system hardware. This makes true multitasking and multiuser operation difficult if not impossible to implement. Nevertheless, because widespread use of OS/2 is still in the future, and many users will continue to use existing versions of DOS, TSRs will continue to be written and used for some time.

Types of TSRs

Let's step back a bit and try to categorize the current flood of TSR programs. First, there are the simplest extensions to MS-DOS itself such as GRAPHICS, MODE, and the various RAMdisk utilities. These programs extend a hardware feature on the IBM PC and do not need to use any MS-DOS function calls. Other examples of this first type would include the various SETCLOCK programs that replace the MS-DOS time function calls to a realtime clock. The MS-DOS ASSIGN utility is a TSR that maps MS-DOS disk calls from logical to actual disk drives in the system. The distinguishing features of this class of TSR is that, once resident, no DOS function calls are made by the TSR.

The second class includes the more complex TSRs that, once resident, must make DOS function calls (such as for file reading and writing). These TSRs are of two types: DOS extension and utility programs and application programs. In the first category are keyboard enhancement programs that allow reading and writing keyboard macro files "on the fly." The second type includes most of the specialty programs that must make DOS function calls and provide some task-switching features. These programs may extend MS-DOS with a printer spooler like PRINT, but more likely they provide some popup application program very conveniently at the touch of a "hot key," as with SideKick.

Well-Behaved Memory-Resident Programs

The main concerns in writing TSRs are trying to create a well-behaved program and making certain that other TSRs already loaded are also allowed to function. The simpler class of TSRs (such as GRAPHICS) are much easier to write than the second class (such as PRINT). Again, the distinguishing feature is whether MS-DOS function calls must be made from the TSR. This fact is reflected in the size of the sample TSRs provided with MS-DOS listed in Table 7-1.

Table 7-1. MS-DOS TSR Program Sizes (bytes)

Program	Version 2.0	Version 3.1	Version 3.3
GRAPHICS	789	3,111	7204
ASSIGN	896	1,509	1530
PRINT	4,608	8,291	8995

The difficulty in TSRs like PRINT, SideKick, Ready, etc., is determining when DOS or an application program is interruptible. This problem exists because MS-DOS function calls are not reentrant or recursive, i.e., you cannot "stack up" several calls. If an MS-DOS function call is in progress and our TSR interrupts and makes another MS-DOS call, the first call will be trashed and lost with unpleasant side effects for the primary application. As well, the ROM BIOS Diskette _IO interrupt INT 13H is also not reentrant. For example, if a disk read was started by the foreground program seeking to a particular track, and we interrupted before the reading took place and invoked an MS-DOS call requiring file access and the disk interrupt, the first seek would be lost upon reentering the Diskette_IO INT 13H routine.

The 8086 and Interrupts on the IBM PC

In order to learn how to write TSR programs, you must understand, in at least a limited way, the underlying hardware and software structure. The IBM PC is based on the Intel 8088 microprocessor chip, which is a member of a family of similar chips including the 8086, 80188, 80186, 80286, and 80386. From a programmer's perspective, all these chips can be programmed as if they were an 8086 microprocessor. The 80186, 80286, and 80386 chips include some enhanced hardware and software features that need not be used. The V20 and V30 microprocessors from NEC (Nippon Electric Corporation) are also extensions to the basic 8086 that have software extensions similar to the 80186.

These chips can all address at least 1024K bytes of memory. The lower 1024 (400h) bytes of memory on all these chips is special, set aside as a table of 256 (100H) possible interrupt vectors. Each interrupt vector consists of a double-word pointer to a location in memory. On the 8086, an interrupt can mean either a hardware interrupt (generated by a device or processor) or a software interrupt (triggered by executing the INT instruction). The INT instruction is a special software instruction on the 8086 CPU family that pushes the CPU's flag register onto the stack, disables hardware interrupts, and invokes the instructions pointed to by the particular interrupt vector in this table. These instructions may be invoked by specific hardware conditions or by software instructions. TSRs are usually interrupt driven.

As an example, we will look at the first few interrupt vectors. Interrupt 0 is invoked if the 8086 chip divides by 0. At address 0 in memory, we would find a pointer to software to handle cases of hardware divided by zero. The first word of this pointer is the offset of the routine to invoke and the second word is the segment. The IBM ROM BIOS sets this interrupt to point to an IRET instruction in the ROM BIOS. This just does nothing and returns from the interrupt. The debug command on an IBM PC under DOS 3.1 will show something like the following:

```
-d0000:0000 000f
```

and the debug output will show

```
0000:0000  E8 4E 2f 01 F0 01 70 00-5F F8 00 F0 F0 01 70 00    .N/
...p._...
```

The Interrupt Vector Interpretation is

```
Location       Offset,Segment        Description

0000    dw    4EE8h, 012Fh     ;INTERRUPT 0 Divide_by_zero (DOS)
0004    dw    01F0h, 0070h     ;INTERRUPT 1 Single-step    (BIOS)
0008    dw    0F85Fh,0F000h    ;INTERRUPT 2 Nonmaskable interrupt (ROM)
000Ch   dw    01F0h, 0070h     ;INTERRUPT 3 Breakpoint     (BIOS)
```

Some of these vectors are special to the microprocessor itself. Intel has reserved vectors 0 through 31 (0-1FH) for internal use, although only a few are used on the 8086. Others are used by the hardware peripheral devices, which interrupt the operation of the microprocessor, for example, when a key is pressed. Finally, most of these vectors are used by the operating system software for invoking various functions and as pointers to special data structures in memory. All communication with the MS-DOS operating system is through the use of these interrupt vectors. When a TSR program is loaded in memory, it replaces some of these existing interrupt vectors with pointers to itself. (See Essay 1, A Guided Tour inside MS-DOS, by Harry Henderson, for a general discussion of interrupts. See Essay 10, Writing a SOUND Device Driver, by Walter Dixon, and Essay 6, Undocumented MS-DOS Functions, by Ray Michels, for discussion of many of the MS-DOS software interrupts. See the last part of Essay 5, Advanced MASM Techniques, by Michael Goldman, for a discussion of interrupt processing.)

When an interrupt is invoked, the 8086 flags register is pushed onto the stack, the current instruction pointer is pushed onto the stack, and hardware interrupts are disabled to prevent a hardware interrupt from breaking into the processing of the current interrupt. Figure 7-1 shows what the stack looks like upon execution of a software or hardware interrupt.

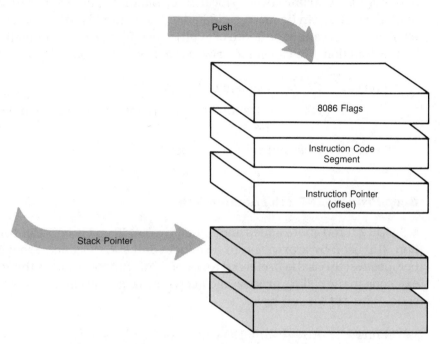

Fig. 7-1.   The 8086 stack upon interrupt.

MS-DOS version 2.0 and above provide several documented as well as undocumented functions that support the TSRs that are provided with the operating system. Based on material I have read, I would assume that most authors of TSRs have determined these undocumented DOS features by disassembling DOS itself and PRINT, for example, and not from information willingly provided by Microsoft. This is how I discovered these hidden features. Let's first look at the documented features.

Documented TSR Support

MS-DOS provides documented support for three functions relating to TSRs.

Terminate and Stay Resident INT 27H

The original function is INT 27H, the Terminal but Stay Resident function that goes all the way back to Seattle Computer Products 86-DOS. This function is the traditional method for MS-DOS programs to remain resident upon termination.

Note that this function affects several other interrupts in the same way as a normal termination (Interrupts 22h, 23h, and 24h are restored to the values that existed before invoking the TSR program), so it cannot be used to install permanently resident Ctrl-Break or Critical Error Handler routines. The maximum size of memory that can be made resident by this method is 64K (it is actually about 63.9K since DX cannot be above 0FFF0H). Open files are not automatically closed by this function. We can summarize INT 27H with the following:

Entry: CS = segment of PSP

          DX = offset of last byte + 1 (relative to PSP) to be made resident

Returns: Does not return to process

Keep Process INT 21H *Function 31h*

MS-DOS 2.0 and above added another equivalent Keep Process call INT 21H (Function 31h) used by a program to terminate and stay resident. From Microsoft's perspective, this is the preferred function. This function allows the return of an exit code to the calling process and allows for larger (greater than 64K) resident code. With INT 21H, we have

Entry: AH = 31h (DOS Function)

          AL = return code

          DX = memory size to reserve in paragraphs (16-byte blocks)

Returns: Does not return to process

Multiplex Interrupt INT 2FH

The least-used documented TSR function is the Multiplex Interrupt INT 2FH also called the Print Spool Control function in some MS-DOS documentation, which may be used for interprocess communication. This interrupt is used by PRINT to pass information to an already resident PRINT spooler (TSR) in memory. However, it may also be used by other processes. Each multiplex interrupt handler is assigned a specific multiplex number. The multiplex number is specified in the AH register. The specific function requested is specified in the AL register. The multiplex numbers AH = 0 through AH = 7Fh are reserved for DOS. Application programs are supposed to use multiplex numbers C0h through FFh. To avoid a conflict between two applications using the same multiplex number, the multiplex number used by a program should be patchable. Function 0 (Get Installed State) is currently the only function that must be defined uniformly by all INT 2FH handlers. INT 2FH is summarized by

Entry: AH = multiplex number

AL = function code

other registers as needed

Returns: AX = error code if unsuccesful (carry set)

Function 0 Get Installed State is summarized by

Entry: AH = multiplex number

AL = 0

Returns: AL = status (0, 1, or FFh)

AL = 0 (not installed, okay to install)

AL = 1 (not installed, not okay to install)

AL = FFh (already installed)

This interrupt was not documented until DOS 3.X versions of the *IBM DOS Technical Reference Manual*, although it was used by the MS-DOS PRINT Utility from MS-DOS 2.0 onward. The MS-DOS 2.0 PRINT utility makes calls with AH = 0 and AH = FFh which are not documented, as well as the documented calls.

Print Spool Multiplex Handler INT 2FH

IBM DOS Technical Reference Manual 3.1 describes the Print Spooler Multiplex (AH = 1), the resident part of PRINT.COM, in detail. DOS version 3.2 added two additional predefined DOS Multiplex Handlers, ASSIGN (AH = 2 is the resident part of DOS 3.X ASSIGN) and SHARE (AH = 10h) is the resident part of SHARE. However, the earlier ASSIGN command in DOS 2.X did not use this interrupt handler. DOS version 3.3 added multiplex handler (AH = B7h), the resident part of APPEND.

Further functions of INT 2FH are summarized by

Entry: AH = 1 (resident Part of PRINT.COM)

AL = 0 (get print spooler installed status)

AL = 1 (submit a file to be printed)

AL = 2 (remove a file from the print queue)

AL = 3 (cancel all files in queue)

AL = 4 (hold print jobs for status read)

AL = 5 (end hold for status read)

DS:DX segment:offset of packet address if Function 1

segment:offset of ASCIIZ file specification if Function 2 (remove file)

Returns: carry clear if successful

             for Function 0

                AL = status (0, 1 or FFh) as defined above

             for Function 4

                DX = error count

                DS:SI   pointer to print queue

Returns: carry set on error

                AX = error code

For Function 1 (submit file to be printed), the packet is five bytes long. The first byte contains the level and the next four bytes contain a double-word pointer of an ASCIIZ file specification (the filename cannot contain wildcards). The level byte under DOS 3.1 through 3.3 is 0. For Function 2, wildcards (* and ?) are permitted in the filespec, allowing multiple files to be deleted. For Function 4, the pointer returned for the print queue points to a linked list of ASCIIZ strings. Each entry in the queue is 64 bytes long, and the last slot has a zero first byte.

Undocumented DOS TSR Support

The following MS-DOS function calls have not been documented in any of the IBM technical reference manuals although they are used by the TSRs supplied with MS-DOS.

IN_DOS *or* DOS_CRITICAL *Function*

The first undocumented MS-DOS function call used by TSR programs returns a byte pointer to a flag in MS-DOS itself. I have seen this function referred to as IN_DOS and also as DOS_CRITICAL in a few articles. If this byte flag is 0, then DOS is not currently active and therefore any DOS call can be made without trashing an active DOS call. This flag is not just a logical flag, but represents a count of recursive calls into MS-DOS. This function cannot be called any time you wish, however. Since it goes through the MS-DOS function entry and stack switch routine with interrupts enabled, allowing interruption, this function cannot be called while MS-DOS is executing another function or interrupts are disabled. Thus a TSR program when it is first loaded by COMMAND.COM during initialization will make an MS-DOS Function 34h call and save the pointer for later use. For some unexplained reason, DOS versions 3.1 and above return a pointer to one byte past this IN_DOS flag byte to a critical error flag byte. The IN_DOS or DOS_CRITICAL function is summarized by

Entry: AH = 34h

          int   21h

Returns: in ES:BX, a pointer to an IN_DOS flag

A second undocumented MS-DOS function supporting TSR programs is the Background Process function, INT 28H. There is one time that MS-DOS can safely be interrupted even when MS-DOS has been called (i.e., the IN_DOS flag is non-zero). If MS-DOS is waiting for keyboard input, the IN_DOS is set to 1, but MS-DOS calls INT 28H continually while waiting. The MS-DOS PRINT utility appears to be the only MS-DOS program that currently uses this interrupt, which would imply that its express purpose was to allow background utilities like spoolers to function. If a TSR program replaces INT 28H and monitors for calls to it, MS-DOS functions below Clear_keyboard_buffer (Function 0Ch) may be safely used.

GET USER_PSP *and* SET USER_PSP *Functions*

Two other undocumented calls are needed for TSRs for file handling using the newer calling conventions added with DOS 2.X and 3.X. These support full directory paths and use *file handles* rather than the FCBs of DOS 1.X and CP/M. DOS stores the file handles being used in the PSP with other operating system information. This *base page* consists of 100h bytes of memory and also includes the command line given for executing the program, the first two filenames given on the command line converted to FCBs, and a default disk buffer address, Data Transfer Area (DTA), that overlays the command-line area.

This pair of undocumented calls provides a way to get and set the PSP of a process in DOS. Before doing any file handling in a TSR, the current user PSP of an interrupted program would first be read from DOS and saved, and then the PSP of the TSR program would be set. The TSR would do any DOS file calls necessary. Finally, the TSR would restore the user PSP in DOS back to the interrupted process. In this way, the TSR would not affect the application programs files or operating system specific information.

The GET USER_PSP function is summarized by:

Entry: AH = 50h

          int   21h

Returns: in BX, the current user-process PSP segment from DOS

The SET USER_PSP function is summarized by:

Entry: AH = 50h

          BX = PSP segment to set in DOS

          int   21h

Under DOS 2.X, if FCBs were used for file handling, file information was not stored in the PSP. As long as only FCB file calls were made, the user's PSP was not required by TSR programs. However, under DOS 3.X, all file handling in DOS is converted internally to file handles. Therefore, these undocumented calls are required when operating under DOS 3.X for all file and device handling calls.

A Simple Memory-Resident Program

Let's make our discussion concrete by showing a TSR in action. The MS-DOS GRAPHICS utility is an example of a very simple TSR program. Upon invocation, GRAPHICS tests to make sure that it was not previously installed. This is done by getting the current INT 5 Print Screen vector and comparing a number of bytes of the current handler with the corresponding bytes in GRAPHICS. Once we know that GRAPHICS isn't there, our new INT 5 vector is installed pointing to GRAPHICS resident code. Now, the code in GRAPHICS will be executed when an INT 5 is invoked (such as by holding down the shift and Print Screen keys). Additionally, GRAPHICS frees up some memory for use of other programs. MS-DOS loads COM programs at 100h, and the memory area in the base page (0 to 0ffh) from 0 to 5ch must be preserved for termination. GRAPHICS goes to the trouble of relocating the resident interrupt handler from 100h down to 60h in the PSP to save 160 bytes of memory. (See Essays 6 and 10 for detailed discussion of the PSP and how it is used.)

Basic Structure of TSRs

Let's illustrate some of the ideas used in GRAPHICS with a simple TSR which allows disabling and enabling the Print Screen key. The basic structure of a TSR program usually consists of two parts: the resident code and the initialization and install routine.

Since we would like to use as little memory as possible, the resident code is normally at the beginning of our program and the initialization code placed at the end, so it may be discarded after use. Again to minimize memory use, TSR programs are often coded in assembly language. However, more sophisticated applications might combine assembly language for certain crucial interrupt routines with code produced from a higher level language compiler.

Here is a "skeleton" showing the basic structure of a TSR program:

```
begin:     jmp  init       ;jump to our initialization routine

new_intx:  .....           ;our resident TSR code
           .......
```

```
       .......

                        ;end of resident code

init:      .....        ;our initialization and install code
                        ;which will be discarded after use
```

The IBM Print Screen Function

Depending on one's perspective, the Print Screen is either a wonderful or a hor-
rible feature. The ROM BIOS keyboard interrupt scans for keystrokes, and if the
Shift key and the Print Screen key are held down at the same time, the keyboard
handler calls a Print Screen function, software Interrupt 5. This is just fine if you
hit those keys on purpose, but that Print Screen key is mighty close to the tiny
Return key on the old-style IBM PC keyboard. Let's say it was an accident, and
hope you have a printer connected and turned on, because that thoughtful Print
Screen routine will wait nearly forever. If no printer is at hand, you can always
reboot the machine and lose the last 30 minutes of the report you've been preparing. With a printer, we only have to turn it on and wait however long it takes
to print out the screen. If we are in the middle of printing in WordStar or
WordPerfect, of course, our printer gets a bunch of gibberish, too. It's clear that
it would be useful to disable Print Screen, except for the few times we might
really want it. But if we *do* want a screen dump, we want to be able to reactivate
the Print Screen key. Thus, making our Print Screen toggle a TSR is appropriate.

The PSOFF Program

The program PSOFF enables or disables the built-in Print Screen routine. It was
written for assembly into a small MS-DOS COM file. The program was written as a
memory-resident procedure, which you might install using a batch file. For example, an AUTOEXEC.BAT file might contain the following for a serial printer:

```
mode com1:9600,8,1,p
mode lpt1:=com1
psoff off
```

This would set up a serial printer as COM1 and disable the Print Screen
function on bootup. At any time, PSOFF may be invoked with either the ON or OFF
option to disable or enable the Print Screen function. For example:

```
A>psoff on
```

would enable this function at some later time.

How It Works

The default Print Screen function is set up when the IBM PC ROM BIOS boots up. The ROM BIOS installs the routine as Interrupt vector 5. Our own PSOFF will be loaded into memory and will install a replacement routine at this interrupt vector and stay resident. When PSOFF is invoked, the ON/OFF parameter will be scanned to determine whether Print Screen will be turned on or off. Once installed, if we invoke PSOFF again, the program must check to see whether it is already installed in memory. If it's already there, the program just changes the ON/OFF setting as specified and exits without staying resident. If the proper ON/OFF parameter is not found, like any good program PSOFF gives a help message describing its use and merely exits.

PSOFF has two basic parts, the initialization code and the interrupt handler itself. In this simple example, almost all of the code is for initialization. The interrupt handler at NEWINT5 is only six bytes long. It has two modes, either on or off. When Print Screen is OFF, the interrupt handler consists of a single IRET instruction (return from interrupt) to complete the function, bypassing the IBM PC Print Screen interrupt handler. When Print Screen is ON, the IRET is replaced with a NOP (no operation) followed by a JMP FAR instruction to the original interrupt handler. The memory resident part of this routine is about 40 bytes long.

The initialization code will be used once and then discarded. It starts at the label INIT. The INIT routine goes through a series of small inline routines. You might note that conditional assembly was used so that slightly different versions could be created for either MS-DOS or CP/M-86. This technique can also be used to accommodate differences in MS-DOS versions if necessary.

Table 7-2 lists a summary of the initialization routines used by PSOFF. Table 7-3 lists subroutines.

Table 7-2.   Inline Initialization Routines

Routine	Operation
init	Set up segment registers and local stack
getparm	Test if proper parameters were given on command line
movint	If good parameters, copy pointer to existing Print Screen function to our own code
testint	Test that PSOFF is not already installed
change	If PSOFF already installed, change its ON/OFF toggle, tell the user, and exit
stint	If PSOFF not installed, install our new INT 5 vector, tell user current status, exit, and stay resident

Table 7-3.   PSOFF Subroutines

Subroutine	Operation
bdos	Call DOS (works with both MS-DOS and CP/M-86)
pchar	Print a single **CHAR** to the screen
pmess	Print a string terminated by a binary 0 to the screen
crlf	Send a carriage return and linefeed to the screen
saystat	Tell user status of Print Screen function

Here is Listing 7-1, PSOFF. You should be able to follow it by reviewing the preceding discussion and noting the comments.

Listing 7-1.   PSOFF

```
TITLE    'Print Screen Off Routine for MSDOS 4-3-85'
         pagewidth          96
;
;        Print Screen Off Routine for MSDOS          :
;        Author:        M. Steven Baker
;        Revision date    March 25, 1985
;        Last revision    April 3, 1985
;
;        Make using the following commands:
;        MASM PSOFF;
;        LINK PSOFF;
;        EXE2BIN PSOFF.EXE PSOFF.COM
;        DEL PSOFF.EXE
;
;        Purpose:
;                installs and stays resident in DOS to revector
;                the print screen routine to an innocuous IRET
;                when invoked with OFF parameter
;
;        Operation:
;                This program must be run first to disable the
;                standard Print Screen Routine for PC-DOS.
;                It revectors the INT5 to this new code.
;                This code stays resident until rebooting
;                to allow a user to either turn ON or OFF
;                the print screen routine.
;
;        E Q U A T E S
```

continued

```
;
cr        equ     0dh
lf        equ     0ah
;
false     equ     0
true      equ     not false
;
cpm86     equ     false
msdos     equ     not cpm86
;
MASM      equ     true          ;using Microsoft or compatible
                                ;assembler
ASM86     equ     not MASM      ;using Digital Research

          if      MASM          ;use some macros
cseg      macro
          CODE    segment
          assume  cs:CODE,ds:CODE,ss:CODE
          endm

jmps      macro   dummy         ;jump short macro
          jmp     short dummy
          endm

rs        macro   count         ;reserve storage
          db      count dup(?)
          endm
          endif                 ;MASM

fcb       equ     05ch          ;file control block for parameters


          cseg

          ORG     0100h
;
; Sign on message
;
begin:    jmp     init          ;jump to initialization code
          jmp     newint5       ;jump to our new interrupt code
;
vernm     db      'Print Screen On/Off Version 1.0  4-3-85',0
;
```

continued

```
newint5 db      90h                 ;NOP space for our IRET
        db      0eah                ;jump far instruction
int5    dw      0,0                 ;kluge jmpf entry point
                                    ;since MASM won't assemble a
                                    ;jump far instruction
;
;       I N I T
;       initialization code for installing our interrupt
;
init:   mov     ax,cs               ;setup segment registers
        mov     ds,ax
        mov     es,ax
        mov     ss,ax
        MOV     SP,Offset stack
;
        CALL    crlf
;
; test if proper parameters are there
;
getparm:
        mov     si,fcb+1
        mov     al,[si]
        cmp     al,' '
        jne     testparm        ;if no parameters, then give help
help:   jmp     givehelp
;
testparm:
        mov     di,offset on_stg ;point to ON string
        mov     cx,4             ;compare four bytes
tparm1: cmpsb                    ;comparison
        jne     tparm2
        loop    tparm1
        mov     byte ptr newint5,90h    ;put NOP at newint5
        jmps    movint
;
tparm2: mov     si,fcb+1                 ;point to parameter
        mov     di,offset off_stg        ;point to OFF string
        mov     cx,4                     ;compare 4 bytes
tparm3: cmpsb                            ;compare them
        jne     help
        loop    tparm3
        mov     byte ptr newint5,0cfh    ;put IRET opcode at newint5
;
```

continued

```
                ; copy print screen interrupt vector to our JUMP FAR return
                ; used to return from our checking code
                ;
        movint: xor     ax,ax               ;zero AX
                mov     ds,ax               ;set DS to segment 0
                cld                         ;set forward direction
                mov     si,14h              ;pointer to int5
                mov     di,offset int5      ;pointer to our JUMP FAR code
                mov     ax,cs
                mov     es,ax               ;set ES to our code segment
                movsw                       ;move offset
                movsw                       ;move segment
        ;
        ; now test that we have not already previously installed this
        ; at the print screen interrupt
        ;
        testint:
                mov     si,14h              ;pointer to int5
                lodsw                       ;get offset to AX
                mov     dx,ax               ;save offset to DX
                lodsw                       ;get segment to AX
                mov     es,ax               ;temporarily store it in ES
                mov     ax,cs               ;restore our DS register
                mov     ds,ax
                mov     ax,offset newint5
                cmp     ax,dx               ;offsets are not equal
                jne     setint
        ;
                mov     si,offset vernm     ;point to version name
                mov     di,si               ;in both SI and DI
                mov     cx,(offset newint5)-(offset vernm)
        testint2:
                cmpsb                       ;compare them for equal
                jne     setint
                loop    testint2
        ;
        change:
                mov     si,offset newint5
                mov     di,si
                movsb                       ;and CHANGE it
                call    saystat             ;give user current status
                jmp     exit
        ;
```

continued

```
; now replace INT5 interrupt vector with pointer to our code
;
setint: mov       ax,cs
        mov       ds,ax    ;setup DS = CS
        mov       bx,ax    ;save our code segment in BX
        xor       ax,ax    ;zero AX
        mov       es,ax    ;setup ES as segment 0
        mov       di,14h   ;point to INT5 vector
;
        cld                ;set forward direction
        cli                ;shut hardware interrupts off
;
        mov       ax,offset newint5         ;setup our int5
        stosw
        mov       ax,bx    ;now set our code segment
        stosw              ;and store it
;
inton:  sti                ;turn back on interrupts
                           ;vector has now been replaced
;
        mov       ax,cs
        mov       ds,ax
;
        call      saystat          ;tell them status
;
;
done:
        if        cpm86
; exit and stay resident under CPM86
        mov       cl,0     ;setup for exit
        mov       dl,1     ;stay resident
        call      bdos
        endif

        if        msdos
; terminate but stay resident under dos
        mov       dx,(offset init)+1
        int       27h
        endif
;
; exit but don't stay resident
;
givehelp:
```

continued

```
                mov     si,offset helpmsg       ;give help message
                call    pmess

                                                ;and fall thru to exit
        exit:
                mov     ax,0
                mov     dx,ax                   ;set DX =0 for CPM86 exit
                call    bdos
        ;
        ;       S A Y S T A T U S
        ;       say status of Print Screen Function
        ;       ENTRY   none
        ;       EXIT    AX and SI are destroyed
        ;
        saystat:
                mov     si,offset endmsg        ;tell them we're done
                call    pmess
                mov     al,byte ptr newint5     ;get value either NOP or IRET
                mov     si,offset onmess
                cmp     al,90h
                je      saystat_2
        ;
                mov     si,offset offmess
                cmp     al,0cfh
                je      saystat_2
                mov     si,offset badmsg
        saystat_2:
                call    pmess
                call    crlf
                ret
        ;
        ; DOS interface
        ;
        crlf:   push    ax
                mov     al,cr
                call    pchar
                mov     al,lf
                call    pchar
                pop     ax
                ret
        ;
        pchar:  push    ax
                push    bx
                push    dx
```

continued

```
            mov     dl,al
            MOV     ah,2
            call    bdos
            pop     dx
            pop     bx
            pop     ax
            RET
;
;           P M E S S
;           print message to screen
;           Entry   SI = pointer to message terminated by null byte
;           Exit    AL and SI destroyed
pmess:  lodsb                   ;get byte
            or      al,al       ;is it zero??
            jnz     pmess2
            ret
pmess2: push    si              ;save pointer
            call    pchar       ;send character
            pop     si          ;restore pointer
            jmps    pmess       ;and continue

bdos:
            if      cpm86
            push    es          ;preserve ES
            push    cx          ;save CX
            mov     cl,ah       ;for cpm86
            int     0e0h
            pop     cx          ;restore registers
            pop     es
            endif
;
            if      msdos
            int     21h
            endif
            ret
;
datast  equ     $
            DSEG
            org     offset datast
;
; message texts
;
helpmsg db      'USAGE as follows:',cr,lf
```

continued

```
          db       '   A>PSCREEN ON    (to ENABLE print screen function)'
          db       cr,lf
          db       '   A>PSCREEN OFF   (to DISABLE print screen function)'
          db       cr,lf,0
;
endmsg    db       'Print Screen Function is ',0
onmess    db       'ENABLED - '
on_stgdb           'ON  ',0
offmess   db       'DISABLED - '
off_stgdb          'OFF ',0
;
badmsg    db       '*** CORRUPTED OR DAMAGED ***'
          DB       cr,lf,'PLEASE REBOOT SYSTEM'
          db       cr,lf,0
;
;
          RS       100h
stack     dw       0
;
intend    equ      $


          if MASM
          CODE     ends
          end      begin
          endif

          if CPM86
          end
          endif
```

A Closer Look at TSRs

Now that we've seen in detail how a simple TSR is implemented, let's look at some more complex examples by examining the MS-DOS ASSIGN and PRINT programs more closely.

The ASSIGN Command

The MS-DOS ASSIGN utility is an example of a more complex TSR program, which modifies MS-DOS itself but does not make any MS-DOS calls when resident. This utility allows the user to assign any logical drive (from A-H in DOS 2.0) to any actual physical drive. Its main purpose is allowing those poorly written programs that absolutely expect their data files to be on drive "B" to run on a hard disk machine. ASSIGN does this logical-to-actual drive mapping by replacing a number of software interrupts, as shown in Table 7-4.

Table 7-4.   Interrupt Vectors Replaced by ASSIGN

Interrupt	Function
INT 21h Dosint	Patches the filespec and disk drive string passed on to the original MS-DOS interrupt
INT 25h Absolute Disk Read	Patches drive number in AL, then passes on to original interrupt vector
INT 26h Absolute Disk Write	Patches drive number in AL, then passes on to original interrupt vector
INT 2Fh Multiplex Interrupt	Provides a way to communicate with the resident part of the ASSIGN program (only replaced in versions distributed with DOS 3.X)

The Diskette__IO (INT 13H) interrupt is not modified, so calls to the ROM BIOS will not be affected by this utility. The memory-resident part of ASSIGN maintains a simple table of 8 bytes that map to actual disk drives. When a drive is assigned, the value in this table is changed to reflect the actual drive to be used as this logical disk. When the ASSIGN command is given without parameters, the default logical to physical drive table is copied into the memory-resident code, as follows:

```
disktabl  db    1,2,3,4,5,6,7,8    ;default disk assign table,
                                   ;ie, logical drive A = disk 1
```

Complex TSR Programs That Make MS-DOS Function Calls

These applications include the more complex TSRs that, once resident, must make MS-DOS function calls used for file reading and writing. Such programs must be much more carefully written to be certain that they interrupt MS-DOS operations and other activities only when it is safe to do so. Some of the hardware interrupts such as the keyboard or timer may be replaced by the TSR. To do this properly requires a greater understanding of the hardware controller (Intel 8259 chip), various machine specific hardware features and the internals of the IBM PC ROM BIOS code.

PRINT: A Model Memory-Resident Program

The MS-DOS PRINT utility can be considered to be a model TSR program. It is a good example in that it uses both documented and undocumented TSR functions in MS-DOS. It also must make MS-DOS calls after becoming memory-resident so it can read disk files and print them in the background. Two hooks are used for background printing, the Background Process INT 28H (MS-DOS software interrupt) and the Timer_tick INT 1CH (a ROM BIOS software interrupt). These two interrupts are vectored to the resident part of PRINT which then tests several other monitors to make certain that MS-DOS is interruptible. These other flags include whether Diskette_IO is in process or the IN_DOS flag is set (i.e., an MS-DOS call was already in process). The following is a rough list of the initialization routine for a TSR (such as the MS-DOS PRINT utility) that must make MS-DOS calls:

1. Test for DOS Version above 2.0 since you will be using some undocumented features not available in MS-DOS 1.X. If not okay, exit.

2. Check to see whether the resident part of PRINT has previously been installed using Multiplex INT 2FH call with AH = 1 and AL = 0 (get installed state). If PRINT already installed, the remaining initialization steps are not executed.

3. Free memory allocated to the environment for the PRINT program.

4. For the PRINT spooler, open the appropriate list device to make certain that it exists.

5. Save old Background INT 28H and install your own.

6. Save old Multiplex INT 2FH and install your own.

7. Save old Diskette_IO INT 13H and install your own.

8. Save existing Printer_IO INT 17H, RS232_IO INT 14H, and Print_Screen INT 5 interrupt vectors and install your own. These replacement interrupt routines will return printer busy if another application tries to print while you are spooling a file to printer.

9. Call IN_DOS function (INT21H Function AH = 34h) and save pointer to the DOS_CRITICAL byte in DOS.

10. Save old Bootstrap INT 19H vector and install your own. This step was only added in DOS 3.3 PRINT. A call to your new INT 19H will restore all the old ROM BIOS vectors and invoke the original INT 19H—reboot the system.

11. Save old Timer_Tick INT 1CH and install new vector. This step is omitted if a NETBIOS interface has already been installed.

12. Set DX pointer to end of resident part of PRINT code, and terminate and stay resident.

When the resident part of PRINT is invoked by one of the two hooks, it checks to make certain that INT 13H (Diskette_IO) was not in progress). Disk operations cannot be interrupted, so if Diskette_IO is occurring, PRINT will return-control to the current application. If entry was by INT 1CH (Timer_Tick), it also checks the IN_DOS flag to make certain a critical MS-DOS function is not being interrupted. The Timer_Tick interrupt is called during each hardware timer tick (18.2 times a second). The INT 1CH entry also sends an End of Interrupt (EOI) command to the interrupt controller chip (Intel 8259) so that other hardware interrupts can occur. If other hardware interrupts are pending, then PRINT returns without printing a character.

PRINT is also careful about saving and restoring certain other parameters before invoking MS-DOS calls which might return an error such as reading a file. If a hardware error occurs, it must be caught by PRINT, not passed on to the interrupted application. The resident part of PRINT has a 512-byte buffer (DOS 2.X) for reading files to spool from disk. MS-DOS version 3.X allows the user the ability to increase this buffer size. The following is a rough list of what is done before and after a file open, disk read, and file close to protect an application program from errors.

1. Save old user PSP segment.

2. Save old INT 24H Critical Error Handler.

3. Save old DTA.

4. Install your own INT 24H vector (Error Handler) to catch any errors.

5. Set DTA to your disk buffer address, set to your PSP in DOS.

6. Make DOS call for disk read.

7. Restore old DTA.

8. Restore old INT 24H Critical Error Handler.

9. Restore old user PSP in DOS.

An UNSPOOL TSR Program

To illustrate some of these considerations, we will outline the structure of a TSR utility to capture output to the printer device and write it to a file. (For space reasons, we cannot include a complete listing.) This program will also incorporate a "hot key" feature to turn on or off this feature at any time. The hot key feature will save the screen and bring up a popup menu. The hot keys could also allow you to change the name of the unspooled file from a default name. After this menu use, we will restore the screen to its condition before the TSR activation.

The basic structure of our program UNSPOOL will be similar to what we have seen already. However, the amount of coding for the resident and initialization parts of the TSR will be much larger. Here is the outline:

```
        jmp   init                    ;our initialization code
        jmp   newint17                ;our replacement Printer_IO
        db    'UNSPOOL Version 1.3  2-20-87',0
;
newint17:

        .....

        .....                         ;resident code ends
;
init:                                 ;our initialization and
                                      ;install routines
        ............
        ..........                    ;TSR ends
```

UNSPOOL Program Structure

Table 7-5 shows the interrupts that we will need to intercept for this TSR. In addition, just before doing any MS-DOS file operations, we will need to save the current DOS user PSP and install our own PSP segment in DOS. Next, we temporarily replace INT 24H to protect and intercept any errors and replace the default DTA—the buffer into which DOS will read the file. After MS-DOS file operations, the original INT 24H handler, the application PSP, and DTA must be restored.

Table 7-5. Interrupts used by UNSPOOL

Interrupt	Function
5	Print Screen interrupt, need to disable if unspooling taking place
9	Keyboard hardware interrupt, sets flag for activation by "hot keys"
13h	Diskette_IO, monitors disk routine to prevent trashing
14h	RS232_IO, for serial printer output
15h	Cassette_IO, determines if UNSPOOL is already memory-resident
16h	Keyboard_IO, watches for a particular character sequence
17h	Printer_IO, for parallel printer output
1Ch	Timer_Tick, vector interrupt for activation
28h	Background Interrupt, vector DOS interrupt for activation
2Fh	Multiplex, monitors calls to printer multiplex

Before bringing up any popup menu, we will need to save the current screen and state of other video parameters. This will require space in the resident part of our TSR for storage of the video parameters and the screen. Then we can bring up our menu and get keyboard input from the user. Finally, the screen will need to be restored along with any video parameters.

Programming Guidelines for TSR Programs

You should now understand the basic procedures for writing various kinds of TSRs. Microsoft has provided a draft specification for TSR programs to developers (Andrews 1986). These draft guidelines define a set of operational rules for TSR programs to minimize conflict when other memory-resident utilities are loaded. They do *not* document or describe the undocumented features of DOS which TSR implementers must know. The gist of the suggestions are that TSR programs should mimic MS-DOS and the ROM BIOS as much as possible. Some valuable basic guidelines are found in the following areas: general issues, the keyboard, video issues, and TSR program interface.

General Issues

You should design your TSR program so it can easily coexist with other TSR programs in memory. It should not be critical that your program be the last interrupt vector in the chain of interrupts. Setting up a local stack in an interrupt routine of your TSR program prevents it from being reentrant. If the interrupt is invoked again, the earlier local stack contents will be written over. Use a local stack only when needed and hardware interrupts are off, or in an area protected from reentry. When using your own MS-DOS Critical Error Handler, do not jump from it to your TSR program code. Instead, set a global error flag that your TSR routines check, issue an `IGNORE` response in the error handler, and return to DOS (using an `IRET` instruction). This assures that the MS-DOS stacks will be cleared properly.

Keyboard Issues

Don't take complete control of `INT 9` (hardware keyboard interrupt). If your TSR program wants to use keystrokes that the IBM PC ROM BIOS doesn't generate (i.e., the CTRL-UP arrow key is not decoded by the original PC or AT ROM BIOS), install your routine, chain into the interrupt, generate a new scan code, and put it into the IBM PC keyboard buffer just as the ROM BIOS does. If you are looking for a single keystroke, set a flag and continue through the interrupt. When the

TSR is running, it should use INT 16H (ROM BIOS Keyboard_IO routine) to get a keyboard input. This allows all TSRs in the chain to see the key request and take any appropriate action.

Video Issues

Use the ROM BIOS whenever possible. If you directly change video modes, cursor types, background intensity, EGA, or VGA registers, save the new values in the appropriate ROM BIOS and video data areas.

TSR Program Interface

This draft guideline also proposes an extensive format of data records for TSR programs and a program interface. The program interface proposed would use Cassette_IO INT 15H (Function AH = 52h) as a method for the nonresident parts of programs to communicate with resident parts. Unfortunately, this TSR format has not been widely implemented and may never be.

The Bottom Line

As a programmer, do I use memory-resident programs myself? Only in special situations. I want as little to interfere with my programming and testing as possible. Oh, I wouldn't mind a good screen-capture utility now and then. But most users do appear to like TSRs and that's a driving force for software development. From my perspective, TSRs do serve a useful purpose when modifying hardware or ROM BIOS routines. I personally prefer to use "program loaders," small programs that load another application and change the MS-DOS or hardware environment. Then, when the application is done, they disappear and go away.

Reading List

Andrews, N. 1986. Moving toward an industry standard for developing TSRs. *Microsoft Systems Journal* 1, no. 2 (December).

Duncan, R. 1986. *Advanced MS-DOS*. Redmond, Washington: Microsoft Press.
▶ The officially sanctioned guide to DOS for assembly language and C programmers.

IBM. 1983. *IBM Technical Reference Manual*. Publication #1502234. North Tarrytown, New York.

▶ The hardware reference to the IBM PC. Section 2 contains a complete listing of the ROM BIOS which is essential for most serious PC work. This is the most heavily used publication on the IBM PC in my library. A version specific to the IBM AT is also available (Publication #636166), but I still use the PC version most often. A later version is available for the IBM PS/2 line; however, it does not contain any BIOS listings, only calling conventions.

————. 1987. *IBM Disk Operating System Technical Reference.* Publication #80X0945. North Tarrytown, New York.
▶ Technical information for a specific version of DOS, the official line. The latest version is for DOS 3.3.

(staff). 1986. Best of BIX. *BYTE Magazine* (September): 380-409.
▶ *BYTE's* online conference for the IBM PC has had discussions on the PRINT.COM program. The Pascal conference has several discussions by staff from Living Videotext (READY) on TSR programs and technology used by READY. Borland's SIG on Compuserve also has an active group of programmers studying TSR software.

M. Steven Baker is currently the technical editor of *Programmer's Journal*, a resource journal for IBM PC programmers and has written on a number of computer and energy-related topics. He holds degrees in architecture and electrical engineering from Massachusetts Institute of Engineering, and Masters degrees in architecture and urban and regional planning from the University of Oregon. Steve works as an energy analyst for the Oregon department of energy and programs on large IBM mainframes, VAX and PRIME minicomputers, and microcomputers.

Related Essays

  3 Adding UNIX Power with PCnix
  6 Undocumented MS-DOS Functions
10 Developing MS-DOS Device Drivers

Keywords

- data security
- encryption
- cryptography
- passwords
- hidden files
- code systems
- cipher systems
- Data Encryption Standard (DES)
- public key cryptosystems

Essay Synopsis: Because of the increasing amount of sensitive data being processed on desktop computers, there is a growing need for improved data security and access control on personal computers and office networks. This essay explains data security strategies, shows how they are implemented, and assesses the value and limitations of each technique discussed. The author explains security-related features of the MS-DOS file system, and how to take advantage of them. Password-checking programs can be installed, sensitive files can be hidden from casual inspection, and different levels of access can be provided to particular users. The ultimate data protection, however, is encryption—making data unusable without the appropriate key. The author explains DES and RSA algorithms, which use mathematical techniques to encrypt and decrypt data.

8

Data Protection and Encryption

Asael Dror

Computer data security is becoming a critical problem, especially with microcomputers. Though it is rarely admitted, a survey reported in *PC WEEK* (June 9, 1987) suggests that more than 80 percent of corporations and agencies have suffered financial loss due to computer security problems.

The same factors which have helped create the microcomputer revolution have also contributed to the data security problem. The availability of inexpensive microcomputers encouraged small businesses and individuals, who had never used computers before, to adopt microcomputers. Meanwhile, in large businesses the concept of *data distribution*—placing the data close to the user— has caused the transfer of information from the traditional mainframes to microcomputers. These trends have been further magnified by technological advances such as fast communication devices, large capacity hard disks, and LANs, which make it easier to transfer, store, and retrieve large amounts of data on microcomputers. Finally, a dramatic increase in computer literacy has given more people the knowledge needed to access the data. Thus, having easy access to large amounts of (often sensitive) data has greatly increased the means and opportunities for such computer security problems as illegal access, data tampering, and computer vandalism.

Three Levels of Unauthorized Data Access

What does illegal data access involve? Unauthorized data access can be classified into three levels. In order of increasing potential for damage, they are

- ▶ Deletion
- ▶ Reading
- ▶ Changing

Deletion

Deletion of data is (surprisingly) the least harmful of the three levels of unauthorized access. Detecting a major deletion is simple—your data is gone. (If the deletion is such that it is not immediately evident, we shall view it as a change to the data rather than deletion.) All that has to be done to recover from deletion is to restore the data. This is an easy matter, assuming you have a recent backup locked away. The only harm caused by the illegal access is that you lose whatever data had been entered since your last backup.

Reading

When people talk about violations of data security, they are most often referring to reading your data. An unauthorized person who wants to read large amounts of your data needs to access your computer for only enough time to copy your hard disk onto diskettes to be read later at leisure. Since reading leaves no marks, you cannot detect the unauthorized access and so will not take measures to minimize the damage.

Changing

The most severe data access violation is changing your data. Someone not only reads your sensitive data but also falsifies it undetectably. While the intruder now has the correct data, you are using a maliciously falsified version. This can cause considerable damage not only to obviously sensitive data but also in lesser areas. Very small changes in the data can make big differences: credit becomes debit, $10 becomes $10 million, a "D" grade becomes an "A," research results become false, the number of your safety deposit box is altered, key people are moved around, and so forth.

Multilayer Protection

To protect data, a three-layer system should be used:

1. Physical security: limiting access to your computer, keeping your backups secured, destroying printed reports, etc.

2. People confidence: ensuring reliability of people who are authorized to access the data

3. Data security: protecting your data on the computer from unauthorized access by someone who has bypassed the physical security

This paper will deal only with the third issue, i.e., the technical means for securing data on MS-DOS machines, but remember that all three elements are important for protecting your data.

MS-DOS Data Structure and Access

Before we can protect the data, let's review how data is organized and accessed in the MS-DOS environment. When DOS allocates and frees disk storage space, it does so in chunks of sectors called *clusters*. A cluster is a fixed number of consecutive sectors the size of which is determined at the time the media is formatted by DOS. For example, when using DOS 3.X with a hard disk of 30MB, a 4-sector (2K) cluster will be used. Space is allocated and deallocated by MS-DOS as needed. When a file grows, more clusters are allocated for it and when the file shrinks, clusters are deallocated.

MS-DOS "sees" a file as an ordered sequence of clusters. The order of the file's clusters is kept in the File Allocation Table (FAT). Other information about the file, such as its name and attributes, are kept in a directory.

Directories

A directory is a collection of entries describing files. There are two types of directories: the root directory is a special area of fixed size and location, and the subdirectory is a DOS file having the subdirectory attribute. Each directory entry is 32 bytes long (see Figure 8-1) and has the format shown in Table 8-1.

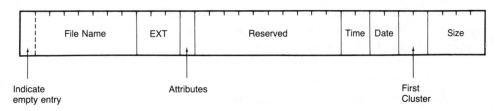

Fig. 8-1.   Directory entry.

The FAT is a collection of entries, each describing one cluster. A FAT entry for a cluster which is allocated to a file has the number of the subsequent cluster of that file. So, to find the chain of clusters making up a file, we find the first cluster in the file's directory entry and then follow the chain. Each cluster's entry in the FAT will tell us what the next cluster of the file is.

Table 8-1.   Directory Entry Format

Byte offset (decimal)	Length in bytes (decimal)	Description
0	8	Filename (without the extension) or an indication that this entry is empty
8	3	Filename extension
11	1	The file's attribute (This is a bit field in which the individual bits are used to indicate that the file has particular attributes: 01H = READ ONLY; 02H = HIDDEN; 04H = SYSTEM FILE; 08H = VOLUME LABEL; 10H = SUBDIRECTORY; 20H = ARCHIVE; 40H and 80H = Reserved, always 0.)
12	10	Reserved
22	2	The time this file was last updated
24	2	The date this file was last updated
26	2	The file's first cluster
28	4	The file's size

Accessing the Data

The MS-DOS data access system is designed as a layered architecture with the following layers: the application program, MS-DOS, BIOS, and the computer's hardware. Each layer has its own "vision" of how the data looks and uses the services of the adjoining (deeper) layer for accessing the data. This design helps to disconnect the higher layers from the hardware implementation details and thus achieve hardware independence.

Application programs use the services of DOS to access the data by performing software Interrupt 21h and passing the required parameters. When DOS is called on to perform data access operations, reference to the data is made by filename and the relative offset of the data within the file. Some common MS-DOS data-handling functions accessed through Interrupt 21h include: open a file (Function 3Dh), close a file (Function 3Eh), read from a file (Function 3Fh), write to a file (Function 40h), delete a file (Function 41h), and move the read/write pointer in the file (Function 42h).

The next layer, DOS, uses the services of BIOS to access the data. BIOS is DOS's interface to the computer's hardware. The call to BIOS is performed via software Interrupt 13h passing the required parameters. When calling BIOS, reference to the data is not made by files, which BIOS does not understand, but by the physical location of the data, i.e., the device, head, track, and sector number. Two of the data-handling functions that BIOS provides are: read a sector (Function 02) and write a sector (Function 03).

The innermost software level, BIOS, communicates directly with the hardware (disk, DMA, timer, and interrupt controllers) via input and output instructions. (See Essay 1, A Guided Tour inside MS-DOS, by Harry Henderson, for further discussion of the three layers of MS-DOS.)

Hiding Your Data

A simple strategy to protect your data is to hide it. If no one knows you have the data or where the data is kept, it cannot be accessed.

Hiding Data with Nonstandard Filenames

One way to hide data is to use nonstandard filenames. MS-DOS specifies that file and subdirectory names may use only the following characters: A-Z 0-9 $ # & @ % ( ) - { } '' _.

In practice, many other nonstandard characters may be used. Some of them cannot be typed directly from the keyboard but may be entered by holding down the ALT key, pressing the character's ASCII code on the numeric keyboard, and then releasing the ALT key. For our purpose, the most useful of those non-standard characters is the null character (which has ASCII code 255). This character appears on the screen as a blank and can be used to create invisible file and subdirectory names such as `<null><null>.<null>`. To access such a file, one must use the exact filename: `<null><null>` is a different filename from `<null><null>.<null>`. It is possible to create 32 different filenames using only this character, but, of course, you too must remember the exact name yourself.

Hiding with Hidden Files

Another way to hide your data is to create an MS-DOS hidden file. A file or sub-directory that has the `HIDDEN` attribute in its directory entry on, will not be listed by the `DIR` command. This is the technique used to make the PC-DOS system files `IBMDOS.COM` and `IBMBIO.COM` invisible. Note that the MS-DOS `ATTRIB` command which can change some of the attributes of a file does not support changing the `HIDDEN` attribute.

Listing 8-1 is a program named HIDE that toggles the `HIDDEN` attribute of a file or subdirectory, that is, it makes a visible file hidden and vice versa. The program reads the current attribute of the file, changes the hidden attribute bit and rewrites the attribute. Note that the program clears the `SUB DIR` attribute. This is done since Function 43h of Interrupt 21h cannot be used to set (or reset) the `SUB DIR` attribute.

Listing 8-1. HIDE

```
        title    'hide'

; This program toggles the hidden attribute of a
; file or subdirectory,
```

continued

```
                ; thus making a visible file hidden or a
                ; hidden one visible

                ; Usage: HIDE filename ¦ subdirectoryname

                ; Written by Asael Dror July 1987


                ; The sequence to generate hide.com is:
                ; masm hide;
                ; link hide;
                ; exe2bin hide.exe hide.com


HIDE_ATTR       EQU   02h          ; HIDDEN file attribute
SUB_DIR_ATTR    EQU   10h          ; SUB. DIR. file attribute
SPACE           EQU   ' '


onlyseg  segment

PARAMLN  equ        80h

         org        100h          ; for .com file


hide     proc       far

         assume     cs:onlyseg,ds:onlyseg,es:onlyseg

         cld
         mov        di,PARAMLN
         sub        ch,ch
         mov        cl,byte ptr[di]   ; get arg len.
         jcxz       fail              ; no arg. given
         inc        di                ; di -> arg.

         mov        al,SPACE
         rep scasb                    ; scan for first nonblank
         je         fail              ; no arg. (filename) given
         inc        cx                ; adjust length and pointer
         dec        di
         mov        si,offset filenm
```

continued

```
        xchg      si,di       ; si->arg. di->filenm
        rep movsb             ; save arg. as filenm


        mov       dx,offset filenm
        mov       ax,4300h
        int       21h         ; get file's attribute
        jc        fail
        xor       cl,HIDE_ATTR  ; toggle HIDDEN attr.

                              ; leave SUB DIR ATTR
                              ; along
        and       cl,(NOT SUB_DIR_ATTR)


        mov       ax,4301h
        int       21h         ; set file's attribute
        jc        fail
        mov       ax,4c00h
        int       21h         ; terminate, errorlevel=0

fail:
        mov       dx,offset failmsg
        mov       ah,09h
        int       21h         ; print fail message
        mov       ax,4c08h
        int       21h         ; terminate, errorlevel=8

filenm  db   64 dup (0)       ; space for the file name
failmsg db   'Cannot change hidden attribute $'

hide    endp
onlyseg ends
        end       hide
```

Protecting data by hiding files may be an effective strategy against a casual observer who uses the DIR command. However, special directory-listing programs (as well as the DOS CHKDSK/V command which lists the tree structure of the entire disk including all hidden files) are able to reveal such hidden files. Here are the results of using HIDE program. The directory as it is shown by the DIR command:

```
Volume in drive D is VDISK  V3.3
Directory of  D:\
```

```
FOO                    9    8-19-87  11:40a
HIDE     COM         162    8-19-87  10:07a
         2 File(s)       386048 bytes free
```

The directory as it is shown by the DIR command after HIDE FOO was used:

```
Volume in drive D is VDISK  V3.3
Directory of  D:\

HIDE     COM         162    8-19-87  10:07a
         1 File(s)       386048 bytes free
```

CHKDSK/V still shows the hidden file FOO:

```
Volume VDISK  V3.3 created Dec 6, 1984 12:00p
Directory D:\
      D:\VDISK  V.3.3
      D:\FOO
      D:\HIDE.COM

   387072 bytes total disk space
      512 bytes in 2 hidden files
      512 bytes in 1 user files
   386048 bytes available on disk

   655360 bytes total memory
   567984 bytes free
```

but DEL FOO will give a File not found when the file is hidden. Entering HIDE FOO a second time cancels the file's HIDDEN attribute and makes it appear in the DIR listing and deletable by the DEL command.

Protecting Files Using the Read-Only Attribute

MS-DOS provides a READ ONLY file attribute that means the file cannot be changed or deleted. The READ-ONLY attribute, like the HIDDEN attribute, is a bit field in the file's directory entry. The READ-ONLY attribute can be changed by using the DOS 3.X ATTRIB command (or by writing a program similar to the one used to toggle the HIDDEN attribute bit). Unfortunately, protecting a file by making it READ-ONLY is really more a precaution against accidental access than a means against intentional malicious access, since the READ-ONLY attribute can be easily turned off and then the data deleted or changed.

Password Protection

The next level of security is the use of password protection. We will build such a protection system starting with the simpler but less effective ways and then gradually improve it. Let's begin with a system that is supposed to protect the whole hard disk from access by unauthorized agents. Such a system should, at a bare minimum, require the user to enter a correct password before any access to the hard disk is allowed.

The simplest (and least effective) way of doing this is by placing a small program in the AUTOEXEC file. This program would be activated when the computer is booted and would request the user to enter the correct password. If the correct password is entered, the program terminates normally and the system can be used. However, if the correct password is not given, the program would halt the computer (switch interrupts off and issue the HLT command to the CPU). Unfortunately, such a program can be bypassed easily. The AUTOEXEC is a batch file, and so can be terminated by pressing BREAK before our password program is even activated.

We could improve this program, by making it immune to BREAK. This can be done by writing the program as a device driver instead of running it from the AUTOEXEC. If we do so, it becomes an extension of DOS and so it is impossible to prevent the program from running. Whenever DOS is booted from the hard disk, the password program will receive control. Since our program does not drive any device, which is what device drivers are really meant to do, we are actually writing a fictitious device driver that does all of its work in its initialization routine. (See Essay 11, Writing a SOUND Device Driver, by Walter Dixon, for a detailed discussion of the structure and function of device drivers.) Now it seems that we have solved the problem. Whenever the system is booted our device driver will "take control," prompt the user for the password and refuse access to the system if the correct password is not given. However, this protection system can be completely bypassed by booting off a diskette instead of the hard disk that contains our device driver.

There are two different approaches to solving this problem: A simple hardware solution is to physically disable the ability to boot off a diskette. This can be done most easily by disconnecting the drive A: diskette. (The drive B: diskette can be left in place.) This solution has the following disadvantages:

▶ We cannot have two internal diskette drives.

▶ Some programs access drive A: directly (such as some copy-protection systems) and so will not work (even if we use the ASSIGN command to substitute another drive for A:).

▶ If our hard disk fails or we want to switch to a new operating system, we have to reconnect drive A:.

▶ If an intruder can connect drive A:, the password system could be bypassed.

A second approach would be to move our password program from the DOS level to the BIOS level. We can develop an adaptor card which will have a CMOS chip with a battery backup for storing the password, and a program in ROM to prompt for the correct password. To have the password program receive control before DOS is booted, the ROM must be located on a 2K boundary in the address space C8000H through E0000H. Also, the ROM must have the following special signature: Byte 0: hex 55; Byte 1: hex AA; Byte 2: the length of our ROM in blocks of 512 bytes; Byte 3: the ROM's entry point. A checksum is done to determine the integrity of the ROM. To be valid, the sum of the bytes in the ROM modula 100h has to be 0.

During POST (the machine's Power On Self Test), the ROM will receive control by a FAR CALL to its entry point.

At last, we have a reasonable protection system. Alas, our system provides protection to our whole hard disk as one unit. We cannot limit different people to different types of access. We have a "go or stop" system: if you know the password you can do everything, if you do not know it you can do nothing. Another limitation of this system is that once the password is given, the system is fully available to anyone. If you take a coffee break and do not turn the power off (or otherwise pass control to the password program), you leave your system totally vulnerable. Also, if the adaptor card can be pulled out, our protection system is not activated, and there is always the possibility of physically removing the hard disk and accessing it on a different computer.

Password Protection of Selected Data

Transforming a system from a whole disk protection system to a protection system for individual files or subdirectories giving different people different access privileges requires intercepting every attempt to access the disk. With a data-protection program that is always memory-resident (either a TSR, device driver, or added ROM, it is possible to redirect all hard disk access attempts to our routine, which will then check for authorization. (See Essay 7, Safe Memory-Resident Programming (TSR), by Steven Baker.) We can intercept access attempts to the hard disk either at the DOS or the BIOS level.

To intercept at the DOS level, we have to reroute the DOS access Interrupt (21h) to point to our routine instead of to DOS. This is done by manipulating the interrupt vector for Interrupt 21h located at address 0:84h. Once the interrupt vector points at our interrupt-handling routine, every time a call is made to DOS, our routine will receive control instead. In the routine, we need to determine whether the function requested is a file access and, if so, check for authorization (i.e., the password check). Afterwards, we have to transfer control over to DOS to finish the work that was originally called for. Intercepting at the BIOS level does not give any significant advantages over intercepting at the DOS level and has many complications, so it is not recommended.

Data Encryption

The major disadvantage of the password protection systems described above is that someone can bypass our intercepting routines, which can be done at least as easily as we intercepted DOS (or BIOS) by simply remanipulating the appropriate interrupt vectors. Furthermore, someone can remove the hard disk and read it on a different machine, giving full access to the data.

The best solution to those problems is to move the protection level down to the data itself. After all, this is really what we want to protect! The most foolproof way to protect the data itself is to scramble (or encrypt) it so that it becomes incomprehensible to unauthorized persons. There are two basic procedures for encrypting data: code systems and cipher systems.

Code Systems

Code systems are based on using a code book to transform the data to its encoded form. There are two basic code book systems: the dictionary type and the key tape type.

Dictionary Systems

Code book systems use a special kind of dictionary code book, to translate the original (plaintext) data to and from its encrypted form (ciphertext). Figure 8-2 shows how a code book would be used to encrypt the message "secret message."

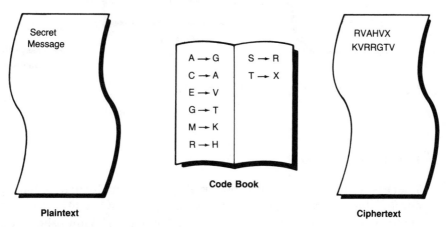

Fig. 8-2.   Simple code book example.

A code book can be devised that will encrypt bytes, letters, words, or phrases. The problem with using a code book is that our data is (usually) not a collection of random information, so it has patterns that are passed on to the encrypted data. The presence of those patterns in the ciphertext gives the codebreaker a great starting point from which to decode the data. For example: the letter e is the most frequently used letter in the English alphabet. If our code book translates every occurrence of the letter e to d, the most frequent letter in our ciphertext will be d. When our ciphertext is analyzed, it will immediately be apparent that d is the most frequent letter, thus leading to the conclusion that it represents the letter e. This is a first step in decrypting our message.

We could improve this technique by changing our code book frequently before the patterns are revealed in the ciphertext (the longer the text the more patterns will emerge). The ideal frequency for changing the code book is to never use the same entry in the code book more than once. For example: first translate e to q, but the second time an e is encountered, translate it to b and so on, never using the same code book entries twice. Figure 8-3 shows how such a nonrepeating code book would be used to encrypt the message "secret message."

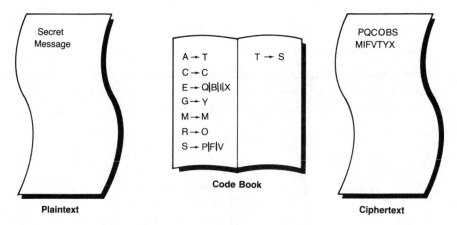

Fig. 8-3.   Nonrepeating code book example.

Key Tape Systems

There is another way to use a code book type system. Instead of having a dictionary (in which some entries will be used many times while others may not be used at all), we could use a code book composed of data to be imposed *on* the plaintext instead of replacing the plaintext. This type of code book is called a key tape. Imposing one type of data on another can be done in many ways. A simple and common way to impose the key tape on the plaintext is by the use of the XOR (exclusive or) function (bit wise modula 2 addition).

The XOR function is defined as follows:

```
0 XOR 0 = 0
0 XOR 1 = 1
1 XOR 0 = 1
1 XOR 1 = 0
```

If our key tape is a random collection of ones and zeros, we could represent our data in a similar form (by using ASCII for example) and then XOR our data with the key tape to generate the ciphertext. To decrypt, we would XOR the ciphertext with the same key tape that was used for encryption. Let's look at an example. Assume "MSDOS" is our plaintext. This is represented in binary (using the ASCII codes of the letters) as

```
0100 1101 0101 0011 0100 0100 0100 1111 0101 0011
```

If our key tape is

```
0100 0110 0111 0011 1001 0000 1100 0110 1011 0100
```

the ciphertext (plaintext XOR key tape) would be

```
0000 1011 0010 0000 1101 0100 1000 1001 1110 0111
```

When we XOR the ciphertext with the key tape again, we get

```
0100 1101 0101 0011 0100 0100 0100 1111 0101 0011
```

which is our original plaintext.

A system such as this, where the key tape is random and is used only once, is called a one-time pad (or tape) system. Such a system is absolutely unbreakable without knowledge of the key tape. The big disadvantage of this type of system is that the length of the key tape must be at least as long as the message we want to encrypt, and if we have a safe way of storing or transmitting the key tape (or code book), why not just use that same means for the message instead? Still, code book and one-time pad systems do have their uses. In the military, for example, the code book (or key tape) could be distributed during peacetime when safe distribution methods were available. Encrypted messages would be transmitted at wartime.

Cipher Systems

The other procedure for encrypting data is by using a cipher system. In a cipher system, there are two elements: an algorithm and keys. The algorithm enables the use of a short key to encrypt a long plaintext.

Before we look at some cipher systems we should look at our "enemy," the one trying to break our system. The following are some assumptions we should make about the enemy if we want to develop a strong cipher system:

- ► He or she is just as intelligent as we are and is familiar with the art of cryptography.

- ► At the enemy's disposal are the tools needed for serious cryptographic work, including such things as letters- and words-frequency information and a high-speed computer.

- ► Our enemy is in no hurry to break our system. Different data have different secrecy durations, but let us assume the data we are protecting should be kept secret for a long time. Of course, if it takes a thousand years to break our system we have a good cipher system—since most data will not be secret or useful by the time the system is broken.

- ► The enemy knows our encryption algorithm. This is a good assumption to make (though there is no need to give the algorithm away on purpose) since we would not like our whole cryptosystem rendered useless if the enemy managed to get one of our encrypting devices (by getting into our embassy, for example). Once the enemy has our encrypting device, it can be reverse engineered and its algorithm revealed.

Data Encryption Standard (DES)

One important cryptosystem is the Data Encryption Standard (DES), a federal standard algorithm for data encryption (U.S. Dept. of Commerce 1977).

Though some may doubt the wisdom of publishing an algorithm for data encryption, we did assume that the enemy knows our algorithm, and by having a standard, there is a way for people to use a good, tested algorithm instead of forcing them to devise their own untested (and usually very weak) method.

DES was originally developed after years of work by IBM, was later adopted as a standard. Before adoption, the algorithm was rigidly tested by the National Security Agency (NSA), and was declared free of any statistical or mathematical weaknesses. This suggests that it is impossible to break the system using statistical methods (such as frequency tables) or to work the algorithm backward using mathematical methods. DES is used by federal departments and agencies to protect all sensitive computer data (excluding some data classified according to the National Security Act of 1947 and the Atomic Energy Act of 1954). DES is also used by many nongovernment institutions, including most banks and money transfer systems.

The DES Algorithm

DES works on blocks of 8 bytes (64 bits), encrypting (or decrypting) them using a 56-bit external (user-supplied) key. Due to the algorithm's complexity and length, we will not go into it in full detail.

First, 16 internal keys ($K_1, K_2 \ldots K_{16}$) are created from the external key using a variety of permutations and left shifts (rotation).

Next, let's consider the block to be encrypted as a collection of bits numbered 1,2,3 . . . 64 (see Figure 8-4). First the block is subject to an *initial permutation* stage, which rearranges the location of the bits. The output is then divided into two parts, left (L_0) and right (R_0), each consisting of 32 bits. The algorithm has 16 steps. Each step receives as input the L and R of the previous stage and outputs a new L and R.

At each stage n (n = 1 to 16) the following is performed:

$$L_n = R_{n-1}$$

The new left part is equal to the previous right part.

$$R_n = L_{n-1} \text{ XOR } f(R_{n-1}, K_n)$$

The new right part is equal to the previous left part XORed with the output of the Function f (whose inputs are the old right part and the nth internal key (K_n)).

The output of the 16th step is then treated by an *inverse of the initial permutation* and is the final encrypted output. Decryption is done by passing the encrypted data through the same algorithm in reverse. The cipher Function f is defined as

1. The 32-bit R (right part) is expanded to 48 bits and is now called ER (this is done by a bit selection table).

2. ER is XORed with K_n (the nth internal key) giving us 48 bits. These are divided into 8 blocks of 6 bits each, which are called $B_1, B_2 \ldots B_8$.

3. There are 8 substitution functions (S boxes) called $S_1, S_2 \ldots S_8$. Every S box gets an 8-bit input and gives a 6-bit output. Thus B_1 would go into S_1 to yield a 6-bit output, B_2 would go into S_2, etc. All the outputs together are the 32-bit output.

4. The output of the last stage is again permutated giving the final output of the Function f.

Note that all the exact permutations, S boxes, bit-selection tables, shifts, substitutions, etc., used in DES are specified in the standard (but are too lengthy to be presented here).

There is no doubt that the DES is a strong cryptosystem. The strength of DES is not only theoretical—it has remained unbroken in spite of many years of widespread use. However, DES does have potential flaws. First, some patterns in the plaintext will be seen in the ciphertext. If we have identical blocks of plaintext (for example, blocks of 8 consecutive blanks), they will be encrypted to identical ciphertext (when we use the same key). Another weakness of the DES has to do with the relatively short key used, only 56 bits. Thus, there are 2^{56} (about 7.2

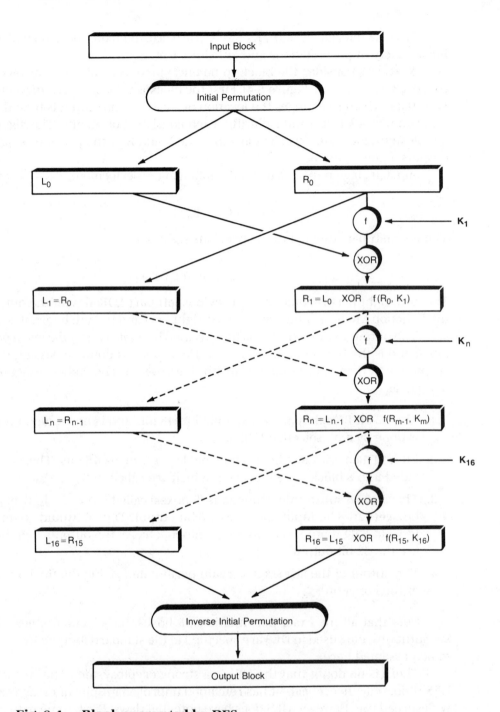

Fig. 8-4.   Block encrypted by DES.

$\times$ 10^{16}) possible keys. It might be possible to devise a special multiprocessor computer that will break messages encrypted by DES by the "brutal force" approach, that is, by generating all possible keys. Such a powerful computer, if it can be developed at all, is only within the development capacity of the security agencies of the superpowers.

The DES is an example of a conventional cryptosystem. In such systems, there is only one key which is used both to encrypt and decrypt the data. If two persons want to pass secret data from one to the other, they must both know the same key, so a safe way to transfer the key is needed.

The following example was created with the `File Encrypt` program. The program is a full DES implementation (that also performs a pre-DES key manipulation to facilitate using the full range of external keys DES can handle).

```
plaintext "MS - DOS" in hex: 4D 53 20 2D 20 44 4F 53
ciphertext (key="DES") in hex: 3F 8D DD 29 E7 80 31 1B
```

Key Selection and Management

For using DES (as well as other encryption and password systems), we must choose secret keys (or passwords). Though this may seem an easy task, it is not. A good key is one which cannot be guessed easily, yet one that we can easily remember. Using a good ciphersystem such as DES will not help us if we keep a written note of our password lying around. On the other hand, forgetting the key used to encrypt data with DES will make decryption absolutely impossible. The worst keys are the most obvious ones: IBMPC, names of people or places, telephone numbers, birthdates, English words (there is only a limited number of words and a computer can try all of them very quickly), etc. Reasonably good keys are those that would seem random to anyone but you, yet you have a method to remember them, for example, the third letter of every word of a famous saying. As a rule of thumb, longer keys and keys that contain different types of symbols (such as letters and numbers) are to be preferred. The best keys are those which are randomly generated, but they are easily forgotten. This problem can be overcome by keeping all the passwords in a file that is encrypted with a master password.

RSA and Public Key Systems

In a public key cryptosystem, keys come in "matching" pairs. One key (the public key) is used to encrypt and the other key (the private key) is used to decrypt data that was encrypted with the matching public key. Obviously, it is critical that the private key cannot be derived from knowledge of the public key. The advantage of a public key cryptosystem over a conventional one is that there is no need to have a safe method to transfer keys between different parties. It is possible to publish a telephone book listing the public keys of all the users of the system. If party A wants to encrypt a message so that only party B can access it, the public key of party B will be used, but only the private (secret) key of party B can be used to decrypt such a message, as shown in Figure 8-5.

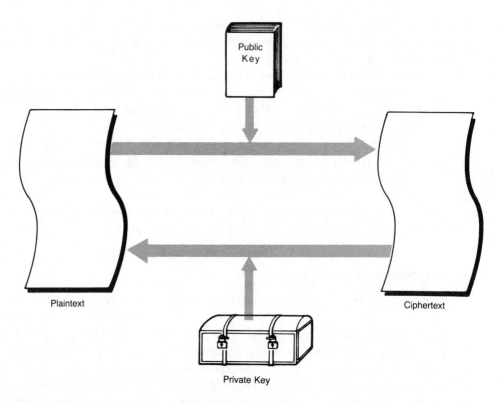

Fig. 8-5. Public key cryptosystem.

Public key cryptosystems are based on the use of trapdoor one-way functions. The term "one-way" suggests that it is easy to compute the function in one way (encrypt the data if you know the public key), but it is very difficult to compute it in the other direction (decrypt the data). The term "trapdoor" suggests that if you have certain secret knowledge (the private key), it becomes easy to compute the function in the other direction (decrypt). The most important public key system today is RSA, named after its inventors: Rivest, Shamir, and Adleman. We will look at the RSA algorithm in some detail. Do not be worried if you get lost in the calculations; you can get the general idea of the algorithm without necessarily following all the calculation's details.

Before we can understand the RSA algorithm we need to define a few terms:

Prime Number. p is a prime number if it has only two divisors (1 and p). Examples of prime numbers are: 3, 5, 7, 11, 13, etc.

Relatively Prime. Two numbers: e and d are called relatively prime if they have no common divisor except 1. For example: 9 (whose divisors are 1, 3, 9) is relatively prime to 10 (divisors 1, 2, 5, 10) while 9 is not relatively prime to 12 since 3 is a common divisor of both.

Modula. If i and j are integers, i modula j is the remainder of dividing i by j using integer division. For example: 31 modula 3 is 1 because 31 ÷ 3 = 10 and 1 remainder; 5 modula 3 = 2 (5 ÷ 3 = 1 and 2 remainder); 20 modula 5 = 0 (20 ÷ 5 = 4 with 0 remainder).

To use the RSA algorithm, we first generate our private and public keys with the following procedure:

1. Choose two very large prime numbers; call them p and q.

2. Define n as the product of p and q (n = p × q).

3. Pick a large random number, to be named d, which is relatively prime to (p − 1) × (q − 1).

4. Define an integer e, so that (e × d) modula ((p − 1) × (q − 1)) = 1.

5. Establish our public key as the set of two numbers n and e, and our private key as the set of numbers n and d.

Now when we want to encrypt data for a person whose public key is (e, n), we would do the following:

First, represent the plaintext as an integer between 0 and n-1. This is done by breaking the plaintext into a series of blocks, and representing each block as an integer. Let's call the number representing our plaintext block M. Next, raise M to the power e. The modula n of this is the ciphertext for this block, and will be named C.

To decrypt the message, using the corresponding private key (d, n), one should raise C to the power d. The modula n of this is the original plaintext.

Here is a simple example using the procedure just listed:

1. Choose p = 3 and q = 11 (in practice we would use much larger primes—100-digit or more primes are suggested).

2. n = 33 (3 × 11)

3. (p − 1) × (q − 1) = 20 so we need a number relatively prime to 20, for example: 3, i.e., d = 3.

4. We need to choose e so that (e × d) modula ((p − 1) × (q − 1)) = 1. In our case (e × 3) modula 20 = 1. So we can use e = 7 (7 × 3 = 21 and 21 modula 20 = 1 because 21 ÷ 20 = 1 and 1 remainder).

5. We publish our public key as n = 20 and e = 7. Our private is (3, 20), meaning n = 20 and d = 3.

Now, suppose someone wants to send us the message

CAB

First, the sender represents the message as blocks of numbers with values 0 to 32. Let's assume the representation is A = 1, B = 2, etc., so the numeric representation of the message is 3 1 2. Next, the sender looks up our public key which is (7, 33) (e, n). Now comes the process of encrypting the message by raising the value of every block to the power 7 modula 33 as shown in Table 8-2. The numeric representation of the encrypted message is: 9 1 29.

Table 8-2.   Encryption Conversion Chart

M block	To the power of 7 (e)	Modula 33 (n)
3	2187	9
1	1	1
2	128	29

When we receive this message we decrypt it by raising every block to the power 3 (d) modula 33 (n) as shown in Table 8-3. The decrypted message is: 3 1 2, the original message.

Table 8-3.   Decryption Conversion Chart

Encrypted block	To the power of 3 (d)	Modula 33 (n)
9	729	3
1	1	1
29	24389	2

The strength of RSA is based on the assumption that it is very hard to derive the private key from the public key. This is based on the fact that the private key can be derived by factoring (finding the divisors of) n. Since n is a very large number (a number with at least 200 digits is recommended) and there are no known effective algorithms to factor such large numbers, it would take very long to do this (requiring over 10^{23} operations). Unfortunately, the fact that until now no efficient algorithm was found to factor very large numbers does not prove that no such algorithm exists, and if such an algorithm is found, this system will become worthless. Also, there might be a yet unknown algorithm to derive at the secret key d without having to factor n.

Data Encryption and MS-DOS

In password protection systems, we found that implementing them at lower access levels (BIOS instead of DOS) improves the system by making bypassing more difficult. On the other hand, in a system based on data encryption, it is better to implement the system at higher access levels, consequently achieving greater control over who has what access to which data. Here, we are not worried about the system being bypassed—anyone is welcome to look at our encrypted data.

An encryption system that works at the BIOS level (intercepts software Interrupt 13h) must treat the hard disk it protects as one whole unit, either granting or denying access to it all. On the other hand, if our encryption system intercepts data access requests at the DOS level, it is possible to give various people different access privileges by encrypting different files with different keys. The ideal place for the encryption software is within the application that uses the data. This enables access control down to a record or even a field level. For example, only the company's directors have access to the president's salary whereas all the secretaries may read the president's home phone number.

Loopholes in MS-DOS Data Security

MS-DOS, unfortunately, was not built with data security in mind, so there are many loopholes which make sensitive data more vulnerable, even when an encryption system is in use.

Deleting a File

When you delete a file using the MS-DOS DELETE command, or if a program deletes a file using the delete file function of DOS, the file is not really deleted, it is only marked as such. The file's data is actually left untouched on the media. For DOS, deleting a file means: marking the FAT entries of the file's clusters as "unallocated clusters," and marking the file's directory entry as "unused."

Since the data that was once your file is still on the media, it may still be accessed (for example, through BIOS using absolute sector addresses) and in some cases, the entire file can be reconstructed. The data is never really deleted, but we hope when the cluster that has your old file's data is allocated to a new file, the new file's data will overwrite it. Why use the word "hope"?

As you recall, the clusters on your hard disk are made up of multiple sectors. When your old file's cluster is allocated to a new file, which only needs the space of some of the sectors, only the data in those sectors will be overwritten by new data. This implies that many of your current files have data of old deleted files appended to them at the end (DOS knows how much data belongs to the current file according to the file length field in the directory).

The solution to this loophole is to physically overwrite the data in your files (with zeros for instance) *before* requesting DOS to DELETE the file (many utility programs can do this, including the Scratch option of File Encrypt).

Formatting a Hard Disk

When MS-DOS formats a hard disk (unlike a diskette), it does not really do a hardware format (the process of creating sectors in the tracks). Although the FAT now indicates that all the clusters are unallocated and the root directory now shows that there are no files, actually, all the data that was on the disk before the format is still there.

My solution: do not rely on the DOS FORMAT command to delete the disk's data. Instead, overwrite the data or use a hardware-formatting program.

Data "Leftovers"

DOS accumulates the data before writing it to the disk in RAM buffers. The smallest amount of data that can be written to a disk is one whole sector (512 bytes). Thus, at a file's end, though DOS may have less data to write, 512 bytes will always be written. The data in this unused part of the buffer is unpredictable. In reality, this will be whichever data just happened to be in the space used as the buffer. This can easily be your secret data that just happened to be in the wrong place at the wrong time.

The obvious conclusion is: do not leave any data "leftovers" in the computer's RAM. When you are finished using a program that accesses sensitive data, turn off the computer and so clear all the RAM. Turning off the power will not only prevent someone who uses the computer after you from looking at the leftover data in RAM, but will also prevent DOS from using your sensitive data as padding for clusters. Of course, programs which are data security-conscious will nullify all the decrypted data left in RAM upon their termination. Regrettably, there are very few such programs.

Summary

In this paper, we reviewed some of the means available to protect your data in the MS-DOS environment. The unavoidable conclusion we have reached is that any efficient data security system must be based on encrypting the data. The algorithm used in an encryption system should preferably be DES or a variation based on DES, but so-called proprietary algorithms should usually be avoided since they are almost always very simple to break.

We can only hope that the increase in computer security problems will motivate more software developers to incorporate strong security measures into their programs. Until then, we can protect our data by the use of stand-alone encryption software.

> The File Encrypt software, a full DES encryption program for the IBM PC written in assembly language for maximum speed, is available for $69.95 (check or money order, California residents add sales tax) from: Wisdom Software, Inc.; P. O. Box 146310; San Francisco, CA 94114-6310 (Phone 415/566-0754. The program runs under both MS-DOS and OS/2 protected mode. For source code availability and integration with other software, contact the author at the above address.

Reading List

Meyer, C. and S. Matys. 1982. *Cryptography: A New Dimension in Computer Data Security*. New York: John Wiley & Sons, Inc.
▶ This book has a strong emphasis on DES. Since one of the authors was a codesigner of DES, the book is obviously biased in favor of DES.

Rivest, R., A. Shamir, and L. Adleman. 1978. A method for obtaining digital signatures and public-key cryptosystems. *Communications of the ACM* 21, no. 2.
▶ This is the original RSA paper written by its inventors. It has more details on the algorithm than we examined here including methods to derive at the large primes needed to implement such a system. This paper is obviously biased in favor of RSA.

U.S. Dept. of Commerce/National Bureau of Stds. 1977. *Data Encryption Standard*. Federal Information Processing Standards Publication 46.
▶ This is the official DES definition and has the algorithm in full detail.

Asael Dror has been programming computers ranging from mainframes to micros for over 11 years. He is an expert in the fields of system and communication software with special interest in computer languages and computer security. He is the author of the File Encrypt program for the IBM PC and the founder of WisdomSoftware, Inc., located in San Francisco.

Related Essays

1 A Guided Tour inside MS-DOS
6 Undocumented MS-DOS Functions
7 Safe Memory-Resident Programs (TSR)
10 Developing MS-DOS Device Drivers

Keywords

► Microsoft Windows

► modeless interfaces

► object-oriented programming

► window functions

► window classes

► messages

► SPY program

Essay Synopsis: To the casual user, Microsoft Windows simply brings a "Mac-like" interface to MS-DOS machines, with windows, pull-down menus, dialog boxes, and other features that make it easy to select and switch between programs. To the programmer, however, MS Windows represents a new way of thinking about the relationship between applications and their environment. This essay will introduce programmers to the Windows way of thinking. Additionally, most of the concepts discussed will carry over directly to the Presentation Manager under OS/2 1.1. Windows offers programmers powerful tools for building user interfaces. However, using Windows effectively demands that programmers break out of the mold of classic MS-DOS programs that run, take input, process, produce output, and then terminate. In Windows, programs must constantly communicate with the environment to keep track of user requests and to manage resources. As both a learning aid and a practical tool, this essay presents a handy program called SPY. This program is your "private eye" on the Windows environment. You will find it useful both for learning about Windows and for helping to debug Windows applications.

9

Inside Microsoft Windows

Michael Geary

Microsoft Windows is an operating environment and software library designed to let you write MS-DOS applications with a modeless, graphical user interface. This user interface bears a striking resemblance to the Macintosh and, likewise, Windows programming and Macintosh programming share many important concepts. In particular, the modeless user interface requires an application program structure that's quite different from traditional DOS applications.

Who's in Charge Here?

What do we mean by a modeless user interface? Many application programs have their user interfaces built around a variety of different modes. A mode is simply a particular state in a program that changes the meaning of the user's input or limits the choices the user has available. For example, some word processors have a menu mode, edit mode, insert mode, delete mode, and perhaps a few others. The menu mode may well have several levels of submodes within itself: you make one menu choice, it leads to another, and another, until you finally select the operation you wanted in the first place. Modes are often used in a well-intentioned attempt to simplify things for the user, but they usually backfire. The novice user is puzzled—and the experienced user irritated—when choices are restricted this way. It's the old problem of, "I'm *here* in the menu tree, now how do I get over *there*?!"

Unfortunately, modes happen to be convenient for the application programmer. As soon as you write a little piece of code like this:

```
printf( "Enter account number:" );
scanf( "%10s", acctnum );
```

you have put the user into enter-account-number mode. If the user has forgotten the account number, it's time to escape out of this section of the program, work through a couple of menus to get to the account number list, exit back out through those menus again, and come back through more menus back to enter-account-number mode. Yet, this kind of code is so easy to write that many applications are programmed this way: prompt the user and input a choice, prompt again and input another choice. At each step, the user is limited to just those options that the program allows at that point.

One of the main goals of MS Windows is to avoid this kind of user interface, replacing it with one in which the user, not the programmer, is in charge. To accomplish this takes a radical restructuring of applications. (See Essay 1, A Guided Tour inside MS-DOS, by Harry Henderson, for a general discussion of approaches to the MS-DOS user interface.)

There are many different kinds of windows you can use, and just choosing how to set up the different windows can be a real challenge. The program we present called SPY can tell you what kinds of windows any application uses, and is also a handy tool for debugging your own applications to see if your windows are set up the way you intended.

Windows and Messages

The way Windows avoids modes and puts the user in control is by doing just the opposite of a traditional DOS application. Instead of letting the program's flow of control be the governing factor, a Windows application spends most of its time waiting for *messages*. In general, each message is directed toward a specific window. Each window in an application has a *window function*, whose job is to process messages for that window.

For example, if the user clicks the left mouse button in a window, Windows generates a `WM_LBUTTONDOWN` message to notify the window function that the button is down, and then a `WM_LBUTTONUP` message when the button is released. These messages are delivered to the window function through calls to that function. Note that the application doesn't "ask" for mouse input—it's the user's action of pressing the button that causes this input. A window function never knows what message it is going to receive next. When it receives any particular message, its job is to process that message and then return as soon as possible. In fact, one good way to think of a window function is as a little machine whose job is to respond to messages generated by the user or by Windows. The fact that window functions process messages generated by the user's actions, instead of asking the user for input, allows the existence of the modeless user interface.

MS Windows generates messages for mouse and keyboard input and also for every other situation where an application needs to be notified of some event. For example, there are messages to let a window know when its size or position has changed, when it needs to have its contents redisplayed, or when a menu selection is made. Messages are one of the most important keys to understanding Windows applications.

Getting the Message: WinMain and Friends

How does a message actually get to a window function? First, each application has a *message queue*, a first-in, first-out (FIFO) queue to hold messages waiting to be processed. A message queue is needed simply to allow type-ahead and "mouse-ahead." (The standard IBM BIOS type-ahead buffer would be inadequate for Windows applications—Windows provides much more extensive keyboard information to the application.)

The main program of any Windows application looks something like this (the example is simplified and will not run in this form):

```
int WinMain()
{
    MSG   msg;

    /* Any initialization would go here */

    /* Main message loop: */
    while( GetMessage( &msg ) ) {
        DispatchMessage( &msg );
    }

    return 0;
}
```

As you can see, there's not much to it—after doing any needed initialization (such as creating the application's windows), the program settles into a loop calling `GetMessage` and `DispatchMessage`. `GetMessage` retrieves the next message from the application's message queue and fills in the `msg` structure with information describing the message. This structure includes

▶ the *window handle* for the window that is to receive this message (When you create a window, Windows assigns a window handle to it and returns that handle to you. Every time you refer to a window, you use its window handle, and each message for a window includes the window handle.)

▶ the *message number*, a numeric code identifying the message (These codes are represented by `#define` constants in C, such as the `WM_LBUTTONDOWN` and `WM_LBUTTONUP` messages we mentioned above.)

▶ two additional parameters, called wParam and lParam (These are a 16-bit value and a 32-bit value, respectively, and contain information that varies depending on the particular message number.)

▶ the mouse position and the time in milliseconds since Windows was started (These two structure fields are usually ignored, since the same information is repeated in wParam or lParam for those messages that deal with mouse position or time of day.)

Strangely, WinMain doesn't do anything with all this information once it's received it except immediately call DispatchMessage, passing it the msg structure. This is where the real work begins, because DispatchMessage calls the window function, passing it the information from the msg structure.

Actually, Windows could have done all this internally. The reason for having this message loop in the application itself instead of down inside Windows is just to give a little more flexibility—there are always those situations where you want to get sneaky and do something a little out of the ordinary with messages. This message loop gives you one more place to do that, by putting extra logic between the GetMessage and DispatchMessage calls. MS Windows provides several functions such as IsDialogMessage that are used this way.

Window Functions

When DispatchMessage receives a message, it calls the window function for the appropriate window. A window function looks something like this:

```
LONG FAR PASCAL ThisWindowFunction( hWnd, wMsg, wParam, lParam )
      HWND      hWnd;       /* Window handle */
      WORD      wMsg;       /* Message number (WM_something) */
      WORD      wParam;     /* 16-bit parameter */
      LONG      lParam;     /* 32-bit parameter */
{
      switch( wMsg )
      {
            case WM_xxxxxxxx:
                  /* process one kind of message */
                  return 0L;

            case WM_yyyyyyyy:
                  /* process another kind of message */
                  return 0L;
      }
```

```
/* default processing for all other messages: */
return DefWindowProc( hWnd, wMsg, wParam, lParam );
}
```

The parameters to the window function correspond to the fields we described for the message structure in `WinMain`; they just happen to be individual parameters instead of structure fields at this point. Note that the window function is quite simple: it's just a big `switch` statement, listing each of the messages that the application wishes to process for this window. After processing any given message, the function returns. (The return value isn't always 0; for some messages, the return value is significant.)

All messages that aren't handled explicitly are passed along to a special Windows function called `DefWindowProc`. This function provides the default processing for all messages. Many messages are simply ignored by `DefWindowProc`—keyboard and mouse messages, for example. If you don't process mouse input, it's ignored. There are some messages that must be processed, however, and `DefWindowProc` takes care of these for you. An example would be the `WM_NCPAINT` message, which causes the border, title bar, and scroll bars for a window to be displayed.

`DefWindowProc` also has defaults for some messages that you might want to handle specially. For example, the `WM_CLOSE` message is a request to destroy (close) a window. `DefWindowProc` calls the `DestroyWindow` function, so the window is immediately destroyed. Many applications' window functions process this message themselves, so they can put up a "Do you want to save . . ." message and call `DestroyWindow` only if the user confirms.

In fact, that is why there is a default window function like this. It would have been possible for Windows to just automatically take the "standard" actions for various messages and never send them to your window function in the first place. Many of the messages passed to `DefWindowProc` are ones you're not likely to be interested in, but passing them through your window function gives you the chance to intercept any and do something special with them when necessary.

Events of the Day

Messages provide a natural way to handle keyboard and mouse (or other pointing device) input without locking the user into different input modes. Windows generates messages for every keystroke, mouse click, and mouse movement, and addresses each message to a particular window.

Mouse Messages

Mouse messages are generally sent to the window underneath the mouse cursor. When the user rolls the mouse around, Windows sends `WM_MOUSEMOVE` messages to each window the cursor moves across. These messages include the mouse cursor position, relative to the window's client area, along with a set of bits telling which mouse buttons are down and whether the Ctrl or Shift keys are down. There's also a message sent each time the user presses, releases, or double-clicks a mouse button. Although many Windows applications use only a single mouse button, Windows supports up to three buttons, and each button can generate those three kinds of messages. The WM_LBUTTONDOWN and WM_LBUTTONUP messages fall into this category.

There is an important exception to the rule that mouse messages go wherever the mouse is pointed. Any window can take over mouse input with the SetCapture function. This function causes all subsequent mouse messages to be directed to a specific window. No other window will get mouse messages until ReleaseCapture is called. These functions are commonly used for "dragging" operations. The application calls SetCapture when the user presses the mouse button and ReleaseCapture when the button is released. In between, the capture window specified in the SetCapture call gets all the WM_MOUSEMOVE messages. The autoscrolling during this lets the window control the dragging without "losing" the mouse if the user happens to roll it past the edge of the window. Text selection in Notepad or Write is an example of this use of SetCapture and ReleaseCapture.

Keyboard Messages

If you have ever struggled with the restricted keyboard interface of DOS and BIOS, you will really appreciate the flexibility of Windows' keyboard handling. Unlike BIOS, which throws away perfectly valid keystrokes like the infamous "5" key on the numeric pad, Windows sends keyboard messages on *every* keyboard event. Your window function gets a WM_KEYDOWN message each time a key is pressed, and a WM_KEYUP message each time a key is released—for every key, even the shift keys. Windows defines a list of virtual key codes, and passes you that code as well as the actual keyboard scan code. Autorepeat keys also generate WM_KEYDOWN messages, but there's a flag passed with the message telling you whether it's an actual keypress or an autorepeat. This gives you complete control over the keyboard handling.

Windows pushbuttons are a good example of the kind of flexibility these keyboard messages can give. When you press the space bar on a pushbutton, the button is highlighted, remains highlighted while you hold the space bar down, and goes back to its normal state when you release the space bar. It also sends the parent window function a notification message (I've been clicked) when you release the space bar. Under DOS, you couldn't have this kind of user interface without writing your own keyboard interrupt handler, because BIOS doesn't tell you when the key is released. With Windows, it's easy: Highlight the button on the first WM_KEYDOWN, ignore the autorepeat WM_KEYDOWN messages (by checking the autorepeat flag), and on the WM_KEYUP, remove the highlight and send the notification message.

Besides this raw keyboard handling, there is an ASCII keyboard message available as well. This message, WM_CHAR, is more like the traditional keyboard input. You get a WM_CHAR message for every actual ASCII character input. For example, if you press Shift-A, you get four raw messages: WM_KEYDOWN of the Shift key, WM_KEYDOWN of the A key (but it doesn't tell you whether it's an upper- or lowercase A!), WM_KEYUP of the A key, and WM_KEYUP of the Shift key. You just get a single WM_CHAR message, with the ASCII code for capital A. You can use the keyboard at whichever level suits your application, or mix and match as needed. It's common to check the WM_KEYDOWN and WM_KEYUP messages for cursor keys and similar functions, and the WM_CHAR messages for actual text input.

Input Focus

One question remains: How does Windows know where to send keyboard input? At any time, one window owns the input focus, and keyboard input is always sent to this window. This is different from the mouse, which sends messages to different windows as you roll across them. Keyboard input goes to the window with the input focus, regardless of where the mouse is located. The user can set the input focus to a window by clicking the mouse in it, by using the Alt-Tab/Alt-Esc keys to switch among the windows, or by calling the SetFocus function to change the input focus to a different window.

When the Windows user changes from one window to another with a mouse click or the Alt keys, that actually doesn't directly set the input focus to that window. First, the window becomes the *active window* and receives a WM_ACTIVATE message. The active window and input focus are closely related, but not the same. The default processing for WM_ACTIVATE does set the input focus to that same window with a SetFocus call, but it doesn't have to be the same. For example, in a dialog box, the active window is the dialog box window itself, but the input focus is directed to one of the items inside the dialog box. This is done by processing the WM_ACTIVATE message. Also, if a window is iconic, it generally doesn't take any keyboard input other than the Alt keys, so the default code for WM_ACTIVATE doesn't set the input focus there if the window is iconic. By the way, Windows sends WM_SETFOCUS and WM_KILLFOCUS messages to your window function to let it know when it is getting and losing the input focus. (If all these messages were telegrams, your Windows application could make Western Union rich!)

Window Rectangles

The screen area for a window is defined by two rectangles: the window and the client. The former gives the window position on the size on the screen and corresponds to the actual border of the window. The client rectangle defines an area within the window rectangle that the application's window function (the "client") will use. The region in between—the title bar, menu bar, scroll bars, fat borders, etc.—is called the "non-client area." Normally, a default window function inside Windows manages this area, but an application program can take over if it needs to. The client area is really a coding convenience, giving the window function a nice, well-defined area it can work in.

Window Styles: Overlapped, Popup, Child

There are three major categories of windows: overlapped, popup, and child. The main difference between them is the screen space they reside in. Overlapped and popup windows share the full screen as their display space, and are defined in terms of absolute screen coordinates. They are clipped at the edge of the screen, and also clipped relative to each other wherever they overlap. This means they won't interfere with each other's display space. If a portion of one window is hidden by another window sitting on top of it, any attempt to display something in the hidden portion is ignored.

What's the difference between an overlapped and a popup window, if they can all overlap each other? Well, "overlapped" is a bit of a misnomer, since popup windows can also overlap. The fact that we even have these two different styles is a holdover from MS Windows 1.X. The overlapped windows used to be tiled windows, which were different from popups. The difference is this: overlapped windows are all independent of each other and can be made iconic. Popup windows cannot be made iconic, and they often have a parent window, which may be either an overlapped window or another popup. If a popup window has a parent, then making the parent iconic will make the popup window disappear until the parent is made visible again. Also, the popup window will always be "on top" of its parent—if the user tries to bring the parent window to the top, the popup will still be on top of it. In most Windows applications, the main application window is an overlapped window and any dialog boxes are popup windows.

Child Windows

A child window always has a parent, and is always displayed within its parent's client area. Child windows can overlap each other, but they are always clipped at the edge of the parent's client area. A child window will never show up outside the boundaries of its parent, and if you move a window, all its child windows come along with it. Child windows are defined in their parent's client coordinates, that is, a child window with an origin of (0,0) would be at the top left corner of its parent's client area.

Child windows are used extensively in Windows applications, as Figure 9-1 shows. The control panel has a main window containing one child window. Inside that child window are several other child windows, the individual components of the control panel. Child windows provide a handy way to provide different kinds of behavior in different areas of a single application window since each child window has its own window function. For example, the MS-DOS Executive has three separate child windows: one for the little disk pictures, one for the current directory path, and one for all the filenames. This way, each child window function can handle its own operations without worrying about the others—you just create the windows and let them run. Child windows are also handy when you want to take advantage of code that's already been written. All the items in a dialog box are child windows and use window functions that have been provided as part of Windows. You don't have to write your own code to put a little edit field inside a dialog box, for example.

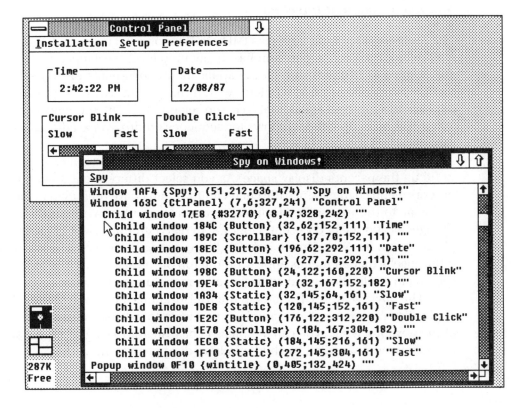

Fig. 9-1.   Windows within windows.

The child windows in the MS-DOS Executive window are not readily apparent to the user. In fact, it takes a program like SPY to reveal them. They are just a coding convenience for the MSDOS.EXE program. The exact same application could have been written with a single window and explicit code to handle things like mouse hit-testing (determining which area the mouse was clicked in). Using child windows, however, helps you modularize your code, and also lets Windows do more of the work for you.

You can also create child windows that the user can directly manipulate. Child windows can have caption bars, sizing borders, and the like, letting the user move and size them. In fact, they can look just like overlapped or popup windows, and can operate much the same except for being located in their parent's client area.

One of the few limitations on a child window is that it can't have any menu of its own. It can have a system menu, but no menu bar of its own. (In Windows 1.X, a child window couldn't even have a system menu, only a close box. That's probably one of the most rarely seen features in Windows 1.X applications.)

Multiple Document Interface

The Multiple Document Interface (MDI) in Windows 2.0 makes extensive use of child windows. Each application has its own top-level overlapped window (and any popups as needed), and all the application's documents or views of documents are opened as child windows within this parent. For example, in a MIDI (Musical Instrument Digital Interface—no relation to MDI!) sequencer program, you might open up child windows for sequence editing, voice editing, MIDI parameters, and a control panel.

The child windows can be moved and sized, and even zoomed (maximized) to fill up the parent's display space. As you select different child windows, the parent's menu changes since the child windows can't have their own menus. This is similar to the way some Macintosh programs operate, wherein the title bar changes as you select different windows. In fact, running a set of Macintosh applications under MultiFinder is much like running Windows. The main visual difference is that all menus appear on the top of the screen on the Mac, where each main application window has its own menu under Windows.

The purpose of MDI is to help the user organize and control the different applications' windows. For example, if you want to get that music program out of the way for a while, you can minimize ("collapse" into a single graphic symbol) its main window, and all its child windows disappear along with it.

Window Classes

Often, you want to have several different windows that operate the same or a similar way. Suppose you have a dialog box with several edit fields. Each one is a window. (In fact, every item in a dialog box is a child window.) Although you need to be able to refer to each one individually, and each one has unique data including its text, the actual program code for each is the same. That suggests they ought to have a common window function and perhaps some common data, along with a block of data unique to each window.

That's exactly what a window class is, defining a collection of windows that share a common window function and have some other attributes in common as well. Windows comes with a number of predefined window classes. Most of these are the various controls or child windows used inside dialog boxes, such as the text editing and pushbutton controls. Applications can also create their own window classes. In fact, nearly every Windows application creates at least one new class for its main window.

You create a window class with the `RegisterClass` function, and thus specify the information that will be common to the windows of this class. `Register-Class` copies this information into Windows' own list of window classes, so that it becomes available for creating windows. This information includes

- the window class name (This is a text string that uniquely names the class. The predefined window classes that come with Windows include Edit (text editing window), Static (background text), Button (push button, radio button, check box), ScrollBar (horizontal or vertical scroll bar), and List (list box).)

- the window function address (This function gets called by Windows whenever there is a message for any window in this class.)

- the icon and cursor to be used for windows in this class

- the default menu and background color (or brush) for these windows

- the class style, several option bits affecting window operation

- two values indicating how much extra space to allocate in the class data structure and in each window data structure (Windows provides functions to read and write this extra data space, giving a convenient place to store additional information for your window functions to use—either data for the class as a whole or data that's unique for each window.)

Creating a Window

Once you've registered a window class, you can create as many windows of that class as you like, using the `CreateWindow` function. The parameters to `CreateWindow` include the information that's unique (or can be unique) to each instance of the window:

- the window title

- the parent window, if this is a child or popup window

- the window's position and size (For a child window, this is relative to the parent window's client area. Otherwise, it's the actual screen position.)

➤ the window's menu (optional, to override class menu)

➤ window style, a set of bit flags like the class style, but unique to this window (These style flags include things like whether the window has scroll bars, a title bar, or a sizing border.)

One remaining parameter to `CreateWindow` is the window class name. The information that was provided with the `RegisterClass` call applies to this window, as well as to the other windows of this class. That includes the window function. In the example we mentioned above, where you have several text edit fields in a dialog box, these are individual instances of the Edit class. Each one has a unique position on the screen and contains different text, but they all share a common window function, containing the code to do the actual text editing.

Where Do Messages Originate?

After you create a window with the `CreateWindow` function, the window function starts receiving all the messages we've been talking about. There are actually two very different ways a message can be originated: `SendMessage` and `PostMessage`. Most of the messages we discussed earlier, including keyboard and mouse input, are created with `PostMessage` calls (or some equivalent functions used internally by Windows). `PostMessage` places a message on an application's message queue, where it will be picked up later by a `GetMessage`/`DispatchMessage` loop, such as the one in `WinMain`.

There are some messages that `CreateWindow` sends directly to the window function during the window creation process, long before `CreateWindow` ever returns. These messages are created with a `SendMessage` call. `SendMessage` is essentially a direct subroutine call to a window function, bypassing the message queue. If you send messages of your own to a window function, the choice of whether to use `SendMessage` or `PostMessage` depends on whether you want the message to be processed immediately or queued up to be processed in sequence with other messages. Some messages return data to the caller—these are always sent with `SendMessage`. For example, you can send an `EM_GETSEL` message to an edit control window, and the return value from `SendMessage` will give you the beginning and end of the current selection in the edit control. `PostMessage` wouldn't work for this.

Graphics Programming in Windows

In Windows, you are doing graphics programming even if your program is text based. Really, that's always true—text is just one kind of graphics—but in Windows, there's no avoiding the fact. You've got to deal with some unfamiliar concepts just to print `Hello, world!`. We're not going to cover all the complexities of graphics here, but will touch on the major concepts needed to make text and simple graphics programs work.

Coordinate Systems and Points

Every time you do any graphics output (in any environment), it takes place in a particular coordinate system that represents either a virtual or physical display surface. For a DOS text-mode application, the coordinate system is the 80 × 25 screen, where you have X coordinates of 0 through 79 and Y coordinates of 0 through 24. A coordinate system is simply some method for relating X and Y coordinates to an actual display, and a point is an (X,Y) coordinate pair.

In Windows, each window has two coordinate systems: device (physical) and logical. Device coordinates refer to actual device pixels, but are normally offset so that (0,0) is the top left corner of the window's client area. Logical coordinates can be assigned in several different ways, either equal to device coordinates or transformed through some formula to scale the coordinate size. This lets you do tricks like the `CLOCK` and `REVERSI` programs, i.e., automatically size your image to fit the window size without having to do all the scaling computations yourself. The mapping mode you use determines how logical coordinates are interpreted.

For a simple text program like SPY, the easiest thing to do is disregard the fancier mapping modes and use the default one, called `MM_TEXT`. In this mode, you are always dealing in terms of actual device pixels, so the one complexity is that you have to find out how large the characters actually are. Since the font size varies with different displays and fonts, Windows provides a function, `GetTextMetrics`, to let you get this information.

Rectangles and Regions

A rectangle is simple. It's defined by a pair of points, the top left and bottom right corners. Although the top left corner is part of the rectangle itself, the bottom right corner is just outside the rectangle by one pixel. In other words, if you had a 2 × 2 rectangle (four pixels total) and its top left corner was (10,10), the bottom right corner would be (12,12), not (11,11).

This is actually rather convenient once you get used to it. For example, you can calculate width = right − left instead of width = right − left + 1. It also lets you represent the empty rectangle (enclosing no pixels at all) as (0,0,0,0). In fact, that's a good way to help keep rectangles straight. Think of them as enclosing a group of pixels instead of describing the edgemost pixels.

A *region* is an arbitrary area of the display space. It can have any shape and size, can have "holes" in it, and can be composed of several discontinuous areas. In other words, a region can be any set of pixels. Internally, regions are represented as a linked list of rectangles, but Windows doesn't let you get at the internal structure. There are a raft of functions to let you create a region, add a rectangle to a region (or remove one), create the intersection or union of two regions, etc.

Regions are powerful tools for graphics programming, and Windows makes extensive use of them. One of the most critical is the clipping region that is in effect whenever you display anything. This is how Windows lets you display inside a window that may have other overlapping windows on top of it. The clipping region includes only the visible portions of your window, and each pixel you try to display is compared with the clipping region and discarded if there's another window on top of it.

Window Painting

For the newcomer to Windows programming, there are many things that must seem pretty strange, and window painting is probably one of the strangest. Even if you're sure you've grasped this idea of message-driven programming, you're likely to try to paint (display) information in your window the wrong way. You discover how to use the TextOut function and successfuly display some text in your window. Things look fine, and then you bring up another window on top of yours momentarily. Then you close that other window, and . . . your window is blank! Or worse yet, part of the text you displayed is still there and part of it has disappeared. What happened?

Well, remember that Windows sends you messages for *everything.* One of the most critical messages—one that nearly every window function needs to handle—is WM_PAINT. This message notifies your window function that all or part of its client area needs to be displayed. In our little mystery above, you displayed something in the window at some other time, but forgot to handle the WM_PAINT message. When the other window covered up your window, the text you had displayed was lost. When the other window was closed, Windows dutifully sent you a WM_PAINT message to tell you to redisplay your client area. The rest was up to you.

Regardless of any other window painting you may do, your window function always has to be prepared to handle a WM_PAINT message, and display whatever part of your client area needs to be refreshed. There's actually a two-step process that leads to a WM_PAINT message being generated. First, part of the window becomes *invalidated.* This simply means that part of the window's screen display may no longer be up to date. This can happen when another window covers it up or as a result of resizing the window. You can also request that all or part of your window be invalidated by calling the InvalidateRect function. Windows doesn't send a WM_PAINT message at that time. It simply accumulates the invalid areas into an update region. Remember, a region can contain any arbitrary area of the screen. The update region contains those portions of your window which have been invalidated.

Later on, when the `GetMessage` call in `WinMain` (or elsewhere) has exhausted all other pending messages, Windows will go ahead and generate a `WM_PAINT` message for any windows that have any accumulated update regions. Then your window function will finally receive the `WM_PAINT` message and call the special `BeginPaint` function. This sets up a data structure telling you what portion of the window needs to be painted, along with other information needed for painting it.

This deferred processing may sound awfully roundabout, but in practice, you generally get the `WM_PAINT` message pretty quickly. The purpose of deferring it is to let your application handle any higher-priority messages, such as keyboard or mouse input, first. For example, the Alt-Tab command in Windows immediately highlights each window frame in sequence, letting the user quickly step through the applications, but doesn't let any `WM_PAINT` messages through until the user releases the Alt key.

Memory Management

Windows has a very powerful—and complex—memory management scheme. There's a heap manager much like the one provided in the C runtime library, except it has the almost magical ability to avoid the problem of memory fragmentation encountered in most dynamic memory management schemes. You know the problem—suppose you allocate several blocks of memory and then free up most of them. You now have plenty of memory free, but it's broken up into small chunks by those blocks that haven't yet been freed. Now if you want to allocate one large block, you can't.

To avoid this problem, Windows uses a *relocatable* memory management system. When you allocate a memory block, using the `GlobalAlloc` function, you don't get back a pointer to it! Instead, you get a *handle* to the memory block. Even though the memory has been allocated, you don't yet know its address. This way, Windows is free to move the block—and other memory blocks— around as needed to avoid fragmentation. If you try to allocate a memory block and there is enough free space but it's broken up into little chunks by other allocated blocks, there is no problem. Windows will simply move those blocks out of the way to bring the free space together into one large block.

What good is a memory block if you don't know its address? Not much! When you want to actually use the memory, you call the `GlobalLock` function, which locks the block down in memory. Windows will no longer move it around. `GlobalLock` returns the current physical address of the memory, so you can use normal C pointer operations to get at it. When you're finished with the memory, you call `GlobalUnlock` to let Windows know that it's okay to start moving it around again if it needs to. The idea is to leave the block unlocked as much of the time as possible, locking it only when you actually access it.

This may seem like a lot of extra work compared to more traditional memory allocation schemes, and it is. But it gives you the advantage of avoiding the old problem of memory fragmentation. In cases where you need instant access to a piece of memory without locking and unlocking it all the time, you can tell `GlobalAlloc` to make the block fixed instead of movable. Then, you get the actual address of the block instead of a handle, and the block will never move. Windows does take the precaution in this case of allocating the block at the low end of memory, where it is less likely to cause fragmentation.

There are a couple of other twists to the memory management. When you allocate a block, you have the option of flagging it as *discardable*. This means that Windows is free to discard this block of memory whenever it runs low on space. On a discardable block, you can request that Windows call back a notification function, that you provide, right before it discards the block. This lets you implement a swapping scheme for memory, even though Windows doesn't have swapping built in.

Windows puts these memory management capabilities to good use in managing program code. Most application code segments, and most of the code that makes up Windows itself, is in relocatable, discardable memory blocks. Windows can move code segments around in memory, discard and reload them as needed, all transparently to the application programs. In effect, this gives you an overlay system for your code, without any of the drawbacks of traditional overlay systems. You don't have to create a tree structure for your overlays, and you don't have to worry about which overlays are in memory at any time. Furthermore, you don't pay the penalty of frequent overlay loading when plenty of memory is available. All you have to do is break up your code into segments, and Windows will take it from there. If there's enough memory available, all your code can fit into it. If Windows starts to run low on memory, it will discard code segments as needed, keeping track of which segments have been executed recently and discarding the oldest.

There are actually two heaps. The functions we just discussed access the global heap, which is shared among all applications and occupies all of memory. Your application also has a local heap, which you can access with a similar set of functions whose names begin with `Local` instead of `Global`. This heap is private to your application and is located in your own DGROUP along with your static data and stack. As in a normal C application, DGROUP is limited to a total of 64K, and can be accessed with near pointers instead of far pointers.

Resources

Nearly every Windows application uses resources, and they're one of those things that sounds unfamiliar at first. But, it's likely you have used them under another name in other programs you've written. Suppose you've built a help facility into an application. Unless you coded all the help text in your program, you probably created a help file containing the different help screens along with some coded information to let your program find the various screens. You may have gone further and included all your error messages in this special file and other little pieces of data your program needs to load in. Of course, this means there's another file for your users to remember to put in the right place for your program to find it. Wouldn't it be nice if you could somehow include all this data in your .EXE file and have an easy way to get to it?

That's exactly what resources are. They're chunks of data incorporated into your `.EXE` file that your program can read in dynamically. Each resource has a type and a name, which are ASCII strings (or numbers) that identify the resource. Any kind of data can be made into a resource. Windows provides predefined resource types and associated functions for the most common data items used by Windows applications. For example, the `LoadMenu` function loads a menu description into memory, `LoadString` loads a text string, etc. There are also the generic `FindResource` and `LoadResource` functions for additional resource types that you define.

Windows includes a Resource Compiler (RC), which reads a text file with the `.RC` extension. This file contains data declarations for the resources you want to include in your program. RC compiles these declarations into a binary format and merges them into your .EXE file. One nice touch here is that RC includes the standard C preprocessor. That lets you use `#include`, `#define` and the other preprocessor directives in your `.RC` file. This is extremely helpful, because you can include a `.H` file in both your C code and your `.RC` file, making the same symbol definitions available in both.

The SPY Program

Now that you've seen how Windows applications work, we can look at our featured application, SPY. SPY is a Windows application that does just what its name suggests. Specifically, SPY scans through all currently existing windows, regardless of which application created them, gathering up all the information it can find about these windows. Then, it displays this information in its own window, letting you scroll through it and view it. SPY is both a tool for developing and testing applications, and a good example of how a Windows application is put together.

Using SPY

SPY's own window shows a list of all existing windows, whether they happen to be currently visible on the screen or not. You can select either a one-line summary of each window or a detailed view that displays all the information SPY has

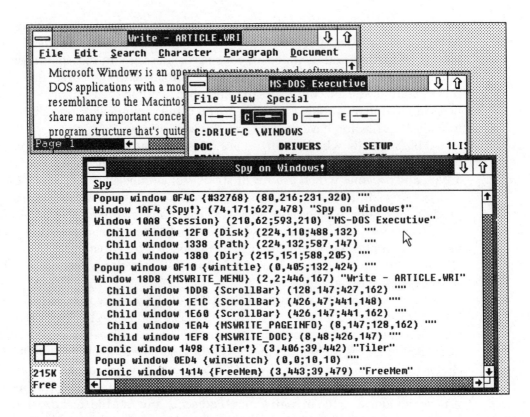

Fig. 9-2.   SPY's summary view.

picked up—the Show Detail command on SPY's menu switches between the two views. The window list doesn't change dynamically—it's a "snapshot" of the state of the Windows system at the time SPY was started up. You can bring the list up to date at any time by selecting New Spy Mission from SPY's menu. Figure 9-2 shows windows owned by the MS-DOS Executive, Write, and SPY itself, along with the Tiler and Freemem programs running as icons. Figure 9-3 shows detailed information about SPY's own window, which can be scrolled up and down to bring the rest of the detailed listing into view. Each line in the summary view shows from left to right:

1. the basic window style: popup, child, iconic, or just plain Window for main application windows (Child windows are indented under their parent.)

2. the window handle, shown as a 4-digit hex number

3. the window class name, shown here in curly braces (The braces aren't part of the actual name.)

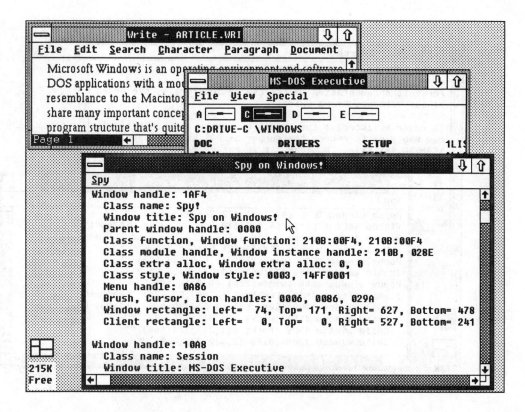

Fig. 9-3. SPY's detail view.

4. the window coordinates, shown as actual screen coordinates, in this order: (left,top;bottom,right)
5. the window title, in quotes

The detailed view shows a number of additional items, and each item is labeled.

One handy use for SPY is to find out just how other applications are setting up their windows. Figure 9-4 shows an example, SPY looking at Notepad. SPY's display reveals that Notepad's main window contains one child window, of the Edit class, which invokes Windows' built-in text editor. That's how Notepad works—it simply creates a multiline edit control inside its main window, just as you could create one inside a dialog box. This is clever. It lets Notepad use the editing code built into Windows, so the Notepad program itself just has to take care of creating the child window, resizing it when the parent window size changes, and handling the file I/O operations and goodies like Search. The actual text editing is handled by the window function for the Edit class, with no effort on Notepad's part.

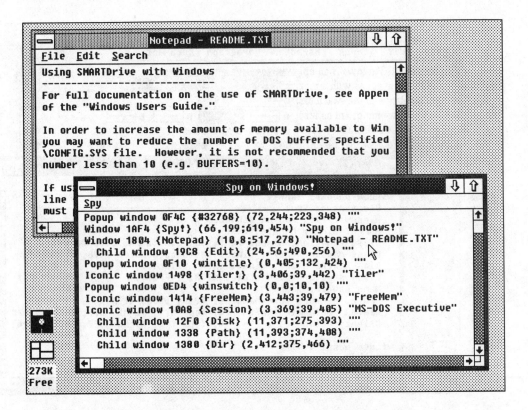

Fig. 9-4.   Notepad reveals a child window of the edit class.

SPY is also handy for debugging your own applications. If you run into a situation where your windows aren't operating correctly, you can have SPY take a look at the situation. In an application like my own SQLWindows database application development system, which creates and destroys all kinds of windows as it executes, I've found this very handy. When things haven't looked quite right, SPY has often pointed the way toward the problem.

How SPY Works

Even though SPY is rather unusual, its programming is typical of a Windows application. Understanding how SPY works will help you understand how any Windows application is put together because, like most Windows applications, SPY is built around its window functions and messages. Let's start at the beginning, with SPY's main program, WinMain. (In reading the listing, you can find functions more easily by noting that they're alphabetized, so don't look at the beginning of the listing for WinMain!)

WinMain

We gave a shortened example earlier of a `WinMain` function, and SPY's main program follows that model. You'll note that `WinMain` has several parameters:

▶ `hInst` and `hPrevInst` are the *instance handles* for this instance and the previous instance of SPY. A Windows user can start up multiple copies of an application, and Windows assigns an instance handle to each. Several Windows functions, such as `CreateWindow`, need your instance handle as a parameter. The reason for giving you the previous instance handle is for cases where you want to copy data over from one instance to the next. A Windows application, just like a DOS application, can have command-line parameters. SPY doesn't happen to use these, so we ignore this parameter.

▶ `nCmdShow` is the parameter that should be passed to a `ShowWindow` call when we create our main window. Normally, a Windows application starts up with its window visible, but the user can request that it be started with an iconic window by holding down the Shift key while starting the program. The `nCmdShow` parameter communicates this to the application.

`WinMain` itself is quite simple. It calls our `Initialize` function to get things started, then falls into the main message loop. This loop is much like the one we looked at before, with one additional function call: `TranslateMessage`. This is a "busywork" function that every Windows application has to call in its main loop. It translates the raw keyboard messages into their ASCII equivalents, and also takes care of some necessary processing for the System (Control) menu.

The main message loop terminates when `GetMessage` returns zero. This doesn't mean there aren't any more messages— `GetMessage` just goes to sleep for a while in that case. The zero return means that a `WM_QUIT` message has been received by `GetMessage`. In SPY, this happens when `PostQuitMessage` is called inside SPY's window function, and that call is made when the window is destroyed.

Windows Naming Conventions

The naming conventions in the SPY program may be unfamiliar to many C programmers. SPY uses the conventions followed in the Windows documentation and many Windows applications. Function names, as you've seen, generally follow a verb-noun model, describing what they do, e.g., `CreateWindow` or `GetMessage`.

Most variable names have a lowercase prefix that tells the variable type. Some of the prefixes used in SPY are listed in Table 9-1. The `np` and `lp` prefixes are often followed by additional prefix letters specifying what is pointed to, as in `lpszCmdLine`, which is a far pointer `lp` to a zero-terminated string `sz`.

Table 9-1.   Variables in SPY

Prefix	Variable Type
h	Handle
n	Integer
b	Boolean value
dw	Double-word (unsigned long integer)
sz	Zero-terminated string
np	Near pointer
lp	Far (long) pointer

Although a Windows application can use any kind of naming convention internally, these conventions turn out to be very handy. It helps to know the type of a variable from looking at its name, and the long, descriptive function and variable names make the code much more readable and maintainable.

Initialize

SPY's `Initialize` function gets everything started. Its main job is to create our window. First, we must register the window class with a `RegisterClass` call. Note, however, that this is done only on the first instance of the program. Subsequent instances can use the same window class. You probably wouldn't want to run multiple instances of SPY, but it's important to program correctly for multiple instances, or else to disallow them completely by exiting out of `WinMain` whenever `hPrevInst` is nonzero.

One other step that's done differently, depending on whether this is the first instance or not, is loading of text string resources. In the first instance, we actually load them from the `.EXE` file with `LoadString` calls, then in subsequent instances use the `GetInstance` function to copy them over from the previous instance. This isn't really necessary, but it speeds up loading of subsequent instances if you can copy over some of the data like this. Also, in a "real" Windows application, every text message should be placed in the `.RC` file and loaded with `LoadString`. This makes it easier to produce foreign-language versions of your program by isolating all the strings in one place outside the actual program code. Then, you can just edit the `.RC` file to change languages. (I cheated to keep the listing size down, and coded most of SPY's strings right in the source code—don't follow my example on this!)

After registering the window class, we create SPY's main window with a `CreateWindow` call, setting the window position and size explicitly and placing the window in approximately the center of the screen. Many programs let Windows assign a default position and size by passing the special value `CW_USEDEFAULT` for the X and nWidth parameters. This is also where we specify that our window will have scroll bars, by giving the `WS_HSCROLL` and `WS_VSCROLL` style options.

After creating the window, we make it visible with a `ShowWindow` call, and post a `WM_COMMAND` message to the message queue. Later, as we pick up messages in our main message loop, this message will get picked up and processed, just as if the user had picked the New Spy Mission menu item. This causes the first information display in the window.

`Initialize` also takes care of a few other details. It determines the character height and width for the system font, necessary information to properly paint and scroll the window. It also preallocates a global memory handle for the `INFO` structure, although it doesn't yet allocate any memory for it (well, it allocates one byte). This simplifies other parts of the program where this handle is used. We don't have to worry later about whether this handle has been initialized or not.

SpyWndProc

This is where the action is. Once we've created our window, the main program settles into its message loop, dispatching messages to `SpyWndProc` as they come in. Like most window functions, this one is a `switch` statement, with one `case` for each message we wish to process. Messages that we're not directly concerned with are passed through to `DefWindowProc` for the standard Windows processing.

WM_COMMAND

We get `WM_COMMAND` whenever the user selects one of the items from our menu, either with the mouse or keyboard. `WM_COMMAND` is also used for notification messages when a window has child windows. (We're not concerned with these here.) For this message, `wParam` contains the command ID number, as assigned in the `SPY.RC` file.

One of the most important menu items is `CMD_SPY`, the New Spy Mission command, which causes the list of windows to be scanned by calling the `Spy-OnAllWindows` function. Figure 9-5 shows SPY's menu just before selecting the New Spy Mission command. Figure 9-6 shows SPY's menu just after selecting the command. The popup window listed at the beginning of SPY's display is the menu from Figure 9-5. Popup menus themselves are windows, and the command was executed before the menu window disappeared. Remember, `CMD_SPY` comes in after initialization even if the user doesn't select it, because we posted it to the message queue in the `Initialize` function. `CMD_EXPAND` (Show Detail) toggles the detail/summary view by toggling our internal flag, `bExpand`, checking or unchecking the menu item with a `CheckMenuItem` call, and invalidating the entire window with an `InvalidateWindow` call so it will get repainted.

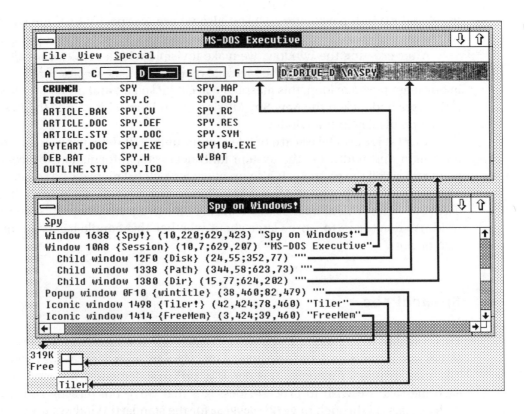

Fig. 9-5. **SPY's menu before selecting New Spy Mission. (The arrows show which window is described by each line of SPY's display.)**

The `CMD_ABOUT` (About Spy . . .) gives an example of how to display a modal dialog box. Despite all the nasty things said about modes earlier, there are still situations where we want to display something or get some user input and suspend the rest of the application temporarily. We do this with a modal dialog box. One caution here, though. Any time you're tempted to put up a modal dialog box, think twice about it and see if a modeless dialog could be used. If so, your users will appreciate it! It gives them more flexibility in using your application. One of the more common design flaws I've seen in Windows and Macintosh applications has been overuse of modal dialogs.

WM_DESTROY

`WM_DESTROY` comes in when our window gets destroyed by a `DestroyWindow` function call. This can happen either by selecting the Exit command on SPY's menu (see `CMD_EXIT` under `WM_COMMAND`), or by selecting Close from the Control menu (the same as double-clicking the Control menu icon). In the latter case, the `DestroyWindow` call is generated inside `DefWindowProc`. Control menu items all

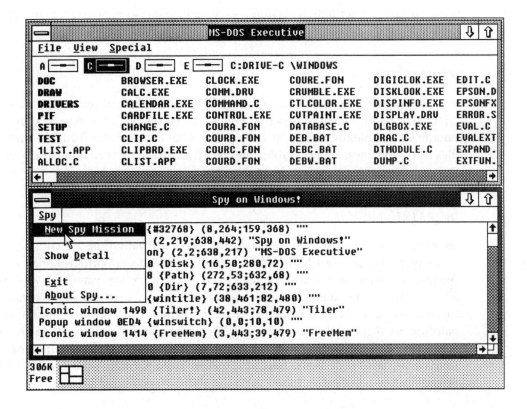

Fig. 9-6. SPY's menu after selecting New Spy Mission.

generate WM_SYSCOMMAND messages, and we pass all those through to DefWindow-Proc for the standard processing. All we do on WM_DESTROY is call PostQuitMessage to terminate the application.

WM_HSCROLL *and* WM_VSCROLL

We get WM_HSCROLL and WM_VSCROLL as a result of any activity in the horizontal or vertical scroll bars, respectively. In both cases, our DoScrollMsg function handles the actual scrolling. This function is fairly lengthy because of the various cases it must handle: clicking in the up-arrow or down-arrow, the page-up or page-down area, or dragging the thumb. But after calculating the new scroll position based on this information, the actual scrolling is simple. We call SetScrollPos to set the scroll bar itself to the new position—this doesn't happen automatically. Then we call ScrollWindow, a very handy function. It optimizes the scrolling by moving the actual window contents if there's any overlap between the old and new positions (as there would be in a single-line scroll), then calls InvalidateRect to cause the remaining area to be repainted. Like all window painting, this part gets deferred until all other activity is done, so we call `UpdateWindow` to force the repainting to happen immediately. This gives a cleaner appearance to the scrolling.

WM_KEYDOWN

`WM_KEYDOWN` indicates that some key has been pressed, and the `wParam` gives the virtual key code. The only keys that SPY is interested in are the cursor keypad, so I made life simple for myself by calling the same `DoScrollMsg` function that handles the scroll bars. I used a table, `CsrScroll`, to convert the virtual key codes into the appropriate parameters for `DoScrollMsg`.

WM_PAINT

`WM_PAINT` is the big one, the message that says it's finally time to paint our window—or, more specifically, the client area of the window. Windows takes care of the title bar, menu bar, and scroll bars for us. There are two ways that we can get a WM_PAINT message. The most common is when `GetMessage` discovers that there aren't any other messages left for us. If any part of our window needs painting, we'll get a `WM_PAINT` message. We can also force an immediate `WM_PAINT` at any time by calling `UpdateWindow` as we do in the scrolling code. (`UpdateWindow` sends a `WM_PAINT` only if any part of the client area actually does need painting.) SPY's window painting is done inside the `PaintWindow` function.

WM_SIZE

`WM_SIZE` lets us know that the size of our window has changed. It's also sent when the window is first created, to tell us the initial size. SPY uses this information to recalculate the scroll bar ranges based on the current client area size.

SpyOnAllWindows

When `SpyWndProc` receives the `WM_COMMAND/CMD_SPY` message, it calls `SpyOnAllWindows` to scan all existing windows and gather up the information on them. We actually make two passes through all the windows here. The first loop counts the total number of windows so that we know how much memory to allocate for the `INFO` structure that holds the window information. After allocating this structure, we make a second loop through the windows to fill in the data for each. This could all be done in one pass, adjusting the memory size of the data structure as needed, but it's a little faster to just calculate the needed size and allocate the correct size structure to begin with.

For each window, `SpyOnAllWindows` calls `SpyOnWindow` to gather up the information about that window and its window class. This is done with with some ordinary Windows functions, notably `GetWindowWord`, `GetWindowLong`, `GetClass-Word`, and `GetClassLong`. These functions extract various pieces of information from the actual window and class data structures that Windows maintains internally. Unlike real-life spies, SPY doesn't have to resort to any devious methods to get its information.

PaintWindow

Finally we get to the point of the whole exercise, displaying something in our window. `PaintWindow` begins by calling the `BeginPaint` function, which lets Windows know that yes, we really are going to go ahead and paint the window. `BeginPaint` "validates" the entire window, that is, it clears out the update region to indicate that no further painting is required. It doesn't throw out that update region completely, though. The intersection of the update region and our window's clipping region becomes the clipping region used for painting, so any painting we do is clipped to the update region.

This new clipping happens because `BeginPaint` creates a new *device context* for us and returns a handle to it. We save this handle in the `hdcPaint` variable for use in the actual painting. Any output you display in Windows is through some device context or another—all the output functions take a device context handle as a parameter. You can always get a device context for your window's client area by calling the `GetDC` function; you don't have to wait for a `WM_PAINT` message. If you do, the clipping region for that device context would be unrelated to any update region the window might have. However, the device context retrieved by `BeginPaint` specifically takes the update region into account.

`BeginPaint` also fills in the `PAINTSTRUCT` structure that we pass as its second argument. This structure contains several pieces of information, in particular a rectangle called `rcPaint`, which is the smallest rectangle that encloses our update region, and tells us just where to start and stop painting. We can either use this information or disregard it—it's just an optimization to speed up painting. In SPY, we use the top and bottom of this rectangle to determine which lines to paint but we don't bother worrying about the left and right edges. We just paint each line of text in its entirety and let Windows figure out which portion of the line needs to be displayed, based on the clipping region.

After calling `BeginPaint`, we set the proper foreground and background colors for our text. The `GetSysColor` function that we use here returns the color values that the user set up with the Control Panel so SPY's display will match the other windows on the screen. Back when we called `RegisterClass`, we specified that the background of our client area should always be erased using the `COLOR_WINDOW` color from Control Panel. We did this by setting the `hbrBackground` field in the window class structure. Here in the paint function, we set the background color of the text itself to match.

Next, we take care of one detail that's crucial to making the window scroll properly. Based on the current scroll bar positions, we calculate just where in the INFO structure to begin picking up data, and where in our window that data should be displayed. If our window were never scrolled, the first record in INFO would always be displayed at the top of our window. However, if the user has scrolled down one line, for instance, we must offset our display by one line. Similarly, if the user has scrolled horizontally, we have to offset our display accordingly. Note that the actual displacement is up to our code to determine. In SPY, I made one scroll bar increment equal to one character height or width, but the actual offsets are all in pixels.

Finally, we loop through the INFO structure, and for each record we paint one line of text (the summary view) or several lines of text (the detail view). We stop the loop when we reach the bottom of the rcPaint rectangle or when we run out of entries in INFO. The INFO structure remains locked for the duration of this loop. We call GlobalLock before the loop and GlobalUnlock after the loop exits.

To display each line on the screen, we can't just do a printf as you might do in an ordinary C program. We have to call the TextOut function provided by Windows. However, we can still take advantage of C's formatting capability in a very convenient way. The Paint function that's called for each line of text is the (almost) exact equivalent of printf, except the actual output is sent to TextOut. We accomplish this trick by calling the vsprintf function within Paint to format the line in a memory buffer, and then pass that buffer as the string parameter to TextOut. vsprintf is really handy in situations like this.

The Resource File: SPY.RC

SPY's resource file contains declarations for the resources that SPY uses. Three are read in during the Initialize function: an ICON statement, naming the icon file where I created SPY's icon (using the ICONEDIT program supplied with the Windows software development kit); a STRINGTABLE statement listing the few text strings that I did make into resources; and a MENU statement, which sets up SPY's menu. Remember, it's better to make all text messages into resources because that makes it easy to translate your application into other languages.

Once you assign the menu command IDs (CMD_SPY, etc.) in a menu, you can fool around with the actual menu layout without changing your C code. Since the command IDs are not related to the actual menu position, you can move menu items around freely if you want to change the menu layout. Furthermore, you can create a complete menu structure and see how it looks in actual operation long before you write any actual code to support those menu items. Any menu command ID codes that you haven't implemented will simply pass through your window function and be ignored. This is handy for prototyping menus.

You might also note the & character used in the menu strings. This specifies which character of a menu command is to be underlined, becoming the mnemonic shortcut character for that command.

One last thing in `SPY.RC` is the DIALOG statement that defines the "About Spy . . . " dialog box. This gives the location, size, and contents of each of the child windows that make up the dialog box. I actually built this definition using the Dialog Editor provided with the Windows SDK—that's a lot more convenient than trying to figure out all those coordinates manually!

The Module Definition File: `SPY.DEF`

Every Windows application has a `.DEF` file, used by the Windows linker LINK4, that specifies several pieces of information Windows needs to know about your application: the module name (which must match the name of your `.EXE` file), descriptions of the code and data segments your program uses, the size of the stack and local heap you want, and a list of the functions that your program "exports."

Each function that you are going to pass along to Windows to be called back, such as a window function or dialog function, must be listed in the EXPORTS list. Dialog functions, like `AboutBox`, must also be run through the `MakeProcInstance` function in your C code, as we do in the `CMD_ABOUT` case in `SpyWndProc`. Forgetting an EXPORTS entry or a `MakeProcInstance` call is one sure way to get your program to crash in very mysterious ways! The problem is that when Windows calls your function back, the DS register will contain the wrong value.

The segment descriptions in the `.DEF` file are also important, but at least LINK4 will set up workable defaults if you leave one out. Since SPY is compiled in small model, we have only a single code segment and single data segment, and we declare them both to be `MOVEABLE`. It's also possible to declare segments as `FIXED`, which can be handy for debugging. It's a good idea to avoid that if possible otherwise.

Have you ever noticed that if you try to run a Windows application outside of Windows, it prints the message: `This program requires Microsoft Windows`? DOS doesn't magically know that. A Windows `.EXE` file is actually two programs in one, a DOS program and a Windows program. The beginning of the `.EXE` file contains an ordinary DOS program, and that's what will run if you try to run the `.EXE` from DOS. The actual Windows program is at the end of the `.EXE` file, past the portion that gets loaded when you run the `.EXE` from DOS. The `STUB` statement in the `.DEF` file gives the name of an ordinary DOS `.EXE` file which is to be included at the beginning of the Windows `.EXE`. The `WINSTUB.EXE` file named here is the program that prints: `This program requires Microsoft Windows.` You could put any program you wanted there, so a single `.EXE` could actually contain both a DOS version and a Windows version of a program.

Conclusion

If you've looked into any OS/2 programming, this discussion of the .DEF file may sound very familiar to you. That's because OS/2 applications use identical .DEF files, and in fact, the same new linker, as Windows applications. The technique of including both a DOS version and a new version of a program is exactly how OS/2's "Family API" works. Windows and OS/2 share a number of other features, such as dynamic linking and relocatable memory management, and, of course, OS/2's Presentation Manager is a direct descendant of Windows.

Besides being a link to the future, Windows is also an exciting system in its own right. It gives applications running on MS-DOS the kind of user interface the Macintosh has always been known for, and provides a great set of tools for a software developer to build quality applications. Programming for Windows is different from traditional application programming and takes some getting used to, but the results are worth it. I find most appealing about Windows the fact that it resolves the old conflict between ease of learning and convenience and utility for the experienced user. In a Windows application, you can have a program that's easy to learn *and* powerful.

Listing 9-1.   SPY

```
The files are:


SPY              MAKE file
SPY.H            Header file for .C and .RC
SPY.C            C source code
SPY.RC           Resource Compiler source code
SPY.DEF          Module definition file


* * * * * * * * * * * *     SPY     * * * * * * * * * * * * * *

# Makefile for SPY.EXE

spy.obj:    spy.c  spy.h
    msc -AS -Gcsw -Oas -u -W3 -Zip $*;

spy.res:    spy.rc  spy.ico  spy.h
    rc -r spy.rc

spy.exe:    spy.obj  spy.res  spy.def
    link4 spy, spy/align:16, spy/co, slibw, spy.def
    rc spy.res
```

continued

```
* * * * * * * * * * * * *     SPY.H     * * * * * * * * * * * * *

/* - - - - - - - - - - - - - - - - - - - - - - - - - - */

/* SPY.H */

/* - - - - - - - - - - - - - - - - - - - - - - - - - - */

#define MAXINT      32767
#define MAXWORD     65535

/* - - - - - - - - - - - - - - - - - - - - - - - - - - */

/* Menu command definitions */

#define CMD_ABOUT    1
#define CMD_EXIT     2
#define CMD_EXPAND   3
#define CMD_SPY      4

/* - - - - - - - - - - - - - - - - - - - - - - - - - - */

/* String table ID numbers */

#define IDS_CLASS    1
#define IDS_TITLE    2

/* - - - - - - - - - - - - - - - - - - - - - - - - - - */

/* Dialog ID numbers */

#define ABOUTBOX     1

/* - - - - - - - - - - - - - - - - - - - - - - - - - - */

* * * * * * * * * * * * *     SPY.C     * * * * * * * * * * * * *

/* - - - - - - - - - - - - - - - - - - - - - - - - - - *\
   *  Spy.c                                         *
   *  Windows Spy Program                           *
   *  Public Domain                                 *
   *  Written by Michael Geary                      *
```

continued

```
*                                                  *
* This program "spies" on all the windows that are *
* currently open in your Windows session, and      *
* displays a window containing all the information  *
* it can find out about those windows. You can     *
* scroll through this window using either the       *
* mouse or keyboard to view the information about   *
* the various windows. The "New Spy Mission"       *
* menu item recaptures the latest  information.     *
\* - - - - - - - - - - - - - - - - - - - - - - - */


#define LINT_ARGS
#include <stdio.h>
#include <stdarg.h>
#include <windows.h>
#include "spy.h"


/* - - - - - - - - - - - - - - - - - - - - - - - */


/*  The display for a single window looks like this in
 *  collapsed mode:
 *
 *  [style] Window H {class} (L,T;R,B) "title"
 *
 *  where [style] is: [Child¦Popup¦Iconic]
 *
 *  or like this in expanded mode:
 *
 *  [style] Window handle: H
 *    Class name: {class name}
 *    Window title: {title text}
 *    Parent window handle: H
 *    Class function, window function: H:H, H:H
 *    Class module handle, Window instance handle: H, H
 *    Class extra alloc, Window extra alloc: D, D
 *    Class style, Window style: H, H
 *    Menu handle: H   -or-  Control ID: D
 *    Brush, Cursor, Icon handles: H, H, H
 *    Window rectangle: Left=D, Top=D, Right=D, Bottom=D
 *    Client rectangle: Left=D, Top=D, Right=D, Bottom=D
 *  {blank line}
 *
 *  Total number of lines for one window display: 13
```

continued

```
    */

#define LINES_PER_WINDOW    13
#define WINDOW_WIDTH        160


/* - - - - - - - - - - - - - - - - - - - - - - - */


/*  The INFO structure contains all the information we
 *  gather up about each window we are spying on. We
 *  allocate an array of INFO structures in the global
 *  heap, with one entry for each window in the
 *  system.
 */


#define CLASSMAX    30
#define TITLEMAX    50


typedef struct {
    HWND     winHWnd;              /* Window handle       */
    char     winClass[CLASSMAX];  /* Class name          */
    HBRUSH   winBkgdBrush;        /* Bkgd brush handle   */
    HCURSOR  winCursor;           /* Cursor handle       */
    HICON    winIcon;             /* Icon handle         */
    HANDLE   winClassModule;      /* Class owner module  */
    WORD     winWndExtra;         /* Window extra data   */
    WORD     winClsExtra;         /* Class extra data    */
    WORD     winClassStyle;       /* Class style word    */
    FARPROC  winClassProc;        /* Class window proc   */
    HANDLE   winInstance;         /* Window owner inst.  */
    HWND     winHWndParent;       /* Parent window       */
    char     winTitle[TITLEMAX];  /* Window title        */
    WORD     winControlID;        /* Ctrl ID/menu handle */
    FARPROC  winWndProc;          /* Window proc         */
    DWORD    winStyle;            /* Window style bits   */
    RECT     winWindowRect;       /* Window rectangle    */
    RECT     winClientRect;       /* Client rectangle    */
    int      winLevel;            /* Child window level  */
} INFO;

typedef HANDLE      HINFO;    /* INFO array handle   */
typedef INFO huge * LPINFO;   /* Far pointer to INFO */


/* - - - - - - - - - - - - - - - - - - - - - - - */
```

continued

```
/*  The CsrScroll array is used for implementing
 *  keyboard scrolling. By looking up the keystroke
 *  in this array, we get the equivalent scroll bar
 *  message.
 */

#define VK_MIN_CURSOR  VK_PRIOR
#define VK_MAX_CURSOR  VK_DOWN

struct {
  char    csBar;  /* Scroll bar this key triggers   */
  char    csMsg;  /* The scroll message for this key */
} CsrScroll[] = {
  { SB_VERT, SB_PAGEUP   }, /* VK_PRIOR: PgUp        */
  { SB_VERT, SB_PAGEDOWN }, /* VK_NEXT:  PgDn        */
  { SB_VERT, SB_BOTTOM   }, /* VK_END:   End         */
  { SB_VERT, SB_TOP      }, /* VK_HOME:  Home        */
  { SB_HORZ, SB_LINEUP   }, /* VK_LEFT:  left arrow  */
  { SB_VERT, SB_LINEUP   }, /* VK_UP:    up arrow    */
  { SB_HORZ, SB_LINEDOWN }, /* VK_RIGHT: right arrow */
  { SB_VERT, SB_LINEDOWN }  /* VK_DOWN:  down arrow  */
};

/* - - - - - - - - - - - - - - - - - - - - - - - - */


/*  Static variables                               */

HANDLE  hInstance;          /* Our instance handle   */
HINFO   hInfo;              /* INFO global handle     */
LPINFO  lpInfo;            /* Far pointer to INFO     */
int     nWindows;          /* Total # of windows      */
BOOL    bExpand = FALSE;    /* Detailed view?         */
int     nLinesEach = 1;    /* 1 or LINES_PER_WINDOW   */
int     nCharSizeX;        /* Char. width in pixels   */
int     nCharSizeY;        /* Char. height in pixels  */
int     nExtLeading;       /* Extra pixels vertically */
int     nPaintX;           /* X coordinate for Paint  */
int     nPaintY;           /* Y coordinate for Paint  */
HDC     hdcPaint;          /* hDC for Paint to use     */
char    szClass[10];       /* Our window class name    */
char    szTitle[40];       /* Our window title         */

/* - - - - - - - - - - - - - - - - - - - - - - - - */
```

continued

```
/*  Declare full templates for all our functions. This
 *  gives us strong type checking on our functions.
 */

BOOL FAR PASCAL AboutBox( HWND, unsigned, WORD, LONG );
void            CountWindow( HWND );
int             DoScrollMsg( HWND, int, WORD, int );
void            HomeScrollBars( HWND, BOOL );
BOOL            Initialize( HANDLE, int );
void     cdecl  Paint( char *, ... );
void            PaintWindow( HWND );
void            SetScrollBars( HWND );
void            SetScrollBar1( HWND, int, int );
BOOL            SpyOnAllWindows( HWND );
void            SpyOnWindow( HWND, int );
long FAR PASCAL SpyWndProc( HWND, WORD, WORD, LONG );
int      PASCAL WinMain( HANDLE, HANDLE, LPSTR, int );


/* - - - - - - - - - - - - - - - - - - - - - - - - - */


/*  Dialog function for the About box.
 *  Since this is a simple box with only one button,
 *  WM_COMMAND is assumed to be a click on that button
 *  (the command number is not checked).
 */

BOOL FAR AboutBox( hDlg, wMsg, wParam, lParam )
  HWND        hDlg;        /* Window handle        */
  unsigned    wMsg;        /* Message number       */
  WORD        wParam;      /* Word parameter       */
  LONG        lParam;      /* Long parameter       */
{
  switch( wMsg ) {

    case WM_COMMAND:
      EndDialog( hDlg, TRUE );
      return TRUE;

    case WM_INITDIALOG:
      return TRUE;
  }
  return FALSE;
}
```

continued

```
/* - - - - - - - - - - - - - - - - - - - - - - - - - */


/*  Count a window for the size calculation. Loops
 *  through its children recursively and counts them
 *  as well.
 */

void CountWindow( hWnd )
    HWND        hWnd;        /* Window handle to count  */
{
    HWND        hWndChild;   /* Child window for loop   */

    /* Count this window */
    ++nWindows;

    /* Loop through children and count them */
    for(
      hWndChild = GetWindow( hWnd, GW_CHILD );
      hWndChild;
      hWndChild = GetWindow( hWndChild, GW_HWNDNEXT )
    ) {
      CountWindow( hWndChild );
    }
}


/* - - - - - - - - - - - - - - - - - - - - - - - - - */


/*  Process a scroll bar message. Calculates the
 *  distance to scroll based on the scroll bar range
 *  and the message code. Limits the scroll to the
 *  actual range of the scroll bar. Sets the new
 *  scroll bar thumb position and scrolls the window
 *  by the necessary amount. Note that the scroll bar
 *  ranges are set in terms of number of characters,
 *  while the window scrolling is done by a number of
 *  pixels. Returns the distance scrolled in chars.
 */

int DoScrollMsg( hWnd, nBar, wCode, nThumb )
    HWND        hWnd;        /* Window handle to scroll */
    int         nBar;        /* SB_HORZ or SB_VERT      */
    WORD        wCode;       /* Scroll bar message code */
    int         nThumb;      /* SB_THUMBPOSITION param. */
```

continued

```
{
  int        nOld;        /* Old scroll bar position */
  int        nDiff;       /* Scroll bar change        */
  int        nMin;        /* Scroll bar range min.  */
  int        nMax;        /* Scroll bar range max.  */
  int        nPageSize;   /* Window height in chars  */
  RECT       rect;        /* Window client rectangle */

  /* Get old scroll position and scroll range */
  nOld = GetScrollPos( hWnd, nBar );
  GetScrollRange( hWnd, nBar, &nMin, &nMax );

  /* Quit if no scrolling (see SetScrollBars) */
  if( nMax == MAXINT )
    return 0;

  /* Calculate horizontal or vertical page size */
  GetClientRect( hWnd, &rect );
  if( nBar == SB_HORZ )
    nPageSize = (rect.right - rect.left) / nCharSizeX;
  else
    nPageSize = (rect.bottom - rect.top) / nCharSizeY;

  /* Select scroll amount, based on scroll message */
  switch( wCode ) {

    case SB_LINEUP:
      nDiff = -1;
      break;

    case SB_LINEDOWN:
      nDiff = 1;
      break;

    case SB_PAGEUP:
      nDiff = -nPageSize;
      break;

    case SB_PAGEDOWN:
      nDiff = nPageSize;
      break;

    case SB_THUMBPOSITION:
```

continued

```
          nDiff = nThumb - nOld;
          break;

        case SB_TOP:
          nDiff = -30000;  /* A kludge but it works... */
          break;

        case SB_BOTTOM:
          nDiff = 30000;
          break;

        default:
          return 0;
     }

     /* Limit scroll destination to nMin..nMax */
     if( nDiff < nMin - nOld )
       nDiff = nMin - nOld;

     if( nDiff > nMax - nOld )
       nDiff = nMax - nOld;

     if( nDiff == 0 )
       return 0;   /* Return if net effect is nothing */

     /* Now we can set the new scroll bar position */
     SetScrollPos( hWnd, nBar, nOld + nDiff, TRUE );

     /* Scroll the actual window contents */
     ScrollWindow(
       hWnd,
       nBar == SB_HORZ ?  -nDiff*nCharSizeX : 0,
       nBar == SB_HORZ ?  0 : -nDiff*nCharSizeY,
       NULL,
       NULL
     );

     /* Force immediate update for cleaner appearance */
     UpdateWindow( hWnd );

     return nDiff;
   }
```

continued

```
/* - - - - - - - - - - - - - - - - - - - - - - - - */

/* Set both scroll bars to the home position (0)
 */

void HomeScrollBars( hWnd, bRedraw )
  HWND        hWnd;      /* Window handle          */
  BOOL        bRedraw;   /* Redraw scroll bars?    */
{
  SetScrollPos( hWnd, SB_HORZ, 0, bRedraw );
  SetScrollPos( hWnd, SB_VERT, 0, bRedraw );
}


/* - - - - - - - - - - - - - - - - - - - - - - - - */

/* Initialize the application. Some of the
 * initialization is different depending on whether
 * this is the first instance or a subsequent
 * instance. For example, we register our window
 * class only in the first instance. Returns TRUE if
 * initialization succeeded, FALSE if failed.
 */

BOOL Initialize( hPrevInst, nCmdShow )
  HANDLE      hPrevInst; /* Prev. instance or 0       */
  int         nCmdShow;  /* ShowWindow parameter      */
{
  WNDCLASS    Class;     /* RegisterClass structure */
  HWND        hWnd;      /* Our window handle         */
  HDC         hDC;       /* Temp display context      */
  TEXTMETRIC  Metrics;   /* System font metrics       */
  int         nScreenX;  /* Screen width in pixels    */
  int         nScreenY;  /* Screen height in pixels */

  nScreenX = GetSystemMetrics( SM_CXSCREEN );
  nScreenY = GetSystemMetrics( SM_CYSCREEN );

  if( ! hPrevInst ) {
    /* Initialization for first instance only */

    /* Load strings from resource file--really, all
     * message strings should be loaded here--we just
     * load a couple as an example. */
```

continued

```
LoadString(
  hInstance, IDS_CLASS, szClass, sizeof(szClass)
);
LoadString(
  hInstance, IDS_TITLE, szTitle, sizeof(szTitle)
);

/* Register our window class */
Class.style         = CS_HREDRAW | CS_VREDRAW;
Class.lpfnWndProc   = SpyWndProc;
Class.cbClsExtra    = 0;
Class.cbWndExtra    = 0;
Class.hInstance     = hInstance;
Class.hIcon         = LoadIcon(hInstance,szClass);
Class.hCursor       = LoadCursor(NULL,IDC_ARROW);
Class.hbrBackground = COLOR_WINDOW + 1;
Class.lpszMenuName  = szClass;
Class.lpszClassName = szClass;

if( ! RegisterClass(&Class) )
  return FALSE;

} else {
  /* Initialization for subsequent instances only */

  /* Copy data from previous instance */
  GetInstanceData(
    hPrevInst, szClass, sizeof(szClass)
  );
  GetInstanceData(
    hPrevInst, szTitle, sizeof(szTitle)
  );
}


/* Initialization for every instance */

/* Allocate an empty INFO structure */
hInfo = GlobalAlloc( GMEM_MOVEABLE, 1L );
if( ! hInfo )
  return FALSE;

/* Create our tiled window, don't display it yet */
hWnd = CreateWindow(
```

continued

```
    szClass,              /* Class name          */
    szTitle,              /* Window title        */
    WS_OVERLAPPEDWINDOW |  /* Window style        */
      WS_HSCROLL | WS_VSCROLL,
    nScreenX * 1 - 20,    /* X: 5% from left     */
    nScreenY * 1 - 10,    /* Y  10% from top     */
    nScreenX * 9 - 10,    /* nWidth: 90%         */
    nScreenY * 7 - 10,    /* nHeight: 70%        */
    NULL,                 /* No parent hWnd      */
    NULL,                 /* Menu handle         */
    hInstance,            /* Owner instance handle */
    NULL                  /* WM_CREATE parameter */
  );

  /* Initialize scroll bars */
  HomeScrollBars( hWnd, FALSE );

  /* Calculate character size for system font */
  hDC = GetDC( hWnd );
  GetTextMetrics( hDC, &Metrics );
  ReleaseDC( hWnd, hDC );
  nExtLeading = Metrics.tmExternalLeading;
  nCharSizeX = Metrics.tmMaxCharWidth;
  nCharSizeY =
    Metrics.tmHeight + Metrics.tmExternalLeading;

  /* Make the window visible before grabbing spy info,
   * so it's included */
  ShowWindow( hWnd, nCmdShow );

  /* Post a message to ourself to trigger the first
   * spy information display */
  PostMessage( hWnd, WM_COMMAND, CMD_SPY, OL );

  return TRUE;
}

/* - - - - - - - - - - - - - - - - - - - - - - - - */

/* Format and paint a line of text. The parameters
 * are the same as for an ordinary printf call, a
 * format string followed by a variable number of
 * arguments to be formatted. We use the vsprintf
```

continued

```
 *   function to format the final string to be
 *   painted. The global variables nPaintX and nPaintY
 *   tell where to paint the line. We increment
 *   nPaintY to the next line after painting. Note the
 *   cdecl' declaration. This forces this function to
 *   use the standard C calling sequence, which is
 *   necessary with a variable number of parameters.
 */

void cdecl Paint( szFormat /* , ... */ )
  char *      szFormat;   /* vsprintf format string  */
{
  va_list     pArgs;      /* vsprintf parameters     */
  int         nLength;    /* Formatted string length */
  char        Buf[160];   /* Temp buffer             */

  va_start( pArgs, szFormat );
  nLength = vsprintf( Buf, szFormat, pArgs );
  va_end( pArgs );

  TextOut(
    hdcPaint,
    nPaintX,
    nPaintY+nExtLeading,
    Buf,
    nLength
  );

  nPaintY += nCharSizeY;
}


/* - - - - - - - - - - - - - - - - - - - - - - - - - */

/*   Paints our window or any portion of it that needs
 *   painting. The BeginPaint call sets up a structure
 *   that tells us what rectangle of the window to
 *   paint, along with other information for the
 *   painting process. First, erase the background
 *   area if necessary. Then, calculate the index into
 *   the INFO array to start with, based on the
 *   painting rectangle and the scroll bar position, and
 *   lock down the INFO. Finally, loop through the
 *   INFO array, painting the text for each entry.
```

continued

```
 *  Quit when we run out of entries or hit the bottom
 *  of the paint rectangle.
 */

void PaintWindow( hWnd )
  HWND          hWnd;         /* Window handle to paint  */
{
  PAINTSTRUCT ps;            /* Painting information    */
  DWORD         rgbOldText;  /* Old text color          */
  DWORD         rgbOldBkgd;  /* Old background color     */
  int           nWin;         /* Index into INFO array   */
  int           X;            /* X position (temp)       */
  int           Y;            /* Y position (temp)       */
  PSTR          pTypeName;   /* Ptr to style string     */

  /* Set up paint structure, store HDC for Paint() */
  hdcPaint = BeginPaint( hWnd, &ps );

  /* Set up painting colors and save old values */
  rgbOldBkgd =
    SetBkColor(
      hdcPaint,
      GetSysColor(COLOR_WINDOW)
    );
  rgbOldText =
    SetTextColor(
      hdcPaint,
      GetSysColor(COLOR_WINDOWTEXT)
    );

  /* Calculate horizontal paint position, based on
   * the scroll bar position */
  X = ( 1 - GetScrollPos( hWnd, SB_HORZ ) )
      * nCharSizeX;

  /* Calculate index into INFO array and vertical paint
   * position, based on scroll bar position and top of
   * painting rectangle */
  Y = GetScrollPos( hWnd, SB_VERT );
  nWin = ( ps.rcPaint.top - nCharSizeY + Y )
         - nLinesEach;
  nPaintY = ( nWin * nLinesEach - Y )
            * nCharSizeY;
```

continued

```
/* Lock down INFO array and set lpInfo pointing to
 * first entry to paint */
lpInfo = (LPINFO)GlobalLock( hInfo );
lpInfo += nWin;

/* Loop through INFO entries, painting each one until
 * we run out of entries or until we are past the
 * bottom of the paint rectangle. We don't worry
 * much about painting outside the rectangle--
 * Windows will clip for us. */
while(
  nWin < nWindows  &&
  nPaintY < ps.rcPaint.bottom
) {

    /* Set X position and indent child windows */
    nPaintX =
      X +
      ( lpInfo->winLevel * nCharSizeX
          * (bExpand ? 4 : 2) );

    /* Set up pTypeName for window style */
    if( lpInfo->winStyle & WS_CHILD )
      pTypeName = "Child window";
    else if( lpInfo->winStyle & WS_ICONIC )
      pTypeName = "Iconic window";
    else if( lpInfo->winStyle & WS_POPUP )
      pTypeName = "Popup window";
    else
      pTypeName = "Window";

    if( ! bExpand ) {

      /* Paint the summary view */
      Paint(
        "%s %04X {%Fs} (%d,%d;%d,%d) \"%Fs\"",
        pTypeName,
        lpInfo->winHWnd,
        lpInfo->winClass,
        lpInfo->winWindowRect.left,
        lpInfo->winWindowRect.top,
        lpInfo->winWindowRect.right,
```

continued

```
        lpInfo->winWindowRect.bottom,
        lpInfo->winTitle
    );

} else {

    /* Paint the detail view, window handle first */
    Paint(
        "%s handle: %04X",
        pTypeName,
        lpInfo->winHWnd
    );

    /* Paint the rest of the info, indented more */
    nPaintX += nCharSizeX * 2;

    Paint( "Class name: %Fs", lpInfo->winClass );
    Paint( "Window title: %Fs", lpInfo->winTitle );
    Paint(
        "Parent window handle: %04X",
        lpInfo->winHWndParent
    );
    Paint(
        "Class function, Window function: %p, %p",
        lpInfo->winClassProc,
        lpInfo->winWndProc
    );
    Paint(
        "Class module handle, Window instance handle: \
%04X, %04X",
        lpInfo->winClassModule,
        lpInfo->winInstance
    );
    Paint(
        "Class extra alloc, Window extra alloc: \
%d, %d",
        lpInfo->winClsExtra,
        lpInfo->winWndExtra
    );
    Paint(
        "Class style, Window style: %04X, %08lX",
        lpInfo->winClassStyle,
        lpInfo->winStyle
```

continued

```
        );
        Paint(
          lpInfo->winStyle & WS_CHILD
            ? "Control ID: %d"
            : "Menu handle: %04X",
          lpInfo->winControlID
        );
        Paint(
          "Brush, Cursor, Icon handles: \
%04X, %04X, %04X",
          lpInfo->winBkgdBrush,
          lpInfo->winCursor,
          lpInfo->winIcon
        );
        Paint(
          "Window rectangle: \
Left=%4d, Top=%4d, Right=%4d, Bottom=%4d",
          lpInfo->winWindowRect.left,
          lpInfo->winWindowRect.top,
          lpInfo->winWindowRect.right,
          lpInfo->winWindowRect.bottom
        );
        Paint(
          "Client rectangle: \
Left=%4d, Top=%4d, Right=%4d, Bottom=%4d",
          lpInfo->winClientRect.left,
          lpInfo->winClientRect.top,
          lpInfo->winClientRect.right,
          lpInfo->winClientRect.bottom
        );

        /* Make a blank line--it's already erased,
         * so just increment Y */
        nPaintY += nCharSizeY;
      }

    /* Increment to next INFO entry */
    ++nWin;
    ++lpInfo;
    }


    /* Unlock the INFO array */
    GlobalUnlock( hInfo );
```

continued

```
   /* Restore old colors */
   SetBkColor( hdcPaint, rgbOldBkgd );
   SetTextColor( hdcPaint, rgbOldText );

   /* Tell Windows we're done painting */
   EndPaint( hWnd, &ps );
}


/* - - - - - - - - - - - - - - - - - - - - - - - - - */


/*  Set horizontal and vertical scroll bars, based on
 *  the window size and the number of INFO entries.
 *  The scroll bar ranges are set to give a total
 *  width of WINDOW_WIDTH and a total height equal to
 *  the number of lines of information available. For
 *  example, if there are 130 lines of information and
 *  the window height is 10 characters, the vertical
 *  scroll range is set to 120 (130 - 10). This lets
 *  you scroll through everything and still have a
 *  full window of information at the bottom. (Unlike,
 *  say, Windows Write, in which scrolling to the
 *  bottom gives a blank screen.)
 */

void SetScrollBars( hWnd )
   HWND         hWnd;        /* Window handle            */
{
   RECT         rect;        /* Window client rectangle */

   GetClientRect( hWnd, &rect );

   SetScrollBar1(
     hWnd, SB_HORZ,
     WINDOW_WIDTH - rect.right / nCharSizeX
   );

   SetScrollBar1(
     hWnd, SB_VERT,
     nWindows * nLinesEach - rect.bottom / nCharSizeY
   );
}
```

continued

```
/* - - - - - - - - - - - - - - - - - - - - - - - */

/*  Set one scroll bar's maximum range. We always set
 *  the minimum to zero, although Windows allows other
 *  values. There is one case we handle specially. If
 *  you set a scroll bar range to minimum==maximum
 *  (maximum = zero for us), Windows does not actually
 *  set the range, but instead turns off the scroll
 *  bar completely, changing the window style by
 *  turning off the WS_HSCROLL or WS_VSCROLL bit. For
 *  example, this is how the MS-DOS Executive makes
 *  its scroll bars appear and disappear. This
 *  behavior is fine if you take it into account in
 *  your programming in two ways. First, whenever you
 *  do a GetScrollRange you must first check the window
 *  style to see if that scroll bar still exists,
 *  because you will *not* get the correct answer from
 *  GetScrollRange if it has been removed. Second, you
 *  must be prepared to get some extra WM_SIZE
 *  messages, because your client area changes size
 *  when the scroll bars appear and disappear. This
 *  can cause some sloppy looking screen painting. We
 *  take a different approach, always keeping the
 *  scroll bars visible. If the scroll bar range needs
 *  to be set to zero, we set it to MAXINT instead so
 *  the bar remains visible. Then, DoScrollMessage
 *  checks for this case and returns without scrolling.
 */

void SetScrollBar1( hWnd, nBar, nMax )
    HWND        hWnd;       /* Window handle          */
    int         nBar;       /* SB_HORZ or SB_VERT     */
    int         nMax;       /* New maximum range value */
{
    int         nOldMin;    /* Previous min value (0)  */
    int         nOldMax;    /* Previous max value     */

    /* Check for a negative or zero range and set our
     * special case flag. Also, set the thumb position
     * to zero in this case. */
    if( nMax <= 0 ) {
        nMax = MAXINT;
        DoScrollMsg( hWnd, nBar, SB_THUMBPOSITION, 0 );
```

continued

```
  }

  /* Get previous range, set it if it has changed */
  GetScrollRange( hWnd, nBar, &nOldMin, &nOldMax );
  if( nMax != nOldMax )
    SetScrollRange( hWnd, nBar, 0, nMax, TRUE );
}


/* - - - - - - - - - - - - - - - - - - - - - - - - - */


/*  Loop through all windows in the system and gather
 *  up information for the INFO structure for each. We
 *  actually loop through them twice:  first, to
 *  simply count them so we can allocate global memory
 *  for the INFO structure, and again to actually fill
 *  in the structure. After gathering up the
 *  information, we invalidate our window, which will
 *  cause a WM_PAINT message to be posted, so it will
 *  get repainted.
 */

BOOL SpyOnAllWindows( hWnd )
  HWND          hWnd;        /* Our window handle      */
{
  HWND          hWndTop;     /* Window handle for loop */

  /* Count up the number of windows */
  nWindows = 0;
  for(
    hWndTop = GetWindow( hWnd, GW_HWNDFIRST );
    hWndTop;
    hWndTop = GetWindow( hWndTop, GW_HWNDNEXT )
  ) {
    CountWindow( hWndTop );
  }

  /* Allocate memory, complain if we couldn't get it */
  hInfo =
    GlobalReAlloc(
      hInfo,
      (DWORD)nWindows*sizeof(INFO),
      GMEM_MOVEABLE
    );
```

continued

```
if( ! hInfo ) {
  nWindows = 0;
  GlobalDiscard( hInfo );
  MessageBox(
    GetActiveWindow(),
    "Insufficient memory!!",
    NULL,
    MB_OK | MB_ICONHAND
  );
  PostQuitMessage( 0 );
  return FALSE;
}


/* Lock down memory and fill it in, then unlock */
lpInfo = (LPINFO)GlobalLock( hInfo );
for(
  hWndTop = GetWindow( hWnd, GW_HWNDFIRST );
  hWndTop;
  hWndTop = GetWindow( hWndTop, GW_HWNDNEXT )
) {
  SpyOnWindow( hWndTop, 0 );
}
GlobalUnlock( hInfo );

/* Set scroll bars based on new window count */
SetScrollBars( hWnd );
HomeScrollBars( hWnd, TRUE );

/* Invalidate our window so it will be repainted */
InvalidateRect( hWnd, NULL, TRUE );

return TRUE;
}

/* - - - - - - - - - - - - - - - - - - - - - - - - - */

/* Gather up the information for a single window and
 * store it in the INFO array entry pointed to by
 * lpInfo. Increment lpInfo to the next entry
 * afterward. Called once for each window.
 */
```

continued

```
void SpyOnWindow( hWnd, nLevel )
  HWND         hWnd;       /* Window handle          */
  int          nLevel;     /* Child window level     */
{
  HWND         hWndChild;  /* Child window for loop  */

  /* Gather up this window's information */
  lpInfo->winHWnd = hWnd;
  GetClassName( hWnd, lpInfo->winClass, CLASSMAX );
  lpInfo->winClass[ CLASSMAX - 1 ] = 0;
  lpInfo->winInstance =
    GetWindowWord( hWnd, GWW_HINSTANCE );
  lpInfo->winHWndParent = GetParent( hWnd );
  GetWindowText( hWnd, lpInfo->winTitle, TITLEMAX );
  lpInfo->winTitle[ TITLEMAX - 1 ] = 0;
  lpInfo->winControlID =
    GetWindowWord( hWnd, GWW_ID );
  lpInfo->winWndProc =
    (FARPROC)GetWindowLong( hWnd, GWL_WNDPROC );
  lpInfo->winStyle =
    GetWindowLong( hWnd, GWL_STYLE );
  GetClientRect( hWnd, &lpInfo->winClientRect );
  GetWindowRect( hWnd, &lpInfo->winWindowRect );
  lpInfo->winLevel = nLevel;

  /* Gather up class information */
  lpInfo->winBkgdBrush =
    GetClassWord( hWnd, GCW_HBRBACKGROUND );
  lpInfo->winCursor =
    GetClassWord( hWnd, GCW_HCURSOR );
  lpInfo->winIcon =
    GetClassWord( hWnd, GCW_HICON );
  lpInfo->winClassModule =
    GetClassWord( hWnd, GCW_HMODULE );
  lpInfo->winWndExtra =
    GetClassWord( hWnd, GCW_CBWNDEXTRA );
  lpInfo->winClsExtra =
    GetClassWord( hWnd, GCW_CBCLSEXTRA );
  lpInfo->winClassStyle =
    GetClassWord( hWnd, GCW_STYLE );
  lpInfo->winClassProc =
    (FARPROC)GetClassLong( hWnd, GCL_WNDPROC );
```

continued

```
/* Move on to next entry in table */
++lpInfo;

/* Now spy on children recursively */
for(
  hWndChild = GetWindow( hWnd, GW_CHILD );
  hWndChild;
  hWndChild = GetWindow( hWndChild, GW_HWNDNEXT )
) {
  SpyOnWindow( hWndChild, nLevel + 1 );
}
}


/* - - - - - - - - - - - - - - - - - - - - - - - - - */


/*  Window function for our main window. All messages
 *  for our window are sent to this function. For
 *  messages that we do not handle here, we call
 *  DefWindowProc, which performs Windows' default
 *  processing for a message.
 */

long FAR PASCAL SpyWndProc(
  hWnd, wMsg, wParam, lParam
)
  HWND      hWnd;        /* Window handle           */
  WORD      wMsg;        /* Message number          */
  WORD      wParam;      /* Word parameter          */
  LONG      lParam;      /* Long parameter          */
{
  RECT      rect;        /* Temp rectangle          */
  FARPROC   lpProc;      /* AboutBox ProcInstance   */

  switch( wMsg ) {

    /* Menu command message - process the command */
    case WM_COMMAND:
      if( LOWORD(lParam) )
        break; /* not a command */
      switch( wParam ) {
        case CMD_ABOUT:
          lpProc =
            MakeProcInstance(
```

continued

```
            (FARPROC)AboutBox,
            hInstance
         );
      if( ! lpProc )
         return 0L;
      DialogBox(
         hInstance,
         MAKEINTRESOURCE(ABOUTBOX),
         hWnd,
         lpProc
      );
      FreeProcInstance( lpProc );
      return 0L;
   case CMD_EXIT:
      DestroyWindow( hWnd );
      return 0L;
   case CMD_EXPAND:
      bExpand = ! bExpand;
      nLinesEach =
         ( bExpand ? LINES_PER_WINDOW : 1 );
      CheckMenuItem(
         GetMenu( hWnd ),
         CMD_EXPAND,
         bExpand ? MF_CHECKED : MF_UNCHECKED
      );
      InvalidateRect( hWnd, NULL, TRUE );
      HomeScrollBars( hWnd, FALSE );
      SetScrollBars( hWnd );
      return 0L;
   case CMD_SPY:
      SpyOnAllWindows( hWnd );
      return 0L;
   }
   break;

/* Destroy-window message - quit the application */
case WM_DESTROY:
   PostQuitMessage( 0 );
   return 0L;

/* Horizontal scroll message--scroll the window */
case WM_HSCROLL:
   DoScrollMsg(
```

continued

```
        hWnd, SB_HORZ,
        wParam, (int)lParam
      );
      return OL;


    /* Key-down message--handle cursor keys, ignore
     * other keys */
    case WM_KEYDOWN:
      if(
        wParam >= VK_MIN_CURSOR  &&
        wParam <= VK_MAX_CURSOR
      ) {
        DoScrollMsg(
          hWnd,
          CsrScroll[ wParam--VK_MIN_CURSOR ].csBar,
          CsrScroll[ wParam--VK_MIN_CURSOR ].csMsg,
          0
        );
      }
      return OL;


    /* Paint message--repaint window as needed */
    case WM_PAINT:
      PaintWindow( hWnd );
      return OL;


    /* Size message--recalculate our scroll bars */
    case WM_SIZE:
      SetScrollBars( hWnd );
      return OL;


    /* Vertical scroll message--scroll the window */
    case WM_VSCROLL:
      DoScrollMsg(
        hWnd, SB_VERT,
        wParam, (int)lParam
      );
      return OL;
  }


  /* All other messages go to DefWindowProc */
  return DefWindowProc( hWnd, wMsg, wParam, lParam );
}
```

continued

```
/* - - - - - - - - - - - - - - - - - - - - - - - - */


/* Application main program. Not much is done here--
 * we just initialize the application, putting up our
 * window, and then go into the message dispatching
 * loop that every Windows application has.
 */

int PASCAL WinMain(
  hInst, hPrevInst, lpszCmdLine, nCmdShow
)
  HANDLE      hInst;        /* Our instance handle    */
  HANDLE      hPrevInst;    /* Previous instance      */
  LPSTR       lpszCmdLine;  /* Command line pointer   */
  int         nCmdShow;     /* ShowWindow parameter   */
{
  MSG         msg;          /* Message structure */

  /* Save our instance handle in static variable */
  hInstance = hInst;

  /* Initialize application, quit if any errors */
  if( ! Initialize( hPrevInst, nCmdShow ) )
    return 1;

  /* Main message processing loop. Get each message,
   * then translate keyboard messages, and finally
   * dispatch each message to its window function. */
  while( GetMessage( &msg, NULL, 0, 0 ) ) {
    TranslateMessage( &msg );
    DispatchMessage( &msg );
  }

  return msg.wParam;
}

/* - - - - - - - - - - - - - - - - - - - - - - - - */


* * * * * * * * * * * *    SPY.RC    * * * * * * * * * * * * * *

/* - - - - - - - - - - - - - - - - - - - - - - - - */
```

continued

```
/* Spy.rc - resource file for SPY.EXE */

/* - - - - - - - - - - - - - - - - - - - - - - - */

#include <style.h>
#include "spy.h"

/* - - - - - - - - - - - - - - - - - - - - - - - */

Spy!    ICON    spy.ico

/* - - - - - - - - - - - - - - - - - - - - - - - */

STRINGTABLE
BEGIN
    IDS_CLASS,      "Spy!"
    IDS_TITLE,      "Spy on Windows!"
END

/* - - - - - - - - - - - - - - - - - - - - - - - */

Spy!    MENU
BEGIN

  POPUP    "&Spy"
  BEGIN
    MENUITEM "&New Spy Mission",  CMD_SPY
    MENUITEM SEPARATOR
    MENUITEM "Show &Detail",      CMD_EXPAND
    MENUITEM SEPARATOR
    MENUITEM "E&xit",             CMD_EXIT
    MENUITEM "A&bout Spy...",     CMD_ABOUT
  END

END


/* - - - - - - - - - - - - - - - - - - - - - - - */

ABOUTBOX DIALOG 25, 25, 180, 85
STYLE WS_DLGFRAME | WS_POPUP
BEGIN
    CTEXT "Spy"                     -1,  0,  5,180, 8
```

continued

```
    ICON  "Spy!"                    -1, 13, 25,  0, 0
    CTEXT "Windows espionage program" -1,  0, 16,180, 8
    CTEXT "Version 1.1"             -1, 58, 38, 64, 8
    CTEXT "Written by Michael Geary" -1,  0, 50,180, 8
    DEFPUSHBUTTON "Ok"   IDOK, 74, 67, 32, 14, WS_GROUP
END


/* - - - - - - - - - - - - - - - - - - - - - - - - */


* * * * * * * * * * * *    SPY.DEF   * * * * * * * * * * * * * * *

NAME    Spy

DESCRIPTION 'Windows Espionage'

STUB    'WINSTUB.EXE'

CODE    MOVEABLE
DATA    MOVEABLE MULTIPLE

HEAPSIZE    1024
STACKSIZE   4096

EXPORTS
    AboutBox       @1
    SpyWndProc     @2
```

Reading List

Geary, M. 1987. Microsoft Windows 2.0. *Microsoft Systems Journal* (July).

———. 1987. Spying on windows. *Byte Extra Edition: Inside the IBM PCs* 12, no. 12.

———. 1988. Converting Windows applications for Microsoft's OS/2 Presentation Manager. *Microsoft Systems Journal* (January).

Grayson, P. 1987. Windows of opportunity. *PC Tech Journal* (February).

Petzold, C. 1986. A step-by-step guide to building your first windows application. *Microsoft Systems Journal* (December).

————. 1988. *Programming Windows*. Redmond, Washington: Microsoft Press.

Wong, W. 1987. Program interfacing to Microsoft Windows. *Micro/Systems Journal* (series starting January/February).

Michael Geary is the principal author of Gupta Technologies' SQLWindows, an interactive application development system for SQL database applications running under MS Windows and the OS/2 Presentation Manager. He has written articles on MS Windows programming for *Byte* and *Microsoft Systems Journal* and is the author of several popular windows utilities, including SPY, Tiler, and Termite (a utility that integrates Notepad and terminal). He is also a technical advisor in Microsoft online support forums.

Related Essays

1 A Guided Tour inside MS-DOS
4 Adding Power to MS-DOS Programming

WORKING WITH THE HARDWARE INTERFACE

The huge existing base of MS-DOS machines offers a stable, lucrative market for those who can extract the maximum speed from RAM memory, board-level registers, and the clever choice of MS-DOS services. The Expanded Memory System, the serial port, the Enhanced Graphics Adapter, and many other devices connect to the main bus through the slots, known as the I/O channel. Such a unifying point in common highlights the contrast in style with which the authors treat their topics. The five essays in this section focus on control of the hardware environment.

Developing MS-DOS Device Drivers

This section's first essay, by Walter Dixon, explains the construction of device drivers and their interface with the DOS kernel and loader. We see how the System File Table, file handles, Device Control Blocks, Current Directory Structure, Program Segment Prefix, and other data structures and workings come into play during the process of loading and using a device driver.

Writing a SOUND Device Driver

Walter Dixon builds on his previous essay and presents a full-blown device driver that turns the PC into a musical instrument, parallel to the PLAY statement in BASIC. The SOUND driver can be played from the MS-DOS user interface or from within an application, the difference being only in writing to the driver.

Programming the Enhanced Graphics Adapter

This essay by Andrew Dumke explains the new latching and bit-map design of this popular display interface. Then he presents a fast dot-drawing program in C, a fast line-drawing algorithm, and ways to read EGA memory, perform Boolean operations on its bit maps, and more.

Programming the Serial Port with C

Naba Barkakati reviews the basics of serial communications and explains the hardware of the serial port. He then discusses error-checking, flow control, buffers, serial interrupts, and use of a circular buffer, and ends with a complete communications program in C.

Understanding Expanded Memory Systems

Ray Duncan explains the rudiments of the bank-switching scheme for EMS, EEMS, and EMS 4.0 and how to test for the Enhanced Memory Manager. He summarizes relevant functions and presents an eight-step strategy for writing applications for Enhanced Memory Systems.

Keywords

- ► device drivers
- ► character devices
- ► block devices
- ► device requests
- ► MS-DOS data structures
- ► file control
- ► IOCTL
- ► driver routines

Essay Synopsis: Device drivers are the essential facilities that allow MS-DOS application programs to control a variety of input and output devices. To become a master programmer of MS-DOS device drivers, you must delve into internal data structures and undocumented features of MS-DOS. The author has painstakingly disassembled the relevant areas of DOS to provide you with a roadmap. The journey begins with a general introduction to the types of drivers and their uses. Next, the author discusses the way drivers are loaded, the data structures they use, and the process by which requests are sent to and handled by the driver.

10

Developing MS-DOS Device Drivers

Walter Dixon

Each MS-DOS application program calls upon DOS to perform services such as opening or writing to a file. Some of these services greatly simplify the task of program development; for example, an application asks DOS to write 10 characters to a printer the same way it would ask that those characters be sent to a disk file. This feature is known as device-independent I/O, a very important service because it frees the application from dealing with the hardware details of different devices.

What we call DOS really is a number of distinct components: the kernel, device drivers, a user interface, and kernel enhancements. (See Essay 1, A Guided Tour inside MS-DOS, by Harry Henderson, for an overview of the MS-DOS components and their interfaces.) The kernel is a basic set of services, most of which are I/O related. Included in the kernel is support for the file system and device-independent I/O. Device drivers are short pieces of code that help DOS deal with hardware such as disks, keyboards, and consoles. Drivers worry about the hardware which controls individual devices and hide these details from the kernel. Kernel enhancements extend the functionality of the kernel. They are needed in special circumstances and should function transparently when they are invoked; for example, `SHARE.EXE` is a kernel enhancement which supports file sharing.

I obtained material for this paper by disassembling PC-DOS version 3.10. As far as I know, much of this information has not been previously documented. Disassembling a complex program such as DOS without access to any of the design documentation is a difficult task. I cannot guarantee that the descriptions are completely accurate or that the operating system design will not change in the future. If you make use of any of this material, you do so at your own risk.

Documentation on the Application/Kernel and Kernel/Driver interface is reasonably good, but the actions of the DOS kernel remain somewhat of a mystery. It loads and locates device drivers and transforms high-level application requests such as read and write into device driver operations. Values in the kernel

I/O data structures affect the way the kernel transforms requests. A side effect of these transformations is that the kernel sends status, flush, and nondestructive read requests to various drivers.

The design of the DOS kernel limits the actions of both drivers and applications. Significant portions of the kernel are nonreentrant and once the kernel begins to execute a nonreentrant section of code, it must complete that section before it can safely process another request. Some of the more subtle implications of this architectural will enable you to bend some of the published rules for writing drivers and create your own background programs like PRINT.COM which can share the processor with other tasks.

This essay concentrates on the transformation process and its side effects. Some exposure to device drivers is necessary if you want to completely understand the interaction of the DOS kernel with drivers. Even if you do not plan to write a driver, you may find this material interesting. DOS is a significant operating system; understanding what goes on behind the scenes has a certain intrinsic value. If you are interested in DOS trivia, many undocumented features of DOS surface in these discussions.

DOS Data Structures

DOS maintains a number of data structures to track systemwide resources like memory and devices. These data structures are created when the kernel boots and are updated as the kernel processes requests. Other resources are application-private, but still must be managed by DOS. Let's look at these data structures and how they are used.

Systemwide Resources

DOS constructs a list of device drivers, a System File Table (SFT), a Device Control Block (DCB) list, and a Current Directory Structure (CDS). The SFT is the focal point for device-independent I/O. DOS uses the DCB list and CDS to help manage disk operations. The CDS is also where DOS stores the current default directory for each drive. Most DOS requests ultimately manipulate one or more of these data structures.

Application-Private Resources in the PSP

When an application starts, the DOS Kernel creates a data structure known as the Program Segment Prefix (PSP) which DOS uses to store application-specific I/O information, to process errors, and to terminate an application gracefully.

DOS deallocates the PSP when the application exits. Listing 10-1 illustrates the format of the PSP. I have arbitrarily assigned names to the various fields in this structure. The comments following each field describe how DOS uses that field. Undocumented fields are marked with an asterisk (*).

Listing 10-1.   Structure of the PSP

```
PSP             STRUC
PSP_W_INT20     DW      0cd20H              ; INT 20 instruction
PSP_W_MemSiz    DW      0                   ; Paragraphs of memory
PSP_B_Unused0   DB      0                   ; Unknown
PSP_T_Call      DB      09aH,0f0H           ; Far call to DOS
                DB      0feH,01dH,0f0H      ; dispatcher
PSP_D_Term      DD      0                   ; Terminate Address
PSP_D_Break     DD      0                   ; Break Address
PSP_D_CritErr   DD      0                   ; Critical error
PSP_W_Parent    DW      0                   ; *Parent PSP*
PSP_T_JFT       DB      20 DUP(0ffH)        ; *JFT Table*
PSP_W_Envron    DW      0                   ; Environment
                DW      0                   ; Unknown
                DW      0                   ; Unknown
PSP_W_JFTSize   DW      20                  ; *JFT Size*
PSP_D_JFTAddr   DD      0                   ; *JFT Address*
PSP_D_Unused1   DW      0ffffH,0ffffH       ; Unused
                DB      16 DUP(0)           ; Unused
PSP_T_Parm1     DB      16 DUP(0)           ; Formatted param 1
PSP_T_Parm2     DB      20 DUP(0)           ; Formatted param 2
PSP_T_DTA       DB      128 DUP(0)          ; Default DTA
PSP             ENDS
```

The Application Interface

Once an application is running, it requests DOS services through the 80X86 interrupt mechanism by placing request-specific information into one or more index registers and executing an interrupt instruction. Different interrupts provide a variety of services.

The Interrupt Mechanism

The general form of an interrupt instruction is INT nn, where nn is a number in the range from 0 to 255. When the processor executes one of these instructions, the contents of the flags, code segment, and instruction pointer registers are pushed on the stack. The interrupt number, nn, becomes an index into a table of double-word pointers in low memory called the Interrupt Vector Table (IVT).

The IVT begins at location 0:0. Each entry contains the address of an interrupt service routine. If the processor had executed an INT 21H instruction, the interrupt number, 21H, would become the index into the IVT. Location 0:84H (84H = 4 × 21H) contains the address of the INT 21H interrupt service routine which will gain control as a result of an INT 21H instruction.

Using the IVT allows DOS to dynamically alter the addresses of the interrupt service routines. This feature is important because it allows for customization. A number of factors, including DOS version, affect where various parts of the operating system get loaded. These services are requested by number and the kernel and the processor convert this number into an address.

When it has completed the request, the interrupt service routine executes an IRET instruction which restores the processor flags and returns to the location following the INT instruction.

INT 21H: *The Application Workhorse*

Applications use a variety of interrupts to request kernel services, but INT 21H is the primary DOS interface. This interrupt provides file and device access, supports device independent I/O, supplies status information, and controls various system resources. The INT 21H interrupt service routine is a significant part of the DOS kernel.

An application places a value in AH to select a particular service, loads service-specific values into other registers, and executes an INT 21H instruction. (As of version 3.1 of DOS, there are 63H different INT 21H functions.) The INT 21H service routine contains a dispatcher which selects an appropriate internal routine to complete the request.

DOS-Device Driver Interface

Just as a precise interface exists between an application and DOS, one exists between DOS and a device driver. Each driver has a device header which helps DOS locate and manage the driver.

The DOS kernel maintains a linked list of device headers. One field in this header contains either the address of the next header or a 0ffffffffH to mark the end of the list. The device header for the NUL device is first on this list, and the kernel implicitly knows the location of the NUL device header.

Whenever DOS needs the services of a device driver, DOS constructs a request header and calls the driver. This structure completely describes what DOS needs done. Listing 10-2 shows the format of a generic request header. There are times when the generic header cannot completely specify a request; in these cases, DOS appends additional fields to the request header.

Listing 10-2.   Generic Request Header Format

```
RH              STRUC
RH_B_Length     DB      0           ;; Length (bytes)
RH_B_Unit       DB      0           ;; Unit code
RH_B_Command    DB      0           ;; Command code
RH_W_Status     DW      0           ;; Operation results
RH_T_Reserved   DB      8 DUP(0)
RH              ENDS
```

What Is a Driver and How Is It Used?

DOS depends on device drivers to deal with the idiosyncracies of specific pieces of hardware; you can think of them as special-purpose extensions of the operating system. Drivers isolate DOS from much of the hardware in your PC, allowing DOS to be ported more easily and simplifying support of new devices.

You can find device drivers in two different places. Some drivers are actually part of DOS and are known as *built-in device drivers*. Other device drivers exist as separate files and are called *loadable device drivers*. Both types of drivers have the same structure.

Built-in drivers support those devices used in the boot process, which include the console and boot disk. Locating driver code within the operating system simplifies the boot process.

Loadable drivers customize and enhance DOS and are added as they are needed. When you configured your system, you probably decided to use ANSI.SYS, which modifies the way DOS deals with the console. Using a new device is as simple as asking DOS to load another device driver. If you selected ANSI.SYS, you enhanced DOS. ANSI.SYS replaces the built-in console driver and provides added function. Loadable drivers also reduce memory requirements. You need only load the drivers required to support your particular hardware configuration.

Each driver has three parts: a device header, a strategy routine, and an interrupt routine. The header is a data structure which the driver shares with DOS. The interrupt and strategy routines contain driver code and data. Whenever DOS needs driver service, it builds a request header, locates the driver, and calls the driver strategy and interrupt routines.

The Device Header

The header is a collection of driver specific information which DOS uses in much the same way as it uses the PSP for an application. In addition to the address of the next header, the device header contains device attributes and the offsets of the strategy and interrupt routines. Listing 10-3 shows the structure of the device header.

Listing 10-3.   Device Header

```
DHD             STRUC
DHD_A_NextDHD   DD      0ffffffffH  ;; Address of next header
DHD_W_Attrib    DW      0           ;; Device attributes
DHD_W_StgyEntry DW      0           ;; Strategy routine offset
DHD_W_IntrEntry DW      0           ;; Interrupt routine offset
DHD_T_Name      DB      ' '         ;; Device name
DHD             ENDS
```

The attributes field (a two-byte word) shown in Figure 10-1 is a summary of device characteristics. This is an important field. It distinguishes between block and character devices, declares a driver's ability to handle optional requests, and identifies devices that require special handling. Table 10-1 lists devices and their functions.

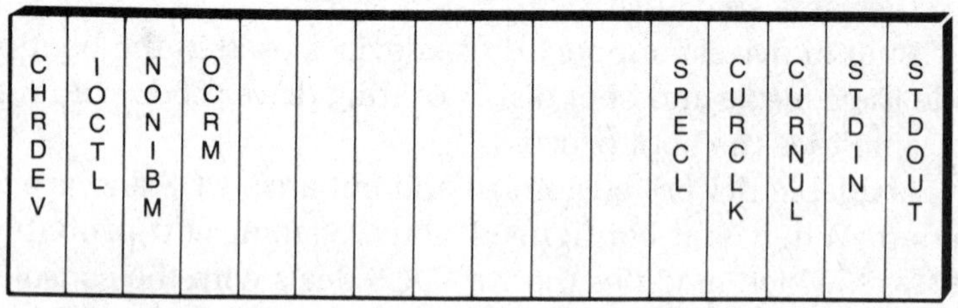

C H R D E V	I O C T L	N O N I B M	O C R M						S P E C L	C U R C L K	C U R N U L	S T D I N	S T D O U T

Fig. 10-1.   Driver attributes word.

A device is either a block device or a character device. Block devices are usually disks and must support the MS-DOS volume structure, which absolutely fixes the location of certain information and establishes rules for naming and organizing files. Character devices, on the other hand, deal with streams of bytes, one byte at a time. The keyboard, display, and printer are character devices.

Strategy and Interrupt Routines

The strategy routine records the address of the request header and returns to DOS. The real work of carrying out the request takes place in the interrupt routine, which recovers the request header address and examines the request type

Table 10-1.   Driver Attributes Field

Device	Characteristics
CHRDEV	Set to indicate a character device. DOS treats character and block devices differently and uses different algorithms to locate their drivers.
IOCTL	Set to indicate driver's ability to respond to I/O Control requests. This support is optional. These requests allow control information such as printer setup or communications parameters to be sent to the device.
NONIBM	A block device is not IBM-format compatible if this bit is set. The media byte takes on special meaning for IBM-format compatible volumes. If this bit is set, a character device can process write-until-busy requests that transfer multiple bytes with one driver request. Normally, characters are sent one at a time.
OCRM	If this bit is set, the driver supports open/close/removable media requests. Driver will be called when a file or device is opened or closed. Removable media requests are sent to block drivers only.
SPECL	Set to indicate that the driver has an **INT 29H** entry point. DOS uses this entry instead of the normal request-passing mechanism to speed output to the current console device. (The current console device has both the STDIN and STDOUT bits set—see below.) This feature has been present in all recent versions of DOS but is not documented. Use at your own risk.
CURCLK	Set to indicate the current clock device. DOS uses the clock device to keep track of the current time and date and to time-stamp files.
CURNUL	If this bit is set, the device is the current NUL device. The NUL device can be written to or read from. Reads always return end of file; writes always succeed. The driver is never actually called to process these requests.
STDIN	Set to indicate that the device is the current standard input device. Certain characters, such as backspace, have special significance. Limited line editing is supported.
STDOUT	If this bit is set, the device is the current standard output device. Certain characters are treated specially. Nonprinting characters are converted to printing and tabs are expanded.

`RH_B_Command`. If the interrupt routine does not support request, it returns an error; otherwise, it processes the request.

Driver Dispatch

After DOS locates the driver and constructs a request header, it places the device header address in DS:SI, the request header address in ES:BX, and calls a driver dispatch routine. With the exception of initialization requests, all driver calls pass through this one routine.

The dispatch routine successively calls the driver strategy and interrupt routines. A side effect of the dispatch logic is that the DS register contains the driver data segment. This feature is not documented and there is no guarantee that future versions of DOS will behave in the same way. Here is the code for the driver dispatch routine:

```
;         DS:SI        has device header address
;         ES:BX        has request header address
;
CallDriver      PROC    NEAR
        mov     ax,[si].DHD_W_StgyEntry ; ax  <== strategy offset
        mov     cs:temp,ax              ; Save strategy offset
        mov     cs:temp+2,ds            ; and segment
        call    cs:DWORD PTR temp       ; Indirect far call to
                                        ; strategy routine
        mov     ax,[si].DHD_W_IntrEntry ; Now fill in interrupt
        mov     cs:temp,ax              ; offset
        call    cs:DWORD PTR temp       ; Indirect far call to
                                        ; interrupt routine
        ret                             ; Return to caller
CallDriver      ENDP
```

Using the DOS INT 21H Application Services Interface

We'll now examine a simple application and its interaction with DOS. The program, LISTER.COM, is shown in Listing 10-4. It uses INT 21H to list a file at on the console. LISTER opens both the file and console device, copies 256 bytes at a time from the file to the console, and returns to DOS after it reaches the end of the input file.

Lines 1 to 14 of LISTER are typical of a COM program. COM programs always begin execution at location 100H. Normally, this location contains a JMP instruction followed by program data and then code. A COM program contains no address references that must be modified when the program loads. This restriction prevents COM programs from making far calls and restricts the way they can initialize segment registers.

LISTER opens the input file (lines 18 to 21) and output device (lines 22 to 27) next. The value placed at AL prior to the open request indicates the access mode—0 for read-only and 1 for write. LISTER opens the input file read-only and the output device for write. A successful open request returns a handle in the AX register that DOS uses to link subsequent requests with a particular file or device.

Lines 30 to 41 read 256 bytes from the input file and write them to the console. Notice how the read and write requests use a handle to specify the target of the read or write operation. Each read request (Line 32) returns the number of bytes read in the AX register. If the length of the file is not a multiple of 256 bytes, the final read will not return the requested number of bytes. Since we do not want to write any more bytes than have been read, the bytes read fixes the size of the next write (Line 36). If the read returns no bytes, LISTER has reached the end of file (lines 33 and 34) and terminates.

Listing 10-4.   LISTER

```
;
;       Copies program source (LISTER.ASM) to console device
;
;       Compile:        MASM LISTER;
;       Link:           LINK LISTER;
;       Convert to COM: EXE2BIN LISTER LISTER.COM
;
bufS    EQU     100H            ; ( 8) Size of program buffer
_text   SEGMENT BYTE PUBLIC 'CODE'
        ASSUME  cs:_text,ds:_text;(10)
        ORG     100H            ; (11) COM programs start here
Lister  PROC    NEAR            ; (12)
        jmp     start           ; (13)
inF     DB      'lister.asm',0  ; (14) name of input file
outF    DB      'con',0         ; (15) name of output device
inH     DW      0               ; (16) handle for input file
outH    DW      0               ; (17) handle for output device
buf     DB      bufS DUP(0)     ; (18) read/write buffer
start:  lea     dx,inF          ; (19) address input filename
        mov     ax,3d00H        ; (20) open for read
        int     21H             ; (21) make request
        mov     inH,ax          ; (22) save handle
        lea     dx,outF         ; (23) address output device
        xor     cx,cx           ; (24) use normal attributes
        mov     ax,3d01H        ; (25) open for write
        int     21H             ; (26) make request
        mov     outH,ax         ; (27) save handle
        mov     cx,bufS         ; (28) buffer size
        lea     dx,buf          ; (29) buffer address
again:  mov     bx,inH          ; (30) input handle
        mov     ah,3fH          ; (31) read function
        int     21H             ; (32) make request
        or      ax,ax           ; (33) end of file?
        jz      done            ; (34) if Z--yes
        mov     bx,outH         ; (35) output handle
        mov     cx,ax           ; (36) bytes read
        mov     ah,40H          ; (37) write function
```

continued

```
          int     21H             ; (38) make request
          jmp     SHORT again     ; (39) repeat read/write
done:     mov     ah,4ch          ; (40) terminate function
          int     21H             ; (41) make request
Lister  ENDP
_text   ENDS
        END     Lister
```

The Boot Process

Now that we see what the DOS kernel can do for us, let's take a look at how some of this magic happens. DOS is a dynamic system, so the best way to see how its parts interact is to see how they are put together. The story begins when DOS boots. The boot process loads the operating system into memory and initializes the major I/O data structures. What we collectively refer to as DOS consists of IBMBIO.COM, IBMDOS.COM, any loadable device drivers, a command line interpreter or shell (normally COMMAND.COM), and possibly some Terminate and Stay Resident (TSR) kernel enhancer like SHARE.EXE.

In the initial stages of the boot process, very few services are available. The ROM code which loads IBMBIO.COM is quite primitive. IBMBIO in turn loads IBMDOS.COM and calls initialization code within IBMDOS which sets up the INT 21H interrupt service routine.

After this IBMDOS initialization code returns to IBMBIO, the customization process can begin. IBMBIO opens and reads CONFIG.SYS using INT 21H requests. Commands in CONFIG.SYS identify loadable drivers and override default values for certain DOS data structures. After CONFIG.SYS has been read, the boot process completes by loading the command line interpreter, COMMAND.COM. COMMAND.COM initializes itself and prompts for user input.

In the Beginning (from ROM to RAM)

When you turn on your system or press control-alt-delete, the processor executes ROM code that verifies the correct operation of your system and figures out what equipment is present. When this Power On Self Test (POST) completes, it executes an INT 19H instruction to invoke the ROM bootstrap routine.

The bootstrap routine tries to read sector 1 track 0 from drive A and then from the hard disk (normally drive C). This sector is the boot sector of an MS-DOS volume. The boot sector contains code and data needed to continue the boot process. Low-level, ROM-based INT 13H requests are used to read the sector. If neither driver responds, control passes to ROM BASIC.

If the boot sector is successfully read, the ROM bootstrap routine jumps to the entry point of the boot-sector code. This code verifies both `IBMBIO.COM` and `IBMDOS.COM` are present in the root directory of the boot disk, and then loads IBMBIO using ROM-based, `INT 13H` requests.

Control passes to IBMBIO which loads `IBMDOS.COM` from disk and calls IBMDOS at its initialization entry point. IBMBIO passes the listhead of a linked list of built-in drivers to IBMDOS; the code for these drivers is part of IBMBIO. This list must contain headers for the disk, clock, and console devices which are needed to finish the boot process. It currently includes drivers for CON (the console), AUX, PRN, CLOCK$ (the clock), COM1, LPT1, LPT2, LPT3, COM2, the floppy disk, and the fixed disk (if present).

`IBMDOS` Initialization

IBMDOS stores the listhead of the driver chain in the next device field of the NUL device header. The NUL device header, which is located in a DOS global table, becomes the new listhead of the driver chain.

IBMDOS scans the driver chain looking for the console and clock devices and records their addresses in the DOS global table. The attributes word of the console driver has both the STDIN and STDOUT bits set; that of the clock driver has the CURCLK bit set. These devices require special treatment.

There are times when DOS must bypass any I/O redirection. Redirection is a function provided by `COMMAND.COM` that allows an application's input and output devices to be changed dynamically. DOS always checks the console device for control-c and reports division overflow (INT 0) to the console device. Using a recorded header address guarantees that these operations are not redirected. Simply naming a device "CON" does not make it the console device. The STDIN and STDOUT bits must be set in the attributes word.

DOS uses the stored address of the clock device header to service explicit time or date requests and to time-stamp certain I/O operations. Recording the address of the clock device header is a performance optimization for time-stamping. The default clock device is named CLOCK$, but DOS uses the CURCLK bit rather than the name to find this device.

Built-in Driver

IBMDOS builds a request header and calls each built-in driver at its strategy and interrupt entry points. The driver initialization code for these built-in devices does very little. Character devices simply set the status word to indicate successful completion. Block device drivers also return a unit count and a table of BIOS parameter block addresses. Each BIOS parameter block provides basic information about disk structure. A block driver can support more than one device. The unit count tells DOS how many devices the driver actually is supporting, and DOS uses this information to initialize the DCB and Cache Block lists.

DCB

The DCB list summarizes the disk structure information returned in the BIOS parameter block and records the address of the device header. The unit count specifies the initial size of the DCB list. Although the DCB entries for the built-in devices are actually contiguous, they are organized as a linked list. DOS records the listhead of the DCB list in the DOS global table.

DOS needs more information about block devices than it does character devices. Where DOS would record the device header address for a character device, DOS records the DCB address for a block device. Since the DCB contains the address of the device header, DOS can find the header if it knows the DCB. Here is the structure of a device control block (none of this is documented, by the way):

```
DCB               STRUC
DCB_B_Drive       DB      0       ; [00] Drive number
DCB_B_Unit        DB      0       ; [01] Unit number
DCB_W_SecSize     DW      0       ; [02] Sector size (Bytes)
DCB_B_ClstMask    DB      0       ; [04] Cluster size -1
                                  ;      Used as mask for finding
                                  ;      cluster boundaries
DCB_B_ClstShift DB        0       ; [05] Sector to cluster shift
                                  ;      mask
                                  ;      Sector >> mask  ==> cluster
DCB_W_FAT1        DW      0       ; [06] LBN of 1st FAT
DCB_B_NumFATs     DB      0       ; [08] Number of FATs
DCB_W_RootSize    DW      0       ; [09] Blocks in root directory
DCB_W_Clst2       DW      0       ; [0B] LBN of first data cluster
DCB_W_LastClst    DW      0       ; [0D] Last cluster in data area
DCB_B_FATSize     DB      0       ; [0F] FAT size (blocks)
DCB_W_RootLBN     DW      0       ; [10] Root Dir LBN
DCB_D_Header      DD      0       ; [12] Device header
DCB_B_MediaCode   DB      0       ; [16] Media code
DCB_B_MediaChgd   DB      0       ; [17] Media changed flag
DCB_D_Next        DD      0       ; [18] Next DCB
DCB_W_Unknown1    DW      0       ; [1C] Unknown
DCB_W_Unknown2    DW      0       ; [1E] Unknown
                  ENDS
```

Cache Block

DOS determines the largest sector size for the built-in block devices by examining the BIOS parameter blocks. This value fixes the size of cache blocks and consequently sets a maximum sector size for all block devices (including loadable devices). IBMDOS allocates a buffer big enough to hold the largest sector and records its address in the DOS global table. This buffer becomes the initial disk cache. The INT 21H disk I/O code requires at least one cache block. DOS uses cache blocks to read File Allocation Table (FAT) and directory blocks and to process partial sector reads and writes.

Contrary to popular opinion, the disk cache is not used to process full block reads and writes for ordinary files. Possibly the designers of DOS felt that it would be unlikely that these complete blocks would be referenced again, and so they would gain newl performance by not having to copy data from cache to a user buffer.

The List of Lists

DOS maintains a table of important information about the I/O subsystem. DOS initially records addresses for the DCB listhead, CONSOLE device header, CLOCK device header, and NUL device header, as well as the largest sector size and current number of block devices. Other information is added later in the boot process.

IBMDOS passes back the address of this global table, which is sometimes referred to as the List of Lists, to IBMBIO. Applications can locate this structure through the undocumented INT 21H (AH = 52H). The following is a listing of the contents of this table; none of it is documented. The labels in this listing refer to offsets in the DOS 3.1 data segment:

```
L0026           DD      0       ; listhead for Device Control
                                ; Blocks (DCBs)
L002A           DD      0       ; System File Table listhead
                                ; (SFT)--handles
L002E           DD      0       ; clock device header
L0032           DD      0       ; console device header
L0036           DW      0       ; largest sector
L0038           DD      0       ; listhead for cache blocks
L003C           DD      0       ; address of Current Directory
                                ; Structure (CDS)
L0040           DD      0       ; System File Table listhead
                                ; (SFT)--FCBs
L0044           DW      0       ; Size of FCB SFT Table
L0046           DB      0       ; drive count
L0047           DB      0       ; last drive
;
;                       Device header for null device
;
L0048           DD      0       ; next device
L004C           DW      8004    ; attributes
```

```
L004E          DW      L1418   ; strategy entry
L0050          DW      L141E   ; interrupt entry
L0052          DB      'NUL    ' ; device name
L005A          DB      0       ; count of joined drives
```

The IBMDOS initialization code fills in a number of entries in the IVT, including the address of the INT 21H interrupt service routine, and returns to IBMBIO, passing back the address of the List of Lists. Much of the memory occupied by this initialization code will be overwritten with DOS data later.

DOS Returns to Its Roots

When IBMBIO receives control again, the console, clock, and disk devices are initialized and INT 21H is operational. IBMBIO uses INT 21H to open and read CONFIG.SYS. Entries in this file customize the boot process by identifying loadable device drivers, controlling the size of various DOS tables, requesting specific processing options, and specifying a shell.

When IBMBIO encounters a "device =" statement in CONFIG.SYS, it loads the driver, inserts its device header immediately after the NUL device in the device header chain, builds an initialization request header, and calls the driver. The driver initialization routine performs any device-specific initialization and returns to IBMBIO.

IBMBIO uses driver-supplied information from the request header to continue the boot process. Each driver initially has all available memory allocated to it. The driver initialization code sets the break address in the request header and IBMBIO uses this information to determine where the next device will be loaded.

Block drivers must also return a unit count and the address of a table of BIOS parameter blocks. IBMBIO adds this unit count to the current number block devices and uses information from the BIOS parameter block table to build a DCB for each unit. IBMBIO adds each new DCB to the linked list of device control blocks.

Adding Some Finishing Touches

After reading CONFIG.SYS, IBMBIO allocates the remaining cache blocks, two SFTs, and the CDS, and inserts their addresses in the List of Lists. Parameters in CONFIG.SYS may affect the size of these data structures.

Completing the Cache

DOS maintains a user-selectable number of memory blocks (a cache) for buffering disk I/O operations. Either a "buffers = " statement in CONFIG.SYS or a default value sets the number of cache blocks. IBMBIO allocates the remaining cache blocks and inserts them in a linked list of available blocks.

There are 16 bytes of overhead for each cache block. DOS uses this space to manage the disk block cache. The next listing illustrates the layout of a cache block. Note that the largest sector on a built-in block device sets the size of the data area. This listing assumes the normal value of 512 bytes. This information is also undocumented.

```
STRUC          CCB
CCB_D_NextCCB  DD      0          ; [00H] Next CCB in linked list
CCB_B_Owner    DB      0          ; [04H] Owning Drive
CCB_B_Status   DB      0          ; [05H] Status of block

CCB_M_IsFAT    EQU     02H        ; This block is a FAT
CCB_M_IsDir    EQU     04H        ; This is a directory Block
CCB_M_IsData   EQU     08H        ; This is a data block
CCB_M_IsValid  EQU     20H        ; This block is valid
CCB_M_IsDirty  EQU     40H        ; This block is dirty

CCB_W_LBN      DW      0          ; [06H] Block number
CCB_W_Count    DW      0          ; [08H] Number of blocks
CCB_D_DCB      DD      0          ; [0aH] DCB of owning drive
CCB_W_Flags    DW      0          ; [0eH] Flags
CCB_T_Data     DB      512 DUP(0) ; [10H] Data from disk
CCB            ENDS
```

The System File Table

The SFT is one of the principal MS-DOS I/O data structures and is the focal point for device independent I/O. Whenever DOS initially accesses a file or device, it creates an SFT entry. This entry records the file/device name, directory attributes, device attributes, context information such as file size and position, and either the DCB (block devices) or Device Header (character devices) address. DOS uses separate SFTs for File Control Block (FCB) and handles. FCBs are another technique for accessing files and devices, providing the same basic capabilities as handles.

The size of the FCB System File Table is fixed by an "fcb = " statement in CONFIG.SYS or a default value. The handle table can grow dynamically. Here is the format for an SFT entry. This information is undocumented.

```
SFT             STRUC
SFT_W_RefCnt    DW       0         ; [00] reference count
SFT_W_Mode      DW       0         ; [02] open mode

SFT_M_FCB       EQU      8000H     ; Entry is for FCB
SFT_M_DenyNone  EQU      0040H     ; Sharing bits (4-6)
SFT_M_DenyRead  EQU      0030H     ;       "
SFT_M_DenyWrite EQU      0020H     ;       "
SFT_M_Exclusive EQU      0010H     ;       "
SFT_M_NetFCB    EQU      0070H     ; This is a network FCB
SFT_M_Write     EQU      0001H     ; File access bits (0-2)
SFT_M_Read      EQU      0000H     ;       "

SFT_B_DirAttrib DB       0         ; [04]
SFT_W_Flags     DW       0         ; [05]

SFT_M_Shared    EQU      8000H     ; Network access
SFT_M_DateSet   EQU      4000H     ; Date set (FILE only)
SFT_M_IOCTL     EQU      4000H     ; IOCTL support (DEVICE only)
SFT_M_IsDevice  EQU      0080H     ; Entry is for a device
SFT_M_EOF       EQU      0040H     ; (DEVICE) end of file on input
SFT_M_Binary    EQU      0020H     ; (DEVICE) transparent mode
SFT_M_Special   EQU      0010H     ; (DEVICE) supports INT 29H
SFT_M_IsClock   EQU      0008H     ; (DEVICE) current clock device
SFT_M_IsNul     EQU      0004H     ; (DEVICE) current nul device
SFT_M_IsStdOut  EQU      0002H     ; (DEVICE) current stdout device
SFT_M_IsStdIn   EQU      0001H     ; (DEVICE) current stdin device
SFT_M_Written   EQU      0040H     ; (FILE) file written
SFT_M_DriveMask EQU      003FH     ; (FILE) mask for drive bits
                                   ;        (0-5)

SFT_D_DCB       DD       0         ; [07] (FILE) DCB address
                                   ;      (DEVICE) Header address
SFT_W_Cluster1  DW       0         ; [0B] (FILE) initial cluster
SFT_W_HHMMS     DW       0         ; [0D] (FILE) Hour, Min, Sec/2
                                   ;             Access time
SFT_W_YYMMDD    DW       0         ; [0F] (FILE) Year, Month, Day
                                   ;             Access date
SFT_D_FilSiz    DD       0         ; [11] File size / EOF location
SFT_D_FilPos    DD       0         ; [15] Current file position
SFT_W_RelClstr  DW       0         ; [19] (FILE) clusters from
                                   ;             beginning of file
SFT_W_CurClstr  DW       0         ; [1B] (FILE) current cluster
SFT_W_LBN       DW       0         ; [1D] (FILE) block number
```

```
SFT_W_DirIndex   DB      0        ; [1F] (FILE) directory index
SFT_T_FileName   DB      0BH DUP(0) ; [20] (FILE) file name
SFT_T_Unknown    DB      04H DUP(0) ; [2B] ????
SFT_W_OwnerMach  DW      0        ; [2F] Machine number of file
                                  ;      owner
SFT_W_OwnerPSP   DW      0        ; [31] PSP of task that
                                  ;      initially accessed file
                                  ;      accessed file
SFT_W_Status     DW      0        ; [33] Status
                 ENDS
```

Building the CDS

The LASTDRIVE statement in CONFIG.SYS or a DOS default value fixes the size of the CDS. There is one CDS entry for each possible drive and all entries are contiguous so the drive number can be used as an index. DOS uses the CDS to process joined, substituted, and network drives, and to maintain current directory information.

Each CDS entry has a device name, current default directory, DCB address, and flags field. The 43H bytes of device and directory information include a drive letter, a colon (:), a backslash (\), and a null to terminate the string. The path-and-filename can be up to 64 (40H) bytes long. The size of the name field is what limits the length of a filename. The flags field identifies joined, substituted, and network devices. The search for a block driver begins by using the drive number as an index into the CDS.

Here is the format of the CDS. None of the information in this listing is documented.

```
CDS              STRUC
CDS_T_Name       DB      43H DUP(0) ; [00] Device and directory
                                    ; name
CDS_W_Status     DW      0        ; [43] Device status

CDS_M_Network    EQU     8000H    ; Network device
CDS_M_Local      EQU     4000H    ; Local device
CDS_M_Joined     EQU     2000H    ; Joined device
CDS_M_Substitue  EQU     1000H    ; Substituted device
CDS_M_Device     EQU     0080H    ; Device

CDS_D_DCB        DD      0        ; [45] Address of DCB
CDS_T_Unknown    DB      8 DUP(0) ; [49] Unknown
                 ENDS
```

DOS at Your Command

At this point IBMBIO has completed all the major DOS I/O data structures. Figure 10-2 illustrates the relationships among these structures. IBMBIO runs the command-line interpreter (shell). The default shell is COMMAND.COM, but a COMSPEC = statement in CONFIG.SYS can select an alternate shell.

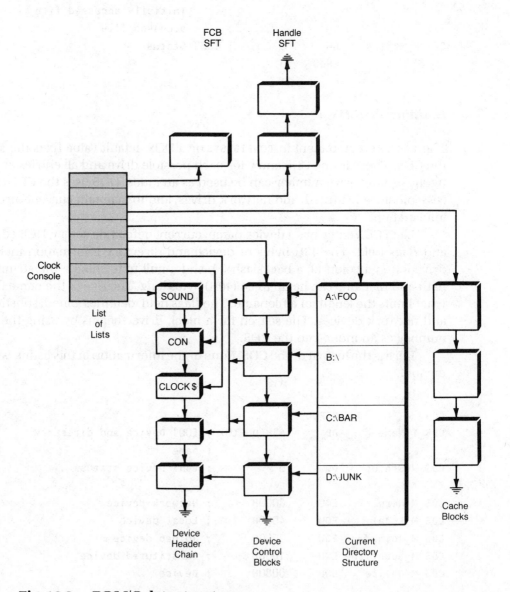

Fig. 10-2.   DOS I/O data structures.

The boot process ends when the shell is run. The shell relies on DOS services to do its job, using INT 21H to display the shell prompt A>, read from the keyboard, and invoke other applications.

The INT 21H Dispatcher: Processing Application Requests

Now that the boot process is finished, DOS stands ready to process application requests, many of which come through INT 21H. The first part of the INT 21H interrupt service routine is a service dispatcher that stores values in static variables, changes to one of three different stacks, and calls a routine to perform the requested function.

Before returning to its caller, the INT 21H dispatcher must restore the static information and stack. If the INT 21H dispatcher is reentered before it can restore this information, DOS may become confused and go off the deep end.

If either a driver or a background process issues an INT 21H request, it can cause the INT 21H dispatcher to be reentered. The architecture of this dispatcher restricts background processing and limits what a driver can do. It is important to understand what happens in this section of code.

Initial Processing

The request type passed in AH is validated. Four requests are serviced immediately—get PSP (AH = 50H and AH = 62H), set PSP (AH = 51H), and get/set/check break state (AH = 33H). The requests corresponding to AH = 50H and AH = 51H are undocumented. These immediately completed requests are always safe to make. We probably would never have occasion to use any of these requests from a driver but they are necessary for background programs.

If the request cannot be immediately satisfied, DOS saves all registers on the current stack and also records contents of the current DS:BX register pair in a static variable (many INT 21H requests pass an address in DS:BX).

INDOS Flag

Most of the remaining code is a critical section which must be completed without interruption. The INT 21H dispatcher increments the infamous INDOS flag when it begins this critical section and decrements the flag at the end.

The purpose of the INDOS flag is support of background programs like PRINT.COM. Background programs initially run from the DOS command prompt, and after performing any initialization, they terminate and stay resident. (See

Essay 7, Safe Memory-Resident Programming (TSR), by Steven Baker, for a thorough discussion of these programs.) Their initialization should record the address of the INDOS flag. The undocumented INT 21H AH = 34H returns the address of this flag in the ES:BX registers. Note that this request can only be safely made when the TSR initializes.

A zero value of the INDOS flag is not an absolute guarantee that it is safe to make an INT 21H request. When DOS processes a critical error, it decrements the INDOS flag and increments a critical error flag. A critical error is an I/O error which cannot be handled by the device driver. The location of the critical error flag varies with DOS version, and both critical error and INDOS flag must be checked. In DOS 3.1, the critical error flag is the byte before the INDOS flag.

Dispatcher Stack Switching

The INT 21H dispatcher works with three separate stacks: user, auxiliary, and disk, and switches among these stacks depending on the request and critical error flag.

The current SS:SP register values are saved in a static variable after saving the previous variable contents in another static variable. This action provides one level of INT 21H recursion needed to support background processing. SS:SP values are also recorded in the PSP of the current task, and are used to restore the stack when the current process terminates.

The current stack is unconditionally changed to the auxiliary stack. If the request is for termination (AH = 0) or get extended error (AH = 59H), it is serviced directly. If the request is in the range 01H to 0CH and a critical error is not in progress, a change is made to the user I/O stack. Critical Error Handlers can safely make INT 21H requests in the range 01H to 0CH because no stack switch is performed. For all other requests, the disk stack is used.

Taking a Break

If the break flag has been set either by a break = on statement in CONFIG.SYS or by an explicit INT 21H request (AH = 33H) and the disk stack is in use, a nondestructive read is issued directly to the console driver to check for control-c. Some of the user-stack requests make an unconditional control-c.

Since control-c checks are sent to the console device, DOS uses the header address from the List of Lists to locate its driver. If a control-c is detected, the DOS kernel executes an INT 23H. COMMAND.COM sets up an INT 23H service routine which terminates the current program, but a program can override this action by declaring its own INT 23H service routine. Because of the way the INT 21H dispatcher switches stacks, it is not safe to issue an INT 21H request from an INT 23H interrupt service routine.

Finishing the Job

For all unsatisfied requests, the dispatcher uses the function code (initial AH value) as an index into a table of internal service routines. In recent versions of DOS, this table begins at offset 0defH of the DOS segment.

When the internal DOS routine returns, the INT 21H dispatcher decrements the INDOS flag, restores the caller's stack pointer, removes the saved registers from the caller's stack, and executes an IRET instruction.

Using FCBs and Handles

The majority of the INT 21H requests are I/O related. There are two basic techniques for requesting a DOS I/O operation: handles and FCBs.

Handles were introduced with version 2.0 of DOS, and they support the hierarchical file system (i.e., directories and subdirectories). Initial access to files and devices is by name, which can include a path. A path contains drive and subdirectory names in addition to the file or device name. Open or create functions return a number called the handle which is used in place of the name for subsequent accesses. When you use handles for read or write, you specify the number of bytes that you want to transfer, a buffer address, and the previously returned handle.

FCBs are an artifact of version 1.0 of DOS and do not support the hierarchical file system. You create the FCB data structure and pass it to the INT 21H dispatcher with each request. Transfers are measured in records instead of bytes; each FCB has its own record size. The Disk Transfer Area (DTA) is a common buffer for all transfers. Here is the format of an FCB (items marked with an asterisk are undocumented FCB fields):

```
;
;               FCB.DEF
;
FCB             STRUC
FCB_B_Drive     DB      0           ; [00] Drive number
FCB_T_Name      DB      '        '  ; [01] Name
FCB_T_Ext       DB      '   '       ; [09] Extension
FCB_W_CB        DW      0           ; [12] Current block
FCB_W_LRS       DW      0           ; [14] Logical Rec Size
FCB_D_FS        DD      0           ; [16] File Size (bytes)
FCB_W_DLM       DW      0           ; [20] Date Last Modified
FCB_W_TLM       DW      0           ; [22] *Time last modified
FCB_B_SFN       DB      0           ; [24] *SFN
FCB_B_Flags     DB      0           ; [25] Modified flags
FCB_A_DHD       DD      0           ; [26] *Device Header/DCB
```

```
                    DW       0        ; [30]
FCB_B_BRR           DB       0        ; [32] Block Relative Rec
FCB_D_FRR           DD       0        ; [33] File Relative Rec
FCB                 ENDS
```

Working with the SFT

Handles and FCBs are application data structures, but, internally, DOS deals with SFT entries, maintaining separate SFTs for handles and FCBs. The entries in each table are assigned a number which ranges from zero to the number of table entries minus one. DOS allocates an SFT entry when the file or device is initially accessed. The number assigned to this entry becomes the System File Number (SFN) and links FCBs and handles to their corresponding SFT entry.

Handles

The handle returned by an open or create is an index into a data structure called the Job File Table (JFT). A handle of 0 references the first element of this table, 1 the second element, etc. The contents of each element of the JFT is the SFN, which is used as an index into the handle SFT.

DOS records the address and size of the JFT in the Program Segment Prefix (PSP) because the JFT and associated handles are application-private resources. The JFT normally holds 20 entries (i.e., there are 20 handles) and can usually be found within the PSP. The size of the JFT sets a limit on the number of open files.

There is not room within the PSP to expand the size of the JFT, but you can allocate a new JFT and update the size and base address in the PSP. DOS never assumes that the JFT is located in the PSP. The capability to grow the JFT this way has existed for some time, but it has not been documented. DOS 3.3 provides an INT 21H function to increase the size of the JFT.

After the initial file or device access, DOS uses the handle as an index into the JFT where it finds the SFN and uses it to find the original SFT entry. Figure 10-3 illustrates the relationship between the handle, PSP, JFT, SFN, and SFT.

FCBs

There is no central structure analogous to the the JFT for File Control Blocks. DOS records the SFN assigned at the initial access in one of the reserved fields of

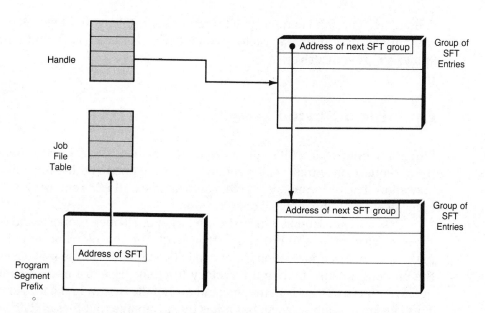

Fig. 10-3.   Program I/O data structures.

the FCB, which is passed back to DOS in subsequent I/O operations. DOS extracts the SFN and locates the corresponding entry in the FCB SFT.

From Driver Request to Call

Now that we have surveyed the general structures involved with file I/O, let's explore the transformation of some of the more common INT 21H requests into driver calls. Operations such as open, close, read, and write originate as either handle or FCB requests, which DOS converts to a standard format before calling a common internal routine to complete the request. This internal routine uses information in an SFT entry to build a request header and locate the device driver. Various important pieces of information are stored in static DOS variables contributing to DOS reentry problems.

Understanding the mechanics of this process is helpful for writing drivers. You will know the types of requests DOS will send to your driver and the circumstances under which they will be sent. It is not exactly obvious when a driver will receive flush, status, and nondestructive read requests. Device attributes have some interesting side effects on the transformation process.

I'll explain how DOS uses the different I/O data structures to locate the driver and complete the request. Familiarity with these structures is an asset for debugging. The information which they contain tells you where DOS loaded your driver, how many characters your driver has processed, and what DOS knows about your driver.

Opening a Device

Either a handle or an FCB request can open a device. The separate routines for these requests eventually call a common internal open routine to complete the operation. The different entry points map handle and FCB requests into the SFT entry needed by the internal open routine.

DOS always assumes a file to be the target of all open requests and concatenates a drive name and directory string with the device name to complete a pathname. If this information is not explicitly contained in the initial reference, the current default drive and directory for that drive are used. The internal open routine parses this pathname and eventually discovers device references. This logic may seem warped, but it has the advantage that files and devices can be treated uniformly. On some systems, the semantics of device names (always ending in a colon or beginning \dev\foo when foo is the name of a device) allow the operating system to recognize a device reference. DOS cannot immediately determine whether a name refers to a file or a device.

Handle and FCB open requests pass through the INT 21H function dispatcher to separate routines that call a common internal open routine. It is this internal open routine which does most of the actual work needed to open a device or file.

A successful open request allocates an SFT entry containing the address of the device header if a device is being referenced, or the address of a DCB containing the address of a device header if a file is being referenced. The SFN identifying the SFT entry is stored in the JFT for handle operations and in the FCB for FCB operations, and will direct subsequent accesses quickly to the correct SFT entry.

Handle Open

The handle open routine allocates an SFT entry from the handle SFT and a handle from the JFT. The SFN corresponding to the newly allocated SFT entry is recorded in the JFT.

If the input file/device name does not contain an explicit device or begin with quotation marks, the current default drive and CDS are used to construct a complete pathname. The flags and status fields in the SFT entry are initialized and the internal open routine is called.

The handle open routine sets the reference count in the SFT entry to 1 if the internal open routine completes successfully; otherwise, it must deallocate the SFT entry and handle and return an error code.

FCB Open

The FCB open routine sets the file open attributes to read/write for compatibility with the handle open. The FCB open routine creates a pathname by concatenating the current default drive and directory from the CDS with the name in the FCB. An SFT entry is allocated from the FCB SFT and the SFT flags field is set to indicate FCB access. A call is made to the internal open routine. If this routine returns successfully, the SFT reference count is incremented, some FCB fields are initialized, and information is copied from the SFT entry back to the FCB.

Whenever an open request is made, a new FCB SFT entry is allocated. Because of the way file sharing is implemented for FCB access, an SFT entry corresponding to the same file may have been previously allocated. The FCB open routine scans the SFT after each request looking for duplicate entries. If there is another SFT entry that references the same file, the reference count and "age" are updated and the new SFT is deallocated. FCB SFT entries are aged, and if an SFT entry is needed and none are available, the oldest one is reused. Sufficient context information is maintained in the FCB to reconstruct the SFT entry at a later time.

The Internal Open Routine

DOS calls a common internal open routine to process both handle and FCB requests. This routine validates the open attributes and examines the SFT flags. Requests for access to a network device are immediately passed to MSNet using INT 2FH; otherwise, a device/file lookup is performed.

The lookup operation is complex and is mainly of interest for processing block device requests. The pathname (drive letter + directory string + file/device name) is scanned from left to right looking for tokens (a string of characters separated by directory delimiters \ or ending with a nul \000). The list of device headers is scanned in an attempt to match the name of a character driver with the token. If the last token from the path (i.e., it ends with a nul) matches the name of a character device, the DOS kernel concludes that this device is the target of the open request.

If a character device is not being referenced, the token must refer to a directory entry. DOS reads directory blocks from disk until it locates the directory corresponding to the token. These steps are repeated for each token until the directory search fails or the end of the path is reached.

Since the header chain is searched starting from the NUL device and working backward, the last device loaded with a particular name is the first one found. Any character device except the NUL device can be replaced by loading a similarly named device driver.

If the open request completes successfully and the device supports open/close/removable media functions, DOS sends an open request to the appropriate device driver. The driver indicates support for these functions by setting the OCRM bit in the device header. Control returns to the handle or FCB open routine.

Reading and Writing

Both handles and FCBs can be used to request read or write operations. Each access method follows a different path through the INT 21H dispatcher, but eventually arrives at common internal read and write routines. The internal routines actually perform the I/O operation using information contained in SFT entries. The various routines along the separate code paths hide the differences between FCB and handle access from the internal I/O routines.

Handle Access

The INT 21H dispatcher calls separate entry points to process read and write requests. This code quickly merges to a common read/write routine.

The read/write routine uses the handle to locate the SFT entry and checks handle ownership by comparing the current PSP to the value recorded in the owner field of the SFT entry. The buffer address is adjusted to minimize "segment wrap" (i.e., the offset is made as small as possible and either the internal read or internal write routine is called to complete the transfer).

FCB Access

There are specific FCB requests for reading and writing records sequentially and randomly. Sequential operations deal with a single record at a time, and random operations can process multiple records. There are different INT 21H requests for each case. These separate routines call a common FCB I/O routine which converts the request size to bytes and the record-oriented FCB position to a byte-oriented file position. Next, the transfer size is adjusted to prevent segment wrap and an SFT element is allocated. Context information is moved from the FCB into this newly initialized SFT element.

Control now passes to the same internal read and write routines used to satisfy handle requests. After the internal routine completes, the file size is copied back to the FCB and the number of records processed is calculated. This number will differ from the requested number if the transfer size was altered.

If a read resulted in transfer of a partial record, DOS zeros the unused part of the buffer. All FCB operations implicitly use the DTA as a buffer. If a write operation is completed, the common FCB I/O routine calls an internal routine to get the current date and time. The time and date routine creates a request header and passes it to the current clock device using the previously recorded device header address. The FCB relative record field is updated regardless of the operation performed. The number of records written and final status are returned.

Internal Read Routine

The internal read routine verifies that read access to the device is allowed (a device such as a printer might be write-only), sets the error locus (for extended error processing) to serial device, and examines the device attributes in the flags word of the SFT entry. Some of these attributes were copied from the device header when the SFT entry was created, and others updated as the device is used. If an end of file has been detected or the device is the current NUL device, the read terminates immediately.

If the flags field indicates that device is in binary or raw mode (set by an Input/Output Control (IOCTL) request), a single read request is sent to the device driver. Binary mode processing can offer a substantial performance advantage, but the request will not terminate until the specified number of characters have been read.

There are two execution paths for text I/O because reads from standard input require special handling. If the device is not standard input, the kernel builds a one-character read request header, makes a control-c check, and calls the driver. If the read request is successful, this routine updates the buffer address and checks for end-of-file (EOF) or carriage routine. If either of these characters is found, the read terminates; otherwise, the steps are repeated until the requested number of characters have been read.

If the device is standard input, the internal read saves the address of the SFT entry in another DOS global variable and converts the request to a buffered read from standard input corresponding to INT 21H (AH = 0AH). The buffered read routine takes care of echo and special character processing and supports limited editing.

The internal read routine updates the SFT entry after the read request completes. It calculates the bytes read and updates the total number of bytes processed since the device was opened. This count, analagous to file position for file operations, is stored in the file position field of the SFT. If an end of file was detected, the SFT flags field is set accordingly. The internal read routine checks the status returned by the device driver in the request header and invokes the DOS Critical Error Handler to deal with any errors.

Internal Write Routine

The internal write routine verifies that write access is permitted, sets the error locus to serial device, and sets the not-at-end-of-file bit in the SFT entry flags field. The internal write routine checks the current mode and device attributes in the SFT entry flags field.

If a device is being accessed transparently, a single write request is passed to the appropriate driver. Since individual characters are not checked in transparent mode, there is no notion of end of file. This mode is useful for sending certain bit-mapped graphics to a printer. The bit pattern corresponding to EOF cannot be sent to a device in text mode. There are also performance advantages with transparent mode since the driver is called only once for each request.

There are two special cases for text mode I/O. If the device is the current NUL device, DOS declares the operation successful and returns without ever calling the driver. Writes to standard output are passed to the DOS display output routine (the same one used to process INT 21H, (AH = 02H) requests) which is described later on.

Text mode I/O of any other device is processed one character at a time. DOS builds a request header for a single character write, makes a control-c check, and passes the request to the driver. If the driver does not return an error, the buffer address and character count are updated. This process continues until either an end of file is written or all the characters have been processed.

The Critical Error Handler processes any errors and may terminate the current process. After the write completes, the internal write routine updates the SFT entry and returns to its caller. The number of bytes written is calculated by subtracting the initial buffer address from the current buffer address. This value will eventually be returned to the application through the INT 21H function dispatcher. The file position is updated by adding the number of bytes written to the old position. (For a device, the file position is the total bytes written since the device was opened.)

Closing a Device

Closing a device releases the resources which DOS allocated when it opened the device. Handle and FCB close requests eventually call a common internal close routine.

The handle close routine is called directly from the INT 21H function dispatcher. It validates handle ownership by comparing the current PSP to the owning PSP stored in the SFT entry; only the handle owner can close a file. If the reference count is 1 or the SFT entry does not correspond to a network FCB, the corresponding SFN is extracted from the Job File Table, and the handle is marked as available. In either case, control passes to the internal close routine.

The FCB close routine retrieves the SFN from the FCB and copies the creation data and time from the FCB to the SFT entry. The flags field of the SFT entry is updated to indicate that the file date has not been set. The date and time will be needed to update directory entries for modified disk files. The internal close routine will complete the FCB close request.

Closing local devices is a simple operation. The reference count in the SFT entry is decreased and when the count becomes zero, the entry is released. If the device supports open/close/removable media requests and the current PSP owns the SFT entry, a close request is sent to the device driver. This ownership requirement can prevent a driver from receiving a close request even if the OCRM bit is set in its header. COMMAND.COM opens PRN, CON, and AUX. Any application run by COMMAND.COM gets access to these devices without opening them through a mechanism known as inheritance. Since COMMAND.COM and not the applications owns these devices, the driver will not be called when an application closes them. The Critical Error Handler is called if the driver reports an error.

IOCTL Requests

IOCTL requests provide some control over DOS/driver interactions. For example, they can return device attribute information or change between binary and text mode. We've seen that mode can affect the transformation of read and write requests.

Applications initiate IOCTL requests with an INT 21H request (AH = 44H); the AL register selects an IOCTL subfunction. Some IOCTL requests are sent only to block devices and are not discussed in this section.

The DOS kernel can satisfy some requests without calling a driver, but it must send either a status or an IOCTL request to complete others. A driver receives the IOCTL request only if the IOCTL bit is set in its header.

Since the DOS kernel needs information from the SFT to satisfy device IOCTL requests, a handle must be passed in the BX register. Applications must either explicitly open a device or reference one that is permanently open such as StdIn or StdOut. DOS validates the handle and then dispatches on the subfunction contained in AL.

Get and Set Device Information

Recall that the Stdin, Stdout, and Binary attributes directly affect request transformation. Applications use IOCTL requests to change these attributes. DOS records device attribute information in the SFT and uses that entry to satisfy these requests. It will process Get or Set Device Attributes (AL = 0 and AL = 1) requests whether or not a driver provides IOCTL support. A driver cannot prevent an application from selecting binary mode and must be prepared to deal with multiple byte reads and writes.

The program in Listing 10-5, BINMODE, illustrates the use of Get and Set Attributes IOCTL requests. Lines 13-15 make an IOCTL Get Attributes request for the current standard output device. The handle for StdOut is permanently assigned, and we do open it explicitly. At line 16, we examine the returned attributes. If StdOut is a device, we issue a set device attributes IOCTL request in lines 18-21.

Listing 10-5.   BINMODE

```
;       BINMODE.ASM
;
;       IOCTL demonstration program
;
;       Create this program in a file called BINMODE.ASM
;       Assemble:       MASM BINMODE;
;       Link:           LINK BINMODE;
;       Make COM file: EXE2BIN BINMODE BINMODE.COM
;
_text   SEGMENT BYTE PUBLIC 'CODE'
        ASSUME  cs:_text,ds:_text
        ORG     100H
BinMode PROC    NEAR
        mov     bx,1            ; [13] bx <== stdout handle
        mov     ax,4400H        ; [14] ax <== IOCTL get attributes
        int     21H             ; [15] make the request
        test    dl,80H          ; [16] is it a device?
        jz      notdev          ; [17] if Z--no
        or      dl,20H          ; [18] put device in binary mode
        xor     dh,dh           ; [19] dh <== 0 (required)
        mov     ax,4401H        ; [20] ax <== IOCTL set attributes
        int     21H             ; [21] make the request
notdev: mov     ah,4cH          ; [22] return to DOS
        int     21H
BinMode ENDP
_text   ENDS
        END     BinMode
```

Use the procedure described in the listing comments to create `BINMODE.COM`; you can use `DEBUG` to demonstrate the effect of this program. *I You must be very careful with* `DEBUG`. `DEBUG` *is cryptic and unforgiving; it can easily trash your hard disk. Make sure that you enter the program and* `DEBUG` *commands exactly as listed.*

`DEBUG` prompts for input with – and occasionally with :. You must enter the responses in italics. Note that you may see different values in your segment registers. At 1544:0117, tabs are no longer expanded; your console (the default StdOut device) is in binary mode.

```
A>DEBUG BINMODE.COM
-g115

AX=4401 BX=0001 CX=001B DX=00F3 SP=FFFE BP=0000 SI=0000 DI=0000
DS=1544 ES=1544 SS=1544 CS=1544 IP=0115 NV UP EI PL ZR NA PE NC
1544:0115 CD21            INT     21
```

```
-g117

AX=44D3 BX=0001 CX=001B DX=00F3 SP=FFFE BP=0000 SI=0000 DI=0000
DS=1544 ES=1544 SS=1544 CS=1544 IP=0117 NV UP EI PL ZR NA PE NC
1544:0117 B44C          MOVoAH,4C

-g
Program terminated normally
-q
A>
```

The console is now in binary mode; you probably don't want to leave it in this condition. You can either reboot your system or restore it with this program. The following DEBUG session will restore your console to text mode.

```
A>DEBUG BINMODE.COM
-g115

AX=4401 BX=0001 CX=001B DX=00F3 SP=FFFE BP=0000 SI=0000 DI=0000
DS=1544 ES=1544 SS=1544 CS=1544 IP=0115 NV UP EI PL ZR NA PE NC
1544:0115 CD21          INTo21
-rdx
DX 00F3
:D3
-g117

AX=44D3 BX=0001 CX=001B DX=00D3 SP=FFFE BP=0000 SI=0000 DI=0000
DS=1544 ES=1544 SS=1544 CS=1544 IP=0117 NV UP EI PL ZR NA PE NC
1544:0117 B44C      MOV     AH,4C

-g
Program terminated normally
-q
A>
```

At 1544:0115, tabs are not yet expanded; the console is still in binary mode. Altering the value in DX (the rdx command) causes the INT 21H instruction to restore the console to text mode. Notice how tabs are expanded at 1544:0117.

Read and Write Control Information

Read and Write Control Information (AL = 2 and AL = 3) IOCTL requests allow applications to exchange arbitrary control information with a driver. An applica-

333

tion might send an IOCTL request whichs sets transmission speed or parity to a communications driver. Programs can send these requests to the SOUND driver to control various music synthesis parameters and retrieve error information. (See Essay 11, Writing a SOUND Device Driver.) DOS will not send these requests to a driver unless the IOCTL bit in the device header attributes word is set.

Get Input and Output Status

IOCTL requests also can cause DOS to send Input and Output Status (AL = 6 and AL = 7) requests to a device driver. Currently, IOCTL requests are the only way to generate an output status request header. The DOS kernel routes these status requests to the driver regardless of the setting of the IOCTL bit in the device header.

Character I/O Routines

The INT 21H interface provides a group of Character I/O (AH = 01H to 0CH) routines which are important because they provide hooks for background processing and frequently can be called from a device driver. These routines support input editing and output logging. Output logging creates a listing of console output on your printer. The internal read and write routines rely on these functions to handle text mode I/O to the standard input and output devices.

Each routine in this group implicitly uses one of the permanently assigned handles (standard input = 0, standard output = 1, standard error = 2, standard auxiliary device = 3, and standard printer = 4) and always verifies the handle before proceeding. Because StdIn amd StdOut can be redirected, any driver should be prepared to receive these requests.

These routines are the source of buffer flush and input status requests. Almost all of the input routines in this group send read/nowait requests to the driver directly or indirectly. A number of these routines call a keyboard poll or background processing routine which are DOS's hooks for background processing.

Display Output

The Display Output (AH = 02H) service writes a single character to the current standard output device; it is also called indirectly by the internal write routine as a result of a text mode write to standard output.

Display Output converts control characters to sequences of printable characters and maintains a current display column. For each printable character, an internal write character routine is called. This routine examines the IsSpecl bit in the device header. If this bit is set, the character is passed to the device driver via the undocumented INT 29H interface instead of using a request header. The INT 29H interface speeds up the process of passing a character to the driver. The write routine places the character in DL and executes INT 29H.

After every fourth character is written, the Display Output routine calls the keyboard poll routine; it also supports screen logging. Each time a character is written, this routine checks the screen logging state. If logging is active and the handle for the standard print device (handle = 4) is valid, the character is written to the printer as well as StdOut.

Buffered Keyboard Input

Buffered Keyboard Input (AH = 0AH) reads one line from the current standard input device and supports limited line editing. This routine can also be called indirectly by the internal read routine as the result of a text mode read from standard input. The line-editing capability is an internal DOS function not associated with a particular device. So long as standard input is a device, DOS will provide editing capability.

Internally, the buffered keyboard input routine calls the console input without echo (INT 21H AH = 8) which repeatedly calls the keyboard poll routine until a character is available. A single character read request is sent to the StdIn device driver.

Keyboard Poll Routine

Several of the character I/O routines call the keyboard poll routine to check for control-c, control-s, and control-p characters. The control-c check is done first. Since a control-c has special significance only if entered from the keyboard, the address of the console device recorded in the boot sequence is used to locate the driver. Control-c checks cannot be redirected. A read/nowait request is sent to the initial console device. If the device returns a control-c in the read/nowait request header, DOS issues an INT 23H. Programs can set up their own INT 23 service routines to trap control-c. By default, the DOS kernel calls the COM-MAND.COM INT 23H service routine which terminates the current program.

If no control-c is found, a read/nowait request is sent to the current standard input device. If the device is busy, the background processing dispatcher is called and the keyboard poll routine exits. If the read/nowait detects a control-s (suspend output), a background processing loop is entered. This loop repeatedly checks the keyboard and calls the background processing dispatcher until keyboard input is detected. If the read/nowait returns a control-p, the keyboard poll routine toggles the print logging flag and validates the handle for the standard printer. If the character is not special, it is returned, and the keyboard poll routine exits.

Background Processing Dispatcher

The background processing dispatcher is one of the hooks added to DOS to support background applications. This routine is called directly from several Keyboard I/O routines as well as from the keyboard poll routine.

If DOS is not currently processing a critical error, the background processing dispatcher issues an INT 28H request. Programs such as PRINT.COM set up INT 28H interrupt service routines. When an INT 28H request is received, it is safe to perform disk I/O. The DOS character I/O routines call this routine on the user I/O stack. If an INT 28H interrupt service routine makes a disk I/O request, the INT 21H dispatcher saves the current stack (user I/O) and switches the disk I/O stack. When the disk I/O completes, the INT 21H dispatcher restores the user I/O stack and completes the character I/O operation. Support for this feature is the reason that the INT 21H dispatcher provides for one level of recursion when it saves the caller SS:SP registers.

Writing Background Programs

Stack switching in the INT 21H dispatcher and recording I/O parameters in static variable makes the INT 21H service routine nonreentrant. Other kernel services including video INT 10H, absolute disk read INT 25H, absolute disk write INT 26H, and Diskette/Disk I/O INT 13H also suffer this limitation. DOS is basically a single-user, single-program operating system, but it does provide some hooks for background programs.

The architecture of the DOS kernel complicates development of these applications. The basic strategy for writing a background program is to load the program normally, perform the necessary initialization to deal with reentrancy restrictions and to insure periodic CPU access, and finally terminate using the DOS TSR request INT 21H (AH = 31H).

A background program can schedule itself two ways. Keyboard I/O requests give background programs access to the processor through the undocumented INT 28H mechanism. Since COMMAND.COM uses these routines for input, background programs will get access to the processor while the user interface awaits input.

There is no guarantee these requests will occur frequently enough once an application starts up. Background programs normally take over the DOS timer interrupt (1cH) as well as INT 28H. Declaring a timer interrupt service routine a program guarantees that it will gain access to the processor 18.2 times a second.

Logic within the background program must decide whether or not it is safe for the application to run when called through either of these interrupts. It is always safe to proceed if the background program does not need any DOS services, but life is hardly ever this simple.

The cleanest scheduling algorithm is for the application to run only at those times when any request for kernel service would be safe. Checking the INDOS and critical error flags and trapping nonreentrant DOS requests provides the application with enough information to make safe scheduling choices.

Initializing a Background Program

Until the background program issues its TSR request, all DOS kernel services are safe. The initialization code should obtain the address of the INDOS flag through the undocumented INT 21H (AH = 34H) request, declare interrupt service routines to trap nonreentrant kernel requests INT 25H, INT 26H, and INT 13H, and establish INT 28H and 1cH interrupt service routines. The interrupt service routines for INT 25H, 26H, and 13H merely note that one of these requests is in progress and then invokes the original interrupt service routine.

The DOS kernel uses the recorded address of the current PSP to locate the JFT. A background program must establish the correct PSP before performing any I/O. When a background program initializes, it must get its own PSP address through INT 21H (AH = 62H) or INT 21H (AH = 51H) (undocumented) for future use.

Any other information available through INT 21H requests should also be obtained at this time, e.g., the address of a device header. Background programs talk directly to the driver to avoid INT 21H reentrancy problems or to minimize the overhead in dealing with a driver. PRINT.COM uses this technique to pass requests to the current print device. An application can get the address of a device header by locating the NUL header using the undocumented INT 21H (AH = 52H) (get List of List address) and walking the device header chain or by using an FCB open.

After completing any other application-specific initialization, the background program issues a TSR request to return control to the user interface. The resident portion of the program will periodically get access to the processor through either INT 28H (background scheduler) or INT 1cH (timer).

Deciding Whether to Run

When the background program is called through one of its interrupt service routines, it must decide whether or not it wants to run. Even if it is safe, a background program might not want to run. Background programs must be careful not to monopolize the processor.

Certain background operations are inherently safe. No special precautions are needed to talk directly to a device driver. If the program is called through INT 28H, it can issue INT 21H requests which are serviced on the disk stack so long as no INT 25H, 26H, or 13H is in progress. If the program gains control through the 1cH timer interrupt it must check the state of the INDOS and critical error flags and verify that none of these interrupts are in progress.

Preparing for the Request

A background program must be careful not to disturb DOS or the current application. It must save any registers that it will modify and initialize its data and stack segments prior to running.

Two significant events can occur in the process of making an INT 21H request: a control-c can be detected or a critical error can occur. The background program must guard against either of these events by setting up control-c INT 23H and critical error INT 24H interrupt service routines. These must be installed any time the background application runs. The background program may also want to disable break (control-c) checks while it is running. INT 21H (AX = 3302H) is useful for this purpose. It exchanges the value in DL with the current break flag. (This particular subfunction is undocumented in some versions of DOS.)

Finally, the application must make sure that the DOS kernel uses the proper JFT to process any handle I/O requests. By loading its own PSP with the undocumented set current PSP INT 21H (AH = 50H BX = PSP) segment, the background program establishes the proper PSP (and hence JFT).

Making the Request

Having made all these preparations, the background application may now safely make an INT 21H request. When this request completes, the application must undo its preparations and return dismiss the interrupt with an IRET instruction.

Debugging a Driver

Writing a device driver is often easier than getting it to work. Normal development aids such as DEBUG will not work on device drivers. You should debug any hardware interrupt service routines as well as the driver strategy and interrupt code. The reliance of DEBUG on INT 21H for input and output prevent its use in a driver strategy or interrupt routine. Unless special precautions are taken, INT 21H cannot be used from within a hardware interrupt service routine. (Rest assured that DEBUG does not take these precautions.)

Starting with a Stub

I like to take a top-down approach to driver development. I begin with a minimal driver which responds properly to initialization requests and returns a success status for all others. I normally use an existing driver as a template for a new driver; the "stub" listed in Essay 11 frequently is a good starting point.

Debugging the Initialization Routine

All initialization routines must return an ending (break) address as a status; block drivers must return some additional information. If you wish, you may print a message from the driver initialization routine using one of the keyboard I/O routines INT 21H (AH = 01H to 0CH).

Recall that IBMBIO sends the initialization request to your driver as part of the boot process. *Errors in your driver can cause your system to hang. You should always boot from a removable media when testing a driver.* If the boot process hangs, reboot with another system disk. Carefully examine the initialization code. Make sure that the driver returns a reasonable break address and that both the strategy and interrupt routines execute *far* returns. Both of these mistakes are common driver errors.

Admiring Your Handiwork

Once you have successfully booted using your new driver, locate your driver code. Make sure your driver really did get loaded and that all its code is intact. It's easy to use the incorrect copy of CONFIG.SYS or to load an old version of your driver. Returning an incorrect break address does not always hang your system; it can cause IBMBIO to overwrite all or part of your driver.

You can use DEBUG and the List of Lists to locate your driver. The next listing shows the sequence used to locate the CLOCK$ driver. I have edited this output to fit in this book; your results won't look exactly like those in the listing. You also may notice different values in the segment registers on your system. As with the previous DEBUG example, user input appears in italics. The commands between a and g104 define and execute a short program. Note that you must end this program with an empty line. (I entered a carriage return in response to the 152A:0105 prompt.) This program returns the address of the List of Lists in ES:BX. The command des:26l40 dumps the first 40H bytes of the List of Lists which includes the NUL device header. The easiest way to locate this header is to look for the string NUL. Working backward from this name, we find the expected value of 8004H for the device attributes. This header corresponds to a character device that is the current NUL device. The next two commands, d901:0l20 and d84d:0l20 walk backward through the driver chain to the CLOCK$ device. If we had wanted to examine driver code, we could have used the DEBUG "u" command to disassemble the driver. From the information contained in this header, we find that the strategy routine starts at 84D:0012 and the interrupt routine at 84D:0024.

```
-a
152A:0100   mov ah,52
152A:0102   int 21
```

```
152A:0104   nop
152A:0105
-g104


AX=5200 BX=0026 CX=0000 DX=0000 SP=FFEE BP=0000 SI=0000 DI=0000
DS=152A ES=012E SS=152A CS=152A IP=0104   NV UP EI PL NZ NA PO NC
152A:0104 90            NOP
-des:26l40
012E:0020                         10 6B          .k
            2E 01 98 00 2E 01 00 00           ........
012E:0030 4D 08 00 00 EA 07 00 02           M...j...
            00 00 F0 0B 00 00 10 10           ..p.....
012E:0040 00 00 B1 09 00 00 06 1A           ..1.....
            00 00 01 09 04 80 18 14           ........
012E:0050 1E 14 4E 55 4C 20 20 20           ..NUL
            20 20 00 90 A5 15 2E 01            ..%...
012E:0060 A9 15 2E 01 A9 15               )...).
-d901:0l20
0901:0000 00 00 4D 08 00 20 4B 00           ..M.. K.
            5A 00 01 52 41 4D 44 49           Z..RAMDI
0901:0010 53 4B 56 44 49 53 4B 20           SKVDISK
            20 56 32 2E 30 08 00 00           V2.0...
-d84d:0l20
084D:0000 00 00 EA 07 08 80 12 00           ..j.....
            24 00 43 4C 4F 43 4B 24           $.CLOCK$
084D:0010 20 20 50 1E B8 D7 08 8E            P.8W..
            D8 89 1E 00 00 8C 06 02           X.......
-q
```

Based on the information presented in this chapter, I have written a program (DEVICES) which lists all block and character devices, displays device information, and prints cache usage statistics. The device information includes
attribute information and the addresses of the device header, strategy, and interrupt routines. DEVICES uses the CDS and the DCBs to locate block devices and
the device header chain to locate character devices. I prefer using this program
to DEBUG because it is easier and provides more information.

Adding Driver Functions

After I am confident that the initialization code is working, I add other driver
functions. I like to use a program that calls the driver directly, bypassing the INT
21H dispatcher. This technique lets me use DEBUG to trace what is happening in
the driver.

The CallDev routine presented in the next listing shows how you can use some undocumented features of DOS to locate and call your driver directly. This program sends a request header directly to the PRN driver causing the message Hello, world to be displayed. Please note that lines 16, 18, 21, 22, and 23 cannot be entered as shown in this listing. I have split these lines so that the listing would fit on this page.

Lines 2-4 reference some include files. The contents of FCB.DEF were given earlier in this essay. The other two files are listed at the end of Essay 11. Lines 13-15 use an FCB to open the "PRN" device. A successful FCB open returns the address of the device header in one of the reserved FCB fields. Lines 16-24 fill in fields in the request header. Lines 25-35 are a bit tricky; they place three addresses on the stack and load ES:BX with the address of the request header. First, the address of done is pushed; next comes the address of the driver interrupt entry. The address of the strategy routine is pushed last. The return_far macro at line 36 executes a far return to the driver strategy routine. When it completes, the strategy routine executes a far routine which transfers control to the interrupt routine. The far return in the interrupt code returns us to done.

```
_text     SEGMENT BYTE PUBLIC 'CODE'      ; [01]
          INCLUDE FCB.DEF                 ; [02]
          INCLUDE DEVICE.DEF              ; [03]
          INCLUDE MACROS.ASM             ; [04]
          ASSUME  cs:_text,ds:_text       ; [05]
          ORG     100H                    ; [06]
CallDev PROC      NEAR                    ; [07]
          jmp     start                   ; [08]
theFCB  FCB       <,'PRN      '>          ; [09]
theRH   RH_IO     <>                      ; [10]
theMsg  DB        'Hello,  world',0dh,0aH; [11]
theMsgSiz         EQU       $-theMsg      ; [12]
          x       x       x       x
start:  mov       ah,0fH                  ; [13] ah <== FCB open
          lea     dx,theFCB               ; [14] dx <== FCB address
          int     21H                     ; [15] do it
          mov     theRH.RH_B_Length,-
                  SIZE RH_IO              ; [16] request header length
          mov     theRH.RH_B_Unit,0  ; [17] unit number = 0
          mov     theRH.RH_B_Command,-
                  RH_C_Output             ; [18] function is output
          mov     theRH.RH_W_Status,0;  [19] initialize status
          mov     ax,OFFSET theMsg   ; [20] add buffer address
          mov     WORD PTR -
                  theRH.RH_A_TransferAddress,ax   ; [21]
          mov     WORD PTR -
```

```
                   theRH.RH_A_TransferAddress+2,ds ; [22]
          mov      theRH.RH_W_Count,-
                   theMsgSiz              ; [23] and message size
          mov      theRH.RH_W_Sector,0; [24] sector = 0
          mov      ax,cs                  ; [25]
          mov      es,ax                  ; [26] es <== SEGMENT theRH
          push     ax                     ; [27] push SEGMENT done
          mov      ax,OFFSET done         ; [28]
          push     ax                     ; [29] push OFFSET done
          mov      bx,OFFSET theRH        ; [30] bx <== OFFSET theRH
          lds      si,theFCB.FCB_A_DHD; [31] ds:si <== device header
          push     ds                     ; [32] SEGMENT Int entry
          push     [si].DHD_W_InterruptEntry; [33] OFFSET Int entry
          push     ds                     ; [34] SEGMENT Stg entry
          push     [si].DHD_W_StrategyEntry ; [35] OFFSET Stg entry
          return_far                      ; [36] call strategy routine
done:     mov      ah,4cH                 ; [37] ah <== terminate
          int      21H                    ; [38]
caller    ENDP
_text     ENDS
          END      CallDev
```

When you use a program such as CallDev, pay particular attention to what happens with the index registers and stack pointer. If any index registers change across the call, make sure you understand why. Forgetting to save a register or restoring registers in the wrong sequence are common errors. It is usually wise to single-step through one driver call. Make sure the ret instructions in the strategy and interrupt routines transfer to the proper place. It is easy to mess up the stack by removing the wrong number of saved values.

Calling Your Driver

The next step in the testing procedure would be to access the driver through DOS. You can use the DOS copy command to test your driver read and write routines.

The copy command uses handles to open, read, and write to a device. The INT 21H dispatcher switches to the disk I/O stack to process these requests. So long as the new device is not the current StdOut device, you can trace execution with INT 21H (AH = 9) messages. The INT 21H dispatcher uses the user stack to process keyboard I/O (AH = 1 to AH = 0cH) requests, and can handle this one level of recursion. Note that this capability is not documented and may break in the future.

If a request appears to complete successfully and DOS dies sometime later, it is a good bet that a register was inadvertantly changed or the driver erroneously overwrote some important DOS variable. (Usually any location accidentally modified by a driver is important to DOS.) The most common cause of trashing a DOS variable is improper initialization of a segment register. Sometimes MASM adds to our confusion by doing something unexpected. You must be very careful with ASSUME statements, or MASM may do you in.

Stack overflow (putting too much information on the stack) or underflow (removing too many items from the stack) can also lock up the system. Stack errors usually show up very quickly. If stack overflow is suspected, switch to a driver-private stack or increase the size of the existing stack.

Unless your driver makes many subroutine calls or saves a lot of information on the stack, you shouldn't need a separate stack. One reason that the INT 21H dispatcher switches stacks is to protect DOS from applications with inadequate stack space. It is easy to switch stacks; you load the SS:SP registers with the address of a data area within your driver. Of course, you must remember to save the original SS:SP values and restore them before your driver returns. The SOUND driver described in Essay 11 illustrates this technique.

Dealing with Hardware Interrupts

Some devices are capable of generating interrupts. They are a way of getting the processor's attention on demand. Your PC has some special hardware to support this feature. When a device generates an interrupt, the same event sequence that occurs when the processor executes an INT nn instruction is followed.

There is one important difference between hardware-generated interrupts and executing an INT instruction: the hardware interrupt can occur at any time. There are times when you don't want to be interrupted. You must take explicit action to avoid an interrupt at an inappropriate time; this process is known as synchronization. (See Essay 11 for a more complete discussion of this topic.)

The PC hardware which supports the interrupt mechanism has some subtle features which you must be aware of, such as adapters that generate a specific interrupt (e.g., 09H) which you must enable. Once an interrupt has been generated, it cannot recur until you say it is OK by sending an End of Interrupt (EOI) message to the hardware.

Adapter interrupt service routines are the most difficult part of the driver to debug. Many interrupt service routine errors, including improper synchronization, tend to be timing sensitive. No BIOS requests can be safely made from an interrupt service routine. Diagnostic information can be written directly to video memory. This technique is not pretty and may introduce enough delay to cause problems or make problems disappear, but it is still worth a try. The printer or COM port may also be used when their slow speed will not cause a problem. Interrupt driven I/O should not be used for diagnostic writes. If the driver does not work and the system does not lock up, sometimes counters can be used to track down a problem. Each time a particular event happens, update a counter. Use a debugger to examine these counters later.

Common interrupt service routine errors include forgetting to send an EOI to the interrupt controller, sending too many EOIs, using a RET instead of an IRET to dismiss the interrupt, not enabling a particular interrupt, forgetting to save a register, and stack overflow. Devices can generate spurious interrupts and interrupts can be missed. Heavy duty hardware aids are often needed to track down these types of errors.

Conclusion

This has been a long journey. We found that in order to understand device drivers we had to look at most of the interfaces and data structures within DOS. (See Essay 6, Undocumented MS-DOS Functions, by Ray Michels, for a reference-type approach to DOS internals focusing on undocumented DOS features.)

The more you know about DOS, the more you can do with it. I have used the information presented in this chapter to write self-loading device drivers and a utility which loads (and unloads) drivers. The key in this age of networks is exploiting the versatility built into DOS. Network devices can be very useful for developing applications in a heterogeneous environment.

Walter Dixon holds degrees in both mechanical and electrical engineering. He is employed at General Electric Corporate Research and Development Center in Schenectady, where he works in the areas of distributed systems and computer networks. Mr. Dixon also teaches graduate computer science at Union College in Schenectady. He has written more than ten device drivers for PC-DOS.

Related Essays

1   A Guided Tour inside MS-DOS
6   Undocumented MS-DOS Functions
8   Data Protection and Encryption
11   Writing a SOUND Device Driver
14   Understanding Expanded Memory Systems

Keywords

- ► device driver
- ► circular buffer
- ► coroutines
- ► finite state machine
- ► synchronization
- ► critical sections

Essay Synopsis: The best way to turn theory into practice in mastering the art of device driver programming is to see how a significant driver is developed and implemented. After a brief recap of the theory discussed in his preceding essay, the author presents and explains a complete, working device driver for generating sophisticated music and other sounds under MS-DOS. The driver uses state of the art programming techniques including circular buffers, coroutines, and finite state machines. Programs are written to test the driver and measure its performance. Many of the concepts used in this essay are applicable to a wide variety of system software.

## 11

Writing a SOUND Device Driver

Walter Dixon

Device drivers are the essential tools that allow your programs to control printers, disk drives, sound generation chips, and many other devices. Writing or modifying device drivers to accommodate new or improved hardware is an important programming task. (See Essay 10, Developing MS-DOS Device Drivers, for a comprehensive discussion of the many MS-DOS data structures and services involved with file and device access.)

Some of the material presented here may be new to you. If your goal is to write a device driver after studying this essay, you'll need to know assembly language, understand MS-DOS, and be familiar with digital logic. This knowledge comes with experience. Even if you are unfamiliar with 8086 assembly language, don't despair. Although the driver and other examples are coded in that language, they are heavily commented, and the accompanying text explains the salient features.

There is a little something for everyone in this essay. The sample device driver turns your PC into a musical instrument, so musically inclined readers will have fun playing with this infrequently exploited PC capability and using it to explore music composition. The more technically minded reader may be interested in the relationship between DOS and device drivers. The programming techniques and performance analysis are useful additions to any programmer's bag of tricks. If you really want to write a device driver, the driver code included at the end of this essay is a good starting point. Although the best way to learn about device drivers is to write one, you can also learn a lot by studying someone else's code.

Setting up the SOUND Driver

The SOUND driver is a sophisticated DOS device driver which converts textual descriptions to musical tones. Commands can be put into a file and sent to the driver with the DOS COPY command or directly written from your own program. They support a superset of the functions provided by the well known BASICA SOUND and PLAY statements.

This section describes the organization of the driver software and the steps needed to create a working version of the SOUND driver. *Please pay special attention to the warning in the next section about installing this driver on your hard disk.* Once I have shown you how to build and install the driver, I will give you an example you can use to try it out.

Creating a Working SOUND Driver

The six files needed to build the SOUND driver are listed in Table 11-1. Listings of these files appear at the end of this chapter. Use EDLIN or a real text editor to create these files. You can also use a word processor if it can save documents as ASCII text. Most word processors normally imbed format information in the file which the assembler (MASM) cannot handle. You need not include the comments that begin with a semicolon and extend to the end of the line.

Table 11-1.   SOUND Driver Files

File	Description
sound.asm	The driver source
macros.asm	Useful macros
device.def	Definitions of device and request headers
hardware.def	Hardware related definitions
values.def	Various driver parameters
fsm.def	Definition of macros for finite state machine

Create a subdirectory and move all these files to it. Do not name this subdirectory SOUND. The driver which you are building is known to DOS by this name and its presence will prevent you from accessing the subdirectory. Use the following commands to create a working SOUND driver. The link command will produce an ignorable warning that there is no stack segment. You now have an executable version of the SOUND driver.

```
masm sound;
link sound;
exe2bin sound \sound.sys
```

Installing and Using the SOUND Driver

I have tested this code on IBM XT and AT computers, but you should not assume that it will work on your system. The driver may not work on certain hardware configurations or in conjunction with programs which manipulate the timer vectors. You should always test a new device driver by booting from a floppy disk. If the driver passes this first test, you can move the driver to your hard disk, but *make sure you have a bootable floppy disk in case something goes wrong.*

Add the following line to your `CONFIG.SYS` file and reboot your system.

```
device=\sound.sys
```

The SOUND driver is now installed and ready to use.

SOUND Driver Commands and Musical Notation

SOUND driver commands control music pitch (frequency) and duration. Each musical note conveys both pitch and duration information. Individual notes are combined to produce a tune.

Pitch and Musical Notes

Pitch specification rules are modeled after the piano keyboard shown in Figure 11-1. (A real keyboard actually has 88 notes.) The SOUND driver can play 84 different notes which are specified by number or name. The command to select a note by number is the letter N followed by the note number `N13` selects the 13th note.

The 84 different notes are divided into seven octaves of 12 notes each. An octave begins with a note named C, followed by C# (C sharp), D, D#, E, F, F#, G, G#, A, A#, and B. Each note in this sequence, known as a chromatic scale, is one half-step above the preceding one. Moving up one half-step increases a note's frequency about six percent. Octaves are numbered from 0 to 6. Moving up one octave doubles a note's frequency. The letter O followed by a number specifies an octave. The command `O3` selects the third octave, the one beginning with *middle C*. The default octave number is 4 `O4`.

Middle C is the key in the middle of a piano keyboard. The note located at zero `N0` is the C three octaves below middle C, and its frequency is ⅛ that of middle C. To completely specify a note, either a number or a name and an octave is required. The commands `O3C` and `N36` both select middle C. Once an octave command appears, subsequent named notes are assumed to be in the same octave. The sequence `O3CDE` selects middle C and then the notes D and E directly above middle C.

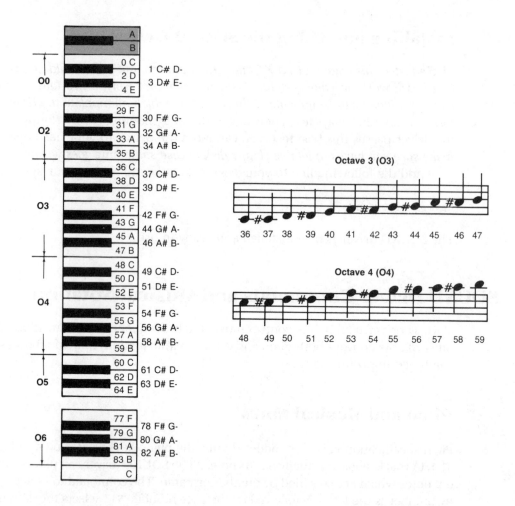

Fig. 11-1.   The piano keyboard.

Sharping a note raises its frequency one half-step and flatting it lowers its frequency by an equal amount. Sharps are indicated by `#` or `+` and flats by `-`. `F#` says take the note F and raise it one half-step. Both BASICA and the SOUND driver support sharps and flats. The SOUND driver accepts double sharps and double flats, which raise or lower, respectively, the frequency one whole-step. `C##` (C double sharp) says to raise C one whole-step. Since D is one whole-step above C, `C##` and D are names for the same note.

Scales and Key Signatures

Notes are grouped into *scales*; each note in a scale has a precise relationship to the preceding one. There are eight notes in a major scale. The third and eighth notes of this scale are one half-step above their predecessors; all others are separated by a whole-step. Each scale has a name taken from its initial note. The simplest major scale is C major whose notes are C, D, E, F, G, A, B, and C. Musical scores use a key signature to select a scale. If there is no explicit signature, the key of C is assumed. The SOUND driver supports multiple keys. The `K` command followed by the key name specifies a key signature; thus, `KF#` selects the key of F sharp. Like the octave command, a key signature remains in effect until it is explicitly changed. BASICA does not support key signatures; all music must be in the key of C.

Key signatures affect the interpretation of music. In the key of C, there are no sharps or flats, and an F sharp must be explicitly written. The G major scale consists of G, A, B, C, D, E, F#, and G. In this key `KG`, an F is played as F sharp. To summarize the effect of a key signature, the sequence `KCOOF` would select F (N6), but `KGOOF` would select F Sharp (N7).

If a sharp or flat is needed in a key where the note would not normally be played this way, the sharp or flat must be explicitly written. Musicians refer to such an occurrence as an accidental. `KCF#` would explicitly ask for F sharp even though that note does not appear in the C major scale. It is sometimes necessary to lower a note which normally would be sharped or raise a note which normally would be flatted. Another accidental, a natural, is used for this purpose. The musical natural symbol does not have an ASCII equivalent; it looks like a square box with two tails. The SOUND driver uses `=` to represent a natural. If a score were written in the key of G (F would normally be sharped) and the composer wanted a normal F (F natural) played, he must explicitly ask for it. The equivalent SOUND driver command would be `KGF=`. This sequence says play in the key of G (KG), but make F unsharped. BASICA does not support naturals.

Duration

Three factors control sound duration: length indicated by the note, time, and tempo. Each note in a musical score has a relative duration implied by how it is written. Scores contain whole-notes, half-notes, quarter-notes, etc. A whole-note lasts twice as long as a half-note and four times as long as a quarter-note. The length command is used to specify default duration, and is written as the letter L followed by a number from 1 to 64. The number 1 corresponds to a whole-note, 2 to a half-note, 4 to a quarter-note, 8 to an eighth-note, etc. L, like O, applies to all following notes. A number following a note indicates the duration of just that note. The sequence `O3L4CDC8` specifies that middle C, D above middle C, and middle C be played in succession. The default duration `L4` makes the first two quarter-notes, but the last note is explicitly labeled as an eighth-note. (The duration of eighth-notes is half that of quarter-notes.) The length of a note may also be *dotted*. A dotted length is 50 percent longer than an undotted one. The sequence `O3L4.CC8.` would play middle C first as a dotted quarter-note (duration 1.5 times a quarter-note) followed by a dotted eighth-note (duration 1.5 times an eighth-note).

Notes may be *tied* together. In musical notation, notes are tied together by connecting them with an arc—the notes must be the same. The arc is also used to indicate something called a *slur*. Tied notes are played as one; the duration is the sum of the individual note lengths. The command 03C1&C1 says play middle C for twice the normal duration of a whole note. BASICA does not support ties.

A second factor affecting note duration is *time* which indicates how many *beats* per measure and what type of note gets one beat. Musical scores are divided into units called measures which contain an equal number of beats; graphically, measures are indicated by vertical bars. If no time is explicitly indicated, a score is assumed to be in ⁴⁄₄ time which means there are four beats to a measure and a quarter-note gets one beat. Neither BASICA nor the SOUND driver support times; however, they could be easily added to the SOUND driver.

Time and Tempo

Tempo is the third factor affecting note duration. Tempo specifies the absolute speed at which a score should be played. Composers specify tempo by indicating that so many of a particular type of note (e.g., quarter-note) must be played in a minute. The note type used to set the tempo depends on the time of the music; BASICA and the SOUND driver use quarter-notes. The tempo command, written as T followed by a number, specifies how many quarter-notes must be played in a minute. The default tempo, T120 says that 120 quarter-notes must be played in one minute. Some scores use a less precise method of specifying tempo. Words like andante (slowly), moderato (moderately), and presto (fast) are used to select a range of tempos. Andante indicates a tempo range of 76-108 quarter-notes per minute, moderato a tempo of 108 to 120, and presto a range of 120-168.

Rests indicate periods of silence. There are whole-rests, half-rests, quarter-rests, etc. These individual rests select different periods of silence. BASICA uses the pause command, P, to indicate a rest. Syntactically, the pause command is treated like a note (except that it cannot be sharped or flatted). The commands P4 and L4P would both indicate a quarter-rest.

Staccato and Legato

Both the SOUND driver and BASICA provide three commands which crudely determine the way music is played. MN asks for "normal" mode, MS selects "staccato" mode, and ML "legato" mode. Music style is implemented by varying the time between notes. (It should be noted that the BASICA implementation used incorrect values for this internote pause.) When a musician changes from one style to the other, he is able to vary volume and harmonic content of the note as well. The sound generation hardware in the IBM PC/XT/AT is rather primitive compared to a musical instrument. The SOUND driver does not support foreground MF and background MB playing.

The SOUND driver supports imbedded comments. A comment begins with an exclamation point (!) and terminates at the end of a line. The delimiter and any subsequent characters are ignored. Comments can be used to imbed lyrics or titles in a tune file; they are not supported by BASICA.

Command Summary

Table 11-2 summarizes the SOUND driver commands. Asterisks indicate SOUND driver enhancements not found in BASICA. Notes (A . . . G) can have trailing accidentals (#, ##, +, + +, −, − −, or =). A dotted length may follow the note name or pause.

Table 11-2.   SOUND Driver Command Summary

Command	Description
−	Flat
− −	*Double flat
#	Sharp
##	*Double sharp
+	Sharp
+ +	*Double sharp
=	*Natural
&	*Tie
!	*Comment
.	Increases duration by 50 percent
A . . . G	Note
Kxx	*Key signature (xx = valid key name)
Lnn	Note length (1 ⟨ = nn ⟨ = 64)
ML	Music legato
MN	Music normal
MS	Music staccato
Nnn	Note number (0 ⟨ = nn ⟨ = 83)
On	Octave (0 ⟨ = n ⟨ = 6)
P	Pause
Tnnn	Music tempo (30 ⟨ nnn ⟨ 300)

Using the SOUND Driver

The first step in using the SOUND driver is to convert a musical score to driver commands. Figure 11-2 illustrates this process for the first 11 notes of "Mary Had a Little Lamb."

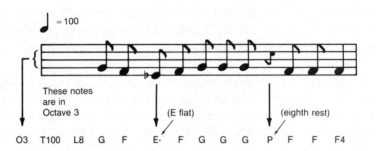

Fig. 11-2.   "Mary Had a Little Lamb."

If you create a file named TUNE.DAT which contains these commands, you can "play" it with the DOS COPY command. COPY TUNE.DAT SOUND. Using the SOUND driver in this way is like playing a record. You start it with the COPY and music continues until the entire file has been processed.

Interactive access to the driver is also possible with commands from the keyboard. Again we use the DOS COPY command, but this time we copy our keyboard input to the driver. Enter the command COPY CON SOUND and then enter the commands and notes you want performed. Either a control-z or F10 terminates the interactive mode. (Both these keys generate an end of file character.) You may find this technique a bit awkward because a note will not start to play until the first character of the next note is entered.

You can also access the driver directly from your own program. The following program plays the first 11 notes of "Mary Had a Little Lamb."

```
_data        SEGMENT WORD PUBLIC 'DATA'
notes        DB      'T100L803GFE-FGGGPFFF4'
num_notes    EQU     $-notes
sound        DB      'SOUND',0
_data        ENDS

_stack       SEGMENT WORD STACK 'STACK' ; "exe" programs
             DW      256 DUP(0)         ; need a stack
_stack       ENDS                       ; segment

_text        SEGMENT BYTE PUBLIC 'CODE' ; start of segment
             ASSUME  cs:_text, ds:_data ; needed by masm

start        PROC    NEAR               ; start of procedure
             mov     ax,_data           ; "exe" programs must
             mov     ds,ax              ; initialize ds
             mov     dx,OFFSET sound    ; dx  <==  addr( sound )
             mov     ax,3d01H           ; ask DOS to open device
```

```
            int     21H                 ; for write
            mov     bx,ax               ; bx  <==  handle
            mov     dx,OFFSET notes ; dx  <==  addr( notes )
            mov     cx,num_notes    ; cx  <==  # characters
            mov     ah,40H              ; ask DOS to write these
            int     21H                 ; characters
            mov     ah,3eH              ; ask DOS to close device
            int     21H
            mov     ah,4cH              ; ask DOS to terminate
            int     21H                 ; program
start       ENDP                        ; end of procedure
_text       ENDS                        ; end of segment
            END     start               ; specify start address
```

You may wish to transcribe printed sheet music into input for the SOUND driver. This takes a little practice, but it's not really hard. As an example, Figure 11-3 illustrates the score to Beethoven's "Ode to Joy," from the last movement of his Ninth Symphony. This listing shows the resulting transcription:

```
KDT12003L4F2GAAGFEDDEFF.E8E2
FFGAAGFEDDEFE.D8D2
E2FDEF8G8FDEF8G8FEDEO2A03F&
FFGAAGFEDDEFE.D8D2
04F2GAAGFEDDEFF.E8E2
F2GAAGFEDDEFE.D8D2
E2FDEF8G8FDEF8G8FEDEO3A04F&
FFGAAGFEDDEFE.L8DDAGFL4
E2FDEF8G8FDEF8G8FEDEO3A04F&
FFGAAGFEDDEFE.D8DP4
```

The SOUND driver maintains an internal buffer (currently 256 notes). Music will continue to play after the copy completes or the device is closed.

Hardware Review

Before we get into the details of writing our SOUND driver, let's consider how the relevant PC hardware is accessed by a device driver. The hardware which controls a device may exist as a separate board called an adapter or may be part of the *mother* board. The board designers provide one or more ports for the CPU to communicate with the device. You can think of these ports as a mailbox. When the CPU wants to tell the device something, it places a message in this mailbox. Similarly, when a device has information for the CPU, it leaves a message in this mailbox. The hardware helps keep track of sender and receiver.

Fig. 11-3. Beethoven's "Ode to Joy."

Some of these devices can perform more than one function. The CPU requests a particular action by sending appropriate data to the device. You can think of what is being sent as a program that the CPU wants the device to execute. The device returns the results of this program to the CPU as a status. Messages placed in these mailboxes may be programs, data, or status.

Controlling a Device

Intel processors use special instructions to communicate with a device. All members of the 80X86 provide IN and OUT instructions. Some have special instructions for reading or writing more than one byte at a time. The IN and OUT instructions move data between the accumulator and the port whose address is in the DX register.

On the IBM PC, COM1 is implemented with an INS8250 UART chip. This chip has several ports. The next listing shows a simplistic approach to reading a character from COM1. Characters are read by specifying the receive buffer pointer as the target of an IN instruction. Actually dealing with COM1 is slightly more involved. We want to read each character only once. The 8250 sets a bit in another register to indicate that a character is available and clears this bit after the receive buffer register is read.

```
COM1    EQU     3f8H                    ; Base for COM1
RBR     EQU     0                       ; Receive buffer register
                                        ; offset
        mov     dx,COM1.RBR             ; dx  <==  addr( RBR )
        in      al,dx                   ; read the character
```

The following example shows how you might actually read a character from COM1. I've omitted some important details from these examples such as establishing communications parameters (speed, parity, etc.) and checking for errors.

```
COM1    EQU     3f8H                    ; Base for COM1
RBR     EQU     0                       ; Receive buffer register

                                        ; offset
LSR     EQU     5                       ; Line status register
                                        ; offset
DR      EQU     1                       ; Data ready flag
        mov     dx,COM1.LSR             ; dx  <==  addr( LSR )
wait:   in      al,dx                   ; read line status
        and     al,DR                   ; new character?
        jz      wait                    ; if Z--not yet
        mov     dx,COM1.RBR             ; dx  <==  addr( RBR )
        in      al,dx                   ; read the character
```

Interrupts Explained

The INS8250 is relatively slow compared to the CPU. The processor will execute many instructions while it waits for a character to arrive. In the previous example, the CPU is doing nothing useful while it awaits the next character. Sometimes we will not want to waste this time. Interrupts help the PC deal with this problem. If a device wants to get the processor's attention (as COM1 would when a character arrived), it can request an interrupt. Under certain conditions, the processor stops what it is doing and deals with the interrupt.

A special chip, the 8259 Interrupt Controller, helps the processor deal with interrupts. This chip controls when an interrupt is serviced and what code will be used to service it. The CPU programs the 8259 by writing control words to one of its registers.

The 8259 deals with up to eight separate devices and assigns a priority to each one. If more than one interrupt has been requested, the 8259 services the one with highest priority first. Once an interrupt begins, no lower priority interrupt can occur until the current one completes, but a higher priority interrupt can suspend the one currently in progress.

The code that gets executed as a result of an interrupt is known as an interrupt service routine. When the processor grants an interrupt, it pushes the processor flags, CS, and IP registers on the stack and transfers control to the interrupt service routine.

When the interrupt service routine begins, all interrupts are disabled. Normally, it will enable interrupts almost immediately. Once interrupts are enabled, this routine can be interrupted by higher priority interrupts.

This routine *must* send the 8259 a control word which indicates that the interrupt has been serviced. Normally, this notification occurs just prior to returning to the interrupted code with an IRET instruction. The following code illustrates a typical interrupt service routine.

```
I8259      EQU     20H         ; Base address
PortA      EQU     0           ; Port offsets
PortB      EQU     1
EOI        EQU     20H         ; Nonspecific end of
                               ; interrupt

ISREntry   PROC    FAR
           STI                 ; Enable higher priority
                               ; interrupts
;
;      Normal ISR Logic:
;
;          (1) Save any registers needed by this routine
;          (2) Deal with interrupt
;          (3) Restore registers saved in step 1
;
           mov     I8259.PortA,EOI ; Say interrupt is over
           iret                    ; pick up where we left
                                   ; off
ISREntry   ENDP
```

The CPU must explicitly enable individual interrupts by sending a control word to the 8259. It can also disable all interrupts with a CLI instruction. The CLI inhibits interrupt recognition until the CPU executes a STI instruction. (There is a special interrupt which is not masked by the CLI instruction, but it is not relevant to our discussion.)

Programming Techniques

The SOUND driver uses circular buffers, coroutines, and finite state machines. It also illustrates synchronization and critical sections. Although these techniques are normally discussed in advanced computer science courses, they are frequently used in system software. Their names may sound exotic, but these techniques are useful and easily implemented.

Circular Buffers

Circular buffers are useful when data is gathered and removed at unpredictable rates. Their implementation requires a storage area, two pointers, and a flag. One pointer specifies where the next data item will be stored and the other identifies which item will be removed next. Data is used FIFO (First In, First Out). Each pointer initially points to the beginning of the storage area. As data is added and removed, each pointer sweeps sequentially through the storage array. At the end of the array, the pointer "wraps" to the first location, hence the name circular buffer (see Figure 11-4).

You can think of this structure as an ordinary array whose beginning and ending location "float." The ending location changes as data is added, and the start changes as data is removed. Each pointer can wrap because the start of the array floats. If we did not allow the beginning location to float, we would have to slide the contents of the buffer down every time we removed an element, which would be time-consuming.

The only trick to implementing a circular buffer is distinguishing between the empty and full states. If we use only two pointers and completely fill the array, we cannot tell whether the buffer is empty or full. Leaving one location unfilled or using an auxiliary variable will solve this problem. The auxiliary variable may be either a boolean or a buffer count. Here is a program that uses a buffer count to distinguish between full and empty:

```
BUF_S_Size      EQU      8
_data           SEGMENT WORD PUBLIC 'DATA'
BUF_A_Remove    DW       BUF_T_Data    ; Both remove and insert
BUF_A_Insert    DW       BUF_T_Data    ; initially point to 1st
                                       ; location
BUF_B_Count     DB       0             ; No elements initially
BUF_T_Data      DB       BUF_S_Size DUP(0)
```

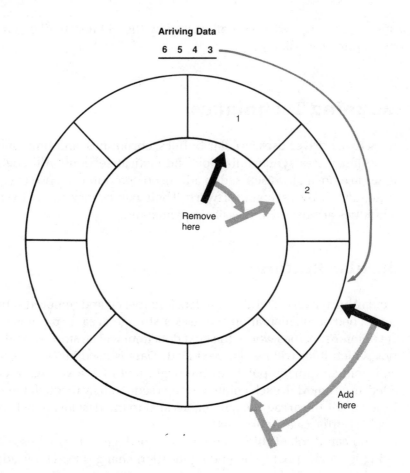

Fig. 11-4. Circular buffer.

```
BUF_A_End      EQU     $                      ; So we can detect wrap

_text   SEGMENT BYTE PUBLIC 'CODE'
        ASSUME  cs:_text, ds:_data
CirBuf  PROC    NEAR
b_succ  clc                                    ; Say we succeeded
        ret                                    ; and returned
b_err   stc                                    ; Say we failed
        ret                                    ; and return

;
;   Inserts byte in AL into circular buffer. Returns with
;   CY=1 if failed (buffer full) or CY=0 otherwise.
;
Insert  LABEL   NEAR
```

```
           cmp     BUF_B_Count,BUF_S_Size  ; Is buffer full?
           jz      b_err                   ; If Z--yes
           xchg    bx,BUF_A_Insert         ; bx  <==  insert address
           mov     BYTE PTR [bx],al        ; Insert it
           call    NextBX                  ; Calc next address
           xchg    BUF_A_Insert,bx         ; Update insert ptr
           inc     BUF_B_Count             ; One more data item
           jmp     SHORT b_succ            ; Take success exit

;
;    Removes byte from circular buffer. Returns with CY=1
;    if failed (buffer empty) or CY=0 and AL=byte otherwise.
;
Remove  LABEL   NEAR
           cmp     BUF_B_Count,0           ; Is buffer empty?
           jz      b_err                   ; If Z--yes
           xchg    bx,BUF_A_Remove         ; bx  <==  remove address
           mov     al,BYTE PTR [bx]        ; Remove byte
           call    NextBX                  ; Calc next address
           xchg    BUF_A_Remove,bx         ; Update remove ptr
           dec     BUF_B_Count             ; One less data item
           jmp     SHORT b_succ            ; Take success exit


NextBX  PROC    NEAR
           inc     bx                      ; Advance to next item
           cmp     bx,BUF_A_End            ; Have we reached end?
           jnz     a0                      ; If NZ--no
           lea     bx,BUF_T_Data           ; Wrap the pointer
a0:        ret                             ; and return
NextBX  ENDP
CirBuf  ENDP
_text   ENDS
```

Coroutines

The familiar programming technique of subroutines is a special case of a more
generalized construction known as a coroutine. The difference between a subroutine and a coroutine is that a subroutine is always invoked at its entry point
and a coroutine is invoked at the instruction following the one last executed.
This concept is confusing until you understand the linkage mechanism. When a
coroutine gives up control, it issues another call rather than executing a return.
This second call leaves the address of the next instruction on the stack.

Coroutines are normally quite complex, and it is difficult to come up with a short example that could not be done more easily with some other technique. The following listing uses coroutines to decompress run length encoded data. In this trivial example, the data consists of zeros and ones. Frequently data contains runs of the same value. Inserting a run length and single value in place of the original run reduces storage requirements. (This technique is common in image processing.) The string 0000111011111000000 would be encoded as 403105160. In this example, the run length must be nine or less.

```
        lea     si,string       ; si  <==  compressed string
        call    Dcmprss         ; set up initial coroutine
nxtch:  pop     bp              ; bp  <==  callback address
        or      al,al           ; end of string?
        jz      done            ; if Z--yes
;
;       We pass through here once for every character in the
;       decompressed string. The character (0 or 1) is in AL
;
        call    bp              ; make coroutine callback
        jmp     SHORT nxtch     ; get the next character
done    LABEL   NEAR            ; end of string reached
;
;       ...                     ; additional processing
;
Dcmprss PROC    NEAR
        pop     bp              ; bp  <==  callback address
;
;       Branch here to look for single value or run
;
d0:     lodsb                   ; al  <==  next byte of
                                ; compressed string
        cmp     al,'1'          ; is it a run length?
        jg      run             ; if G--yes
        call    bp              ; make coroutine callback
;
;       Return here if not in the middle of a run
;
        jmp     SHORT Dcmprss   ; get another character
;
;       Branch here at start of a run
;
s_run:  cbw                     ; convert run length to
        mov     cx,ax           ; binary integer
        sub     cl,'0'          ; (ascii to binary conversion)
```

```
        lodsb                     ; al  <==  repeated byte
;
;       Branch here to resume run processing
;
c_run:  push    ax                ; save repeated value
        call    bp                ; make callback
;
;       Return here to continue processing a run
;
        pop     bp                ; bp  <==  callback address
        pop     ax                ; recover repeated value
        loop    n2                ; continue processing run
        jmp     SHORT d0          ; look for run length or
                                  ; single value
Dcmprss ENDP
```

The advantage of using coroutines in this example is that the calling program is unaware of the run length decompression. The decompression routine Dcmprss uses the program counter to maintain state information implicitly. The callback address which Dcmprss leaves on the stack indicates whether or not a run is being processed.

Finite State Machines

Finite state machines are common in compilers, communications protocols, and pattern-searching. They provide a way of dealing with data that must be processed according to certain rules or that must arrive in a predetermined sequence. Finite state machines manipulate abstract entities called *tokens* which may be characters, words, sentences, or program statements. The collective set of sequencing rules is called a *grammar*. A token may be acceptable at one time and not at another. The grammar specifies when a token is acceptable. The set of all possible tokens is called the alphabet.

A finite state machine is in a particular *state* while it is waiting for a token. When the token arrives, the finite state machine checks to see if the token is acceptable. The grammar specifies when a particular token arriving at a given time conforms to the rules. If the token is acceptable, the finite state machine makes a *transition* to a new state where a different set of tokens may be legal. (It may also stay in the same state.)

The SOUND driver uses a finite state machine to recognize the sequences MN, MS, and ML (see Figure 11-5). In fact, it uses a state machine to recognize all sequences. In this case, the alphabet consists of the letters L, M, N, and S. The state machine immediately rejects a token which is not in its alphabet. The finite state machine initially looks for an M, in this first state, the only legal token. The arrival of an M causes a transition to a new state where N, S, or L are acceptable. The arrival of one of these three letters causes the finite state machine to accept or recognize the string. It is common to use a picture to represent what happens in a finite state machine. Figure 11-5 describes recognition of the `MS`, `MN`, and `ML` sequences. Circles represent states and arcs represent transitions. Arcs are labeled with the token which causes the transition. Some arcs are not labeled. After recognizing `ML`, `MN`, or `MS`, the state machine in this example resets itself. It is then ready to look for another M.

Synchronization

Cooperation is needed when multiple processes work on the same problem. If we were to write two separate programs—one which inserted characters into a circular buffer and another that removed them—we would immediately recognize the importance of this requirement. The program which removes characters must recognize an empty buffer, and the program which inserts characters must be smart enough to deal with a full buffer. This scenario is the basis for a classical computer science problem, the Producer-Consumer Problem, which is solved by synchronization. The consumer, in this case, the remove routine, must wait for a new character if the buffer is empty. Similarly, the producer must wait for a character to be removed if the buffer is full. Each program can use the buffer count to stay in sync with its partner.

The same problem also occurs in a single program with multiple execution threads such as interrupt-driven device drivers. A program which fills a circular buffer at a noninterrupt level and removes characters from within an interrupt service routine has two execution threads.

Relegating an execution thread to an interrupt service routine adds an interesting twist to this problem. The producer, which operates at the noninterrupt level, can enter a busy wait loop if it finds the buffer full. At some time in the future, an interrupt will occur and the consumer will remove a character. After the interrupt is dismissed, the producer will notice that the buffer is no longer full and insert its character. The consumer cannot use this strategy. Since it is operating at an interrupt level, the consumer blocks the producer's execution. A busy wait loop in the interrupt service routine (see the next example) would never terminate, resulting in a condition known as a deadlock. The consumer must dismiss the interrupt and depend on the consumer to somehow cause an interrupt after it places a character in the buffer.

```
test:   cmp     count,size              ; is the buffer full
        jz      test                    ; if Z--yes
;
;       There's at least one empty location now.
;
```

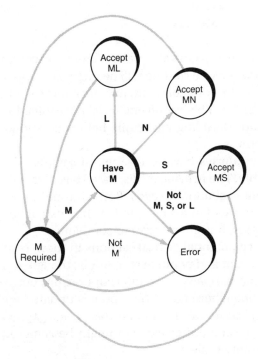

Fig. 11-5.   Finite state machine.

Critical Sections

The following example illustrates what happens when two execution threads
try to alter a common variable:

```
;
;       noninterrupt level code
;
        mov     ax,value        ; [a] put value in accumulator
        add     ax,10           ; [b] make an adjustment
        mov     value,ax        ; [c] update value
;
;       ...
;


;
;       Interrupt service routine
;
        mov     ax,value
```

```
sub      ax,10
mov      value,ax
```

If an interrupt occurs after [a] but before [c] completes, the alteration made in the interrupt service routine will be overwritten as [c] executes. For these two code fragments to work correctly, no interrupts can occur between the load and store instructions. This requirement of guaranteed completion is known as a critical section. Disabling interrupts before [a] and enabling them after [c] insures correctness.

We don't always have to disable interrupts when two threads update a shared variable. The previously discussed circular buffer routines may be called from different execution threads. Both routines alter BUF_B_Count, but this adjustment occurs within a single, indivisible instruction. Once the INC or DEC instruction begins, it is guaranteed to complete.

There are potential critical sections in these routines. If Insert is called at both the interrupt and noninterrupt levels, the BUF_A_Insert may be corrupted. (Consider what happens if the interrupt occurs between the two xchg instructions.) Changing where the buffer count is updated will introduce a critical section. If BUF_W_Count were changed before BUF_A_Insert or BUF_A_Remove was updated, the wrong buffer element might be removed. (Look at the buffer full and buffer empty cases.)

Identifying and dealing with critical sections is a very important part of writing a device driver. When handled incorrectly, critical sections often result in nasty bugs that can be very difficult to isolate. You'll see examples of critical sections in the SOUND driver.

DOS Internals

In this section, we will review driver structure and DOS/driver interaction. You can find more complete descriptions of this material in the *Disk Operating System Technical Reference Guide* (1984), the *MS-DOS Technical Reference Encyclopedia* (1986), the *MS-DOS Developer's Guide* (Angermeyer et al. 1986), and in Essay 10 of this book.

Every device driver has three parts—device header, strategy routine, and interrupt routine. Whenever DOS needs to access a device, it creates a structure called a request header and passes its address to the driver, which uses it to return status information to DOS.

Device Header

The device header supplies a device name, a summary of driver capabilities, and the addresses of two driver entry points. The following example illustrates the header. Because of the way in which DOS loads device drivers at boot time, the device header must be at the beginning of the driver.

```
DHD                  STRUC
DHD_A_NextDHD        DD    -1        ;; Address of next device
DHD_W_Attrib         DW    0         ;; Device attributes
DHD_W_SrategyEntry   DW    0         ;; Strategy entry offset
DHD_W_InterruptEntry DW    0         ;; Interrupt entry offset
DHD_T_Name           DB    8 DUP(' ')
DHD                  ENDS
```

DOS builds a linked list of device headers. The head of this chain is the NUL device, and each DHD_A_NextDHDfield contains the address of the next header in this chain. The DHD_W_Attribfield identifies the driver as block or character, describes the driver's ability to respond to optional requests, and specifies certain special devices. The next two fields specify the offsets for the strategy and interrupt entry points. Since these fields are only 16 bits, both entry points must be in the same segment as the header. The final header field contains the name of a character device. Although IBM documentation and various other sources suggest that block drivers set the first byte of the name field to a unit count, DOS does not use this value.

Strategy Entry

The strategy entry currently does very little. When DOS needs to access a device, it passes a request header to the driver strategy entry which stores this address and returns.

Interrupt Entry

The real work of completing the request happens in the interrupt entry code. This code recovers the address of the request header and completes the requests. In most cases, the interrupt entry code sets the status field of the request header to indicate the results of its processing.

Request Header

DOS constructs a request header like the one illustrated in the next example to describe a driver request. This structure is not sufficient to describe all possible driver requests. DOS appends information to this basic structure for certain requests.

```
RH                        STRUC
RH_B_Length               DB      0     ;; Length (bytes) of this
                                        ;; request header
RH_B_Unit                 DB      0     ;; Unit code
RH_B_Command              DB      0     ;; Command code
RH_W_Status               DW      0     ;; Operation results
RH_T_ReservedDOS          DB      8 DUP(0)
RH                        ENDS
```

RH_B_Length specifies the total length of the request header. DOS always sets this field, but it is never used. A block device driver can control multiple units. The RH_B_Unit field identifies which unit is the target of the request. DOS keeps track of the driver address and unit number for each block device. RH_B_Command specifies the requested operation. The driver normally sets RH_W_Status to indicate the results of an operation. This field is also used to indicate that a device is busy.

IOCTL Requests

A BIOS call initiates IOCTL requests which allow direct device control and access to device status information. The next example demonstrates this technique. DOS can satisfy some of these requests without driver intervention and supports them regardless of the state of the IOCTL bit. Get and set device information (AL = 0 or AL = 1) manipulates DOS tables. The set function can change mode as well as current standard input and output. These operations affect the way DOS passes requests to the driver (see Essay 10). DOS sends input and output status requests to the driver in response to IOCTL status operations.

```
        mov     al,function     ; there are several functions
                                ; (see Tech ref manual)
        mov     ah,44h          ; BIOS IOCTL request
;
;       Request dependent info in BX and CX
;
        int     21H             ; issue BIOS request
```

Other requests require explicit driver support. The driver indicates it is able to handle these requests by setting the IOCTL bit in the device attributes word. If this bit is set, DOS creates the appropriate request header and passes its address to the driver, which is free to interpret these requests as it sees fit.

Prototype Driver

The prototype character driver upon which the SOUND driver is built does no useful work. It returns a successful status for each character device operation and an error status for all others. Code for this prototype driver is listed next. Because it is so simple, the prototype driver is a good introduction to my programming style and driver structure in general.

```
        TITLE   DriverStub
        INCLUDE MACROS.ASM      ; useful macros
        INCLUDE DEVICE.DEF      ; Driver data structures


_ff     = DHD_M_Character OR DHD_M_IOCTL
dFlags  = _ff OR DHD_M_OCRM


_text   SEGMENT BYTE PUBLIC 'CODE'
        ASSUME  cs:_text,ds:_text
        ORG     00H             ; Drivers begin at 00H
Driver  PROC    NEAR

begin:  DHD   <-1,dFlags, StgyEntry, IntEntry,'SOUND   '>

RQ_T_Table:
        DW      SoundInit            ; Device Initialization
        DW      SoundNOP             ; Media check
        DW      SoundNOP             ; Build BIOS parameter
                                     ; block
        DW      SoundInIOCTL         ; Input IOCTL request
        DW      SoundError           ; Input (read) request
        DW      SoundError           ; Nondestructive input
        DW      SoundError           ; Input status
        DW      SoundError           ; Input Flush
        DW      SoundWrite           ; Output (write)
        DW      SoundWrite           ; Output write verify
        DW      SoundStatus          ; Output status
        DW      SoundFlush           ; Output flush

        DW      SoundNOP             ; Output IOCTL request
        DW      SoundOpen            ; Device open request
        DW      SoundClose           ; Device close request
        DW      SoundNOP             ; Removable media
        DW      SoundWriteTilBusy    ; Write until busy
```

```
RQ_S_Table      = (RQ_T_Table-$)/2


                DW      256 DUP(0)           ; Private stack for driver
DriverSP  DW          $-2                    ; Current top of stack
DosSS     DW          0                      ; DOS stack segment
DosSP     DW          0                      ; DOS stack pointer
RqOffset  DW          0                      ; OFFSET of request hdr
RqSegment DW          0                      ; SEGMENT of request hdr


                SUBTTL  Process Driver Requests

DriverRequest   PROC    NEAR

SoundError:
        mov     ax,DHD_C_ErrUnknownCommand
        ret


SoundNOP:
SoundInIOCTL:
SoundWrite:
SoundWriteTilBusy:
SoundStatus:
SoundFlush:
SoundOpen:
SoundClose:
        mov     ax,DHD_M_StsDone
        ret
DriverRequest   ENDP

        PAGE
        SUBTTL  DOS Entry Points

DriverExit:
        les     bx,DWORD PTR RqOffset     ; ES:BX <== DOS request
        mov     es:[bx].RH_W_Status,ax    ; Return status to DOS
        mov     DriverSP,SP               ; Save driver stack
        mov     SS,DosSS                  ; Restore dos stack
        mov     SP,DosSP
        popf                              ; Restore processor flags
        pop_all                           ; Restore all registers
        return_far                        ; and return to DOS

StgyEntry:
        mov     CS:RqOffset,bx            ; Save request address
```

```
        mov     CS:RqSegment,es
        return_far                      ; and return to DOS

IntError:
        mov     ax,DHD_C_UnknownCommand ; Say command is bad
        jmp     SHORT DriverExit

IntEntry:
        push_all                        ; Save all registers
        pushf                           ; Save processor status
        mov     ax,cs                   ; Set driver DS
        mov     ds,ax                   ; (DOS currently does
                                        ;   this for us)
        mov     DosSS,ss                ; Save DOS stack
        mov     DosSP,sp
        mov     ss,ax                   ; Establish driver stack
        mov     sp,DriverSP             ; Restore driver SP
        cld                             ; Set direction flag
        les     bx,DWORD PTR RqOffset   ; ES:BX <== DOS Request
        mov     al,es:[bx].RH_B_Command ; AL <== command
        cmp     al,RQ_S_Table           ; Is it in range?
        jge     IntError                ; If GE--out of range
        cbw                             ; Make command a word
        add     ax,ax                   ; Convert to word index
        mov     si,ax                   ; SI <== function table
                                        ;  index
        call    RQ_T_Table[si]          ; Dispatch on function
        jmp     DriverExit

SoundInit:
        mov     WORD PTR es:[bx].RH_A_Break, OFFSET SoundInit
        mov     WORD PTR es:[bx+2].RH_A_Break,cs
        mov     ax,DHD_M__StsDone
        ret

driver  ENDP
_text   ENDS
        END     begin
```

Coding Style

In some of the previous code fragments you may have noticed variable names of
the form XXX_Y_Zzzzzz. These names arise from the technique I use to label

data structures. Each of these structures has a 2- to 5-character name which is a prefix to the name of a structure element. One of the type-specifiers listed in Table 11-3 follows this prefix. The final part of each name identifies an individual field. Underscores separate these components. For example, the DHD structure defines the device header. The attributes field of the header is a word; the complete field name is `DHD_W_Attrib`.

Table 11-3.   Naming Conventions

Specifier	Meaning
A	Address
B	Byte Field
C	Constant (Byte or Word)
M	Mask (Bit field)
S	Size of a structure
T	Text Field (arbitrarily long)
V	Bit Number
W	Word (2-byte) field

You may notice that comments begin with one, two, or three semicolons. Normal comments begin with a single semicolon. I use double semicolons in macro definitions to suppress comments in their expansions. Whenever interrupts are disabled, I begin comments with three semicolons to remind myself of the interrupt state.

Driver Structure

The prototype driver begins with references to two include files. These two files, which I include in every device driver, define MASM STRUCs and macros, and appear in the listings at the end of this essay. (See Essay 5, Advanced MASM Techniques, by Michael Goldman, for more information on STRUCs and macros.)

The `MACRO.ASM` file includes definitions for push_all and pop_all. Performing these operations in a macro ensures that I save all the registers and restore them in the correct order. It is easy to forget to save a register or to restore one out of order. Macro definitions for explicit near and far returns are also defined in this file. On more than one occasion, MASM has generated a near return when I really wanted a far return. Of course, this error was one that I created, but the macro definitions prevent MASM from helping me make mistakes.

The `DEVICE.DEF` file defines the device and request headers as well as specifying symbolic values for the various fields within these structures.

Data declarations follow the include statements. The first declaration is the device header which begins at `ORG 0`. The PSP causes normal applications to start at ORG 100H, but the driver does not have a PSP. A dispatch table follows the header. It is a very common practice to have separate routines for every driver function and to use the request code RH_B_Command as an index into a table of routine addresses.

Driver code follows the data section. Notice that the code and data are in the same segment. Although separate segments are possible, it is common to combine code and data into a single segment.

The strategy code records the request header address and returns. The real work happens in the interrupt code, which saves all registers and the current processor flags, sets up the driver data segment, switches to a private driver stack, and dispatches on the request code. After completing all request-specific processing, the driver returns a status in the request header and restores all registers.

Sound Generation Hardware

The remainder of this chapter deals specifically with the SOUND driver. The SOUND driver manipulates sound generation hardware and the system clock. Before I could design the SOUND driver, I had to understand how this hardware worked.

Sound Generation

A frequency generator, filter, and speaker make up the sound generation hardware. The square wave output of the frequency generator drives the speaker through a filter (see Figure 11-6).

The PC uses an 8253-5 programmable interval timer as the frequency generator. This chip can perform different functions depending on its initialization. The frequency generator divides a 1.139180MHz fixed-frequency, square-wave clock input by a software selectable 16-bit value. To produce the A above middle C (440Hz) you would load a value of 2712 (1,193,180 ÷ 440) into the counter. The counter output is a 440Hz square wave.

You may know that a square wave can be represented as the sum of many sine waves. The frequency of the second and all following sines in this sum are integer multiples of the first whose frequency matches that of the square wave. Each sine wave has an associated amplitude which determines its contribution to the final sum. Mathematicians call this representation a Fourier series.

Removing the higher frequency sine waves and sending what is left to a speaker produces music. On the PC, the filter removes the high-frequency sound waves. Technically, this filter is called a *low-pass* filter because it allows the low-frequency waves to pass and stops the higher-frequency ones.

Changing the divisor while the speaker is on results in an unpleasant tone.

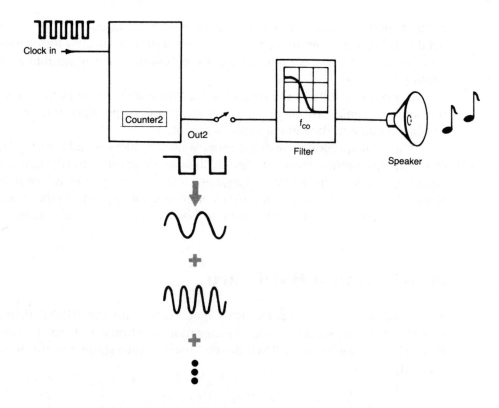

Fig. 11-6.   Sound generation hardware.

The speaker can be turned on and off under software control. Whenever we want to change the sound frequency or produce a period of silence, we must turn off the speaker. This listing illustrates use of the sound generation hardware.

```
          INCLUDE  HARDWARE.DEF      ; SOUND driver hardware def'ns
_m1       =        (SelCtr2 SHL SC)    ; select counter
_m2       =        (LSBMSB SHL RL)     ; select read/load
_m3       =        (Mode3 SHL M)       ; select mode
cntrlW    EQU      _m1 OR _m2 OR _m3   ; 8253 control word
_text     SEGMENT  BYTE PUBLIC 'CODE'
          ASSUME   CS:_text,DS:_text
          ORG      100H
a440      PROC     NEAR
          mov      al,cntrlW         ; Set up 8253 to function
          out      I8253.Mode,al     ; as a tone generator
          call     TurnOff           ; Turn off speaker
          mov      ax,2712           ; ax <==  frequency divisor
          out      I8253.Ctr2,al     ; Write LSB of divisor
          jmp      SHORT $+2         ; Delay for AT
```

```
           xchg    al,ah              ; al  <==  MSB divisor
           out     I8253.Ctr2,al      ; Write MSB of divisor
           call    TurnOn             ; Turn speaker on now
           xor     cx,cx              ; Delay for a while
  x:       loop    x                  ; (Period depends on CPU speed)
           call    TurnOff            ; Turn speaker off
           mov     ah,4cH             ; Return to DOS
           int     21H
  a440     ENDP
  Speaker PROC     NEAR
           out     I8255.PortB,al     ; Update 8255
           ret                        ; and return
  TurnOff LABEL    NEAR               ; Turn off speaker
           in      al,I8255.PortB     ; Read current port settings
           and     al,SpeakerOff      ; Turn off the speaker
           jmp     SHORT Speaker      ; Update 8255 (jmp req'd for AT)
  TurnOn LABEL     NEAR               ; Turn on speaker
           in      al,I8255.PortB     ; Read current port settings
           or      al,SpeakerOn       ; Enable the speaker
           jmp     SHORT Speaker      ; Update 8255 (jmp req'd for AT)
  Speaker ENDP
  _text    ENDS
   END     a440
```

System Clock

The programmable interval timer chip (8253) actually contains three independent down counters. One of these counters (Counter 2) is part of the sound generation hardware and another (Counter 0) drives the system clock. DOS sets up Counter 0 the same as I programmed Counter 2 in the previous example. DOS uses a frequency divisor of 65536. (This value is actually loaded into the counter as 0. The 8253 decrements the counter first and then tests for 0.) The output of the counter, a 1.139180MHz/65536Hz ($\sim$ 18.2) square wave, is connected to channel 0 (IRQ 0) of the 8259 interrupt controller chip. DOS programs the 8259 so that Counter 0 generates an interrupt 18.2 times a second.

Overview of the SOUND Driver

Now that we've reviewed driver basics and looked at the hardware used by our SOUND driver, let's see how the driver is implemented. There are three distinct parts to the SOUND driver—a DOS interface, a compiler, and a player. The DOS interface is similar to the previously discussed prototype. The compiler and player expand this prototype to a fully functional character driver.

DOS Interface

The DOS interface consists of the device header, strategy entry, and interrupt entry. The attributes word of the device header DHD_W_Attrib declares the SOUND driver to be a character driver which supports WriteUntilBusy, IOCTL, and OCRM requests. The strategy code records the address of the request header. The interrupt code saves all registers, switches to an internal stack, and dispatches on request header function to a specific subroutine which completes the request. The driver saves information on its private stack between calls. Before returning to DOS, the interrupt code switches back to the DOS stack, restores all processor registers, and sets a completion status in the request header.

Compiler

The interrupt entry code calls the SOUND driver output routines (SoundWrite and SoundWriteTilBusy), which pass characters from a buffer in the DOS request header to the compiler. The compiler converts ASCII text to note pitch and duration information and stores the compiled data in a circular buffer. The compiler encodes pitch as an 8253 programmable interval timer frequency divisor and duration as ticks of the system clock. A finite state machine implements the compiler.

Player

The player is driven by interrupts from the system clock. It removes compiled notes from the circular buffer and manipulates the PC sound generation hardware to produce music. The player loads pitch information into the 8253 Programmable Interval Timer and initializes a counter with duration information. This counter is decremented on every tick of the system clock. When the tick count goes to zero, the player gets another note from the circular buffer.

SOUND Driver Finite State Machine

There are three parts to the SOUND driver finite state machine: macros which describe the translation rules or grammar, subroutines which recognize specific musical constructs, and an interpreter. The FSM.DEF include file defines all macros and internal data structures which the finite state machine uses; you will find a listing of this file at the end of the chapter.

Macros

STATE and TRAN macros specify the rules for music compilation. The STATE macro identifies the start of a particular state, and the TRAN macro defines legal transitions out of this state. One or more TRAN macros follow each STATE macro. These two macros build the state transition table which drives the interpreter.

The only argument for the STATE macro is a state name. The TRAN macro has four arguments: class, data, nstate, and action. Class is the name of a subroutine which recognizes a particular token such as a note or key signature. Certain class routines use the data argument. Nstate specifies the state which will be entered if a transition is successful. If the nstate argument is omitted, a default value of the next state in the transition table is used. Action is the address of an action routine, which can contribute to the decision of whether or not to accept a transition or perform some special processing if a transition is successful. Action routines are a hook for decisions that cannot be described easily by the state table.

Class Routines

Class routines assemble and examine tokens and they decide whether or not to make a transition. The class routines referenced in the TRAN macro are specific to music compilation. Every class routine returns with an unprocessed character in the AL register.

Class routines recognize notes which include a name (A . . . G) and possibly an accidental, numbers, key signatures, and commands. The command routine compares the current input character to the value in the data field; it is normally used in conjunction with the SubState class routine.

SubState is a special class routine which saves the current state and enters the state specified by nstate—you can think of it as a subroutine call. SubState is used when a transition must be described in terms of other transitions. A transition to `S_exit` causes a successful exit from SubState, a transition to `S_fail` causes an unsuccessful exit from SubState. The following example shows the state table entry which defines the Tempo command. This definition says that tempo is defined by the letter T, followed by a number. Notice how the Command class routine recognizes the letter T. If the current letter is not a T, the substate, `s_t`, returns a failure; otherwise, the Number class routine looks for a number. If a number is found, the TempoDone routine is called and a successful exit is taken from the substate `s_t`.

```
state    s_t
tran     Command,'T'
state
tran     Number,,s_exit,TempoDone
```

Interpreter

The state machine interpreter keeps track of the current state, which is no more than a list of legal transitions. The interpreter passes the current character to each class routine which may need more characters to complete a token. At some point, the class routine will either recognize the token or return with a failure status. If the class routine returns success, the interpreter calls the optional action routine (if present). If this routine does not reject the transition, the interpreter enters the state specified by the nstate argument. A failure status causes the interpreter to process the next transition (if there is another one).

SOUND Driver Coroutines

The finite state machine analyzes characters which come from either Sound-Write or SoundWriteTilBusy requests. SoundWrite requests are one character long unless the SOUND driver is in binary mode. Binary mode and write-until-busy requests are arbitrarily long.

Coroutines simplify the relationship between multiple entry points and the finite state machine. The finite state machine calls NextCharacter when it needs another character. In an effort to satisfy this request, NextCharacter makes a coroutine callback to the original driver entry point. The target of this callback is a loop within either SoundWrite or SoundWriteTilBusy. The loop logic removes a single character from the buffer specified in the request header and makes a coroutine callback to NextCharacter. If the current request header cannot provide another character, the SOUND driver returns to DOS. Information saved on the driver-private stack ensures that processing will be resumed properly on the next driver call. Initialization code in the ResetExit routine sets up the initial call; normal coroutine processing propagates the calls.

Synchronization and Circular Buffers

All circular buffer operations occur in BufferInsert and BufferRemove. Class routines call BufferInsert whenever a note or a rest has been completed. The player calls BufferRemove from the timer interrupt service routine when it is time to play another note. Neither of these operations is indivisible. Both routines manipulate a common data structure which must be kept in a consistent state.

The SOUND driver architecture makes synchronization between compiler and player easy. The player manipulates the next available note pointer, and the compiler handles the next free space pointer. Access to these pointers is completely independent and does not require synchronization. Both routines make indivisible adjustments to the buffer count. The increment operation used by the compiler and the decrement option used by the player are guaranteed to complete once started.

Speeding up the System Clock

We have tacitly assumed that DOS would provide clock ticks for the SOUND driver. It turns out that the system clock does not provide sufficient resolution. At the standard clock rate of 18.2 ticks per second, a quarter-note played at the default tempo of 120 lasts nine ticks (60 ÷ 120 * 18.2). An eighth-note (half as long as a quarter-note) would last only five ticks. Since we need short periods of silence between notes, we actually would play an eighth-note as four audible ticks followed by one tick of silence. Because the tick per note is so small, we cannot accurately deal with tempo or the relative durations of short notes. The faster the tempo, the worse the problem becomes.

An obvious solution is to increase the system clock speed, but this approach might cause the processor to spend excessive time servicing timer interrupts. Since the ability to speed up the system clock was important, I created a prototype interrupt service routine. By the time I wrote this prototype code, I had designed all the driver data structures and decided how to implement the compiler; the interrupt service routine interface was completely specified. Using a factor of 16 speedup, I analyzed the time required to execute this prototype code. It was apparent from this analysis that I could safely increase the frequency of the system clock.

Space constraints prevent a discussion of the prototype code, but it was almost identical to the code finally used in the SOUND driver. The estimate was so accurate because it was made after the interrupt service routine interface was completely specified.

New Clock Interrupt Service Routine

The following example illustrates the interrupt service routine code, which has some subtle aspects. We cannot just change the frequency of the system clock. On every clock tick, the clock interrupt service routine in ROM gets called. This code updates the time of day, checks the status of the diskette timers, issues an INT 1CH, sends an EOI to the 8259 interrupt controller, and dismisses the clock interrupt with an IRET. If the ROM BIOS routine were called too frequently, the system clock would gain time and diskette operation would be impaired. Any other device driver or TSR program which linked to the INT 1CH vector would also be called too often. It is difficult to predict the effects of more frequent calls to these linked routines, but a significant percent of the available CPU cycles could be spent servicing the timer interrupt and traversing the INT 1CH chain.

```
ClkISR0:
            cmp     cs:NoteTicks,0   ;;; [ABC(22)]Playing a note?
            jz      clk0             ;;; [ABC(16/4]If Z--no
            dec     cs:NoteTicks     ;;; [BC(31)]Decrement note count
            jnz     clk0             ;;; [BC(16/5)]If NZ not note end
            call    PlayNextNote     ;;; [C(23+496)]Play another note
clk0:       dec     cs:ClockTicks    ;;; [ABC(31)]Dec clock ticks
            jz      clk3             ;;; [ABC(16/4)]Not time for old
                                     ;;; clock isr
ClkIntExit:
            push    ax               ;;; [ABC(15)]Save ax
            mov     al,EOI           ;;; [ABC(4)]Send Nonspecific EOI
            out     I8259.PortA,al   ;;; [ABC(10)]EOI to 8259
            pop     ax               ;;; [ABC(12)]Restore ax
            iret                     ;;; [ABC(32)]and exit ISR
clk3:       cs:                      ;;; (22)Reset counter
            mov     ClockTicks,FastTickCount
            cs:                      ;;; (32) Call old clock isr
            jmp     OldInt8Vector


ClkISR1:
            cmp     cs:ClockTicks,1 ;;; Can clock frequency change?
            jl      clk2             ;;; If L--no reset ClockTicks
            jg      clk1             ;;; If G--not yet
            call    SetClockSlow     ;;; Enter slow mode
            cs:                      ;;; Say not busy
            and     DriverStatus,NOT MASK Busy
clk1:       dec     cs:ClockTicks    ;;; One more tick
            jmp     SHORT ClkIntExit;;; and exit ISR
clk2:       cs:                      ;;; Set ticks to wait
            mov     ClockTicks,FastTickCount
            jmp     SHORT ClkIntExit;;; and exit ISR

SetAltISR:
            and     DriverStatus,NOT MASK EOFPending  ;;; EOF not
                                                      ;;; pending
            or      DriverStatus,(1 SHL ChangePending);;; but vector
                                                      ;;; change is
            mov     ax,OFFSET ClkISR1         ;;; Played last note
            call    SetISR                    ;;; Swap clock ISR
            ret                               ;;; and return
```

When we change the frequency of the system clock, we must also change the clock interrupt service routine. Changing the clock frequency is easy. We change the frequency divisor from 65536 to 16384 (0x1000) to get a factor of 16 speedup. We also must change the clock interrupt vector to point to the new clock interrupt service routine.

The first action performed by the Clk0ISR code is to check the value of NoteTicks. If a note is currently being played, NoteTicks will be nonzero. Only nonzero values are decremented. When NoteTicks becomes zero, it is time to play a new note. Whether any note processing took place or not, ClockTicks is decremented. When this value becomes zero, it is reset to 16 (the clock speedup factor), and the old INT 8 service routine is invoked with a JMP instruction.

Invoking the old INT 8 routine every 16th-fast clock tick maintains the proper delay between calls. The transfer of control is done with a JMP instruction to ensure that only one EOI gets sent to the 8259 interrupt controller. (Remember, the ROM BIOS interrupt service routine wants to send an EOI.)

Driver Performance

Estimating driver performance is done by calculating execution times for worst case code paths. These estimates provided assurance that DOS could handle the clock speedup and that the driver could play notes in real time. At the faster clock rate, there are 3432800 ns (nanoseconds) between interrupts (1193180 ÷ 4096 = 291 interrupts/sec = .0034328 sec/interrupt = 3432800 ns/interrupt).

In the previous example of the clock interrupt service routine, the numbers in parentheses are instruction times in clock cycles and the letters inside square brackets are code paths.

When no note is playing and the BIOS interrupt service routine does not need to be invoked, code path A is followed. This path takes 197 clock cycles (51 + 22 + 16 + 31 + 4 + 15 + 4 + 10 + 12 + 32). The PC runs at a clock speed of 210 ns; this path requires 41370 (210 × 197) ns or 1.2 percent (41370 ÷ 3432800 × 100) of the available CPU cycles (to a first approximation).

When a note is playing and the ROM BIOS interrupt service routine is not called, code path B is followed. The processor overhead for this path is 1.4 percent. When a new note has to be played (path C), overhead goes up to 4.5 percent. No estimates were made on how much time was required to execute the original BIOS interrupt service code or compile the text. The number of routines chaining to the 1CH interrupt is unpredictable and can have a drastic effect on the length of this code path. So long as this path takes less than 6 percent (100 × 1/16) of the total CPU cycles, we should not miss any "fast ticks."

A significant portion of the time available for compile is spent in DOS code. If we make a worst case assumption that BIOS code and resident timer routines take up 6 percent of the CPU cycles and that playing a note takes up 4.0 percent (certainly a very conservative assumption since notes are changed relatively infrequently), we still have 90 percent of the processor cycles available. There should be no problems playing most scores in real time. When the completed driver was tested by copying a score to it, it was found that the copy command completed before the music stopped confirming this analysis. Isn't all this science wonderful!

Adding Refinements

The system clock can be permanently sped up by changing the counter frequency and interrupt vector in the SOUND initialization routine (SoundInit), or the clock frequency can be altered when music is being played. The former approach would work at the expense of some wasted CPU cycles when the SOUND driver is not being used, but, as our performance analysis shows, its impact should not be noticed. The SOUND driver uses the latter technique. This approach is more elegant and provides further examples of driver synchronization as well as illustrating nonstandard uses for open and close routines. The system clock is sped up in the open routine and slowed down in the close routine.

The OCRM bit is set in the device header. When the device is closed either explicitly or implicitly by process termination, DOS sends a close request to the SOUND driver. The Interrupt code dispatches to the SoundClose routine which informs the state machine that a close operation has been requested (an EOF is passed through the NextCharacter coroutine). With interrupts disabled, the driver state is set to end of file pending and NoteTicks is tested. It is important that both actions are taken with interrupts disabled. Note playing is interrupt driven and will always take precedence over compiling. If NoteTicks ever goes to 0, the compiler is sure that the Player has nothing to do. If the Player has nothing to do and a close has been sent to the driver, SoundClose resets the clock speed to slow and restores the original interrupt service routine (call SetAltISR). If NoteTicks is nonzero, the Player is currently busy. Eventually the Player will run out of notes, notice that a close has been requested (driver state will be end-of-file pending), and reset the clock speed and interrupt service routine.

If interrupts are not disabled while the driver state is changed and Note-Ticks is checked, an interrupt could occur between the two instructions. If the final note completed between these two instructions, SetAltISR would be invoked twice. If the order of these two instructions were reversed, SetAltISR might never get called. It is important that the two instructions be executed without interruption. The CLI instruction ensures that this critical section completes without interruption.

The actual swap of interrupt vectors is slightly more involved than what has been previously described. We want to change vectors and slow down the clock on the 16th-fast tick so we do not lose any time (on the average 25 ms per close). To avoid time loss, SetAltISR sets the driver state to change pending and changes the interrupt service routine to ClkISR1. ClkISR1 waits for the Clock-Ticks to go to one, then slows down the clock and restores the interrupt vector to its original value.

Since the OCRM is set in the device header, the SOUND driver is called each time the device is opened. The SoundOpen routine processes open requests. It immediately clears the end of file pending driver state. If a vector change is pending, a busy wait loop is entered. SoundOpen could back out of the vector change, but very little would be gained and the code complexity would increase. If two songs are played in quick succession, it is possible that the interrupt vectors will not change and the clock speed will not be altered between songs. Whenever the vector and clock speed are in their original state, the driver state is InitNeeded. If SoundOpen finds the driver in the InitNeeded state, it changes the interrupt vector to Clk0ISR and speeds up the clock.

Finishing Touches

The open routine (SoundOpen) speeds up the clock and copies the CErr.ERR_L_Bytes and CErr.ERR_A_Text values. These variables describe the last error and identify where it occurred. SoundOpen then resets the error description and initializes some driver parameters. It also initializes the driver stack and calls ResetExit to set up the initial coroutine callback.

The SOUND driver supports both input and output IOCTL routines. These routines allow the user to read or modify the default tempo, octave, and style. They also allow the user to interrogate the driver about the most recent compiler errors. Error information is read-only.

As I mentioned previously, the driver is free to interpret the IOCTL information as it sees fit. The SOUND driver expects to be passed a list of requests. Each list element has a request identifier, request length, buffer address, and a return length address. Both addresses are specified with a segment and an offset. The optional return length address is the address of a variable which will be set to the actual number of bytes returned. The following listing requests the current default note length, octave, and the text of the last compiler error.

```
ITEM            STRUC
ITEM_W_Code     DW      0       ; Request code
ITEM_W_Length   DW      0       ; Allocated size
ITEM_A_Address  DW      0       ; Address of item buffer
                DW      0
ITEM_A_RetLen   DW      0       ; Address of actual length
                DW      0       ; (ignored if segment=0)
```

```
ITEM            ENDS

IOCTL_K_CBytes  EQU     0       ; Get     current bytes read
IOCTL_K_PBytes  EQU     1       ; Get     previous bytes read
IOCTL_K_CError  EQU     2       ; Get     text of current error msg
IOCTL_K_PError  EQU     3       ; Get     text of previous error msg
IOCTL_K_Length  EQU     4       ; Get/Set default note length
IOCTL_K_Octave  EQU     5       ; Get/Set default octave
IOCTL_K_Tempo   EQU     6       ; Get/Set default tempo
IOCTL_K_Style   EQU     7       ; Get/Set default style

stack   SEGMENT WORD STACK 'STACK'
        DW      256 DUP(0)
stack   ENDS


_data   SEGMENT WORD PUBLIC 'DATA'
sound   DB      'SOUND',0
itmlst  ITEM    <IOCTL_K_Length, 2,OFFSET Length,SEG _data,0,0>
        ITEM    <IOCTL_K_Octave, 2,OFFSET Octave,SEG _data,0,0>
;
;       Note that you cannot actually wrap structure reference
;
        ITEM    <IOCTL_K_CError,50,OFFSET Text,   SEG _data,
                                OFFSET TLength,SEG _data>
itmend  EQU     $
Length  DW      0               ; Return default length here
Octave  DW      0               ; Return default octave here
TLength DW      0               ; Length of Text
Text    DB      50 DUP(0)       ; Error text here
_data   ENDS

_text   SEGMENT BYTE PUBLIC 'CODE'
        ASSUME  cs:_text,ds:_data
main    PROC    NEAR
        mov     ax,_data        ; Establish data segment
        mov     ds,ax
        mov     dx,OFFSET sound ; Open device (need handle)
        mov     ax,3d01H        ; Say write-only access
        int     21h
        mov     bx,ax           ; bx <== handle
        mov     dx,OFFSET itmlst; dx <== item list
        mov     cx,itmend-itmlst; cx <== length of item list
        mov     ax,4402H        ; issue a read IOCTL
        int     21H
```

```
            mov      ah,4cH          ; Return to dos
            int      21H
main        ENDP
_text       ENDS
            END      main
```

Coroutines are also used to implement the list processing. The read or write IOCTL routines call FirstItem to process the first IOCTL item; coroutines satisfy the remaining requests.

Conclusion

In this essay, I have introduced some new programming techniques and shown how they are used in a real device driver. A listing of this driver and its include files appears next. The techniques I have described and much of the code is directly applicable to other drivers.

To write your own device driver, you will need to understand the hardware you are controlling. Most purchased hardware comes with a technical description similar to what is provided in the *IBM Hardware Technical Reference Manual*. Usually, this description does not include sufficient information to write a device driver, and you will have to consult the component data catalogs provided by chip vendors. These catalogs usually contain a complete description of how a chip works and many also provide sample circuits and code.

Listing 11-1 gives the complete source listings for the SOUND driver. The main program PLAY.ASM is followed by its supporting include files, which are presented in the order they appear in the INCLUDE statements. This listing is thoroughly commented.

Listing 11-1.   Sound Driver

```
            TITLE    SoundDriver
            SUBTTL   Basica 3.0 Compatible Sound Driver
;
;   SOUND.ASM
;
;       Source for SOUND device driver
;


;
;       © 1987 W. V. Dixon. All rights reserved.
```

continued

```
;
;        May be freely copied for personal, nonprofit use
;        so long as this copyright notice and disclaimer are
;        retained and usage restrictions are observed. This
;        software may not be used in whole or in part in any
;        program which is sold without prior written consent
;        of the author.
;
```

```
;
;        DISCLAIMER
;        ==========
;
;        This software is furnished as an example of a character
;        device driver. The author will assume no responsibility
;        for any direct or indirect damages resulting from the use
;        of this code. You are using this software ENTIRELY AT
;        YOUR OWN RISK.
;


                INCLUDE MACROS.ASM          ; Useful macros
                INCLUDE DEVICE.DEF          ; Device driver data structures
                INCLUDE VALUES.DEF          ; Limits and parameters
                INCLUDE HARDWARE.DEF        ; PC hardware definitions
                INCLUDE FSM.DEF             ; Finite state machine definitions


                SUBTTL  Driver-specific macro definitions
                PAGE
;
;        Macro to associate text with message number. The message
;        number is defined as the address of the text string.
;
error_msg   MACRO   number,text
                LOCAL   x
                LOCAL   y
x               DB      y-x-1,text,0        ;; Define message text
y:
number          EQU     OFFSET x            ;; Define error number
                ENDM                        ;; MACRO error_msg


;
```

continued

```
;                 Signal that an error occurred.
;
signal           MACRO   x
                 mov     cx,x                    ;; cx  <==  error number
                 jmp     WriteFaultExit          ;; and take error exit
                 ENDM                            ;; MACRO signal


;
;                 Define a musical scale
;
defscale         MACRO   name,scale,sharps,flats
name:            DB      scale                   ;; Specify notes in scale
                 IRPC    y,<sharps>              ;; Specify which notes are sharp
                 DB      &y
                 ENDM                            ;; IRPC sharps
                 IRPC    y,<flats>         ;; Specify which notes are flats
                 DB      &y
                 ENDM                            ;; IRPC flats
                 ENDM                            ;; MACRO defscale



                 SUBTTL  Data Structures
                 PAGE
;
;                 Define driver status summary word
;
DSS              record  InitNeeded:1,Busy:1,ChangePending:1,EOFPending:1,InComment:1,
InTie:1,HasNote:1


DSS_M_HasNote             EQU    1 SHL HasNote         ; Compiler has note
DSS_M_InTie               EQU    1 SHL InTie           ; Compiler processing tie
DSS_M_InComment           EQU    1 SHL InComment       ; Compiler processing comment
DSS_M_EOFPending          EQU    1 SHL EOFPending      ; End file pending
DSS_M_ChangePending       EQU    1 SHL ChangePending   ; Vector change pending
DSS_M_Busy                EQU    1 SHL Busy            ; Device is in use
DSS_M_InitNeeded          EQU    1 SHL InitNeeded      ; Clock speedup needed



;
;       Define Score (SCR) structure
;
SCR              STRUC
SCR_W_Length     DW      SCR_K_DLength        ; Note length
```

continued

```
SCR_W_Octave      DW      SCR_K_DOctave         ; Octave
SCR_W_Tempo       DW      SCR_K_DTempo          ; Tempo
SCR_W_Key         DW      0                     ; Key signature
                                                ; NB Must fill in when defined

SCR_W_Style       DW      SCR_K_DStyle          ; Style
SCR_W_Ticks       DW      SCR_K_DTicks          ; Current tick count
SCR_W_TTicks      DW      0                     ; Tied tick count
SCR_W_TFreq       DW      0                     ; Tied frequency divisor
SCR_W_NTicks      DW      SCR_K_DTicks          ; Note ticks
SCR_W_NFreq       DW      0                     ; Note frequency divisor
SCR               ENDS
SCR_S_Size        EQU     SIZE SCR


;
;        Define Error structure
;
ERR               STRUC
ERR_L_Bytes       DW      0,0                   ; Bytes read
ERR_A_Text        DW      0                     ; Address of error text
                                                ; NB Must fill in when defined

ERR               ENDS
ERR_S_Size        EQU     SIZE ERR


;
;        Define IOCTL item list structure. List is array of ITEM
;        elements.
;
ITEM              STRUC
ITEM_W_Code       DW      0                       ; Request code

ITEM_W_Length     DW      0                       ; Allocated size
ITEM_A_Address    DD      0                       ; Address of item buffer
ITEM_A_RetLen     DD      0                       ; Address of actual length
                                                  ; (ignored if segment=0)
ITEM              ENDS
ITEM_S_Size       EQU     SIZE ITEM



                  SUBTTL  Constant Definition
                  PAGE
;
;        Miscellaneous ASCII symbols
```

continued

```
;
BELL            EQU     07H
LF              EQU     0aH
CR              EQU     0dH
EOF             EQU     1aH                 ; Used to tell state machine
                                            ; about end of file
;
;       Item codes for IOCTL requests
;
IOCTL_K_CBytes  EQU     0                   ; Get      current bytes read
IOCTL_K_PBytes  EQU     1                   ; Get      previous bytes read
IOCTL_K_CError  EQU     2                   ; Get      text of current error msg
IOCTL_K_PError  EQU     3                   ; Get      text of previous error msg
IOCTL_K_Length  EQU     4                   ; Get/Set default note length
IOCTL_K_Octave  EQU     5                   ; Get/Set default octave
IOCTL_K_Tempo   EQU     6                   ; Get/Set default tempo
IOCTL_K_Style   EQU     7                   ; Get/Set default style


;
;       Driver parameters
;


;
;       Driver attributes word
;
_temp_          =       DHD_M_IsCharacter OR DHD_M_IOCTLSupport
_temp_          =       _temp_              OR DHD_M_WriteBusySupport
DHD_C_Attrib    EQU     _temp_              OR DHD_M_OCRMSupport



                SUBTTL  IVT Definition
                PAGE
IVTSegment      SEGMENT AT 0                ; To reference interrupt vectors
                DD      8 DUP(0)            ; Don't care about these
Int8Vector      DD      0                   ; Timer (8253 Counter 0) interrupt
IVTSegment      ENDS



                SUBTTL  Driver Data Declarations
                PAGE
_text           SEGMENT BYTE PUBLIC 'CODE'
                ASSUME  cs:_text,ds:_text
                ORG     00H
```

continued

```
driver          PROC    NEAR


;
;       Declare device header
;
begin:          DHD     <-1,DHD_C_Attrib, StgyEntry, IntEntry,'SOUND    '>


;
;       Driver action table used to dispatch to appropriate processing routine
;       based on request type.
;
RQ_T_Tabl       DW      SoundInit               ; Device Initialization
                DW      SoundNOP                ; Media check
                DW      SoundNOP                ; Build BIOS parameter block is
                DW      SoundInIOCTL            ; Input IOCTL request
                DW      SoundError              ; Input (read) request
                DW      SoundError              ; Nondestructive input
                DW      SoundError              ; Input status
                DW      SoundError              ; Input Flush
                DW      SoundWrite              ; Output (write)
                DW      SoundWrite              ; Output write with verify
                DW      SoundStatus             ; Output status
                DW      SoundFlush              ; Output flush
                DW      SoundOutIOCTL           ; Output IOCTL request
                DW      SoundOpen               ; Device open request
                DW      SoundClose              ; Device close request
                DW      SoundNOP                ; Removable media
                DW      SoundWriteTilBusy       ; Write until busy
RQ_S_Table      EQU     ($-RQ_T_Table)/2


;
;       Table used for processing IOCTL requests
;
;                       Address         Length
;                       =======         ======
;
IOCTL_T_Table   DW      CErr.ERR_L_Bytes,   4
                DW      PErr.ERR_L_Bytes,   4
                DW      CErr.ERR_A_Text,    0
                DW      PErr.ERR_A_Text,    0
                DW      DScore.SCR_W_Length,2
                DW      DScore.SCR_W_Octave,2
```

continued

```
            DW         DScore.SCR_W_Tempo, 2
            DW         DScore.SCR_W_Style, 2
IOCTL_S_Table  EQU     ($-IOCTL_T_Table)/4


;
;       State table. Defines state transitions for device driver state
;       machine.
;
            state    s_main                        ; This is the main state
            tran     lambda,,,CompileNote          ; Compile note (if completed)
            state
            tran     substate,s_note,s_main        ; Note
            tran     substate,s_l,s_main           ; Length (Lnn)
            tran     substate,s_p,s_main           ; Rest
            tran     substate,s_o,s_main           ; Octave (On)
            tran     substate,s_n,s_main           ; Numeric note (Nnn)
            tran     substate,s_t,s_main           ; Tempo (Tnnn)
            tran     substate,s_key,s_main         ; Key signature
            tran     substate,s_music,s_main       ; Music style (ML, MN, MS)
            tran     Command,EOF,s_main            ; Gracefully terminate state machine
            state    s_l                           ; Process length
            tran     Command,'L'                   ; Need 'L' first
            state                                  ; 'L' must be followed by
            tran     DottedNumber,,s_exit,LengthDone    ; dotted number
            state    s_t                           ; Process tempo
            tran     Command,'T'                   ; Need 'T' first
            state                                  ; 'T' must be followed by
            tran     Number,,s_exit,TempoDone      ; number
            state    s_n                           ; Process numeric note
            tran     Command,'N'                   ; Must begin with 'N'
            state                                  ; 'N' must be followed by
            tran     Number,,s_exit,NoteDone0      ; a number
            state    s_o                           ; Process octave
            tran     Command,'O'                   ; Must begin with 'O'
            state                                  ; 'O' must be followed by
            tran     Number,,s_exit,OctaveDone     ; a number
            state    s_key                         ; Process key signature
            tran     Command,'K'                   ; Must begin with 'K'
            state                                  ; 'K' must be followed by
            tran     Signature,,s_exit,SignatureDone   ; a valid signature
            state    s_music                       ; Process music command
            tran     style,,s_exit,StyleDone       ; Must be a valid style
            state    s_p                           ; Process a pause (rest)
```

continued

```
          tran     Command,'P',np_length,PauseDone      ; Must begin witn 'P'
          state    s_note                               ; Process a note
          tran     Note,,np_length,NoteDone1            ; Must begin with valid note
          state    np_length                            ; Length of note or rest
          tran     Dots,,s_tie,NPDone0                  ; Dots may follow
          tran     DottedNumber,,s_tie,NPDone1          ; Dotted number may follow
          tran     lambda,,s_tie,NPDone2                ; Anything else ends note
          state    s_tie                                ; Look for ties
          tran     Command,'&',s_exit,TieDone0          ; '&' starts a tied note
          tran     lambda,,s_exit,TieDone1              ; Anything else ends note
          state_end                                     ; End of driver state table
```

```
;
;          Style table is used to define various music styles. These styles are
;          indicated by MN (Normal), ML (Legato), and MS (Staccato).
;
StyleTable      DB        'MNLS',StyleStaccato,StyleLegato,StyleNormal
```

```
;
;          Define scales for each key signature. There are 12 positions in
;          each scale beginning with C flat (C-) and extending to B sharp (B+).
;          The position of the note name indicates whether it is sharped or
;          flatted in the key signature in question. (Note that the notes of
;          the scale are in reverse order so we can conveniently use a scab
;          instruction. The scale column is used to determine a notes pitch.
;          The sharps and flats column also tell whether the note is normally
;          sharped or flatted; they are used in processing accidentals.
;
;                     Key      Scale           Sharps          Flats
;

;                     #=#=#=#==#=#=#  #B#A#G#FE#D#C# #B#A#G#FE#D#C#
          defscale C    ," B A G FE D C ",01010101101010,01010101101010
          defscale G    ," B A GF E D C ",01010100101010,01010102101010
          defscale D    ," B A GF E DC ",01010100101000,01010102101020
          defscale A    ," B AG F E DC ",01010000101000,01010202101020
          defscale E    ," B AG F ED C ",01010000100000,01010202102020
          defscale B    ," BA G F ED C ",01000000100000,01020202102020
          defscale FSharp," BA G FE D C ",01000000000000,01020202202020
          defscale CSharp,"B A G FE D C ",00000000000000,02020202202020
;                     -=-=-=-==-=-=  -B-A-G-FE-D-C- -B-A-G-FE-D-C-
```

continued

```
            defscale F     ,"  BA G FE D C ",02010101101010,00010101101010
            defscale BFlat ,"  BA G F ED C ",02010101201010,00010101001010
            defscale EFlat ,"  B AG F ED C ",02020101201010,00000101001010
            defscale AFlat ,"  B AG F E DC ",02020101202010,00000101000010
            defscale DFlat ,"  B A GF E DC ",02020201202010,00000001000010
            defscale GFlat ,"  B A GF E D C",02020201202020,00000001000000
            defscale CFlat ,"  B A G FE D C",02020202202020,00000000000000
```

```
;
;       Define the key signatures. The order in this table corresponds to
;       the previous scale definitions. Again we reverse the order for
;       convenience in using the scasw instruction.
;
Keys        DB      'C-G-D-A-E-B-F C+F+B E A D G C ' ; note reverse order


;
;       The following table defines the counter (8253 counter 3) value for each
;       note. Values are calculated by dividing the input oscillator frequency
;       (1193180) by the note pitch (in Hz).
;
;                       C    C#    D    D#    E     F    F#    G    G#    A    A#    B
FreqDivTable DW     36156,34090,32248,30594,29101,27117,25386,24350,22945,21694,20572,19244
            DW      18356,17292,16124,15297,14550,13714,12829,12175,11472,10847,10198, 9700
            DW       9108, 8584, 8007, 7648, 7231, 6818, 6449, 6087, 5736, 5423, 5120, 4830
            DW       4554, 4307, 4058, 3836, 3615, 3418, 3224, 3043, 2875, 2711, 2560, 2415
            DW       2281, 2153, 2032, 1918, 1810, 1709, 1612, 1521, 1435, 1355, 1280, 1207
            DW       1140, 1075, 1015,  958,  904,  854,  806,  760,  718,  677,  642,  603
            DW        570,  538,  507,  479,  452,  427,  403,  380,  359,  338,  321,  301


;
;       Associate message text with error number. The error number is actually
;       the address of the text string defined in the following table. The
;       message text is returned in an OutputIOCTL request.
;
            error_msg   BadStateTable,'Driver internal error: state table bad'
            error_msg   NumberTooLarge,'Number is too large'
            error_msg   BadSignature,'Key signature is bad'
            error_msg   BadLength,'Length is out of range'
            error_msg   BadOctave,'Octave is out of range'
            error_msg   BadTempo,'Tempo is out of range'
            error_msg   BadNote,'Note is out of range'
            error_msg   BadTie,'Tied notes must be the same'
            error_msg   Successful,'No errors encountered'
```
continued

```
LocalStack      DW      256 DUP(0)                      ; Private stack for driver
DriverSP        DW      $-2                             ; Current top of stack
DosSS           DW      0                               ; DOS stack segment on entry
DosSP           DW      0                               ; DOS stack pointer on entry
RqOffset        DW      0                               ; OFFSET of DOS i/o request
RqSegment       DW      0                               ; SEGMENT of DOS i/o request

;
;       Circular buffer for storing notes as they are compiled. Notes are
;       put in at one end (BUF_A_NextFree) and removed from the other
;       (BUF_A_NextData). When the buffer is empty,  BUF_W_Count=0,
;
BUF_T_Notes     DD      BUF_S_Notes dup(0)              ; Buffer for note duration and pitch
BUF_W_Count     DW      0                               ; Notes currently in buffer
BUF_A_NextFree  DW      BUF_T_Notes                     ; Next free buffer location
BUF_A_NextData  DW      BUF_T_Notes                     ; Next data item in buffer

OldInt8Vector   DD      0                               ; Original timer (8253) interrupt
vector
ClockTicks      DW      0                               ; Used to count clock ticks
NoteTicks       DW      0                               ; Used to measure note duration

PErr            ERR     <,Successful>                   ; Previous error bytes and text
CErr            ERR     <,Successful>                   ; Current error bytes and text
CScore          SCR     <,,,SCR_K_DKey>                 ; Current values
InitialCErr     ERR     <,Successful>                   ; Initial CErr values
DScore          SCR     <,,,SCR_K_DKey>                 ; Default Values


;
;       IO request state information
;
SavedCX         DW      0                               ; Bytes left to read
SavedSI         DW      0                               ; Buffer OFFSET
SavedDS         DW      0                               ; Buffer SEGMENT

DriverStatus    DSS     <>                              ;  Device driver status summary

                PAGE
                SUBTTL  Driver Exit Routines
;
;       WriteFaultExit  - Come here when want to return a WriteFault error
```

continued

```
;
WriteFaultExit: mov     ax,DHD_C_ErrWriteFault          ; Say a write fault occurred


;
;       ResetExit       - Come here to reset driver state. Error code in ax.
;
ResetExit:      mov     sp,OFFSET DriverSP-2            ; Reset driver stack
                mov     bx,OFFSET StateMachine          ; To get to state machine
                push    bx
                sub     sp,6                            ; For NextCharacter registers
                mov     bx,OFFSET nc4                   ; To set up initial coroutine
dispatch
                push    bx
                jmp     SHORT DriverExit                ; and take common exit


;
;       SuccessExit     - Come here to return successful completion to DOS.
;
SuccessExit:    mov     ax,DHD_M_StsDone                ; Say we were successful
;
;       DriverExit      - Common driver exit code. Returns error code and
;                         restores DOS state.
;
DriverExit:     les     bx,DWORD PTR RqOffset          ; ES:BX  <== DOS request
                mov     es:[bx].RH_W_Status,ax         ; Return exit status to DOS
                mov     DriverSP,SP                     ; Save driver stack
                mov     SS,DosSS                        ; Restore dos stack
                mov     SP,DosSP
                popf                                    ; Restore flags
                pop_all                                 ; Restore all registers
                return_far                              ; and return to DOS

                PAGE
                SUBTTL  Get Next Character (Coroutine)
;
;       Called by state machine to read next character. The driver will have
;       previously set up a coroutine call back (in BP). NextCharacter makes
;       a coroutine callback to appropriate driver write routine. The write
;       routine makes a call back to NextCharacter thus propagating the call
;       back address.
;
NextCharacter:  pushr   <bx,cx,di>                      ; Save nonvolatile registers
                jmp     SHORT nc3                       ; Skip special cases
```

continued

```
nc0:            or      DriverStatus,DSS_M_InComment    ; Say we're in a comment
                jmp     SHORT nc3                        ; and get another character
nc1:            mov     al,'+'                           ; Change '#' to '+'
                jmp     SHORT nc5                        ; and exit with '+'
nc2:            and     DriverStatus,NOT MASK InComment ; Say comment has ended
                cmp     al,EOF                           ; Was it an EOF that ended it?
                jz      nc5                              ; If Z--yes (Exit with EOF)
nc3:            call    bp                               ; Return to coroutine for next char
nc4:            pop     bp
                cmp     al,' '                           ; Is this a printing character?
                jl      nc2                              ; If L--nonprinting
                test    DriverStatus,MASK InComment      ; Are we in a comment?
                jnz     nc3                              ; If NZ--we are
                cmp     al,'!'                           ; Are we starting a comment?
                jz      nc0                              ; If Z--yes
                cmp     al,'#'                           ; Is ths a '#'?
                jz      nc1                              ; If Z--yes (Convert to '+')
                job     al,'a','z',nc5                   ; If not lowercase, exit directly
                sub     al,20h                           ; Convert to uppercase
nc5:            popr    <di,cx,bx>                       ; Restore nonvolatile registers
                exit    success                          ; and return to caller


                PAGE
                SUBTTL  Driver State Machine
;
;       Come here when state machine gets confused
;
StateError:     signal  BadStateTable                    ; Say the state table is bad
StateMachine:   mov     bx,-1                            ; Mark initial state
                push    bx                               ; and put on stack
                mov     bx,OFFSET s_main                 ; bx  <==  initial state
main0:          call    [bx].FSM_A_Class                 ; Dispatch on class
                jnc     main2                            ; Transition successful
main1:          lea     bx,[bx].FSM_A_Ntrans             ; Take next transition
                jmp     SHORT main0                      ; and dispatch on transition
main2:          test    [bx].FSM_A_Action,0ffffh         ; Any action routine?
                jz      main3                            ; If Z--no action routine
                call    [bx].FSM_A_Action                ; and call action routine
                jc      main1                            ; Action routine rejected transition
main3:          mov     bx,[bx].FSM_A_Nstate             ; Transition successful
                                                         ; Move to next state
                jmp     SHORT main0                      ; and dispatch
```

continued

```
                PAGE
                SUBTTL  State Machine Class Processing

;
;       Defines class processing action. BX has current state. Values are
;       returned in CX. If class action is unsuccessful,  the character
;       causing failure is in AL. If the action is successful,  AL has a
;       new,  unprocessed character.
;
Classes         PROC    NEAR

Substate:       add     sp,2                        ; Remove return address
                push    bx                          ; Put current state on stack
                mov     bx,[bx].FSM_W_Data          ; Get next state
                jmp     main0                       ; And return to state dispatcher
Command:        cmp     al,byte ptr [bx].FSM_W_Data ; Look for a character match
                jz      s0                          ; If Z--found one
                exit    failure                     ; No match--say we failed
s0:             call    NextCharacter               ; Get a new character
                exit    success                     ; and say match occurred
Lambda:         exit    success                     ; Lambda transition always
successful
exit_failure:           stc                         ; Say transition failed
;
;       Common state transition exit. Restores state. Makes sure that stack
;       is not messed up. Previous state is returned in BX.
;
state_exit:     popr    <si,bx>                     ; Recover state and return address
                pushf                               ; Remember carry state
                cmp     bx,-1                       ; Popped too many states?
                jnz     se0                         ; If NZ--we're still OK
                mov     si,OFFSET StateError        ; Force error exit
se0:            popf                                ; Restore carry state
                jmp     si                          ; Return to caller or StateError
exit_success:           clc                         ; Say transition successful
                jmp     SHORT state_exit            ; and take common exit


;
;       Process a string of one or more dots (.)
;
d0:             call    NextCharacter               ; Get next character
d1:             cmp     al,'.'                      ; Is character a dot?
                loopz   d0                          ; It is a dot. Get another character
```

continued

```
                   neg      cx                      ; Convert loop count to dot
                   dec      cx                      ; count
                   clc                              ; Assume successful
                   or       cx,cx                   ; Was there a dot?
                   jnz      d2                      ; Must have at least 1 dot
                   stc                              ; Say we failed
d2:                ret                              ; Return with status (success or
failure)
Dots:              xor      cx,cx                   ; Initialize loop count
                   jmp      SHORT d1                ; Look at current character


;
;         Convert an ascii number '0' to '9' to a binary value. Return with
;         cy=1 if not a number.
;
bd0:               exit     failure                 ; Say this isn't a digit
BinaryDigit:       job      al,'0','9',bd0
                   sub      al,'0'                  ; Ascii to binary conversion
                   xor      ah,ah                   ; Byte to word conversion
                   mov      cx,ax                   ; cx  <==  converted digit
                   ret                              ; and return to caller
;
;         Process a number. Number is returned in CX. CY=1 if no digits found.
;
Number:            call     BinaryDigit             ; Convert first digit
                   jc       NoNumber                ; If c--no number
                   push     cx                      ; Save number (first digit)
n1:                call     NextCharacter           ; Get next character
                   call     BinaryDigit             ; Convert to binary
                   jc       NumberExit              ; Not a digit--we are done
                   mov      ax,10                   ; Accumulate digit
                   pop      dx                      ; Old number
                   mul      dx                      ; ax:dx  <==  old number*10
                   or       dx,dx                   ; Product > 64K?
                   jnz      NumberError             ; If NZ--yes (too large)
                   add      cx,ax                   ; cx  <==  digit + 10*old number
                   jc       NumberError             ; If c--number too large
                   push     cx                      ; Save number
                   jmp      SHORT n1                ; and get next digit
NumberExit:        pop      cx                      ; cx  <==  number
                   exit     success                 ; Say we succeeded and return
NumberError:       signal   NumberTooLarge          ; Say number too large
NoNumber:          exit     failure
```

continued

```
;
;       Process a dotted number. A dotted number consists of a number followed
;       by 0 or more dots. Each dot scales number by ¾. Scaled number returned
;       in CX.
;
DottedNumber:   call    Number              ; Look for number
                jc      NoNumber            ; If c--no number
                push    cx                  ; Save number
                call    Dots                ; Look for one or more dots
                jc      NumberExit          ; Only number (no dots)
                pop     dx                  ; Recover number
                call    DotTheNumber        ; Scale for dots seen
                jc      NumberError         ; If c--number too large
                ret                         ; Return (cx = scaled number)


;
;       Process key signature.
;
SignatureError: signal  BadSignature        ; Say signature bad
Signature:      mov     ah,' '              ; Assume no sharp or flat follows
                mov     cx,ax               ; cx  <==  key signature
                call    NextCharacter       ; Get another character
                mov     si,ax               ; Save this character
                cmp     al,'-'              ; Is it a flat?
                jz      sig0                ; If Z--it is a flat
                cmp     al,'+'              ; Is it a sharp?
                jnz     sig1                ; If NZ--neither sharp nor flat
sig0:           mov     ch,al               ; Add sharp or flat to signature
sig1:           mov     ax,15               ; Number of key signatures
                xchg    ax,cx
                mov     di,OFFSET Keys      ; List of valid signatures
        repne   scasw                       ; Try to match cx with valid
signature
                jnz     SignatureError      ; If NZ--no match
                cmp     ah,' '              ; Did we use this character
                mov     ax,si               ; Recover last character
                jz      sig2                ; If Z--last character not used
                call    NextCharacter       ; Get another character
sig2:           exit    success             ; and return indicating success


;
;       Process note. Note returns relative position within current scale
```

continued

```
;         in CX.
;
NoNote:         exit    failure                 ; Character is not a note
NoteExit0:      call    NextCharacter           ; So AX will have unprocessed
character
NoteExit1:      exit    success                 ; Return (Found note)
Note:           mov     di,CScore.SCR_W_Key     ; di  <== address of scale
                mov     cx,14                   ; Number of notes in scale
        repne   scasb                           ; See if this is a note
                jnz     NoNote                  ; If NZ--no (not a note)
                call    NextCharacter           ; Get another character
                cmp     al,'+'                  ; Is this a sharp?
                jz      DoSharp                 ; If Z--yes
                cmp     al,'-'                  ; Is this a flat?
                jz      DoFlat                  ; If Z--yes
                cmp     al,'='                  ; Is this a natural?
                jnz     NoteExit1               ; If NZ--not an accidental
DoNatural:      sub     cl,byte ptr [di+13]     ; Subtract one if sharped
                add     cl,byte ptr [di+27]     ; and add one if flatted
                jmp     SHORT NoteExit0         ; Success exit
DoSharp:        add     cl,byte ptr [di+13]     ; Sharp may add one to note
                call    NextCharacter           ; Get next character
                cmp     al,'+'                  ; Double sharp?
                jnz     NoteExit1               ; If NZ--no (success exit)
                inc     cl                      ; Double sharp always adds one
                jmp     SHORT NoteExit0         ; Get next character and exit
DoFlat:         sub     cl,[di+13]              ; Flat may subtract one
                call    NextCharacter           ; Get next character
                cmp     al,'-'                  ; Double flat?
                jnz     NoteExit1               ; If NZ--no (Success exit)
                dec     cl                      ; Double sharp always lowers one
                jmp     SHORT NoteExit0         ; Get next character and exit

;
;       Process style (MS, MN, or ML.
;
StyleFailure:   exit    failure                 ; Say style is invalid
Style:          mov     di,OFFSET StyleTable    ; di  <== style table
                mov     cx,1                    ; Look at first character
        repnz   scasb                           ; in style table ('M')
                jnz     StyleFailure            ; If NZ--not Music command
                call    NextCharacter           ; Get next character
                mov     cl,3                    ; Look at next three characters
```

continued

```
        repnz   scasb
                jnz     StyleFailure              ; If NZ  didn't find L, N, or P
                mov     cl,es:[di+3]              ; cl  <==  appropriate style
                call    NextCharacter             ; Get another character
                exit    success                   ; and say we were successful


CLASSES         ENDP


                PAGE
                SUBTTL  Utility Routines


Utility         PROC    NEAR

;
;       Save previous byte count and error message. These fields are zeroed when
;       file is opened. We want to be able to return these in response to IOCTL
;       request. Before IOCTL can be issued,  another open may have occurred.
;
SetDefaults:    push    es                        ; Save current ES
                mov     cx,cs
                mov     es,cx                     ; ES  <==  driver segment
                lea     di,PErr
                lea     si,CErr
                mov     cx,ERR_S_Size/2           ; Copy current error to
        rep     movsw                             ; previous error
                add     si,SCR_S_Size             ; si <== Initial CErr value
                mov     cx,(SCR_S_Size+ERR_S_Size)/2 ; Initialize both SCR and
        rep     movsw                             ; CErr
                pop     es                        ; Restore ES
                ret                               ; and return


;
;       Get current INT 8 ISR address
;
GetISR:         xor     dx,dx                     ; dx  <==  IVTSegment
                mov     es,dx                     ; es  <==  IVTSegment
                assume  es:IVTSegment
                les     dx,es:Int8Vector          ; es:dx  <==  Int8 vector
                assume  es:_text
                ret                               ; and return


;
;       Set INT 8 ISR to address in ds:ax
```

continued

```
;
SetISR:         pushf                                   ; Save current flags (to restore int
  state)
                cli                                     ; Disable interrupts while changing
vector
                pushr   <dx,es>                         ;;; Save nonvolatile registers
                xor     dx,dx                           ;;; dx  <==  IVT Segment
                mov     es,dx                           ;;; ds  <==  IVT Segment
                ASSUME  es:IVTSegment
                mov     es:WORD PTR Int8Vector,ax       ;;; Set INT8 ISR OFFSET
                mov     es:WORD PTR Int8Vector+2,ds     ;;; and segment
                popr    <es,dx>                         ;;; Restore nonvolatile registers
                ASSUME  es:_text
                popf                                    ;;; Restore interrupt state
                ret                                     ; and return


;
;       Sets 8253 counter 0 to value in AX register.
;
SetCounter0:    out     I8253.Ctr0,al                   ; Write LSB of count
                jmp     SHORT $+2                        ; Delay (for AT)
                xchg    al,ah                           ; AL  <==  MSB of count
                out     I8253.Ctr0,al                   ; Write MSB of count
                xchg    al,ah                           ; Return with count intact
                ret


;
;       Set the clock to run slow (normal speed)
;
SetClockSlow:   pushr   <ax,ds>                         ;;; Save nonvolatile registers
                mov     ax,SlowTickDivisor              ;;; ax  <==  count down value (64K)
                call    SetCounter0                     ;;; Use normal countdown value
                lds     ax,cs:OldInt8Vector             ;;; ds:ax  <==  original int vector
                call    SetISR                          ;;; Make this the int vectir
                or      cs:DriverStatus,DSS_M_InitNeeded;;; Say vector must change
                and     cs:DriverStatus,NOT MASK ChangePending;;; and that a change is in
progress
                popr    <ds,ax>                         ;;; Restore nonvolatile registers
                ret


;
;       Speed up clock. We make clock tick FastTickCount times faster. We
;       do this to increase the resolution in timing note duration.
```

continued

```
;
SetClockFast:   pushr   <ax,es>                         ; Save nonvolatile registers
                pushf                                   ; Save int enable flag
                cli                                     ; Disable interrupts while setting
up
                call    GetISR                          ;;; Get current int 8 vector
                mov     WORD PTR OldInt8Vector,dx       ;;; and save it
                mov     WORD PTR OldInt8Vector+2,es
                mov     ClockTicks,FastTickCount        ;;; Initialize clock tick count
                mov     ax,FastTickDivisor              ;;; ax  <==  Countdown value for
timer
                call    SetCounter0                     ;;; Set clock fast
                mov     ax,OFFSET ClkISR0               ;;; Setup new clock ISR
                call    SetISR
                and     cs:DriverStatus,NOT MASK InitNeeded  ;;; Don't need to change ISRs
                popf                                    ;;; Restore interrupt state
                popr    <es,ax>                         ; Restore nonvolatile registers
                ret                                     ; and return


;
;       Converts a number to a dotted number. Dot count is in CX and number
;       is in DX. Dotted number is returned in CX.
;
DotTheNumber:   push    ax                              ; Save nonvolatile register
dtn0:           mov     ax,dx                           ; Copy of number
                shr     ax,1                            ; Number / 2
                shr     ax,1                            ; Number / 4
                sub     dx,ax                           ; 3/4 number
                loop    dtn0                            ; More dots to process
dtn1:           mov     cx,dx                           ; cx  <==  scaled number
dtn2:           pop     ax                              ; Recover nonvolatile register
                ret                                     ; and return


Utility         ENDP

                PAGE
                SUBTTL  State Machine Action Routines


Actions         PROC    NEAR

LengthError:    signal  BadLength                       ; Say length was bad
TempoError:     signal  BadTempo                        ; Say tempo was bad
LengthDone:     job     cx,MinLength,MaxLength,LengthError ; Range check length
```

continued

```
                mov     CScore.SCR_W_Length,cx          ; Save length
                jmp     SHORT lt0                       ; Take common exit
TempoDone:      job     cx,MinTempo,MaxTempo,TempoError ; Range check tempo
                mov     CScore.SCR_W_Tempo,cx           ; Save tempo
lt0:            push    ax                              ; Save nonvolatile register
                mov     ax,4352                         ; dx:ax  <== 69888
                mov     dx,1
                div     CScore.SCR_W_Tempo              ; Calculate 69888 ÷
(CScore.SCR_W_Length *

                xor     dx,dx                           ; Zero remainder
                div     CScore.SCR_W_Length
                mov     CScore.SCR_W_Ticks,ax           ; Call result CScore.SCR_W_Ticks
                mov     CScore.SCR_W_NTicks,ax          ; Update CScore.SCR_W_NTicks too
                pop     ax                              ; Restore nonvolatile register
                exit    success                         ; and return successfully

;
;       Dotted note or rest. CX has dot count. Length specified by
;       CScore.SCR_W_Length. Calculate dotted length (result in CX).
;
NPDone0:        mov     dx,CScore.SCR_W_Length          ; dx  <==  default note length
                call    DotTheNumber                    ; Calc dotted length (cx = dots)


;
;       CX has total length (including dots). Either fall through from NPDone0
;       or called as a result of DottedNumber processing.
;
NPDone1:        push    ax                              ; Save nonvolatile register
                mov     ax,4352                         ; dx:ax  <==  69888
                mov     dx,1
                div     CScore.SCR_W_Tempo
                xor     dx,dx                           ; Zero remainder
                div     cx                              ; Calculate 69888 ÷ (NoteLength *
CScore.SCR_W_Tempo)
                mov     CScore.SCR_W_NTicks,ax          ; Call result CScore.SCR_W_NTicks
                pop     ax                              ; Restore nonvolatile register

;
;       Either we're using default tick count (CScore.SCR_W_Ticks) or we have
;       set CScore.SCR_W_NTicks to proper value. CScore.SCR_W_NTicks is set to
;       CScore.SCR_W_Ticks after note has been compiled.
;
```

continued

```
NPDone2:        exit    success                         ; Exit successfully


;
;       Complete octave processing by checking range and saving value.
;
OctaveError:    signal  BadOctave                       ; Say octave was bad
OctaveDone:     job     cx,MinOctave,MaxOctave,OctaveError  ; Check octave range
                mov     CScore.SCR_W_Octave,cx          ; Save value
                exit    success                         ; Exit successfully


;
;       Complete processing of a note. If it was specified by a letter,  convert
;       to absolute number by considering octave. Convert absolute note number
;       (either letter or Nxx) to pitch. Say there is a valid note.
;
NoteError1:     signal  BadTie                          ; Say tie is bad
NoteError:      signal  BadNote                         ; Say this wasn't a note
NoteDone2:      cmp     cx,CScore.SCR_W_TFreq           ; Is this note same freq?
                jnz     NoteError1                      ; If NZ--No
                exit    success                         ; Tie is good
NoteDone1:      push    ax                              ; Save nonvolatile register
                dec     cx                              ; Tables start with A- instead of A
                mov     ax,12                           ; 12 notes in an octave
                mul     CScore.SCR_W_Octave             ; ax  <== base note of octave
                add     cx,ax                           ; cx  <== absolute note
                pop     ax                              ; Restore nonvolatile register
NoteDone0:      job     cx,MinNote,MaxNote,NoteError    ; Range check note
                mov     si,cx                           ; Convert note to word index
                add     si,cx
                mov     cx,FreqDivTable[si]             ; cx  <== Frequency Divisor
                mov     CScore.SCR_W_NFreq,cx           ; Save frequency divisor
                test    DriverStatus,DSS_M_InTie        ; Processing tied note
                jnz     NoteDone2                       ; If NZ--yes
                exit    success                         ; Take successful return


;
;       Complete processing of a rest. Say there is a valid note.
;
PauseDone:      or      DriverStatus,DSS_M_HasNote      ; and say we have a complete note
                exit    success                         ; Take successful return


;
;       Complete processing of style
```

continued

```
;
StyleDone:        mov      CScore.SCR_W_Style,cx          ; Record the stype
                  exit     success                       ; and take success exit


;
;         Complete processing of signature


;
SignatureDone:    pushr    <ax,dx>                       ; Save nonvolatile registers
                  mov      ax,cx                         ; ax  <==  signature number
                  mov      dx,42                         ; Size of scale + sharps + flats
                  mul      dx                            ; Offset of scale
                  add      ax,OFFSET C                   ; Address of scale
                  mov      CScore.SCR_W_Key,ax           ; Save scale
                  popr     <dx,ax>                       ; Restore nonvolatile registers
                  exit     success                       ; Take successful return


;
;         Note ends in &
;
TieError:         signal   BadLength                     ; Note is too long
TieDone0:         push     ax                            ; Save nonvolatile registers
                  mov      ax,CScore.SCR_W_NTicks        ; Add tick count for this note
                  add      CScore.SCR_W_TTicks,ax        ; to accumulated ticks
                  jc       TieError                      ; If C--too big
                  or       DriverStatus,DSS_M_InTie      ; Say we're processing a tie
                  mov      ax,CScore.SCR_W_NFreq         ; Remember frequency
                  mov      CScore.SCR_W_TFreq,ax
                  pop      ax                            ; Receiver nonvolatile register
                  exit     success                       ; and exit
TieDone1:         push     ax                            ; Save nonvolatile register
                  xor      ax,ax                         ; New CScore.SCR_W_TTicks value
                  xchg     ax,CScore.SCR_W_TTicks        ; New CScore.SCR_W_TTicks  <==  0
                                                         ; AX  <==  old(CScore.SCR_W_TTicks)
                  add      CScore.SCR_W_NTicks,ax        ; AX  <==  Total note length
                  jc       TieError                      ; If CY--note too big
                  and      DriverStatus, NOT DSS_M_InTie ; Say no longer in tie
                  or       DriverStatus,DSS_M_HasNote    ; Say we have a valid note
                  pop      ax                            ; Restore nonvolatile register
                  exit     success                       ; Exit successfully
Actions           ENDP


                  PAGE
```

continued

```
                SUBTTL  Buffer Manipulation Routines


BufferRoutines PROC    NEAR


;
;       When pointer has reached end of buffer,  wrap it around to the start.
;       SI is current pointer.
;
CheckForWrap:   cmp     si,OFFSET BUF_W_Count        ; Is pointer at end of buffer?
                jl      cfw0                         ; If L--not at end
                mov     si,OFFSET BUF_T_Notes        ; At end. Wrap to start
cfw0:           ret                                  ; Return with pointer to next item


;
;       Try to insert note into buffer. If the buffer is full,  we wait for
;       a note to be removed. AX has note duration and DX has note pitch.
;
BufferInsert:   cmp     BUF_W_Count,BUF_S_Notes      ; Is there any room?
                jge     BufferInsert                 ; If GE--no room (Busy wait loop)
                mov     di,BUF_A_NextFree            ; di  <==  next free slot
                stosw                                ; Store Counter value
                xchg    ax,dx                        ; ax  <==  duration
                stosw                                ; Save duration in buffer
                xchg    ax,dx
                xchg    di,si                        ; si  <==  buffer pointer
                call    CheckForWrap                 ; Adjust pointer for wraparound
                xchg    di,si
                mov     BUF_A_NextFree,di            ; Update next free pointer
                inc     BUF_W_Count                  ; Say one more note in buffer
                ret                                  ; and return


;
;       Remove a note from the buffer. On return, Z=1 ==> buffer empty.
;       Z=0  ==>  we were able to remove a note. DX has duration and AX
;       has pitch.
;
BufferRemove:   cmp     BUF_W_Count,0                ; Anything in buffer?
                jz      br0                          ; If Z--no (buffer empty)
                mov     si,BUF_A_NextData            ; si  <==  address of next note
                lodsw                                ; ax  <==  note duration (ticks)
                mov     dx,ax                        ; dx  <==  note duration
                lodsw                                ; ax  <==  frequency divisor
                dec     BUF_W_Count                  ; One less note in buffer
```

continued

```
                call    CheckForWrap             ; Make sure pointer wraps at end
                mov     BUF_A_NextData,si        ; Update pointer
                or      si,si                    ; Return with Z=0 (have data)
br0:            ret


BufferRoutines  ENDP


                PAGE
                SUBTTL  Compile and Play Music


NotePrepPlay    PROC    NEAR


;
;       Check note status. If we have a complete note,  the note state informa-
;       tion is converted to a duration and pitch. The converted note is stored
;       in the note buffer.
;
CompileExit:    ret                              ; Compilation done
CompileNote:    test    DriverStatus,DSS_M_HasNote   ; Do we have a valid note?
                jz      CompileExit              ; If Z--no note yet
                push    ax                       ; Save nonvolatile register
                mov     ax,CScore.SCR_W_Ticks    ; Set CScore.SCR_W_NTicks =
CScore.SCR_W_Ticks
                xchg    ax,CScore.SCR_W_NTicks   ; and ax = old note tick count
                xor     dx,dx                    ; Set Frequency divisor back to 0
                xchg    dx,CScore.SCR_W_NFreq    ; (rest) and dx = old frequency
divisor
                mov     cx,CScore.SCR_W_Style    ; cx  <==  style
                cmp     cl,StyleLegato           ; Playing in Legato?
                jz      cn0                      ; If Z--yes (no gap between notes)
                or      dx,dx                    ; Are we playing a rest?
                jz      cn0                      ; If Z--yes (no gap between notes)
                mov     si,dx                    ; si  <==  frequency divisor
                mov     dx,ax                    ; dx  <==  note duration
                shr     dx,cl                    ; dx  <==  gap between notes (rest
duration)
                sub     ax,dx                    ; ax  <==  audible duration
                xchg    dx,si                    ; dx  <==  frequency divisor,  si
<== (rest duration)
                call    BufferInsert             ; Insert audible portion in buffer
                mov     ax,si                    ; ax  <==  rest duration
                xor     dx,dx                    ; dx  <==  frequency divisor (0 ==>
rest)
```

continued

```
cn0:            call    BufferInsert                    ; Insert legato note or rest into
buffer
                cli                                     ; Begin critical section
                cmp     NoteTicks,0                     ;;; Is an interrupt expected?
                jnz     cn1                             ;;; If NZ--yes
                call    PlayNextNote                    ;;; No note playing. Play one.
cn1:            sti                                     ;;; Interrupts ok now
                and     DriverStatus,NOT MASK HasNote   ; Say we've played this note
                pop     ax                              ; Restore nonvolatile register
                ret                                     ; and return


;
;       Play the next note. If the buffer is empty,  check for end of
;       file. After an end of file and the buffer is empty,  the clock
;       is set back to slow mode so as not to consume CPU cycles.
;
PlayNoteExit0:  test    DriverStatus,MASK EOFPending    ;;; Have we hit end of file?
                jz      PlayNoteExit1                   ;;; If Z--no EOF yet
                call    SetAltISR                       ;;; Start swap of interrupt vectors
PlayNoteExit1:  popr    <ds,si,dx,ax>                   ;;; Restore nonvolatile registers
                ret                                     ;;; and return
PlayNextNote:   pushr   <ax,dx,si,ds>                   ;;; Save nonvolatile registers
                in      al,I8255.PortB                  ;;; Read current 8255 outputs
                mov     si,cs                           ;;; Do this now in case slow adapter
                mov     ds,si                           ;;; ds  <==  driver segment
                and     al,SpeakerOff                   ;;; Turn off speaker
                out     I8255.PortB,al
                call    BufferRemove                    ;;; Get next note from buffer
                jz      PlayNoteExit0                   ;;; If Z--no (buffer empty)
                or      ax,ax                           ;;; Is this a rest?
                jz      pn1                             ;;; If Z--yes (Don't enable speaker)
                out     I8253.Ctr2,al                   ;;; LSB of frequency divisor
                in      al,I8255.PortB                  ;;; Overlap with I8253 access
                xchg    al,ah                           ;;; ah  <==  8255 latch settings
                out     I8253.Ctr2,al                   ;;; MSB of frequency divisor
                xchg    al,ah                           ;;; al  <==  8255 latch settings
                or      al,SpeakerOn                    ;;; Turn speaker back on
                out     I8255.PortB,al
pn1:            mov     NoteTicks,dx                    ;;; and set durations
                jmp     SHORT PlayNoteExit1             ;;; Take common exit


NotePrepPlay    ENDP
```

continued

```
                  PAGE
                  SUBTTL   Interrupt Service Routines

ClockISRs         PROC     NEAR

;
;          Normal ISR when clock is in fast mode. (Clock frequency has been
;          increased FastTickCount times). If NoteTicks >0,  we are playing
;          a note. In this case decrement NoteTicks. If result is 0,  its time
;          to turn off the speaker and get another note. Every FastTickCount
;          times through,  we call the old ClockISR to update date and time
;          and make any INT 1ch calls.
;
ClkISR0:          cmp      cs:NoteTicks,0              ;;; Are we playing a note?
                  jz       clk0                        ;;; If Z--no
                  dec      cs:NoteTicks               ;;; Decrement note count
                  jnz      clk0                        ;;; If NZ--not at note end
                  call     PlayNextNote               ;;; Play another note
clk0:             dec      cs:ClockTicks              ;;; Decrement clock tick counter
                  jz       clk3                        ;;; Not time to do old clock isr
ClkIntExit:       push     ax                          ;;; Save ax
                  mov      al,EOI                      ;;; Send nonspecific EOI to
                  out      I8259.PortA,al             ;;; 8259 Interrupt controller
                  pop      ax                          ;;; Restore ax
                  iret                                 ;;; and exit ISR
clk3:             mov      cs:ClockTicks,FastTickCount ;;; Reset the counter
                  jmp      cs:OldInt8Vector           ;;; and call old isr to do int 8
things

;
;          An end of file was detected and the sound buffer is empty. We are
;          waiting for the ClockTick count to go to 1,  so we can put the clock
;          back in slow mode. (If we didn't wait,  we would lose an average
;          of 27 ms each time we did change).
;
ClkISR1:          cmp      cs:ClockTicks,1            ;;; Can we change clock frequency
yet?
                  jl       clk2                        ;;; If L--no must reset ClockTicks
                  jg       clk1                        ;;; If G--not time yet
                  call     SetClockSlow               ;;; Put the clock in slow mode
                  and      cs:DriverStatus,NOT MASK Busy ;;; Say driver is not busy
clk1:             dec      cs:ClockTicks              ;;; Count one more tick of the clock
```

continued

```
               jmp     SHORT ClkIntExit              ;;; and exit ISR
clk2:          mov     cs:ClockTicks,FastTickCount   ;;; Wait ClockSpeedUp ticks
               jmp     SHORT ClkIntExit              ;;; and exit ISR


;
;      Switch Timer ISR from ClkISR0 (Fast clock) to ClkISR1 (Fast,  waiting
;      for tick count to go to 1.
;
SetAltISR:     and     DriverStatus,NOT MASK EOFPending ;;; EOF no longer pending
               or      DriverStatus,DSS_M_ChangePending ;;; but vector change is
               mov     ax,OFFSET ClkISR1                 ;;; Have played last note
               call    SetISR                           ;;; Swap clock ISR
               ret                                      ;;; and return


ClockISRs      ENDP

               PAGE
               SUBTTL  Process Driver Requests



DriverRequest  PROC    NEAR

SoundNOP:      jmp     SuccessExit



SoundError:    mov     ax,DHD_C_ErrUnknownCommand
               jmp     DriverExit



;
;      IOCTL request processing...
;


;
;      IOCTL Exits
;
;      Inputs
;
;      bx      address of next IOCTL list item
;
ItemTooShort:  popr    <es,bx,cx>
ItemBad:       mov     ax,DHD_C_ErrGeneralFailure       ; ax <== error code
               jmp     SHORT ioctl_exit_0
```

continued

```
LastItem:        mov      ax,DHD_M_StsDone              ; ax <== successful completion
ioctl_exit_0:    les      di,DWORD PTR RqOffset         ; es:bx <== request header
                 les      di,es:[di].RH_A_BufferAddress ; es:di <== ioctl item list
                 sub      bx,di                         ; bx <== bytes processed
                 les      di,DWORD PTR RqOffset         ; es:di <== request header
                 mov      es:[di].RH_W_Count,bx         ; Return count
                 jmp      DriverExit                    ; Take common driver exit


;
;        IOCTL Item List Coroutines
;
;        Outputs:
;
;        al       item code
;        es:di    item address
;        cx       allocated item length
;        dx       required item length


;
;        Initialize coroutine processing
;
;        Inputs:
;
;        es:bx - request header
;
FirstItem:       pop      bp                            ; bp <== coroutine return
                 mov      cx,es:RH_W_Count[bx]          ; cx <== size of item list
                 les      bx,es:[bx].RH_A_BufferAddress ; es:bx <== item list
;
;        Get next list item
;
;        Inputs:
;
;        es:bx    next item address
;
NextItem:        sub      cx,ITEM_S_Size                ; cx <== bytes left in item list
                 jl       LastItem                      ; If L--at end
                 mov      ax,es:[bx].ITEM_W_Code        ; ax <== item code
                 cmp      al,IOCTL_S_Table              ; Is it legal?
                 jge      ItemBad                       ; If G--no
                 pushr    <cx,bx,es>
                 shl      ax,1                          ; Convert code to word index
                 shl      ax,1
```

continued

```
                mov     si,ax                       ; Use si for index
                mov     dx,IOCTL_T_Table+2[si]      ; dx <== length of item
                mov     si,IOCTL_T_Table[si]        ; si <== address of item
                or      dx,dx                       ; Is it a string
                jnz     ni_0                        ; If NZ--no
                mov     si,[si]
                xchg    al,dl                       ; Save item code
                lodsb                               ; al <== length of error text
                xchg    al,dl                       ; Put values where they belong
ni_0:           mov cx,es:[bx].ITEM_W_Length        ; cx <== allocated bytes
                cmp     cx,dx                       ; Enough bytes allocated?
                jl      ItemTooShort                ; If L--no
                les     di,es:[bx].ITEM_A_Address   ; es:di <== item address
                call    bp                          ; Make coroutine callback
;
;       Return here to process next item
;
                pop     bp                          ; bp <== callback address
                popr    <es,bx,cx>
                push    ds
                lds     si,es:[bx].ITEM_A_RetLen    ; ds:si <== return length address
                mov     ax,ds                       ; See if return length givem
                or      ax,ax                       ; (not given if segment = 0)
                jz      ni_1                        ; If Z--not needed
                mov     [si],dx                     ; Return bytes moved
ni_1:           pop ds
                add     bx,ITEM_S_Size             ; bx <== address of next item
                jmp     SHORT NextItem             ; Process next item



;
;       IOCTL processing routines. Input routine (SoundInIOCTL) read
;       information from device. Information is returned to buffers
;       passed in IOCTL request. Output routine (SoundOutIOCTL) writes
;       information to device. Information comes from buffers passed
;       in IOCTL request.
;
;       Inputs:
;
;       es:bx   Request header
;
SoundOutIOCTL:  call    FirstItem                   ; Get first item in list
soi_0:          pop     bp                          ; bp <== callback address
```

continued

413

```
                cmp     al,IOCTL_K_Length               ; Legal output item?
                jl      ItemBad                         ; if L--no
                xchg    si,di                           ; swap es:di and ds:si
                pushr   <ds,es>
                popr    <ds,es>
        rep     movsb                                   ; copy item
                mov     ax,es                           ; restore ds
                mov     ds,ax
                call    bp                              ; get next item
                jmp     SHORT soi_0


SoundInIOCTL:   call    FirstItem                       ; Get first item in list
sii_0:          pop     bp                              ; bp <== callback address
        rep     movsb                                   ; copy item
                call    bp                              ; Get next item in list
                jmp     SHORT sii_0



;
;       Process write requests (Write, WriteVerify, WriteTilBusy,,,
;


;
;       Utility routines...
;
WriteSetup:     mov     cx,es:[bx].RH_W_Count           ; cX <==  transfer size
                lds     si,es:[bx].RH_A_TransferAddress ; dS:SI <==  buffer address
                mov     cs:SavedDS,ds                   ; Save xfer buffer segment
                ret                                     ; Return (to state machine)
WriteRestore:   mov     cx,SavedCX                      ; Restore transfer count
                lds     si,DWORD PTR SavedSI            ; Restore Buffer offset
                ret                                     ; and return
WriteUpdate:    mov     dx,cs                           ; Reset our data segment
                mov     ds,dx
                mov     es,dx
                mov     SavedCX,cx                      ; Update count remaining
                mov     SavedSI,si                      ; and current buffer offset
                add     CErr.ERR_L_Bytes,1              ; Count total characters transferred
                adc     CErr.ERR_L_Bytes+2,0            ; MSW of character count
                ret                                     ; Return to request processing
WriteDone:      mov     bx,cs                           ; Restore driver ds
                mov     ds,bx
```

continued

```
            les     bx,DWORD PTR RqOffset       ; es:bx  <==  request header
            sub     es:[bx].RH_W_Count,cx       ; Calculate bytes processed
            jmp     SuccessExit                 ; and take success exit
;
;       Process Write and WriteVerify
;
SoundWrite: call    WriteSetup                  ; Copy transfer parameters (size and
 address)
sw0:        lodsb                               ; al  <==  next byte to write
            call    WriteUpdate                 ; Update transfer parameters
            pop     bp                          ; Coroutine callback address
            call    bp                          ; Call coroutine
            call    WriteRestore                ; Restore transfer paramters
            loop    sw0                         ; and process next byte
            jmp     SHORT WriteDone             ; Common write exit
;
;       Process WriteTilBusy
;
SoundWriteTilBusy:
            call    WriteSetup                  ; Copy transfer parameters (size and
 address)
sw1:        cmp     BUF_W_Count,BUF_S_Notes-1   ; Is buffer (almost) full?
            jge     WriteDone                   ; If Z--yes (Don't wait)
            lodsb                               ; al  <==  next byte to write
            call    WriteUpdate                 ; Update transfer parameters
            pop     bp                          ; Coroutine callback address
            call    bp                          ; Call coroutine
            call    WriteRestore                ; Restore transfer paramters
            loop    sw1                         ; and process next byte
            jmp     SHORT WriteDone


SoundStatus: mov    ax,DHD_M_StsDone            ; Assume not busy
            cmp     BUF_W_Count,BUF_S_Notes-1   ; Is buffer full?
            jl      ss_0                        ; If l--no
            or      ax,DHD_M_StsBusy            ; Say operation would wait
ss_0:       jmp     DriverExit                  ; and exit


SoundFlush: cli                                 ; Begin critical section
            or      DriverStatus,DSS_M_EOFPending ;;; Say EOF is pending
            mov     BUF_W_Count,0               ;;; Reset count and buffer
            mov     BUF_A_NextFree,OFFSET BUF_T_Notes;;; pointers
            mov     BUF_A_NextData,OFFSET BUF_T_Notes
            cmp     NoteTicks,0                 ;;; Are we doing anything?
```

continued

```
                jnz     sf0                             ;;; If NZ--yes
                call    SetAltISR                       ;;; Done. Change to slow mode
sf0:            sti                                     ;;; Interrupts OK now
                jmp     SuccessExit


SoundOpen:      call    SetDefaults                     ; Set driver default values
                and     DriverStatus,NOT MASK EOFPending; EOF is no longer pending
so0:            test    DriverStatus,MASK ChangePending ; Is a vector change pending?
                jnz     so0                             ; If NZ--yes (wait for it)
                test    DriverStatus,MASK InitNeeded    ; Does clock need to be set fast?
                jz      so1                             ; If Z--no (back to back copies)
                call    SetClockFast                    ; Set clock in fast mode
so1:            or      DriverStatus,DSS_M_Busy         ; Say device is busy
                mov     al,(SelCtr2 SHL SC) OR (LSBMSB SHL RL) OR (Mode3 SHL M)
                out     I8253.Mode,al
                mov     ax,DHD_M_StsDone                ; Say operation was successful
                jmp     ResetExit                       ; and reset driver


SoundClose:     mov     ax,cs                           ; Set ES  to driver segment
                mov     es,ax
                mov     al,EOF                          ; Tell state machine we're done
                pop     bp                              ; Set up coroutine
                call    bp                              ; and make call
                jmp     SuccessExit                     ; Take success exit
DriverRequest   ENDP


                PAGE
                SUBTTL  DOS Entry Points


StgyEntry:      mov     CS:RqOffset,bx                  ; Save request address
                mov     CS:RqSegment,es
                return_far                              ; and return to DOS


IntError:       mov     ax,DHD_C_ErrUnknownCommand      ; Say command is bad
                jmp     ResetExit                       ; and reset driver
IntEntry:       push_all                                ; Save all registers
                pushf                                   ; Save flags
                cld                                     ; Set direction flag
                mov     ax,cs                           ; Set driver DS
                mov     ds,ax                           ; (DOS currently does this for us)
                mov     DosSS,ss                        ; Save DOS stack
                mov     DosSP,sp
                mov     ss,ax                           ; Establish driver stack
```

continued

```
                mov     sp,DriverSP                     ; Set SP to where we left off
                les     bx,DWORD PTR RqOffset           ; es:bx  <==  Request Header
                mov     al,es:[bx].RH_B_Command         ; AL  <==  command
                cmp     al,RQ_S_Table                   ; Is it in range ?
                jge     IntError                        ; If GE--out of range
                cbw                                     ; Make command a word
                add     ax,ax                           ; Convert to word index
                mov     si,ax                           ; SI  <==  function table index
SoundDispatch:  jmp     RQ_T_Table[si]                  ; Dispatch on function code

SoundInit:      mov     WORD PTR es:[bx].RH_A_BreakAddress, OFFSET SoundInit
                mov     WORD PTR es:[bx+2].RH_A_BreakAddress,cs
                or      DriverStatus,DSS_M_InitNeeded
                mov     dx,OFFSET Copyright
                mov     ah,9
                int     21h
                mov     ax,DHD_M_StsDone
                jmp     ResetExit
Copyright       DB      BELL,"SOUND v2.0",CR,LF
                DB      "© W. V. Dixon 1987",CR,LF
                DB      "   All rights reserved",CR,LF,'$'
driver          endp
_text           ends
                end     begin




;;
;;      MACROS.ASM
;;
;;      Common device driver macro definitions
;;
```

```
;;
;;      © 1987 W. V. Dixon. All rights reserved.
;;
;;      May be freely copied for personal,  nonprofit use
;;      so long as this copyright notice is retained and usage
;;      restrictions are observed. This software may not be
;;      used in whole or in part in any program which is sold
;;      without prior written consent of the author.
;;
```

continued

```
;;
;;      Macros for pushing and popping registers
;;


;;
;;      Push an arbitrary number of registers
;;
pushr           MACRO   x               ;; x is register list
                                        ;; (enclosed within <>)
                IRP     y,<x>           ;; For all registers in list
                push    y               ;; Push it on the stack
                ENDM                    ;; IRP
                ENDM                    ;; MACRO pushr


;;
;;      Push all registers onto stack
;;
push_all    MACRO
                pushr   <ax,bx,cx,dx,di,si,bp,ds,es>
                ENDM                    ;; MACRO pusha


;;
;;      Pop an arbitrary number of registers
;;
popr            MACRO   x               ;; x is register list
                                        ;; (enclosed within <>)
                IRP     y,<x>           ;; For all registers in list
                pop     y               ;; Pop the register
                ENDM                    ;; IRP
                ENDM                    ;; MACRO popr



;;
;;      Pop all registers from stack
;;
pop_all             MACRO
                popr    <es,ds,bp,si,di,dx,cx,bx,ax>
                ENDM                    ;; MACRO popa



;;
```

continued

```
;;      Macros for near and far returns
;;
return_far   MACRO
             DB      0cbh              ;; Opcode for far return
             ENDM                      ;; MACRO return_far


return_near  MACRO
             DB      0c3h              ;; Opcode for near return
             ENDM                      ;; MACRO return_near


;;
;;      Macros for return with status
;;
;;           CY=0    ==> SUCCESS
;;           CY=1    ==> FAILURE
;;
exit    MACRO   x                      ;; x is success or failure
        IFIDN   <x>,<success>            ;; If x is success
             clc                       ;; Set CY=0
        ELSE                           ;; x is not success
             IFIDN   <x>,<failure>       ;; If x is failure
                  stc                  ;; Set CY=1
             ELSE                      ;; x is not failure
                  %OUT   "Invalid exit argument - failure assumed"
                  stc
             ENDIF                     ;; x is not failure
        ENDIF                          ;; x is not success
        ret                            ;; Return with status in carry
        ENDM                           ;; MACRO exit


;;
;;      Unconditional return with failure status
;;
ret_failure  MACRO   x                 ;; x is argument count
             stc                       ;; Say we failed (CY=1)
             ret     x                 ;; and return
             ENDM                      ;; MACRO ret_failure


ret_success  MACRO   x                 ;; x is argument count
             clc                       ;; Say we succeeded (CY=0)
             ret     x                 ;; and return
             ENDM                      ;; MACRO ret_success
```

continued

```
;;
;;      Macro to do range check
;;
;;              If value is less than minvalue or greater than maxvalue,
;;              jump to outrange;  otherwise fall through to next statement
;;              unless inrange is not blank. If inrange is not blank and
;;              value is within range,  jump to inrange.
;;
job     MACRO   value,minvalue,maxvalue,outrange,inrange
        cmp     value,minvalue          ;; Value less than minimum?
        jl      outrange                ;; If L--yes (jump outrange)
        cmp     value,maxvalue          ;; Value greater than maximum?
        jg      outrange                ;; If G--yes (jump outrange)
        IFNB    <inrange>               ;; If inrange label is specified
        jmp     inrange                 ;; Jump to it
        ENDIF                           ;; Inrange nonblank
        ENDM                            ;; MACRO job


;;
;;      Macro to trace driver execution
;;
trace   MACRO   msg                     ;; Message to display
        LOCAL   x                       ;; We need some local labels
        LOCAL   y
        jmp     SHORT x                 ;; Jump over text
y       DB      msg                     ;; Define message text
        DB      0dh,0ah,'$'             ;; Append <CR><LF> and "$"
x:      pushr   <ax,dx,ds>              ;; Save nonvolatile registers
        pushf                           ;; Remember flags
        mov     ax,cs
        mov     ds,ax                   ;; ds  <==  current CS
                                        ;; (message segment)
        mov     dx,OFFSET y             ;; dx  <==  message address
        mov     ah,9                    ;; Issue bios request to display
        int     21h                     ;; Message
        popf                            ;; Restore flags
        popr    <ds,dx,ax>              ;; Restore registers
        ENDM                            ;; MACRO trace
```

continued

```
;;
;;   DEVICE.DEF
;;
;;       Common device driver definitions
;;
```

```
;;
;;       © 1987 W. V. Dixon. All rights reserved.
;;
;;       May be freely copied for personal,  nonprofit use
;;       so long as this copyright notice is retained and usage
;;       restrictions are observed. This software may not be
;;       used in whole or in part in any program which is sold

;;       without prior written consent of the author.
;;
```

```
;;
;;       Bit settings for device header (DHD) attributes word
;;
DHD_M_IsCharacter        EQU     8000h    ;; Character device
DHD_M_IsBlock            EQU     0000h    ;; Block device
DHD_M_IOCTLSupport       EQU     4000h    ;; Supports MS-DOS IOCTL functions
                                          ;; (INT 21H  AH = 44H)
DHD_M_NonIBMFormat       EQU     2000h    ;; Media is not IBM format compatible
DHD_M_IBMFormat          EQU     0000h    ;; Media is IBM format compatible
DHD_M_WriteBusySupport   EQU     2000h    ;; Write until busy supported
DHD_M_IsNetwork          EQU     1000h    ;; Network device
DHD_M_OCRMSupport        EQU     0800h    ;; Open / Close / Removable media
                                          ;; supported
DHD_M_LogDevSupport      EQU     0040h    ;; Get / Set logical device supported
DHD_M_IsSpecial          EQU     0010h    ;; Supports INT 29H output
DHD_M_IsCurClk           EQU     0008h    ;; Device is current clock
DHD_M_IsCurStdOut        EQU     0004h    ;; Device is current stdout
DHD_M_IsCurStdIn         EQU     0002h    ;; Device is current stdin
DHD_M_IsCurNul           EQU     0001h    ;; Device is current nul
DHD_M_GenIOCTLSupport    EQU     0001h    ;; Supports MS_DOS generic IOCTL function
                                          ;; (INT 21H  AX = 440DH)

;;
```

continued

```
;;        Driver return status values
;;        (MSB of Request Header status word)
;;
DHD_M_StsDone            EQU     100h    ;; Successful completion
DHD_M_StsBusy            EQU     200h    ;; Device is currently busy
DHD_M_StsError           EQU     8000h   ;; Unsuccessful completion


;;
;;        Specific driver error codes
;;        (LSB of Request Header status word)
;;
DHD_C_ErrWriteProtect    EQU     DHD_M_StsError OR 0     ;; Write protection error
DHD_C_ErrUnknownUnit     EQU     DHD_M_StsError OR 1     ;; Illegal unit number
DHD_C_ErrNotDriveReady   EQU     DHD_M_StsError OR 2     ;; Drive is not ready
DHD_C_ErrUnknownCommand  EQU     DHD_M_StsError OR 3     ;; Illegal driver command
DHD_C_ErrCRC             EQU     DHD_M_StsError OR 4     ;; CRC error on drive
DHD_C_ErrBadStructure    EQU     DHD_M_StsError OR 5     ;; Bad request structure length
DHD_C_ErrSeek            EQU     DHD_M_StsError OR 6     ;; Error on seek
DHD_C_ErrUnknownMedia    EQU     DHD_M_StsError OR 7     ;; Media unknown
DHD_C_ErrSectorNotFound  EQU     DHD_M_StsError OR 8     ;; Sector not found
DHD_C_ErrPaperOut        EQU     DHD_M_StsError OR 9     ;; No paper in printer
DHD_C_ErrWriteFault      EQU     DHD_M_StsError OR 0ah   ;; Error writing
DHD_C_ErrReadFault       EQU     DHD_M_StsError OR 0bh   ;; Error reading
DHD_C_ErrGeneralFailure  EQU     DHD_M_StsError OR 0ch   ;; Catchall error
DHD_C_ErrInvDiskChange   EQU     DHD_M_StsError OR 0fh   ;; Invalid disk change



;;
;;        Device Header (DHD)
;;
DHD                STRUC
DHD_A_NextDHD      dd      -1      ;; Address of next device
DHD_W_Attrib       dw      0       ;; Device attributes
DHD_W_StrategyEntry dw     0       ;; Offset to strategy routine
DHD_W_InterruptEntry dw    0       ;; Offest to interrupt routine
DHD_T_Name         db      '      ' ;; Device name
DHD                ENDS


;;
;;        Request Header (RH)
;;

;;
```

continued

```
;;      Generic request header.  Directly used for:
;;
;;               Input Status        (RH_C_InputStatus)
;;               Input Flush         (RH_C_InputFlush)
;;               Output Status       (RH_C_OutputStatus)
;;               Output Flush        (RH_C_OutputFlush)
;;               Device Open         (RH_C_Open)
;;               Device Close        (RH_C_Close)
;;               Removable Media (RH_C_RemovableMedia)
;;
RH                      STRUC
RH_B_Length      DB      0       ;; Length (bytes) of request
RH_B_Unit        DB      0       ;; Unit code
RH_B_Command     DB      0       ;; Command code
RH_W_Status      DW      0       ;; Status
RH_T_ReservedDOS DB      8 DUP(0);; Reserved for DOS
RH                      ENDS


;;
;;      Request Header commands
;;
RH_C_Init          EQU    00H    ;; Device initialization
RH_C_Media         EQU    01H    ;; Media check
RH_C_BuildBPB      EQU    02H    ;; Build BIOS Parameter block
RH_C_InputIOCTL    EQU    03H    ;; Input IOCTL
RH_C_Input         EQU    04H    ;; Input
RH_C_InputNoWait   EQU    05H    ;; Nondestructive input
RH_C_InputStatus   EQU    06H    ;; Input status
RH_C_InputFlush    EQU    07H    ;; Input flush
RH_C_Output        EQU    08H    ;; Output
RH_C_OutputVerify  EQU    09H    ;; Output and verify
RH_C_OutputStatus  EQU    0aH    ;; Output status
RH_C_OutputFlush   EQU    0bH    ;; Output flush
RH_C_OutputIOCTL   EQU    0cH    ;; Output IOCTL
RH_C_Open          EQU    0dH    ;; Device / File open
RH_C_Close         EQU    0eH    ;; Device / File close

RH_C_RemoveableMedia   EQU    0fH    ;; Check for removable media
RH_C_OutputTilBusy     EQU    10H    ;; Output until busy
RH_C_GenIOCTL          EQU    13H    ;; Generic IOCTL request
RH_C_GetLogDevice      EQU    17H    ;; Get Logical device
RH_C_SetLogDevice      EQU    18H    ;; Set logical device
```

continued

```
;;
;;      Initialization request (RH_C_Init)
;;
RH_INIT                   STRUC
                DB        TYPE RH DUP(0)
RH_B_UnitCount    DB      0       ;; Number of units
RH_A_BreakAddress DD      0       ;; Ending address of driver
RH_A_BPBTable     DD      0       ;; Pointer to BPB array
RH_B_Drive        DB      0       ;; Drive number
RH_INIT                 ENDS


;;
;;      Media Check (RH_C_Media)
;;


;;
;;      Returned MediaStatus values
;;
RH_C_MediaChanged         EQU     -1  ;; Media has changed
RH_C_MediaNotChanged      EQU     +1  ;; Media has not changed
RH_C_MediaNotSure         EQU      0  ;; Not sure whether media has
                                      ;; changed


RH_MEDIA              STRUC
                DB        TYPE RH DUP(0)
RH_B_MediaCode    DB      0       ;; Current media code
RH_B_MediaStatus  DB      0       ;; Media status
RH_A_MCVolumeID   DD      0       ;; Pointer to volume id
RH_MEDIA           ENDS



;;
;;      Build BIOS Parameter Block (RH_C_BuildBPB)
;;
RH_BUILD_BPB         STRUC
                DB        TYPE RH DUP(0)
                DB        0       ;; Current media code (RH_B_MediaCode)
RH_A_BufferAddress DD     0       ;; Buffer address / FAT Sector
RH_A_BPB          DD      0       ;; Address of BPB table
RH_BUILD_BPB         ENDS
```

continued

```
;;
;;      Input or output request. Used for:
;;
;;              Input                   (RH_C_Input)
;;              Output                  (RH_C_Output)
;;              Output and Verify       (RH_C_OutputVerify)

;;              Input IOCTL             (RH_C_InputIOCTL)
;;              Output IOCTL            (RH_C_OutputIOCTL)
;;              Output til busy         (RH_C_OutputTilBusy)
;;
RH_IO                   STRUC
                        DB      TYPE RH DUP(0)
                        DB      0       ;; Current media code (RH_B_MediaCode)
RH_A_TransferAddress    DD      0       ;; Transfer address
RH_W_Count              DW      0       ;; Byte/sector count
RH_W_Sector             DW      0       ;; Starting sector
RH_A_VolumeID           DD      0       ;; Pointer to volume id
RH_IO                   ENDS


;;
;;      Nondestructive Input No Wait (RH_C_InputNoWait)
;;
RH_RNW                  STRUC
                        DB      TYPE RH DUP(0)
RH_B_ByteRead           DB      0       ;; Byte just read
RH_RNW                  ENDS




;;
;;  VALUES.DEF
;;
;;      Specifies min/max, constants, and default values for
;;      SOUND driver.
;;


;;
;;      © 1987 W. V. Dixon. All rights reserved.
;;
```

continued

```
;;      May be freely copied for personal, nonprofit use
;;      so long as this copyright notice is retained and usage
;;      restrictions are observed. This software may not be
;;      used in whole or in part in any program which is sold
;;      without prior written consent of the author.
;;


MinTempo        EQU     35              ;; Minimum tempo
MaxTempo        EQU     256             ;; Maximum tempo
MinOctave       EQU     0               ;; Lowest octave
MaxOctave       EQU     7               ;; Highest octave
MinLength       EQU     1               ;; Longest note (whole)
MaxLength       EQU     64              ;; Shortest note (sixty-fourth)
MinNote         EQU     1               ;; Lowest note
MaxNote         EQU     88              ;; Highest note


BUF_S_Notes     EQU     256             ;; Internal buffer size


StyleLegato     EQU     0               ;; Play Legato
StyleNormal     EQU     4               ;; Play Normal
StyleStaccato   EQU     3               ;; Play Staccato


SCR_K_DLength   EQU     4               ;; Default note length (quarter-note)
SCR_K_DOctave   EQU     4               ;; Default octave
                                        ;; (octave above middle C)
SCR_K_DTempo    EQU     120             ;; Default tempo
                                        ;; (quarter-notes per second)
SCR_K_DKey      EQU     OFFSET C        ;; Default key
SCR_K_DStyle    EQU     StyleNormal     ;; Default style
SCR_K_DTicks    EQU     146             ;; Default note length in ticks
                                        ;; 69888 ÷ (DefaultTempo * DefaultLength)


FastTickCount   EQU     16              ;; Speed up timer by factor of 16
FastTickDivisor EQU     1000h           ;; Counter preset for speedup
SlowTickCount   EQU     0               ;; Normal timer
SlowTickDivisor EQU     0               ;; Counter preset for normal speed
```

continued

```
;;
;;   HARDWARE.DEF
;;
;;        Hardware definitions for SOUND driver
;;


;;
;;        © 1987 W. V. Dixon. All rights reserved.
;;
;;        May be freely copied for personal,  nonprofit use
;;        so long as this copyright notice is retained and usage
;;        restrictions are observed. This software may not be
;;        used in whole or in part in any program which is sold
;;        without prior written consent of the author.
;;


;;
;;        8259 Interrupt Controller
;;
I8259          EQU     20H              ;; Base address
EOI            EQU     20H              ;; Nonspecific end of interrupt
                                        ;; control word



;;
;;        8255 PPI
;;
I8255          EQU     60H              ;; Base address
PortA          EQU     00               ;; Port A offset (base = 0x60)
PortB          EQU     01               ;; Port B offset (base = 0x61)
PortC          EQU     02               ;; Port C offset (base = 0x62)
Control        EQU     03               ;; Control port  (base = 0x63)


;;
;;        Speaker control
;;
PB0            Record  SpeakerData:1,SpeakerGate:1

SpeakerOn      EQU     MASK SpeakerData OR MASK SpeakerGate
```

continued

```
SpeakerOff       EQU     NOT SpeakerOn


;;
;;      8253 Timer / Counter
;;
I8253            EQU     40H            ;; Base address
Ctr0             EQU     0              ;; Counter 0 (base = 0x40)
Ctr1             EQU     1              ;; Counter 1 (base = 0x41)
Ctr2             EQU     2              ;; Counter 2 (base = 0x42)
Mode             EQU     3              ;; Control   (base = 0x43)


;;
;;      Control word format
;;
ModeWord         Record  SC:2,RL:2,M:3,BCD:1


;;
;;      Control word values
;;
CounterLatch     EQU     0
MSBOnly          EQU     2
LSBOnly          EQU     1
LSBMSB           EQU     3

SelCtr0          EQU     0
SelCtr1          EQU     1
SelCtr2          EQU     2

Mode0            EQU     0
Mode1            EQU     1
Mode2            EQU     2
Mode3            EQU     3
Mode4            EQU     4
Mode5            EQU     5



;;
;; FSM.DEF
;;
;;      Macros for generating state transition table
```

continued

```
;;


;;
;;      © 1987 W. V. Dixon. All rights reserved.
;;
;;      May be freely copied for personal,  nonprofit use
;;      so long as this copyright notice is retained and usage
;;      restrictions are observed. This software may not be
;;      used in whole or in part in any program which is sold
;;      without prior written consent of the author.
;;



;;
;;      Macros for generating state labels
;;


;;
;;      Generates label for current state
;;
this_s          MACRO   x               ;; Create label for
s_&x:                                   ;; s_xxx (current state)
                ENDM                    ;; MACRO this_s


;;
;;      Generates label for next state
;;
next_s          MACRO   x               ;; Generate reference to
                DW      s_&x            ;; s_xxx (next state)
                ENDM                    ;; MACRO next_s



;;
;;      Define state table entry
;;
FSM             STRUC                   ;; Define state table entry
FSM_A_Class     DW      0               ;; Class processing routine
FSM_W_Data      DW      0               ;; Class data
FSM_A_Nstate    DW      0               ;; Next state
FSM_A_Action    DW      0               ;; Action routine
FSM_A_Ntrans    DW      0               ;; Offset of next transition
FSM             ENDS
```

continued

```
;;
;;      State definition counter
;;
nnn=0                                   ;; Make sure state count
                                        ;; set to 0



;;
;;      Define transition macro (tran)
;;
tran    MACRO   t_class,t_name,t_nstate,t_action
        DW      t_class                 ;; Class always present

        IFNB    <t_name>                ;; Name is optional
                DW      t_name          ;; Use it if present
        ELSE                            ;; Otherwise
                DW      0               ;; say not present
        ENDIF                           ;; IFNB <t_name>

        IFNB    <t_nstate>              ;; Next state optional
                DW      t_nstate        ;; Use next state if present
        ELSE                            ;; Otherwise
                next_s      %nnn        ;; Default to next state
        ENDIF                           ;; IFNB <t_state>


        IFNB    <t_action>              ;; Action routine optional
                DW      t_action        ;; Use it if present
        ELSE                            ;; Otherwise
                DW      0               ;; say no action routine
        ENDIF                           ;; IFNB <t_action>



        ENDM                            ;; MACRO trans



;;
;;      Define state macro (state)
;;
state   MACRO   sname                   ;; State macro definition
```

continued

```
        IFE     nnn                             ;; If first invocation
s_exit:             tran    exit_success,0,0 ;; Make sure that s_exit defined
nnn=1                                           ;; We've defined one state
s_fail:             tran    exit_failure,0,0 ;; Make sure s_fail defined
nnn=2                                           ;; We've defined two states
        ENDIF                                   ;; IFE nnn


        tran    exit_failure,0,0                ;; Final transition for previous
                                                ;; state. (Forces error exit
                                                ;; because no matching transition)
        IFNB    <sname>                         ;; If optional name present
sname:                                          ;; Define it as a symbol
        ENDIF                                   ;; IFNB <sname>
        this_s      %nnn                        ;; Always define s_xxx style name

nnn=nnn+1                                       ;; One more state defined
        ENDM                                    ;; ENDM state



;;
;;      Define state end (state_end) macro
;;      Forces completion of last state (specifically appends
;;      failure transition to previously built transition table).
;;
state_end       MACRO                   ;; Declare end to state table
                state                   ;; Final state forces last tran
                ENDM                    ;; For previous state to be
                                        ;; defined
```

An executable version of the SOUND driver and all driver source code is available on IBM 5-¼″ DSDD diskette. Also included on this diskette are sources and executables for DEVICES and a self-loading RAMdisk device driver. These are written primarily in Microsoft C. All the programs on this disk have been tested under PC-DOS version 3.10. The author believes they work correctly but makes no guarantees to this effect. The software is provided strictly on an as-is basis and you are using it entirely at your own risk. The author will assume no responsibility for any damage that the software may cause. All code carries a copyright notice similar to the SOUND driver in this essay. The diskette is available for $10.00 (check or money order) from Walter Dixon; RR#2, Box 581; Delanson, NY 12053.

Reading List

Angermeyer, J., and K. Jaeger/The Waite Group. 1986. *MS-DOS Developer's Guide*. Indianapolis: Howard W. Sams & Company.

IBM. 1984. *Disk Operating System v. 3.00 Technical Reference Guide*. North Tarrytown, New York.

Lai, R./The Waite Group. 1987. *Writing MS-DOS Device Drivers*. Reading, Massachusetts: Addison-Wesley Publishing Company, Inc.

Microsoft. 1986. *MS-DOS Technical Reference Encyclopedia*. Redmond, Washington.

Walter Dixon holds degrees in both mechanical and electrical engineering. He is employed at General Electric Corporate Research and Development Center in Schenectady, where he works in the areas of distributed systems and computer networks. Mr. Dixon also teaches graduate computer science at Union College in Schenectady. He has written more than ten device drivers for PC-DOS.

Related Essays

6 Undocumented MS-DOS Functions
10 Developing MS-DOS Device Drivers

Keywords

- Enhanced Graphics Adapter (EGA)
- graphics memory organization
- EGA registers
- Bresenham's Algorithm
- pixel values
- bit planes
- color palettes

Essay Synopsis: The Enhanced Graphics Adapter (EGA) has effectively become the standard for graphics on MS-DOS systems. Although many programming languages contain high-level graphics routines, direct access to the EGA registers and memory is needed for many demanding applications. Due to its increased capabilities, the EGA is considerably more complex to program than are the CGA or monochrome displays. You will learn how to program the EGA through basic routines for reading and writing pixels, drawing lines, printing the screen, and setting the color palette registers. The examples use access through C pointers, but the same principles can be used by programs in assembly or other languages. The author also discusses performance considerations.

12

Programming the Enhanced Graphics Adapter

Andrew Dumke

The Enhanced Graphics Adapter (EGA) has established a new standard for high-resolution graphics on the IBM PC and compatibles. The EGA is more flexible and powerful than the Color Graphics Adapter (CGA) it replaces, but also more complex to program. This paper is intended to show how to program the EGA, the similarities and differences between it and previous adapters, and a few graphics routines to make using the EGA much easier. Basic graphics routines will be presented for reading and writing pixels, drawing lines, printing the screen, and manipulating the palette registers. As each of these routines is developed, the different methods of controlling the color and shapes written to the EGA's memory will be covered. These concepts are easily extended to a future programming project of your own.

Inside the EGA

Most of the routines in this paper use EGA output ports and direct memory access for maximum performance. Although there are more than 60 EGA output registers, the few ports covered here are enough for most programming projects. The EGA BIOS is also more involved than the few calls covered here would indicate, but not many graphics programs need to use any more than the most basic BIOS functions.

While many of the improvements over the CGA have to do with text, only the EGA graphics modes will be examined in detail. Every code listing in this paper is EGA-specific, and does not apply at all to the CGA. The routines use C pointers for direct memory access. If pointers are unfamiliar to you, you may want to brush up on them before modifying any of these routines.

Compiling the Examples

The examples included were developed using Microsoft C version 4, and Borland's Turbo C version 1. These two compilers are source code compatible. There may be some syntactic differences with other compilers but the concepts are the same. All the EGA functions have been separated into separate C functions. As you read this paper, keep two separate files. The first, `ega.c`, should contain the EGA C functions covered in this paper. Each code listing has a comment to remind you to add the functions to `ega.c` that are used later. The second file, `ega.h`, will contain the function prototypes for the functions in `ega.c` and EGA-specific macros.

Once `ega.c` has been compiled, the EGA-specific functions in `ega.obj` may be called by any program by linking that program with `ega.obj`.

Microsoft C

To compile all examples under Microsoft C, use:

```
MSC example.c /W 3 ;
LINK example ;
```

The `/W 3` compiler switch turns on strong type-checking to help you catch errors. If you keep the EGA functions in a separate source code file, compile with these statements:

```
MSC ega.c /W 3 ;
MSC example.c /W 3 ;
LINK example + ega ;
```

If you use Microsoft C version 3.0, add the `/Ze` compiler switch to enable the `far` keyword.

Borland Turbo C:

The Borland Turbo C compiler will compile and link in a single step. To compile with Turbo C, use:

```
TCC EXAMPLE
```

If you keep the EGA functions separate, use:

```
TCC EXAMPLE EGA
```

where `EXAMPLE` is the file with your code, and `EGA` contains EGA-specific graphic functions. Strong type-checking is the default with Turbo C so no compiler switches are necessary.

History of the EGA

IBM introduced the EGA in 1984. It is well on the way to becoming the dominant color graphics display adapter for the IBM PC. The EGA is compatible with the two other popular IBM display adapters, the CGA and the Monochrome Display Adapter (MDA). With the introduction of the new PS/2 systems, IBM introduced three new video standards: the MCGA on the PS/2 model 30, the Video Graphics Array (VGA) on all other PS/2s, and the optional high-resolution 8514/A. The MCGA is compatible with the older CGA standard but not the EGA. The VGA and 8514/A both support most EGA programs. The MCGA may be upgraded to a VGA. Essentially, the EGA is the new lowest common denominator for IBM color graphics, replacing the older CGA.

The original EGA from IBM comes with 64K of graphics memory on the card which may be expanded in 64K increments to 256K. The more EGA memory, the greater the graphics capabilities. EGA compatible cards from other manufacturers often come with the full 256K memory already installed.

Video functions on the IBM PC are called with the BIOS Interrupt 10h. These video functions allow a program to set text or graphics modes, read or write single pixels, and place characters on the screen. The EGA has a new BIOS that replaces all the original PC video functions, and adds several new BIOS functions. The new EGA functions allow new characters to be defined, more control over the palette, and text strings to be printed. Several of the new BIOS function calls relating to graphics will be covered later, but the new EGA BIOS calls for text functions will not be covered in this essay.

Monitors and EGA Capabilities

The EGA is designed to work with one of three different monitors—the IBM Color Display (CD), the IBM Enhanced Color Display (ECD), or the IBM Monochrome Display (MD)—and their equivalents from other manufacturers. The monitor used determines the graphics resolution, the maximum number of colors, the color palette, and the number of pixels that make up each character.

The IBM Color Monitor has a maximum resolution of 640x200 pixels. The Color Monitor is limited to 200 scan lines vertically by only being able to use one vertical scan rate. The EGA is compatible with all the text and graphic modes of the Color Graphics Adapter when used with the Color Monitor. There are two new graphics modes, modes 13 and 14, that use up to 16 colors with 320x200 and 640x200 resolution. However, the Color Monitor is limited to a 16-color fixed palette and 200 scan lines vertically. The fixed palette uses the same 16 colors used by the CGA in text mode. The default character box is 8x8 pixels. The modes available with the IBM Color Monitor are listed in Table 12-1.

Table 12-1. IBM Color Monitor Modes

Mode Number	Type	Maximum Colors	Size (Col. × Row)	Box Size	Maximum Pages	Buffer Segment	Resolution
0	Text	16	40x25	8x8	8	B800	320x200
1	Text	16	40x25	8x8	8	B800	320x200
2	Text	16	80x25	8x8	4/8/8*	B800	640x200
3	Text	16	80x25	8x8	4/8/8*	B800	640x200
4	Graphics	4	40x25	8x8	1	B800	320x200
5	Graphics	4	40x25	8x8	1	B800	320x200
6	Graphics	2	80x25	8x8	1	B800	640x200
13	Graphics	16	40x25	8x8	2/4/8*	A000	320x200
14	Graphics	16	80x25	8x8	1/2/4*	A000	640x200

* Depends on amount of installed EGA memory

Enhanced Color Display

The IBM Enhanced Color Display is compatible with all the modes used with the Color Monitor, and uses one more high-resolution mode. The Enhanced Color Display is able to use two vertical scan rates, one for 200 line modes and one for 350 line modes. The new multisync-type monitors are able to use the two standard EGA-generated vertical scan rates as well as even higher frequencies for higher resolution. The high-resolution mode, mode 16, can be used *only* with the IBM Enhanced Color Display, an equivalent monitor, or a multisync monitor since the vertical resolution is 350 scan lines and the Color Display can only display 200 lines. The EGA can display 16 colors from a 64-color palette in most modes when used with the Enhanced Color Display. The 16 colors are only available in mode 16 if there is more than 64K on the EGA card. Modes 4 through 6, the CGA compatible graphics modes, are limited to the same 16-color fixed palette as the CGA. The text modes on the Enhanced Color Display use 8x14 pixels for each character, which gives a higher-resolution character than used on the CGA. The modes for the Enhanced Color Display (and multisync equivalents) are listed in Table 12-2.

Monochrome Graphics Modes

The IBM Monochrome Display is used primarily as a text-only display. The text mode is compatible with the IBM Monochrome Adapter. However, there is a new mode that adds 640x350 graphics with four "colors": black, video, flashing video, and intensified video. If a Monochrome Monitor is connected to the EGA, it is unable to use any of the color graphics modes, but may use the new monochrome graphics mode.

The EGA converts the 8x14 font used with Enhanced Color Monitor into an MDA-compatible 9x14 font. This is accomplished by extending any line draw characters into the 9th pixel position.

Table 12-2.   Enhanced Color Display Modes

Mode Number	Type	Maximum Colors	Size (Col. × Row)	Box Size	Maximum Pages	Buffer Segment	Resolution
0	Text	16 of 64	40x25	8x14	8	B800	320x350
1	Text	16 of 64	40x25	8x14	8	B800	320x350
2	Text	16 of 64	40x25	8x14	4/8/8*	B800	640x350
3	Text	16 of 64	80x25	8x14	4/8/8*	B800	640x350
4	Graphics	4	40x25	8x8	1	B800	320x200
5	Graphics	4	40x25	8x8	1	B800	320x200
6	Graphics	2	80x25	8x8	1	B800	640x200
13	Graphics	16 of 64	40x25	8x8	2/4/8*	A000	320x200
14	Graphics	16 of 64	80x25	8x8	1/2/4*	A000	640x200
16	Graphics	4/16 of 64*	80x25	8x14	1/2*	A000	640x350

* Depends on amount of installed EGA memory

The addition of multiple video pages is a subtle change in the standard MDA mode 7, the text mode, with the EGA. The original Monochrome Adapter uses only one page. The EGA can store up to eight individual video pages, depending on the amount of EGA memory. The page number is specified in the 8086 register BH when using the BIOS functions for text. If older software uses BH for other data, or fails to initialize it, the final text output may not appear on the desired page.

EGA-compatible cards from other manufacturers may offer a Hercules-compatible graphics mode when used with a Monochrome Display. The two modes for the Monochrome Display are listed in Table 12-3.

Table 12-3.   Monochrome Display Modes

Mode Number	Type	Maximum Colors	Size (Col. × Row)	Box Size	Maximum Pages	Buffer Segment	Resolution
7	Text	4	80x25	9x14	4/8*	B000	720x350
15	Graphics	4	80x25	8x14	1/2*	A000	640x350

* Depends on amount of installed EGA memory

Installation Considerations and Presence Test

Notice that the capabilities of the EGA are dependent on the monitor and the amount of memory on the EGA board. The monitor determines which video mode to use for graphics or text, and the amount of EGA memory determines the number of colors and pages available. It is very important for your programs to determine whether there is an EGA present in the PC before you try to use it, and which monitor and memory were used if one is found.

EGA BIOS routine: Return EGA Information (INT 0x10)

The program we will show next does just that. The function `get_ega_info(&info)` is called with a pointer to a structure to hold EGA information. The function first retrieves a byte from the BIOS data area. That byte, at 0x40:0x87, has encoded information about the EGA hardware configuration, memory, and monitor. It is one of several status bytes kept by the EGA BIOS for its internal use and to provide information to programs. The bits we are interested in are bits 5 and 6 which indicate total EGA memory, bit 3 which indicates whether the EGA is the active display, and bit 1 which indicates the type of monitor. The Function calls one of the EGA's new BIOS calls, alternate Function 10, which returns EGA information. This function is called by placing 0x12 in register AH and 0x10 in BL, and using `INT 10H`. Since the PC's BIOS does *not* use a video function 0x12, this call can be used as an EGA presence test. The PC's BIOS will safely reject unknown `INT 10H` calls with the registers unchanged, so if the outgoing registers are unchanged by the call, or the incoming registers do not match the data in the EGA information byte, there is simply no EGA present. Here is the EGA BIOS call which returns the information:

Call with:	AH =	0x12 To Select EGA Alternate Functions
	BL =	0x10 Alternate Function for EGA Information
Returns:	BH =	0 = Color Monitor
		1 = Monochrome Monitor
	BL =	Encoded EGA Memory:
		0 = 64K
		1 = 128K
		2 = 192K
		3 = 256K
	CH =	Feature Bits
	CL =	EGA Board Switch Settings

The `egacheck.c` Program and Macros

This program will check for an active EGA display card. (There may be another display card in the system. If another card is active, bit 3 of the byte at 0x40:0x87 will be 1.) If an active EGA card is found, some information about the setup is saved.

Notice the macro `PEEK_BYTE(seg,off)`, which allows this program to retrieve a byte from anywhere in the PC's memory. It works by shifting the value for the segment left one word (16 bits), and then bit ORing the offset to form a long int. This long int is then cast to a far pointer.

Also notice the definition #define LINT_ARGS. If you wish to use the Microsoft C's built-in lint on the library functions, you must define this before all the #include directives. You also must compile with the /W 3 compiler option to use the Microsoft lint. With LINT_ARGS at the top, before the #includes, the compiler will check all library function calls for argument-type agreement and number of arguments.

```c
/* egacheck.c */
/* Checks for an EGA */
/* If one is found, information is saved */
#define LINT_ARGS    /* Enable strong type checking */
#include <conio.h>
#include <dos.h>
#include <stdio.h>

#define PEEK_BYTE(seg,off) \
     (*(char far *) ( (long)(seg)<<16 ¦ (off) ) )

/* Add this template to "ega.h" */
struct Ega_info
{
  char monitor ; /* to hold the type of monitor */
  int  memory ;  /* amount of memory: 64, 128, 192, 256K */
  char high_res_graphics ;
  char text_mode ;
} ;              /* Template to hold information about EGA */

/* Add this function prototype to "ega.h" */
int get_ega_info(struct Ega_info *) ;

main()
{
struct Ega_info info ;

if(get_ega_info(&info))       /* test for EGA */
 {
   printf("\n\nEGA in use.") ;
   printf("\nConnected to a") ;
   switch(info.monitor)
   {
     case 'C': puts(" Color Monitor") ;
               break ;
```

```
        case 'M': puts(" Monochrome Monitor") ;
                break ;
        case 'H': puts("n Enhanced Color Monitor") ;
                break ;
        default: break ;    /* undefined */
    }
    printf("\n%iK bytes of EGA Memory.", info.memory) ;
    printf("\nMode %#2i is the highest resolution graphics mode.",
        (int)info.high_res_graphics) ;
    printf("\nMode %#2i is the text mode.\n\n",
        (int)info.text_mode) ;
 }
else
 puts("\nNo active EGA.") ;
}                          /* End of main() */


int get_ega_info(info)
struct Ega_info *info ;

/* This function tests if an active EGA is in the system */
/* Add this function to ega.c */
/* Be SURE to use "get_ega_info(&info)" IE USE THE "&"
   IN FRONT OF "INFO" */
{
    union REGS regs ;
    int i ;
/* Get the EGA information byte from the BIOS data area */
    char bios_info = PEEK_BYTE(0x40,0x87) ;

    /* Bit 3 indicates if the EGA is active or not
    ** it is NOT a test for presence */
    if(bios_info & 0x8)
        return (0) ;    /* if bit 3 is 1, EGA is NOT active */

    regs.h.ah = 0x12 ; /* EGA Alternate BIOS Function */
    regs.h.bl = 0x10 ; /* Get Info */
    regs.h.bh = 0xFF ; /* An impossible return value */
    int86(0x10, &regs, &regs) ;   /* EGA BIOS Video Call */

/* bios_info bits 5 + 6 and BL(encoded EGA memory) and */
/* bios_info bit 1 and BH must be equal if there is an EGA */
if((regs.h.bl != ((bios_info & 0x60) >> 5)) || /* Memory */
   (regs.h.bh != ((bios_info & 0x2) >> 1)) || /* Monitor */
```

```
    (regs.h.bh == 0xFF))                              /* BH != FF */
     return(0) ; /* if any test fails, return, no EGA */


 /* OK, there is an EGA, save the type of monitor */
 /* The monitor type code is:
      'C' for color,
      'M' for mono,
      'H' for highres */
 switch(regs.h.cl) /* cl has the EGA switch settings */
 {
     case 0:   /* mono primary, EGA color 40x25 */
     case 6:   /* mono second, EGA color 40x25 */
         info->monitor = 'C' ;
         info->high_res_graphics = 0xD ;
         info->text_mode = 0x1 ;
         break ;
     case 1:   /* mono primary, EGA color 80x25 */
     case 2:   /* same as 1 */
     case 7:   /* mono second, EGA color 80x25 */
     case 8:   /* same as 7 */
         info->monitor = 'C' ;
         info->high_res_graphics = 0xE ;
         info->text_mode = 0x3 ;
         break ;
     case 3:   /* mono primary, EGA high res */
     case 9:   /* EGA high res primary, mono second */
         info->monitor = 'H' ;
         info->high_res_graphics = 0x10 ;
         info->text_mode = 0x3 ;
         break ;
     case 4:   /* color 40 primary, EGA mono */
     case 5:   /* color 80 primary, EGA mono */
     case 10:  /* EGA mono primary, color 40 second */
     case 11:  /* EGA mono primary, color 80 second */
         info->monitor = 'M' ;
         info->high_res_graphics = 0xF ;
         info->text_mode = 0x7 ;
         break ;
     default:  /* Reserved Switch Settings */
     return (0) ;
 }
 /* EGA is active in this system, return the memory */
 return(info->memory = 64 * (regs.h.bl + 1) ) ;
}
```

EGA BIOS Routine: Write Dot (INT 0x10)

Now that we know what mode to use for graphics, we can draw something on the display. The EGA BIOS has the same write dot call as the PC BIOS. This call is slow, but usable on all IBM graphics cards. Here is the specifics of the EGA BIOS Write Dot:

Call With: AH = 0xC To Select Write Dot Function

BH = Page

DX = Row Number

CX = Col Number

AL = Color Value

Returns: Nothing

Notice the addition of a page value in BH. If you are converting older soft-ware to run on the EGA, make sure the page number is in BH before calling INT 10H. Programs written for the monochrome adapter, or the CGA in graphics mode, are especially vulnerable to this oversight.

The BIOS call to switch to a graphics mode is precisely the same as on the PC, namely Function 0 of INT 10H. *However, the BIOS does not check that the mode you select will not damage your monitor.* A monochrome monitor, connected to an EGA, may be damaged by a color text or graphics mode signal, so it is important to check for monitor and mode compatibility. The function get_ega_info(&info) from the EGACHECK program is used to check the moni-tor and find the high-resolution mode that is safe to use. The program in the next listing demonstrates the use of set_crt_mode() to set a graphics mode, and dot() which uses the BIOS write dot function. The program will draw a series of parallel diagonal lines.

```
/* diagonal.c */
/* Demonstrates the EGA high res graphic mode */
#define LINT_ARGS
#include <conio.h>
#include <dos.h>
#include <stdio.h>
#include "ega.h"

void set_crt_mode( char ) ; /* Add this to "ega.h" */
void dot( int, int, int, int ) ;

main()
```

```
{
    register i,j ;
    struct Ega_info info ;
    if(get_ega_info(&info))
        set_crt_mode(info.high_res_graphics) ;
    else
        return(1) ;

    for(j = 0; j <= 500; j += 5)
    for(i = 0; i <= 100; ++i)
        dot(i,i+j,13,0) ;
    getch() ;          /* wait for a character to be typed */
    set_crt_mode(info.text_mode) ;
}


/*====================================*/
void dot(row,col,color,page)
int row, col, color, page;
{
    union REGS regs ;
    regs.x.dx = row ;
    regs.x.cx = col ;
    regs.h.al = (char)color ;
    regs.h.ah = (char)0xC ;        /* Write Dot call */
    regs.h.bh = (char)page ;       /* NEW TO THE EGA! */
    int86(0x10, &regs, &regs) ;
}


/*====================================*/
void set_crt_mode(mode)
/* Add this function to ega.c */
char mode ;
{
    union REGS regs ;
    regs.h.al = mode ;             /* al=mode to set */
    regs.h.ah = (char)0 ;          /* Set Mode Function */
    int86(0x10, &regs, &regs) ;    /* execute BIOS int 10h */
}
/*====================================*/
```

When you see how slow the BIOS write dot function is, you will probably wonder about making it faster. To do that requires bypassing the EGA BIOS and putting pixels directly into the EGA's memory. However, you first must understand how the EGA's memory is organized, and how to control it.

Memory Organization

The EGA uses two different display memory organizations for graphics. In modes 4 through 6, the EGA uses the same memory organization as the CGA. In these modes, the display memory segment starts at 0xB800 and uses 80 bytes per scan line. Since there are 200 scan lines, 16,000 bytes are used. In the medium resolution 320x200 mode, each byte represents four pixels with one of four colors, or two bits per pixel. In mode 6, each byte represents eight pixels with two colors, or one bit per pixel. If a bit is 1, the corresponding pixel is on, and if a bit is 0 the corresponding pixel is off. Additionally, the even-numbered scan lines are in the first 8K of the display memory, and the odd-numbered scan lines are in the second 8K of memory. The split scan line memory requires every pixel's offset to be tested if it is in the even or odd bank.

The display memory for modes 13 through 16 starts at segment 0xA000 and uses up to 64K of the 8086 CPU address space. (Where is the 256K of EGA memory I paid for? More on that in a minute.) Each byte represents eight pixels with the most significant bit being the leftmost. The scan lines are not separated in memory like they are in the CGA modes, so the byte offset of a pixel is easier to calculate. In mode 16, the EGA has a maximum resolution of 640x350, or 224,000 pixels. Since there are up to 16 colors, each pixel uses four bits to specify the color. This is a total memory usage of (640 $\times$ 350 pixels $\div$ 8 pixels/byte $\times$ 4 bits/pixel $\div$ 1024 bytes/K) = 109K. But the 8086 CPU used in the PC can only address a segment of 64K. The EGA fits into the 64K segment limit by dividing 128K of its 256K memory into four 32K bit planes. Each bit plane (or bit map) corresponds to one bit of a pixel's color. Imagine these four bit planes as being stacked on top of each other at the same CPU address. Each CPU display memory address is actually four bytes of EGA memory.

Latch Registers

Reading or writing four different bytes (one for each bit plane) at the same address presents a problem. To overcome this problem, the EGA has four *latch registers*. These hold one byte from each of the four bit planes temporarily. Each of the four latch registers is filled with a byte from each of the bit planes at the address last read by the CPU. When the CPU sends a byte to the address last read, each of the four latch register contents may be unchanged, modified, or entirely replaced by the CPU data. The latch register contents are then written back to the EGA's bit planes. When the latch registers are written back to the EGA's bit planes, they are again "stacked," with each bit of the four bytes forming the four-bit color for eight pixels. The relationship between the latch registers and the bit planes is shown in Figure 12-1. The state of the EGA's memory and the contents of the four latch registers after the CPU reads the byte at A000:0000 are represented. The 8 pixels in the byte contain colors 0 through 7. It is important to understand that the byte returned to the CPU after reading A000:0000 has no use. That byte is read only to establish which pixels to work with (in this case pixels 0 through 7 in row 0), and to "prime" the latch registers, allowing the individual bytes of the bit planes to be manipulated by CPU data. Then the eight pixels contained in the four bytes can be modified, replaced, or cleared by the PC's CPU. To work with pixels in a different row or column, the offset from A000 is changed and a new byte containing the pixels is read by the CPU.

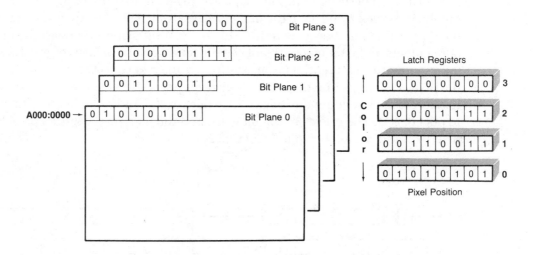

Fig. 12-1.   EGA bit maps and latch registers.

Whether the latch registers are modified, replaced, or unchanged by the CPU depends on the settings of several EGA control registers. These registers are accessed through one of five indexed Very Large Scale Integration (VLSI) chips on the EGA. These VLSI chips are set by sending an index number corresponding to the function desired, followed by the data for that function. Essentially, the index corresponds to one of many registers internal to the EGA, but mapped to a single PC output port. Data for these registers are sent using the 8086 OUT instruction or the C library's outp() function. For example, the EGA has a bit-mask register that will allow individual bits of the latch registers to be protected from change. Setting a bit to 0 in this register masks out the corresponding bit in the latch registers, and setting a bit to 1 allows that bit to be changed by CPU writes. The bit-mask register allows individual pixels to be changed without altering an adjacent pixel's address by the byte. In other words, the bit-mask register allows individual pixels to be changed rather than the entire byte full of pixels. The bit-mask register is Function number 8 on the EGA's Graphics ~ 1&2 chip. It is programmed by sending an index of 8 to port 0x3CE followed by the bit-mask data to port 0x3CF. The following C statements would set the bit-mask register to protect all bits except bit 2:

```
outp(0x3CE, 8) ;      /* The index of the bit mask */
outp(0x3CF, 0x2) ;    /* All bits, except bit 2, to 0 */
```

But these statements give no clue, except for the comments, to what they do. In the next section, we will cover a C macro to make setting the EGA registers easier.

A second EGA register that affects how the latch register contents are re-written is the map-mask register. If any of the four bits of the map-mask register are zero, the corresponding bit maps are protected from change. Sending a number between 0 and 15 to the map-mask register will allow that color corresponding to that number to be written to the EGA's bit planes. However, the previous contents of the bit maps are not cleared, and must be before setting the map mask—but after setting the bit mask—by writing a zero to the byte containing the pixel to change. The map-mask register is part of the EGA's Sequencer chip. It is accessed by sending the index of 2 to port 0x3C4 and sending the map mask to port 0x3C5. The effects of the bit mask and the map mask, setting pixel 2 on map 0, 2, and 3, are shown in Figure 12-2.

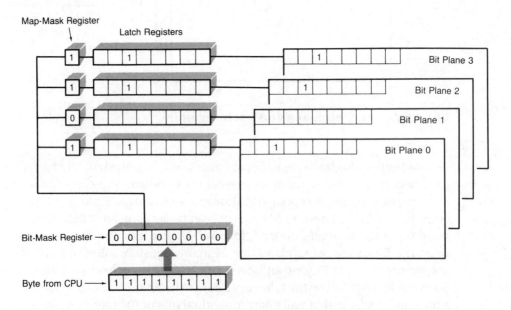

Fig. 12-2. Bit-mask and map-mask registers.

With these two registers, and an understanding of the EGA latch registers, we have enough information to create a routine in C that will directly write a dot into screen memory. This routine is faster than the same routine in the EGA's BIOS. On an 8MHz AT, the EGA BIOS will put 2.65 dots on the display in one millisecond (2.65 dots/ms). The routine in the listing in the next section FASTDOT.C puts 7.55 dots/ms on the display, or an increase in speed of 185 percent. The drawback is that `fastdot()` will work only in EGA graphics modes and would have to be rewritten for another display card.

More Macros

The first thing we need to do is define some routines to access the EGA's VLSI controllers. These macros will allow the routine to set the bit mask, the map mask, and other internal EGA registers.

```
#define EGA_GRFX(index, value)  { outp(0x3CE, index) ; \
                                  outp(0x3CF, value) ;}
#define EGA_SQNC(index, value)  { outp(0x3C4, index) ; \
                                  outp(0x3C5, value) ;}
```

The first macro, `EGA_GRFX`, takes as arguments the index number corresponding to the function desired on the Graphics ~ 1&2 controller chip, as well as the value to send to the chip. The EGA's Graphics 1&2 chips control the access to the bit planes. Although there are actually two chips at the same address, you can treat the Graphics ~ 1&2 chips as one chip. The address to index the Graphics ~ 1&2 chip is 0x3CE, and the data address is 0x3CF. The macro expands into two C statements. The first statement sends the index value to the chips using the library function `outp()`. The second statement sends the data.

The second macro, `EGA_SQNC`, is similar to `EGA_GRFX`. However, `EGA_SQNC` accesses a different chip, the EGA's Sequencer chip, by sending the index and data to different output ports. The Sequencer chip's main interest here is the map-mask register.

The next two macros will allow the routine to access a segment:offset address anywhere in the PC's address space:

```
#define PEEK_BYTE(s,o)  (*(char far *) ( (long)(s)<<16 ¦ (o) ) )
#define PEEK_WORD(s,o)  (*(int far *) ( (long)(s)<<16 ¦ (o) ) )
```

The final macros give a name to some common uses of the previous macros. The `GET_CRT_COLS()` macro returns the value to use for the number of bytes per line in the EGA graphics modes. `EGA_BIT_MASK` and `EGA_MAP_MASK` set the bit-mask and the map-mask registers, respectively.

```
#define GET_CRT_COLS()  PEEK_WORD(0x40, 0x4a)
#define EGA_BIT_MASK(mask)  EGA_GRFX(8, mask)
#define EGA_MAP_MASK(mask)  EGA_SQNC(2, mask)
```

These macros make the following code written to manipulate EGA hardware far easier to read and understand. The six macros: EGA_GRFX, EGA_SQNC, PEEK_BYTE, PEEK_WORD, EGA_BIT_MASK, and EGA_MAP_MASK should be added to ega.h. These macros are used in all the routines in the rest of this paper.

```c
/* fastdot.c */
#include <conio.h>
#include "ega.h"

fastdot(row, col, color)
/* add this function to ega.c */
/* This routine will put a dot in the EGA's display buffer
** Use only in EGA graphics modes (13,14,15, or 16)
** and on an EGA with 128K memory or greater */
int    row, col, color;
{
char latch ;
/* establish the address of the byte to change */
/* buffer byte is A000:((row * bytes/row) + col/8) */
   unsigned char far *rgen = (char far *)(0xA00000000L +
                               (col >> 3)  +
                               (row * GET_CRT_COLS()) ) ;
/* Calculate the bit to change: */
   char bit_mask = (char)(0x80 >> (col & 7)) ;
   EGA_BIT_MASK(bit_mask) ;         /* set the bit mask */
   latch = *(rgen) ;                /* prime the EGA latches */
   *(rgen) = 0 ;                    /* clear the bit */
   EGA_MAP_MASK(color) ;            /* set the color */
   *(rgen) = 0xFF ;                 /* set the bit */
   EGA_MAP_MASK(0xF) ;              /* reset the map mask */
   EGA_BIT_MASK(0xFF) ;             /* reset the bit mask */
}
```

Write-Only Register in the EGA

Notice the last two lines where the map mask and the bit mask are reset. The majority of EGA registers are write-only. Any concurrent or subsequent program that uses the display needs to make assumptions about the state of the EGA, because a write-only register cannot be read. Therefore, the safest state to leave the EGA registers in is the EGA BIOS default state. Additionally, the EGA BIOS assumes the EGA registers are in the default state when writing characters on the display. If the bit-mask register is set to mask bits, the characters will be unreadable. For the bit mask and the map mask, the default is no mask at all, so a "mask" of 0xF and 0xFF restores the default state.

Also notice how the byte address of the pixel is calculated:

```
char far *rgen = (char far *)(0xA0000000L +
                 (col >> 3) +
                 (row * GET_CRT_COLS()) );
```

The address of the byte is ((row × bytes per row) + cols ÷ 8 bits per byte). For the division of cols by 8, C's shift right operator, the >> is used for greater speed. Since 8 = 2 × 2 × 2 = 2 << 3, then cols ÷ 8 = cols >> 3. To calculate the number of bytes per row, which can be 40 bytes in video mode 13 or 80 bytes in modes 14 through 16, look at the number of characters per row in the BIOS data area (address 0x40:0x4A). The number of bytes per row and the characters per row are the same in the EGA graphics modes. The result of the total calculation is added to 0xA0000000L, which is the segment of the EGA graphics modes. The entire value is then cast to a far pointer.

The bit number in the byte that corresponds to the pixel to change is calculated by (col~&~7). Once the bit number is known, the bit mask is set to 0x80 >> bit number. The value 0x80 is 010000000b.

The routine above assumes that page 0 is used. To add the ability to address a page other than page 0, add these lines:

```
while(page){
  rgen += PEEK_WORD(0x40, 0x4c) ;   /* add the page length */
  --page ;}
```

where page is the number of the page to address. The word at 0x40:0x4C contains the length of the CRT Display buffer in bytes used by the EGA's BIOS routines.

Try the DIAGONAL.C program after replacing dot with fastdot(). It is two to three times faster than the BIOS routine.

Lots of Dots

For maximum performance on the EGA, many functions need to be written to take advantage of unique EGA hardware. For example, the fastdot routine above set the bit mask and map mask to the needed values at the beginning of the routine, then reset those registers to the BIOS default state at the end. If a function calls the fastdot routine repeatedly, the register reset at the end of the fastdot routine is repeated unnecessarily. That slows the function down. The program BRES.C shown next includes a line drawing routine that is based on Bresenham's Algorithm. Bresenham's Algorithm was originally used to control digital plotters, but it is equally suited for bit/map CRT graphics. The algorithm always increments (or decrements) by 1 in either the x or y direction. The x or y direction is selected by the magnitude of the slope of the line. If the rise (y direction) is greater, increment (or decrement) y; if the run (x direction) is greater, increment (or decrement) x. Whether to increment or decrement x and y is decided by the direction of the line. A cumulative error term is used to decide when to increment or decrement in the perpendicular direction. Instead of calling the fastdot routine above, the dots are placed on the display directly. The EGA registers are reset only once at the end, and the function is much faster than the same one written based on a calling `fastdot()`.

```c
/* bres.c */
/* Draws a pattern to demonstrate the line() function */
#define LINT_ARGS
#include <conio.h>
#include <dos.h>
#include <stdio.h>
#include "ega.h"

void line(int,int,int,int,int) ;  /* Add this to ega.h */
/*=============================================================*/
main()
{
    int x1, y1, x2, y2 ;
    int step = 10, color = 13, scan_lines ;
    struct Ega_info info ;

    if(get_ega_info(&info) >= 128) /* Active EGA? Memory? */
    {
        set_crt_mode(info.high_res_graphics) ;
        scan_lines = (PEEK_BYTE(0x40, 0x84) + 1)
                        * PEEK_WORD(0x40, 0x85) ;
        y2 = (scan_lines - 1) - ((scan_lines - 1) % step) ;
        for (y1 = 0, x1 = 0, x2 = 0;
                y1 <= y2;
                y1 += step, x2 += step)
            line(x1,y1,x2,y2,color) ;
        getch() ;       /* Wait for a key press */
        set_crt_mode(info.text_mode) ;
    }
    else
        puts("\nEGA adapter not active or not installed.\n") ;
}
/*=============================================================*/
void line(x1,y1,x2,y2,color)
```

```
int x1,y1,x2,y2,color ;
/* A fast line function - uses Bresenham's algorithm. */
/* row(y's) and col(x's) and are assumed not equal */
#define sign(x) (((x) < 0) ? (-1) : (1))
#define qabs(x) (((x) < 0) ? -(x) : (x))
{
int dx = qabs(x2 - x1) ; /* run */
int dy = qabs(y2 - y1) ; /* rise */
int s1 = sign(x2 - x1) ; /* direction to increment/decrement */
int s2 = sign(y2 - y1) ;
int dx2, dy2, bytes_per_line = GET_CRT_COLS() ;
register error_term, i ;
unsigned char far *rgen = (char far *)(0xA0000000L) ;
unsigned char exchange = (char)0 ;


/* The larger of rise or run determines
** which to increment in the loop */
if(dy > dx)
  { int temp = dx; dx = dy; dy = temp; exchange = (char)1;  }

dx2 = (dx << 1) ;          /* Used repeatedly, calculate now */
dy2 = (dy << 1) ;          /* Use shifts for speed */
error_term = (dy - dx) << 1 ; /* Initialize error_term */
EGA_GRFX(0, color) ;  /* Use the EGA's Set/Reset Register */
EGA_GRFX(1, 0xF) ;    /* Enable all bit planes */
for (i=1; i<=dx; ++i) /* All the pixels along the line */
  {
  EGA_BIT_MASK(0x80 >> (x1 & 7) ) ;
  rgen[ ((x1 >> 3) + (y1 * bytes_per_line)) ] += 0x1 ;
    while (error_term >= 0)  /* loop until another pixel */
    {
     if (exchange)
         x1 += s1 ;
     else
         y1 += s2 ;
    error_term -= dx2 ;
    }
    if (exchange)
        y1 += s2 ;
    else
        x1 += s1 ;
    error_term += dy2 ;
  }
EGA_GRFX(1, 0) ;       /* Disable the Set/Reset register */
```

```
EGA_BIT_MASK(0xFF) ; /* Reset the bit mask */
}
/*===============================================================*/
```

To keep the graphic image on the screen, a program should have the height and width of the display in pixels. The width is given by `GET_CRT_COLS()` * 8 pixels/byte. The height could be determined exactly with a table containing scan line counts for each mode. However, there is a quicker but less accurate way. Both the number of character rows and the point size (bytes per character) are programmable on the EGA, and therefore, either one can change. The height, however, of the character box in bytes and the number of scan lines determine the number of rows. Since the word at 0x40:0x85 has the bytes per character and the byte at 0x40:0x84 has the number of rows, they can be used to calculate the number of scan lines for any video mode. The C statement:

```
scan_lines = (PEEK_BYTE(0x40, 0x84) + 1)
                * PEEK_WORD(0x40, 0x85) ;
```

calculates the approximate value for total scan lines—approximate since the number of rows is rounded down and may or may not be off by 1. Once the EGA data are known, the program draws a pattern of lines that is independent of the EGA graphics mode used.

Using the Set/Reset Register

The `line()` function uses a different method to specify the color of dots on the display than the `fastdot()` routine. The `fastdot()` routine uses the map-mask register to specify the color, but since specifying a mask to the map-mask register does not clear the previous dot, the dot must be cleared with the map mask first reset to 0xF and then set to the color of the new dot. In other words, both the map mask and EGA memory must be accessed twice for every dot to set to a specific color. The `line()` function uses the set/reset register and the enable set/reset register to specify the color. The set/reset register will set a byte to 0xFF in each EGA bit plane where a bit is on in the set/reset register, and will reset a byte to 0 in each EGA bit plane where a bit is off. Therefore, the previous contents of the latch registers are replaced with the color number corresponding to the value set in the set/reset register. The map-mask register has no effect on the set/reset register but the bit-mask register is usable to protect adjacent pixels. To use the set/reset register, you must first enable it with the enable set/reset register. The BIOS default state for the enable set/reset register is 0, which means that the set/reset register is turned off. Each bit of a four-bit value sent to the enable set/reset register corresponds to an EGA bit plane. If a bit in the enable set/reset register is 0, the corresponding bit plane is protected from change by the set/reset register. The set/reset register and the enable set/reset register are part of the EGA's graphics controller. The set/reset register is accessed by first sending an index of 0 to port 0x3CE, then sending the four-bit color code to port 0x3CF. The set/reset register only affects the bit planes enabled in the enable set/reset register. The enable set/reset register is accessed by sending an index of 1 to port 0x3CE, then sending the four-bit map mask to port 0x3CF.

Notice the statement `rgen[ ((x1>>3) + (y1 * bytes_per_line)) ] += 0x1 ;`. Since the EGA display buffer is linear, it can be easily addressed as an array. The expression inside the brackets calculates the buffer offset of the byte to change. The right side of the statement would seem to be adding 1 to that byte, and that is what the CPU thinks it is doing. However, the actual purpose is to preserve the adjacent pixels contained in the byte. When the bit-mask register is used, the display buffer must be read first to fill the latch registers so that the other bits in the byte may be preserved. Unlike the map-mask register, when the set/reset register is used, the byte sent by the CPU has no meaning beside establishing addressability of the byte to change. So the `+= 1` does two things: It reads the display buffer in order to prime the latch registers, and then sends a byte back which triggers the set/reset register. The 1 could be any value as long as the C compiler translates the operation into an 8086 instruction that first reads and then stores a byte in the EGA's display memory.

Using the EGA Write Modes

The EGA has three write modes: 0, 1, and 2. Changing the EGA write mode will change the way EGA hardware reacts when the CPU sends a byte to the display buffer. Each write mode is optimized for a different use. Write mode 0 is the general-purpose write mode, write mode 1 is optimized for copying EGA memory regions, and write mode 2 is best used for color fills. Changing the write mode can speed up an operation dramatically.

Write mode 0 is the mode used by the EGA BIOS. It is the most general-purpose write mode. In write mode 0, the color of a pixel may be set by using either the map-mask register or the set/reset register. The map-mask register is used by the EGA BIOS and by the `fastdot()` routine. The `line()` function uses the set/reset register to specify a color. When using the map-mask register, individual pixels may be set by the CPU sending a byte, with the corresponding bits in the byte set to 1. However, adjacent pixels in the byte must be protected with the bit-mask register. When using the set/reset register, the bits in a CPU byte sent to the EGA display do not correspond to pixels. The byte is written only to determine the offset of the pixels to change. The color is specified in the set/reset register, and the bit-mask register allows individual control of pixels.

Write mode 2 is the most similar to write mode 0. Write mode 1 has a special use and will be covered later. In write mode 2, the byte sent from the CPU sets the color rather than individual pixels. The bit-mask register gives control over individual pixels, and, if the bit-mask register is not set, the entire byte of pixels is filled with the color from the CPU. The write mode is specified in bits 0 and 1 of a byte sent to the mode register on Graphics ~ 1&2 chips. The index of the mode register is 5. The program `rect.c` shown next demonstrates write mode 2. The `rect()` routine uses write mode 2 to fill a rectangle with a given color.

```
/* rect.c */
/* this program demonstrates write mode 2 */
#define LINT_ARGS
#include <conio.h>
#include <dos.h>
#include <stdio.h>
#include "ega.h"

void rect(int,int,int,int,char);  /* add to ega.h */

main()
{
int i,j;
set_crt_mode(16); /* Make sure you have the
                  ** right monitor/memory! */
printf("\nColor #:\n");
for (i=0,j=0;i<16;++i,j+=40)
{
    printf(" %2i  ",i);
    rect(50,j,349,j+39,(char)i);
}
getch();
set_crt_mode(3) ;
}

void rect(row1,col1,row2,col2,color)
int col1,row1,col2,row2 ;
char color ;
/* add this function to "ega.c" */
{ /* This Function generates a filled rectangle */
   /* It is assumed that row1 < row2, and col1 < col2 */
unsigned char far *rgen = (char far *)(0xA0000000L) ;
int rows = row2 - row1 ;            /* number of rows */
int cols = (col2 >> 3) - (col1 >> 3) - 1 ; /* total columns */
char left = (char)(0xFF >> (col1 & 7)) ;   /* left bit mask */
char rght = (char)~(0xFF >> (col2 & 7)) ;  /* right bit mask */
```

```
char next_row ;
char bytes_per_line = (char)GET_CRT_COLS() ;
register x,y ;
char latch ;

if (cols < 0)   /* Test if col1 and col2 are in the same byte */
    left &= rght, cols = 0, rght = 0 ;
rgen += bytes_per_line*row1 + (col1 >> 3) ;   /* EGA offset */
next_row = bytes_per_line - cols - 2 ;   /* next row offset */

EGA_GRFX(5,2);              /* Set Write Mode 2 */
for(y = 0 ; y < rows ; y++) /* do every row */
{
  EGA_BIT_MASK(left) ;    /* Set the bit mask for left */
  latch = *(rgen) ;       /* Latch the EGA bit planes */
  *(rgen++) = color ;     /* Set the color, point to next byte */
  EGA_BIT_MASK(0xFF) ;    /* No mask in the center */
  for(x = 0; x < cols; x++) /* do every column */
    {
        latch = *(rgen) ;
        *(rgen++) = color ;
    }
  EGA_BIT_MASK(rght) ;    /* Set the right bit mask */
  latch = *(rgen) ;       /* Latch the EGA bit planes */
  *(rgen++) = color ;     /* Set the color */
  rgen += next_row ;      /* Go to the next row */
}
EGA_BIT_MASK(0xFF) ;      /* Reset the Bit Mask */
EGA_GRFX(5,0) ;          /* Reset the Write Mode */

}
```

Write mode 2 is set with the macro `EGA_GRFX(5,2)`. You must be careful not to send a value other than 0, 1, or 2 since the other bits of the byte sent to the mode register are significant to the EGA. The map-mask register and the bit-mask register are effective in write mode 2, but the set/reset register is not usable. Write mode 0, the BIOS default write mode, is set with `EGA_GRFX(5,0)`. The write mode must be reset to 0 before other programs or BIOS calls are used.

Write mode 1 is used to copy one area of EGA memory to another area rapidly. This is most useful for scrolling, animation, or saving and restoring areas of the screen. Write mode 1 allows you to copy the four bytes in each of the four bit planes with only one CPU read and write. The EGA memory offset containing the eight pixels to copy is read to prime the latch registers, then the offset containing the destination for the eight pixels is written to by the CPU. When

the CPU writes a byte, and the write mode is set to 1, the EGA discards the byte
from the CPU and copies the latch registers to each of the bit planes. Write mode
1 is many times faster than reading the four individual bytes from the bit planes
and then writing the four bytes back at the new address. The bit-mask register is
not usable with write mode 1. All four bytes in the latch registers are written to
all four bit planes regardless of the setting of the bit mask. The map-mask register can be used to protect individual bit planes.

The next program, mode1.c, demonstrates write mode 1. A pattern of lines
is drawn at the top of the screen. That pattern is then copied using write mode 1.
Finally, the edge of the pattern is redrawn rapidly to demonstrate the potential
for animation.

```
/* mode1.c */
/* This program demonstrates EGA write mode 1 */
#define LINT_ARGS
#include <conio.h>
#include <dos.h>
#include <stdio.h>
#include "ega.h"

void copy( int,int,int,int,int,int ) ;

void main()
{
    register i,j;
    int k = 0;
    set_crt_mode(16) ; /* Enhanced Monitor Only! */
    /* Draw an interesting pattern: */
    for(k = 0; k <= 4; ++k)
    for(j = 0+k; j <= 500+k; j += 5)
    for(i = 0+k; i <= 100+k; ++i)
        fastdot(i,i+j,13) ;
    for(k = 0; k <= 3; ++k)
    for(j = 0+k; j <= 500+k; j += 5)
    for(i = 0+k; i <= 100+k; ++i)
        fastdot(i,i+j,3) ;
    /* Copy the pattern 120 rows down: */
    copy(0,0,105,639,    120,0) ;
    while(!kbhit())
    {
/* copy the edge repeatedly,
** gives the illusion of motion: */
        copy(99,100,106,592,    219,100) ;
        copy(99,100,106,592,    219,108) ;
```

```
    }
    set_crt_mode(3) ;
}


void copy(r1_1, c1_1, r2_1, c2_1, r1_2, c1_2)
int        r1_1, c1_1,      /* Upper left corner of source */
           r2_1, c2_1,      /* Lower right corner of source */
           r1_2, c1_2 ;     /* Upper left corner of destination */
{
/* Copies one screen region to another rapidly. Uses
** write mode 1. Only the upper corner of the destination
** needs to be given. */
    char far *source = (char far *)(0xA0000000L) ;
    char far *destination = (char far *)(0xA0000000L) ;
    int rows = r2_1 - r1_1 ;
    int cols = (c2_1 >> 3) - (c1_1 >> 3) ;
    int bytes_per_line = GET_CRT_COLS() ;
    int next_row = bytes_per_line - cols ;
    register x,y ;

    source += bytes_per_line * r1_1 + (c1_1 >> 3) ;
    destination += bytes_per_line * r1_2 + (c1_2 >> 3) ;

    EGA_GRFX(5,1) ;                   /* Set write mode 1 */
    for(y = 0 ; y < rows ; y++)
    {
        for(x = 0; x < cols; x++)
            *(destination++) = *(source++) ;  /* copy four bytes */
        source += next_row ;
        destination += next_row ;
    }
    EGA_GRFX(5,0) ;                   /* Reset the write mode */
}
```

Since the bit-mask register is not usable in write mode 1, the copy() routine
will copy all eight pixels in the source bytes to the destination bytes. In other
words, write mode 1 is only usable on bytes rather than pixels. Write mode 1 can
be used to save an area of the screen to a nonvisible page, which is useful for
implementing pull-down menus. The area under the pull-down menu can be
saved to a nonvisible page, then restored after the user has finished with the
menu. Write mode 1 can only copy to another part of the EGA's memory. Reading
a color from EGA memory requires reading the four bit maps individually.

Reading the Bit Maps

Since each byte of address space in the EGA represents four bytes of graphics memory, EGA memory cannot be read by the CPU directly. The EGA will return the byte from the bit plane selected in the read map select register. The map to read must be set before reading the EGA offset containing the pixels you are interested in. Determining the color of a given pixel requires a separate read from each of the four bit planes. Each bit of the four-bit color value is on one of the four bit planes. The most significant bit of the color value is on bit map 3, and the least significant bit is on bit map 0. The read map select register is index 4 on the EGA's Graphics ~ 1&2 chip. Since each of the EGA's bit maps must be read individually, the value in the read map select register corresponds to only one EGA bit map at a time.

The function readdot returns the color of a pixel on the display. Like fastdot(), it is several times faster than the equivalent BIOS routine to read the color of a dot.

```
/* return the color of a pixel */
int readdot(row,col)
int row,col;
{
    register color = 0 ;
    register latch ;
    unsigned char far *rgen = (char far *)(0xA0000000L +
                            (col >> 3)  +
                            (row * GET_CRT_COLS())) ;
    int bit_number = (col & 7)^7 ;
    int bit_mask = (1 << bit_number) ;
    int plane ;
    /* step through each plane 3,2,1,0 */
    for(plane = 3; plane >= 0; plane--)
    {
        EGA_GRFX(4,plane) ;             /* select plane to read */
        latch = *(rgen) & bit_mask ;    /* bit from that plane */
        latch >>= bit_number ;          /* right justify the bit */
        color <<= 1 ;                   /* make room for new bit */
        color |= latch ;                /* add the bit */
    }
    return(color) ;
}
```

The offset of the byte containing the pixel is determined in exactly the same way as in the fastdot() routine. A value for a bit mask is calculated by determining the bit number of the byte to change. But the bit-mask value is not sent to the EGA's bit-mask register. The EGA's bit-mask register has no effect on bytes read from the EGA. The bit mask is used to isolate the pixel from the byte read from the EGA's bit plane. The bits are then added plane by plane to the pixel's color code. The read map select register selects the map to read from. The bit maps are read backward, (3, 2, 1, 0), since that makes the color code translation easier. Notice that the read map select register is not reset at the end of the routine. The last time through the loop sets the read map select register to 0, which is the default value.

A Print Screen Routine with Dithering

Although the readdot() routine could be used for a graphics print screen routine, it would be very slow (over three minutes). The reason readdot() is so slow for multiple pixels is that each EGA byte is read 32 times to return the color of the eight pixels (8 pixels × 4 bit planes). A print screen routine can be made much faster by reading the EGA four bit planes only once and keeping the values in an array that can then be accessed much quicker. This technique is used in the print screen routine in the next listing. The print screen is written for a Hewlett-Packard LaserJet printer. Since the LaserJet cannot print colors, the prtsc() function uses an array of dither patterns, each unique to one of 16 colors. The array of dither patterns is indexed by the color of the pixel and the row the pixel is on.

```
/* prtsc.c */
/* This function will print a graphics screen to
** an HP LaserJet Printer */
#include <dos.h>
#include <string.h>
#include <stdio.h>
#include <stdlib.h>
#include "ega.h"
prtsc(res)
int res ;
{
/* The array contains 8x8 dither patterns for each EGA color */
    static unsigned char dither[16][8] =
        {
            { 0x00,0x00,0x00,0x00,0x00,0x00,0x00,0x00 },  /* 0 */
            { 0x88,0x44,0x22,0x11,0x88,0x44,0x22,0x11 },  /* 1 */
            { 0x88,0x11,0x22,0x44,0x88,0x11,0x22,0x44 },  /* 2 */
            { 0x18,0x24,0x42,0x81,0x18,0x24,0x42,0x81 },  /* 3 */
```

```
            { 0xAA,0xAA,0xAA,0xAA,0xAA,0xAA,0xAA,0xAA },  /* 4 */
            { 0xFF,0x00,0xFF,0x00,0xFF,0x00,0xFF,0x00 },  /* 5 */
            { 0x88,0x00,0x22,0x00,0x88,0x00,0x22,0x00 },  /* 6 */
            { 0xEE,0xFF,0xBB,0xFF,0xEE,0xFF,0xBB,0xFF },  /* 7 */
            { 0xAA,0x55,0xAA,0x55,0xAA,0x55,0xAA,0x55 },  /* 8 */
            { 0x77,0xBB,0xDD,0xEE,0x77,0xBB,0xDD,0xEE },  /* 9 */
            { 0x77,0xEE,0xDD,0xBB,0x77,0xEE,0xDD,0xBB },  /* 10 */
            { 0xE7,0xDB,0xBD,0x7E,0xE7,0xDB,0xBD,0x7E },  /* 11 */
            { 0xCC,0xCC,0xCC,0xCC,0xCC,0xCC,0xCC,0xCC },  /* 12 */
            { 0xFF,0xFF,0x00,0x00,0xFF,0xFF,0x00,0x00 },  /* 13 */
            { 0xFF,0x00,0xFF,0x00,0xFF,0xFF,0xFF,0x00 },  /* 14 */
            { 0xFF,0xFF,0xFF,0xFF,0xFF,0xFF,0xFF,0xFF }   /* 15 */
        } ;
    union REGS inregs, outregs ;
    int scan_lines = get_scan_lines() ;
    unsigned char far *rgen = (char far *)(0xA0000000L)
                    + (PEEK_WORD(0x40,0x4C)
                    *  PEEK_BYTE(0x40,0x62)) ;
    unsigned char bit_planes[4] ;
    static char start_raster_graphics[] = { "\x1B*r1A" } ;
    static char end_raster_graphics[] = { "\x1B*rB" } ;
    char transfer_graphics[7] ;
    char set_resolution[16] ;
    char buffer[7] ;
    char *cp ;
    int row, col, line, line_multiple ;
    char color, plane ;
    int bit_mask,byte,bit ;
    char crt_mode = PEEK_BYTE(0x40,0x49) ; /* CRT graphics mode */
    int bytes_per_line = GET_CRT_COLS() ;

    if (crt_mode < 13)              /* EGA modes only */
        return(0) ;
    if (crt_mode ==  14)
    /* 640x200 mode, print each line twice */
        line_multiple = 1 ;
    else
        line_multiple = 0 ;

    strcpy(set_resolution,"\x1B*t") ;
    strcat(set_resolution,itoa(res,buffer,10)) ;
    strcat(set_resolution,"R") ;
    cp = strcat(set_resolution, start_raster_graphics) ;
    inregs.x.dx = 0 ;                     /* LPT1 */
```

```
inregs.h.ah = 0 ;                    /* Print character call */
while(inregs.h.al = *cp++)           /* Print the string */
      int86(0x17,&inregs,&outregs) ;
strcpy (transfer_graphics,"\x1B*b") ;
strcat (transfer_graphics,itoa(bytes_per_line,buffer,10)) ;
strcat (transfer_graphics,"W") ;


EGA_GRFX(3,24) ;                     /* Set the EGA to XOR */
for (row = 0; row < scan_lines; ++row)
for (line = 0; line <= line_multiple; ++line)
{
   cp = transfer_graphics ;          /* Set the LaserJet for */
   while(inregs.h.al = *cp++)        /*    a line of graphics */
      int86(0x17,&inregs,&outregs) ;
   for (col = 0; col < bytes_per_line; ++col)
   {
      /* First, read the EGA bit planes. */
      for(plane = 0; plane <= 3; ++plane)
      {
         EGA_GRFX(4,plane) ;
         bit_planes[plane] = rgen[(col + row * bytes_per_line)]
;
      }
      /* XOR the byte just read: */
      if(line || crt_mode != 14)
         rgen[(col + row * bytes_per_line)] = 0xFF ;

      for (byte = 0, bit = 7; bit >= 0; --bit)
      {
         bit_mask = 1 << bit ;
      /* calculate the color of ONE pixel masked by bit_mask: */
         color = (((bit_planes[3] & bit_mask) >> bit) << 3) |
                 (((bit_planes[2] & bit_mask) >> bit) << 2) |
                 (((bit_planes[1] & bit_mask) >> bit) << 1) |
                 (((bit_planes[0] & bit_mask) >> bit) ) ;
      /* Read a byte from dither based on the row and color: */
         byte |= (dither[color][(row & 7)] & bit_mask ) ;
      }
      /* Print the byte: */
      inregs.h.al = (char)byte ;
      int86(0x17, &inregs, &outregs) ;
      /* Restore the previous row: */
      if((row) && (!line))
      {
```

```
                    byte = rgen[(col + (row-1) * bytes_per_line)] ;
                    rgen[(col + (row-1) * bytes_per_line)] = 0xFF ;
              }
        }
}
cp = end_raster_graphics ;          /* set the LaserJet for text */
while (inregs.h.al = *cp++)
        int86(0x17,&inregs,&outregs) ;

/* Restore the last line: */
for(col = 0; col <= bytes_per_line; ++col)
    {
        byte = rgen[(col + (row-1) * bytes_per_line)] ;
        rgen[(col + (row-1) * bytes_per_line)] = 0xFF ;
    }
EGA_GRFX(3,0) ;                        /* Reset the EGA */
return(1) ;
}


/*=========================================================*/
int get_scan_lines()
{
int scan_lines ;
 switch(PEEK_BYTE(0x40,0x49))       /* video mode is at 40:45 */
 {
   case 13:
   case 14: scan_lines = 200 ;  /* a 200 line mode */
            break ;
   case 15:
   case 16: scan_lines = 350 ;  /* a 350 line mode */
            break ;
   default: scan_lines = 0 ;    /* Unknown mode */
 }
return(scan_lines) ;
}
```

If you compile and run prtsc(), you will notice a line advancing from the top of the screen to the bottom, showing how much of the screen has been printed. This line is created by XORing the contents of all the EGA bit maps with 0xFF. But how do you XOR all four bit maps without reading and storing each one? The answer is to use the EGA's data rotate register. This register allows the contents of the latch registers to be rotated, ANDed, ORed, or XORed with the data from the CPU. The meaning of each bit of the data rotate register is shown in Figure 12-3.

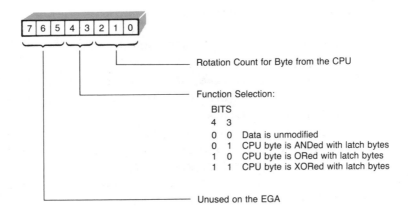

Fig. 12-3.   The data rotate register.

Using the data rotate register to rotate the byte from the CPU is of limited use. The latch registers are not rotated by this function, only the CPU data. The CPU is just as able to rotate the byte before sending it. However, the AND, OR, and XOR functions are very useful for quick logical operations on the bytes in the latch registers.

The stream I/O functions from the C library (such as `fprintf()` or `fputs()`) are not used in `prtsc()` because any byte (0 − 0xFF) may be sent to the printer as graphics data. Some values, such as EOF (0x1A), have special meaning to MS DOS. If the `prtsc()` routine tried to send 0x1A to the printer using one of the stream I/O functions, MS-DOS would terminate I/O rather than printing the byte. Even opening the device for binary output will not cure this. To get around this problem, each byte is printed directly using the PC BIOS print character call `INT 0x16`.

If you do not have a LaserJet printer, you should be able to adapt the `prtsc()` function to another printer easily. The main thing to change is the printer control strings. The other potential change is the method used to send graphics data to the printer. The LaserJet, and most other new printers, take graphics one horizontal line at a time. Older printers may need graphics sent in 8x8 chunks. As an example, here is an equivalent print screen for an Epson printer:

```
#include <dos.h>
#include <string.h>
#include <stdio.h>
#include <stdlib.h>
#include "ega.h"
prtsc()
/* This print screen is for an Epson FX-80 */
{
```

```
static unsigned char dither[16][8] =
  {
    { 0x00,0x00,0x00,0x00,0x00,0x00,0x00,0x00 },   /* 0 */
    { 0x88,0x44,0x22,0x11,0x88,0x44,0x22,0x11 },   /* 1 */
    { 0x88,0x11,0x22,0x44,0x88,0x11,0x22,0x44 },   /* 2 */
    { 0x18,0x24,0x42,0x81,0x18,0x24,0x42,0x81 },   /* 3 */
    { 0xAA,0xAA,0xAA,0xAA,0xAA,0xAA,0xAA,0xAA },   /* 4 */
    { 0xFF,0x00,0xFF,0x00,0xFF,0x00,0xFF,0x00 },   /* 5 */
    { 0x88,0x00,0x22,0x00,0x88,0x00,0x22,0x00 },   /* 6 */
    { 0xEE,0xFF,0xBB,0xFF,0xEE,0xFF,0xBB,0xFF },   /* 7 */
    { 0xAA,0x55,0xAA,0x55,0xAA,0x55,0xAA,0x55 },   /* 8 */
    { 0x77,0xBB,0xDD,0xEE,0x77,0xBB,0xDD,0xEE },   /* 9 */
    { 0x77,0xEE,0xDD,0xBB,0x77,0xEE,0xDD,0xBB },   /* 10 */
    { 0xE7,0xDB,0xBD,0x7E,0xE7,0xDB,0xBD,0x7E },   /* 11 */
    { 0xCC,0xCC,0xCC,0xCC,0xCC,0xCC,0xCC,0xCC },   /* 12 */
    { 0xFF,0xFF,0x00,0x00,0xFF,0xFF,0x00,0x00 },   /* 13 */
    { 0xFF,0x00,0xFF,0x00,0xFF,0xFF,0xFF,0x00 },   /* 14 */
    { 0xFF,0xFF,0xFF,0xFF,0xFF,0xFF,0xFF,0xFF }    /* 15 */
  } ;
union REGS inregs, outregs ;
int scan_lines ;
unsigned char far *rgen = (char far *)(0xA0000000L)
                    + (PEEK_WORD(0x40,0x4C)
                    *   PEEK_WORD(0x40,0x62)) ;
unsigned char bit_planes[4] ;
static char start_raster_graphics[] = { "\xD\xA\x1b\x33\x18"
} ;
char transfer_graphics[7] ;
char *cp ;
int row, col, line_multiple ;
char color, plane ;
int bit_mask,byte,bit ;
char crt_mode = PEEK_BYTE(0x40,0x49) ; /* CRT graphics mode */
int bytes_per_line = GET_CRT_COLS() ;
int n1, n2 ;

if (crt_mode < 13)              /* EGA modes only */
    return(0) ;
switch(crt_mode)
  {
  case 13:    line_multiple = 2 ;
              scan_lines = 200 ;
              break ;
  case 14:    line_multiple = 4 ;
```

```
                  scan_lines = 200 ;
                  break ;
        case 15:
        case 16:    line_multiple = 2 ;
                  scan_lines = 350 ;
                  /* falls through! */
        }


cp = start_raster_graphics ;
inregs.x.dx = 0 ;                        /* LPT1 */
inregs.h.ah = 0 ;                        /* Print character */
while(inregs.h.al = *cp++)               /* Print the string */
      int86(0x17,&inregs,&outregs) ;
strcpy (transfer_graphics,"\x0D\x0A\x1B\x4c") ;
n2 = (line_multiple * scan_lines) / 256 ;
n1 = (line_multiple * scan_lines) - n2 * 256 ;
transfer_graphics[4] = (char)n1 ;
transfer_graphics[5] = (char)n2 ;
transfer_graphics[6] = (char)0 ;


EGA_GRFX(3,24) ;                          /* Set the EGA to XOR */

for (col = 0; col < bytes_per_line; ++col)
{
cp = transfer_graphics ;
while(inregs.h.al = *cp++)                /* Print the string */
      int86(0x17,&inregs,&outregs) ;
   for (row = scan_lines - 1; row >= 0; --row)
   {
      /* First, read the EGA bit planes. */
         for(plane = 0; plane <= 3; ++plane)
         {
          EGA_GRFX(4,plane) ;
          bit_planes[plane] = rgen[(col + row * bytes_per_line)] ;
         }
         /* XOR the byte just read: */
         rgen[(col + row * bytes_per_line)] = 0xFF ;

         for (byte = 0, bit = 7; bit >= 0; --bit)
         {
            bit_mask = 1 << bit ;
            /* the color of ONE pixel masked by bit_mask: */
            color = (((bit_planes[3] & bit_mask) >> bit) << 3) |
                    (((bit_planes[2] & bit_mask) >> bit) << 2) |
```

```
                        (((bit_planes[1] & bit_mask) >> bit) << 1) ¦
                        (((bit_planes[0] & bit_mask) >> bit) ) ;
            /* byte from dither based on the row and color: */
            byte ¦= (dither[color][(row & 7)] & bit_mask ) ;
        }
        /* Print the byte: */
        for(n1 = 1; n1 <= line_multiple; ++n1)
            {
                inregs.h.al = byte ;
                int86(0x17,&inregs,&outregs) ;
            }
        if(col != 0)
            {
                byte = rgen[(col-1 + row * bytes_per_line)] ;
                rgen[(col-1 + row * bytes_per_line)] = 0xFF ;
            }
    }
}
for (row = scan_lines - 1 ; row >= 0; --row)
{
    byte = rgen[(col - 1 + row * bytes_per_line)] ;
    rgen[(col - 1 + row * bytes_per_line)] = 0xFF ;
}
EGA_GRFX(3,0) ;                         /* Reset the EGA */
return(1) ;
}
```

A print screen generated from the color bar program (rect.c) is shown in Figure 12-4. This print screen took about 16 seconds to print with a parallel LaserJet, printed with Prtsc.c. Each color is shown dithered.

EGA Color Palettes

When used with an Enhanced Color Monitor, the EGA can display any 16 colors from a 64-color palette. It takes four bits to represent 16 colors. Each of these bits corresponds to one of the EGA's four bit planes. On the CGA, and with the EGA's default palette, the four bits correspond to red, green, blue, and intensity (IRGB). But once the EGA palette is changed from the default, the four-bit color code is simply an index to the new palette.

The 64-color palette has the same three basic colors (red, green, blue) as the 16-color palette, but there is no intensity bit. Instead, each color has two bits for individual intensity, giving three intensity levels for each color. The total 64-

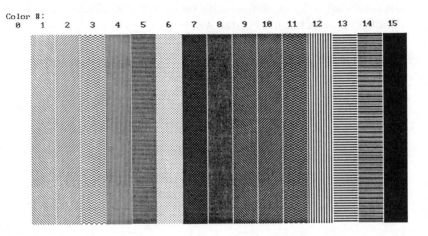

Fig. 12-4.   Color bar print screen.

color palette may be represented with six bits. The bits for the lower intensity of the three colors are the most significant bits in the six-bit value, and are usually abbreviated as lowercase rgb for red, green, and blue. The least significant three bits are the brighter red, green, and blue and are abbreviated as RGB. The total six-bit value, rgbRGB, is used to select one of the 64 colors. Once one of the 16 colors is set to an rgbRGB value, that color may be selected with a four-bit IRGB value. The bits of an rgbRGB value will always indicate the red, green, and blue components of the resulting color, but an IRGB value is simply an index to the current palette.

The RGB colors can only be used with an EGA connected to an Enhanced Color Monitor. When the EGA is connected to a Color Display, only the 16 colors from the default palette may be used. In text modes and the EGA graphics modes, individual palette registers may be set to any of the 16 default colors. In the CGA compatible modes, the palette must be changed using the CGA compatible BIOS calls.

The EGA also has an overscan register. The color value sent to the overscan register is displayed as a border. However, the overscan is usable only in the 200 scan line modes.

EGA BIOS Routine: Set Palette (INT 0x10)

The EGA's palette registers are most often set with a new EGA BIOS call. The BIOS call can set either one of the 16 colors, or all 16 at once. The BIOS call is Function 0x10 of Interrupt 0x10. There are four subfunctions: 0 sets individual palette registers to any rgbRGB value (or any IRGB value if the EGA is not connected to an ECD); 1 sets the overscan register; 2 sets all the palette registers and the overscan register; and 4 toggles between text blinking and intensity. The sub-function is selected in register AL.

Call with: AH = 0x10

AL = 0, Set Individual Palette Register
BL = color number (IRGB) to change
BH = rgbRGB value to set

AL = 1, Set Overscan Register
BH = color number to set

AL = 2, Set All Palette Registers and Overscan
ES:DX points to a 17-byte table
Bytes 0—15 has the 16 rgbRGB values for colors 0—15
Byte 16 is a color number for the Overscan Register

AL = 3, Toggle Intensity/Blinking Bit
Changes the meaning of bit 7 of the text attribute byte.
BL = 0, allow background intensity
BL = 1, allow foreground blinking

Unfortunately, the palette registers are write-only. It is not normally possible to determine what rgbRGB value a given color number represents. The EGA BIOS will check for the existence of a 256-byte table called the parameter save area when changing the palette registers. The BIOS will save the rgbRGB values in that table if it exists. The creation and maintenance of a parameter save area will not be covered here, but it is important to use BIOS calls to set the palette so that a parameter table will be updated.

The following is a program that demonstrates the uses of the palette registers. It will only work with an EGA/ECD combination. The program will first draw 16 colored rectangles using the rect() function. The palette is then continuously changed.

```
/* palette.c */
/* demonstrates the 64 color palette */
#define LINT_ARGS
```

```
#include <conio.h>
#include <dos.h>
#include <stdio.h>
#include "ega.h"


void set_all_pal(char *) ;
void gotoXY(int,int) ;


main()
{
int i,j,ch = 0;
char palette[17]] ;       /* This array holds the palette */
set_crt_mode(16) ;        /* Make sure you
                          ** have the right monitor! */


/* Draw some color bars: */
printf("\nColor #:\n") ;
for (i=0,j=0;i<16;++i,j+=40)
{
   printf(" %2i  ",i);
   rect(50,j,300,j+39,i);            /* from listing 5 */
   palette[i] = (char)i;             /* initialize the array */
}
   gotoXY(15,22) ;
   printf("rgbRGB of color 7") ;
   printf("%c%c%c%c%c%c",205,205,205,205,205,190) ;
   gotoXY(20,0) ;
   printf("Press Space to single space, Esc to exit") ;

   palette[16] = (char)0 ;
   while(ch != 27)                   /* while not ESC */
      {
      if (kbhit())                   /* If a key is hit, */
        ch = getch() ;               /*    get the character */
      for (i = 1; i<=15; ++i)
          {
          palette[i]++;
          if (palette[i] == 64)    /* max rgbRGB value */
                palette[rl]i] = 1 ;
          }
        set_all_pal(palette) ;       /* Set the palette */
```

```
        gotoXY(15,23) ;

        /* Convert the rgbRGB value to binary: */
        for(i = 5;i>=0; --i)
            if(palette[7] & 1<<i)
                putchar('1') ;
            else
                putchar('0') ;
        if(ch == 32)                      /* single space mode */
            while(!kbhit());
    }

set_crt_mode(3) ;
}


/*=========================================*/
void set_all_pal(palette)
char *palette ;
/* This function sets the entire palette */
{
 union REGS regs ;                 /* the 8086 registers */
 struct SREGS segregs ;            /* the 8086 segment registers */
 char far *fp = (char far *)palette ;
 regs.h.ah = 0x10 ;                /* EGA BIOS call set palette*/
 regs.h.al = 2 ;                   /* Function to set all */
 segregs.es = FP_SEG(fp) ;         /* ES to segment of palette */
 regs.x.dx = FP_OFF(fp) ;          /* DX to offset of palette */
 int86x(0x10, &regs, &regs, &segregs) ;
}


/*==========================================*/
void gotoXY(x,y)
int x,y ;
/* This function moves the text cursor to x,y */
{
    union REGS regs ;
    regs.h.ah = 2 ;                /* set cursor function */
    regs.h.bh = 0 ;               /* page 0 */
    regs.h.dh = (char)y ;         /* row */
    regs.h.dl = (char)x ;         /* col */
    int86(0x10, &regs, &regs) ; /* call int 0x10 */
}
```

Making Everything Faster

Remember the macros `EGA_GRFX` and `EGA_SQNC`? They are reproduced here:

```
#define EGA_GRFX(index, value) { outp(0x3ce, index) ; \
                                 outp(0x3cf, value) ;}
#define EGA_SQNC(index, value) { outp(0x3c4, index) ; \
                                 outp(0x3c5, value) ;}
```

Each of these macros sends an index to one of the EGA's ports followed by a byte of data. `EGA_GRFX` sends the index to 0x3CE and the data byte to 0x3CF. `EGA_SQNC` sends the index to 0x3C4 and the data byte to 0x3C5. In both cases, the address of the index port is one port below the data port. You can take advantage of this arrangement to make every code listing that uses these macros up to 30 percent faster. The key is to output a word (two bytes) to the lower of the two addresses, rather than a byte to each address.

Borland's Turbo C already has the library function to output a word to a port. It is called `outport()`. The macros only need to be slightly rewritten to take advantage of `outport()`. Since Turbo C already produces much faster code than the Microsoft compiler, the speed improvement is not dramatic. However, the change is easy to make, and does increase the speed of the example programs about 10 percent.

The Microsoft C library only includes the function `outp()`, and will only send a byte at a time. To send a word requires writing a new function in assembly:

```
; out.asm
; does word outs with the Microsoft Compiler
; This example is for the small model only

; assemble with :   MASM  out /ML
; link with your program with:   LINK yours.obj out.obj
; The /ML makes lower case labels
ret_sequence equ 4


_TEXT segment byte public 'CODE'  ; use the Microsoft segments
       assume cs:_TEXT
       public _outport            ; this is called

_outport proc near                ; small model uses near calls
       push bp                     ; save the stack frame
       mov bp, sp                  ; point to the arguments
```

```
        add bp, ret_sequence       ; skip over the return

        mov dx, [bp]               ; the port
        mov ax, [bp+2]             ; the data to send
        out dx, ax                 ; send the data
        pop bp                     ; recover the stack frame
        ret                        ;
_outport endp

_TEXT ends
        end
```

The word output function is named outport() to provide compatibility with Turbo C. When word outs are done, the byte in AL is first written to the port number in DX, and then the byte in AH is written to the port DX + 1. That means the data byte must be the byte in AH, and the index byte needs to be in AL. The macros are rewritten like this:

```
#define EGA_GRFX(index, value) \
            outport(0x3ce, (((int)value << 8) | (index)) )
#define EGA_SQNC(index, value) \
            outport(0x3c4, (((int)value << 8) | (index)) )
```

Conclusion

With the EGA, everything is complicated. IBM was locked in to supporting two very different previous display standards (the CGA and MDA) when designing the EGA. The result now is supported in the even more complicated VGA. Your best bet for designing software to run on the EGA without sacrificing future compatibility is to separate hardware-dependent code into logically independent functions. For example, the fastdot() routine should be easy to rewrite for all future IBM displays. A more complicated plotting routine that calls fastdot() to plot dots would not need to be rewritten as long as fastdot() supports the display. Also consider how easy it was to upgrade all the routines in this paper simply by rewriting the EGA_GRFX and EGA_SQNC macros. Now every routine is faster since they all can do word outs rather than byte outs.

This essay has developed several basic graphics functions: line(), fastdot(), readdot(), prtsc(), and rect(). Many of the EGA peculiarities, such as latch registers, have been examined. The three ways of setting a color on the EGA, the map-mask register, the set/reset register, and write mode 2, have also been shown. Although the routines in this paper are fast, there are many improvements that could be made. High performance graphics routines on the EGA tend to be found only though exploration.

Reading List

Newman, W., and R. Sproull. 1979. *Principles of Interactive Computer Graphics.* New York: McGraw-Hill Book Co.

Rogers, D. 1985. *Procedural Elements for Computer Graphics.* New York: McGraw-Hill Book Co.

A complete technical reference manual with an EGA BIOS listing and complete EGA description may be ordered from IBM by calling 800/IBM-PCTB (800/426-7282). The EGA technical directory is $9.95 and is part no. 6280131.

Andrew Dumke is the author of an EGA-based desktop publishing program, Laser GT, and an EGA print screen utility, Laser PR, both released by Sterling Pacific Inc. Mr. Dumke is currently a San Francisco-based fulltime computer industry investor with interests in microcomputers. He has owned a variety of microcomputer systems since 1978, and has programmed in C since 1983.

Related Essays

  1 A Guided Tour inside MS-DOS
10 Developing MS-DOS Device Drivers

Keywords

- asynchronous serial communications
- Universal Asynchronous Receiver Transmitter (UART)
- RS-232-C standard
- error-detection methods
- communications protocols
- XON/XOFF flow control
- interrupts
- polling

Essay Synopsis: Most MS-DOS computers these days need to use serial communications to transfer messages, programs, and data with other computers. Since many applications programs require serial communications capability, these functions belong in every programmer's toolkit. This essay begins by covering the basic concepts of asynchronous serial communication, including a discussion of error-detection methods and common communications protocols. This is followed by a look at the actual serial port hardware and how it can be used to control modems, to manage XON/XOFF flow control, and to handle interrupts. Finally, the author presents a complete interrupt-driven, buffered serial communications package implemented in Microsoft C.

13

Programming the Serial Port with C

Nabajyoti Barkakati

The PC and data communications are rapidly becoming an integral part of our lives. PC users routinely expect to be able to share programs, send messages and use their PCs to talk to other computers, large and small. An increasing number of computers are now hooked up in networks and various protocols and standards have been developed to guarantee that all computers in a network can communicate with each other and even with other networks. If you develop applications for the PC, chances are that you will one day be required to exploit its communications capabilities.

Luckily for us, enough standardization exists in the PC arena to allow us to write a single software package to handle most communications chores. To summarize in a single jargon-laden sentence: In the PC world, we normally communicate by asynchronous serial data transfers using the ASCII encoded character set and Universal Asynchronous Receiver Transmitter (UART) based hardware connected to a telephone line via an RS-232-C port and a modem. If all of these terms are too technical for you, don't despair—we will explain each and guide you through the design and implementation of a small but very functional serial communications package written in C.

Basics of Asynchronous Data Communications

Textual information is stored in computers by representing each character by a pattern of bits as prescribed by the ASCII code (ANSI standard X3.4-1977). The code uses seven bits per character, stored in the rightmost seven bits of an eight-bit byte. The ASCII code provides for 128 characters, which allows us to represent all upper- and lowercase letters, the numerals, and the punctuation symbols. In addition, there are 32 nonprintable characters (*control characters*) that are often used to signal special conditions—carriage return, line feed, form feed, etc. Two of these characters, Control-S and Control-Q, are used in what is known as the XON/XOFF flow control during asynchronous communications.

In data communications, we are interested in transferring the bytes from one device to another, e.g., from the PC to an electronic Bulletin Board System (BBS). If we had eight lines between the two points, we could let each line correspond to a bit and send the data one byte at a time. This would be a *parallel* transfer. The parallel port on the PC works this way, though in addition to the eight data lines there are other signals to assist in the data transmission. On the other hand, if we have only a single line, we would send each byte of data *serially*, one bit at a time. In addition to these options, we may also decide to send the data *synchronously* so that every byte is sent at a predetermined time (e.g., once every x seconds), or *asynchronously* at a rate that is not necessarily uniform. Serial communications is cheaper than parallel because it requires only one data line. Also, the asynchronous mode of transmission makes much less demand on hardware because there is no need for special hardware to maintain synchronism between the transmitter and the receiver. Thus, asynchronous serial communications is the preferred solution. Of course, in this mode of data transmission we must have a means to convert each data byte into a series of bits and indicate to the receiver the beginning and the end of each byte. Figure 13-1 illustrates the concept of asynchronous serial communication.

For the moment, let us assume that we have some means of converting each byte into a stream of 1s and 0s, bits that can be transmitted over the communications medium (for example, the telephone line). In fact, the UART performs precisely this function, as we will see in the next section. It is normal practice to indicate that a line is "okay" by keeping it at a logical 1 when it is idle. In this case, the line is said to be *marking*. On the other hand, when the line is at a logical 0, it is said to be *spacing*. Thus, logical 1 and 0 are also referred to as MARK and SPACE respectively. In asynchronous communications, a change in the condition of the line from MARK to SPACE indicates the start of a character (see Figure 13-2). This is referred to as the START bit. A pattern of bits follows the START bit, representing the character and a bit known as the PARITY bit. Finally, the line transitions to its idling MARK condition which represents the STOP bit and indicates the end of the current character. The number of bits used to represent the character is known as the *wordlength* and is usually either seven or eight. The PARITY bit is used to perform rudimentary error detection.

How does the transmitter (or the receiver) know how long each bit lasts? In fact, both must have some knowledge of this duration or the detection of the bits would be impossible. The duration of each bit is determined by data clocks at the receiver and the transmitter. Note, however, that while the clocks at the receiver and the transmitter must have the same frequency, they are not required to be synchronized. The selection of the clock frequency depends on the *baud rate*, which essentially refers to the number of times the line changes state every second. Nominally, a clock rate of 16 × baud rate is used so that the line is sampled often enough to detect a bit reliably.

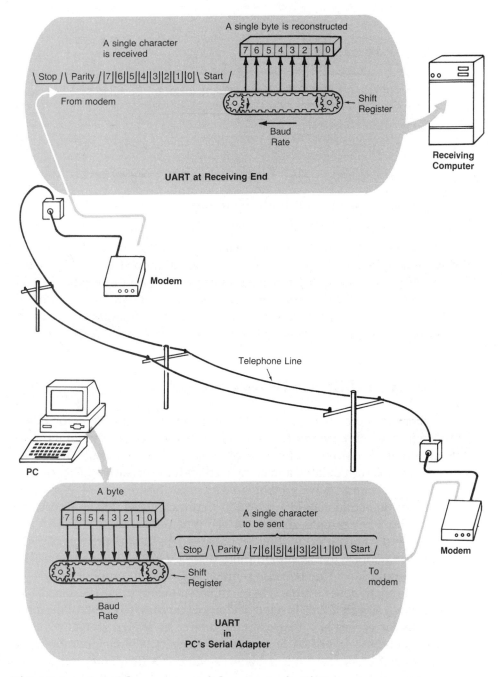

Fig. 13-1.   Asynchronous serial communications.

In addition to the ASCII characters used for information exchange, there is one particular condition of the line that is sometimes used to gain the attention

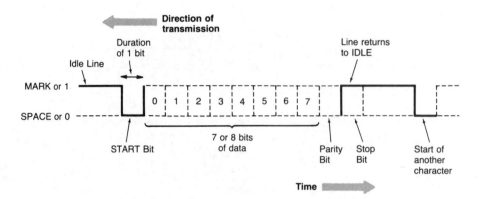

Fig. 13-2. Format of a single character.

of the receiver. Remember, the normal state of the line is MARK (1) and the beginning of a character is indicated by a transition to SPACE (0). If the line stays in the SPACE condition for a period longer than the time it would have taken to receive all the bits of a character, we say that a BREAK condition has occurred. There is no ASCII representation of BREAK—it is essentially the line "dropping dead" for a short duration of time that constitutes a BREAK.

Parity and Error Detection

Earlier, we mentioned the PARITY bit as being useful for error detection. For example, when *even parity* is selected, this bit is set so the total number in the current word is even. (A similar logic applies for odd parity.) At the receiving end, the parity is recalculated and compared with the received parity bit. If they disagree, the receiver declares that a parity error has occurred. A major drawback of error detection via parity check is that it can only detect errors that affect a single bit. For example, the bit pattern 0100 0001 0 (ASCII A, with a 0, or even parity bit) transmitted with eight-bit wordlength and even parity may change (due to say, noise in the line) to 0100 0111 0 (ASCII G), but to the receiver, everything would seem fine because there is still an even number of ones.

A much more reliable scheme of detecting errors is the so-called Cyclic Redundancy Check (CRC). Instead of checking errors in a single character, the CRC checks for errors in a block of characters. As shown in Figure 13-3, the CRC calculation treats a block of characters as a single binary number (with a large number of bits!) and finds a 16-bit remainder after dividing this number by a prespecified 17-bit divisor, for example, the CCITT polynomial:

$$X^{16} + X^{12} + X^5 + 1$$

Since the remainder after a division is always less than the divisor, by choosing a

17-bit divisor we are guaranteed, at most, 16 bits in the remainder. The remainder is known as the CRC checkvalue and often referred to as the CRC of that block. The two-byte CRC checkvalue is then sent at the end of the block of characters and, at the receiver, the CRC is recalculated and compared with the received CRC to check for transmission errors. Thus, each block of characters would have two more bytes appended and these would be the CRC (or the Block Check) characters. How good is this method of error detection? Research has shown that the CRC can detect a burst of errors shorter than 16 bits with 100 percent accuracy. CRC is widely used in hard disks for error detection. File transfer protocols such as XMODEM and KERMIT also use CRC.

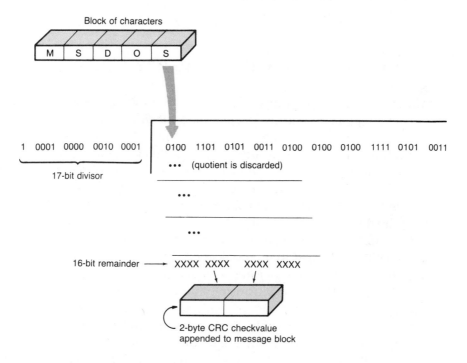

Fig. 13-3. Computing the CRC bytes.

Since a detailed discussion of this topic is beyond the scope of this essay, we refer the reader to chapter 3 of Campbell (1987) and chapter 13 of McNamara (1982). Both authors provide a thorough analysis of several CRC techniques and, more importantly, present algorithms to compute CRCs.

So far we have talked about sending and receiving individual characters. The serial communications package that we will develop operates at this level. However, there are other higher-level protocols (or conventions) used when transmitting files from one computer to another that send data in the form of *packets* of characters with additional information to help the receiver answer such questions as

➤ Was the packet received without errors?

➤ How do I construct the original file out of the received packets?

➤ How do I decode the information in case it is encoded?

The two most widely used file transfer protocols in the PC world are XMODEM and KERMIT. Once again, we are taking the easy way out by referring the reader to books that describe these protocols. The recent book by da Cruz (1987), who was one of the original authors of the KERMIT protocol, has a very complete discussion of KERMIT. The XMODEM protocol, originated by Ward Christensen in 1977, is also discussed (pp. 303-309). Campbell (1987) also describes both of these protocols.

Communicating with the RS-232-C Standard

Although in the PC we represent the 1s and 0s by voltage levels, the signals carried in a telephone line are usually tones of different frequencies. The device that sits between the PC's hardware and the transmission line, and makes data communication possible, is the modem (modulator/demodulator). A modem can convert information back and forth between the voltage/no voltage representation of digital circuits and analog signals (for example, tones) appropriate for transmission through the telephone lines. Standards such as the RS-232-C, set forth by the Electrical Industry Association (EIA), specify a prescribed method of information interchange between the modem or data communications equipment (DCE), and the PC's communications hardware or data terminal equipment (DTE). A modem can be operated in one of two modes: half duplex or full duplex. Half duplex mode can only transmit in one direction at a time while full duplex operation permits independent two-way communications. The RS-232-C standard provides control signals such as Request To Send (RTS) and Clear To Send (CTS) that may be used to coordinate the transmission and reception of data. As shown in Figure 13-4, the RS-232-C standard is evident in the cable and connectors used to connect the PC to the modem. The arrows in the figure point to equipment for which the signal is intended. Table 13-1 lists the acronyms and their meanings.

Various other configurations of the cables are shown in Campbell (1987).

Flow Control with XON/XOFF

In addition to the "handshaking" via the hardware RTS/CTS signals, special ASCII control characters (Control-Q/Control-S or XON/XOFF) are used to achieve flow control in software. Flow control is necessary because sometimes either the transmitter or the receiver may not be able to keep up with the rate of transmission and should be able to inform the other party to stop while it catches up.

Table 13-1.   RS-232-C Signals

Acronym	Meaning
TD	Transmitted Data
RD	Received Data
RTS	Request To Send
CTS	Clear To Send
DSR	Data Set Ready
RLSD	Receive Line Signal Detector
DTR	Data Terminal Ready

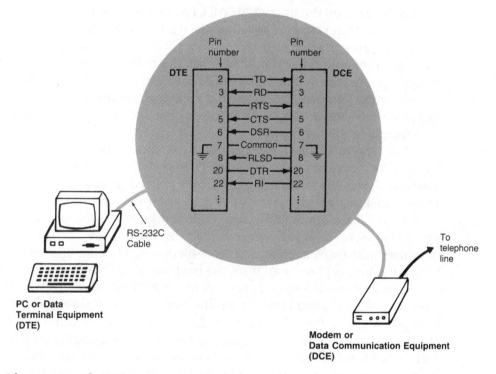

Fig. 13-4.   The RS-232-C connection.

Suppose the receiver has a buffer to store incoming characters. As the buffer gets close to full, the receiver can send an XOFF character to the transmitter to indicate that transmission should stop. Of course, the transmitter must understand the meaning of XOFF and cease sending characters. Then when the receiver processes characters (e.g., puts them in a disk file) and the buffer empties, it can send an XON to indicate that transmission can proceed. This scheme of flow control is widely used because of its simplicity. In the serial communications package we will develop, we will be primarily concerned with full duplex communication with XON/XOFF flow control.

Now that we have gone over some of the basics of asynchronous serial communications, let us roll up our sleeves and see how we can program the PC's communications hardware.

Taming the UART

The most common communications hardware on the IBM PC and compatibles is the serial or asynchronous communications adapter or *serial adapter*. This adapter is based on the Intel 8250 UART, has an RS-232-C port for connecting to the communication channel (for example, the telephone line) via a modem, and, like the graphics adapter, is programmable through a set of registers. The registers are accessible from the 8086 or 80286 microprocessor in the IBM PC through predefined I/O port addresses. Note that the information presented in this section is, of necessity, somewhat technical. However, everything will fall into place once you go through the C code presented later and correlate it with the material in this section.

The Intel 8250 UART is controlled by writing to or reading from a set of internal data locations called registers. Each register can hold a byte. These registers are accessible to the programmer via port addresses. The port addresses are assigned sequentially, so it is enough to know the address of the first port to be able to find any other. This is also commonly known as the *base address* of the serial adapter. In the IBM PC, the two serial ports COM1 and COM2 are assigned base port addresses 3F8h and 2F8h respectively. Thus for the serial adapter COM1, the first register is at 3F8h, the next one at 3F9h and so on.

There are seven physical registers in the 8250 which we will investigate in the order of increasing offsets from the base address (see Figure 13-5). At the base port address, there is a single register which doubles as the *receive buffer register* and the *transmit holding register* used to store a single character that is received or is being transmitted. Next comes the *interrupt enable register* which is used to enable, by setting the bit to 1, or disable interrupts that the serial adapter is capable of generating. The third register, the *interrupt identification register*, contains the UART's report on the identity of an interrupt. In the 3-bit interrupt ID (bits 0-2), 110 means line status, 100 means received data, 010 means transmit buffer empty, and 000 means modem status. Then comes the *line control register* used to set up various communications parameters such as word-length, number of stop bits, parity, and baud rate. In bit 6, 1 sets the line to SPACE. (See Essay 5, Advanced MASM Techniques, by Michael Goldman, for examples showing how to manipulate these bits in assembly language.) The fifth register is the *modem control register*, which is used to send signals such as DTR and RTS to the modem. Bit 3 must be 1 for interrupt I/O on PC. Finally, the last two registers, the *line status register* and the *modem status register* indicate the status of the line and the modem, respectively.

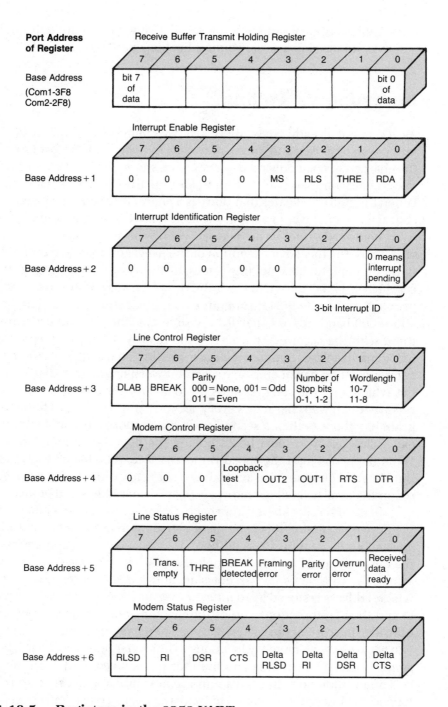

Fig. 13-5. Registers in the 8250 UART.

The first two registers are also used in setting baud rates, but for the sake of brevity, we will skip over some of these details, focusing our attention on only those aspects of programming the serial adapter that have a direct bearing on our goal—to develop a serial communications package for the PC.

Interrupts vs. Polling

As you might already know, there are two common methods of I/O in any computer system: *polled* and *interrupt-driven*. In polled I/O, the program requesting the character repeatedly reads a status register in the I/O device until it indicates that a character is available for input (or until the program decides to "time out"). When the status indicates that there is a character ready, the program reads the character from the appropriate register in the I/O device. A similar sequence of "wait until ready, then write" is used when writing characters out to the I/O device. Thus, the thread of execution of the program is held up until the I/O operation is complete. The polling refers to the repeated checking of the status register of the I/O device to see if the desired transaction can be initiated. A big problem with polled I/O through the communication port is that, at baud rates above 300 baud, there is hardly any time available for the program to do anything with the received character, even display it on the screen. Consider the following example. Suppose you are reading characters at 300 baud and the communication parameters are seven-bit wordlength, even parity, and one stop bit, which with the start bit adds up to 10 bits per character. So you expect to receive roughly 30 characters every second. After reading a character, your program has about 1/30th of a second to do other chores. If you do not want to miss any characters you must begin polling the port again before this time is up. What happens when the speed is increased to 9600 baud? You guessed it! The time interval between characters is too short to even put the received character up on the display let alone interpret special characters and emulate a terminal.

In the interrupt-driven approach, the program enables interrupts from the I/O device, assuming it is capable of signaling interrupts to the CPU, and then goes about its own business without any concern about the device. Whenever the device is ready for I/O, it signals the CPU via hardware. Upon receiving this signal, the CPU saves its current *state* and invokes an *interrupt service routine* whose address is stored in an *interrupt vector table*. This routine performs the I/O and then restores the state of the machine and returns control to the CPU. Consider the case of characters arriving at the communication port of the PC. If you set aside some memory locations to hold characters (a buffer), you can use a simple interrupt handling routine that quickly reads the character from the communication port and saves it in the next available location in the buffer. As long as the interrupt handler can read and save a character before another one arrives, no characters will be lost. This simple task is easy enough to complete even in the short time interval between characters at 9600 baud. The beauty of this method is that it does not matter how long the main program takes to manipulate the characters saved in the buffer. Of course, there is the risk of filling up the buffer, but this can be remedied by simply increasing the size of the buffer. If this is not good enough, there is XON/XOFF flow control to help us out.

From our discussion, it is clear that an interrupt-driven, buffered communication package with XON/XOFF flow control is preferred over a polled implementation, so we will develop an interrupt service routine that will, depending on the cause of the interrupt, either read a character from the adapter and save it in a *receive queue* or send out a character from a *transmit queue*. That way, our main program (which may be a terminal emulator) can feed itself off the receive queue and send out characters by simply placing them in the transmit queue. How are interrupts enabled and and how are they serviced? Let's explore the possibilities.

Servicing Interrupts from the Serial Adapter

The serial adapter on the PC can be programmed to interrupt the CPU whenever one of four things happens (see Figure 13-6). The UART assigns a priority to each of these events. Table 13-2 lists the four interrupts.

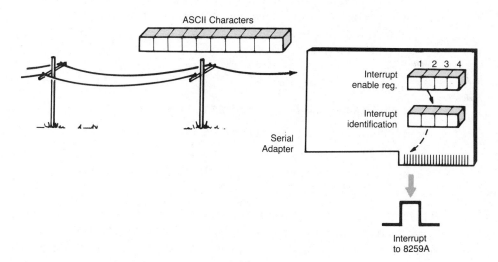

Fig. 13-6.   Interrupts from the serial adapter.

The event with highest priority is the receive line status (RLS) interrupt. This occurs when one of the following happens: the line goes dead (logical 0) for a period longer than that necessary to receive a character, a character is received before the last one was read (an overrun error), there is a parity error, or

Table 13-2. Serial Adapter Interrupts

Priority	Interrupt ID
1	Receive line status (RLS)
2	Receive data available (RDA)
3	Transmit holding register empty (THRE)
4	Modem status (MS)

no stop bit was found while assembling a character out of the received bits (a framing error). This interrupt is processed by reading the line status register.

Next comes the receive data available (RDA) interrupt that occurs when a character is ready in the receive buffer register. It can be cleared by reading the character from that register. Of course, in our scheme of things, the character will be squirreled away into a receive queue.

The transmit holding register empty (THRE) interrupt has the next priority. As the name suggests, it occurs when the register assigned to hold the character to be transmitted (same port address as the receive buffer register) is empty. This interrupt is processed by writing into this register or by reading from the interrupt identification register. The second method of clearing this interrupt is necessary because sometimes, even though the UART interrupts to say the transmit buffer is empty, there may not be anything to transmit.

The lowest priority interrupt is the modem status (MS) interrupt, and is caused when the modem

▶ asserts (sends) the CTS signal

▶ indicates its readiness by setting the DSR line

▶ receives a call, in which case the RI line becomes a logical 1

▶ detects a carrier signal (the tone you hear when you dial a number and a modem answers), which means the RLSD line is set to 1

This interrupt can be cleared by reading the modem status register.

Each of these interrupts may be turned on or off individually by setting appropriate bits in the *interrupt enable register*. On the IBM Serial/Parallel Adapter (as well as the IBM Asynchronous Adapter) the bit named OUT2 in the modem control register must also be set to 1 before interrupts from the UART can reach the CPU. When interrupts occur, the serial adapter arranges them according to priority and indicates the pending interrupt of highest priority in the *interrupt identification register*. The adapter stops responding to further interrupts of equal or lower priority until it determines that the current one has been serviced by the interrupt service routine.

8259A: The CPU's Receptionist

In the IBM PC (and compatibles) the CPU does not directly accept interrupts from hardware devices such as the serial adapter. Rather, hardware interrupts are first fielded by an Intel 8259A Programmable Interrupt Controller (PIC) chip. The 8259A acts as the CPU's "receptionist." A programmable device, the 8259A accepts up to eight distinct interrupts and can mask (i.e., ignore) interrupts individually. The 8259A responds to each unmasked or allowed interrupt and forwards it to the CPU, provided no other interrupt of higher priority is being serviced at that moment.

How does the 8259A assign priorities? Just as the UART has its method of determining priorities of interrupts generated from the serial adapter, the 8259A also has its own scheme of assigning priorities to interrupts. The serial adapter is only one of several hardware devices that can interrupt the 8259A. Each device is hardwired or jumpered into distinct inputs known as *interrupt request* (IRQ) inputs in the 8259A. That's why it is customary to talk about the IRQ assigned to a hardware interrupt. Another feature is also tied to the IRQ of an interrupt—the *interrupt number* used in referring to that particular interrupt. On the IBM PC, this number is eight plus the IRQ. This is the number used by the CPU when looking up the address of the interrupt handling routine from the interrupt vector table. Since the 8259A associates higher priorities with lower IRQs, the hardware devices needing maximum attention have lower IRQ. Thus the system timer gets IRQ0, the keyboard has IRQ1 and so on. The two communication ports COM1 and COM2 are respectively assigned IRQ4 and IRQ3, resulting in interrupt numbers 12 and 11 (decimal). By the way, the interrupt numbers must be known so that DOS function call (software Interrupt 21h) with Function numbers 35h and 25h can be used for get and set interrupt vectors, respectively. (See Essay 5, Advanced MASM Techniques, by Michael Goldman, for a discussion on avoiding pitfalls in interrupt handling.)

A few more details to note: The CPU automatically disables all interrupts when it transfers control to the actual software service routine for the current interrupt. So unless we do something, while we are processing a character from the serial port, the system timer, the keyboard and the disk will *not* be serviced. Since many vital system functions rely on interrupts (for example, updating of the system time), it is important to turn interrupts back on as soon as the service routine gets control—with an STI SeT Interrupt flag instruction. Although during the servicing of an interrupt the 8259A inhibits further interrupts of the same or lower priority, higher priority interrupts are still acknowledged, and if the interrupt flag is set, our serial service routine will be interrupted. This will then allow the timer, the keyboard, and the disk to interrupt our routine, allowing them to function properly.

How do we tell the 8259A when the serial interrupt processing is complete? Our service routine has to send an end-of-interrupt EOI command to the 8259A before returning control to the CPU. Although there are ways of indicating an end-of-interrupt for a specific IRQ, for the priority scheme used in the PC it is enough to send what is known as a nonspecific end-of-interrupt (code 20h) to the 8259A, nonspecific because it does not specify which interrupt has been serviced but simply tells the 8259A that the servicing is complete for the highest-priority interrupt that has been acknowledged. This reenables acknowledgment of further interrupts at that IRQ or lower.

Programming the 8259A

How do we program the 8259A? As with any hardware in the PC, the 8259A is programmed via two command words (registers) at I/O port addresses 20h and 21h, respectively (see Figure 13-7). The register at 21h is used solely for masking interrupts. An interrupt is masked (i.e., not acknowledged) if the bit correspond-ing to its IRQ (counting from right to left with the rightmost bit assigned to IRQ0) is a logical 1. The port at 20h is used to send the end-of-interrupt command to the 8259A. As we noted earlier, on the PC this is done by writing 20h to this port.

Various programming tricks follow from this scheme of things. The first serial port in the IBM PC (known as COM1: to MS-DOS) is assigned IRQ4 (Inter-rupt number 12), and the second one (COM2:) has IRQ3 (Interrupt 11). Thus, the 8259A can be programmed to acknowledge interrupts from COM1: by reading from the port at 21h and writing back the contents logically ANDed with EFh. Interrupts from COM1: may be masked by repeating the above step but ORing with 10h in place of the logical AND. Programming devices in this manner, by first reading the contents of a register and then writing back again with the ap-propriate bit altered, is recommended because that way we do not disturb any prior bit settings.

Sorry, We Don't Do Much BIOS

After being swamped by all this information, you are probably wondering if we could do all these via the BIOS? Unfortunately, the answer is no. Unlike the mini-mal support for the graphics adapter, the BIOS provides hardly anything in the way of controlling the serial adapter for us. The BIOS does have a function, Inter-rupt 14h, to access the serial adapter. Unfortunately, this function only supports polled I/O which is not much help because of the drawbacks of polling we have outlined earlier. However, this function is ideal for the initial setting up of the parameters of the communication port, and we will make use of this function in our package to save code. Another useful built-in feature of the BIOS is that dur-ing the Power On Self Test (POST) phase, it checks for the existence of serial adapters COM1 and COM2 and if it finds either, the address of the first register

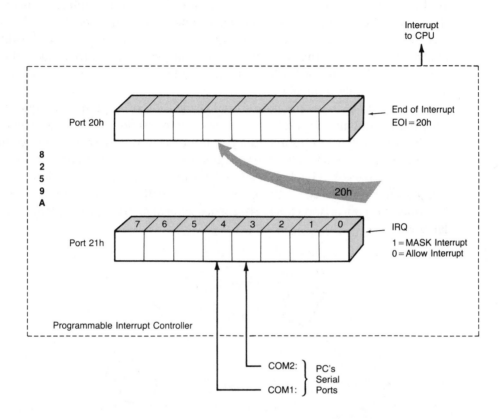

Fig. 13-7. **The 8259A programmable interrupt controller.**

of each adapter is stored in an area of memory beginning at offset zero of segment 40h. Since, in the PC, a 20-bit physical address equals 10h × 16-bit segment + 16-bit offset, if your PC has a single serial adapter designated as COM1:, the physical location 400h would contain 3F8h. So in our interrupt-driven package, we will get the port address of the serial adapter from this BIOS data area at offset 0 and segment 40h.

We need to go over just a few more details before we can design the communications package. The serial adapter in the PC supports full duplex communication (that means, we can transmit and receive simultaneously) with the following programmable parameters. Using BIOS Interrupt 14h, the baud rate can be set to 110, 150, 300, 600, 1200, 2400, 4800, or 9600 baud. The parity can be one of none, odd, or even, but the line control register may be directly programmed for space or mark parity as well. Either one or two stop bits are allowed and the wordlength can be seven or eight bits.

Queues for the Interrupt Handler

We have mentioned the use of buffers to save received characters. Conceptually, the buffer should behave like a checkout line at the supermarket cash register. The incoming characters line up one after another and the program reading the characters takes the first one in the line and processes it, then takes the next, and so on. This type of buffer is known as First In First Out or FIFO buffers. They are also called *queues*.

Figure 13-8 shows the conceptual realization of a queue. The queue naturally has a front and a rear. In an actual implementation, the queue size, i.e., the maximum number of characters it can hold, is fixed. It is convenient to think of the storage locations assigned to the queue as a circle so that once we go past the last location we come back to the first one again. This makes efficient use of the limited space available in the queue, and is called circular implementation. Tremblay and Sorenson (1984, 217-23) describe algorithms to implement a circular queue.

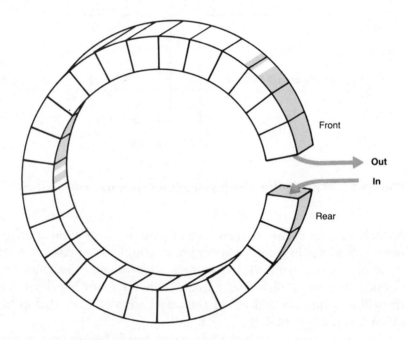

Fig. 13-8.   A circular FIFO buffer (queue).

Summary

Programming the serial adapter for interrupt-driven I/O requires that we do the following:

1. Get the base port address of the selected communication port from BIOS data area at segment 40h and offset 0.

2. Using MS-DOS Function, 35h, get the address of the old interrupt service routine for the interrupt number corresponding to this adapter and save it.

3. Using MS-DOS Function 25h, install our own interrupt service routine for that interrupt number.

4. Set up the communication parameters of the adapter using BIOS Function 14h.

5. Set up the receive and transmit queues to hold incoming and outgoing characters.

6. Turn on signals needed by modem (e.g., DTR and RTS in the modem control register).

7. Enable all interrupts from the adapter (by setting bits 0 through 3 of the interrupt enable register to 1).

8. Turn on the bit OUT2 in the modem control register to enable interrupts from the serial adapter.

9. Program the 8259A to recognize interrupts with the IRQ of this adapter (by setting the appropriate bit to zero in the interrupt mask register accessed through the port address 21h).

At some point, when the user decides to terminate the communication session, a "cleanup" routine should be called involving the following steps:

1. Turn off interrupts from the serial adapter.

2. Reset the bits in the modem control register.

3. Restore the old interrupt service routine.

4. Mask the interrupts for this IRQ in the 8259A.

Specifications for Our Serial Communications Package

Based on what we know so far, the specifications for our serial communication package are fairly simple. We want to be able to perform interrupt-driven, buffered I/O from the serial communications adapter configured as either COM1 or COM2. We need one buffer to store received characters and another one for characters waiting to be transmitted. The buffers ensure that the interrupt handler has some place to save characters and return control to other processing as quickly as possible. In case the buffer should fill up, we want to allow XON/XOFF flow control. As we mentioned earlier, many installations respond only when a BREAK signal is received so our software must be able to send a BREAK. This requires that the line be held in a spacing state for a period longer than the time it takes to send all the bits of a character at the current baud rate. (Generally, 250 milliseconds is long enough.) The user should be able to set communications parameters such as baud rate, wordlength, number of stop bits and parity easily. Some computers often play games with the unused eighth bit in a byte representing a character. For example, one might set the eighth bit to 1, another might require that this bit be always 0. In order to be able to keep up with these inconsistencies, the software should have the ability to selectively turn the eighth bit of each byte to 1 or to 0 while transmitting or receiving. In order to test the package, we also need a main routine. We will go over the major pieces one by one. You may find it convenient to consult the listings at the end of this essay as we go through the design.

Since there will be a lot of reference to the listings, Tables 13-3 through 13-6 show the sequence in which they appear and a short description of the functions contained in Listings 13-2 through 13-5. (There is no table for Listing 13-1, Makefile for Microsoft MAKE, because it is short.)

Table 13-3.   Listing 13-2: Main Program COMTEST.C

Function	Description
main()	Main routine to test package
connect()	Connects over serial line as a dumb terminal
sendfile()	Sends file to serial port
newparams()	Changes communications parameters
showparams()	Displays current settings of communications parameters

Table 13-4.   Listing 13-3: Assembly Language Portion of Package

Function	Description
_s_saveds	Saves current contents of DS register in a location in its code segment, invoked from C as s_saveds().
_s_inthndlr	Interrupt handler for serial port, calls s_mainhndlr() in Listing 13-5.
_s_cli	Disables interrupts
_s_sti	Enables interrupts

The main program in Listing 13-2 shows typical usage of the functions in our communications package. Listing 13-1 has the makefile that can be used with Microsoft's MAKE to prepare the executable version of the test program

COMTEST. The package itself consists of some assembly language routines shown in Listing 13-3, the C routines in Listing 13-4 that provide the capability to buffer characters, and the C routines in Listing 13-5 to handle interrupts and perform setup and cleanup operations.

Table 13-5.   Listing 13-4: The Circular Buffer (Queue) Package

Function	Description
q—setup()	Allocates storage and initializes circular queue
q—reset()	Deallocates queue
q—getfrom()	Returns next element in queue
q—puton()	Inserts new element into queue

Table 13-6.   Listing 13-5: C Portion of Package, SERIAL.C

Function	Description
s—mainhndlr()	Handles interrupts from PC's serial port
s—rls()	Handles receive line status interrupt
s—rda()	Handles receive data available interrupt
s—trmty()	Handles transmit holding register empty interrupt
s—ms()	Handles modem status interrupt
s—setup()	Sets up serial port and the 8259A for interrupt-driven I/O
s—intinit()	Enables interrupts from serial port
s—cleanup()	Cleans up before exiting to DOS by disabling interrupts from serial port and restoring old interrupt vector
s—intoff()	Disables interrupts from serial port
s—setcommparams()	Sets up communications parameters of serial port using BIOS Function 14h
s—setvals()	Internal utility routine to set new value for a parameter
s—vtblsrch()	Routine to search internal table for a string
s—getvals()	Returns string containing value of a parameter
s—sendchar()	Places character on transmit queue
s—rcvchar()	Returns character from receive queue
s—txqempty()	Returns 1 if transmit queue is empty
s—sendbreak()	Sends BREAK signal
s—delay()	A coarse timer used by `s_sendbreak()`

Overview

Figure 13-9 shows a flow chart for the program COMTEST.C (Listing 13-2). This program is provided so you can test the serial communications package. The main program accepts optional command line arguments specifying communications parameters such as baud rate, parity, port number, etc. First it goes over these arguments and calls the function `s_setvals()` to enter the name of each

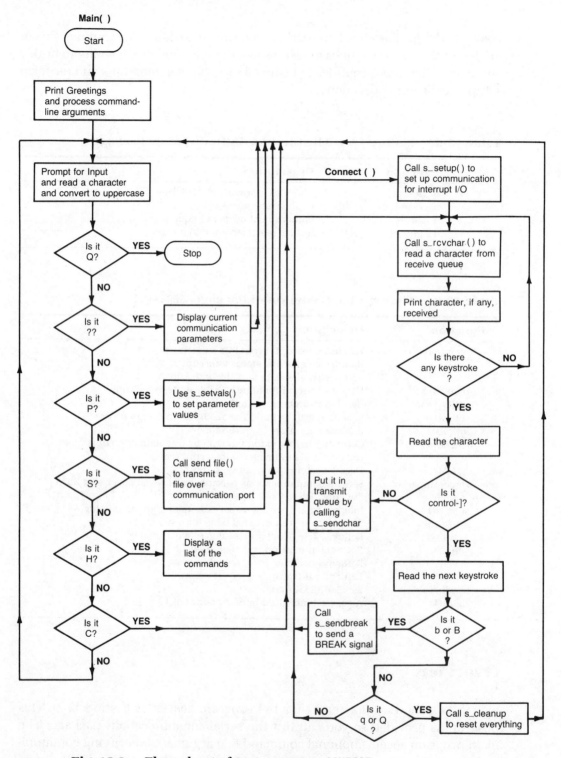

Fig. 13-9. Flow chart of test program COMTEST.

parameter and its value into an internal table maintained in the file SERIAL.C (Listing 13-5). This table is used to translate the value of each parameter entered by the user into an internal form. For example, this allows us to enter the string "even" as the value of the parameter named parity even though internally "even parity" is denoted by the integer 3. The internal forms are dictated by what BIOS accepts, but we see no reason to burden the user with these details. So, s_setvals() essentially hides the details and makes it easy for us to enter new values for the parameters.

After processing the command-line arguments, the program enters an endless loop to accept single character commands and process them until it receives the command q. You can get a list of the commands by typing h. (Commands can be entered in either lower- or uppercase, and are converted to uppercase.) A ? displays the current parameter settings by calling the function showparams() to do this. New communication parameters can be entered by typing p. The C function newparams() will prompt you for the names and the values of the parameters you want to change. Two commands follow that are more interesting because they actually perform serial communications.

The s command calls the function sendfile() to transmit a file over the serial port. If you happen to have your printer hooked up to the serial port, you can use this function to print files. This can be very handy because most printers with a serial interface require the use of XON/XOFF flow control but the PRINT command under MS-DOS does not use XON/XOFF. In other words, using this function as a model, you can write your print utility for printers hooked up to the PC's serial port.

The last and most interesting command is c that calls the C function connect() which emulates a "dumb" terminal. This is the typical way a package like this might be used. The following is a detailed description of how connect() works.

First, the communication port is set up by the routine s_setup(). This gets the address of the serial port from the BIOS data area in segment 40h and sets up various masks for enabling and disabling interrupts from the serial adapter. It uses DOS Function 35h to get and save the address of the current interrupt handler for serial interrupts, following which it installs our package's interrupt handler s_inthndlr() using the DOS function call with Function 25h. Then it calls the routine s_setcommparams() which uses the RS232 interrupt (14h) of the BIOS to set the communication parameters. Next the value of the DS register is saved by calling s_saveds() (Listing 13-3). This is a crucial step because, as you will see, our interrupt handler calls a C routine to do the actual work. All important variables are in the C function's data segment. That is why we must save the value of DS in the assembly code so that data is accessible during interrupt handling. After this step, memory is allocated for the transmit and the receive queues and some internal variables are initialized to default values. Finally, interrupts are enabled by calling s_intinit().

After setting up the serial port, connect() falls into an endless loop that first calls s_rcvchar() which returns a character if there are any in the receive queue or returns a 1 otherwise. If a character is returned, it is simply displayed and the keyboard is checked for any unprocessed keystrokes. If there are none, the routine returns to the beginning of the loop. If a character is found waiting in the keyboard buffer, it is read. As long as this character does not match a predefined special character (DEFAULT_ESC in the listing), the character is placed on the transmit queue by calling the routine s_sendchar() from the package, and then the loop is repeated.

Why is there a predefined special character? It allows us to exit from the endless loop and provides a way to send a BREAK signal. If a match with the special character is found, the routine waits for one more character, and if that character is a q it exits after performing the necessary cleanup functions by calling the routine s_cleanup(). If it is a b, a BREAK signal is sent by calling s_sendbreak().

The routine s_cleanup() is used to reset everything at the end of a communication session. This routine calls s_intoff() to turn off all interrupts from the serial adapter and mask the interrupt at the 8259A. Then the original interrupt vector for the serial interrupt is restored. Finally, the storage allocated to the transmit and receive queues is released.

How is the BREAK signal sent? The routine s_sendbreak() first puts the line in a spacing state by setting bit 6 of the line control register (LCR) to a logical 1. The BIOS time-of-day interrupt (number 1Ah) is used to achieve a delay of approximately 250 milliseconds, at the end of which bit 6 of LCR is reset to logical 0. This delay is achieved by calling the C routine s_delay() (Listing 13-5).

The other two routines we mentioned, s_sendchar() and s_rcvchar(), are high-level interfaces to the communications package. Using these routines, you can place characters in and retrieve characters from the transmit and the receive queues.

How are the characters magically appearing in the receive queue and disappearing from the transmit queue? All this is happening behind the scenes courtesy of our friendly interrupt handler that was duly installed as the guardian of the serial port when s_setup() was called.

FIFO Buffers

For buffered I/O, there must be some FIFO buffers set up to hold incoming and outgoing characters while they are waiting to be processed. As described earlier, we have chosen to implement a circular queue. Listing 13-4 shows QPAC.C— an implementation of a generic circular FIFO buffer. The routine q_setup() is used to allocate memory for a queue and initialize some internal variables such as front and rear indices of the queue. Notice that the number of elements in the queue and the size of each element are selected by the programmer by passing them as parameters when calling `q_setup()`. The queue is deallocated by `q_reset()`.

Of course, there must be a way to put elements on the queue and retrieve the first element in the queue. These functions are performed by the routines `q_puton()` and `q_getfrom()`, respectively.

Serial Interrupt Handler

Now let us jump right into the heart of the package—the interrupt service routine for the serial adapter. In the previous sections, we outlined the actions that should be performed by this interrupt service routine. It should first turn on interrupts (with an STI instruction) and save the current state of the machine (by pushing all the registers onto the stack), then read the interrupt identification register of the 8250 UART to determine which one of four events caused the interrupt. Next, it should perform the action necessary to clear the interrupt. If it is either a line status interrupt or a modem status interrupt, the handler simply reads the line or the modem status register. If there is received data available, the handler reads the character from the UART's receive buffer and inserts it into the receive queue. If the interrupt indicates that the transmit holding register is empty and if the transmit queue is not empty, a character is retrieved and written out to the transmit holding register. After the processing is complete, an EOI (20h) should be sent to the 8259A and the registers should be restored. Then the routine should return by using an IRET (return from interrupt) instruction. (This is one reason why we must have some assembly language routines in our package.) Remember, an IRET instruction is necessary to return from interrupts.

The C routine `s_mainhndlr()` (serial main handler) services the interrupts from the serial port by calling one of the routines: `s_rls()` for line status interrupt, `s_rda()` for receive data available, `s_trmty()` when the transmit holding register is empty, and `s_ms()` for modem status changes. Figure 13-10 is a flow chart for the complete interrupt handler.

The installed interrupt handler in our package is the assembly language routine `s_inthndlr()` shown in Listing 13-3. Immediately after saving the registers, this routine calls `s_mainhndlr()` in SERIAL.C (Listing 13-5) which services the interrupt as outlined above. There is only one tricky part in this arrangement. The compiled version of the C routines in SERIAL.C will use the segment register DS to point to the area in memory where the variables and data are stored. At the time when the interrupt from the serial port occurs, there is no certainty that the DS register contains a value appropriate for the routines in SERIAL.C. We call this the problem of "establishing the addressability of the data." This problem can be solved by saving the value of the DS register (appropriate for the routines in file SERIAL.c) at a location in the code segment of the assembly language routine during the setup (i.e., when `s_setup()` is called). From then on, whenever the assembly language routine `s_inthndlr()` gets called because of an

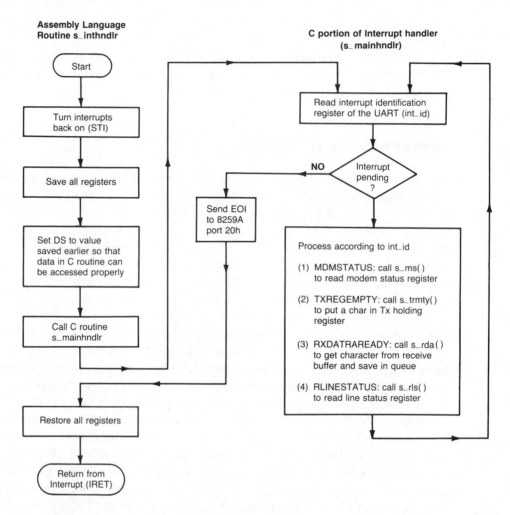

Fig. 13-10.   Flow chart of interrupt handler.

interrupt, the 80X86 microprocessor will load the CS register with the code segment of this routine and the saved value will always be accessible for loading the DS register before calling the C routine s_mainhndlr(). Specifically, we call the assembly language routine s_saveds() (Listing 13-3) from the C routine s_setup() (Listing 13-5) during setup. This is the routine that saves the DS register (corresponding to the segment address of the data in the file SERIAL.C) in a location in the code segment of the assembly language routine.

Notice that in s_mainhndlr(), interrupts are processed until no further interrupts are pending. This ensures that interrupts from the serial adapter, that may have occurred while an earlier interrupt was processed, don't get lost.

There are two more assembly language routines in the file SERASM.ASM. These routines, s_sti() and s_cli(), are used to set and clear the interrupt flag, respectively. It is necessary to disable interrupts in some parts of the serial package. For example, suppose you are installing an interrupt handler for the serial port. This means you are inserting the segment and the offset address of your routine into the CPU's interrupt vector table. What if an interrupt from the serial port should occur just after you've changed the segment address in the vector table, but before the offset is altered? With the CPU jumping off to this indeterminate address, the results could be unpredictable and most likely, very unwelcome. So it is important to disable all interrupts during these crucial periods.

Our Package and Microsoft C

One of our goals was to implement as much of the communications package as possible in Microsoft C (we used version 4.0). As you can see by examining the listings, this is quite possible. Assembly language routines are only needed to perform the functions return from interrupt and set/clear interrupt flag because Microsoft C has no functions to do these. We make use of the Microsoft C library functions inp() and outp() to read from and write to port addresses. The communications parameters are set up by accessing BIOS via the function int86(). Similarly, DOS functions are accessed through intdosx(). The DOS functions are used to get (Function number 35h) and install (Function 25h) interrupt vectors.

A note on memory models available in Microsoft C. The "large" memory model in the Microsoft C compiler uses full 32-bit (16-bit segment and 16-bit offset) data and code pointers. This makes it slow compared to, for example, the "small" model which assumes that everything fits into two physical segments—one for code and one for the data. The large model has the benefit of allowing truly large-scale programs. To keep things simple, we have used the large model. Since the package works at 9600 baud with this model, it should also work with the small memory model. To change to the small model, you will have to replace the keyword FAR in the assembly language routines with the keyword NEAR. Also, in the makefile (Listing 13-1), the line MODEL=L should be replaced with MODEL=S before reconstructing the executable. Other variations such as "mixed" memory models are also possible, but we will not consider them here.

Our serial communications package and this essay were prepared prior to the release of version 5.0 of the Microsoft C compiler. Prerelease announcements and "beta test" reports indicate that the run-time library will be expanded considerably in version 5.0 with the inclusion of many new routines, most notably in the categories of graphics, memory allocation, and MS-DOS/BIOS interface. Among the new routines for interfacing with the hardware are ones that can enable and disable 80X86 interrupts. There will also be a new attribute (named interrupt) for functions that tells the compiler to treat the function as an interrupt handler. This will instruct the compiler to use a "return from interrupt" instead of a "return from subroutine call" as the last instruction in the compiled code. With these new features, it should be possible to write the serial communications package entirely in Microsoft C 5.0 with no need for routines written in Assembler.

Testing the Package

Listings 13-3, 13-4, and 13-5 constitute our serial communications package. Use the makefile COMTEST in Listing 13-1 to prepare the executable COMTEST.EXE.

The routines were compiled with Microsoft C 4.0 using the large memory model and tested on an IBM PC AT (PC-DOS 3.1) with an IBM Serial/Parallel Adapter. The dumb terminal was used at 9600 baud to communicate with a VAX/ VMS system without any problem. COMTEST also successfully printed files at 9600 baud on an Imagen laser printer using XON/XOFF flow control.

Conclusion

Our serial communications package supports interrupt-driven, buffered I/O through the serial port, and may be used in application programs such as terminal emulators, file transfer utilities, and smart interfaces for minis and mainframes. The way it relies on a minimal amount of assembly language programming and uses C routines to service the interrupts could serve as an example if you want to develop C-based interrupt handlers. The information presented in this essay may serve as a reference guide to those who are interested in developing other interrupt-driven applications, especially those involving asynchronous communications.

Of course there is much room for improvement in the package. One obvious function we can add is an XMODEM file transfer protocol with CRC error-checking, but we will have to save that for another time.

The routines have been tested at speeds of 1200 through 9600 baud and found to work properly. However, the testing was far from thorough, so you may very well find some bugs. If you do, feel free to fix them and drop us a line.

Program Listings and the Makefile

Listing 13-1.   Makefile for Microsoft MAKE

```
#################################################################
#
```

continued

```
#    File:   C O M T E S T
#
#    Makefile for COMTEST.EXE--a program to test an asynchronous
#    communications package for IBM PC and compatibles.
#
#    Copyright © 1987 Nabajyoti Barkakati
#    Copies may be made for noncommercial, private purposes only.
#
#################################################################

MODEL=L

SRC=.
INC=.

CFLAGS=-A$(MODEL) -I$(INC) -Gs      -Od
#        modelsize   incl. nostkchk noopt.


MSC=msc $(CFLAGS)
ASM=masm

# General inference rules
# Rule to make .OBJ files from .C files

.C.OBJ:
$(MSC) $*.C,,,;

.ASM.OBJ:
$(ASM) $*.ASM,,,;

# Make object files

COMTEST.OBJ: $(SRC)\COMTEST.C

SERIAL.OBJ: $(SRC)\SERIAL.C

QPAC.OBJ: $(SRC)\QPAC.C

SERASM.OBJ: $(SCR)\SERASM.ASM

# Make the executable
```

continued

```
COMTEST.EXE: $(SRC)\COMTEST.OBJ $(SRC)\SERIAL.OBJ $(SRC)\QPAC.OBJ\
$(SRC)\SERASM.OBJ
LINK  $**, $@;
ERASE $(SRC)\*.LST
ERASE $(SRC)\*.COD


################## End of File: COMTEST #########################
```

Listing 13-2.   Main Program, COMTEST.C

```
/*--------------------------------------------------------------*/
/*
 * Filename:     C O M T E S T . C
 * Purpose:      Test an asynchronous communication package for
 *               IBM PC and compatibles.
 *               This version was developed on an IBM PC-AT with
 *               an IBM Serial Card. DOS version 3.1 was used.
 * Language:     Microsoft C 4.0
 * Usage:        Use makefile COMTEST with Microsoft MAKE.
 *
 *               Sample invocation:
 * "comtest baud 9600 parity none wordlength 8 stopbits 1"
 *
 *               When you run COMTEST.EXE you can set the
 *               communication parameters, send a file over
 *               the communication line, and connect to the
 *               serial port as a "dumb" terminal.
 *
 * Copyright © 1987 Nabajyoti Barkakati
 *  Copies may be made for noncommercial, private purposes only.
 *
 * Date Started:     10-JAN-1987
 * Revisions: V1.00   9-FEB-1987 -- First working version. (NB)
 */
/*--------------------------------------------------------------*/
#include <stdio.h>
#include <conio.h>
#include <ctype.h>

#define TRUE    1
#define FALSE   0
#define BUFSIZE 512
```

continued

```
#define CONTROL(x)  (x-0x40)
#define DEFAULT_ESC CONTROL(']')

extern int  s_setup(), s_sendchar(), s_rcvchar(), s_setvals(),
            s_cleanup(), s_txqempty();
extern void s_sendbreak();
extern char *s_getvals();

static char buffer[BUFSIZE];

static char helplist[] =
"\n\
    q -- exit.\n\
    c -- connect to serial port.\n\
    s -- send a file over serial port.\n\
    ? -- show status.\n\
    p -- set new communication parameters.\n\
    h -- print this list.\n";

main(argc, argv)
int argc;
char *argv[];
{
    static void connect(), newparams(), sendfile(), showparams();
    int ch, i, code;
    printf("\nCOMTEST 1.0 -- Testing Serial Communications\n");
    printf("Type H for help, ? for parameters.\n");

/* Setup communication port. Use parameters specified by user
 * on command line, if any. Sample invocation:
 *     comtest baud 9600 parity none wordlength 8 stopbits 1
 */
    if (argc > 1) {
        for (i = 1; i < argc; i += 2) {
            if (s_setvals(argv[i], argv[i+1]) == 0) {
                fprintf(stderr,
                    "Error setting parameter: %s to value: %s\n",
                    argv[i], argv[i+1]);
            }
        }
    }
/* Accept and respond to user command */
```

continued

```
        while (TRUE) {
            printf("\nCOMTEST> ");
            ch = getche();
            code = toupper(ch);
            switch (code) {
                case 'Q': exit(0);
                case 'C': connect();
                          break;
                case 'S': sendfile();
                          break;
                case 'P': newparams();
                          break;
                case '?': showparams();
                          break;
                case 'H': printf(helplist);
            }
        }
}
/*----------------------------------------------------------------*/
/*  c o n n e c t
 *  Connect over serial port as a dumb terminal.
 */
static void connect()
{
    int ch, nxt;
    printf("\nConnecting...\n");
/* First set up the serial port */
    s_setup();
/* The following endless loop simulates a very dumb terminal.
 * We first get a character from the receive queue, print it,
 * then check if any keystrokes are waiting. If a key was
 * struck, it's read in and sent out to the transmit buffer.
 * This sequence of steps is repeated until user hits the
 * ^] (CTRL and ]) keys together)--then a 'b' sends out
 * a BREAK signal and a 'q' cleans up everything and returns.
 */
    while (TRUE) {
        if ((ch = s_rcvchar()) != -1) putch(ch);
        if ( kbhit() != 0) {
            ch = getch();
            if (ch == DEFAULT_ESC) {
                printf("\n'b' to send BREAK, 'q' to quit\n");
                nxt = getch();if (nxt == 'b' || nxt == 'B') {
```

continued

```
                    s_sendbreak();
                }
                if (nxt == 'q' || nxt == 'Q') {
                    s_cleanup();
                    return;
                }
            }
            else {
                s_sendchar(ch);
            }
        }      /* End of kbhit() check */
    }
}
/*------------------------------------------------------------*/
/* s e n d f i l e
 * Send a file over the serial port.
 */
static void sendfile()
{
    register int i, j;
    int readcount;
    unsigned long bytecount;
    char filename[40];
    FILE *infile;

    printf("\nEnter name of file to be transmitted: ");
    scanf("%s", filename);
/* Open file for binary read only */
    if ((infile = fopen(filename, "rb")) == NULL) {
        fprintf(stderr, "Error opening file: %s\n", filename);
        return;
    }
    printf("Transmitting file...\n");
/* First set up the communications port */
    s_setup();
    bytecount = 0;
    j = 0;
    while (TRUE) {
/* Read in a "chunk" from the file into a buffer */
        readcount = fread(buffer, sizeof(char), BUFSIZE, infile);
        bytecount += readcount;
        for (i=0; i < readcount; i++) {
/* Keep sending each character until successful */
```
continued

```
            while ((s_sendchar(buffer[i])) != 1);
        }
        j++;
        if (j == 10) {
            j = 0;
            printf("%lu", bytecount);
        }
        else {
            putch('.');
        }
        if (readcount < BUFSIZE) {
            printf("(end)\nTransmitted %lu characters.\n",

            bytecount);
/* Now wait until the transmit queue is emptied out */
            while (s_txqempty() != TRUE);
/* Close comm port and return */
            s_cleanup();
            return;
        }
    }
}
/*------------------------------------------------------------*/
/* n e w p a r a m s
 * Set new parameters in the communications package.
 */
static void newparams()
{
    int ch;
    char pname[20], pvalue[20];
    while (TRUE) {
        printf("\nParameter name (Q to quit): ");
        scanf("%s", pname);
        ch = pname[0];
        if (toupper(ch) == 'Q') return;
        printf("Change %s from %s to: ", pname,
                                s_getvals(pname));
        scanf("%s", pvalue);
        if (s_setvals(pname, pvalue) == 0) {
            fprintf( stderr,
                "Error setting parameter: %s to value: %s\n",
                pname, pvalue);
        }
```

continued

```c
    else {
        printf("%s is now %s\n", pname, pvalue);
    }
  }
}
/*------------------------------------------------------------*/
/*  s h o w p a r a m s
 *  Show current parameters.
 */
static void showparams()
{
    printf("\n  Current Settings\n");
    printf("  Name         Value\n");
    printf("port          = %s\n", s_getvals("port"));
    printf("baud          = %s\n", s_getvals("baud"));
    printf("wordlength    = %s\n", s_getvals("wordlength"));
    printf("stopbits      = %s\n", s_getvals("stopbits"));
    printf("parity        = %s\n", s_getvals("parity"));
    printf("xonxoff       = %s\n", s_getvals("xonxoff"));
    printf("null_ignore   = %s\n", s_getvals("null_ignore"));
    printf("del_ignore    = %s\n", s_getvals("del_ignore"));
    printf("8thbit0_on_rx = %s\n", s_getvals("8thbit0_on_rx"));
    printf("8thbit1_on_rx = %s\n", s_getvals("8thbit1_on_rx"));
    printf("8thbit0_on_tx = %s\n", s_getvals("8thbit0_on_tx"));
    printf("8thbit1_on_tx = %s\n", s_getvals("8thbit1_on_tx"));
}
/*------------------ END OF FILE: COMTEST.C ------------------*/
```

Listing 13-3.   Assembly Language Portion of Package

```asm
;-------------------------------------------------------------
; Filename:    S E R A S M . A S M
; Purpose:     Assembly language routines to support interrupt
;              handling in an asynchronous communication package
;              for IBM PC and compatibles.
; Usage:       Routines called from Microsoft C 4.0 programs.
;
; Copyright © 1986, 1987 Nabajyoti Barkakati
;                      Silver Spring, MD 20904
; Right to use, copy, and modify this code is granted for personal
; noncommercial use, provided that this copyright disclosure is
; retained on all copies. All other rights reserved.
```

continued

```
;
;  Date Started:      10-DEC-1986
;  Revisions:  V1.00   9-FEB-1987--First working version. (NB)
;-------------------------------------------------------------------
TITLE           SERASM
SERASM_TEXT     SEGMENT BYTE PUBLIC 'CODE'
SERASM_TEXT     ENDS
;
EXTRN           _s_mainhndlr:FAR
ASSUME CS:SERASM_TEXT
SERASM_TEXT     SEGMENT
PUBLIC          _s_saveds
PUBLIC          _s_inthndlr
PUBLIC          _s_cli
PUBLIC          _s_sti
;
save_ds:        DW   0                       ; Storage for DS
;
_s_saveds       PROC FAR
                CLI
                PUSH ax
                MOV  ax,ds
                MOV  WORD PTR cs:save_ds,ax
                POP  ax
                STI
                RET
_s_saveds       ENDP
;
_s_inthndlr     PROC FAR
                STI
                PUSH bp
                PUSH ds
                PUSH es
                PUSH ax
                PUSH bx
                PUSH cx
                PUSH dx
                PUSH si
                PUSH di
                MOV  ax, WORD PTR cs:save_ds ; Set DS to value
                MOV  ds, ax                  ; saved earlier
                CALL _s_mainhndlr            ; Call C int handler
                POP  di
```

continued

```
                   POP   si
                   POP   dx
                   POP   cx
                   POP   bx
                   POP   ax
                   POP   es
                   POP   ds
                   POP   bp
                   IRET
_s_inthndlr        ENDP
; The following routine turns off interrupts.
_s_cli             PROC FAR
                   CLI                    ; Turn off interrupts
                   RET                    ; and return.
_s_cli             ENDP
; The following routine turns on interrupts.
_s_sti             PROC FAR
                   STI                    ; Interrupts back on
                   RET                    ; and return.
_s_sti             ENDP
SERASM_TEXT        ENDS
END
;------------------ END OF FILE:  SERASM.ASM --------------------
```

Listing 13-4.   The Circular Buffer (Queue) Package

```
/*---------------------------------------------------------------*/
/*
 *  Filename:      Q P A C . C
 *  Implements a circular queue in Microsoft C 4.0.
 *
 *  Copyright © 1986, 1987 Nabajyoti Barkakati
 *  Copies may be made for noncommercial, private purposes only.
 *
 */
/*---------------------------------------------------------------*/
#include <stdio.h>
#include <malloc.h>

typedef struct QTYPE {
```

continued

```
      int   count;
      int   front;
      int   rear;
      int   elemsize;
      int   maxsize;
      char  *data;
} QTYPE;

QTYPE *q_setup();
char  *q_getfrom();
int   q_puton(), q_reset();

/*-------------------------------------------------------------*/
/*  q _ s e t u p
 *  Allocate a queue with room for specified number of characters.
 *  The argument elemsize is the size of each data element.
 */
QTYPE *q_setup(maxsize, elemsize)
unsigned maxsize, elemsize;
{
    QTYPE *queue;
    if ((queue = (QTYPE *) calloc(1,sizeof(QTYPE))) == NULL){
        fprintf(stderr,"Ran out of memory in queue setup!\n");
        return(NULL);
    }
    queue->maxsize = maxsize;
    queue->elemsize = elemsize;
    if ((queue->data = calloc(maxsize,elemsize)) == NULL){
        fprintf(stderr,"No room for data in queue setup!\n");
        return(NULL);
    }
/* Initialize queue */
    queue->front = neg]1;
    queue->rear = -1;
    queue->count = 0;
    return(queue);
}
/*-------------------------------------------------------------*/
/*  q _ r e s e t
 *  Deallocate a queue and its data area.
 */
int q_reset(queue)
QTYPE *queue;
```

continued

```
{
    free (queue->data);
    free ((char *)queue);
}
/*-----------------------------------------------------------*/
/*  q _ g e t f r o m
 *  Copy next data element in queue to specified location.
 *  Also return the pointer to this element.
 */
char *q_getfrom( queue, data )
QTYPE *queue;
char  *data;
{
    register int i, j;
    char *current;
    current = NULL;
    if(queue->front == -1) return(current);
/* Else retrieve data. Copy elemsize characters into data. */
    if (queue->elemsize == 1){
        current = &(queue->data[queue->front]);
        *data = *current;
     }
    else {
    for(i=0,j=queue->front * queue->elemsize;
            i<queue->elemsize;  i++, j++){
        *(data+i) = queue->data[j];
    }
    current =
        &(queue->data[queue->front * queue->elemsize]);
     }
    queue->count--;
    if(queue->count == 0) {
/* The queue is empty. Reset front and rear, and the count. */
        queue->front = queue->rear = -1;
        return(current);
    }
/* Increment front index and check for wraparound */
    if(queue->front == queue->maxsize-1) {
        queue->front = 0;
    }
    else {
        queue->front++;
    }
```

continued

```
        return(current);
}
/*-------------------------------------------------------------*/
/*  q _ p u t o n
 *  Put a data element into queue.
 */
int q_puton( queue, data)
QTYPE *queue;
char  *data;
{
    register int i, j;
/* First check if queue is full. Return 0 if full. */
    if(queue->count == queue->maxsize) return(0);
/* Else, adjust rear and check for wraparound */
    if(queue->rear == queue->maxsize-1){
        queue->rear = 0;
    }
    else {
        queue->rear++;
    }
/* Save data in queue. Copy elemsize characters */
    if (queue->elemsize == 1){
        queue->data[queue->rear] = *data;
    }
    else {
        for(i=0,j=queue->rear * queue->elemsize;
                i<queue->elemsize;   i++, j++){
            queue->data[j] = *(data+i);
        }
    }
    queue->count++;
    if(queue->front == -1) queue->front = 0;
    return(1); /* Successfully inserted element */
}
/*-------------------- END OF FILE:  QPAC.C --------------------*/
```

Listing 13-5.   C Portion of Package, SERIAL.C

```
/*-------------------------------------------------------------*/
/*
```

continued

```
*  Filename:      S E R I A L . C
*  Purpose:       An asynchronous communication package for
*                 IBM PC and compatibles. Supports asynchronous
*                 communication adapters based on Intel 8250
*                 UART (or compatible).
*                 This version was developed on an IBM PC-AT with
*                 an IBM Serial Card. DOS version 3.1 was used.
*  Language:      Microsoft C 4.0
*  Usage:         This a set of routines that provides basic
*                 functions for asynchronous communication.
*                 Call s_setvals to set parameters and s_getvals
*                 see parameter values. Call s_setup to setup
*                 port for communications. Use s_sendchar and
*                 s_rcvchar to send and receive characters
*                 respectively. A BREAK may be sent by calling
*                 s_sendbreak.
*
*  Copyright © 1986, 1987 Nabajyoti Barkakati
*                        Silver Spring, MD 20904
*  Right to use, copy, and modify this code is granted for personal
*  noncommercial use, provided that this copyright disclosure is
*  retained on all copies. All other rights reserved.
*
*  Date Started:      10-DEC-1986
*  Revisions:  V1.00   9-FEB-1987--First working version. (NB)
*/
/*--------------------------------------------------------------*/
#include <stdio.h>
#include <ctype.h>
#include <string.h>
#include <dos.h>
#include <conio.h>

#define TRUE 1
#define FALSE 0
#define EOS  '\0'

/* Definitions for the 8259 Programmable Interrupt Controller */
#define P8259_0    0x20    /* Address of int control register */
#define P8259_1    0x21    /* Address of int mask register    */
#define END_OF_INT 0x20    /* Nonspecific EOI                 */

/* Define some ASCII characters */
```

continued

```
#define NUL_ASCII    (0)
#define XON_ASCII    (0x11)
#define XOFF_ASCII   (0x13)
#define DEL_ASCII    (0x7f)

/* Address of BIOS data area (segment 40h, ofset 0) */
#define BIOS_DATA    ((int *)(0x400000L))

/* Some interrupt vectors */
#define BIOS_RS232   0x14
#define BIOS_TOD     0x1a

/* Defines for BREAK */
#define BREAK_ON   0x40
#define BREAK_OFF  0xbf

/* Time of day interrupts occur once every 18.2 seconds */
#define TOD_INTERVAL (1000.0/18.2) /* Interval in milliseconds */

/* The address of the comm port is in the integer
 * 'comport'. This variable is initialized by reading from
 * the BIOS data area at segment 0x40.
 */
#define IER         (comport + 1)  /* Interrupt Enable Register */
#define IIR         (comport + 2)  /* Interrupt Identification  */
#define LCR         (comport + 3)  /* Line Control Register     */
#define MCR         (comport + 4)  /* Modem Control Register    */
#define LSR         (comport + 5)  /* Line Status Register      */
#define MSR         (comport + 6)  /* Modem Status Register     */

/* Individual Interrupt Enable Numbers */
#define RDAINT  1
#define THREINT 2
#define RLSINT  4
#define MSINT   8

/* Modem Control Register value */
#define MCRALL 15          /* (DTR, RTS, OUT1 and OUT2 = 1)  */
#define MCROFF 0           /* Everything off                 */

/* Interrupt Enable Register value to turn on/off all int.  */
#define IERALL  (RDAINT+THREINT+RLSINT+MSINT)
#define IEROFF  0
```

continued

```c
/* Some masks for turning interrupts off */
#define THREOFF 0xfd

/* Interrupt identification numbers */
#define MDMSTATUS   0
#define TXREGEMPTY  2
#define RXDATAREADY 4
#define RLINESTATUS 6

/* Some flags */
#define XON_RCVD  1
#define XOFF_RCVD 0
#define XON_SENT  1
#define XOFF_SENT 0

/* Hi and low percentages for xon-xoff trigger */
#define HI_TRIGGER(x)  (3*x/4)
#define LO_TRIGGER(x)  (x/4)
/* Function to get bit 0 of an integer */
#define bit0(i)        (i & 0x0001)

/* Function to turn on interrupt whose "Interrupt Enable Number"
 * is 'i', in case it has been disabled. For example, the
 * THRE interrupt is disabled when an XOFF is received from the
 * remote system.
 */
#define turnon_int(i,j)  if(((j=inp(IER))&i)==0)outp(IER,(j¦i))

#define report_error(s)  fprintf(stderr,s)

typedef struct QTYPE {
    int   count;
    int   front;
    int   rear;
    int   elemsize;
    int   maxsize;
    char *data;
} QTYPE;

typedef struct VTBLTYPE {
    char *vname;
    int   value;
```

continued

```
    } VTBLTYPE;

    typedef struct NTBLTYPE {
        char     *pname;
        VTBLTYPE *vtblentry;
        int      *p_value;
        VTBLTYPE *p_vtable;
        int       vtblsize;
    } NTBLTYPE;

    /* Functions accessible by user */
    int  s_sendchar(), s_rcvchar(), s_setvals(), s_setup(),
         s_cleanup(), s_txqempty();
    void s_sendbreak(), s_delay();
    char *s_getvals();

    /* Global status indicators */
    int  s_linestatus, s_modemstatus, s_rbocount, s_totalcount,
         s_rlscount, s_rdacount, s_trmtycount, s_mscount;

    extern  QTYPE *q_setup();
    extern  char  *q_getfrom();
    extern  int   q_puton(), q_reset();
    extern  void  s_inthndlr(), s_cli(), s_sti(), s_saveds();

    static  void  s_rls(), s_rda(), s_trmty(), s_ms();
    static  void  (*p_newhndlr)();
    static  QTYPE *txq, *rxq;
    static  union REGS xr, yr;
    static  struct SREGS sr;

    static  VTBLTYPE b_table[] = {
        "110", 0,
        "150", 1,
        "300", 2,
        "600", 3,
        "1200", 4,
        "2400", 5,
        "4800", 6,
        "9600", 7
    };

    static  VTBLTYPE p_table[] = {
```

continued

```
    "none",  0,
    "odd",   1,
    "even",  3
};

static  VTBLTYPE s_table[] = {
    "1",  0,
    "2",  1
};

static  VTBLTYPE w_table[] = {
    "7",  2,
    "8",  3
};

static  VTBLTYPE port_table[] = {
    "1",   0,
    "2",   1
};

static  VTBLTYPE onoff_table[] = {
    "off",   0,
    "on",    1
};

static   int    port_number = 0,
                comport=0,
                baudrate = 4,
                parity = 0,
                stopbits = 0,
                wordlength = 3,
                txqsize = 1024,
                rxqsize = 2048,
                enable_xonxoff = 1,
                rcvd_xonxoff = XON_RCVD,
                sent_xonxoff = XON_SENT,
                null_ignore = TRUE,
                del_ignore = TRUE,
                bit7_1_rx = FALSE,
                bit7_0_rx = TRUE,
                bit7_1_tx = FALSE,
                bit7_0_tx = FALSE,
                send_xon = FALSE,
```

continued

```
                    send_xoff = FALSE,
                    seg_oldvector = 0,
                    off_oldvector = 0,
                    pckd_comparams = 0x83,
                    int_number = 12;
                    int_enable_mask = 0xef,
                    int_disable_mask = 0x10;


    static  NTBLTYPE pname_table[] = {
        "baud",            &(b_table[4]),    &baudrate,
                b_table, (sizeof(b_table)/sizeof(VTBLTYPE)),
        "parity",          &(p_table[0]),    &parity,
                p_table, (sizeof(p_table)/sizeof(VTBLTYPE)),
        "stopbits",        &(s_table[0]),    &stopbits,
                s_table, (sizeof(s_table)/sizeof(VTBLTYPE)),
        "wordlength",      &(w_table[1]),    &wordlength,
                w_table, (sizeof(w_table)/sizeof(VTBLTYPE)),
        "port",            &(port_table[0]), &port_number,
                port_table, (sizeof(port_table)/sizeof(VTBLTYPE)),
        "xonxoff",         &(onoff_table[1]), &enable_xonxoff,
                onoff_table, (sizeof(onoff_table)/sizeof(VTBLTYPE)),
        "null_ignore",     &(onoff_table[1]), &null_ignore,
                onoff_table, (sizeof(onoff_table)/sizeof(VTBLTYPE)),
        "del_ignore",      &(onoff_table[1]), &del_ignore,
                onoff_table, (sizeof(onoff_table)/sizeof(VTBLTYPE)),
        "8thbit0_on_rx",   &(onoff_table[1]), &bit7_0_rx,
                onoff_table, (sizeof(onoff_table)/sizeof(VTBLTYPE)),
        "8thbit1_on_rx",   &(onoff_table[0]), &bit7_1_rx,
                onoff_table, (sizeof(onoff_table)/sizeof(VTBLTYPE)),
        "8thbit0_on_tx",   &(onoff_table[0]), &bit7_0_tx,
                onoff_table, (sizeof(onoff_table)/sizeof(VTBLTYPE)),
        "8thbit1_on_tx",   &(onoff_table[0]), &bit7_1_tx,
                onoff_table, (sizeof(onoff_table)/sizeof(VTBLTYPE))
    };


    #define  pnmtbl_size  (sizeof(pname_table)/sizeof(NTBLTYPE))
    /*----------------------------------------------------------------*/
    /* s _ m a i n h n d l r
     * Main interrupt handler for all serial port interrupts.
     * Called by the assembly routine s_inthndlr.
     */
    int s_mainhndlr()
    {
```

continued

```
int c;
    register int int_id, intmask;
    while (TRUE) {
/* Read the interrupt identification register, IIR */
        int_id = inp(IIR);
        if (bit0(int_id) == 1) {
/* If bit 0 is 1, then no interrupts pending. Send an end of
 * interrupt signal to the 8259A Programmable Interrupt
 * Controller and then return.
 */
            outp(P8259_0, END_OF_INT);
            return;
}
s_totalcount++;
if (int_id >= RXDATAREADY) turnon_int(THREINT,intmask);

/* Process interrupt according to id.
 * The following list is in increasing order of priority.
 */
        switch (int_id) {
            case MDMSTATUS:   s_ms();
                              break;
            case TXREGEMPTY:  s_trmty();
                              break;
            case RXDATAREADY: s_rda();
                              break;
            case RLINESTATUS: s_rls();
                              break;
/* Just fall through if id is none of the above */
        }
    }
}
/*------------------------------------------------------------*/
/* s _ r l s
 * Process a "receive line status" interrupt
 */
static void s_rls()
{
    register int intmask;
/* Read line status and save it in 's_linestatus' */
    s_linestatus = inp(LSR);
    s_rlscount++;
}
```

continued

```
/*-------------------------------------------------------------------*/
/*  s _ r d a
 *  Process a "receive data available" interrupt
 */
static void s_rda()
{
    register int intmask;
    char c;
/* Read from comport */
    c = inp(comport);
    s_rdacount++;
    if(enable_xonxoff) {
        if(c == XON_ASCII) {
            rcvd_xonxoff = XON_RCVD;
/* Turn on THRE interrupt if it's off. */
            turnon_int(THREINT,intmask);
            return;
        }
        if(c == XOFF_ASCII) {
            rcvd_xonxoff = XOFF_RCVD;
/* Turn off THRE interrupts. */
            intmask = inp(IER);
            if (intmask & THREINT) outp(IER, intmask & THREOFF);
            return;
        }
    }
    if(null_ignore && c == NUL_ASCII) return;
    if(del_ignore && c == DEL_ASCII) return;
    if(bit7_1_rx) c |= 0x80;
    if(bit7_0_rx) c &= 0x7f;
    if( q_puton(rxq, &c) == 0){
/* Increment receive buffer overflow count */
        s_rbocount++;
    }
/* Check if queue is almost (75%) full */
    if(enable_xonxoff){
        if(rxq->count >= HI_TRIGGER(rxqsize)  &&
            sent_xonxoff != XOFF_SENT ) {
/* Set flag to send XOFF */
            send_xoff = TRUE;
/* and turn on THRE interrupts so that we can send the XOFF */
            turnon_int(THREINT,intmask);
        }
```

continued

522

```
        }
}
/*------------------------------------------------------------*/
/*  s _ t r m t y
 *  Process a "transmit holding register empty" interrupt
 */
static void s_trmty()
{
    char c;
    register int ierval;

    s_trmtycount++;

    if (send_xoff == TRUE) {
        outp(comport, XOFF_ASCII);
        send_xoff = FALSE;
        sent_xonxoff = XOFF_SENT;
        return;
    }
    if (send_xon == TRUE) {
        outp(comport, XON_ASCII);
        send_xon = FALSE;
        sent_xonxoff = XON_SENT;
        return;
    }

/* Put a character into the transmit holding register */
    if( q_getfrom(txq, &c) != NULL){
        if(bit7_1_tx) c |= 0x80;
        if(bit7_0_tx) c &= 0x7f;
        outp(comport, c);
        return;
    }
/* Nothing to send--turn off THRE interrupts */
    ierval = inp(IER);
    if (ierval & THREINT) outp(IER, ierval & THREOFF);
}
/*------------------------------------------------------------*/
/*  s _ m s
 *  Process a "modem status" interrupt
 */
static void s_ms()
{
```

continued

```
/* Read modem status and save in 's_modemstatus' */
    s_modemstatus = inp(MSR);
    s_mscount++;
}
/*-------------------------------------------------------------*/
/* s _ s e t u p
 * Sets up everything for communication. Call this routine
 * after parameter values have been specified (by s_setparams).
 * Return 1 if setup successful, else return 0.
 */
int s_setup()
{
int i;
    static void s_intinit();

    if (port_number < 0 || port_number > 1)
                report_error("Invalid port number!\n");
/* Get port address from BIOS data area and save in 'comport' */
    comport = *(BIOS_DATA + port_number);
    if (comport == 0){
        report_error("BIOS could not find port!\n");
        return(0);
     }
/* Set up masks for 8259A PIC. To enable interrupt from the
 * port this mask is ANDed with the mask register at 21h.
 * To disable, OR the disable mask with the mask register.
 * The interrupt number is 8+the IRQ level of the interrupt.
 * Com port 1 has IRQ 4, port 2 has IRQ 3.
 */
    if (port_number == 0) {
        int_enable_mask = 0xef;
        int_disable_mask = 0x10;
        int_number = 12;
    }
    if (port_number == 1) {
        int_enable_mask = 0xf7;
        int_disable_mask = 8;
        int_number = 11;
    }
/* Get old interrupt vector and save it. Use DOS function 35h */
    xr.h.ah = 0x35;
    xr.h.al = int_number;
    segread(&sr);
```

continued

```
    intdosx(&xr, &yr, &sr);
    off_oldvector = yr.x.bx;
    seg_oldvector = sr.es;

/* Install new interrupt service routine, use DOS function 25h */
    p_newhndlr = s_inthndlr;
    xr.h.ah = 0x25;
    xr.h.al = int_number;
    xr.x.dx = FP_OFF(p_newhndlr);
    segread(&sr);
    sr.ds = FP_SEG(p_newhndlr);
    intdosx(&xr, &yr, &sr);

/* Set up communication parameters */
    s_setcommparams();

/* Call assembly language routine to save current value of DS */
    s_saveds();

/* Setup the transmit and receive queues */
    if ( (txq = q_setup(txqsize, sizeof(char))) == NULL   ){
        report_error("Error creating transmit queue!\n");
        return(0);
    }
    if ( (rxq = q_setup(rxqsize, sizeof(char))) == NULL   ){
        report_error("Error creating receive queue!\n");
        return(0);
    }

/* Reset all counts and flags. */
    s_rbocount = 0;
    s_totalcount = 0;
    s_rlscount = 0;
    s_rdacount = 0;
    s_trmtycount = 0;
    s_mscount = 0;

    rcvd_xonxoff = XON_RCVD;
    if (sent_xonxoff == XOFF_SENT) {
        send_xon = TRUE;
    }
    else {
        send_xon = FALSE;
```

continued

```
    }
    send_xoff = FALSE;

/* Turn on interrupts from the comm port and setup 8259A */
    s_cli();
    s_intinit();
    s_sti();

    return(1);
}
/*------------------------------------------------------------*/
/*  s _ i n t i n i t
 *  Start up interrupts from the serial board. Also set up
 *  8259A to accept the interrupts. This routine should be
 *  invoked with the interrupts turned off, i.e., inside a
 *  (CLI---STI) pair.
 */
static void s_intinit()
{
    int intmask;

/* Set up modem control register (port = MCR) */
    outp(MCR, MCRALL);

/* Enable all interrupts on the serial card (port = IER) */
    outp(IER, IERALL);

/* Read 8259A's interrupt mask register and write it back after
 * ANDing with int_enable_mask.
 */
    intmask = inp(P8259_1) & int_enable_mask;
    outp(P8259_1, intmask);
}
/*------------------------------------------------------------*/
/*  s _ c l e a n u p
 *  Cleanup after comm session is done. Turns off all interrupts.
 */
int s_cleanup()
{
    static void s_intoff();

/* Turn off interrupts from serial card */
    s_cli();
```

continued

```
    s_intoff();
    s_sti();

/* Restore orginal interrupt vectors */
    xr.h.ah = 0x25;
    xr.h.al = int_number;
    xr.x.dx = off_oldvector;
    sr.ds = seg_oldvector;
    intdosx(&xr, &yr, &sr);

/* Deallocate space used by the transmit and receive queues */
    q_reset(txq);
    q_reset(rxq);
}
/*-------------------------------------------------------------*/
/* s _ i n t o f f
 * Turn off all interrupts after comm session is done.
 * Should be called with interrupts cleared.
 */
static void s_intoff()
{
    int intmask;

/* First reset the Interrupt Enable Register on the comm card  */
    outp(IER, IEROFF);

/* Turn off all bits of Modem Control Register */
    outp(MCR, MCROFF);

/* Next disable 8259A from recognizing ints at this IRQ level   */
    intmask = inp(P8259_1) ¦ int_disable_mask;
    outp(P8259_1, intmask);
}
/*-------------------------------------------------------------*/
/* s _ s e t c o m m p a r a m s
 * Set up basic communication parameters by using BIOS interrupt
 * number 14h, function 0 (ah=0).
 */
int s_setcommparams()
{
/* Set up communication port parameters. Use BIOS INT 14h, AH=0 */
    pckd_comparams = (baudrate << 5) ¦ (parity << 3) ¦
                (stopbits << 2) ¦ (wordlength);
```

```
        xr.h.ah = 0;
        xr.h.al = pckd_comparams;
        xr.x.dx = port_number;
        int86(BIOS_RS232, &xr, &yr);

/* Copy status into "s_linestatus" and "s_modemstatus" */
        s_linestatus = yr.h.ah;
        s_modemstatus = yr.h.al;
}
/*------------------------------------------------------------*/
/*  s _ v t b l s r c h
 *  Searches a value string in specified table. Returns index if
 *  found. Returns -1 if string not in table. (Internal Routine)
 */
static int s_vtblsrch(string, table, size)
char *string;
VTBLTYPE *table;
int size;
{
    int i;
    for (i = 0; i < size; i++) {
        if ( (strcmpi(string, table[i].vname)) == 0) {
            return(i);
        }
    }
    return(-1);
}
/*------------------------------------------------------------*/
/*  s _ s e t v a l s
 *  Set the value string for a named parameter.
 *  Return 1 if ok, 0 otherwise.
 */
int s_setvals(name, vals)
char *name, *vals;
{
    static int s_vtblsrch();
    int i, j, retval;

    retval = 0;
/* First search table for parameter name */
    for (i=0; i<pnmtbl_size; i++) {
        if (strcmpi(pname_table[i].pname, name) == 0) {
/* Now search the table for the value string */
```

continued

```
            if ((j = s_vtblsrch(vals, pname_table[i].p_vtable,
                        pname_table[i].vtblsize)) != -1) {
                *(pname_table[i].p_value) =
                    (pname_table[i].p_vtable)[j].value;
                pname_table[i].vtblentry =
                    &((pname_table[i].p_vtable)[j]);
                retval = 1;
            }
            break;
        }
    }
    return(retval);
}
/*--------------------------------------------------------------*/
/* s _ g e t v a l s
 * Return the value string corresponding to a named parameter.
 * Returns NULL in case of error.
 */
char *s_getvals(name)
char *name;
{
    int i;
    for (i=0; i<pnmtbl_size; i++) {
        if (strcmpi(pname_table[i].pname, name) == 0) {
            return((pname_table[i].vtblentry)->vname);
        }
    }
    return(NULL);
}
/*--------------------------------------------------------------*/
/* s _ s e n d c h a r
 * Puts a character into transmit queue. Returns 1 if all's ok,
 * 0 if there were problems.
 */
int s_sendchar(ch)
int ch;
{
    int retval, intmask;

    retval = q_puton(txq, &ch);
/* Turn on THRE interrupt if it's off and an XOFF was not received*/
    if (rcvd_xonxoff != XOFF_RCVD)turnon_int(THREINT,intmask);
    return(retval);
```

continued

```
    }
/*-------------------------------------------------------------*/
/*  s _ r c v c h a r
 *  Returns a character from the receive queue.
 *  Returns -1 if queue is empty.
 */
int s_rcvchar()
{
    int ch, intmask;
/* If we had sent an XOFF earlier, we might have to send an XON */
    if(enable_xonxoff){
        if(rxq->count <= LO_TRIGGER(rxqsize)  &&
            sent_xonxoff != XON_SENT ) {
            send_xon = TRUE;
            turnon_int(THREINT,intmask);
        }
    }
    if (q_getfrom(rxq, &ch) == NULL) {
        return(-1);
    }
    else {
        return(ch);
    }
}
/*-------------------------------------------------------------*/
/*  s _ t x q e m p t y
 *  Returns 1 if txq (transmit queue) is empty, else returns 0.
 *  Need when sending file.
 */
int s_txqempty()
{
    if (txq->count == 0) {
        return (TRUE);
    }
    else {
        return (FALSE);
    }
}
/*-------------------------------------------------------------*/
/*  s _ s e n d b r e a k
 *  Send a break signal (hold line in spacing state for 250 ms).
 */
void s_sendbreak()
```

continued

```
{
    int lcrval;
/* Turn on bit 6 of LCR to initiate BREAK signal */
    lcrval = inp(LCR) | BREAK_ON;
    outp(LCR, lcrval);
    s_delay(250.0);
/* Turn off bit 6 of LCR to end the BREAK signal */
    lcrval = inp(LCR) & BREAK_OFF;
    outp(LCR, lcrval);
}
/*-----------------------------------------------------------*/
/*  s _ d e l a y
 *  Delay for 'd_ms" milliseconds. Resolution ~55 milliseconds.
 *  WARNING : This is a very "coarse" timer.
 */
void s_delay(d_ms)
double d_ms;
{
    int ticks;
    long oldcount, newcount;
/* Get timer ticks for this delay */
    ticks = (int)(d_ms / TOD_INTERVAL + 0.5);
    xr.h.ah = 0;
    int86(BIOS_TOD, &xr, &yr);
/* On return CX has high count and DX has low count.
 * The high count is incremented every 65,536 low counts.
 */
    oldcount = (long)(( (long)(yr.x.cx) << 16) |
              (unsigned) yr.x.dx);
    newcount = oldcount;
/* Now keep checking count until difference between new and
 * old counts is 'ticks'.
 */
    while ((newcount - oldcount) < ticks) {
        int86(BIOS_TOD, &xr, &yr);
        if (yr.h.al != 0) {
/* The timer has crossed 24 hours */
            newcount = (long)(( 24L << 16) | (unsigned) yr.x.dx);
        }
        else {
            newcount = (long)(( (long)(yr.x.cx) << 16) |
                      (unsigned) yr.x.dx);
        }
```

continued

```
    }
  }
  /*------------------ END OF FILE:  SERIAL.C ------------------*/
```

> The source code for the serial communications package described in this article is available on a 360KB double-sided double-density IBM PC diskette (DOS 3.1) for $9.95. (check or a money order) from LNB Software, Inc.; 2005 Aventurine Way; Silver Spring, MD 20904.

Reading List

Note that although we have presented all pertinent details necessary to develop a serial communications package, we could not discuss all aspects of data communications. For your convenience, we are including this list of references. The recent book by Campbell (1987) discusses "communications programming" from the viewpoint of C programmers working with MS-DOS or CP/M machines. McNamara's book (1982) has a wealth of technical information on all aspects of data communications in general. The book by LaFore (1984) is an excellent guide on assembly language programming for the IBM PC, and Prata's book (1986) is very helpful if you are a programmer trying to make the most of the PC and MS-DOS. For detailed information on the serial adapter and interrupt handling in the PC, you can consult the IBM reference manuals directly, but we hope that after having read this essay, you will not find it necessary to do so—at least not until you need information on exact meanings of the internal registers of the asynchronous communications hardware on the PC. The book on data structures by Tremblay and Sorenson (1984) has algorithms on pp. 219-223 to implement a circular queue. Campbell, J. 1987. *C Programmer's Guide to Serial Communications.* Indianapolis: Howard W. Sams & Company.

da Cruz, F. 1987. *KERMIT—A File Transfer Protocol.* Bedford: Digital Press.

IBM. 1984. *Personal Computer AT Technical Reference Manual.* Part #1502243. North Tarrytown, New York.

———. 1984. *Options and Adapters Technical Reference Manual.* Part #6322509. North Tarrytown, New York.

Intel Corporation. 1981. *iAPX 86,88 User's Manual.* Publication #21201-001. Santa Clara, California.

LaFore, R. 1984. *Assembly Language Primer for the IBM PC*. New York: New American Library (Plume/Waite).

McNamara, J. 1982. *Technical Aspects of Data Communications*. Bedford: Digital Press.

Prata, S./The Waite Group. 1986. *Advanced C Primer + +*. Indianapolis: Howard W. Sams & Company.

Tremblay, J., and P. Sorenson. 1984. *An Introduction to Data Structures with Applications*. New York: McGraw-Hill Book Co.

Nabajyoti Barkakati works as an electronics engineer for a well-known research laboratory. He began his programming career in 1975, and has worked extensively with FORTRAN, C and several assembly languages (PDP-11, 80X86). He remains an avid programmer, primarily interested in developing communications and graphics software on the IBM PC and the Macintosh. He has a Ph.D. in electrical engineering from the University of Maryland.

Related Essays

  1 A Guided Tour inside MS-DOS
  6 Undocumented MS-DOS Functions
 10 Developing MS-DOS Drivers

Keywords

- ▶ expanded memory systems
- ▶ Expanded Memory (EMS)
- ▶ Enhanced Expanded Memory (EEMS)
- ▶ expanded memory manager
- ▶ device drivers
- ▶ memory management

Essay Synopsis: Today's applications often press against the 640K limit for addressable memory under MS-DOS, especially when memory is being shared with several memory-resident programs. Expanded memory systems offer the opportunity to use main memory as a window onto megabytes of additional memory. The demand for expanded memory support is growing, and programmers are often called upon to provide it with new or revised products. This essay explains different standards for expanded memory (EMS and EEMS) and provides a summary of the function calls needed for a program to access and manage expanded memory. He gives an outline of the strategy needed for recognizing the type of EMS support present, and provides example listings of key routines.

14

Understanding Expanded Memory Systems

Ray Duncan

The Intel 8086 and 8088 microprocessors, which serve as the heart of the original IBM PC and most of its compatibles, can directly address up to one megabyte of memory. In the IBM PC architecture, the bottom 640K of this address space is available for use by MS-DOS and the programs which run under its control. The upper 384K are reserved for use by various adapter boards and for test programs and device drivers in read-only memory (ROM). Personal computers based on the Intel 80286 and 80386 microprocessors are physically capable of addressing much larger amounts of RAM, but run MS-DOS in so-called real mode (8086 emulation mode) where they are still subject to the same one-megabyte limitation.

In the early days of the IBM PC and MS-DOS, a 640K program space seemed simply enormous. After all, most of the first MS-DOS programs were ported from 8080 and Z-80 systems running under CP/M, where 64K of memory was the maximum and 32K systems were not unusual. But within three years, several events conspired to make the 640K space seem suddenly crowded after all. Completely new applications were written that were able to take full advantage of the larger address space, a new class of immensely popular applications called Terminate and Stay Resident (TSR) emerged, and MS-DOS itself rapidly grew larger as it was enhanced to support networks and fixed disks. (See Essay 1, A Guided Tour inside MS-DOS, by Harry Henderson, for a general discussion of changes in MS-DOS, and Essay 7, Safe Memory-Resident Programming (TSR) by Steven Baker.)

Lotus, Intel, Microsoft EMS

In order to prolong the useful life of the 8086/88-based PCs, Lotus Development Corporation and Intel Corporation worked together on a method to increase the amount of fast storage available to MS-DOS applications. The result of their collaboration, the Expanded Memory Specification (EMS) version 3.0, was announced at the Spring COMDEX in 1985. Shortly afterward, Microsoft announced support for the EMS, and that Microsoft Windows would be upgraded to use the memory made available by EMS hardware and software. EMS version 3.2, modified from 3.0 to add support for multitasking operating systems, was released in August 1985 as a joint effort of Lotus, Intel, and Microsoft and is commonly referred to as the LIM EMS.

Enhanced Expanded Memory

In response to the first Intel and Lotus announcement, AST Research, a manufacturer of popular add-on memory boards for IBM PC compatibles, formulated a competitive memory expansion approach called the Enhanced Expanded Memory Specification (EEMS). The AST design was upward compatible from the original EMS, but technically more complex and specifically directed at improving the performance of multitasking operating systems. It was subsequently endorsed by Ashton-Tate and Quadram, modified for compatibility with the LIM EMS version 3.2, and became popularly known as the AQA EEMS.

In August 1987, Lotus, Intel, Microsoft, and the other interested parties announced Expanded Memory Specification version 4.0. EMS 4.0 reconciles the previous EMS 3.2 and EEMS specifications, is upward compatible from EMS 3.2, raises the limit on the maximum amount of expanded memory which may be installed in a system, and adds many new capabilities for the benefit of multitasking program managers such as DESQView and Microsoft Windows.

It is apparent, as this book goes to press, that the Expanded Memory Specification has been a tremendous success. EMS compatible expansion boards are available from scores of manufacturers, and an incredible variety of software products, including all of the most popular spreadsheets and integrated environments, have been revised to take advantage of EMS memory when it is available. (Representative products that support Lotus/Intel/Microsoft EMS and/or AST Research/Quadram/Ashton-Tate EEMS are included in the Reading List at the end of this essay.)

What Is Expanded Memory?

The Lotus/Intel/Microsoft EMS and the AST/Quadram/Ashton-Tate EEMS are functional specifications of bank-switched memory subsystems. Bank-switching is a technique whereby one out of many logical memory pages can be made available for access by the central processor in a window at a predetermined physical address, somewhat like bringing one card out of a deck to the top where it can be read. It was first widely employed on Apple II and S-100 bus computers in the late 1970s, to overcome the memory size limitations and the slow floppy disk access times on those machines.

An EMS or EEMS compatible memory subsystem consists of one or more user-installable expanded memory boards which are plugged into the IBM PC expansion bus and resident driver program—the Expanded Memory Manager (EMM)—provided by the board manufacturer. Together, the boards and driver allow an application program to gain access to as much as 8 megabytes of random access storage (32 megabytes in the case of EMS 4.0) in a hardware-independent manner. The application calls on the driver to map 16K pages of expanded memory in and out of the microprocessor's usual 1-megabyte address space as they are needed (see Figure 14-1). The driver accomplishes this mapping by writing expanded memory logical page numbers to specific CPU I/O ports, which are in turn physically connected to page registers on the memory boards.

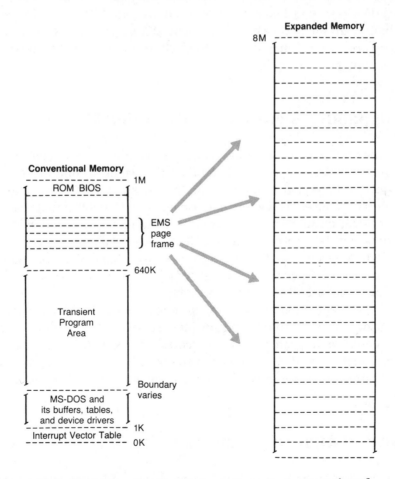

Fig. 14-1. Relationship of expanded memory to conventional memory.

The EMS 3.2, EEMS, and EMS 4.0 specifications differ mainly in where the expanded memory pages may be mapped to main memory, and how many pages may be so mapped simultaneously. LIM EMS 3.2 allows four 16K pages to be mapped at a time into a contiguous 64K area called a *page frame.* The location of the page frame is user-configurable so that it will not conflict with other hardware expansion options, but it is always located above the 640K area controlled by MS-DOS. Thus, since the expanded memory pages lie outside the area recognized by the operating system, they cannot be used for the execution of programs but only for storage of data.

In the AQA EEMS or EMS 4.0 design, on the other hand, more than four expanded memory pages can be mapped into memory at once, and the pages can be mapped anywhere within the CPU's one-megabyte address space. This makes it possible for specially designed multitasking managers (such as Quarterdeck System's DESQView) or operating systems (such as Digital Research's Concurrent PC-DOS) to use expanded memory for storage of executable program code and very fast switching between processes. However, for upward compatibility with the LIM EMS 3.2, the AQA EEMS and EMS 4.0 require that the memory area used to map the first four 16K pages (referred to in the the AQA EEMS as windows) be contiguous.

Expanded Memory vs. Extended Memory

Expanded memory should not be confused with extended memory. Although the two terms sound almost identical, they refer to completely different types of storage. Extended memory is the term used by IBM to refer to the memory at physical addresses higher than 1 megabyte (100000H) that may be accessed by an 80286 or 80386 microprocessor executing in protected mode. Since MS-DOS runs on these processors in real mode, extended memory is not directly accessible to MS-DOS-based application programs. Most machines contain ROM BIOS routines and special hardware support that allow it to be used for storage by electronic disk (RAMdisk) drivers, however.

Protected mode operating systems such as Microsoft's XENIX or OS/2, on the other hand, can take full advantage of extended memory for storage of both executable programs and data. Protected-mode 80386 virtual machine managers, such as Windows/386, can even take advantage of the 80386's page registers to simulate the presence of expanded memory by remapping extended memory.

Expanded Memory Manager

The EMM provides the hardware-independent interface between application programs and the expanded memory board(s). The EMM is supplied by the manufacturer in the form of an installable device driver compatible with MS-DOS version 2.0 or later. (See Essay 10, Developing MS-DOS Device Drivers, by Walter Dixon, for the theory and practice of installable device drivers.) The EMM itself is not sensitive to the version of MS-DOS that is running, but installable device drivers were not supported under MS-DOS versions 1.0 and 1.1.

The user installs the EMM by copying the file containing the driver to his boot disk, adding a `DEVICE=` directive to the `CONFIG.SYS` file, and restarting the system. Internally, the EMM is divided into two distinct components: the driver and the manager.

The driver portion contains some of the elements of a genuine installable character device driver, in that it includes Initialization and Output Status subfunctions and a valid device header. These elements allow the EMM to be incorporated into the environment in an orderly way, and provide a means for application software to test for the driver's presence using conventional operating system services.

The manager element of the EMM is the true interface between application software and the expanded memory hardware. The LIM EMS defines the services to be provided by the EMM, including

- status of the expanded memory subsystem
- allocation of expanded memory pages
- mapping of logical pages into physical memory
- deallocation of expanded memory pages
- support for multitasking operating systems
- diagnostic routines

The EMS also specifies how the EMM services are invoked, what parameters they accept, and what results they will return.

The AQA EEMS redefines the software interface between application software and the EMM from that used in LIM EMS 3.2 only slightly, extending the definition of one of the EMS 3.2 functions and adding one new function in order to remove the restrictions on the mapping regions and the number of pages which may be mapped simultaneously.

The LIM EMS 4.0, in its turn, defines about 40 new functions and subfunctions. Since the EMS 4.0 functions are mainly used by program managers and operating systems, they will not be described in detail in this essay.

Application programs communicate with the EMM directly via a software interrupt `INT 67H`. The MS-DOS operating system kernel does not take part in expanded memory manipulations and does not make any use of expanded memory for its own purposes. However, some multitasking manager programs that run on top of MS-DOS, such as Microsoft Windows and Quarterdeck System's DESQview, are able to use expanded memory for swapping program code and/or data.

Testing for Expanded Memory

Before it attempts to use expanded memory for storage, an application program must establish that the Expanded Memory Manager is present and functional, and then it must call the driver to check the status of the memory boards themselves. There are two methods a program can use to test for the existence of the EMM.

The first technique is to issue an open file or device request INT 21H (Function 3DH), using the guaranteed device name of the EMM driver, EMMXXXX0. If the open operation succeeds, either the driver is present or there is a file with the same name in the current directory of the default disk drive. The application can then issue IOCTL Get Device Information INT 21H (Function 44H Subfunction 00H) and IOCTL Get Output Status INT 21H (Function 44H Subfunction 07H) requests to further qualify the existence and status of the driver. In any case, the handle that was obtained from the open function should be closed INT 21H (Function 3EH) so it can be reused for another file or device. The open method is demonstrated in the following listing:

```
            .
            .
            .
                                   ; attempt to "open" EMM
     mov  dx,seg emm_name          ; DS:DX = addr. of name
     mov  ds,dx                    ; of Expanded Memory Manager
     mov  dx,offset emm_name
     mov  ax,3d00h                 ; Function 3DH, Mode=00H
                                   ; = open, read-only
     int  21h                      ; transfer to MS-DOS
     jc   error                    ; jump if open failed

                                   ; open succeeded, make sure
                                   ; it was not a file
     mov  bx,ax                    ; BX = handle from open
     mov  ax,4400h                 ; Function 44H Subfunction 00H
                                   ; = IOCTL Get Device Information
     int  21h                      ; transfer to MS-DOS
     jc   error                    ; jump if IOCTL call failed
     and  dx,80h                   ; Bit 7 = 1 if character device
     jz   error                    ; jump if it was a file

                                   ; EMM is present, make sure
                                   ; it is available...
                                   ; (BX still contains handle)
```

```
        mov   ax,4407h                  ; Function 44H subfunction 07H
                                        ; = IOCTL Get Ouput Status
        int   21h                       ; transfer to MS-DOS
        jc    error                     ; jump if IOCTL call failed
        or    al,al                     ; test device status
        jz    error                     ; if AL=0 EMM is not available

                                        ; now close handle
                                        ; (BX still contains handle)
        mov ah,3eh                      ; Function 3EH = Close
        int 21h                         ; transfer to MS-DOS
        jc  error                       ; jump if close failed
        .
        .
        .
emm_name db 'EMMXXXX0',0                ; guaranteed device name for
                                        ; Expanded Memory Manager
```

The second method of testing for the driver is to use the address that is found in the vector for INT 67H to inspect the device header of the presumed EMM. The contents of the vector can be obtained conveniently with INT 21H (Function 35H). If the EMM is present, the name field at offset 0AH of the device header contains the eight-byte ASCII string, EMMXXXX0. This method is highly reliable and it avoids the overhead of an open operation, but it is considered less "well-behaved" because it involves inspection of memory that does not belong to the application. The get interrupt vector technique is illustrated in the following listing:

```
emm_int    equ    67H                  ; Extended Memory Manager
                                        ; software interrupt
        .
        .
        .
                                        ; first fetch contents of
                                        ; EMM interrupt vector...
        mov   al,emm_int                ; AL = EMM int. number
        mov   ah,35h                     ; fxn 35H = get vector
        int   21h                       ; transfer to MS-DOS
                                        ; now ES:BX = handler addr.

                                        ; assume ES:00000 points
                                        ; to base of the EMM...
        mov   di,10                     ; ES:DI = addr. of name
                                        ; field in Device Header
```

```
        mov   si,offset emm_name
        mov   cx,8                      ; length of name field
        cld
        repz  cmpsb                     ; compare names...
        jnz   error                     ; jmp if driver absent
          .
          .
          .
emm_name  db   'EMMXXXX0'               ; guaranteed device name for
                                        ; Expanded Memory Manager
```

Using Expanded Memory

It is not uncommon for several programs, such as electronic disks (RAMdisks), TSR utilities, and foreground application programs, to be using expanded memory for storage at the same time. Accordingly, it is important that each program treat expanded memory as a system resource like a file or peripheral device, and employ only the documented EMM services to allocate, access, and release expanded memory pages. Otherwise, the data belonging to one or more of the programs may be corrupted or destroyed.

Once it has established that the Expanded Memory Manager is present, the application program bypasses MS-DOS and communicates with the EMM directly via software INT 67H. The general calling sequence is

```
mov   ah,function    ; AH selects EMM function

  .                  ; load other registers with
  .                  ; values specific to the
  .                  ; requested service

int   67h            ; transfer to EMM
```

In general, registers ES:DI are used to pass the address of a buffer or an array, and register DX holds an expanded memory handle, a 16-bit token returned by the EMM when a program first allocates some expanded memory pages and used by the program for subsequent access to those pages. Some EMM functions also use the AL and BX to pass such information as logical and physical page numbers.

Upon return from an EMM function call, register AH contains zero if the function was successful. Otherwise, AH contains an error code with the most significant bit set, from the selection listed in Table 14-1.

Table 14-1. **Expanded Memory Manager Error Codes**

Error Code	Significance
00H	Function was successful
80H	Internal error in the expanded memory manager software (Possible causes include a logical error in the driver itself or damage to the memory image of the driver.)
81H	Malfunction in the expanded memory hardware
82H	Memory manager is busy (It is already processing an expanded memory request.)
83H	Invalid expanded memory handle
84H	Function requested by the application is not defined
85H	No more expanded memory handles available
86H	Error in save or restore of mapping context
87H	An allocation request specified more logical pages than are physically available in the system (No pages were allocated.)
88H	An allocation request specified more logical pages than are currently available in the system (The request does not exceed the physical pages that exist, but some are already allocated to other EMM handles; no pages were allocated.)
89H	Zero pages cannot be allocated
8AH	The logical page that was requested for mapping is outside the range of logical pages assigned to the handle
8BH	Illegal physical page number in mapping request (not in the range 0-3)
8CH	The save area for mapping contexts is full
8DH	Save of mapping context failed, because save area already contains a context associated with the requested handle
8EH	Restore of mapping context failed, because save area does not contain a context for the requested handle
8FH	Subfunction parameter not defined

Other values are typically returned in registers AL and BX or in a user-specified buffer. The parameters and returned results for the various functions supported by the EMS and EEMS compatible EMMs are summarized in Tables 14-2 and 14-3. EMS Functions 49H and 4AH (not listed) were defined in EMS version 3.0 and are "reserved" in later EMS versions.

Table 14-2. **Expanded Memory Manager Interface**

Function Name	Action	Call With	Returns	Comments
Get Manager Status	Test whether the expanded memory software and hardware are functional.	AH = 40H	AH = status	This call is used after the program has established that the Expanded Memory Manager is present in the system.
Get Page Frame Segment	Obtain the segment address of the EMM page frame.	AH = 41H	AH = status BX = segment of page frame, if AH = 0	The page frame is divided into four 16K pages, which are used to map logical expanded memory pages into

Table 14-2.   (cont.)

Function Name	Action	Call With	Returns	Comments
				the physical memory space of the 8086/8088 processor.
Get Expanded Memory Pages	Obtain the number of logical expanded memory pages present in the system and the number of pages that are not already allocated.	AH = 42H	AH = status BX = unallocated pages, if AH = 0 DX = total EMS pages in system	The application need not have already acquired an EMM handle to use this function.
Allocate Expanded Memory	Obtains an EMM handle and allocates logical expanded memory pages to be controlled by that handle.	AH = 43H BX = logical pages to allocate	AH = status DX = EMM handle, if AH = 0	Equivalent of a file open function for the EMM. The handle that is returned is analogous to a file handle, and owns a certain number of EMM pages. The handle must be used with every subsequent request to map memory, and must be released by a close operation.
Map Memory	Map one of the logical pages of expanded memory assigned to a handle onto one of the four physical pages within the EMM's page frame.	AH = 44H AL = physical page (0-3) BX = logical page (0 . . . n − 1) DX = EMM handle	AH = status	The logical page number must be in the range (0 . . . n − 1), where n is the number of logical pages previously allocated to the EMM handle with Function 43H. To actually access the memory once it has been mapped to a physical page, the application also needs the segment of the EMM's page frame, obtained with Function 41H.
Release Handle and Memory	Deallocate the logical pages of expanded memory currently assigned to a handle, and then release the handle itself for reuse.	AH = 45H DX = EMM handle	AH = status	This function is the equivalent of a close operation on a file. It notifies the EMM that the application will not be making further use of the data it may have stored within expanded memory pages.
Get EMM Version	Return the version number of the Expanded Memory Manager software.	AH = 46H	AH = status AL = EMM version, if AH = 0	The returned value is the version of the EMS with which the driver complies. The version number is encoded as BCD, with the integer part in the upper four bits, and the fractional part in the lower four bits.
Save Mapping Context	Save the contents of the expanded memory page-map-	AH = 74H DX = EMM handle	AH = status	This function is designed for use by interrupt handlers and resident drivers or utili-

Table 14-2.   (cont.)

Function Name	Action	Call With	Returns	Comments
	ping registers on the expanded memory boards, associating those contents with a specific EMM handle.			ties that must access expanded memory. The handle supplied to the function is the handle that was assigned to the interrupt handler during its initialization sequence, not to the program that was interrupted.
Restore Mapping Context	Restore the contents of all expanded memory hardware page-mapping registers to the values associated with the given handle.	AH = 48H DX = EMM handle	AH = status	Use of this function must be balanced with a previous call to EMM function 47H. It allows an interrupt handler or resident driver which used expanded memory to restore the mapping context to its state at the point of interruption.
Get Number of EMM Handles	Return the number of active EMM handles.	AH = 4BH	AH = status BX = number of EMM handles, if AH = 0	If the number of handles returned is zero, none of the expanded memory is in use. The number of active EMM handles never exceeds 255. A single program can make several allocation requests and therefore own several EMM handles.
Get Pages Owned by Handle	Return the number of logical expanded memory pages allocated to a specific handle.	AH = 4CH DX = EMM handle	AH = status BX = logical pages, if AH = 0	The number of pages returned is always in the range 1-512 if the function is successful. An EMM handle never has zero pages of memory allocated to it.
Get Pages for All Handles	Return an array that contains all the active handles and the number of logical expanded memory pages associated with each handle.	AH = 4DH DI = offset of array to receive information ES = array segment	AH = status BX = number of active EMM handles IF AH = 0, array is filled in as described in comments column	The array is filled in with two-word entries. The first word of each entry contains a handle, and the second word contains the number of pages associated with that handle. The value returned in BX gives the number of valid two-word entries in the array. Because 255 is the maximum number of EMM handles, the array need not be larger than 1020 bytes.
Get/Set Page Map	Save or set the contents of the page-mapping registers on the expanded memory boards.	AH = 4EH AL = subfunction number DS:SI = array holding mapping information (subfunctions 1, 2) ES:DI	AH = status AL = bytes in page-mapping array (subf. 3) Array pointed to by ES:DI receives mapping infor-	Subfunctions: 0 = get mapping registers into array 1 = set mapping registers from array 2 = get and set mapping registers in one operation 3 = return needed size of page-mapping array (This

Table 14-2.   (cont.)

Function Name	Action	Call With	Returns	Comments
		= array to receive information (subfunctions)	mation, for subfunctions 0 and 2	function was added in EMS version 3.2 and is designed to support multitasking. It should not ordinarily be used by application programs.) The content of the array is hardware.

Table 14-3.   Modified or Additional Expanded Memory Manager Functions Defined by the AST/Quadram/Ashton-Tate EEMS

Function Name	Action	Call With	Returns	Comments
Map Memory	Map one of the logical pages of expanded memory assigned to a handle onto one of the EMM's physical windows.	AH = 44H AL = window no. (see comment) BX = logical page (0 . . . n − 1) DX = handle	AH = status	The logical page number must be in the range (0 . . . n − 1), where n is the number of logical pages previously allocated to the EMM handle with Function 43H. The window number must be within the range returned by the EEMS function 60H (see below). The first four windows are mapped contiguously for EMS compatibility.
Get Physical Window Array	Obtain the number of mapping windows and an array containing the addresses of those windows.	AH = 60H ES:DI = address of array	AH = status AL = number of windows Array receives window-mapping information	This function fills in the array with a list of the physical page windows available. Each entry in the array is one byte in length and corresponds to a physical page number that contains the most significant six bits of the segment address.

Strategy for Using Expanded Memory

Although the EMM software interface may appear somewhat forbidding at first glance, it is really very easy to use. The general strategy for use of expanded memory by an application program is quite straightforward:

1. Establish the presence of the EMM by one of the two methods demonstrated in the earlier examples. If the EMM cannot be found, the application must either terminate or proceed using conventional memory resources only.

2. Once the driver is known to be present, check its operational status with EMS Function 40H. This function verifies that the EMM has been properly initialized during the system boot process, and that the EMS hardware is functioning correctly.

3. Check the version number of the EMM with EMS Function 46H to ensure that all services the application will request are available. For example, if the application makes use of EMS Function 4EH, it must ensure that it is running with version 3.2 or greater of the EMM rather than 3.0. The algorithm to be used by the program is as follows:

    a. Issue `INT 67H` with AH = 46H. If AL = 40H, the EMM is compatible with EMS version 4.0. If AL = 30H, the EMM is compatible with EMS version 3.0. If AL = 32H, proceed to step 3b.

    b. Issue `INT 67H` with AH = 60H. If an error is returned (AH not zero), the EMM is compatible with LIM EMS version 3.2. If AH is zero upon the return, the EMM is compatible with the AQA EEMS.

4. Obtain the segment of the EMS compatible page frame used by the EMM with EMS Function 41H. Applications exploiting the additional mapping capabilities of the EEMS must obtain the additional window addresses with EEMS Function 60H.

5. Allocate the desired number of expanded memory pages with EMS Function 43H. If the allocation is successful, the EMM returns a handle that is used by the application to refer to the expanded memory pages that it owns. This step is exactly analogous to opening a file and using the handle obtained from the open function for read/write operations on the file.

6. If the requested number of pages are not available, the application can query the EMM for the actual number of pages available (EMS Function 42H) and determine whether it can continue in a degraded fashion.

7. Once the application has successfully allocated the number of expanded memory pages it needs, it uses EMS Function 44H to map logical pages in and out of the physical page frame, in order to store and retrieve data in expanded memory.

8. When the program finishes using its expanded memory pages, it must release them by calling EMS Function 45H before it terminates and returns control to MS-DOS. Otherwise, the pages will be lost to use by other programs until the system is restarted.

The following is a program skeleton that illustrates this general approach to the use of expanded memory. This code assumes that the presence of the EMM has already been verified with one of the techniques shown earlier.

```
    .
    .
    .
mov   ah,40h          ; test EMM status
int   67h
or    ah,ah
jnz   error           ; jump if bad status from EMM

mov   ah,46h          ; check EMM version
int   67h
or    ah,ah
jnz   error           ; jump if couldn't get version

cmp   al,030h         ; make sure it is at least ver. 3.0
jb    error           ; jump if wrong EMM version

mov   ah,41h          ; get page from segment
int   67h
or    ah,ah
jnz   error           ; jump if failed to get frame
mov   page_frame,bx   ; save segment of page frame

mov   ah,42h          ; get no. of available pages
int   67h
or    ah,ah
jnz   error           ; jump if get pages error
mov   total_pages,dx  ; save total EMM pages
mov   avail_pages,bx  ; save available EMM pages
or    bx,bx
jz    error           ; abort if no pages available
mov   ah,43h          ; try and allocate EMM pages
mov   bx,needed_pages
int   67h             ; if allocation is successful
or    ah,ah
jnz   error           ; jump if allocation failed

mov   emm_handle,dx   ; save handle for allocated page
    .
    .                 ; now we are ready for other
    .                 ; processing using the EMM pages
```

```
        .
                        ; map in EMS memory page...
mov  bx,log_page        ; BX <- EMS logical page number
mov  al,phys_page       ; AL <- EMS physical page (0-3)
mov  dx,emm_handle      ; EMM handle for our pages
mov  ah,44h             ; Function 44H = map EMS page
int  67h
or   ah,ah
jnz  error              ; jump if mapping error
        .
        .
        .

                        ; program ready to terminate,
                        ; give up allocated EMM pages...
mov  dx,emm_handle      ; handle for our pages
mov  ah,45h             ; EMS Function 6 = release pages
int  67h
or   ah,ah
jnz  error              ; jump if release failed
```

To ensure that it will not be terminated unexpectedly by events that are not under its control, any program that uses expanded memory should replace the system's default handlers for Control-C and Critical Error exceptions with its own handlers, the addresses of which are stored in the vectors for INT 23H and INT 24H, respectively. These new handlers would be responsible for releasing expanded memory pages owned by the application and cleaning up any other loose ends before returning control to MS-DOS and allowing the application to be terminated.

Device Drivers, TSRs, and Expanded Memory

A TSR, interrupt handler, or installable device driver (such as an electronic disk) that uses expanded memory follows the same general procedure outlined above, but with a few minor variations. These variations are imposed by the fact that the program may be executing as a result of a hardware interrupt or during the system boot process.

If the program is a device driver, it will need to test for the existence of the EMM and allocate expanded memory pages during its Initialization routine, which is called when the driver is loaded into memory and before the operating system is fully functional. Consequently, the driver must use a modified version of the get interrupt vector method of testing for the existence of the EMM, fetching the contents of the INT 67H vector directly rather than using INT 21H (Function 35H). Of course, the user must be warned to place the DEVICE=line that loads the

EMM before the `DEVICE=` line that loads the driver that uses expanded memory services.

TSRs and interrupt handlers are usually initialized in a more normal system context (i.e., they are typically first loaded as though they were normal programs from COM or EXE files). Therefore, they can test for the EMM's presence like any other application program.

When a TSR, device driver, or interrupt handler acquires control and needs to access its expanded memory pages, it must first save the EMM context with a call to EMM Function 47H. This function stores the current contents of the page-mapping registers on the EMS hardware and any other hardware-dependent information, which will be needed later to restore the exact same state of the EMS subsystem, into an internal buffer. Note that the EMS context which is being saved belongs to the foreground application program that was interrupted, but the context is saved in association with the EMM handle owned by the background program, handler, or driver which has asserted control.

When the background program is finished using expanded memory, it calls EMM Function 48H, which restores the expanded memory hardware to its state at the point of interruption, so that the expanded memory page-mappings previously requested by the foreground program are again valid. This is an absolutely vital step since the foreground program assumes that its expanded memory pages are always available within the page frame after it has requested them to be mapped. It has no way to know that it has been temporarily suspended by a background program that also used the same page frame for expanded memory access.

A driver, interrupt handler, or TSR typically owns its expanded memory pages on a permanent basis (until the system is restarted) and never deallocates them. For example, an electronic disk which is using expanded memory to emulate a physical disk device would have no reason to ever change its initial page allocation, since block devices do not change size dynamically while the system is running!

C Interface to Expanded Memory

As a practical example of the use of expanded memory pages, Listing 14-1 contains an assembly language subroutine package `EMSPROCS.ASM` that allows C programs to test for the existence of the EMM, test its status, and allocate, map, and deallocate expanded memory pages. The package is compatible with EMS 3.2, EEMS, or EMS 4.0. The functions supported are listed in Table 14-4.

When an error occurs on an EMM function call, the actual error code returned by the expanded memory manager is stored in the variable `_emserr`, which can be declared external in the C program and then accessed as the static integer variable `emserr`.

Table 14-4.   Functions of `EMSPROCS.ASM`

Function	Description
EMSInst	Returns flag indicating whether the EMM is installed in the system (A value of 0 indicates that the manager is present, a value of 1 is returned if the manager cannot be found.)
EMSReady	Returns a flag indicating whether the EMM and the expanded memory hardware are functional (A value of 0 indicates that the subsystem is usable and ready, a value of 1 is returned if the subsystem should not be used. Use of this function assumes a previous successful call to EMSInst.)
EMSPages	Returns total number of expanded memory pages installed in the system (Use of this function assumes that the presence of the EMS driver and hardware has been established by previous successful calls to EMSInst and EMSReady.)
EMSAvail	Returns number of expanded memory pages currently available (Use of this function assumes that the presence of the EMS driver and hardware has been established by previous successful calls to EMSInst and EMSReady.)
EMSAlloc	Allocates expanded memory pages and returns an EMM handle that can be used for subsequent mapping of those pages (If the pages cannot be allocated, 1 is returned. Use of this function assumes that the presence of the EMS driver and hardware has been established by previous successful calls to EMSInst and EMSReady.)
EMSMap	Called with an EMM handle, a logical expanded memory page number, and physical page number within the page frame (0-3) (It maps a previously allocated expanded memory page to the requested physical page within the page frame, returning a far pointer to the mapped page.)
EMSFree	Called with an EMM handle and releases the previously allocated EMM pages.

The subroutine package, Listing 14-1, can be assembled with the command: `MASM /Mx EMSPROCS`. The `/Mx` switch must be included so that the function names are not folded to uppercase (failure to use the `/Mx` switch will result in "unresolved" messages when you attempt to link the package to a C program). The assembly language code shown for these procedures assumes that the C programs which call it are being compiled as small model programs, but should be easy to convert for use with other memory models or high level languages.

Listing 14-1.   EMSPROCS

```
        name    emsprocs
        page    55,132
        title   EMS support functions for C


;
; Expanded memory support functions for Microsoft C
```
continued

```
;
; Copyright © 1987 Ray Duncan
;
; To assemble:  MASM /Mx /Zi EMSPROCS;
;

args     equ    4              ; offset of arguments, small model
emm_int  equ    67h            ; expanded memory manager interrupt
DGROUP   group  _DATA          ; automatic data group


_DATA    segment word public 'DATA'

         public  _emserr
_emserr  dw     0              ; status from last EMS operation

emmname  db     'EMMXXXX0'     ; logical device name for EMM

emframe  dw     0              ; segment of EMS page frame

_DATA    ends


_TEXT    segment word public 'CODE'

         assume cs:_TEXT,ds:_DATA

         public  _EMSInst,_EMSReady
         public  _EMSPages,_EMSAvail
         public  _EMSAlloc,_EMSMap,_EMSFree

;
; status = EMSInst();
;
; status is 0 if expanded memory manager is present, 1 if not.
;
_EMSInst proc    near

         push    bp             ; establish stack frame,
         mov     bp,sp          ; save register variables
         push    di
         push    si
```

continued

```
        mov    _emserr,0          ; initialize EMS error status

                                  ; fetch contents of
                                  ; EMM interrupt vector...
        mov    al,emm_int         ; AL = EMM int. number
        mov    ah,35h             ; fxn 35H = get vector
        int    21h                ; transfer to MS-DOS
        mov    di,10              ; ES:DI = presumed addr. of
                                  ; name field in device header
                                  ; DS:SI = guaranteed EMM name
        mov    si,offset DGROUP:emmname
        mov    cx,8               ; length of name field
        cld
        repz cmpsb                ; compare names...
        mov    ax,0               ; assume return false flag
        jz     _EMSInst1          ; jump if driver present
        inc    ax                 ; else return true flag

_EMSInst1:
        pop    si                 ; restore register variables
        pop    di                 ; and return to C program
        pop    bp
        ret

_EMSInst endp


;
; status = EMSReady();
;
; status is 0 if EMS subsystem operational, 1 if not
;
_EMSReady proc   near

        push   bp                 ; establish stack frame,
        mov    bp,sp              ; save register variables
        push   di
        push   si

        mov    ah,40h             ; call EMM to get status
        int    emm_int

        xchg   ah,al              ; fix up status and save it
```
                                        continued

```
        and     ax,0ffh         ; and set Zero flag
        mov     _emserr,ax

        mov     ax,0            ; assume returning false flag
        jz      _EMSReady1      ; jump if status ok
        inc     ax              ; otherwise return true flag

_EMSReady1:
        pop     si              ; restore register variables
        pop     di              ; and return to C program
        pop     bp
        ret

_EMSReady endp


;
; pages = EMSPages();
;
; returns number of expanded memory pages installed in the system,
; returns 0 pages if operation failed.
;
_EMSPages proc  near

        push    bp              ; establish stack frame,
        mov     bp,sp           ; save register variables
        push    di
        push    si

        mov     ah,42h          ; call EMM to get total pages
        int     emm_int

        xchg    ah,al           ; fix up status and save it
        and     ax,0ffh         ; and set Zero flag
        mov     _emserr,ax

        mov     ax,0            ; assume returning zero pages
        jnz     _EMSPages1      ; jump if bad status
        mov     ax,dx           ; otherwise return total pages

_EMSPages1:
        pop     si              ; restore register variables
        pop     di              ; and return to C program
```

continued

```
        pop     bp
        ret


_EMSPages endp


;
; pages = EMSAvail();
;
; returns the number of expanded memory pages currently available,
; returns 0 pages if operation failed.
;
_EMSAvail proc  near

        push    bp              ; establish stack frame,
        mov     bp,sp           ; save register variables
        push    di
        push    si

        mov     ah,42h          ; call EMM to get available pages
        int     emm_int

        xchg    ah,al           ; fix up status and save it
        and     ax,0ffh         ; and set Zero flag
        mov     _emserr,ax

        mov     ax,0            ; assume returning zero pages
        jnz     _EMSAvail1      ; jump if bad status
        mov     ax,bx           ; otherwise return available pages

_EMSAvail1:
        pop     si              ; restore register variables
        pop     di              ; and return to C program
        pop     bp
        ret


_EMSAvail endp


;
; EMM_handle = EMSAlloc(pages);
;
; EMM_handle is -1 if pages could not be allocated
;
_EMSAlloc proc  near
```

continued

```
        push    bp                  ; establish stack frame,
        mov     bp,sp               ; save register variables
        push    di
        push    si

        mov     ah,41h              ; first get page frame segment,
        int     emm_int             ; we'll need it for mapping calls
        xchg    ah,al               ; fix up status and save it
        and     ax,0ffh             ; and set Zero flag
        mov     _emserr,ax

        mov     ax,-1               ; assume returning -1 signal
        jnz     _EMSAlloc1          ; jump if bad status

        mov     emframe,bx          ; else save page frame address

        mov     bx,[bp+args]        ; attempt to allocate pages
        mov     ah,43h
        int     emm_int

        xchg    ah,al               ; fix up status and save it
        and     ax,0ffh             ; and set Zero flag
        mov     _emserr,ax

        mov     ax,-1               ; assume returning -1 signal
        jnz     _EMSAlloc1          ; jump if bad status
        mov     ax,dx               ; otherwise return EMM handle

_EMSAlloc1:
        pop     si                  ; restore register variables
        pop     di                  ; and return to C program
        pop     bp
        ret

_EMSAlloc endp

;
; char far *pageptr = EMSMap(EMM_handle,logical_page,physical_page)
;
; maps the requested logical expanded memory page into the
; specified physical page, and returns a far pointer to the
; physical page, or a NULL pointer if the mapping failed.
```
                                        continued

```
;
_EMSMap proc    near

        push    bp              ; establish stack frame,
        mov     bp,sp           ; save register variables
        push    di
        push    si

        mov     dx,[bp+args]    ; EMM handle
        mov     bx,[bp+args+2]  ; logical page
        mov     ax,[bp+args+4]  ; physical page
        mov     ah,44h
        int     emm_int         ; request mapping
        xchg    ah,al           ; fix up status and save it
        and     ax,0ffh         ; and set Zero flag
        mov     _emserr,ax
        jnz     _EMSMap1        ; bad status, return NULL ptr

                                ; mapping OK, calculate pointer
        mov     ax,[bp+args+4]  ; get physical page again
        mov     dx,4000h        ; multiply it by 16 KB
        mul     dx              ; to set AX = offset in page frame
        mov     dx,emframe      ; get segment of page frame
        jmp     _EMSMap2        ; and return far pointer

_EMSMap1:                       ; if error, return NULL pointer
        mov     dx,0
        mov     ax,0

_EMSMap2:
        pop     si              ; restore register variables
        pop     di              ; and return to C program
        pop     bp
        ret

_EMSMap endp

;
; status = EMSFree(EMM_handle);
;
; status is 0 if pages deallocated successfully, 1 otherwise.
;
_EMSFree proc   near
```

continued

```
        push    bp                  ; establish stack frame,
        mov     bp,sp               ; save register variables
        push    di
        push    si

        mov     dx,[bp+args]        ; get EMM handle
        mov     ah,45h              ; and try to release it
        int     emm_int

        xchg    ah,al               ; fix up status and save it
        and     ax,0ffh             ; and set Zero flag
        mov     _emserr,ax

        mov     ax,0                ; assume returning false flag
        jz      _EMSFree1           ; jump if status was ok
        inc     ax                  ; otherwise return true flag

_EMSFree1:
        pop     si                  ; restore register variables
        pop     di                  ; and return to C program
        pop     bp
        ret

_EMSFree endp


_TEXT   ends

        end
```

Finally, we will present a brief C program EMSDEMO.C, Listing 14-2, that demonstrates use of some of the EMS access subroutines. EMSDEMO.C can be compiled into the file EMSDEMO.OBJ and then linked with EMSPROCS.OBJ to form the executable file EMSDEMO.EXE with the following command line (for Microsoft C): CL EMSDEMO.C EMSPROCS.

Listing 14-2.   EMSDEMO.C

```
/*

        EMSDEMO.C   Demonstrate use of EMS support
                    functions in EMSPROCS.ASM
```
continued

```
        Ray Duncan, August 1987

        To compile and link to EMSPROCS, with CodeView info:

            MASM /Mx /Zi EMSPROCS;
            CL /Zi EMSDEMO.C EMSPROCS
*/

#include <stdio.h>

extern unsigned EMSInst();        /* prototypes for EMS functions */
extern unsigned EMSReady();       /* provided by EMSPROCS.ASM */
extern unsigned EMSPages();
extern unsigned EMSAvail();
extern unsigned EMSAlloc(unsigned);
extern char far *EMSMap(unsigned, unsigned, unsigned);
extern unsigned EMSFree(unsigned);

extern int emserr;                /* contains status of most recent
                                     expanded memory operation */

static char *ErrorMsg[] = {   "EMM internal error",
                              "EMS hardware malfunction",
                              "Memory manager busy",
                              "Invalid EMM handle",
                              "Function not defined",
                              "Out of EMM handles",
                              "Mapping context error",
                              "Insufficient pages installed",
                              "Insufficient pages available",
                              "Zero pages allocation error",
                              "Invalid logical page number",
                              "Invalid physical page number",
                              "Context save area full",
                              "Duplicate context save",
                              "Context restore not found",
                              "Subfunction parameter undefined" };

main(argc, argv)
    int    argc;
    char   *argv[];
```

continued

```
{   int status,handle;          /* miscellaneous variables */
    char far *pageptr;          /* far pointer for mapped page */

    puts("\nSimple Demo Program for EMSPROCS");

    if( EMSInst() )             /* test if EMM is installed in system */
    {   puts("\nExpanded memory manager not found");
        exit(1);
    }

    if( EMSReady() )            /* if installed, make sure it is ready
*/
    {   puts("\nExpanded memory manager not ready");
        DisplayError();
    }

    status = EMSPages();        /* report total pages in system */
    printf("\nExpanded memory pages installed = %d", status);
    DisplayError();

    status = EMSAvail();        /* report pages not yet allocated */
    printf("\nExpanded memory pages available = %d\n", status);
    DisplayError();

    handle = EMSAlloc(3);       /* allocate some expanded memory */
    printf("\nAllocating 3 pages, handle returned = %xh", handle);
    DisplayError();

                                /* demonstrate page mapping */
    pageptr = EMSMap(handle,2,3);
    puts("\n\nMapping logical page 2 to physical page 3,");
    printf("Page pointer = %lxh", pageptr);
    DisplayError();

    status=EMSFree(handle);     /* now release our pages */
    puts("\n\nDeallocating pages");
    DisplayError();

    exit(0);
}

DisplayError()                  /* show EMM error no. & message */
{   if(emserr)
```

continued

```
{   printf("\nEMS error: %xh, %s", emserr, ErrorMsg[emserr&0x7f]);
    exit(1);
}
}
```

Reading List

▶ The Lotus/Intel/Microsoft Expanded Memory Specification version 3.2 (part no. 300275-003) or Expanded Memory Specification version 4.0 (part no. 300686-001) can be obtained from Intel Corp.; 3065 Bowers Ave.; Santa Clara, CA 95051.

▶ The AST Enhanced Expanded Memory Specification can be obtained by writing to Product Marketing, AST Research; 2121 Alton Ave.; Irvine, California 92714.

▶ The following are representative products that support LIM EMS and/or AQA EEMS.

Spreadsheets:

Lotus Development Corp. *1-2-3*

Javelin Software. *Javelin*

Computer Associates. *SuperCalc*

Lifetree Software. *Words & Figures*

Daybreak Technologies. *Silk*

Databases:

Ansa. *Paradox*

Borland International. *Reflex*

Information Builders. *PC/Focus*

Software Publishing. *Pfs:Professional File*

Software Solutions. *DataEase*

Symantec. *Q&A*

Integrated Products:

Ashton-Tate. *Framework II*

Lotus Development Corp. *Symphony*

Innovative Software. *Smart*

CAD:

Autodesk. *AutoCAD*

T&W Systems. *VersaCAD*

Program Managers and Operating Systems:

Microsoft. *Windows*

Quarterdeck Systems. *DESQview*

Digital Research. *Concurrent PC-DOS*

Softlogic Solutions. *Software Carousel*

Utilities:

Bourbaki Inc. *1DIR +*

Living Videotext *Ready!* and *ThinkTank*

Multisoft. *Super PC Kwik*

PC Support Group. *Lightning*

Phoenix Technology. *PDisk*

Polytron. *PolyBoost* and *PolyDesk III*

Software Masters. *Flash*

Ray Duncan is the author of *Advanced MS-DOS* (Microsoft Press 1986) and numerous articles and columns in *Dr. Dobb's Journal* and other publications. Ray is founder of Laboratory Microsystems Inc., a software house specializing in Forth interpreters and compilers.

Related Essays

1 A Guided Tour inside MS-DOS

10 Developing MS-DOS Device Drivers

Index

A

AboutBox function (Windows), 269
Absolute Disk Read interrupt, 37, 209, 336
Absolute Disk Write interrupt, 209, 336
Accidentals with SOUND driver, 351
Active windows, 247
Adaptor cards for data protection, 226
Adjust Block Size function, 160–162
Age of SFT entries, 327
Allocate Expanded Memory function (EMM),
   544
Allocate Memory function, 160–161
Alphabets for finite state machines, 363
ALT key for entering nonstandard filenames,
   221
Ampersands (&)
   with SOUND driver, 352
   for substitute operator, 127–128
Ancient system call, 151
AND operator, 119–120
Andante tempo with SOUND driver, 352
ANSI.SYS console driver, 30
   replacement for, 76
APPEND command, 13
Application programs
   batch file calling by, 17
   data access by, 220
   INT 21H for, 306, 310–312, 321–323
   interface for, 305–306
   and MS-DOS, 21–29
AQA EEMS, 536, 539, 547
Arc file tool (PCnix), 81
Archiver, 81
Arithmetic with EBL, 96
Arrow keys with keydo.com program, 62

ASCII code
   conversion of bytes and words to, 181–182
   and data communications, 477–478
   window messages for, 247
ASSIGN program, 189–191, 208–209
Assignments with EBL, 96
Asterisks (*)
   in EBL, 96, 98
   as wildcards and metacharacters, 86–87
Asynchronous data communications, 477–484
At sign character (@)
   with batch echoing, 59
   with VC, 105
Atget function (VC), 102–103
Atsay function (VC), 102
Attributes
   character, 104
   device, 308–309, 329, 331
   file, 39
Auto repeat, keyboard, 62
AUTOEXEC.BAT file, 92–93
   in booting, 10
   passwords for, 225
AUX, opening of, 331
Auxiliary stack, 322

B

B + trees, 107–112
Background Process function, 197, 210, 336
Background programs, 336–338
Backslashes (\) in file paths, 18, 58–59, 71
Bank-switching with expanded memory,
   536–537
Base address of serial adapters, 484

Base page, 197
Batch files, 17–18, 91–93
    ECHO commands in, 59–61
    and environment, 156–157
    for on-line help, 66–67
    for PCnix commands, 62–67
Baud rate
    in data transfer, 478
    with serial adapter, 491
Beats with SOUND driver, 352
BEEP command (EBL), 96
BEGIN/END command (EBL), 96
BeginPaint function (Windows), 255, 267
BEGSTACK/.END command (EBL), 96
BEGTYPE/END command (EBL), 96
BINARY device attribute, 331
Binary files
    locating text strings in, 76
    phone transmission of, 84–85
    reading of, 329
BIOS, 6–8
    for data access, 220
    for EGA, 437
    hardware access by, 29
    loading of, 312–313
    module for, 10
    for serial adapter, 490–491
    software interrupts with, 25–26
BIOS function (EBL), 97
BIOS parameter blocks and built-in drivers,
        313
Bit-mapped graphics and transparent write
        mode, 329–330
Bit maps, reading of, 460–461
Bit-mask register, 447–448, 454, 456–459, 461
Bit-oriented data structures with MASM,
        117–120
Bit planes, 446–447
Block devices, 308, 313–314, 316
Block length in PSP, 150–151
Block size, function for, 160–162
Booting of MS-DOS, 8–11
    and device drivers, 312–321
    and DPB, 173
    sector for, 8, 312
Borland International
    integrated programming environments by,
        28
    Turbo languages, linking of files in, 13
BREAK
    in data transfer, 480
    disabling of, 225
Break flag and INT 21H, 322
Break-out switch debugger, 147
Bresenham's Algorithm with line drawing,
        451–452
Buffers

Buffers—cont
    flushing of, 177, 334
    for keyboard input, 335
    size of, with EBL, 95
    See also Cache; Circular buffers
BUFFERS = command, 10, 92, 317
Built-in device drivers, 10, 307
    and IBMDOS initialization, 313
Busy flag, 170

C

C
    compiling with, 436
    expanded memory interface for, 550–551
    forward declarations in, 42–43
    libraries for, 28–29, 100–105
    and PCnix, 85
    and Resource Compiler, 257
    system calls with, 77
C-INDEX + , file access with, 108–110
Cache
    blocks for, 314–317
    for file I/O, 10
    pointer to, 171
Cache Block list and block drivers, 313
Calendar with PCnix, 73–74
CALL command (batch), 17, 64
CALL command (EBL), 95, 96
CALL.PURGE function (EBL), 97
Cassette_IO interrupt for TSRs, 214
Cat command (UNIX) and p PCnix tool, 76
CD (Color Display), 437
CDS (Current Directory Structure), 304, 319
CGA (Color Graphics Adapter), 437
Ch command (PCnix), 64–65
Chaining of programs, 158–159
Char_out subroutine, 180
Characters
    attributes of, 104
    devices for, 308
    I/O routines for, 334–336
CheckMenuItem function (Windows), 263
Child process, creation of, 158–159
Child windows, 248–250
    in Notepad, 259
CHKDSK/V command and hidden files,
        223–224
Chmod file tool (PCnix), 81
Chn file tool (PCnix), 81–82
CHRDEV driver attribute, 309
CICS (Customer Information Control System),
        100
Cipher systems, 229–230
Circular buffers, 80, 359–361
    for serial adapter, 492, 498–499

Circular buffers—cont
    for SOUND driver, 378–379
Class routines for SOUND driver, 377
Classes, window, 250–252
Clear To Send signal, 482
CLI instruction, 358
Client rectangles, 247–248
Clipping regions, 254, 267
Clock
    with PCnix, 73–74
    pointer to, 171
Clock devices
    header for, in List of Lists, 315
    and IBMDOS initialization, 313
    initialization of, 316
Clock interrupt service routine for SOUND
    driver, 379–381
Close file function, 220
Closing of devices, 330–331
CLS command (EBL), 96
Clusters, 219
Code macros, 129–136
Code segments with interrupts, 26, 139
Code systems for data protection, 227–229
CodeView, 28
    with MASM, 140
Color
    monitors for, 437–439
    palettes of, 468–472
    of pixels, 460–461
    and set/reset register, 454
COLOR command (EBL), 96
Color Display, 437
Color Graphics Adapter, 437
COM files
    using debug to create, 67–68
    PSP segment address for, 149
    structure of, 23
COM1
    base port address of, 484
    and INS8250 IC, 357
    interrupt request for, 489
COM2
    base port address of, 484
    interrupt request for, 489
Combining of commands, 64–66
COMMAND.COM file, 7–8
    for batch file subroutines, 64
    environment for, 158
    loading of, 10, 312
    operation of, 11–16
Command lines
    editing of, 62
    parsing of, 13–15, 46–48
    in PSP, 152
    slashes in, 18, 58–59
Command processor

Command processor—cont
    back door to, 179–180
    MS-DOS, 6
Commands
    combining of, 64–66
    driver, 353
    EBL, 96–98
    renaming of, 63
    repeating of, 63
    user, processing of, 11–16
Comments
    with EBL, 96, 98
    with SOUND driver, 353
Commit File function, 177
Communal declarations with MASM, 140
Compatibility and BIOS, 29
Compilation
    of SOUND driver, 376
    of whereis, 52
Compressor, file, 81
COMSPEC environment variable, 16, 155–156
    command for, 320
CON, opening of, 331
Configuration and CONFIG.SYS file, 8–11, 92
    in booting, 10
    and environment size, 157–158
    and installable device drivers, 30
    loading of, 312
Console Device Drivers, pointer to, 171
Console devices
    ANSI.SYS drivers for, 30
    handles for, 152–153
    header for, in List of Lists, 315
    and IBMDOS initialization, 313
    initialization of, 316
    INT 2AH for, 179
Control-C
    checking for, 322, 335
    and expanded memory systems, 549
    and INT 23H, 338
    and PSP, 151
Control characters, 477–478
Control functions, EBL, 97
Control-P, processing of, 335
Control-Q, with asynchronous
    communications, 478, 482
Control-S
    with asynchronous communications, 478,
    482
    with keyboard polling, 335
Controller chips, EGA, 449
Coordinates, window, 248, 253
COPY command for sequential files, 107
Copying of files with whereis, 39
Coroutines, 361–363
    for SOUND driver, 378
Cp command (UNIX), emulation of, 65–66

CP/M
  and PSPs, 149–151
  and TSRs, 187
CRC (Cyclic Redundancy Check), 480–481
Create PSP block function, 158–159
CreateWindow function (Windows), 251–252
.CREF directive (MASM), 134
Critical errors
  and background programs, 337–338
  and expanded memory systems, 549
  flag for, 322
  handlers for, 213, 330, 331
Critical sections, handling of, 365–366
Cross-reference listings with MASM, 134
Cruz, Frank, Kermit protocol by, 84
CTS (Clear To Send) signal, 482
CURCLK driver attribute, 309, 313
CURNUL driver attribute, 309
Current Directory Structure, 304, 319
Current drive, function for, 70
Customer Information Control System, 100
CW_USEDEFAULT message (Windows),
    262–263
Cyclic Redundancy Check in data transfer,
    480–481

D

Dadd function (C-INDEX), 111
Data communications of binary files, 84–85
  See also Serial ports
Data Encryption Standard, 230–236
Data entry with VC, 102–103
Data macros, 126–129
Data protection and encryption, 220
  hiding data, 221–224
  and MS-DOS data access, 219–220
  and MS-DOS loopholes, 237–238
  passwords for, 225–237
  unauthorized access, levels of, 217–219
Data rotate register, EGA, 464–465
Data segments with interrupts, 139
Data structures. *See* Tables
Data Transfer Area, 37–38, 323, 328
Date
  and clock device header, 313
  on directories, 220
  in DTA buffer, 328
  function for, 84
  handling of, with whereis, 50–52
DCB. *See* Device Control Blocks
Dclose function (C-INDEX), 110
Dcreate function (C-INDEX), 110
Ddelete function (C-INDEX), 111–112
Deadlocks and wait loops, 364
Debug

Debug—cont
  cautions for, 332
  for creating .COM files, 67–68
  for PSP examination, 149
  scripts with, 60–61
Debugging
  break-out switch for, 147
  with CodeView, 28
  of drivers, 338–344
  of windows, 260
.DEF window files, 269
DefWindowProc function (Windows), 245,
    264–265
Delete key
  with keydo.com program, 62
  with VC, 103
Deletion of files
  and data protection, 218, 237–238
  function for, 220
  with whereis, 39
DES (Data Encryption Standard), 230–236
Desk accessories, TSR, 185
Desq function (C-INDEX), 111
DestroyWindow function (Windows), 245, 264
Device contexts, 267
Device Control Blocks, 10, 304, 314
  and device openings, 326
  listhead for, in List of Lists, 315
Device coordinates, 253
Device drivers, 29–30, 303–304, 307–310
  and background programs, 336–338
  in BIOS, 10
  and boot process, 312–321
  debugging of, 338–344
  DEVICE = command for, 30, 316
  and DOS tables, 304–307
  in DPB, 172
  and expanded memory, 549–550
  and FCBs and handles, 323–324
  and hardware interrupts, 343–344
  and INT 21H, 321–323
  routines for, 325–336
  and SFT, 324–325
  See also SOUND driver
Device headers, 306–308, 313, 315
  for SOUND driver, 366–367
Device Parameter Blocks, 171–177
Dfind function (C-INDEX), 111
Diagonal lines, program to draw, 444–445
Dictionary code book systems, 227–228
Diff text tool (PCnix), 75–76
Direct access of hardware, 29
Directives, EBL, 97
Directories
  and DPB, 173
  entries in, 173, 219–220
  ls PCnix tool for, 82–84

Directories—cont
    reading of, in open routines, 327
    renaming of, 82
    searching of, with whereis, 39, 44–46
    tree-structured, 35–36
DIRINFO structure, 37–38, 40–41
Discardable blocks, 256
Disk devices
    information for, in DPB, 171–172
    initialization of, 316
    logical, 172–173, 189, 209
    in UNIX, 58
Disk I/O
    buffer for, 317
    interrupt for, 336
Disk organizer, 81
Disk stack, 322
Diskette_IO interrupt, 191
Dispatch routine for device drivers, 309–310
DispatchMessage function (Windows),
    243–244
Display. *See* Screen display
Display Output routine, 334–335
Dog file tool (PCnix), 81
Dopen function (C-INDEX), 110
DOS
    data access by, 220
    loading of, 312
    for SOUND driver, 376
    variables for, function for, 171–172
DOS_CRITICAL function, 196–197
DOS Safe Interrupt, 178–179
Dotted notes with SOUND driver, 351–352
Down arrow key with VC, 103
DPB (Device Parameter Blocks), 171–177
Dread function (C-INDEX), 111
DTA (Data Transfer Area), 37–38, 323, 328
Du file tool (PCnix), 81
Dummy functions, 169–170
Dummy labels, with MASM, 132
Dupdate function (C-INDEX), 112
DUPKEY label (C-INDEX), 109
Duplicate handles, function for, 177–178
Duplicate PSP block function, 159
Duration with SOUND driver, 351–352

E

EBL (Extended Batch Language), 18, 94–99
ECD (Enhanced Color Display), 437–438
ECHO command (batch), disabling, 59–61
ECHO command (UNIX), xp PCnix tool for, 85
Ed text tool (PCnix), 75
Editing
    of character input, 334
    of command lines, 62

Editing—cont
    with standard devices, 335
EEMS (Enhanced Expanded Memory
        Specification), 31, 536–540
EGA. *See* Enhanced Graphics Adapter
Eline text tool (PCnix), 75–76
ELSE directive (MASM), 129
EM_GETSEL message (Windows), 252
EMM (Expanded Memory Manager), 537–540
EMS. *See* Expanded memory systems
Encryption, data, 227–237
End of Interrupt instruction, 343, 489–490
End key
    with keydo.com program, 62
    with VC, 103
Endline.c program, 79
ENDM directive (MASM), 127
Enhanced Color Display, 437–438
Enhanced Expanded Memory Specification,
        31, 536–540
Enhanced Graphics Adapter, 435–440
    bit maps with, 460–461
    checking for, 440–443
    line drawing with, 451–454
    memory in, 446–449, 455, 457
    palettes for, 468–472
    print screen routine for, 461–468
    set/reset register in, 454–455
    speeding up of, 473–474
    write modes for, 455–459
    write-only register in, 450–451
Environments
    and PSP, 22, 151
    segment for, 156–158
    setting of, 92–94
EOI (end of interrupt) instruction, 343,
        489–490
Epson printers, print screen routine for,
        465–468
Equ directive (MASM), 134
EQUAL parameter with C-INDEX, 111
Equal sign (=)
    with MASM, 134
    with SOUND driver, 351
Errors and error codes
    with C-INDEX, 110
    in data transfer, 480–482
    for device drivers, 339
    with EBL, 97–98
    with expanded memory systems, 543
    and read and write routines, 329
ESC key with VC, 103
Even parity in data transfer, 480
Events, window, 245–247
Exclamation point (!) with SOUND driver, 353
EXE files
    PSP segment address for, 149

EXE files—cont
  structure of, 23–24
EXEC function
  and batch files, 17
  for program loading, 22
Execution of programs, 15–16
EXIT command (EBL), 96
Exit routine (MS-DOS) and PSP, 151
Expanded memory systems, 31, 535–538
  C interface to, 550–551
  control with, 542–550
  EEMS, 536
  Expanded Memory Manager for, 537–540
  LIM, 535–536, 539, 547
  testing for, 540–542
EXPORTS lists, 269
Expression operator, MASM, 128
Extended Batch Language, 18, 94–99
Extended memory compared to expanded,
    538
Extensions in directories, 220

F

FAT. See File Allocation Table
Fatal Error routine and PSP, 151
FCB. See File Control Blocks
FCB = command, 317
Ffind file tool (PCnix), 81
FHT (File Handle Table), 151
Fields
  bit, 119–120
  with VC, 102–104
FIFO buffers, 492, 498–499
File Allocation Table
  and cache blocks, 315
  for clusters, 219
  and DPB, 173
  and file deletion, 237
  and PCnix mv command, 82
File Control Blocks, 26–27
  access routine with, 328
  close routine with, 330–331
  and device drivers, 323–324
  open routine with, 327
  in PSP, 152
  and SFT, 324–325
File Handle Table, 151
File handles, 152–155
  duplication of, 177–178
  and PSP, 151, 197
Filecopy.c program, 77–78
Filenames
  with commands, 15
  in directories, 220
  limitation of, 19

Filenames—cont
  nonstandard, for hiding data, 221
Files, 18–20
  access of, with PSP, 152
  attributes for, 39
  batch. See Batch files
  binary. See Binary files
  closing of, 330
  copying of, 39
  deletion of, and data protection, 237–238
  with EBL, 97
  EXE, 23–24, 149
  FCBs for, 26–27
  handles for. See File handles
  include, 40, 125–126
  key access systems for, 107–112
  linking of, 13
  listing of, 310–312
  names for. See Filenames
  opening of, 220, 540
  options with, 38–39
  password protection of, 226–227
  PCnix tools for, 81–84
  random, 107, 328
  sequential, 107, 328
  size of, on directories, 220
  system, 7–8
  tree-structured, 18–20
  See also Whereis directory search program
FILES = command, 92, 153
Filling of rectangle, program for, 456–457
Filter for SOUND driver, 373
Filter programs, 14
FIND commands in MS-DOS vs. UNIX, 20
FindResource function (Windows), 257
Finite state machines, 363–364
  for SOUND driver, 376–378
Flats for SOUND driver, 350–351
Flushing of buffers, 177, 334
Folders in graphic environments, 19
FOR command with batch files, 17
Formatting
  of hard disks, for data protection, 238
  of input, with VC, 103
Forward declarations with C, 42–43
Fragmentation
  of hard drives, program for, 81
  of memory, and windows, 255–256
Free Memory function, 160–161
Frequency generator for SOUND driver, 373
Full duplex
  in data transfer, 482
  with serial adapter, 491
Function 02H, 330, 334–335
Function 0AH, 329, 335
Function 0BH, 131
Function 17H, 82

Function 19H, 70
Function 1DH, 170
Function 1EH, 170
Function 1FH, 177
Function 20H, 170
Function 25H, 137, 489
Function 26H, 158–159
Function 2AH, 84
Function 2CH, 84
Function 31H, 25, 61, 194
Function 32H, 177
Function 33H, 321, 338
Function 34H, 170, 179, 196, 322, 337
Function 35H, 137, 489, 541
Function 37H, 59, 170
Function 3DH, 220, 540
Function 3EH, 220, 540
Function 3FH, 154, 220
Function 40H, 153–154, 220
Function 41H, 220
Function 42H, 220
Function 44H, 331, 540
Function 45H, 177–178
Function 46H, 177–178
Function 48H, 160–161
Function 49H, 160–161
Function 4AH, 160–162
Function 4BH, 151, 162, 179
Function 4CH, 150
Function 4EH, 37
Function 4FH, 37
Function 50H, 159–160, 197, 321, 338
Function 51H, 159–160, 321, 337
Function 52H, 163, 171–172
Function 55H, 159
Function 56H, 82
Function 57H, 84
Function 62H, 159–160, 321, 337
Function 68H, 177
Functions
    dispatcher of, 22
    for whereis, 41–42
    window, 242
    See also specific functions

G

Gersbach, J., keydo.com program by, 62
Get Device Attributes, 331, 540
Get DOS Variables function, 171–172
Get _ega_info function, 440
Get EMM Version function (EMM), 544
Get Expanded Memory Pages function (EMM),
    544
Get Input Status, 334
Get Manager Status function (EMM), 543

Get MS-DOS Busy Flag function, 170
Get Number of EMM Handles function (EMM),
    545
Get Output Status, 334
Get Page Frame Segment function (EMM), 543
Get Pages for All Handles function (EMM), 545
Get Pages Owned by Handle function (EMM),
    545
Get Physical Window Array function (EMM),
    546
Get PSP function, 321
Get/set/check break state function, 321
Get/Set Page Map function (EMM), 545–546
Get/Set Switch Char function, 170
GET USER _PSP function, 197–198
GetClassLong function (Windows), 267
GetClassWord function (Windows), 267
GetDC function (Windows), 267
Getenv function, 156
GetInstance function (Windows), 262
GetMessage function (Windows), 243–244, 261
GetSysColor function (Windows), 267
GetTextMetrics function (Windows), 253
GetWindowLong function (Windows), 267
GetWindowWord function (Windows), 267
Global filenames, C, tglob PCnix program for,
    85
Global list. *See* List of lists
Global options with MASM, 133
GlobalAlloc function (Windows), 255–256
GlobalLock function (Windows), 255, 268
GlobalUnlock function (Windows), 255, 268
GOTO command (EBL), 96
Grammars for finite state machines, 363
Graph in a Box, 186
Graphic interfaces, folders in, 19
GRAPHICS (TSR program), 189, 191
    and INT 05H, 198
Graphics with windows, 252–255
GREAT parameter (C-INDEX), 111
GREATEQ parameter (C-INDEX), 111
Greater than sign (>)
    with EBL, 97
    with IRP directive, 135
    for redirection, 14
Grep text tool (PCnix), 75–76

H

Half duplex in data transfer, 482
Handles
    access routine with, 328
    close routine with, 330
    and device drivers, 323–324
    duplication of, function for, 177–178
    file. *See* File handles

Handles—cont
    instance, 261
    open routine with, 326
    window, 243, 255
Hard drives
    formatting of, for data protection, 238
    organizer for, 81
Hardware interrupts, 136
    and device drivers, 343–344
    kernel access by, 25–26
    keyboard, and TSRs, 213–214
Hashing with random files, 107
Headers
    device, 306–308, 313, 315, 366–368
    for EXE programs, 23
Heap manager with windows, 255–256
Help screens, 105–106
    batch files for, 66–67
    HELPGEN.EXE program (VC), 106
Hex_to_ascii subroutine, 181
Hexb_to_ascii subroutine, 181–182
HIDDEN attribute for hiding data, 221–224
Hierarchical files,18–20. *See also* Whereis
    directory search program
Home key
    with keydo.com program, 62
    with VC, 103
Horton, Mark, programs by, 84–85
Hyphen (-)
    for command options, 18, 58–59, 71
    with SOUND driver, 350

I

IBMBIO.COM file, 7–8, 312–313
IBMDOS.COM file, 7–8, 312–316
IF command with batch files, 17
IF/THEN . . . ELSE command (EBL), 96
IFE directive (MASM), 129
IFIDN directive (MASM), 132
IFNB directive (MASM), 132
IN instruction, 357
IN_DOS function, 196–197
Include files
    with MASM, 125–126
    for whereis, 40
Index sequential files, 107
Indexes for help files, 106
INDOS flag, 211
    and background programs, 337
    and INT 21H, 321–322
Inheritance with devices, 331
INKEY command (EBL), 96
Inp function, 501
Input editing with character I/O, 334
Input focus with windows, 247

INS8250 UART IC, 357
Insert key with VC, 103
Installable device drivers, 30, 307
    in CONFIG.SYS file, 10
    See also Device drivers
Instance handles, 261
Instant Recall, 186
Instruction pointer and interrupts, 26
INT 05H, 198–199
INT 09H, 213–214
INT 10H, 26, 336, 437
    Function 0CH, 444
    Function 10H, 469–472
    Function 12H, 440
INT 13H, 191, 220, 336, 337
INT 14H, 490–491
INT 15H, 214
INT 16H, 214
INT 19H, 312
INT 1CH, 210–211, 336–337
INT 20H, 150
INT 21H (general dispatcher), 26
    for applications, 306, 310–312, 321–323
    and ASSIGN, 209
    for device drivers, 321–322, 329–330,
        334–335, 337–338
    for directories, 37, 82
    for files, 84, 220
    for handles, 153–154, 177–178
    for JFT size, 324
    for keyboard, 131
    for List of Lists location, 315
    for opening devices, 326
    and passwords, 226
    and PSPs, 150–152, 158–163, 197–198
    for switch character, 59, 170
    for TSRs, 25, 61, 194, 196–197
    undocumented, 170–172
    See also specific functions
INT 22H, 22, 151, 194
INT 23H, 151, 194, 322, 335, 338, 549
INT 24H, 151, 194, 338, 549
INT 25H, 37, 209, 336, 337
INT 26H, 209, 336, 337
INT 27H, 193–194
INT 28H, 159, 178–179, 197, 210, 336–337
INT 29H, 335
INT 2AH, 179
INT 2EH, 179–180
INT 2FH, 194–196, 209, 327
Int 4BH, 22
INT 4CH, 67
INT 67H, 539, 541–549
Int86 functions, 501
Intdos function, system date, 51
Intdosx functions, 501

Integrated programming environments, 28,
113
Intel 8250 UART, 484–492
Intel 8253–5 programmable timer, 373–375
Intel 8259A PIC chip, 489–490
Interfaces
for device drivers, 306–307
uniform, 28
user, 20–21, 241
Internal commands
COMMAND.COM, 12
for devices, 327, 329–330
Interrupt Controller (8259), 358, 375
Interrupt enable register, UART, 484–485, 488
Interrupt entry for SOUND driver, 376
Interrupt identification register, UART,
484–485, 488
Interrupt requests, UART, 489
Interrupt Vector Table, 26, 62, 191–192, 306
Interrupts, 62
with applications, 305–306
and COM1, 357–359
for device drivers, 308–309
for expanded memory, 540–546
handlers for, 44, 136–139, 499–501
INT instruction for, 26, 191
for I/O, 486–487
kernel access by, 25–26
problems with, 27
for serial adapter, 487–488
and TSRs, 25, 191–193
undocumented, 178–182
See also specific interrupts
InvalidateRect function (Windows), 254
InvalidateWindow function (Windows), 263
IO.SYS file, 7–8
loading of, 10
IOCTL driver attribute, 309
IOCTL requests, 331–334, 368, 540
IRET instruction, 306
IRP directive (MASM), 135–136
IRQ (interrupt request), 489
Isblank function (VC), 104
IsDialog Message function (Windows), 244

J

JFT (Job File Table), 324, 326
and background programs, 338
and closing of files, 330

K

K command (SOUND driver), 351
/K directive (EBL), 97

Keep Process function, 194–196
Kegel, Dan, nansi.sys by, 75–76
KERMIT file transfer protocol, 481–482
Kermit tool (PCnix), 84
Kernel, 6–8
device driver support in, 303–304
features of, 21–22
interrupts for, 25–26
and IOCTL requests, 331
relocation of, by SYSINT, 10
Key file access systems, 107–112
Key signatures with SOUND driver, 351
Key tape code book systems, 228–229
Keyboard
auto repeat with, 62
buffered input of, 335
function for, 131–132
input by, with EBL, 96
and INT 28H, 197
interrupt request for, 489
poll routine for, 335
and shells, 11
and TSRs, 186, 213–214
with VC, 103–104
window messages for, 246–247
Keydo.com program, 62
Kneller, D.G., make utility by, 84
Korn shells (ksh), 18

L

L command (SOUND driver), 351–352
/L directive (EBL), 97
Labels, MASM, 132
Large memory model for Microsoft C, 501
LaserJet printer, print screen routine for,
461–465
LASTDRIVE in CONFIG.SYS file, 319
LASTFIELD label (C-INDEX), 109–110
Latch registers, EGA, 446–449, 458, 464
Learning curves, 20–21
LEAVE command (EBL), 96
Left arrow key with VC, 103
Legato mode with SOUND driver, 352–353
Length command with SOUND driver,
351–352
LESS parameter (C-INDEX), 111
Less than sign (<)
with EBL, 97
with IRP directive, 135
LESSEQ parameter (C-INDEX), 111
Libraries for C, 28–29, 100–105
LIM expanded memory system, 535–536, 539,
547
Line control register, UART, 484–485
Line-editing with standard devices, 335

Line feeds with debug, 60
Line status register, UART, 484–485
Lines, program to draw, 452–454
Linked lists for DCBs, 10
Linking of files, 13
List of Lists, 10
   and device drivers, 313–316
   pointer to, 171
LISTER.COM program, 310–312
Loadable device drivers, 10, 30, 307
   See also Device drivers
Loading of programs, 22
LoadMenu function (Windows), 257
LoadResource function (Windows), 257
LoadString function (Windows), 257, 262
Local area networks, C-INDEX with, 108
LOCAL directive (MASM), 132
Local memory management function, 256
Local stacks for TSRs, 213
Logical coordinates, 253
Logical disk drives
   and ASSIGN, 189, 209
   in DPB, 172–173
Logical operators, 119–120
Loop functions, VC, 104
Low-pass filter for SOUND driver, 373
LParam parameter (Windows), 244
Ls file tool (PCnix), 81–84

M

Macintosh, learning curves for, 20–21
Macros
   code, 129–136
   data, 126–129
   for EGA, 449–450
   and ProKey, 186
   for SOUND driver, 377
   with whereis, 41–42
Make tool (PCnix), 84
MakeProcInstance function (Windows), 269
Map-mask register, 448, 454, 457
Map Memory function (EMM), 544, 546
Map select register, EGA, 460
Mapping modes, window, 253
MARK in data transfer, 478
MASK directive (MASM), 119
MASM techniques
   code macros, 129–136
   data macros, 126–129
   include files, 125–126
   records, 117–120
   structures, 120–124
MCB (Memory Control Block), 162–163
MCGA, 437
MD (Monochrome Display), 437–439

MDA (Monochrome Display Adapter), 437–439
MDI (Multiple Document Interface), 250
Media descriptor byte in DPB, 173
Memory
   allocation of, 22–24, 152, 160–169, 255–256
   configuration of, with SYSINT, 10
   in EGA, 446–449
   and PSP, 151–152
   with windows, 255–256
   See also Expanded memory systems
Memory Control Blocks, 162–163
Memory models for Microsoft C, 501
Memory resident programs. *See* Terminate
   and Stay Resident programs
Menus
   batch file generation of, 18
   benefits of, 93–94
   and child windows, 250
   disadvantages of, 241–242
Messages, window, 242–248
Metacharacters, UNIX, 86–87
Microsoft and TSRs, 189–190
Microsoft C, 28
   compiling with, 436
   for data transfer package, 501–502
Microsoft Quick languages, linking of files in,
   13
Microsoft Windows, 30, 241–242
   classes of, 250–252
   graphics with, 252–255
   learning curve with, 20
   memory management of, 255–256
   messages for, 242–248
   resources for, 256–257, 268–269
   SPY program for, 257–269
   styles of, 248–250
Minus sign (–)
   for command options, 18, 58–59, 71
   with SOUND driver, 350
MKDIR command with PCnix, 72–73
MKS Toolkit, 18
ML command (SOUND driver), 352
MM_TEXT message (Windows), 253
MN command (SOUND driver), 352
Modal dialog boxes, 264
MODE program, 188
Modeless dialog boxes, 264
Modeless programs, 31
Modeless user interfaces, 241
Modems for data transfer, 482
   registers for, 484–485
   status interrupt for, 488
Moderato tempo with SOUND driver, 352
Modularity of MS-DOS, 6
Module Definition Files, 269
Monitors
   damaging of, 444

Monitors—cont
    for EGA, 437–440
Monochrome Display, 437–439
Monochrome Display Adapter, 437–439
Morris, G. Allen, Jr., dog program by, 81
Mouse window messages, 245–246
Move read/write pointer function, 220
MS command (SOUND driver), 352
MS (modem status) interrupt, 488
MS-DOS, 5
    2.0 compared to 3.3, 7
    applications level of, 21–29
    hardware level with, 29–30
    learning curves for, 20–21
    structure of, 6–11
    user level of, 11–21
MSDOS.SYS file, 7–8
    See also Kernel
MSNet and network devices, 327
Multilanguage programming, 28
Multilayer data protection, 218–219
Multiple Document Interface, 250
Multiple programs, 25
Multiple shells, 17–18
Multiple structures with MASM, 123–124
Multiplex Interrupt, 194–196, 209
Multisync monitors, 438
Multitasking
    expanded memory for, 535–536, 538
    and file handles, 154
    and Function 55H, 159
    operating system for, 27
    and PSP, 22, 152
    and TSRs, 189–190
    and UNIX, 57
    and VC, 104
Multiuser systems, C-INDEX with, 108
Musical notes, 349–350
    See also SOUND driver
Mv file tool (PCnix), 81–82

N

N command (SOUND driver), 349
%NAME% variable (EBL), 97
Nansi.sys display driver, 75–76
National Security Agency, DES approval by, 230
Naturals with SOUND driver, 351
Nesting of macros, 131–133
Network devices and open routines, 327
NONIBM driver attribute, 309
NONKEY label (C-INDEX), 109–110
Nonstandard filenames for hiding data, 221
NOT operator, 119–120
Notepad, 259–260

Notes (musical) with SOUND driver, 349–350
Now tool (PCnix), 84–85
NUL device
    driver for, in DPB, 172
    header for, 306, 313, 315
    writing to, 330
Null characters in filenames, 221
Number sign (#)
    with SOUND driver, 350
    for VC fields, 103

O

O command (SOUND driver), 349
Object-oriented programming, 30–31
OCRM driver attribute, 309, 327, 331
Octaves with SOUND driver, 349–350
Odd parity in data transfer, 480
-ON.ERROR (EBL), 98
On-line help, batch files for, 66–67
Open file function, 220, 540
Opening of devices, 326–327
Option switches with COMMAND.COM, 14, 18, 58–59
    with whereis, 38–39
OR operator, 119–120
OS/2, 31–32
    and windows, 270
%OUT directive (MASM), 129
OUT instruction, 357
    with EGA, 447
Outline processor, TSR, 186
Outp function, 501
    with EGA, 447, 473
Outport function, 473
Output logging with character I/O, 334
Overlapped windows, 106, 248
Overscan register, EGA, 469–470

P

P command (SOUND driver), 352
/P directive (EBL), 95, 97
P text tool (PCnix), 75–76
Packets, data transfer of, 481–482
Page frames, 538
Painting of windows, 254–255, 267–268
PaintWindow function (Windows), 267–268
Palettes, 468–472
Paragraphs, 151, 160–161
Parallel data transfer, 478
Parameter save area and EGA, 470
Parent process, id for, in PSP, 151
Parity in data transfer, 478, 480–482
PARSE command (EBL), 96

Parsing
  of command-line options, 46–48
  of user commands, 11, 13–15
Password protection, 225–237
PATH environment variable, 13, 156
Paths, 13
  for opening devices, 326
  separators for, 18, 58–59, 71
  setting of, 92–93
PAUSE batch command, 95
Pauses with SOUND driver, 352
PC-DOS, 8, 187–188
PCnix
  batch files for, 62–74
  with MS-DOS functions, 58–62
  tools for, 75–86
  and UNIX, 55–58
  and wildcards, 86–87
Percent sign (%)
  for batch variables, 97, 156
  for expression operator, 128
  for UNIX prompt, 58
Permanent part of COMMAND.COM, 15
PgDn key with VC, 103
PgUp key with VC, 103
Physical security of data, 218
PIC (Programmable Interrupt Controller) chip,
  489–490
Piping, 14
  with batch files, 156
  with UNIX, 57
Pitch (musical), 349–350
Pixels
  addresses of, 451
  color of, 460–461
  height and width of, 454
Placeholders with batch files, 17
Plus sign (+) with SOUND driver, 350
Polling of I/O, 486
Popup windows, 248
Port addresses, 484
Portability
  and C, 100
  and device drivers, 307
Ports, I/O, 490
  See also Serial ports
POST. *See* Power On Self Test
PostMessage function (Windows), 252
PostQuitMessage function (Windows), 261
Power On Self Test, 8, 312
  and passwords, 226
  and serial adapters, 490–491
Pr text tool (PCnix), 75–76
Predefined equates with MASM, 140
Presto tempo with SOUND driver, 352
PRINT.COM program
  and INT 21H, 337

PRINT.COM program—cont
  and INT 28H, 179, 336
  and INT 2FH, 194
  as TSR, 188–189, 191, 210–211
Print Screen key, disabling of, 198–208
Print screen routine, 461–468
Print Spooler Control interrupt, 194–196
Printer and control-p, 335
Printing of characters, subroutine for, 180
PRN, opening of, 331
Process Id in PSP, 151
Program Segment Prefix, 148–152
  and background programs, 337
  command line in, 14
  construction of, 22
  functions for, 158–160
  JFT in, 324
  resources in, 304–305
  and TSRs, 197–198
Programmable Interrupt Controller chip,
  489–490
Programmable interval timer (8253-5) chip,
  373–375
Programs
  execution of, 15–16
  loading of, 22
  multiple, 25
  object-oriented, 30–31
  structure of, 22–24
  termination of, 150
ProKey, 186
PROMPT environment variable, 156
Prompts
  in booting, 10
  for PCnix, 58
  setting of, 93
Protection, data. *See* Data protection and
  encryption
PS/2, video adapters for, 437
PSOFF program, 199–208
PSP. *See* Program Segment Prefix
Public key cryptosystems, 233–236
Pushbuttons, window, 246
Pwd file tool (PCnix), 81

Q

/Q directive (EBL), 97
%Q variable (EBL), 97
Qk.com program, 62
Question marks (?) as wildcards and
  metacharacters, 86–87
Queues
  for interrupt handler, 492
  with serial data transfer, 487
  for window messages, 243–244

QuickBASIC, 28
QuickC, 28

R

/R directive (EBL), 97
%R variable (EBL), 97
RAM function (EBL), 97
RAMdisk
 drivers for, 30
 with PCnix, 71–72
Random files, 107, 328
RC (Resource Compiler), 257
RDA (receive data available) interrupt, 488
READ command (EBL), 96
Read Control Information, 333–334
Read from file function, 220
READ-ONLY attributes for hiding data, 224
READ.PARSED command (EBL), 96
Read sector function, 220
Reading
 of data, unauthorized, 218
 of devices, 328–329
READSCRN command (EBL), 96
READSCRN.PARSED command (EBL), 96
Ready outline processor, 186
Receive buffer register, UART, 484–485
Receive data available interrupt, 488
Receive line status interrupt, 487–488
Receive queues for data transfer, 487
Records
 locking of, with C-INDEX, 108–109
 with MASM, 117–120
Rectangles, window, 247–248, 253–254
Recursive methods for directory searching,
  19, 36–37
Redirection, 14
 and file handles, 153–154
 and Function 46H, 178
 and IBMDOS initialization, 313
 with MODE, 188
Regions, window, 253–254
RegisterClass function (Windows), 251–252,
  262, 267
Registers, UART, 484
Release Handle and Memory function (EMM),
  544
ReleaseCapture function (Windows), 246
Relocatability of EXE programs, 23
Relocatable memory management with
  windows, 255
Renaming
 of commands, 63
 of directories, 82
Repeating
 of commands, 63

Repeating—cont
 of keystrokes, 62
REPT directive (MASM), 127
Request headers
 and IBMDOS, 313
 for SOUND driver, 367–368
Request To Send signal, 482
Reserved functions, 169–170
Resident part of COMMAND.COM, 15
Resource Compiler, 257
Resources, window, 256–257, 268–269
Restore Mapping Context function (EMM), 545
Rests with SOUND driver, 352
RESUME (EBL), 98
Ret variable (C-INDEX), 110
Ret variable (VC), 106
RETURN command (EBL), 96
Right arrow key with VC, 103
RLS (receive line status) interrupt, 487–488
Rm command (UNIX), approximation of, 63
Rollins, Dan, qk.com program by, 62
Root directory, 219
 and DPB, 173
RS-232-C data transfer standard, 482–484
RSA cryptosystems, 234
RTS (Request To Send) signal, 482

S

/S directive (EBL), 97
%S variable (EBL), 97
Save Mapping Context function (EMM),
  544–545
Scales (musical) with SOUND driver, 350–351
Scrambling of data, 227–237
Screen display, 99–107
 dumping of, 189
 and INT 10H, 437
 memory for, 446–449
 printing of, 461–468
 programming of, 91
 and TSRs, 214
Screen logging, 335
ScrollWindow function (Windows), 265
Search for First directory function, 37,
  545–546
Search for Next directory function, 37
Search paths, 13
Seattle Computer Products, MS-DOS by, 187
Sector size in DPB, 171, 173
Security. *See* Data protection and encryption
Semicolons (;) with MASM comments, 134
SendMessage function (Windows), 252
Sequencer chip, EGA, 448–449
Sequential files, 107, 328
Serial adapters, 484

Serial adapters—cont
    interrupts for, 487–488
Serial ports
    and asynchronous data communications,
       477–484
    program using, 493–532
    and UART, 484–492
SET command, 13, 155
Set Current PSP function, 159
Set Device Attributes, 331
Set Palette routine, 469–472
Set PSP function, 321
Set/reset register, EGA, 454–455, 457
SET USER_PSP function, 197–198
Setattr function (VC), 104
SetCapture function (Windows), 246
SETCLOCK programs, 190
SETDTA macro (whereis), 38
SetFocus function (Windows), 247
Setloop function (VC), 105
SetScrollPos function (Windows), 265
SFN (System File Number), 324–326
SFT. *See* System File Table
Sharps for SOUND driver, 350–351
Shells, 320
    commands for, 10, 96
    multiple, 17–18
    UNIX, 18
    See also COMMAND.COM file
ShowWindow function (Windows), 261
SideKick, 185
SKIP command (EBL), 96
Slashes (/)
    for command options, 18, 58–59
    with EBL commands, 97
    in file paths, 18, 58–59, 71
Slurs with SOUND driver, 352
Small memory model for Microsoft C, 501
SmartKey, 186, 187
Software interrupts
    kernel access by, 25–26
    and TSRs, 191–193
    See also specific interrupts
SOUND driver
    DOS internals for, 366–368
    file creation for, 353–355
    finite state machine for, 376–378
    hardware for, 355–359, 373–375
    listing of, 385–431
    musical notation for, 349–353
    performance evaluation of, 381–382
    programming techniques for, 359–366
    prototype for, 369–373
    refinements for, 382–385
    setting up, 347–349
SPACE in data transfer, 478
SPECL driver attribute, 309

Spelling checker, TSR, 186
Split text tool (PCnix), 75
Spoolers, TSR, 188–189
Spotlight, 185
SPY program for windows, 257–269
Sr text tool (PCnix), 75
Staccato mode with SOUND driver, 352–353
STACK command (EBL), 96
STACK.LIFO command (EBL), 96
STACK.OFF function (EBL), 97
STACK.ON function (EBL), 97
STACK.PURGE function (EBL), 97
Stack segment and PSP, 151
Stacks
    with interrupts, 26, 138, 192–193, 213
    overflow of, with device drivers, 343
    switching of, with INT 21H, 322–323
Standard auxiliary device with character I/O,
    334
Standard error with character I/O, 334
Standard I/O handles, 152
Standard input
    with character I/O, 334
    devices for, 130, 335
    reading from, 329
Standard interface, CICS as, 100
Standard output
    with character I/O, 334
    devices for, 180
    writing to, 330, 334–335
Standard printer with character I/O, 334
START bit in data transfer, 478
Startup, DOS, 8–11
STATEOF command (EBL), 96
States in finite state machines, 363
STDIN driver attribute, 309, 313, 331
#stdio.h file for C, 100
STDOUT driver attribute, 309, 313, 331
STI instruction, 358, 489
STOP bit in data transfer, 478
Str text tool (PCnix), 75
Strategy routines for device drivers, 308–309,
    376
STRING label (C-INDEX), 109
String_out subroutine, 180–181
Strings, handling of, by EBL, 96
Strings program (UNIX) and str PCnix tool, 76
Structures
    with MASM, 120–124
    as subroutine parameters, 136
Subdirectories, 219
    password protection of, 226–227
Subroutines, 180–182
    in batch files, 157
    batch files as, 64
    coding of, as macros, 134
    compared to coroutines, 361

Subroutines—cont
    compared to macros, 130
    parameters for, structures as, 136
SUBST command with PCnix, 68–71
Substitute operator (&), MASM, 127–128
SuperKey, 186
Switch tool (PCnix), 84–85
SWITCHAR
    changing of, 59
    function for, 170
    with SUBST, 71
    switch PCnix program for, 85
Synchronization
    of interrupts, 343
    of multiple processes, 364–365
    of SOUND driver, 378–379
Synchronous data transfer, 478
SYSINT module, 10
System calls from C, 77
System clock, speeding up of, 379–382
System date, function to convert, 51
System File Number, 324–326
System File Table, 26–27, 152–153, 304
    aging of entries in, 327
    building of, 317–319
    and closing of devices, 330
    and device drivers, 324–326
    and IOCTL requests, 331
    pointer to, 171
    and read routine, 329
System files, 7–8
System kernel. *See* Kernel
System timer, interrupt request for, 489

T

T command (SOUND driver), 352
Tables, 26–27
    and device drivers, 304–307
    of files open, 171
    MS-DOS, building of, 10
Tail text tool (PCnix), 75–77
Task-switching, 25
Tempo with SOUND driver, 352
Temporary part of COMMAND.COM, 15
Terminate and Stay Resident programs,
        185–186
    and busy flag, 170
    and expanded memory, 549–550
    function calls with, 61, 209–211
    guidelines for, 213–214
    interrupt for, 193–194
    and memory allocation, 23–25, 158
    origin of, 186–190
    PSP functions for, 159–160
    sample of, 198–208

Terminate and Stay Resident programs—cont
    with UNIX-like shells, 56
    UNSPOOL program, 211–213
    well-behaved, 190–198
Termination handler, 22, 151, 194
TEST command (MASM), 119–120
Text, PCnix tools for, 75–80
Text mode, writing in, 330
Tglob tool (PCnix), 84–85
Thesaurus, TSR, 186
THRE (transmit holding register empty)
        interrupt, 488
Time
    and clock device header, 313
    on directories, 220
    in DTA buffer, 328
    function for, 84
    interrupts for, 336, 489
Timer_Tick interrupt, 210–211
Tokens for finite state machines, 363
Toscreen.c program, 77
Touch tool (PCnix), 84
Tr text tool (PCnix), 75–76
TRACE.OFF function (EBL), 97
TRACE.ON function (EBL), 97
Transitions in finite state machines, 363
TranslateMessage function (Windows), 261
Transmit holding register, UART, 484–485
Transmit holding register empty interrupt,
        488
Transmit queues for data transfer, 487
Transparent write mode, 329
Trapdoor functions, 234
Tree command, 19
Tree-structured files, 18–20
    See also Whereis directory search program
TSR programs. *See* Terminate and Stay
        Resident programs
Turbo C, compiling with, 436
Turbo Lightning, 186
Turbo Pascal, 28
TYPE command (EBL), 96
TYPE operator (MASM), 135
.TYPE operator (MASM), 135

U

/U directive (EBL), 97
UART (Universal Asynchronous Receiver
        Transmitter), 357, 484–492
Uniform, 187
Uniform interfaces, 28
Uniq text tool (PCnix), 75–76
Universal Asynchronous Receiver Transmitter,
        357, 484–492

UNIX
  file path separators in, 18, 58–59
  learning curves for, 20–21
  shells for, 17
  See also PCnix
UNSPOOL program, 187, 211–213
Up arrow key with VC, 103
UpdateWindow function (Windows), **266**
User interaction with EBL, 95
User interface
  improving, 20–21
  modeless, 241
  See also Command processor
User stack, 322
Uudecode tool (PCnix), 84
Uuencode tool (PCnix), 84

V

%V variable (EBL), 97
Variables
  batch, with EBL, 96–98
  Dos, function for, 171–172
  in environment, 156–157
VC (Vitamin C) library, 100–106
VDISK.SYS driver, 30
Vertical bar (¦)
  with batch files, 156
  for piping, 14
VGA (Video Graphics Array), 437
Video and TSRs, 214
Video Graphics Array, 437
Video interrupt, 336, 437
Video services, BIOS, interrupt for, 26
Virtual windows with VC, 107
Vitamin C library, 100–106
VSAM files, 107

W

Wc text tool (PCnix), 75–76
Well-behaved TSRs, 190–198
Whereis directory search program, 35
  analysis of, 39–52
  compilation of, 52
  functions in, 37–38
  options in, 38–39
  using recursion, 36–37
White, Nat, RAMdisk system by, 71
Wildcards
  commands with, 15

Wildcards—cont
  compared to UNIX metacharacters, 86–87
  with directories, 19, 37
Windows, creation of, with VC, 106–107
  See also Microsoft Windows
WinMain function (Windows), 243, 261
WM_ACTIVATE message (Windows), 247
WM_CHAR message (Windows), 247
WM_CLOSE message (Windows), 245
WM_COMMAND message (Windows), 263
WM_DESTROY message (Windows), 264–265
WM_HSCROLL message (Windows), 263, 265
WM_KEYDOWN message (Windows),
    246–247, 266
WM_KEYUP message (Windows), 246–247
WM_KILLFOCUS message (Windows), 247
WM_LBUTTONDOWN message (Windows),
    242, 246
WM_LBUTTONUP message (Windows), 242,
    246
WM_MOUSEMOVE message (Windows),
    245–246
WM_NCPAINT message (Windows), 245
WM_PAINT message (Windows), 254–255,
    266
WM_QUIT message (Windows), 261
WM_SETFOCUS message (Windows), 247
WM_SIZE message (Windows), 266
WM_SYSCOMMAND message (Windows),
    265
WM_VSCROLL message (Windows), 263, 265
Wordlength in data transfer, 478
WordStar and p PCnix tool, 76
WParam parameter (Windows), 244, 266
Write Control Information, 333–334
Write Dot routine, 444
Write modes, EGA, 455–459
Write-only register, EGA, 450–451
Write sector function, 220
Write to file function, 220
Writing to devices, 328–330
Wselect function (VC), 106

X

Xatget function (VC), 104
Xcopy command, 19
.XCREF directive (MASM), 134
XMODEM file transfer protocol, 481–482
XON/XOFF data flow control, 478, 482–484
XOR operator, 119
Xp tool (PCnix), 84–85

The Waite Group's MS-DOS Developer's Guide, Second Edition

John Angermeyer, Kevin Jaeger,
The Waite Group

[Expa]nding upon the first edition, *MS-[DOS] Developer's Guide* covers the MS [and] PC DOS operating systems, concen[trati]ng on techniques for developing ap[plica]tions programs. Ideally suited for [progr]ammers, developers, and "power [user]s," the book highlights the specifics [of th]e operating system's internal [beha]vior which is so essential to [syste]m integration and software [deve]lopment.

[This] revised guide includes special em[phas]is on undocumented DOS functions [as w]ell as coverage of MS-DOS file [struc]tures and their differences.

[Topic]s covered include:

[■ T]ools for Structured Coding
[■ T]he Design and Implementation of
[M]odular Programs
[■ P]rogram and Memory Management
[■ R]eal-Time Programming
[■ I]nstallable Device Drivers
[■ W]riting Programs for the Intel 8087/
[8]0287 Math Coprocessor
[■ L]ANs and MS-DOS
[■ D]isk Layout and File Recovery
[In]formation
[■ R]ecovering Data Lost in Memory
[■ Di]fferences Between MS-DOS
[V]ersions
[■ Hi]gh-Level Languages
[■ De]bugging Techniques
[■ Mi]crosoft Windows
[■ Ap]pendices: Development Tools,
[Bib]liography, ASCII Cross-Reference
[an]d Number Conversions, Product
[En]hancements

[XXX P]ages, 7½ x 9¾, Softbound
[ISBN:]0-672-22630-8
[No. 22]630, $24.95

The Waite Group's Understanding MS-DOS®

Kate O'Day and John Angermeyer,
The Waite Group

MS-DOS is a very powerful and intricate operating system with millions of users. This operating system can be explored by beginning programmers in a hands-on approach, at the keyboard.

Understanding MS-DOS introduces the use and operation of this popular operating system for those with little previous experience in computer hardware or software. The fundamentals of the operating system such as EDLIN, tree-structured directories and pathnames, and such advanced features as redirection and filtering are presented in a way that is easy-to-understand and use.

Topics covered include:

■ Organizing Data into Files
■ Redirecting Input and Output
■ Using the Text Editor EDLIN to
  Create and Edit Files
■ Using Commands to Manage Files
■ Special Function Keys and Key
  Combinations
■ Creating Batch Files of Often
  Repeated Commands
■ Create and Use Tree Structured
  Directories

300 Pages, 7 x 9, Softbound
ISBN: 0-672-27067-6
No. 27067, $17.95

The Waite Group's Tricks of the MS-DOS® Masters

John Angermeyer, Rich Fahringer,
Kevin Jaeger, and Dan Shafer,
The Waite Group

This title provides the personal user (not necessarily the programmer or software developer) with a wealth of advanced tips about the operating system and tricks for using it most successfully.

Also included are advanced tips on using popular software packages such as WordStar.®

Topics covered include:

■ Secrets of the Batch File Command
  Language
■ Secrets of Pipes, Filters, and
  Redirection
■ Secrets of Tree-Structured Directories
■ Discovering Secrets: A Debugger
  Tutorial
■ Secrets of DOS Commands
■ Secrets of Files
■ Secrets of Free and Low-Cost
  Software
■ Secrets of Add-on Software, Boards,
  and Mass Storage
■ Secrets of System Configuration
■ Secrets of Data Encryption

568 Pages, 7½ x 9¾, Softbound
ISBN: 0-672-22525-5
No. 22525, $24.95

The Waite Group's Discovering MS-DOS®

Kate O'Day, The Waite Group

This comprehensive study of MS-DOS commands such as DEBUG, LINK, and EDLIN begins with general information about operating systems. It then shows how to use MS-DOS to produce letters and documents; create, name, and manipulate files; use the keyboard and function keys to perform jobs faster; and direct, sort, and find data quickly.

It features a command summary card for quick reference.

Topics covered include:

■ Introduction to MS-DOS
■ What is a Computer System?
■ What is an Operating System?
■ Getting MS-DOS off the Ground
■ System Insurance
■ Editing
■ Filing
■ Batch Files
■ Paths
■ Input/Output
■ Hard Disks
■ Appendices: Error Messages,
  Reference Card

296 Pages, 7½ x 9¾, Softbound
ISBN: 0-672-22407-0
No. 22407, $19.95

Visit your local book retailer, use the order form provided, or call 800-428-SAMS.

MS-DOS® Bible, Second Edition
Steven Simrin, The Waite Group

This revised edition of the best seller is ideally targeted for the intermediate level user and programmer of the operating system, especially those who have upgraded to the new version 3.3. The comprehensive tutorial emphasizes the new features found in DOS 3.3 and provides expanded coverage of batch files, device drivers, memory management, and network commands.

The new expanded batch language, disk structure, terminate and stay resident programs (TSRs), and the Lotus-Intel expanded memory model 4.0 are highlighted. The new commands are explained in detail, and a unique "Information Jump Table" is included and enhanced for easy reference.

Topics covered include:

- Starting MS-DOS
- MS-DOS Files and Batch Files
- Directories, Paths, and Trees
- Installing a Fixed Disk
- Redirection, Filters, and Pipes
- EDLIN
- Extended Keyboard and Display Control
- Debug
- Link
- Disk Structure
- MS-DOS Device Drivers
- MS-DOS Commands
- Appendices: Undocumented Features; MS-DOS Interrupts and Function Calls; Practical Batch Files; ASCII Cross Reference Table

568 Pages, 7½ x 9¾, Softbound
ISBN: 0-672-22617-0
No. 22617, $22.95

Hard Disk Management Techniques for the IBM®
Joseph-David Carrabis

This is a resource book of in-depth techniques on how to set up and manage a hard disk environment directed to the everyday "power user," not necessarily the DOS expert or programmer.

Each fundamental technique, based on the author's consulting experience with Fortune 500 companies, is emphasized to help the reader become a "power user." This tutorial highlights installation of utilities, hardware, software, and software applications for the experienced business professional working with a hard disk drive.

Topics covered include:

- Introduction to Hard Disks
- Hard Disks and DOS
- Backup and What You Need to Know
- Service and Maintenance
- Setting Up a Hard Disk
- Organizing a Hard Disk
- Hard Disk Managers
- Utilities to Find Files, Get Overlays, unERAse Files, Recover Damaged Files, Speed Up Disk Access, and Restore and Backup Disks
- Maintenance Utilities
- File Security Utilities
- Security Utilities

250 Pages, 7½ x 9¾, Softbound
ISBN: 0-672-22580-8
No. 22580, $22.95

IBM® PC AT User's Reference Manual
Gilbert Held

Includes everything you need to know about operating your IBM PC AT—how to set the system up, write programs that fully use the AT's power, organize fixed-disk directories, and use IBM's multitasking TopView.

Includes a BASIC tutorial for beginners and includes several fixed disk organizer programs—all clearly described, explained, and illustrated.

Topics covered include:

- Hardware Overview
- System Setup
- Storage Media and Keyboard Operation
- The Disk Operating System
- Fixed Disk Organization
- BASIC Overview
- Basic BASIC
- BASIC Commands
- Advanced BASIC
- Data File Operation
- Text and Graphics Display Control
- Batch and Shell Processing
- Introduction to TopView
- Appendices: ASCII Code Representation, Extended Character Codes, BASIC Error Messages, Programming Tips and Techniques

453 Pages, 7 x 9¼, Softbound
ISBN: 0-8104-6394-6
No. 46394, $29.95

IBM® PC & PC XT User's Reference Manual, Second Edition
Gilbert Held

Expanded to include the more powe[r] PC XT, this second edition contains most up-to-date information availabl[e] the IBM PC. From setup through a[pply]ing and modifying the system, this continues to provide users with cle[ar] step-by-step explanations of IBM PC hardware and software—complete w[ith] numerous illustrations and example[s].

Highlights of the second edition inc[lude] instructions for using DOS 3.1 and upgrading a PC to an XT; informati[on] on the customized hardware config[ura]tion of the PC and XT; explanation[s of] how to load programs on a fixed d[isk] and how to organize directories; an[d] material on available software, incl[uding] compilers.

Topics covered include:

- Hardware Overview
- System Setup
- Storage Media and Keyboard Op[eration]
- The Disk Operating System
- Fixed Disk Organization
- BASIC Overview
- BASIC Commands
- Data File Operations
- Text and Graphics Display Con[trol]
- Batch Processing and Fixed Disk Operations
- Audio and Data Communicatio[n]
- Introduction to TopView
- Appendices: ASCII Code Representation, Extended Character Codes, BASIC Error Messages, and Programming Ti[ps] and Techniques

496 Pages, 7 x 9¼, Softbound
ISBN: 0-672-46427-6
No. 46427, $26.95

Visit your local book retailer, use the order form provided, or call 800-428-SAMS.

The Waite Group's Desktop Publishing Bible
James Stockford, Editor

Publish high-quality documents right on your desktop with this "bible" that tells you what you need to know—everything from print production, typography, and high-end typesetters, to copyright information, equipment, and software.

In this collection of essays, experts from virtually every field of desktop publishing share their tips, tricks, and techniques while explaining both traditional publishing concepts and the new desktop publishing hardware and software.

Topics covered include:

- Publishing Basics: Traditional Print Production, Conventional Typography, Case Studies in Selecting a Publishing System, and a Comparison of Costs for Desktop and Conventional Systems
- Systems: The Macintosh, PC, MS-DOS, An Overview of Microsoft Windows, Graphics Cards and Standards, Monitors, Dot and Laser Printers, UNIX, and High-End Work Stations
- Software: Graphics Software, Page Layout Software, Type Encoding Programs, PostScript, and JustText
- Applications: Newsletters, Magazines, Forms, Comics and Cartooning, and Music

480 Pages, 7½ x 9¾, Softbound
ISBN: 0-672-22524-7
No. 22524, $24.95

Personal Publishing with PC PageMaker®
Terry M. Ulick

Here is everything you need to know about PC PageMaker to design publications. It shows you how to select and use type, work in multicolumn and multipage layouts, create graphs, and merge text with graphic elements.

Hands-on instruction at the terminal, numerous visual examples, and a detailed explanation of typesetting terms provide the information necessary to help the beginning to intermediate PC user produce attractive copy.

Topics covered include:

- Assembling a Personal Publishing System
- Selecting the Right Hardware and Software
- Pages on the IBM®
- Electronic Page Assembly
- Working with Type
- PostScript™ and LaserJet Plus™ TypeStyles
- Formatting Type
- Working with PageMaker
- Building Master Pages
- Placing Elements on a Page
- Adding Graphic Elements
- Linking PageMaker Files
- Printing Page Files
- High-Volume Printing
- Multicolored Pages
- Grids and Sample Pages

304 Pages, 7½ x 9¾, Softbound
ISBN: 0-672-22593-X
No. 22593, $18.95

Micro-Mainframe Connection
Thomas Wm. Madron

Focusing on the organizational environment, this book explores the opportunities, technologies, and problems involved in implementing the transfer of data between the mainframe and the micro workstation—more comprehensively than any other book on the market.

Designed to help managers and technical support people design and implement micro-mainframe networks, it gives complete information about features, facilities, and requirements, including cost considerations.

Topics covered include:

- The Micro-Mainframe Link
- Features, Facilities, and Problems in the Micro-Mainframe Connection
- Local Area Networks in the Micro-Mainframe Connection
- Micros as Mainframe Peripherals: Mainframes as Micro Peripherals
- Micros and IBM® Mainframes in a Synchronous Network
- Asynchronous Devices in a Synchronous Network: Protocol Conversion
- File Transfer
- Data Extraction, Data Format, and Application Specific File Transfers
- Making the Micro-Mainframe Connection

256 Pages, 7½ x 9¾, Hardbound
ISBN: 0-672-46583-3
No. 46583, $29.95

The Waite Group's Modem Connections Bible
Curtis and Majhor

This book describes modems, how they work, and how to hook ten well-known modems to nine name-brand computers. A handy Jump Table shows where to find the appropriate connection diagram and applies the illustrations to eleven more computers and seven additional modems. It also features an overview of communications software, an explanation of the RS-232C interface, and a section on troubleshooting.

Topics covered include:

- Types of Modems
- How Modems Work
- Connecting Equipment
- The RS-232 Connector
- The Progress of a Call
- Full Duplex and Half Duplex Mode
- Types of Communications Programs
- Features and Uses
- Voice/Data Switching
- How to Read the Charts
- Jump Table
- Appendices: Types of Online Services and Costs, The RS-232C Interface, Further Reading, Glossary, Troubleshooting, Communications Software for Microcomputers

192 Pages, 7½ x 9¾, Softbound
ISBN: 0-672-22446-X
No. 22446, $16.95

Visit your local book retailer, use the order form provided, or call 800-428-SAMS.

The Waite Group's
Printer Connections Bible
Marble and House

This book contains all the information necessary to make the proper connections to get a printer printing. It focuses on the hardware side of connecting, particularly the main interface—the cable itself.

Avoid hours of frustration with this easy-to-follow format including tables and diagrams, information about various printers, computers and software, printer technology, and cables and connectors.

Topics covered include:

- Types of Printers
- Cable and Connector Types
- Soldering
- The ASCII Code
- Binary Numbers
- Serial and Parallel
- Centronics Parallel
- More Complex Parallel Interfaces
- RS-232 Serial Interface
- Speed Considerations in RS-232
- Printer Drivers
- Hardware versus Software Handshaking
- DIP Switches
- Jump Table
- Connection Diagrams

240 Pages, 7½ x 9¾, Softbound
ISBN: 0-672-22406-2
No. 22406, $16.95

The Waite Group's
Microsoft® C Programming
for the IBM®
Robert Lafore

Programmers using the Microsoft C compiler can learn to write useful and marketable programs with this entry level book on Microsoft C programming.

This title is a tutorial geared specifically to the IBM PC family of computers. Unlike other introductory C titles, it is written for the Microsoft C compiler. It provides special coverage of IBM features such as sound, color graphics including CGA and EGA, keyboard, variable storage, and character graphics.

Topics covered include:

- Getting Started
- Building Blocks
- Loops
- Decisions
- Functions
- Arrays and Strings
- Pointers
- Keyboard and Cursor
- Structures, Unions, and ROM BIOS
- Memory and the Monochrome Display
- CGA and EGA Color Graphics
- Files Preprocessor
- Serial Ports and Telecommunications
- Larger Programs
- Advanced Variables
- Appendices: Supplemental Programs, Hexadecimal Numbering, IBM Character Codes, and a Bibliography

640 Pages, 7½ x 9¾, Softbound
ISBN: 0-672-22515-8
No. 22515, $24.95

The Waite Group's
Turbo C® Programming for
the IBM®
Robert Lafore

This entry-level text teaches readers the C language while also helping them write useful and marketable programs for the IBM PC, XT, AT, and PC/2.

This tutorial is based on Borland's new Turbo C compiler with its powerful integrated environment that makes it easy to edit, compile, and run C programs. The author's proven hands-on intensive approach includes example programs, exercises, and questions and answers and covers CGA and EGA graphic modes.

Topics covered include:

- C Building Blocks
- Loops
- Decisions
- Functions
- Arrays and Strings
- Pointers
- Keyboard and Cursor
- Structures, Unions, and ROM BIOS
- Memory and the Character Display
- CGA and EGA Color Graphics
- Files
- Larger Programs
- Advanced Variables
- Appendices: References, Hexadecimal Numbering, Bibliography, ASCII Chart, and Answers to Questions and Exercises

608 Pages, 7½ x 9¾, Softbound
ISBN: 0-672-22614-6
No. 22614, $22.95

IBM® PC and Macintosh®
Networking Featuring: TOPS™
and AppleShare™
Stephen L. Michel

IBM PC and Macintosh owners and users who want to combine the power of their machines will welcome this complete resource for networking the IBM PC and the Macintosh using TOPS and AppleShare.

This book details the specifics of using the Macintosh and the IBM PC on the same network, including transferring files, sharing printers, transporting data from IBM software to Mac and vice versa, and mixing word processing and spreadsheet programs.

Topics covered include:

- How the Macintosh and PC Really Differ
- TOPS
- AppleShare
- Coexistence
- Managing the Network
- Appendices: Glossary, ASCII Characters Sets, Using PostScript Printers

328 Pages, 7¾ x 9¼, Softbound
ISBN: 0-672-48405-6
No. 48405, $21.95

Visit your local book retailer, use the order form provided, or call 800-428-SAMS.